A
DICTIONARY OF HINDUSTANI PROVERBS

Important Books of Interest Published Recently

Enchclopaedia of Indian Folk Literature, in 12 Volumes
written by Several Authors

Encyclopaedia of Indian Proverbs, in 7 Volumes & 9 Parts
Written by Several Authors

THE BUDDHISTS.
Encyclopaedia of Buddhism, in 5 Volumes
Edited by Subodh Kapoor

THE HINDUS.
Encyclopaedia of Hinduism, in 5 Volumes
Edited by Subodh Kapoor

Encyclopaedia of Indian Mysticism, in 12 Volumes
Edited by Sadhu Santideva

The Secret Lore of India
W.M. Teape

The Contribution of Women to Sanskrit Literature,
in 3 Volumes
J. B. Choudhari

Encylopaedia of Commonwealth Literature, in 2 Volumes
H.H. Anniah Gowda

The Best of Premchand, in 2 Volumes
Madan Gopal

A
DICTIONARY OF HINDUSTANI PROVERBS

A Classified Collection
Including many Marwari, Punjabi, Maggah.
Bhojpuri and Tirhuti Proverbs, Sayings,
Emblems, Aphorisms, Maxims and Similes

BY

S. W. Fallon

Edited and Revised By

R. C. Temple

Assisted By

Lala Faqir Chand

GYAN

Published by

Gyan Publishing House
5, Ansari Road
Daryaganj, New Delhi-110002
Phone: 011-47034999, 9811692060
E-mail: books@gyanbooks.com

Distribution Network
gyanbooks.com
India, USA, Canada, UK, Australia, France

ISBN : 978-81-212-3323-1 (PB)
First Published, 2002

2nd Impression 2020

Printed at: Gyan Press, Delhi.

PREFACE.

There has been a great, but unavoidable, delay in finally producing this work. It is hoped, however, that it will be found to have been carefully compiled to the end·

All the quotations in it belong to Dr. Fallon's Collection of Proverbial Phrases, etc. I have not added to them from outside sources. The form in which they are presented in the vernacular is also Dr. Fallon's, and so is the system of transliteration, being adopted to that used in his well-known *New Hindustani Dictionary*. Readers will at once understand why it is I have not ventured to interfere with the *forms* of the proverbs,—that being too delicate a matter for a foreigner, however familiar with a language, to attempt, I am, however, responsible for the renderings and explanations attached, because the collection was handed over to me practically untranslated and without annotation. As to these all I can says is, I have taken every care to make them correct.

I have been assisted in my labors by Lālā Faqir Chand and Thakur Das, who did so much in helping Dr, Fallon in his *Dictionaries* and whose efficient and conscientious aid I now cordially acknowledge. Another fellow-worker has been Chaina Mal, whose assistance in other work I have already frequently had occasion to acknowledge, and to whose able assistance I once more have the great pleasure of publicly testifying. Faqir Chand and Thakur Das live at Dehli and Chaina Mal at Ambala, as a matter of fact these have worked quite independently, so that I have had the benefit of advice given me from perfectly separate sources,—a point of considerable importance in a work such as this.

Dr. Fallon made his collection between 1870 and 1880 while his Dictionary was being compiled and his object was mainly to illustrate by their laws the real life of the people, and also the methods by which they expressed their thoughts. His assistants numbered about a dozen ; one of those above mentioned, worked on to the end with me. I should state that I had no share in working the collection, nor took any part in the work until I undertook to bring it out after Dr. Fallon's lamented death.

The comprehensive title of the work makes it clear that Dr. Fallon's intention was to cover both the dialects and the lore of Northern India as widely as he could. To say that he altogether succeeded in his aim would be far from the truth, but I must here say that the vastness of the work he accomplished has often excited my admiration, as I proceeded with the task of translation into English and explanation. Incomplete as it really is, this work contains upwards of 12,500 proverbial phrases !

Like Spain, India is a land of proverbial sayings :—their name is legion and their use constant and never ending. The natives employ them in their daily intercourse, in their commercial and social correspondence, in all the many vicissitudes of every day life, even in the very Courts of Law. I have often heard a witness reply to a question put by a pleader with a proverb, and in altercations and disputes the natives hurl them at each other by the dozen. The closely connected with real Indian proverbs are the religious and philosophical aphorisms, always attributed to some *bhagat*, or saint, which so nearly approach the former as to be almost indistinguishable from them. They are habitually used on every possible occasion of daily life, especially in seasons of trouble. They are familiar to all; the women sing them as they do their household work; the men employ them for purposes of condolence and congratulation; the children are taught them as soon as they can speak; many persons largely interlard their conversation with them. Taken all in all, therefore, there is no study—as a study—that I know of, that will render the student of the natives of India so deeply conversant with their thoughts and mode of life as that of their proverbial and aphoristic lore.

I have been influenced as to the actual form in which this book has been printed principally by the necessity of making it uniform with Dr. Fallon's *New Hindustani Dictionary*, and to some extent by certain main considerations, which I will explain at greater length. In the first place comes the method of record. Dr. Fallon made his collection alphabetic, *i. e.* he arranged the proverbs in alphabetical order according to their first words. In a language like Hindustani, the "small" words and pure grammatical expressions are not likely to be numerous in the beginnings of sentences, and so this method is not so objectionable as it would be in English, for instance. The question is, is it the best? or rather, what is the best method? This is a very old question, and still remains pretty much in the same condition as when it puzzled Ray, the collector of English proverbs, two hundred years ago. The object of all such collections is, of course, to present the proverbs and sayings so as to make them readily accessible to the student, and so as to avoid redundancy, or, in other words, repeating the same proverb over and over again in the book under different heads. Now a proverb is a sentence of several words, often capable of more than one application and heading and nearly always of variable form. Again, be the collector as careful as he may in his selection of headings, he will find that many proverbs will properly group themselves under more than one of them. Ray held that no collection of proverbs was really usefully complete without an index as long as itself. I am afraid he was quite right, and feel sure that a complete collection is only that one, which is accompanied by a concordance. In this way alone can a proverb be readily found when wanted. But it is quite clear that few publishers would stand the expense and few authors find the time and energy necessary. As regards Eastern proverbs the alphabetical method is that invariably pursued by Orientals themselves, and it is, I think, practically the most useful one.

Secondly, as to language. In India the same proverb is found to exist in several languages and in many different dialects without deviation as to meaning. This, of course, arises from identity of surrounding social condition among peoples speaking separate tongues. The consequence is that there is just that difference in form as is necessitated by difference of dialect, and no more. So that by comparing the same proverb, as expressed in different dialects one learns almost the exact amount of linguistic difference there is between them. In this sense, as indicators of philological differentiation, lists of identical proverbs in several dialects are extremely valuable.

Thirdly, as to rendering and illustration, literal translations would not only give a wrong impression of the meaning of the originals, but would altogether miss their force and pungency. The method I followed, therefore, was to turn the vernacular into as racy English as I could command without losing the sense. But it is impossible to always avoid baldness. Rhyme and cadence are necessarily lost in a translation, and it must be borne in mind that many an aphorism and many a saying in every language charms and attracts, not because it conveys any particularly taking idea, but simply because of the excellence of the rhythmical form in which it is expressed. Again, proverbs and sayings are often capable of more than one application, as above said, and consequently, in different localities, they are used in different senses. Such variations are a great trouble to the translator. My assistants, who as I have already explained, resided in places far apart from each other, not unfrequently differed as to the application of a proverb and in such cases put down each variant signification. Frequently also, the application is entirely arbitrary, and so much is this the case, that it seems to me to be quite hopeless for any European to attempt to render into a European tongue, or to essay to illustrate Oriental proverbs, without using to the full the best native assistance he can procure. Illustration and explanation too, are always a great difficulty in this connection. I was aware that it is best to assume ignorance on the part of the reader in such matters and to explain everything, and acting extensively on this idea I always rather feared I had overdone explanation ; quite lately however, a gentleman, not very conversant with things Oriental but of considerable general culture, complained that he could not take to Fallon's, *Proverbs*, because he did not sufficiently understand the allusions. This shows that, so far from giving too much illustration, I have not done enough in that line. The lesson, I take it, is that a recorder of proverbs cannot be too lavish in wealth of annotation,

With this I take leave of the reader, trusting that errors in record and errors in translation may be alike lightly censured in consideration of the task being one of the most difficult that either recorder or translator could undertake.

The Nash, Worcester. R. C. TEMPLE.

December 1886

ABBREVIATIONS.

Agric.	stands	for	Agricultural.
Bhoj.	"	"	Bhojpurī.
E.	"	"	Eastern.
Hin.	"	"	Hindus.
Mag.	"	"	Maggah.
Mah.	"	"	Mahammadans.
Mar.	"	"	Mārvāṛī.
Ped.	"	"	Pedantic.
Panj.	"	"	Panjābī.
Pers.	"	"	Persian.
Rus.	"	"	Rustic.
Tir.	"	"	Tirhūtī.
Wom.	"	"	Women.

FALLON'S
HINDUSTANI PROVERBS.

A

Āb āb kar mar gayā, sirhāne rahā pānī.
With water by his side he died crying *l'eau l'eau.*

☛ The story goes that a Persian scholar kept on crying out at his death '*āb āb*,' but as none of the attendants understood him he died of thirst, while all the time the water (*pānī*) was by his bedside.

Ā bail, mujhe mār.
Come bull, and gore me.
(Said of one who wilfully brings misfortune on himself.)

Ā balā, gale lag.
Come misfortune and embrace me.
(The point is the same as in the preceding.)

Ā, baṛe bāp kī beṭī hai, to panjah kar le.
Come on then; if you are the daughter of such a strong father, try your five fingers' strength against mine.
(Said to a woman boasting of her strength. The feat is to interlace the fingers backs upwards and to see which can make the other kneel first by mere pressure).

Ab bhī merā murdah tere zindah par bhārī hai. Mah.
Still my dead is more than a match for your living.
(My family, etc, are more respectable.)

Abhī Dillī dūr hai.
Dillī is still a long way off.
(It is a far cry to Loch Awe. It is said to those who pretend to have done a great deal when they have really done but little.)

Abhī ek biṅṭ kī do dāl nahīṅ huī haiṅ.
The pea is not yet divided into two equal halves.
(The dispute is not yet satisfactorily settled.)

Abhī hoṅṭoṅ kā dūdh bhī nahīṅ sūkhā hai.
The milk is not yet dry on your lips.
(Said in reproof to a young man who asserts his opinions confidently.)

Abhī kaë din, kaë rāt?
How many days and nights (have) as yet (passed over you)?
(Said to one who claims a right before it is due by prescription.)

Abhī ser meṅ pūnī bhī nahīṅ katī hai.
Of the pound of cotton not a skein is yet spun.
(Scarce a fraction of the work is yet done.)

Abhī to tumhāre dūdh ke dāṅt bhī nahīṅ ṭūṭe haiṅ.
You have not yet shed your milk teeth.
(Who are you that you boast?)

Abhī to tum mā kā dūdh pīte ho.
You are still drinking your mother's milk.

Ab jīne kā kuchh savād nahīṅ.
There is no zest in life now.

Ab ke bache to sab ghar rache.
Saved once, saved for ever.

Ab ke muṛiheṅ, ho rājā. E.
Come back and be king.

Ab ke sāhe ham na byāhe, phiṭ paṛo woh sāhe! Hin.
The marriage season come and I not wed! out on the season that hath sped!
(Cursing the stick that beats you.)

Ab ke wār meṅ beṛā pār hai.
This time my boat will cross over.
(Gamblers: this throw I am going to win: also when success is expected.)

Ab kī ab ke sāth, jab kī jab ke sāth.
The present for the present; the future for the future.
(Sufficient for the day is the evil thereof. Mat. vi. 34.)

Ab kī chhai kī nirālī bāteṅ.
The queer conversation of the rising generation.

Āb na dīdah, mozah kashīdah. P.
No water to be seen, and his stockings pulled off.
(Crying out before you are hurt.)

Ab pachhtāë kyā hot hai, jab chiṛyāṅ chug gaīṅ khet.
What's the good of crying when the birds have eaten up the field?
(Crying over spilt milk.)

Abrā kī joṛū sab kī bhaujāī. E.
The poor man's wife is every one's sister-in-law.
(It is customary in India to jest with the wife of an elder brother.)

Abre kī bhaiṅs byāïl, sagro gāoṅ maṭyā le dhāïl Bhoj.
When the poor man's buffalo calves every one runs with his pail (for milk).
(Grinding the poor and defenceless.)

Ābrū jag meṅ rahe, to jān jānā pashm hai.
Keep your honor, but count your life as cast off hair.
(Honor is more than life.)

Ab satvantī ho-kar baiṭhī, lūṭ-kar sansār. Wom.
She sits a saint, grown rich on a world's plunder.

Ab se āë, ghar se āë.
Coming from there I came from home.
(Said by one on returning home, who has experienced no inconvenience in strange place.)

Ab to pathar ke nīche hāth dabā hai.
I have got my hand under a stone.
(To be in a fix, or to undertake a difficult matter.)

Ab to rupaë kī zāt hai.
Caste is now money.
(Upstart a churl, and gathered good, And thence did spring his gentle blood.)

Achchhā kīyā Khudā ne, burā kīyā bande ne.
Good is God's, evil is man's.

Achchhā kīyā Rahmān ne, burā kiyā Shaitān ne.
Good is God's, evil is the Devil's.

Achchhe bhaë aṭal, prān gaë nikal.
A life is well lost that is lost in gorging sweets.
☞ This proverb is applied jestingly to the Chobā Brāhmans of Mathurā, who are credited with eating to excess. The good work of feeding the poor has degenerated into the custom of inducing each man to eat till he bursts, by the offer of a money reward, rising from 4 *ānās* up to a gold *mohar* for every sweetmeat eaten on a full stomach.

Achchhe bure meṅ chār ungal kā farq hai.
Between good and evil there is but a handbreadth.

Achchhe ghar bayānā dīyā.
You have given earnest money for a good house.
(Said especially when the parents of a boy have secured for his future bride a girl of good family.)

Achchhe haiṅ, par Khudā pālā na ḍāle!
He is a very good man, but heaven keep me from him!
(Often used ironically of the Police.)

Achchhī bhaī, guṛ sathrāṅ ser.
Hurrah! seventeen pounds of treacle for the rupee.
(Very low prices; a good bargain; treacle (*guṛ*) sells at ten *sers* the rupee usually.)

Achchhī chīz sab ko pasand hai.
Every body loves a good thing.

Āchhe din pāchhe gaë, Har se kīyā na het, Ab pachhtāë kyā hot hai, jab chiryāṅ chug gaiṅ khet?
Your best days passed and you loved not God, What boots repentance now, when the birds have eaten your field?
(Remember now thy Creator in the days of thy youth, while the evil days come not, nor the years draw nigh, when thou shalt say I have no pleasure in them. Eccl. xii. 1.)

Adālat kā baṛā nāzuk muāmlā hai.
Going to law is a very delicate matter.

Ā, daliddar, kāndhe chaṛh baiṭh.
Come, poverty, sit on my shoulders.
(Said to the idle.)

Ādam āyā, dam āyā.
When Adam came, *dam* (breath) came.

Ādar baṛhal gajādhar bahu ke. E. Wom.
A rich man's wife is always respected.

Ādar nā bhāo, jhūṭhe māl khāo.
Great cheers, little welcome.

Ādhā āp ghar, ādhā sab ghar.
Half for himself, and half for all the rest.
(The lion's share.)

Ādhā Miyāṅ Shekh Sharfuddīn, ādhā sārā gāoṅ.
Half to Shekh Sharfuddīn, half to the village.
(The lion's share to the great man.)

Ādhā taje paṇḍit, sarbas taje gaṅvār.
The wise man gives half, the fool gives all.
(Said of the improvident and spendthrift.)

Ādhā tītar, ādhī baṭer.
Half partridge, half quail.
(Applied to mixed speech, or jargon. Neither fish, nor flesh, nor good red herring.)

Ādhe Asāṛh to bairī kā bhī barse. Agric.
The July rains fall even on the enemy's field.
(Equal justice.)

Ādhe gāoṅ Dīvālī, ādhe gāoṅ Phāg.
One half the village plays Dīvālī, and the other half Holī.
(Half the village is at feud with the other half:—the season for Divālī is Autumn and for Holi Spring, so the two festivals cannot be held together.)

Adhelā na de, adhelī de.
He'll give half a rupee, but not half a pie.
(Penny wise, pound foolish.)

Ādhe Māghe, kamlī kāṅdhe. Rus.
In the middle of February coats go over the shoulders.
(The winter is past.)

Ādhe Qāzī Quddūh, ādhe Bābā Ādam. Mah.
Half the world are Bābā Ādam's, and half are Qazī Qudduh's.
(Applied to one who has a large family, in allusion to the tale that Qāzī Qudduh's wife had 70 sons at a birth. He is therefore considered to have a large share in the population of the world.)

Ādhī ko chhoṛ-ke sārī ko dhāve, aisā ḍūbe, thā nā pave.
Leave half to run after the whole, and you will be drowned beyond finding.
(All covet, all lose.)

Ādhī murgī, ādhī baṭer.
Half hen, half quail.
(Said of the hypocritical and double-faced.)

Ādhī rāt ko jaṅbhāī āve, shām se mūṅh phailāve.
He sets his mouth ajar at sunset in order to gape at midnight.
(Commencing with unnecessary preparation.)

Ādhī roṭī bas, Kāyath haiṅ ki pas?
Half a loaf's enough, I am a Kāyath not a beast.

Ādh ser ke pātr meṅ kaise ser samāë?
How can a half pound measure hold a pound?

Ād Hindū, bād Musalmān. Hin.
First Hindū, then Musalmān.
(Allusion to the conversion of many Hindūs to Islām.)

Ādī ke chandan, lilār charcharāī. E.
Put ginger for sandalwood, and your forehead will smart.
(Pounded sandalwood is a common cooling remedy.)

Ādī mirchāī kā kaun sāth? E.
Chillies don't go with ginger.

Ādmī ādmī antār, koī hīrā, koī kankar.
Amongst men some are gems, and some are pebbles.
(Or, there are men and men, as every stone is not a gem.)

Ādmī anāj kā kīṛā hai.
Man is a grain worm.
(He cannot live without corn.)

Ādmī apne matlab meṅ andhā hai.
Man is blind in his own interest,
(i. e. blind to every thing else. Men are blind in their own cause.)

Ādmī ashraf ul-makhlūqāt hai.
The noblest of creatures is man.

Ādmī hai, ki ghanchakkar?
Is he a man or a top?
(Said of one who is always wandering about.)

Ādmī hai yā ābnūs kā kundah?
Is he a man or a block of ebony?
(Said of a negro.)

Ādmī hai yā bijlī?
Is he a man or lightning?
(So sharp.)

Ādmī ho, yā be dāl ke būdam?
Are you a man or a *būdam* without the *d*?
(The Persian *būdam* without the *d* means an owl (*būm*.)

Ādmī ho, yā sang-i-be-nūn?
Are you a man or a stone without the *n*?
(The Persian *sang* is a stone, and *sag* is a dog: a joke of the *literati*.)

Ādmī jāne base, sonā jāne kase.
Know a man by his company and gold by a touchstone.

Ādmī kā shaitān ādmī hai.
Man's enemy is man.

Ādmī kī davā ādmī hai.
Man's remedy is man.

Ādmī kī kasauṭī muāmlā hai.
The touchstone for man is dealing with him.

Ādmī kī peshānī dil kā āinah hai.
The countenance is the reflection of the heart.

Ādmī kī qadr mare par hotī hai.
A man's worth is found out when he is dead.

Ādmī ko ādmī se sau dafā kām paṛtā hai.
Man needs man's aid a hundred times.

Ādmī ko ādmīyat lāzim hai.
Humanity is the characteristic of human beings.

Ādmī ko ḍhāī gaz zamīn kāfī hai. Mah.
Man wants but seven feet of earth.
(His grave.)

Ādmī ko ḍhāī gaz kafan kāfī hai.
Man wants but seven feet of cere-cloth.

Ādmī kuchh kho-kar sīkhtā hai.
To lose is to learn.
(Man learns by experience.)

Ādmī kiyā hai? ābnūs kā kundah hai.
He is not a man, but a log of ebony.
(Said of a very black man.)

Ādmī kiyā hai? sarāṅche kā bāṅs hai.
He is not a man, but a long bamboo.
(Said of a very tall person.)

Ādmī māl kī khātir pahāṛ sir par uṭhātā hai.
A man will carry a mountain on his head for the sake of gain.

Ādmī ne ākhir kachchā shīr piyā hai.
Man after all is a creature reared on mother's milk.
(Human weakness. The natives have a saying that man is *kachchā* (crude and liable to err) because he is reared on (*kachchā dūdh*) mother's milk.)

Ādmī pānī kā bulbulā hai.
Man's life is but a water bubble.

Ādmī par jaisī paṛtī hai, waisī sahtā hai.
What befalls a man must be borne.
(Man is born to bear.)

Ādmī peṭ kā kuttā hai.
Man is the dog of his stomach.
(Man is the slave of his stomach.)

Ādmī sā pakherū koī nahīṅ.
There is no bird like a man.
(*i. e*, so volatile and unsteady.)

Ādmī ṭhokar khā-kar saṅbhalta hai.
Man stumbles and gets sense.

Āē ām, jāē lebedā.
The mango is down, but the stick is gone.
(To gain your end you needs must spend.)

Āē Chait suhāvan, phūaṛ mail chhuṛāvan. Wom.
When April comes her dirt leaves her.
(*i. e.* she is only clean when the heat makes her perspire. Said of a dirty, lazy woman.)

Āēgā kuttā to pāēgā ṭikā. Wom.
When the dog comes he will get his share.
(Who works gets.)

Āē kanāgat phūlā kāṅs, Bāman uchhleṅ nau nau bāṅs. Hin.
When the *kanāgats* come, the long grass blooms, And the Brāhman dances nine poles high.
☞ The *kanāgat* at the *sharādh* is the feasting of Brāhmans with oblations made to appease the souls of the dead :—*kāṅs phūlnā*, is an idiom to express a wild luxuriant growth; flourishing as the green bay tree.

Āē kī shādī, na gaē kā gam.
Neither glad for its coming, nor sorry at its going.
(An even-tempered man; a well balanced mind. 'My mind to me a kingdom is.')

Āë mere agle, man māne so kar le. Wom.
My husband, you can do with me as you choose.
(Said by a woman when ill treated by her husband, meaning 'I am completely at your mercy.')

Āë Mīr, bhāge pīr.
When *Mīr* comes the *pīrs* retire.
☞ To understand this proverb it is necessary to premise that a person named Shekh Saddo, or Mīrāñjī, who lived at Amrohā, pretended to great skill in the art of making amulets, fortune telling, etc., called *Ilm-i-taskhīr*. One day in ploughing, he turned up a lamp which had been constructed by a famous magician of former times, with four wicks, and endowed with such properties, that whenever it was lighted, four *genii*, or familiar spirits, appeared to the person who lighted it, (invisible to all besides) and were ready to perform his orders. The first time that he lighted it, he was alarmed at the appearance of the *genii* and endeavoured to extinguish the lamp, but the *genii* informed him, that being once summoned, they could not retire till he had given them some order to perform. The Shekh, being a man of a lascivious disposition, ordered them to bring a beautiful woman, whom he had seen at a distant place. This was immediately performed, and the lady who was of high rank was much astonished and alarmed to find herself in such a place with a stranger. When, however, he was proceeding by force or persuasion to gratify his impure desire, one of the *genii* informed him that their obedience to him would only continue while his actions were confined within the bounds of virtue, and that whenever he transgressed those they were to put him to death. He desisted for that time, and the same scene was several times repeated, till at last the violence of his passion got the better of his fear, and he perpetrated the act, whereupon he was immediately put to death by the *genii*. Though in fact a profligate character, he obtained the reputation of being a saint or prophet, through the supernatural power which he exerted by means of his familiar spirits, and a superb *dargāh*, or shrine, is dedicated to his memory at Amrohā. After his death he is said to have become a powerful Spirit or *Jinn*, who occasionally descends upon, or inspires human beings, particularly women, who are then endued with a knowledge of futurity and other preternatural powers. There are other spirits of departed seers, which exercise similar power, such as Shāh Daryā, Zain Khāñ, Nannhe Miyāñ, etc., but they are of inferior rank to Mīrāñ, so that when he comes in person they all retire: hence the proverb. It expresses that when the chief in any employment appears, the inferior agents withdraw.

Aëre gaëre fasl bahotere.
The harvest of dregs is very great.
(I shall find a mouthful somewhere or other.)

Aëre gaëre pach kalyān.
Out-casts are among the five good things.
(Ironical; the scum or dregs of society: the *panch kalyān* are the five pure pleasures.)

Āë terī qudrat!
How wondrous is thy power, (Oh God)!

Āë the Har bhajne ko, aur otan lage kapās.
Came to sing hymns, but set to pick oakum.
(He reckoned on the easy services of the temple, but was set to pick cotton.)

Āë, to jāë kahāñ?
When it comes, where will it go?
(You cannot tell how a matter will end).

Afīmchī tīn manzil se pahchānā jātā hai.
An opium-eater is known three stages off.

Afīmī mīṭhās barī ragbat se khātā hai.
Who opium eats devours sweets.

Afīm yā khāë amīr, yā khāë faqīr.
Only a beggar or a rich man can eat opium.
(It is very expensive and therefore can only be bought by the rich or begged by the poor.)

Aflātūn ke nātī (yā sāle) bane hai.
Got up like a relative of Plato.
(Said to one who is proud and haughty.)

Afsos! dil garhe meñh!
Alas! my heart is deep in a pit!
(Excessive grief.)

Āftāb par thūko, apne hī muñh par pare.
Spit at the sun, and your spittle will fall in your own face.
(Speaking evil of the great will injure yourself.)

Afyūnī janūnī.
The opium eater is mad.

Āgā Mīr kī dāī sab sikhī sikhāī.
The nurse of Agā Mīr knows every thing.
(Rich people get good servants.)

Agarche gandah, magar ijād-i-bandah.
Though born of dirt he is still full of wits.

Agar koh ṭalle, na ṭalle faqīr.
Though the mountain move, the *faqīr* won't.
(The mountain to Muhammad.)

Āg aur bairī ko kam nā samjhe.
Despise neither fire nor foe.

Āg aur pānī ko kam nā samjhe.
Despise neither fire nor water.

Āg aur phūñs kā bair hai.
Fire and straw cannot agree.
(Moral:—be careful of the company of the other sex.)

Āg bin dhuāñ nahīñ.
No smoke without fire.

Āge Āgrā pīchhe Lāhor.
Āgrā before and Lāhor behind.
☞ The story goes that a man going to Lāhor turned his face in ignorance towards Āgrā; hence, the proverb means going the wrong way about a thing.

Āge chalte haiñ, pīchhe kī khabar nahīñ.
They go ahead without knowing what's in the rear.

Āge daur, pīchhe chaur.
Fast run fast lose.
(Applied to one who learns rapidly, but soon forgets what he has acquired.)

Āge hāth pīchhe pāt. Wom.
A hand before and a leaf behind.
(Spoken of one so wretchedly poor, that he has not clothes enough to cover his nakedness.)

Āge jāve ghuṭne ṭūṭeṅ, pīchhe dekhe āṅkheṅ phuṭeṅ. Wom.
Go ahead and break your knees, look behind and turn blind.
(On the horns of a dilemma.)

Āge Khudā kā nām.
There is nothing left but God's name.
(Come to the last resource.)

Āge kuā, pīchhe khāī.
A well before, and a ditch behind.
(On the horns of dilemma.)

Āge nāth nā pīchhe pagā, Sab se bhalā kumhār kā gadhā.
Nor halter, nor heel ropes; Who so lucky as the potter's ass?

Āge pag rakhe pat baṛhe, pīchhe pag rakhe pat jāe.
To advance is honor, to turn back is disgrace.

Āge pīchhe sab chal baseṅge.
Sooner or later all die.

Āge rok, pīchhe ṭhok, sasur saṛke nā jāe to kiyā ho?
A block ahead and driven from behind; if that old brute won't leave the road what can I to do?
(Give me room; I prefer your room to your company.)

Aggam buddhī Bānyā, pachchham buddhī Jāṭ. Rus.
The most wit to the Bānyā, the least wit to the Jāṭ.

Aghānā bagulā pothyā tīt. E. Rus.
To the surfeited heron all fish is bad.
(Said of the *blasé*; sick of a good thing.)

Aghan, chulhe adhan.
Hearths are lighted in December.
(Said of things in season).

Agil khetī āge āge, pachhila khetī bhāg jāve. E. Agric.
A crop in time and good produce, a crop too late and failure.

'Āg' kahte mūṅh nahīṅ jaltā.
You don't burn your mouth by saying 'fire.'

Āg kā jalā āg hī se achchhā hotā hai.
Burnt by fire is cured by fire.
(Like cures like: application; treat a man as you find him.)

Āg ke āge sab bhasam hai.
After the fire it's all ashes.
(Cause and effect.)

Āg khāegā so aṅgāre hagegā.
Eat fire and pass live coals.
(As you brew so drink.)

Āg khāe mūṅh jare, udhār khāe peṭ jare.
Eat fire and your mouth will burn, live on credit and your belly will burn.

Āg ko dāman se ḍhāknā.
Covering a fire with your skirt.
(To cherish a serpent in your bosom.)

Āg lagante jhopre, jo nikle so lābh.
When the house is on fire, what is saved is so much gained.

Āg lagāe pānī ko dauṛnā.
To run for water after setting fire to the house.
(Hypocrisy.)

Āg lagāe tamāshā dekhe.
He sets fire to his house and enjoys the fun.
(Downright folly; also applied to great expenditure in fireworks, and hence in any extravagance.)

Āg lage mandhe, bajr paṛe barāt.
Fire burn the nuptial bower and lightning strike the procession.
(A curse.)

Āg lage pe billī kā mūt ḍhūṅḍnā.
To look for cat's urine when the house is on fire.
(To go far in quest of small and rarely found remedies to meet a present and great danger.)

Āg lage par kuāṅ khodnā.
To dig a well after the house is on fire.
(To shut the stable door when the horse is stolen.)

Āg lage to bujhe jal se, jal meṅ lage to bujhe kaise?
Fire you can quench with water, but how will you quench it if the water's on fire.
(You can reform the young criminal, but not the habitual:—old habits stick.)

Āg lage, to ghūr batāve.
It is a fire, but he calls it smoke.
(A cheat.)

Aglā kare, pichhle par āve.
The superior's mistakes fall on the subordinate.

Aglā līpā gayā sarāhā, ab kā līpā āge āyā.
Past acts are done and gone, commence the present.
(Said to one who claims rewards for long past services.)

Agle ko ghās, nā pichhle ko pānī.
Nor grass for the living, nor water for the dead.
(Said of the selfish or miserly.)

Āg lene āe the, kiyā āe? kiyā chale?
Come for fire is come and gone.
(Said of a short visit.)

Agle pānī, pichhe kīch.
First water, then mud.
(Delays are dangerous; the early bird gets the worm; the point is that those first at a well get water, those who come last get mud.)

Agī bhailī pachhlī, pachhlī paradhān. E. Wom.
The first became last and the last first.

Āg meṅ mūt yā Musalmān ho!
Make water on the fire or become a Musalmān.
☞ This proverb is said to have originated in the tyrannical reigns of the Mugal Kings who

forced Hindūs to embrace Islām. No Hindū will make water on fire as the latter is regarded as a god.

Āg pānī kā bair hai.
Fire and water won't agree.

Agṛam bagṛam, kaṭh kāṭhambar.
A chaotic heap of old wood and planks.
(Rubbish.)

Ahār chūke, woh gaë; beohār chūke, woh gaë; Darbār chūke, woh gaë; susrāl chūke, woh gaë.
Who fails to eat is undone, who fails in trade is undone, who fails at Court is undone, who fails with his mother-in-law is undone.
(The mother-in-law controls the gifts to the bridegroom in India.)

Ahāre, beohāre lajjā nā kāre.
In eating and trading there is no shame.

Āh-i-mardāṅ na ūhī zanāṅ. Mah.
Not a man's *āhe*, nor a woman's *ūhī* in him.
(He is neither man nor woman; said to a great coward: can't say 'bo' to a goose.)

Ahīr dekh gaḍaryā mastānā.
The shepherd got drunk, when he saw the neatherd drunk.
(Said of a poor man who imitates the follies of one more wealthy.)

Ahīr gāṛī jāt gāṛī, nāī gāṛī kujāt gāṛī.
The Ahīr's cart is a proper cart, the barber's cart is an improper cart.
(Every cobbler to his last.)

Ahīr kā kiyā jijmān? aur lapsī kā kiyā pakwān?
Who is client to an Ahīr? And what dainty is gruel?
(*Jijmān* is a client to a *prohit* or Brāhman family priest.)

Ahīr kā peṭ gahīr, Bāman kā peṭ madār.
The Ahīr's belly is deep, and the Brāhman's is a pit.
(Both classes are noted for voracity.)

Ahīr kī daheṅḍī, maṭṭyā surkhrū. Rus.
The churner is more valuable than the milkman's pail.
(The workman is worthier than his tools.)

Ahīr se jab gun nikle, jab bālū se ghī.
Good will come out of an Ahīr when butter comes out of sand.
(Can any good thing come out of Nazareth?)

Ahmad kī ḍāṛhī baṛī yā Mahmūd kī?
Is Ahmad's or Mahmūd's beard the largest?
(What care you or I?)

Ahmad kī pagṛī Mahmūd ke sir par.
Ahmad's turban on Mahmūd's head.
(Robbing Peter to pay Paul.)

Ahmaq se paṛī bāt, kaṛho aiṅṭa, toṛo dāṅt.
In dealing with a fool take your club and break his teeth.

Āī bahū, āyā kām; gaī bahū gayā kām.
The wife come, and work come; the wife gone, and work gone.

Āī bāt kā rakhnā kund-sahn honā.
It is stupid to suppress what comes into the mind.
(Used as an apology for saying something that is likely to be disagreeable to another person.)

Āī bāt ruktī nahīṅ.
The word in the mouth is hard to suppress.
(Out of the fullness of the heart the mouth speaketh.)

Aib karne ko bhī hunar chāhiye.
Even vice requires art.
(No royal road to learning.)

Āī gaī, pār paṛī.
What's come and gone is gone away.
(Spoken to one who would recall past transactions: Let by-gones be by-gones.)

Āī hai jān ke sāth, jāegī janāze ke sāth. Mah.
Come with your life, it leaves but with your corpse.
(A bad habit.)

Aile gaile, goṛ halukaile, pile kaur haluk. Bhoj.
With coming and going his knees shook, and what little he got he vomited.
(To work hard and fail.)

Aile joṛlā parkhore. F.
A relative has come, go and recognize him.
(Look before you leap.)

Aile kul ke agaro, dīyā butaile sagaro. E. Wom.
The girl came to the family and put out all the lamps.
(Said of a wife who brings ill-luck.)

Ail tiharvā, kharchaë ke gharbā, nā koi chinhe jāne, nāhīṅ etibarvā. Bhoj. Wom.
The cost of the festival has come on us, but no one knows and trusts us here.
(Natives look on it as a bounden duty to keep up the fixed festivals at any cost, the proverb therefore applies to a poor stranger.)

Āī māī ko kājar nahīṅ, bilāī ko bhar mangā. E. Wom.
To his mother not even lamp-black, to the cat as much as she asks.
(Said of the debauchee.)

Āī mauj faqīr kī, dīyā jhopṛā phūk.
When frenzy comes on the *faqīr* he burns down his own hut.
(Indifferent to the world's goods.)

Āī na gaī, chhochho ghar hī meṅ rahī. Mah. Wom.
A chance guest, she stuck to the house.
(A leech.)

Āī na gaī, kaule log gyāban huī. Wom.
A chance passenger, she leant against the pillar and became pregnant.
(Spoken of one who has incurred blame without cause. It is also a riddle, the solution of which is a loaf of bread (*roṭī*.)

Āī na gaī, kaun nāte bahin? E. Wom.
Never even seen, how she is sister?

Aiṅtvār jab jānye, jab haṭṭī līpeṅ bānye. Hin.
Know it's Sunday when the shopman leeps his shop.
(It being the invariable custom.)

Āī par chūke nahīṅ.
Lose no opportunity.

Aisā chāṭā ki dhoē kā chāchhā.
He licked it like the uncle of washing.
(*Chāchhā* is a superior; the proverb means therefore he licked it cleaner than it could be washed; said of a very sharp man.)

Aisā jaise rupaē ke ṭake bhunā liye.
As you change your rupee to please yourself.

Aisā kīyā dil gurdah, ki rupayā kīyā khurdah. Mah.
Such spirit and liberality! he has actually changed a rupee!
('Bang went six pence!')

Aisan buṛbak kaun hai jo khāt nahīṅ aghāē? E. Rus.
Every fool knows when his stomach is full.

Aisan suhāg morā nit uṭh holā. E. Wom.
May such good fortune be ever mine!

Aise ādmī ke dīde meṅ satthi kī pīch pasā dījye.
Fill such a man's eyes with rice water!
(For fear of the evil eye.)

Aise būṛhe bail ko kaun bāndh bhūs de?
Who would feed up such a decrepit old ox?

Aise chūtyā Shikārpūr meṅ rahte haiṅ.
Such fools live in Shikārpūr.
(Allusion to the custom of regulated illegitimacy in Shikārpūr.)

Aise gaē jaise gadhe ke sir se sīṅgh.
Clean gone as horns from the head of a donkey.

Aise gaē jaise mahfil meṅ se jūtā.
Vanished as shoes from a party.
☞ Shoes have to be left outside a house and therefore have a way of vanishing at parties, like umbrellas in England.

Aise hī tum ne soṅṭh bechī hai?
You haven't sold me ginger? Have you?
(*Soṅṭh* is a valuable article; said to those who demand money for doing nothing.)

Aise hote to Īd Baqrīd ko kām āte. Mah.
Had you been of any use you would have been used at the Īd and Baqrīd.
(The two great Mahammadan festivals. Said to the absolutely worthless.)

Aise par tīn harf bhejte haiṅ.
We send him three letters.
(*lām, ain, nūn*, spelling *lān*, a curse; a saying of the *literati*.)

Aise pe to aisī, kājal dīye pe kaisī? Wom.
So beautiful! how will she be with her eyes touched up with lamp black?

Aise ūt revāṛī jāēṅ, āṭā bech-ke gājar khāēṅ.
Send this fool to the sheep, he has sold his flour to eat carrots!

Aisī aisī chhaṭī bal bal jāēṅ, nau nau patrī bhatāīṅ khāeṅ. E. Wom.
Accept the invitation where you'll get nine plates of rice.

Aisī bahū siyānī, je paiṅchā māṅge pānī. E. Wom.
Such a clever wife! She asks for water on loan.

Aisī hotī kātanhārī, to kāhe phirtī mārī mārī? Wom.
Had you spun well, would you have been deserted and forlorn?

Aisī kahī kī dhoē na chhūṭe.
So said that it can't be washed off.
(The cap fits.)

Aisī laṭkī ki bhuī meṅ paṭkī. Wom.
So degraded as to touch the earth.

Aisī mekh mārī ki pār nikal gaī.
He struck the nail so that it went through.
(Said of an injury received from another.)

Aisī tere hī tale Gangā bahe hai?
O yes! you can make the Ganges flow?
(Said to a boaster: would you set the Thames on fire?)

Āī to ramāī, nahīṅ faqat chārpāī.
If she come, welcome; if not, at any rate bed.
(Half a loaf is better than no bread.)

Āī to rozī, nahīṅ rozah. Mah.
Earn and dine, or else fast.

Ajab Terī qudrat, ajab Terā khel, Chhachhūṅdar bhī ḍāle chaṅbelī kā tel.
Wondrous God's power! wondrous God's caprice! The musk-rat oils his head with jasmine essence!
(The beggar on horseback.)

Āj baservā niar, kal baservā dūr. E.
To-day's home is near, to-morrow's home is far.
(This world and the next.)

Ajgar kare na chākrī, panchhī kare na kām,
Dās Malūkā yūṅ kahe, sab ke dātā Rām.
The python doth no service, the birds no toil, But God giveth to them all, said Malūkā Dās.
("Consider the lilies of the field how they grow, they toil not, neither do they spin." Matthew vi. 28.)

Ajgar ke dātā Rām.
God gives even to the python.
(Said by a lazy fellow who spends his money, but will do no work when required.)

Āj hamārī, kal tumhārī; dekho, logo, pherā phārī.
To-day mine, to-morrow thine; see my friends, how changeable she is.
(*Varium et mutabile est fœmina.*)

Āj hai so kal nahīṅ.
To-day is and to-morrow is not.

Ajīran ko ajīran hī ṭhele, nahīṅ sir chauhaṭṭe khele. E.
Let the strong contend with the strong, or your head shall be a foot-ball for the wayfarer.

Ājizī sab ko piyārī hai.
Humility pleases every one.

Āj kā kām kal par mat rakho.
Don't put off to-day's work till to-morrow.

Āj kal kī kanyā apne mūnh se bar māngtī hain. Hind.
The girls of the period choose their own husbands.
(Very shocking in India.)

Āj kal rozgār unqā hai.
Now-a-days a livelihood is but a name.
(*Unqā* is a fabulous bird.)

Āj kal sher bakri ek ghāṭ pānī pīte hain.
Now-a-days the goat and the tiger drink at the same stream.
(The wolf also shall dwell with the lamb. Isaiah, xi. 6.)

Āj kal to tumhāre hī nām kamān charhī hai.
Now-a-days the bow is drawn in your name.
(The power is with you.)

Āj ke banyā, kal ke seṭh.
To-day a tradesman, to-morrow a merchant-prince.

Āj ke thāpe āj nahīn jalte.
To-day's cowpats are not burnt to-day.
(Dung fuel must of course be dry.)

Āj kī āj, āj kī baras din men!
To-day is to-day, or within a year!

Āj kidhar kā chānd niklā hai?
Which side is the moon to-day?
(An unexpected visit from a rich man.)

Āj kyā ghoṛe bech-ke soë ho?
Have you sold your horse that you sleep so soundly to-day?
(Free from the cost and care of keeping a horse. Uneasy lies the head that wears a crown.)

Āj main hūn aur woh hai.
To-day it's he and I!
(I will settle with him to-day.)

Āj main, kal tū.
I to-day, you to-morrow.
(The ups and downs of the world; every dog has his day.)

Āj mere mangnī, kal mere byāh, Parson laundyā ko koī lejā.
Betrothed to me to-day, wed to me to-morrow, who knows who will get the girl the day after?
(The uncertainty of the future.)

Āj mere mangnī, kal mere byāh, Tūṭ gāī ṭangṛī, rah gayā byāh.
To-day my betrothal, to-morrow will be my wedding, Broken thy leg and the wedding will be put off.
(The uncertainty of the future; don't count your chickens until they are hatched.)

Āj mue kal dūsrā din.
Dead to-day, to-morrow is but another day.
(Dead to-day and forgotten to-morrow.)

Āj nahīn, kal.
Not to-day, to-morrow.
☞ This proverb is founded on the story of an ultra pious Musalmān who used every night to pray under a tree that God in his love would draw him to himself. (*Khudā, apnī mohabbat men khench!* Prov.). One night a wag sitting on a branch overhead, let down a noose with which he began to haul up the devotee. "Not to-day," roared the pious man, 'to-morrow.'

Āj napūtī, kal napūtī, ṭesū phūlā sadā napūtī. Wom.
To-day barren, to-morrow barren; even when the *palās* tree blossoms still barren.
(This tree blossoms only in spring, when all nature teems with life. Used to express the total relinquishment of hope.)

Āj se kal neṛe hai.
To-morrow is not far off from to-day.

Āj tak paṛe hīng hagte hain.
His stools are still foul.
(Not cured yet.)

Ākal-khurā, jag se burā.
The envious man is the worst in the world.

Akāl mirt kī muktī nahīn.
There is no salvation for the suicide.

Akāl nahīn hai, kāl hai.
Not famine now, but black death.
(A long famine.)

Ākās bāndhen, Pātāl bāndhen, ghar kī ṭaṭṭī khulī!
He controls Heaven and Hell, and leaves his own door open!
(*Akās bāndhnā*, etc, 'to bind heaven and hell' the ordinary cry of an Indian charmer; the proverb is said of those that find fault.)

Akelā chale nā bāṭ, jhāṛ baiṭhe khāṭ.
Don't travel alone and dust the bench before you sit on it.
(Look before you leap.)

Akelā chanā bhāṛ nahīn phoṛ saktā.
A single pea can't break the oven.

Akelā hanstā bhalā nā rotā.
It is not good to laugh or weep alone.

Akelā Hasnū rove, ki qabr khode! Mah.
Let lonely Hasnū weep or dig the grave?
(You can't do two things at once.)

Akelā pūt kamāū kare, ghar kā kare, yā kachahrī kare.
When an only son is bread winner, let him work at home or at the office.
(He can't do both: Jack of all trades fails.)

Akele dukele kā Allah belī.
God protects the friendless and forlorn.
☞ A story is told of an old *ṭhag* who, on seeing a solitary traveller, made use of the proverb to intimate the fact to his comrades, who thereupon issued from their hiding place to rob and kill their victim. Also used in its obvious sense.

Akelī kahānī guṛ se mīṭhī.
One story is sweeter than treacle.
(One story is good till it is capped by a better one.)

Akelī lakaṛyā nā jare nā bare, nā ujārā hoï. Rus.
A single stick nor burns, nor lights, nor makes a flame.

Akelī lakṛī kahān tak jale? Wom.
How long will a single stick burn?
(One man cannot do the work of ten.)

Akelaā gail maidān phire, log kahil kī hardē gaile. Bhoj. Wom.
If she go out by herself they say she is with a stranger.
(Moral; a woman should go out of her house in company, or she risks her character.)

Ākhir apnī zāt par ā gayā.
After all his low birth asserted itself.
(Scratch the Russian and you will find the Tartar.)

Ākhir maroge, rupayā jor jor kiyā karoge?
You'll die in the end, so why hoard up your rupees?

Ākhthū, khatte hote hain!
I say, how sour they are!
(Sour grapes.)

Ālā de nivālā. Mah. Wom.
O niche, give a morsel.
☞ It is said that a certain king enamoured of a beautiful beggar girl, married her. In the midst of regal pomp, she could not relinquish the habit of begging, and therefore put morsels of food into the niches in the walls of her apartment and begged from them. The proverb is used to express that early habits cannot be rooted out. What is bred in the bone, will never come out of the flesh.

Ā lagā bhurbhure chane-vālā.
The street cryer is here again.
(Said of a noisy intruder; *bhurbhure chane* is the street cry of the seller of parched peas.)

Alakh Purakh kī māyā! kahīn dhūp, kahīn chhāyā!
How wondrous are God's mysteries! Here sunshine, there shade!
(Image drawn from the sun shining through a shower.)

Alā lūn, balā lūn, sahnak sarkā lūn. Mah. Wom.
I'll love you, and I'll serve you, but I'll steal your dinner.
(Said of a hypocrite.)

Ālamgīr Sānī, chūlhe āg, nā ghare pānī.
In the reign of Ālamgīr II nor fire in the stove, nor water in the pitcher.
(Misgovernment: Ālamgīr II was Emperor from 1754 to 1759 A. D.)

Ālas, nindra, aur jambhāī, Yeh tīnon hain kāl ke bhāī.
Sloth, sleep and yawning, Are the three brothers of death.

Al bal Khudā bal. Mah.
God's strength is the greatest strength.

Albelī ne pakāī khīr, dūdh kī jagah ḍālā nīr. Wom.
The ninny made *khīr* of water instead of milk.
(*Khīr* is a dish of rice and milk.)

Al farbah khuāh-makhuāh mard-i-ādmī. Mah.
A fat man is undoubtedly one of the first consequence.
(In appearance.)

Al gaī, bal gaī, jalve ke vaqt ṭal gaī. Mah. Wom.
She loves and she serves, but in the time of need she's off.

Alif Allah. Mah.
God is *Alif*.
☞ *Alif* is the first letter of the alphabet; hence, the proverb means 'I am the alpha and the omega.' *Alif* is always written alone, hence it means unconnected, lonely.

Alif ke nām Be nahīn jānte.
He doesn't know A from B.

Alif ke nām khutkā bhī nahīn jāntā.
He doesn't know *alif* from a stick.
(He doesn't know a B from a bull's foot.)

Ālī himmat sadā muflis.
A speculator is always poor.

Alīl kī rāē alīl.
The body sick, the mind sick.
(The opinion of a sick man is not to be relied upon.)

Ālim voh kyā, amal na ho jis kā kitāb par?
Is he learned, who does not act up to his books?
(Practise what you preach.)

Al jāūn, bal jāūn, jalve ke vaqt ṭal jāūn. Mah. Wom.
I'll love her and serve her, but when it comes to presents I'll run way.
(The niggardly.)

Al khāmoshī nīm razā.
Silence is half consent.

Allah Allah karo, khair māngo. Mah.
Call on God and ask his blessing.

Allah Allah, khair sallah. Mah.
Thank God, it is well over.
(All's well that ends well.)

Allah de, Allah dilāve, bandah de murād pāve. Mah. Wom.
God gives, and God makes man give, but man gives that he may obtain.

Allah de, bandah pāē.
God gives and man receives.

Allah do singh deve to woh bhī qabūl hain.
If God should even give me two horns, I should be contented.
(Spoken by one in misfortune, to express resignation to the divine will.)

Allah hai, to kiyā gam hai?
There is a God, so why do you grieve?

Allāh hī Allāh hai!
God is indeed God!
(An exclamation expressing astonishment or despair.)

Allah hī kī chorī nahīn, to bande kā kiyā ḍar hai?
As nothing can be hid from God, why fear man?

Allah kā diyā sab kuchh.
God's gift is every thing.

Allah kā diyā sir par.
God's gifts are on my head.
(Contentment and resignation: also a riddle, with a pun on the word *diyā*, meaning 'God's lamp is over our heads'—'the moon.')

Allah kā nām lo!
Take the name of God!
(Have the fear of God in you; said to one who tells a lie.)

Allah kā nām sachchā, sab jhūṭā hai jotān.
God alone is truth, all else is false.

Allah kare bāṅkā pakṛā jāë, Lāl Khāṅ ke lakṛe se jakṛā jāë. Mah, Wom.
Please God, the swell will be caught and put in the stocks.
(*Bāṅkā* is a vicious fop.)

Allah kare so ho.
It will be as God wills.
(*Deo volente.*)

Allah ho Akbar!
God is great. (Good god!)

Allah re, dīde kī safāī!
Good God! how shameless her eyes are!

Allah re, maiṅ!
Good God! what a fine fellow I am!
(Like me, God bless the example!)

Allah yār hai, to beṛā pār hai.
If God be our friend we have already succeeded.

Al qabz o dalīl ul-milk. A.
Possession presumes the right.
(Possession is nine points of the law.)

Ālsī sadā rogī.
A lazy fellow is always ill.

Amānat meṅ khāyānat to zamīn bhī nahīṅ kartī, Mah.
Even the earth does not commit breach of trust.
(*i. e.* it yields what is sown in it.)

Amānī, abadānī, ijārah ujāṛah.
Government collection is prosperity, farming is depopulation.
(*Amānī* is the direct collection of revenue by a collector on the part of Government in opposition to *ijārah*, or farmed revenue.)

Ām bo, ām khāo, imlī bo imlī khāo.
Plant a mango and eat a mango, plant a tamarind and eat a tamarind.
(As you sow so you will reap.)

Āmdanī ke sir sehrā hai.
Income is a marriage wreath.
(*i. e.* glory depends on wealth.)

Ām imlī kā sāth hai.
The mango is become the companion of the tamarind!
(*i. e.* is ripening at the same time. Used to express some very rare event, because the mango ripens in the hot season, the tamarind in the cold.)

Amīr kā ugāl, garīb kā ādhār.
The rich man's vomit is the poor man's food.

Amīr ko jān pyārī, faqīr ko ek dam bhārī.
The rich man loves life, the poor man grudges each breath.

Amīr ne pādā, sehat huī; garīb ne pādā be-adabī huī.
If the rich man offend it is well, if the poor man offend it is impertinent.
(The rich man's wealth covers a multitude of sins. "What in the captain's but cholerie word, Is in the soldier deemed rank blasphemy.")

Ām jhaṛe paṭāī, laṛikā rove 'dāī dāī.' E.
Only the mango blossoms are falling, and the child cries 'give, give! (mangoes.)'
(Crying for the moon.)

Ām ke ām, guṭhlīon ke dām.
The mangoes are mangoes, and the stones are money.
(You can eat the one, and sell the other; said of a good bargain, one that pays any way.)

Am khāne yā peṛ ginne?
Will you eat the mangoes or count the trees?
(We should enjoy the good things that are presented to us, without puzzling ourselves with fruitless enquiries about them.)

Ām machhlī kā sāth hai.
Mangoes and fish are fast friends.
(The unripe mango is often dressed with fish in native cooking.)

Āmne sāmhne ghar karūṅ, aur bīch karūṅ maidān. Wom.
I will take up my abode right in front, and there shall be no screen between us.
(Said of an impudent, shameless woman.)

Ām phale neo chale, aranḍ phale itrāë.
The mango in fruit bends down, the castor in fruit goes up.
(The wise man in office is humble, Jack in office is offensive.)

Ānand ke tār bajāte hain.
He plays on pleasure's harp.

Ānāṛī kā saudā bārā bāt.
Dealing with a clodhopper is confusion.

Ānāṛī kā sonā bārā bānī.
The clodhopper's gold is quite pure.
(Said of one who overrates the articles he has to sell: all his geese are swans.)

Anarth karat tāhe ḍar nāhīṅ. So jaiheṅ thoṛe din māhīṅ.
Who has no fear of doing evil, his days and months are few.

Ān banī sir āpne, chhoṛ parāī ās.
It's on your own head now, give up trusting to others.

An-birtak birat ghamlor bajāī.
The irregular priest makes a noise.
(Dissenters are always noisy.)

Andar chhūt nahīṅ, bāhar kaheṅ 'dūr, dūr.' Hin.
Within no abstinence, without he says 'away.'
(Hypocrisy.)

Anḍā sikhāve bachche ko ki chīṅ chīṅ mat kar.
The egg teacheth the chick not to chirp.
(Don't teach your grandmother to suck eggs.)

Anḍe hoṅge to bachche bahutere ho jāeṅge.
Have the eggs, and you will have plenty of chicks.
(Capital brings wealth.)

Ande kā Shahzādah.
The Prince of an egg.
(Simple or inexperienced.)

An-dekhā chor bāp barābar.
The undetected thief is (as honored) as your father.
(The greatest sin is being found out.)

An-dekhā chor sāle barābar.
An undetected thief is like a brother-in-law.
(He has free access to all parts of the house.)

Ande seve koī, bachche leve koī.
One hatches the eggs and another carries off the chickens.
(One beats the bush, another catches the bird: fools build houses for wise men to live in.)

Andhā āṅkh pāe hī patyāe.
When the blind man sees he believes.
(Seeing is believing.)

Andhā baglā kīchaṛ khāe.
The blind heron eats dirt.
(The ignorant always live in misery and wretchedness.)

Andhā bāṅṭe shīrnī hīr phīr apnoṅ hī ko de.
The blind man distributes his sweets among his own family.
(Spoken of one who gives every thing in his gift to his own relations. Nepotism.)

Andhā be-īman.
The blind man is unbelieving.
☞ It is related that a blind man at a feast, suspecting that the other guests might be eating with both hands, began to do likewise. It then occurred to him that they might be eating with their mouths too. So he applied his mouth to the dish as well. Finally he thought that the others might be running away with their dishes so he took his dish and ran away.

Andhā be-īman, bahrā bahishtī.
Blind is faithless, deaf is heavenly.
(The deaf man hears no evil.)

Andhā chūhā, thothe dhān.
The blind rat gets hollow grain.

Andhā dhund manohrā gāe.
Under misrule, they play the fool.
(When the cat's away the mice may play).

Andhā gāe, bahrā bajāe.
The blind man sings, while the deaf man plays.

Andhā gurū, bahrā chelā, māṅge haṛ de baheṛā.
A blind teacher and a deaf disciple ask for myrobolans and get gall-nuts.

Andhā hādī, bahrā murshid. Mah.
A blind guide and a deaf follower.

Andhā jāne āṅkhoṅ kī sār.
The blind man knows the value of eyes.

Andhā kahe 'maiṅ surag chaṛh mūtūṅ, aur mujhe koī na dekhe.'
The blind man says he will mount the sky to make water, that no one may see him.

Andhā kyā chāhe? do āṅkheṅ!
What does the blind man want? Two eyes!
(Spoken by one who is offered the thing which he most wishes for.)

Andhā kyā jāne basant kī bahār?
What does a blind man know of the beauty of spring?

Andhā kyā jāne lāl kī bahār?
What does a blind man know of the beauty of the tulip?

Andhā lakṛī ek bār khotā hai.
The blind man loses his staff but once.

Andhā mullā, ṭūṭī masīt.
A blind *mullā*, and a ruined mosque.

An dhan anek dhan, sonā rūpā katek dhan?
Wealth in corn is true wealth, wealth in gold and silver is vain wealth.

Andhā rājā, chaupaṭ nagrī.
A blind king and darkness in the city.

Āṅdhar ke gāe byāil, ṭahrī leke daurlan. Bhoj.
The blind man's cows calved, and every one ran with his milk-pail.

Āṅdhar kūkar batāse bhūke. E.
The blind dog howls at the wind.

Āṅdhar kūṭe, bahar kūṭe, chāval se kām. E.
Whether a blind man pound, or a deaf man pound, the rice is pounded.
(The work is done whoever does it.)

Andhā sipāhī, kānī ghoṛī, Bidhnā ne āp milāī joṛī.
Between the blind soldier and his wall-eyed mare, Providence hath created friendship.
(Companions in misfortune.)

Andhe āge roye, dono dīde khoye.
To weep before the blind is to lose both your eyes.
(Applied to one who makes his complaints to persons who will not attend to them: ye may cry your eyes out ere ye melt the heart of a wheel-barrow.)

Andhe Hāfiz, kāne Navāb.
Blind is Hāfiz, one-eyed is Nawāb.
(The title 'Hāfiz,' properly speaking one who knows the Qurān by heart, is given by courtesy commonly to the blind, and likewise Nawāb, my Lord, to the one-eyed.)

Andhe kā Ḳhudā hāfiz.
God protects the blind.

Andhe ke hāth baṭer lagī.
The blind man chanced on a quail.
(Said of one who comes in unexpectedly for something good).

Andhe kī dād nā faryād, andhā mār baiṭhegā.
There is no redress against a blind man, he will still strike all in his way.

Andhe ke hisāb rāt din barābar.
Day and night, it's all the same to the blind man.

Andhe kī jorū kā Allah belī!
God protect the blind man's wife!
(Her husband cannot look after her.)

Andhe kī lakṛī.
A blind man's staff.
(An only son.)

Andhe ko bhāgnā kiyā zurūr?
Blind men must not run.

Andhe ko jūā muāf hai.
The blind are excused from gambling.
(Used in excuse of an omission committed through ignorance or inadvertence.)

Andhe ne chor pakṛā, dauṛyo 'Miyāṅ Langṛe!'
A blind man caught a thief and asked a lame man to run after him!

Andhe rasyā āīne pe maren!
A blind bean dying for a looking-glass.

Andhere ghar kā dīyā.
The lamp of a dark house (a son).

Andhere ghar meṅ dhiṅgaṛ nāche.
The bugaboo dances in a dark house.

Andhere ghar meṅ sāṅp hī sāṅp.
The dark house is full of snakes.

Andheri rain meṅ baṛī jeoṛī sāṅp.
A rope is a snake on a dark night.

Andher nagrī, abūdh rājā, ṭake ser kakṛī, ṭake ser khājā.
When the city is dark and the king a fool greens and sweets both sell for a farthing.
(*i. e.* cheap and expensive things are sold at one price: gross injustice, downright anarchy:—the story is told of *Harbong kā rāj.* Elliot's *Glossary.*)

Āndhī āē baiṭh jāē, menh āē bhāg jāē.
When it blows sit down, when it rains run away.

Āndhī ke āge bene kī batās!
Using a fan in a high wind!

Andhī ke ām.
Storm mangoes.
(A windfall; a godsend.)

Andhī mā pūtoṅ kā nij mūṅh dekhe.
A blind mother never sees the faces of her sons.

Andhī nāyan, āine kī talāsh.
A blind barber's-wife searching for a looking glass.

Andhī pīse, kuttā khāē.
The blind woman grinds and the dog eats.
(Spoken of a person who does not take care of his gains: a fool and his money are soon parted.)

Andhoṅ meṅ kānā rājā.
A one-eyed man is a king among the blind.

Andhoṅ ne bāzār lūṭā.
The blind have plundered the market.
(To express something wonderful.)

Andhoṅ ne gāoṅ mārā, 'dauṛyo, be laṅgṛe.'
The blind are plundering the village, 'come on ye lame, (and help!)'

Andhrī gaīyā, dharam rakhwālī. Rus.
A blind cow, and faith her keeper.

Andhyārī gaī, ki chor?
Has darkness gone or the thief?
(Thieves of course work only in the dark.)

An-dokhī ko dokh, jis kī gatī na mokh.
To the slanderer of the innocent neither burial or salvation.
(Thou shalt not bear false witness.)

Andwā bail jīū kā zavāl. Rus.
An entire ox is the worry of one's life.

Aṅgrez bhī aql ke putle haiṅ.
Clever puppets these English are!
(Made up of, or bristling with inventions: *aql kā putlā*, idiom, inventive or clever.)

Aṅgrezī rāj, tan ko kapṛā, nā peṭ ko nāj.
The English reign, no clothing for the body, no food for the stomach.
(Said of direct taxation.)

Aṅgrez kī naukrī aur bandar nachānā barābar hai.
To serve the English is to tease a monkey.
(The meaning is that to serve the English is as dangerous as to make a monkey dance; every moment you are in danger of being clawed and kicked. The English are commonly described as having the waspish and uncertain temper of the monkey, and so being dangerous to approach.)

Angrezoṅ ne charsā bhar zamīn se sārā Hindustān apnā kar liyā.
From a plot of land the English got possession of all India.

An-honī hotī nahīṅ, honī hovan-hār.
What's not to happen never happens, what is to happen is going to happen.
(The doctrine of the fatalist.)

An-hot meṅ aulād.
The posterity of want.
(The poor man with a pile of children.)

Anī ke tale hazār baras.
A thousand years are at the sword-point.
(While there is life there is hope.)

An-jān kī maṭṭī kharāb.
The stranger is always unfortunate.

An-jān su-jān sadā kalliyān.
Fools and the wise are ever happy.

An kā goṛvā dhoē naunyā, āpan dhovat lajāē. E.
The barber washes others' feet, but is ashamed to wash his own.

An-kar chukkar, an-kar ghī, pāṅḍe bāp kā lāgā kī? E.
Another's flour, another's butter, what do they cost the cook?
(*Pāṅḍā*, a Brāhman cook: allusion to their borrowing flour and *ghī* for their sacrifices.)

Ankar dhan par Lachhmī Nārāyan.
On another's wealth he is Lachhmī Nārāyan.
(Master of wealth.)

Ankar khetī, ankar gāē, woh pāpī jo māran jāē.
Another's the field, and another's the cow: he is the sinner that beats her.
(Unwarrantable interference.)

Ankar sendūr dekh, āpan kapār phoṛe! E.
Seeing another's position he ruins himself.

Ankar sir kaddū barābar.
Another's head is a pumpkin.
(You may cut it off.)

Ankar sughar bar pānī ke halkor, apnā kubuj bar sutboṅ bhar korā. E. Wom.

Another's clever husband is like a splash of water; one's own foolish husband is like a plate full of meal.
(One's own little is better than another's all.)

Anke dhan par chor rājā.
On others' wealth the thief is a king.

Anke panyā main bharūn, mere bhare Kahār. E. Wom.
I fetch water for others, a *Kahār* fetches it for me.
(The greater fleas have lesser fleas upon their backs to bite 'em, The lesser fleas have smaller fleas and so *ad infinitum.*)

Ānkh bachī, māl doston kā.
Eyes off and your goods are your friends'.
(You must keep an eye on your property yourself.)

Ānkh chaupaṭ, andhere nafrat!
Blind of his eyes he hates the darkness!

Ānkh eko nahīn, kajrautī das ṭhāīn! E. Wom.
Eyes she has none, but she has ten pots of lamp-black (for her eyes)!

Ānkhen hain yā bhains ke chūtar?
Are they eyes or a buffalo's buttocks?
(Said of one who can't see what's before his nose.)

Ānkhen hūīn chār, man men āyā piyār; ānkhen hūīn eṭ, man men āyā khoṭ.
When eyes meet he is your friend: when eyes are turned he finds fault.
(The hypocrite.)

Ānkhen to khulī rah gaīn, aur mar gaī bakrī.
The she-goat died with her eyes open.
(A sudden death: arising from the custom of decapitating goats by one blow of a sword or a knife, which leaves the eyes open.)

Ānkh gaḍḍū, nāk maddū, Sohnī nām!
Hollow eyes and swollen nose, and Beauty her name!

Ānkh hai jab tak, to khush ātī hai bhaun:
Ānkh hī phūṭī, to kab bhātī hai bhaun?
The eye-brow pleases while the eye remains: doth the eye-brow please if the eye be broken?
(The brother-in-law is regarded with tenderness for the sake of the wife, when the wife is dead her brother is no more treated with affection. The *dāmād* or son-in-law is also called the eyebrow (*bhaun*) of his wife.)

Ānkh kā andhā, gānṭh kā pūrā.
Blind eyes and a full purse.
(A rich fool for customer: the Banyā's morning prayer.)

Ānko kā pānī ḍhal gayā.
The water of his eyes is spilt.
(He is lost to all sense of shame.)

Ānkh ke āge nāk, sūje kyā khāk?
With your nose before your eyes you can't see a bit.
☞ It is related that a man without a nose pretended that, relieved of this obstruction, he was enabled to see fairies and even the Supreme Being; and thus, like the fox who had lost his tail, he induced others to cut off their noses. When the disappointed victim complained of the imposture he was told that the new *panth* (sect) into which he was now admitted was in itself a distinction of which he should be proud. As no man liked to proclaim his own inferiority, he labored henceforth to increase the numbers and importance of the new sect of the noseless.

Ānkh kī badī bhaun ke sāmhne.
The fault of the eyes before the eye-brows.
(Spoken of one who mentions the faults or defects of another before his relation or intimate friend.)

Ānkh lajāī aur dahī parāī.
Cast down your eyes and the curds will be another's.
(Spare to speak, spare to speed: very shy won't succeed.)

Ānkh men lor, dānt nipor.
Weeping eyes and laughing teeth.
(Crocodile's tears.)

Ānkh men mail aur is men mail nahīn.
Dirt can get into the eyes but not into this.
(Very clean.)

Ānkh na dīdah, kārhe kashīdah! Wom.
Blind of the eyes the needle plies!

Ānkh na nāk banno chānd sī!
Nor eyes, nor nose, yet fair as the moon!

Ānkh ojhāl, pahaṛ ojhal.
Out of sight is over the hills.
(Out of sight, out of mind.)

Ānkhon dekhā ghaṭ paṛe! main ne kānon sunā thā!
Never mind what you saw! I heard it with my own ears!
(Used in reproof, to one who brings only reports in opposition to ocular demonstration: hearsay evidence.)

Ānkhon dekhī mānūn, kānon sunī na mānūn. Wom.
I believe what I see, but not what I hear.
(Seeing is believing.)

Ānkhon kā andhā, nām Nain Sukh!
Blind of the eyes and called Nain Sukh.
(Eyes' delight!)

Ānkhon kā andhā, nām Shekh Raushan!
Blind of the eyes and called Mr. Bright.
(Said of one who plumes himself on qualities which he does not possess.)

Ānkhon kā dekhā dūr kar, bhale mānas kā kahnā kar.
Don't belive what you have seen, but trust what a good man says.
(Winking at a trifling fault.)

Ānkhon kā kājal churātā hai!
He would steal the lamp-black from your eyes.
(He would steal the teeth out of your head: he would rob his own father.)

Ānkhon kā nūr, dil kī ṭhanḍak,
The light of my eyes, and my heart's delight.

Ānkho kā tārā.
The star of the eyes.
(The apple of the eye.)

Ānkhoṅ kā tel nikālnā.
Taking the oil out of the eyes.
(To strain or try the eyes.)

Ānkhoṅ kī sūiyāṅ nikālnī bāqī haiṅ.
Only the needles in the eyes remain to be extracted.
(The best part of the work has been done, only a small portion remains.)

☞ This proverb is based on a common superstition, among native women especially, that if an effigy be made of flour and pricked all over with needles and left in the *marghaṭ* or place of cremation the object of their enmity will be similarly pierced to death. They however believe that if the needles be again extracted from the figure by the aid of magic the dead person returns to life. The following variant of the story of the calumniated wife is very common, that once upon a time the wife of a man, thus slain, having extracted all the needles but those in the eyes was obliged to suspend her work in order to go to prayers, the hour for which had arrived. Her slave girl happening to come in drew out the remaining needles. The man returned to life, and believing that it was she who had drawn out all the needles, forthwith married the slave and repudiated his wife.

Ānkhoṅ meṅ charbī chhāī hai.
There's fat in his eyes.
(He is too proud to recognise his old friends: he can't see for smoke.)

Ānkhoṅ meṅ ghar kartā hai.
He takes up his abode in the eyes.
(He deceives, or he is beloved.)

Ānkhoṅ meṅ khāk!
Dust in the eyes!

Ānkhoṅ meṅ khāk ḍālnā.
Throwing dust into the eyes.
(To deceive one.)

Ānkhoṅ meṅ sarsoṅ phūlnā.
Mustard is growing in his eyes,
(He is blind drunk.)

Ānkhoṅ pe palkoṅ kā bojh nahīṅ hotā.
The eyes don't feel the weight of the eyelashes.
(One does not feel the burden of one's own belongings.)

Ānkhoṅ pe ṭhīkrī rakhnā.
To keep a potsherd on the eyes.
(To pretend blindness; to ignore.)

Ānkhoṅ sukh kaleje ṭhanḍak. Wom.
The delight of the eye, the joy of the heart.
(A son.)

Ānkh phaṛke dahnī, maiyā mile ki bahnī,
Ānkh phaṛke bāīṅ, bhaiyā mile ki sāīṅ. Wom.
Superstition.
When the right eye throbs it's mother or sister coming;
When the left eye throbs it's brother or husband coming.

Ānkh phere toṭe kī sī, bāt kare mainā kī sī.
Her eyes restless as a parrot's, she jabbers like a *mainā.*
(A prostitute.)

Ānkh phūṭegī to kyā bhauṅ se dekhenge?
When your eyes are out will you see with your eyebrow?
(How will you live when the breadwinner's gone? Commonly said to the daughter-in-law when she curses her husband.)

Ānkh phūṭī pīṛ gaī.
When the eye is out the pain is gone.
(Better an eye out than one which is always aching.)

Ānkhoṅ se sukhī, nām Hāfiz jī!
Blessed with eyes and called Mr. Hāfiz!
(*Hāfiz* is a term of respect toward blind men.)

Ānkhyoṅ-vāle, ankhyāṅ baṛī nemat haiṅ!
Sight is a great blessing, O ye that can see.
(The blind beggar's street cry.)

An-mile ke tyāgī, rānḍ mile bairāgī.
With a wife he is an ascetic, without a wife a monk.
(The *bairāgī* is a celibate with a wife living, the *tyāgī* is he who has no wife at all.)

An-mile kī kusal hai.
Loneliness is safety.
(Spoken of or by a person who has travelled a road infested by robbers without meeting any one.)

Annukh ghar meṅ nātī bhatār. E.
In a stranger's house the grandson is lord.
(Be civil to a cock on his own dunghill.)

Anokhe gāoṅ meṅ ūnṭ āyā, logoṅ ne jānā Panmeshar āyā.
A camel wandered into a strange village and the people took him for a God.
(By *anokhā gāoṅ* understand a village in which a camel had never been heard of.)

Anokhe ghar kaṭorī.
A cup in a strange house.
(Where it had never been seen before: applied to a mean person having acquired some trifle of which he is unreasonably proud.)

Anokhī jurvā, sāg meṅ shurvā. Mah Wom.
The silly hussy has made broth of the greens.
(*Shorba* is soup made of meat.)

Anokhī ke hāth lagī kaṭorī, pānī pī pī marī padoṛī.
An ignorant woman got hold of a cup and drank water till she burst.
(Set a beggar on horse-back and he will ride to the devil.)

Ān se māre, tān se māre, phir bhī na mare to rān se māre.
She'll try her voice, she'll try her eyes, if these should fail she'll try her thighs.

Ānsū ek nahīṅ, kalejā ṭūk ṭūk.
Not a tear in her eye, yet her heart is breaking.

Āntā titā, dāntā non, peṭ bharan ko tin hī kon,
Ānkhe pānī, kānhe tel, kahe Ghāg, baidāī gel.

Bitter for the guts, salt for the gums, stomach three parts full, water for the eyes, and oil for the ears, and there is no need for the doctor, says Ghāg.

Ant bhale kā bhalā.
The end of a good man is good.

Ānt bhārī to māth bhārī.
When the stomach is sick the head is sick.

Ant bure kā burā.
The end of an evil man is evil.

Ant matā so matā.
The last conclusion is the best.
(Second thoughts are best: the allusion is to the doctrine of the transmigration of the soul, by which a man becomes that thing in the next life which he last thought of in this.)

Antṛī meṅ rūp, buqchī meṅ chhab. Mah. Wom.
Your beauty is in your stomach, and your grace in your bundle.
(The complexion depends on the food you eat, and *chhab* or grace on the clothes you wear).

Antriyāṅ qulhu Allah paṛh rahī haiṅ.
The bowels are saying grace.
(The phrase implies excessive hunger: the belly chimes, it's time to go to dinner. *Qulhu Allaha Ahad*, Qurān, S 37 s 30, "say God is one," the ordinary Muhammadan grace before dinner.)

Āo, dugānah, chuṭkī kheleṅ, khālī se begār bhalī.
Come, Neighbour, let us twirl our thumbs, any occupation is better than doing nothing.

Āo jāo ghar tumhārā, khānā māṅge dushman hamārā.
Come and go, for my house is yours, but ask a dinner and you are my enemy.
(Sham hospitality.)

Āo, pīr, ghar kā bhī le jāo!
Come, father, take away the chattels too!
(*Pīr*, spiritual guide: a slap at the rapacity of these people.)

Āo, pūt sulāchhne, ghar hī kā le jāo!
Come, my sweet son, bring ruin on the house!

Āpam dhāp kaṛākaṛ bīte, jo māre so jīte.
Be quick yourself to strike; who strikes first wins.

Āpan bhal hoit, to jagattar parīt gārī.
If you are good, the whole world is your friend.

Āpan de-ke, buṛbak bane ke! Bhoj.
Give up your all, and be a fool!
(Benevolence spells bankruptcy.)

Āpan khet bambh loṭe, pāhī joṭe jāī la. Bhoj.
His own fields lie fallow while others' lands he ploughs.

Āpan māmā mar mar gailan, jolhā dhunyā māmā bhailan. Bhoj.
Leave your own uncles and make uncles of weavers and carders.
(Low people: a man is known by the company he keeps.)

Āpan peṭ to kuttā bhī bhartā hai. E.
Even a dog fills his stomach.

Ā, paṛausan, laṛeṅ. Wom.
Come, neighbour, let us fight.
(It is more painful to do nothing than something.)

Ā, pāṛausan, mujh sī ho!
Come, neighbour, and be as I am. Wom.
(Uttered as an imprecation by an unfortunate person, implying a wish that others may experience similar misfortunes.)

Āpat kāle marjādo nāstī. Ped.
Black calamity destroys orthodoxy.
(A man will drop his religious customs in time of need.)

Āp bhalā to jag bhalā.
A good man finds a good world.
(Good mind, good find.)

Āp bhūle, ustād ko lagāē.
For the mistakes of the pupil the master is blamed.
(No one owns his fault:—and the woman said 'the serpent beguiled me and I did eat' Gen. iii, 13.)'

Āp bītī kahūṅ yā jag bītī?
Shall I tell my own story or another?

Āp chale bhuīyāṅ, shekhī gāṛī par.
He goes afoot and his grandeur on a cart.

Āp ḍūbā to jag ḍūbā.
When I am drowned, the world is drowned.

Āp ḍūbe Bāmnā jijmāne le ḍūbe.
When the Brāhman drowns he takes his clients with him.
(Spoken of one who ruins himself and involves others in his disgrace.)

Āp ek kaheṅge, maiṅ das sunāūṅgā.
Abuse me once and I'll abuse you ten times.

Āp gaē aur ās pās.
He ruined himself and his neighbours.

Ā phaṅsī kā muōmlā hai.
Caught unawares.

Āp hāre, bahū ko māre.
He loses and beats his wife.
(Unreasonable anger: to injure the helpless in order to relieve one's temper.)

Āp har fan maulā haiṅ!
You are master of every art!
(Ironical: a Jack of all trades, but master of none.)

Āp hī apnī qabr khodtā hai.
He digs his own grave himself.
(He is the cause of his own misfortune.)

Āp hī kī jūtiyoṅ kā sadqa hai.
Your own shoes are your entertainers.
☛ The story goes that a wag, taking advantage of the religious obligation (*sunnat*) which requires Mahammadans to accept every invitation to an entertainment, once invited a number of Mullās to a feast. After they were assembled he gave secret orders to sell all the shoes left outside according to custom, and to provide the entertainment from the proceeds. His guests were profuse in compliments, saying: *Ap ne baṛī taklīf kī!* You have taken a deal of trouble. The host replied in the polite language of etiquette, *Ap hī kī jūtiyon kā sadqā hai.* Your shoes (you) have enabled me to be your entertainer!

Āp hī miyāṅ mangte, bāhar khaṛe darvesh.
The beggar is kept standing at the beggar's door.
(To express that he can not serve others who is always asking favours for himself.)

Āp hī nāk choṭī giriftār haiṅ. Mah. Wom.
His very nose and hair are captives.
(He is hemmed in with difficulties.)

Āp jāneṅ, aur āp kā īmān.
I leave it to you and to your conscience.

Āp kāj, mahā kāj.
Self done is well done.
(If you want a thing done well, do it yourself.)

Āp khāē, bilāī batāē.
He eats and accuses the cat.
(Say it's the cat!)

Āp khurādī, āp murādī.
Self eating and self regarding.
(Wrapt up in self.)

Āp kī khijālat mere sir aṅkhoṅ par.
Your shame is on me.
(I feel ashamed for you: your shame is my shame.)

Āp kī ṭikkī yahāṅ nahīṅ lagne kī.
Your loaf can't be baked here.
(Said to a person who expects something.)

Āp ko fazīhat, gair ko nasīhat.
Vicious yourself you preach to others.
(Practise what you preach.)

Āp mare jag parlo, or, *Āp mare sansār nās.*
When I am dead the world is gone.
(*Apres moi le deluge.*)

Ap Mīyāṅ Sūbedār, ghar meṅ bībī jhoke bhāṛ.
Abroad my Lord Governor, at home his wife fills the oven.

Apnā apnā ḍhaṅg hai.
To each his own way.
(*Quot homines tot sententiæ.*)

Apnā apnā dukhṛā sab rote haiṅ.
Each recites his doleful lay.

Apnā apnā gholo, apnā apnā pīo.
Each must make his own sherbet and drink it.

Apnā apnā hī hai, parāyā parāyā hī hai.
Your own is your own, a stranger's is a stranger's.
(Render under Cæsar the things that are Cæsar's, and unto God the things that are God's. Math. xxii, 21.)

Apnā apnā kamānā, apnā apnā khānā.
The earnings of each for the expenses of each.

Apnā apnā lahnā hai.
Each has his own fate.

Apnā bail kulhāṛī nāthab. Bhoj.
My own ox's nose I can bore with an axe.
(If I please, as he is my property: I can do as I will with my own.)

Apnā 'bismilla,' dūsre kā 'nauz bi'llah.' Mah.
One's own 'God bless him,!' to the other's 'God preserve me from him!'
(Allusion to the rhyming Arabic sayings.)

Apnā de-kar laṛāī mol lenā hai.
To part with your own and buy a quarrel.
(To lend money is to lose a friend.)

Apnā dīje, dushman kīje.
Give your own and make an enemy.

Apnā ghar, apnā bāhar.
Your own house is your own, inside or out.

Apnā ghar dūr se sūjhtā hai.
A man knows his own house a long way off.
(We have all sharp eyes for our own interests.)

Apnā ghar hag bhar, dūsre kā ghar thūkne kā ḍar.
You may foul your own house, but must not even spit in another's.

Apnā ghar sanjhaut nā, ankar ghar mūsar aisan bātī. Wom. Tir.
No wick in her own house, she sets another's house on fire.
(Enjoys others' property.)

Apnā ghar sattū nā, ankā ghar peṛā!
No barley-meal at home, but cake in others' houses.
(Said of the sponger.)

Apnā gū bhojan barābar.
One's own dirt is as good as food.
(One's own vices seem virtues.)

Apnā hārā, aur mehrī kā mārā, kaun kahtā hai?
Who tells of his own losses, or of the slaps of his wife?

Apnā hāth Jagan Nāth.
His own hand is Lord of the land.
(Said of a person with whom no one interferes; being allowed to have his own way.)

Apnā hī māl jāē, āp hī chor kahlāē.
His property stolen, and himself called a thief.
(An allusion to the practice of the Police of throwing the blame on the complainant when they can't find the thief.)

Apnā hī paisā khoṭā, to parakhne-vāle kā kiyā dosh?
If your money is bad the assayer is not to blame.
(Applied to one who resents the just censures of another on his worthless son or other relation.)

Apnā haiye hī nā, dusre ke dānī. E.
With nothing of his own he is generous to others.
(A vain boaster.)

Apnā ke birī birī, dūsre ke khīr pūrī. E.
She drives people away herself and begs dainties from others.

Apnā ke jure nā, ankā ke dānī. Bhoj.
With nothing of his own, he is generous to others.

Apnā ke roṭī tīn gīt gautī! E. Wom.
With one loaf for herself only, she sings a song of three!

Apnā koī nahīṅ.
No one is your friend.

Apnā kuttā barjo, ham bhīk se bāz āë.
Call away your dog, I have not come to beg!

Apnā lāl ganvāë-ke dar dar mānge bhīk.
Having lost his ruby, he begs from door to door.
(The results of extravagance.)

Apnā lenā kyā, parāyā denā kyā?
Is it difficult to take your own, or to give away another's property?

Apnā māl apnī chhātī tale.
Your own property is under your own breast.
(Eng. idiom, under your own thumb.)

Apnā maran jagat kī hānsī.
What's death to you is fun to the world.
(Thoughtlessness.)

Apnā mīṭh, ankar tīt. E.
Your own is sweet, another's bitter.
(One's own geese are always swans.)

Apnā mūnh to dekho.
Look at your own face!
(Before you abuse mine.)

Apnā nainā mujhe de, tū ghūm phir-ke dekh. E. Wom.
Lend me your eyes, while you go about blinded!
(Selfishness.)

Apnā nikāl, mujhe ḍālne de.
Take out yours and let me put in mine.
(Selfishness.)

Apnā pūt, parāyā ḍhaṭīngṛā!
One's own is a son, another's is a lout.
(Every one thinks his own child a prodigy of excellence.)

Apnā rakh, parāyā chakh!
Save your own, and spend another's!

Apnā sā mūnh le-kar rah jānā.
To take your own face and keep it.
(To hang down one's head, or hide one's face through shame.)

Apnā so naberā, parāyā so ḍhaṭkerā.
He has spent his own property and sets no value on others.'

Apnā ṭeṭar dekhen nahīn, dūsre kī phūllī nihāren. E.
He can't see the cataract in his own eye, but he sees the stye in another's.
("Thou hypocrite, first cast out the beam that is in thine own eye and then shalt thou see clearly to cast out the mote out of thy brother's eye." Math. vii, 5.)

Apnā ṭhīk nā, ankar nīk nā. E.
His own is not right, nor another's good.
(A fool himself he takes no advice.)

Apnā toshā, apnā bharosā.
Look to yourself for your own support.

Apnā ullū kahīn nahīn gayā.
My pigeon has not flown away yet.
(I have still some one to cheat.)

Apnā vohī jo apne kām āve.
He is a friend who renders essential service.
(A friend in need is a friend indeed.)

Apne aib sab līpte hain.
Every one whitewashes his own blemishes.

Apne apne khayāl men sab mast hain.
Every one is pleased with his own ideas.

Apne apne qadeh kī sab khair manāte hain.
Every one prays that his own cup be full.

Apne bachche ke dānt koson se mālūm hote hai.
The teeth of one's own calf are visible a long way off.

Apne bachche ke dānt har koī jāntā hai.
Every body knows the teeth of his own calf.

Apne bachche ko aisā mārūn paṛausan kī chhātī phaṭ jāë. Wom.
I will beat my child to break my neighbour's heart.
(To cut off the nose to spite the face.)

Apne bāolon roiye, aur ke bāolon hansye. Wom.
Cry over your own idiot (son), but laugh over another's.

Apne ḍhig paisā, to parāyā āsrā kaise?
With money in your pocket why seek another's help?

Apne dil kī gavāhī ko sach jān!
Believe what your own conscience says!

Apne ghar ke sab pādshāh hain.
Every one is a king in his own house.
(An Englishman's house is his castle.)

Apne ghar men ātā kis ko burā lagtā hai?
Who would refuse to let (money) come into his house?

Apne jhopṛe kī khair māngo!
Pray for the welfare of your own hut!
(Keep your breath to cool your own porridge.)

Apne kīye kā kyā ilāj?
There is no remedy for one's own acts.

Apne kīye ko bhugto!
As you do so must you rue!

Apne ko nā, ante, khablā khablā bante. E. Wom.
He gives to others and not to his own, and so is boiling water.
(A man who is surly to his own family and civil to strangers is as dangerous to touch as boiling water.)

Apne lage to deh men, aur ke lage to bhīt men.
If he strikes you, he strikes your body, if you strike him you strike a wall.
(Thoughtless of another's pain.)

Apne man se jānye parāë man kī bāt.
You know what's in another's mind from what's in your own.
(You judge others by yourself.)

Apne mare bagair surag nahīn.
You cannot see heaven without dying.

Apne Mīyān dar Darbār, apne Mīyān chūlhe duār.
My Lord goes to Court, and my Lord goes to the kitchen.
(Jack of all trades.)

Apne mūe Rām nahīn.
When you 're dead there 's no Rām (God).
(Invoke him whilst you live.)

Apne mulk kī bhalāī chāh.
Be loyal to your own country.

Apne mūṅh Dhannā Bāī. Or, *apne mūṅh Miyāṅ Miṭṭhū.*
According to herself my Lady Bountiful. *Or* according to himself my Lord Pleasant.

Apne mūṅh shādī mubārak.
He congratulates himself on his own marriage.
(Blowing one's own trumpet.)

Apne nain ganvāē-ke dar dar māṅge bhīk.
Putting out his own eyes, he begs from door to door.
(Having squandered away his own substance he now begs from others.)

Apne nain mujhe de, tū ghulātā phir.
Give me your eyes and go about begging yourself.
(Said in reply to one who makes an unreasonable demand.)

Apne pāoṅ meṅ āp hī kulhāṛī mārte haiṅ.
He cuts his own feet with his axe.
(He is the cause of his own misfortunes: he is his own enemy.)

Apne pūt kuāre phireṅ, paṛausī ke phere. Wom.
Leaving her own sons bachelors she marries off others' sons.

Apne se bache to aur ko deṅ.
Give to others when you can spare.
(Charity begins at home.)

Apne suī bhī na jāne do, dūsre ke bhāle ghuseṛ do!
Don't put a needle into your own (body), but thrust a spear into another's!

Apnī apnī chāl ḍhāl hai.
Every one has his own ways.
(*Chacun a son goût.*)

Apnī apnī chāl hai.
Every one has his own gait.

Apnī apnī khāl meṅ sab mast haiṅ.
Every one is pleased with his own skin.

Apnī apnī sab gāte haiṅ.
Every one sings his own song.

Apnī apnī samajh hai.
Many men, many minds.
(*Quot homines tot sententiæ.*)

Apnī apnī tuntunī, apnā apnā rāg.
Every one on his own pipe, and each his own song.

Apnī aql aur parāī daulat baṛī mālūm hotī hai.
One's own sense and another's wealth are always great.

Apnī aql ke āge kisī ko samajhtā hī nahīṅ.
He considers no one's wisdom before his own.

Apnī asal pe ā gayā hai.
His origin is asserting itself.
(To show the cloven foot.)

Apnī balā aur ke sir.
He lays his misfortune on others heads.
(He lays his troubles at another's door.)

Apnī ber ko gholam ghālā, hamrī ber ko bhūkam bhākā. E.
You make cakes for yourself, but I starve.

Apnī beṭī ko aisā mārūṅ, ki potoh trās kar jāē. Wom.
I will beat my daughter, that my daughter-in-law may learn to fear.
(*Pour encourager les autres.*)

Apnī chhāch ko koī khaṭṭā nahīṅ kahtā.
No one calls his own butter-milk sour.
(No one cries stinking fish.)

Apnī chilam bharne ko merā jhopṛā jalāte ho?
You burn my hut to light your pipe.

Apnī ḍāṛhī sab bujhāte haiṅ.
Every one extinguishes the fire in his own beard.

Apnī galī meṅ kuttā bhī sher.
A dog is a lion in his own lane.
(Every cock fights best on his own dunghill.)

Apnī garaz bāolī.
Need drives mad.

Apnī garaz ko gadhe charāte haiṅ.
For one's own ends the asses are fed.
(Allusion to the Hindū custom of feeding up asses with boiled pulse (*ghunghunyaṅ*) during the decline of an attack of small pox.)

Apnī garaz ko gadhe ko bāp banāte haiṅ.
To gain one's ends a donkey is called father.

Apnī guṛyā saṅvārnā.
To dress up one's own doll.
(Spoken of a father who defrays the whole expense of his daughter's marriage, her dress, ornaments, etc., without any charge to the bridegroom or his family.)

Apnī hāī aur par ganvāī.
To credit others with one's own feelings.
(To judge others by one's self.)

Apnī harāī marāī koī nahīṅ bhūltā.
No one forgets his own disasters.

Apnī izzat apne hāth hai.
Your honor is in your own hands.

Apnī jān sab ko piyārī hai.
Every one loves his own life best.
(Dear life: life is precious to all: greater love hath no man than this, that a man may lay down his life for his friends. John. xv, 13.)

Apnī karnī, pār utarnī.
Your own deeds will bring you to salvation.

Apnī kokh kā pūt nausādar. Wom.
The son of your own womb is invaluable.
(*Nausādar* is *sal ammoniac*, and is a very expensive and useful article for household purposes.)

Apnī liṭṭī par sab āg rakhte haiṅ.
Every one keeps a fire for his own bread.
(Each for himself.)

Apnī maslahat har shakhs khūb jāntā hai.
Each knows his own affairs best.

Apnī nīṅd sonā, apnī nīṅd uṭhnā.
Sleeping his own sleep, and waking at his own time.
(Independent.)

Apnī or nibāhiye, vā kī woh jāne.
Keep up your feelings, *he* knows about himself.
(Don't be the first to break up a friendship.)

Apnī pagṛī apne hāth hai.
Your turban (honor) is in your own hands.

Apnī Rādhā ko yād karo.
Attend to your own Rādhā.
(Spoken by way of reproof. Mind your own business. Rādhā is the name of Krishna's wife.)

Apnī ṭāṅg ughārye aur āp hī lājoṅ marye. Wom.
Expose your leg and die of shame.
(To wash the family dirty linen in public.)

Apnī to yeh deh bhī nahīṅ.
Not even these bodies are our own.
(Put not your trust in the things of this world.)

Apnoṅ kī ār koī nahīṅ uṭhātā.
No one will owe an obligation to his own relations.

Āp raheṅ uttar, kām kareṅ pachchham.
He lives in the north, and works in the west.
(A bungler.)

Āp rāh rāh, dum khet khet.
Himself in the road and his tail in the fields.
(His hand behind him plucks the fruit as he walks: a large business.)

Āp se āve to āne de.
What comes of itself let it come.
☞ The story is told of the wife of a strict Musalmān, who had forbidden the use of fowls for food, recounting to him with great glee how she had captured a fat capon for his dinner. The pious man was greatly shocked and desired her to throw away the unlawful thing. But the thrifty housewife remonstrated that she had spent a great deal of *ghī* and spices on the meal and his scruples were so far overcome that he consented to partake of the gravy only. Accordingly in deference to the good man's scruples, every bit of meat that came along with the gravy was being carefully put back, when he cried out in the words of the proverb 'What comes of itself let it come!' The story is also told of an orthodox *paṇḍit* who preached that egg-fruit (*baiṅgan*) is strictly forbidden as food. One day he was presented with a basket of them. He ordered them to be returned, whereon his wife suggested that what comes of itself is acceptable in the words of the proverb, to which the Paṇḍit agreed.

Āp se bhalā Khudā se bhalā.
Who is good in his own eyes is good before God.

Āp se gayā, jahān se gayā.
Gone from myself is gone from the earth.

Āp sune rāg se, faqīr sune bhāg se.
You hear (music) by paying, the poor hear by good luck.

Āp to garm karke sharbat pilāte haiṅ.
You put me in a rage first and then give me a cooling draught.
(Good at excuses.)

Āp zindah, jahān zindah.
While you're alive the world's alive.

Āqilāṅ pairavī-i-nuqat na kunand. Pers.
The learned don't need the dots.
(Allusion to the Persian character in which the diacritical dots settle the powers of the letters.—In the rough writing of the scribes, however, these are left out.)

Āqil ko ek harf bahut hai.
A letter is enough for the wise.

Aql baṛī ki bahs (Fac. *bhains*)?
Which is best, sense or talk? (Fac. a buffalo).

Aql chih kuttīst, ki pesh-i-mardāṅ bi-āyad. Pers.
Who is that bitch, sense, that she should come to heroes!
(Brute force.)

Aql kā dushman.
The enemy of wisdom (a fool).

Aql ke ghoṛe dauṛānā.
To gallop on the horse of inner consciousness.
(To soar on the wings of fancy.)

Aql ke nākhūn lo!
Pare the nails of your sense.
(Sharpen your wits.)

Aql ke pīchhe laṭh līye phirtā hai.
He is hunting down reason with a club.
(He is a sworn enemy to reason.)

Aql ke tote uṛ gaë.
The parrot of wisdom is flown away.
(He looks blank or foolish.)

Aql kī kotāhī, aur sab kuchh hai.
He has every thing but sense.

Aql-mand ko ek ishārah kāfī hai.
One hint is enough for the wise.

Aqlmandoṅ kī dūr balā.
Calamity keeps away from the sensible.

Aql nā gyān, thappaṛ khāë samajh bihān. E.
Nor sense nor wisdom, but he 'll learn by blows.

Āras, nindrā, aur jamhāī, yeh tīnoṅ haiṅ kāl ke bhāī.
Sloth, sleep and yawning, these three are the brothers of death.

Aṛhāī din kī saqqe ne bhī bādshāhat kar lī.
A water-carrier once reigned for two days and a half.
(Allusion to a well known incident in the *Alif Laila* (Arabian Nights). Said of one unexpectedly raised to power which he uses tyrannically: Jack in office.)

Aṛhāī hāth kī kakṛī nau hāth kā bīj.
Two and half ells of cucumber, and nine ells of seed.
(Spring wedded to winter.)

Arhar kī ṭaṭyā aur Gujrātī tālā!
A screen of pea-stalks and a Gujrātī padlock!
(Gujrāt in the Panjāb is celebrated for its locksmiths. Therefore it is obviously useless to lock a screen of pea-stalks, instead of a door, by so good a padlock.)

Aṛī dhaṛī Qāzī ke sir paṛī. Mah.
Whatever happens the Qāzī is responsible.
(Shifting responsibility on to others' shoulders.)

Arī javānī bāorī, ek bār phir ā!
Come once more, my bloom of youth!

Arkā nāin, bāṅs kī naharnī! E.
The inexperienced barber has bamboo nail scissors.
(These should be of steel.)

Armān bharī ghūghā. E.
A shell full of desires.

Arsaṭh tīrath kar āī tomṛī, tau bhī na gaī kaṛvāī.
The ascetic's gourd went on sixty eight pilgrimages, its bitterness remained nevertheless.
(Shall the leopard change his spots or the Ethiopian his skin?)

Ārsī men munh dekho,
Look at your own face in the mirror.
(Spoken to a person who seems to have forgotten himself and to betray an unreasonable pride: ārsi is a mirror worn on the thumb as a ring by married women.)

Aṛte se aṛ jāiye, chalte se chal dūr.
Fight with those who fight, but let the peaceable alone.

Arzān ba-illat, garān ba-hikmat. Pers.
Cheap and nasty, dear and good.

Ārzū aib hai.
Desire is a sin.

Asal asal hai, naql naql.
Real is real, a copy is a copy.

Asal kahe so dārī jār! E.
Speak the truth and be abused!

Asal ke asal hote hain.
Good stock, good issue.

Asal se khatā nahīn, kam asal se wafā nahīn.
Gentility has no flaw, base birth no fidelity.

Āsā mare, nirāsā jīve.
Want too much dies, want nothing lives.

Āsān nahīn hai rishta-i-ulfat kā toṛnā,
Mushkil hai bāle-pan kī mohabbat kā chhoṛnā.
It is not easy to break the bonds of love, even as it is hard to give up the love of one's childhood.

Asbāb men asbāb, ek chang ek rabāb!
His whole stock of goods, a jew's harp and a fiddle!

Ās birānī jo tāke woh jīwat hī mar jāe.
Who looks to others for help is a ruined man.

Ās buṛhāpā āyān huā sūt ku-sūt,
Yā ho paisā gānṭh kā, yā ho pūt sapūt.
When old age comes and you wax feeble, You'll need money or a dutiful son.
(Moral: lay up against a rainy day.)

Ashrafyān luṭen, aur koelon pe mohar!
Seal up the charcoal; never mind the gold coins!
(Penny wise, pound foolish.)

Āshiq andhā hotā hai.
The lover is blind.

Āshiqī aur khālā jī kā ghar!
The lover in his own aunt's house.
(He may do as he likes there with any girl, for his aunt will protect him: said to one under the protection of the powerful.)

Āshiqī aur māmā jī kā ḍar!
You a lover and afraid of my uncle!
(Her father he hath barred the door, Her mother keeps the key, But neither bolt nor bar shall keep My own true love from me.)

Āshiqī khālā jī kā ghar nahīn.
Loving is not like living in my aunt's house.
(The course of true love never does run smooth.)

Āshiq kī ābrū hai gālī aur mār khānā.
A libertine's honor is in abuse and buffets.

Āshiq ko Khudā zar de, nahīn, kar de zamīn ke parde!
God give the libertine cash, or hide him in the earth!

Āshiqī nā kīje to kiyā ghās khodiye?
If you have no right feelings go and cut grass.

Āshnāī karnā āsān, nibāhnā mushkil.
It is easy to make friends, but difficult to remain so.

Ashrāf ke laṛke bigaṛte hain to bhaṛve bante hain.
A nobleman's son in bad company is no better than a pimp.

Āshtī aur jān jī kā ḍar!
You a hero and afraid of your life!
(Spoken of a person who having undertaken a difficult and perilous enterprise, still looks for ease and safety.)

Asīl kī murgī ṭake ṭake!
A penny for a game-bird!
(Said of unappreciated merit.)

Āskatī girā kuen men, kahā, 'abhī kaun uṭṭhe'?
A sluggard fell into a well, 'Who's going to get up yet?' quoth he.
(The voice of the sluggard.)

Āskatī girā kuen men, kahā, 'yahān hī bhale'!
A sluggard fell into a well, 'I am all right here,' quoth he.

Āsmān kā thūkā munh par ātā hai.
Spit at heaven and the spittle will fall in thy face.
(Used to him who abuses those in a higher position: pride goes before a fall.)

Āsmān ke phaṭe ko kahān tak theglī lage?
If heaven break who will patch it up?
(Used towards the hopeless and spendthrift.)

Āsmān men theglī lagātī hai.
She claps a patch on to the sky.
(Said generally of a procuress very smart at her trade.)

Āsmān ne ḍālā, dhartī ne jhelā.
Cast down from the sky, and supported by the earth.
(Said of a deserted forlorn wretch who is not taken care of or looked after by any body.)

Āsmān se girā, khajūr men aṭkā.
Come down from the skies, and stuck in a palm tree.
(Said of a person who commences great things and is stopped by trifles. To swallow an ox and be choked with the tail.)

Assī baras kī umar aur nām Miyān Māsūm!
Eighty years of age and called Mr. Child!

Assī kī āmad chaurāsī kā kharch !
Income eighty and expenses eighty four.
(Spoken of one who spends more than his income: playing the prodigal; outrunning the constable.)

Assī, lassī.
(A man of) eighty is curdled milk and water.
(Second childhood.)

Astabal kī balā bandar ke sir.
The mischances of the stable are all upon the monkey's head.
(It is always the cat that did it.)

Āstīn kā sāṅp.
The snake in his sleeve.
(A secret enemy; the serpent in his bosom.)

Āstīn meṅ sāṅp pālā hai.
He is cherishing a serpent in his sleeve.

Ātā ho to use hāth se na dīje, jātā ho to us kā gam na kīje.
If it comes don't let it go, if it goes don't grieve for it.

Atāī nān khaṭāī, jab jī meṅ āī toṛ khāī.
Nature's cakes are eaten when the heart desires.
(Genius obeys its own instincts and will not be controlled.)

Āṭā nahīṅ to ḍalyā jab bhī ho jāegā.
If it won't grind into good flour it will at least be coarse flour.
(Better get it wrong than not try at all.)

Āṭā nibṛā, būchā saṭkā.
When the flour is spent, the cur is off.
(Spoken of one who deserts his friends when they have it no longer in their power to serve him.)

Ātā to sab hī bhalā, thoṛā, bahutā, kuchh,
Jāte to dohī bhale, dāliddar aur dukh.
All things coming are good, little, some, or great: Two things going are good, penury and pain.

Āte āo, jāte jāo.
Come when you will, go when you will.

Āte bhale, ki jāte?
Is it best to come or go?
(Said of a person disliked.)

Āte jāte mainā nā phaṅsī, aur tū kiyoṅ phaṅsā, re kavve?
The accustomed *mainā* escapes the snare, why art thou caught, O crow?
(A fool who knows a particular danger will escape when a wise man who does not know will fall into it.)

Āṭe kā chirāg ghar rakkhūṅ to chūhā khāe, bāhar rakkhūṅ to kavvā le jāe.
If I put the dough-lamp into the house the rats will eat it, if I put it outside the crows will eat it.
(To be between the horns of a dilemma: lamps made of dough are used by women when they make a vow to Devī, etc.)

Āte kā nām Sahjā, jāte kā nām Muktā.
When coming its name is Forbearance, when going its name is Relief.
(A coming misfortune must be borne with patience, when it is gone you are liberated.)

Āṭe ke sāth ghun pīsā.
The worm is ground up with the flour.
(Spoken of the poor when involved in the misfortunes of the great.)

Āṭe meṅ non.
Salt in the flour.
(To express a very small proportion.)

Āṭh bār, nau teohār.
Eight days and nine holidays.
(Luxury.)

Āṭh gāoṅ kā chaudharī, aur bārah gāoṅ kā rāo.
Apne kām na āe, to apnī aisī taisī meṅ jāo.
Chief of eight hamlets, and lord of twelve,
Out on him if he is of no good to me!
(Said of a disobliging rich man.)

Āṭh julāhe nau huqqā, jis par bhī thukkam thukkā.
Eight weavers quarrelling over (the equal distribution of) nine *huqqās*.
(To illustrate the stupidity of the weavers.)

☞ A story goes that a party of 10 weavers came across a mirage in the desert and thinking it a river they prepared to cross: on crossing of course the mirage disappeared, but they counted themselves over to see if they were all safe. Each man omitted to count himself, so that whoever counted made one missing. So they all began to howl over this until a stranger put them straight. Another story is that a crow, perched on the housetop, carried off a weaver's child's bread: before giving the child any more the weaver took the precaution to remove the ladder, thinking that the crow had come up by it! Another story is that a weaver being told by a Mah. soothsayer (*rammal*) that it was written in his fate that his nose would be cut off by an axe, was incredulous, and taking up an axe, he kept moving it about, saying. '*yūṅ karba to gor kaṭbā, yūṅ karbā to hāth kaṭbā, aur yūṅ karbā tab nā*'—If I do so I cut my leg, if I do so I cut my hand, but unless I do so' (but his nose was off)!

Āṭh kaṭhautī maṭhā pīye, solah makunī khāe,
Us ke mare nā roiye, ghar kā daliddar jāe.
Who drinks eight cups of tyre, and eats sixteen cakes, Weep not at his death, (for with him) the poverty of the house departs.
(Said of the glutton.)

Āṭh mile kāṭh, Tulsī mile jāt.
Let eight kinds of wood unite, and Tulsī has a caste!
(*Tulsī*, the sacred basil: a skit at the readiness with which a Hindū 'caste' can be formed.)

Āṭhoṅ gāṅṭh kummet.
Bay in all his eight joints.
(Horses of that colour are esteemed hardy and active. The phrase is used to express that a person is very cunning and wicked.)

Āṭhoṅ pahar Kāl kā ḍaṅkā sir par bājtā hai.
The Angel of Death drums night and day over our heads.

Atī aur Narāyan se bair hai.
God is an enemy to excess.

Āṭī bahu, janamtā pūt.
The arrival of a wife is the beginning of posterity.

Aṭkā banyā saudā de.
The entangled shopman does business.
(As the only means of obtaining payment for previous transactions.)

Atkā bhalā nā bolnā, atkī bhalī nā chup,
Atkā bhalā na barsnā, atkī bhalī na ḍhup.
Too much speaking, too much silence, Too much rain, too much sun are not good.
(Too much of a good thing.)

Aṭkal pachchū gair muqarrar.
All guess and no certainty.

Atkā phūlā soṅjhnā ḍāl pāt se jāē.
If the horse-radish tree flower heavily both wood and leaf are gone.
(Excess is ruin: the horse-radish tree has an excessively brittle wood, which constantly breaks under the weight of its flowers.)

Aṭkegā so bhaṭkegā.
To doubt is to be lost.

Ātmā meṅ pare to Parmātmā kī sūjhe.
When the belly is full you may see the Supreme Soul.
(*i. e.* God: when the belly is empty you are of course thinking of *it*.)

Attār kā shīshā, aur madārī kā piṭārā.
The druggist's bottle is the juggler's bag of tricks.
(The one professes to heal every disease, and the other can work all sorts of wonders.)

Aughaṭ chale, na chaupaṭ gire.
If you don't go a difficult road you won't fall headlong.
(Don't beat about the bush.)

Auṅdhā khāē lauṅḍā.
The child has fallen backwards.
(Attempting anything beyond one's powers.)

Auṅdhe mūṅh, chirāg pāoṅ!
May you be turned upside down!
(A curse: both the phrases *auṅdhe mūṅh* and *chirāg pāoṅ* mean topsy-turvy.)

Auṅdhe mūṅh dūdh pīte haiṅ.
He still drinks milk with his face downwards.
(He is yet a child: said to a fool.)

Auṅdhe mūṅh Shaitān kā dhakkā!
A headlong fall pushed by the Devil!
(A curse.)

Auṅdhī khoprī, ulṭī mat.
Crooked brains in a crooked skull.

Aurat aur ghoṛā rān tale kā.
A horse and a woman are yours while in your power.

Aurat aur kakṛī kī bel jaldī baṛhtī hai.
A woman and a cucumber grow fast.
(Allusion to the early maturity of women in India.)

Aurat kā khasam mard, mard kā khasam rozgār.
The husband of the woman is man, the man's husband is his livelihood.

Aurat kā kyā etebār?
What reliance is there on a woman?
(*Varium et mutabile est fœmina.*)

Aurat kā rāj hai.
A woman's kingdom.
(A hen-pecked husband.)

Aurat ke nāk na hotī to gū khātī.
Had a woman no nose she would eat dirt.
(Had not a woman a nose to be cut off for immorality she would go wrong shamelessly.)

Aurat kī aql guddī pīchhe hotī hai.
A woman's sense always lies in the back of her neck.
(She has always an after thought. She is wise when it is too late.)

Aurat kī mat mān.
Don't act on your wife's advice. *Or,* accept your wife's advice.
(According to the sense of the words.)

Aurat kī salāh pe jo chale woh chūtyā.
He is a downright fool who acts according to his wife's advice.

Aurat kī sāt be-wafā hotī hai.
Womankind is perfidious.

Aurat ko nā-dārī meṅ jāṅchye.
A woman is tested by poverty.

Aurat mard kā joṛā hai.
The woman is the pair to the man.

Aurat nā mard, muā hījṛā hai,
Haḍḍī nā paslī, muā chhīchṛā hai. Mah. Wom.
Nor man nor woman, but a dead eunuch,
Nor bones nor ribs, but stale offal.
(Abuse.)

Aurat par hāth uṭhānā achchhā nāhīṅ.
It is not right to lift one's hand to a woman.

Aurat pe jahāṅ hāth phirā aur woh phailī.
Caress a girl and she develops.

Aurat rahe to āp se, nahīṅ jāē sage bāp se.
A woman is chaste if it's in her, if not she would go with her own father.

Aur dinaṅ khīr pūrī, parab ke din dāṅt nipori. Wom.
On week days she lives on tit bits, on holidays she grinds her teeth.
(The eccentric woman; one who goes her own way.)

Aur kī burāī apne āge āī.
I have to pay for others' misdeeds.

Aur kī phullī dekhte haiṅ, apnā ṭeṭar nahīṅ nihārte.
He sees a speck in another's eye, but not the film on his own.
("Why beholdest thou the mote that is in thy brother's eye; but considerest not the beam that is in thine own eye. Math. vii, 3.)

Aur kī bhūk na jāne, apnī bhūk āṭā sāne. Wom.
She cares nought for others' hunger, for herself she kneads the flour.

Aur mazāq bhūl gaë, mere pīs āīyo!
You have forgotten all your jokes but beating me!

Aur rang kā gilahrā.
A squirrel of another colour.
(Change of subject, or appearance in an unusual dress.)

Ausar chūkī ḍomnī gāve tāl be tāl.
The songstress misses the tune and sings out of tune.
(Spoken of one who commits blunders from agitation of mind.)

Ausar kā chūkā ādmī, aur ḍāl kā chūkā bandar nahīṅ sañbhalte.
The man who misses his chance and the monkey that misses his branch cannot be saved.

Āvat hā hī, jāvat santokh.
Rejoicing when it comes, patience when it goes.
(The Lord giveth, and the Lord taketh away, Blessed be the name of the Lord!)

Āve nā jāve, Brihaspat kahlāve.
He knows nothing and he calls himself Brihaspat.
(Vanity: *Brihaspat* was a Rishi and regent of the planet Jupiter.)

Avval khesh, bādhū darvesh. Pers.
First yourself, then the beggar.
(Charity begins at home.)

Avval marnā, ākhir marnā, phir marne se kyā hai ḍarnā?
Sooner or later you must die, why then fear to die?

Avval taām, bādhū kalām. Pers.
Eat first and talk afterwards.

Āyā bandah, āī rozī, gayā bandah gaī rozī. Mah.
Come man, come food, gone man, gone food.
(With the birth of the child the mother's milk begins to flow.)

Āyā kar, tū jāyā kar, ṭaṭṭī mat khuṛkāyā kar.
Come and go as you please, but don't bang the door.

Āyā Kātak, uṭṭhī kutyā.
October has come, for the bitches are on heat.

Āyā kuttā le gayā, tū baiṭhī ḍhol bajā.
While she beats the drum, the dog eats her food.
(The story is told of a *mirāsan* or professional player.)

Āyā Mangsir, jāṛā rangsir.
November's come, now Winter's in his prime.

Āyāṅ rā chih bayāṅ? Pers.
Why explain the obvious?

Āyā Rājā Poh, jāṛe ko chaṛhā chhoh.
When King Poh comes the winter is at its coldest.
(*Poh* or *Pūs* is January.)

Āyā Ramzān, bhāgā Shaitān. Mah.
When *Ramzān* comes, the Devil flies.
(*Ramzān* is the Mahammadan's lent, during which the greedy mendicant has a bad time of it.)

Āyā to nosh, nahīṅ farāmosh.
If it comes I have a dinner, if not I don't care.

Āzādī Khudā kī nemat hai.
Liberty is the gift of God.

B

Bābā āë, tālī baje.
Father has come, let us clap our hands (rejoice).

Bābā āveṅ nā ghanṭā bāje.
Neither the father comes, nor the bell rings.
(A disappointment—the father of the house has to pray before any food can be eaten.)

'*Bābā jī! chele bahut ho gaë haiṅ.*' '*Bachchā, bhūke mareṅge to āp chale jāeṅge.*'
'Reverend father! how many are the disciples about thee!' 'My son, they 'll go of themselves as soon as they are hungry.'
(A rich man and his dependents.)

Bābā jī kā ṭhevas baṛ. E.
My lord has a very long thumb.
(He is overweening.)

Bābā jī ke bābā jī, bajantarī ke bajantarī.
He is both a priest and a drummer.
(Serves two purposes.)

Bābā ke rāje satuā mahgal, saīyāṅ ke rāje sab sahtal. Bhoj. Wom.
In my father's house I could hardly get flour, in my husband's house every thing is easy.
(Allusion to the frequent marriages of poor girls to rich men.)

Bābā mare, nihālū jāme, vohī tīn ke tīn.
Grandfather's dead, grandson is born, and still we are three (to feed).

Bābhan hūe, to kyā hūe? Gale lapeṭā sūt.
If he became a Brahman, what is it? Only the winding of string round his neck.

Bābhan ke baduā kahle, nān jāt latyāole. Bhoj.
Call a churl a gentleman and he kicks his own brethren.
(A jack in office overawes his old acquaintances.)

Bach, be Jummā, āndhī āī!
Get out of the way, Jummā, there is a storm brewing!

Bachche te khilāṅde dūdh te bhāt, baṛe hue to mār de lāt. Panj.
You feed a child on milk and rice, and when he's grown up he kicks you.
(The ingratitude of youth.)

Bache nar, hazār ghar.
Save a hero, save a thousand homes.

Bachhṛā khūṅṭī hī ke bal kūdtā hai.
The young calf skips at his tether.
(He dances to another's piping: said of a man who trades upon the interest of his friends.)

Bachnoṅ kā bāṅdhā khaṛā hai āsmān.
The sky is bound by its word (to stand firm).

Bad achchhā, bad-nām burā.
A bad man is better than a bad name.
(Give a dog a bad name and hang him.)

Badan meṅ dam nahīṅ, nām Zorāvar Khāṅ!
No strength in his body and he calls himself Mr. Strong-i'-th'-arm!

Badan pe nahīṅ lattā, pān khāēṅ albattā. Wom.
Not a rag to her body and she eats betel.
(Cheap swagger.)

Badāūṅ ke lālā.
Children of Badāūṅ.
(A city where all the people are said to be fools.)

Bad badī se na jāē, to nek nekī se bhī nā jāē.
If the wicked man will not depart from his wickedness, let not the good man abandon his goodness.

Bad ghoṛe kī mekh.
The peg of a vicious horse.
(A very vicious man.)

Bāḍhe pūt pitā ke dharmā, khetī upje apne karmā.
The father's good works prosper the son, but fate prospers the field.

Baḍhyā marī to marī, Āgrā to dekhā.
What if the ox did die, I saw Āgrā.
(I got something out of my journey.)

Bādlā maṅḍhe se nīm nahīṅ chhuptā.
You will not hide the *nīm* leaf by a covering of embroidery.
(It will still be bitter: murder will out.)

Badlī kī chhāṅ kiyā?
The shadow of a cloud!
(It is soon past.)

Badlī kī dhūp jab nikle jab tez.
Sunshine on a cloudy day when out is hot.

Badlī meṅ din nā dise, phūhaṛ baiṭhī pīse. Wom.
Not seeing thé day-light for the clouds the booby goes on grinding.
(Native women usually grind their corn in the very early morning.)

Bādshāhī riāyā se hai.
No subjects, no king.

Bādshāhoṅ kī bāteṅ bādshāh hī jāneṅ.
Only kings can understand kings' affairs.

Bagair sīkhe kuchh nahīṅ ātā.
Nothing can be learnt without learning.
(There is no royal road to learning.)

Bagal meṅ chhurī, mūṅh meṅ Rām Rām. Hin.
A dagger in his bosom, and politeness in his mouth.
(To describe a treacherous foe professing friendship: to smile in your face and cut your throat.)

Bagal meṅ īmān dāb-kar bāt karte haiṅ.
You are talking with your faith hidden under your arm.
(Talking against your conscience.)

Bagal meṅ laṛkā, shahar meṅ dhaṅḍhorā.
The child is in her arms, and she is crying through the city.
(The butcher looked for his knife, when he had it in his mouth.)

Bagal meṅ mūṅh ḍālo.
Put your head under your arm.
(Look to yourself.)

Bagal meṅ soṅtā, nām Garīb Dās.
A club under his arm, his name Mr. Innocent!

Bagal meṅ tūtī kā pinjrā, 'Nabī jī, bhejo!'
A parrot's cage under his arm and he calls on the Prophet to send another.
(Avarice: always asking for more.)

Bagaṛ meṅ bagaṛ tīn ghar, telī, dhobī, nāī.
Three are houses in the yard: an oilman's, a washerman's and a barber's.
(Low society.)

Bāgh bakrī ek ghāṭ pānī pīte haiṅ.
The lion and the lamb drink at the same stream.
(Said of a good government:—the wolf shall also dwell with the lamb and the leopard shall lie down with the kid......and a little child shall lead them. Isaiah xi, 6.)

Bāgh kī mausī, bilāī.
The cat is the aunt of the tiger.
(*i. e.* of the same breed.)

Bāgh mār nadī meṅ ḍārā, bilāī dekh ḍarānī. Rus. Wom.
She killed a tiger and threw it into a stream, and now she fears a cat!
(Loss of nerve.)

Bāgho ke mūṅh kehū dhoal he? Bhoj.
Who ever washed a tiger's face?
(Allusion to the habit of not washing a child's face for the first six or seven years to keep off *nazar*, the evil eye.)

Baglā bhagat.
A saintly heron.
(Spoken of a hypocrite who pretends to great piety and virtue, while he is in reality rapacious and wicked: allusion to the habits of the bird which stands silently motionless while watching for its prey, looking all the while as if it were meditating on holy things.)

Baglā bhī dhobī kā bhāī hai.
The heron is the washerman's brother.
(Always standing in water.)

Bāg lāgal nā, maṅgrā ḍerā del. Bhoj.
The garden not laid out and the mendicant has pitched his tent.
(The *faqir* of India has a habit of taking up his abode in any garden he fancies.)

Baglā māre, pankh hāth.
Kill a heron and you'll get feathers.
(Spoken of one who injures others without

benefit to himself : you can get nothing out of a cat but her skin.)

Baglī ghūnsa.
A blow under the arm.
(An unfair and secret enemy : a blow under the belt.)

Bahan kahe merā bīr pyārā, kāl kahe merā hai yeh chārā.
The sister says 'he is my dear brother,' death says 'he is my prey.'

Bahan ke ghar bhāī kuttā, sāsre jaṅvāī kuttā, kuttā pāle woh kuttā: sab kutton kā woh sardār, jo bāp rahe beṭī ke bār.
A brother living on his sister, a son-in-law living on his father-in-law, and he who keeps dogs, is a dog : but a father living on his daughter is a dog of dogs.

Bāhar ke khāeṅ, ghar ke gīt gāeṅ. Wom.
While strangers eat, the household starves.
(Said to a spendthrift and extravagant man making a show beyond his means.)

Bāhar lambī lambī dhotī, bhītar maṛve kī roṭī.
For going out an ample robe, at home the coarsest fare.

Bāhar miyāṅ alalle talalle, ghar meṅ chūhe pakkeṅ. Mah. Wom.
Abroad my lord has cakes and wine, at home he cooks rats.

Bāhar miyaṅ chhail chikanyā, ghar meṅ libṛī joë. E.
My lord abroad is a dandy, but at home there is a draggle-tailed wife.

Bāhar miyāṅ jhaṅg jhaṅgāle, ghar meṅ naṅgī joë. Wom.
Abroad my lord goes in gorgeous array with a naked wife at home.

Bāhar Miyāṅ Paṅj-hazārī, ghar meṅ bīvī karmoṅ mārī. Wom.
Abroad he is my Lord Governor, at home his wife is a victim of fate.
(A poor miserable creature.)

Bāhar miyāṅ sūbedār, ghar meṅ bīvī jhoke bhāṛ. Wom.
My lord abroad is a captain, but at home his wife feeds the oven.
(The occupation of a menial.)

Bāhar tyāg, bhītar suhāg.
Celibate abroad, he is married at home.
(Only saints are celibate in India.)

Bah mareṅ bail, baiṭhe khāeṅ turang.
The oxen labor and the stallion eats at his ease.

Bahrā bahishtī, andhā dozakhī.
The deaf for Heaven, the blind for Hell.
(The blind man is very suspicious, the deaf can hear no evil.)

Bahrā so gahrā.
Deaf is deep.

Bahrā sune Dharam kī kathā ?
Shall the deaf hear the word of the Law ?

Bahre āge gāonā, aur gūṅge āge gal, andhe āge nāchnā, tīnoṅ al bilal.
To sing to the deaf, to talk to the dumb, and to dance to the blind, are three foolish things.

Bahtā pānī nir-malā, bandhā gandhīlā hoë: Sādhū jan ramtā bhalā, dāg na lāge koë.
Running water is pure, stagnant water is foul : a wandering *jogī* is pure, no stain pollutes his soul.
(Because he is doing what he should.)

Bahte daryā meṅ jis kā jī chāhe hāth dho le.
All who will may wash in the running stream.
(Make hay while the sun shines.)

Bahte ko bah jān de, mat batlāve ṭhaur, Samjhāë samjhe nahīṅ, to dhakkā dede aur.
Let a man go to ruin in his own way, don't give him advice.
If a man heed not advice thrust him away.
(Quem deus vult perdere prius dementat.)

Bahū beṭī sab rakhte haiṅ.
All have wives and daughters.
(Said in reproof to one who casts amorous glances at another's female relatives.)

Bahū lālī, dhan ghar ghālī.
A flaunting bride is the ruin of the family.
(A nice wife and a back door do often make a rich man poor.)

Bahū sharam kī, beṭī karm kī.
A modest wife, and a fortunate daughter.
(Are the best.)

Bahuryā ke baṛ dulār, hāṅḍī basan chhūahī nā pāvas ! Tir. Wom.
Many caresses to his wife, but she must not touch the house vessels !
(Sham love.)

Bahut atahtāī, jūī ke kāl hā. Rus.
A great oppressor is always in danger of his life.

Bahut atīt, maṭh kharābah.
Many monks ruin the monastery.
(Too many cooks spoil the broth.)

Bahut aulād bhī gazab hai.
Many children are a misery.

Bahut gaī, thoṛī rah gaī.
Most of life has gone, and but little remains.
(Have mercy then ! A prayer.)

Bahut kathnī, thoṛī karnī.
Saying much, doing little.
(Much ado about nothing.)

Bahut sonā daliddar kī nishānī.
Much sleep is the forerunner of poverty.

Baid kare baidāī, changā kare Khudāī.
It is God that cures the patient, but it is the Doctor that takes the fee.
Or The physician tries his art, but God cures the patient.
(God healeth and the physician hath the thanks.)

Baid kī baidāī gaī, kānṛī kī ānkh gaī.
The one-eyed woman lost her eye, and the oculist his fee.
(Allusion to the native custom of only paying for cures.)

Bail badhiyā, sājhe adhyā. Agric.
The bull and the ox go half shares.
(The poorer cultivators generally have to go shares in the ploughing of their fields, and so go shares also in the produce.)

Bail kā bail gayā, nau hāth kā paghā gayā.
The bullock went taking his nine yard rope with him.
(A heavy and complete loss.)

Bail na kūdā, kūdī gaun : yeh tamāshā dekhe kaun ?
The panier has jumped in without the ox, who ever saw such a thing before ?
(Said to one who obtrudes himself where he is not required.)

Bail sarkārī, yāroṅ kī ṭiṭkārī !
The bullock is Government's and I enjoy the driving ! [hūṅ.

Bāingnoṅ kā naukar nahīṅ hūṅ, āp kā naukar
I am not the egg-plant's servant, but yours.
☛ The master was one day enjoying a dish of egg-fruit and extolling its excellence, when the servant chimed in and said it was indeed most excellent. One day, however, the egg-fruit having disagreed with him the master began to abuse it as a very unwholesome vegetable, and his servant then observed, that it was very unwholesome truly. 'Why' said the master, 'did you praise it before' ? 'I am your servant' he replied, 'not the egg-plant's !
(Sambo, it is a fine day. Is massa, it am berry fine day. Sambo, it is raining hard ! Is, massa, it am raining like de berry debbil !)

Bairī bol ghināone, marye apne kāl.
Your enemy's words are terrible, but death comes at its appointed hour.
(Threats don't kill.)

Bairī kā bol, basole kā chhol. [axe.
Your enemy's remarks are blows with an.

Bairī se bach, pyāre se rach.
Associate with your friend, and keep aloof from your foe.

Baisākh, Jeṭh dutiyāyām, Uttar ūncho chānd,
Yeh nehche kar jāniye, pirthī menh sulabh. Agric.
If the new moons of April and May have the northern horns high, there will be plenty of rain for the earth.

Baiṭhā baniyā kyā kare ? is koṭhī ke dhān us koṭhī men dhare !
The chandler has nothing to do, so he carries his grain from one store to another.

Baiṭhe baiṭhe to Qārūṅ kā khazāna bhī khālī ho jātā hai.
Even Qārūn's treasury would be dissipated by continued idleness.
(Qārūn, Korah, is the conventional oriental Mahammadan miser.)

Baiṭhe se begār bhalī. [idle.
To work without pay is better than sitting

Baiṭhī buṛhyā mangal gāe.
The old hag sits and sings away.

Bajā de, khanyā, ḍholkī ! Miyāṅ khair se āe.
Beat the drum, my songstress ! My lord has come in safety.

Bajā kahe jise ālam, use bajā samjho.
Āvāzah-i-khalq ko naqqārah-i-Khudā samjho.
What the world calls proper deem to be proper. The voice of the people is the word of God.

Bajā naqqārah kūch kā ukhṛan lāgī mekh.
Chalne-hāre chal base, khaṛā hūā tū dekh.
The drums for the march have sounded, the tents are struck. The army has started and you are still staring.

Bakhshī ke dhaggaṛ.
The *protegé* of the Lord Chancellor.

Bakhsho, bī billī ! chūhā lanḍūṛā hī jīyegā.
Forgive me, madam puss ; even a tail-less mouse can live.
(Though you have already pulled off my tail, spare my life : I am content to live without it. Spoken by one who has been injured by the calumnies of another, and entreats her to desist.)

Bakhtāvar kā āṭā gīlā, kambakht kī dāl gīlī.
The rich man's flour goes bad and so does the poor man's pulse.
(But it is nothing to the former and is ruin to the latter.)

Bakht deṅ yārī, to kar ghoṛe asvārī,
Bakht na deṅ yārī, to kar khā charve-dārī.
If fortune favours, own the horse.
If fortune favours not, be its groom.

Bakhtoṅ ke balyā, pakāī khīr ho gayā dalyā.
Such is the power of my fate that I cook rice and milk and obtain split peas.
(Ill-luck : *khīr* being much more expensive than *dalyā*.)

Bakht uṛ gae, bulandī rah gaī.
Great fortune is gone, greatness only remains.

Bakrā muṭāe tab lakṛī khāe.
When the goat waxes fat he gets beaten.
(Because he gets pugnacious : used to a jack in office.)

Bakre kī mā kab tak khair manāe ?
How long will the buck goat's mother pray for his life ?
(Buck goats are killed off early in India : the pitcher that often goes to the well will be broken at last.)

Bakrī jān se gaī, khāne-vāle ko maza na āyā.
The goat has lost its life, and the palates of the guests have not been pleased.
(Applied to a case in which one person has incurred a loss, without any advantage to the others.)

Bakrī kare ghās se yārī, to charne kahāṅ jāe ?
If a goat forms friendship with the grass, what will he eat ?

Bakrī kā sā mūṅh chaltā hī rahtā hai.
His jaws are always working like a goat's.
(A glutton.)

Bakrī ke nasībon chhurī hai.
The butcher's knife is the goat's fate.

Bakrī ne dūdh dīyā meṅgnī bharā.
The goat gave milk, but filled it with droppings.
(Applied to one who has conferred a favour with a very bad grace.)

Bakrī se hal chaltā to bail kaun rakhtā?
If goats could draw the plough who would keep oxen?

Bakrī yā sasse kī tīn hī ṭāṅgeṅ!
Goats and hares have only three legs!
(Applied to a person who having once asserted a thing however absurd, persists in it to the last without regard to argument or consequence. The saying is said to have been originated by a thief who, having stolen a leg of one of the above animals, and being charged with the theft defended himself with this absurd assertion.)

Bālak jāne hīyā, mānas jāne kīyā.
A child judges by the heart, a man by deeds.

Bālakoṅ ko sikhānā bālak-pan hī se chāhiye.
Teach a child from its earliest childhood.
(Teach a child betimes in the way he should go.)

Bāl bāl gunah-gār. Mah. Wom.
Faulty in every hair.
(That is, full of faults and imperfections. Generally used as an expression of humility by one who confesses his own faults.)

Bāl bāṅdhā chor.
An expert thief.
(Taken from the practice of shooting at a mark hung up by a hair.)

Bāl bāṅdhā gulām hai.
He is a slave tied up by the hair.
(Hopeless slavery.)

Bāl bāṅdhī kauṛī mārtā.
He can knock down a shell hung up by a hair.
(A good shot.)

Bal, be Jummā, terī dhaj!
Bravo, Jummā! I admire your tricks (*or* your figure.)
(Spoken in contempt: attitude is everything.)

Bāl haṭ, tiryā haṭ, rāj haṭ.
The obstinacy of a child, a woman and a king (is not to be overcome.)

Bal jāë rāj ko, motī lageṅ pyāz ko!
Perish the kingdom, where onions are as dear as pearls!

Bāl jinjāl, bāl singār.
The hair is a plague and an ornament too.

Bāl jinjāl: pale to pāl; nahīṅ, to mūchhoṅ ko ṭāl.
The hair is a trouble: if you can keep it in order, do so; if not, throw away even your moustache.

Bāl kā kambal karnā.
To make a blanket of a hair.
(To make a mountain of a mole-hill.)

Bāl kī khāl, hindī kī chindī.
He can skin a hair, and split a word into fragments.
(To describe one of a very subtle intellect: splitting hairs.)

Bāloṅ hāth chhināla, aur kāgoṅ hāth sandesā. Wom.
An assignation through a child is a message through a crow.
(Allusion to the notion that crows carry messages for women to their lovers.)

Bal to apnā bal, nahīṅ jāë jal.
Your strength is your own strength, another's is useless (to you).

Bālū kī bhīt, ochhe kā sang; pāturyā kī prīt, titlī kā rang.
A wall of sand is the base man's friendship; a harlot's love is the gorgeous hue of the butterfly.

Balvān kā hal bhūt jote.
The devil drives the strong man's plough.

Bāman bachan parvān!
The Brāhman is a true prophet!

Bāman beṭā loṭe poṭe, mūr byāj dono ghoṭe. Rus.
A Brāhman will twist and turn, till he does you out of both interest and principal.

Bāman jīme hī patyāë.
(1) The Brāhman has faith when he has eaten.
(The proof of the pudding is in the eating.)
(2) Trust a Brāhman when he has eaten.
(Allusion to the difficulty of feeding a Brāhman before satisfying his claim to a cash present (*dakshinā*). The proverb is capable of either construction.)

Bāman kā beṭā bāvan baras tak bauṅgā.
A Brāhman's son is a fool for fifty two years.
(Allusion to the habit of the caste of living on alms.)

Bāman kī beṭī kalma paṛhe.
A Brāhman's daughter would repeat the Muhammadan creed for this.
(To describe anything so delicious as to make one renounce one's religion for it.)

Bāman mantrī, bhāṭ khavās, us rājā kā hove nās.
With a Brāhman for minister and a bard for favorite the Rājā was ruined.

Bāman nāche, dhobī dekhe.
A Brāhman dances and the washerman looks on.

Bāman se dān māṅgte haiṅ!
To ask the Brāhman for alms!
(To make an improper request, as it is a duty to make gifts to Brāhmans.)

Ban ā kutte kī jo pālkī baiṭhā jāë.
It is a favored dog that rides in a carriage.

Banaj kareṅge Bāniye, aur kareṅge rīs.
Banaj karā thā Bhāṭ ne sau ke rah gaë tīs.
The Baniyā can trade, others can only imitate. A bard once traded and his hundred became thirty.

Banaj kare to ṭoṭā āve, baiṭh khāë dhan chhīje.
Kahe Kabīr, suno, bhāī santo, māṅg khāë so jīte.

Who trade suffer losses, who sit at home waste their wealth. Saith Kabīr, hear brother saints! who live by begging prosper.

Banaj men kyā bhāī-bandī?

What friendship is there in trade?

(Every one is for himself.)

Ban, bālak, aur bhains, ukhārī, Jeṭh mās yeh chār dukhārī. Agric.

Trees, babies, buffaloes and sugarcanes, These four suffer in the month of May.

(From the hot winds.)

Bandah ājiz hai. Mah.

A slave is powerless.

(Expressing resignation.)

Bandah bashar hai.

Man is but man.

(Apt to err.)

Bandah joṛe palī palī, Rahmān luṛhāē kuppe.

Man collects by spoonfuls, but God dissipates the whole jar at once.

(*L'homme propose mais le Dieu dispose!* Applied to the sudden destruction of wealth acquired by long and sordid parsimony.)

Bandar bhapkī.

The menace of a Monkey.

(A hollow threat.)

Bandar ek nisācharī layā karī apnī ardhangī:
Lāl Dās, Raghunāth dayā se, utpan hue Farangī:

A demon took a monkey to wife saith Lāl Dās, the result, by the grace of God, was the English race.

(Allusion to the belief that Raghunāth or Rāmchandar had promised Hanumān, the monkey king, in gratitude for the help given him, that the monkey race should reign in the Kāljug, or the present age, over Hindūstān.)

Bandar kā hāl muchhandar jāne.

Monkey-leaders understand monkeys.

Bandar kā zakhm (yā ghāo.)

A monkey's wound.

(Applied to those who constantly irritate a wound by rubbing and scratching.)

Bandar ke gale men motiyon kī mālā!

A pearl necklace round a monkey's neck!

(Pearls before swine.)

Bandar ke hāth āīnā!

A looking-glass in a monkey's hands.

(What's the use of it as he is so ugly!)

Bandar ke hāth nāryal.

A cocoa-nut in a monkey's hand.

(Said when a thing of value has fallen into the hands of one who cannot estimate its worth: Pearls before swine.)

Bandar kī āshnāī, ghar men āg lagāī.

Friendship with a monkey is setting your house on fire.

Bandar kī āshnāī kiyā?

What is a monkey's friendship worth?

(Said of any feeble or treacherous acquaintance.)

Bandar kī dostī, jī kā ziyān.

The friendship of an ape is the loss of life.

Bandar kī sannyā.

The army of monkeys.

(The British nation: also used to a large family with which it is dangerous to interfere, as they can all back each other up.)

Bandar kī ṭopī.

A monkey's cap.

(Applied to a restless person continually in motion. St. Vitus's dance.)

Bandar kī turat, phurat, surat, mashhūr hai.

The monkey's dexterity, agility and cunning are notorious.

Bandar kyā jāne ādī kā savād? E.

What does a monkey know of the flavour of ginger?

Bandar nāche, ūnt jal mare.

The monkey dances, and the camel is dying with envy.

Bande kā chāhā kuchh nahīn hotā, Allāh kā chāhā sab kuchh hotā hai.

What man wishes never happens, what God wishes ever happens.

Bandgī aisī, aur inām aisā!

Such service and such a reward!

(Spoken in reproach to one who makes a poor return for service done him.)

Bandgī bechārgī.

Service is helplessness.

Bandhī muṭṭhī lākh barābar.

A shut fist contains a *lākh* (for all you know).

(The value of the present made with the closed fist is exaggerated by the receiver, who wants to show how highly he was appraised.)

Bandhī rahe, na ṭake bikāē.

It remains tied up, and doesn't fetch a penny.

(Sold too late.)

Bāndh khīsā, le hissah.

Close your pocket, and keep your share.

Bāndhe sakelā, phire akelā.

An armed man may wander alone.

Bāndī jab shādī kartī hai, tab aisī hī kartī hai. Mah. Wom.

When her slave celebrates a wedding she does it as well as this.

(Said in contempt of an entertainment.)

Bāndī ke āge bāndī āī, logon ne jānā āndhī āī! Wom.

A slave girl got a handmaid, and the people thought a storm had come!

Bāndī ke āge bāndī, menh gine na āndhī. Wom.

When a slave girl gets a handmaid she takes no thought of rain or storm.

(Makes her work any how. No indulgence is shewn by low born people to their servants! Put a beggar on horse back and he will ride to the devil.)

Band ke jāē band men nahīn rahte. Wom.

Born in bondage does not remain in bondage.

(Misfortune will not always cling to one.)

Bane sab kī sarāhen, bigre kahen kambakht!
All the world praises success, and says that failure is ill-luck!

Bangālā jādū kā ghar hai!
Bengal is the abode of witchcraft!

Bangāle kī Bangālan jādū bharī.
The Bengal women are full of witchery.

Bangālī jo ādmī, to paret kaho kis ko?
If a Bengali is a man, what is a devil?

Bāngā men sayār gaile, kā orh aile, kā penh aile? Mag.
A jackal in a cotton field; what can he wear and what can he put on?
(Cotton is of no use to the jackal.)

Bānh chhurāē jāt ho, nibal jān ke moe;
Hirde men se jāoge to mard badāngī toē. Wom.
Shake yourself off and go, and think me powerless; If you go out of my heart then think yourself a man.

Bānh gahe kī lāj.
The shame of taking by the arm.
(And letting go: protect for ever or not at all.)

Bānh pakre kī or nibāhnā.
To take by the hand and support through life.

Banī ke sab yār hain.
Every body is friendly towards a rich man.

Banī ke sau sāle, bigrī kā ek bahnoī bhī nahīn.
A rich man has a hundred brothers-in-law, a poor man none.
(Hundreds will give their sisters to a rich man, but no one will marry the sister of a poor man.)

Banī phir besvā, khole phir kesvā. Wom.
A woman with her hair down is a harlot.

Banī to banī, nahīn Dāūd Khān Panī.
If I manage it, well; if not, there is Dāūd Khān Panī.
(I can go to him: that is if I cannot get employment in one place, I may in another.)

Banī to bhāī, nahīn dushmanāī.
If you agree you are my friend, if not my enemy.

Baniyā bhī apnā gur chhipā-kar khātā hai.
Even the grocer eats his own sugar in secret.
(Spoken in reproof to one who indulges in vice publicly without shame.)

Baniyā detā hī nahīn, kahe 'zarā pūrā toliyo.'
The merchant refuses to give and the other says 'give me full weight.'
(Applied to one who, so far from taking a refusal, goes on to insist on something better than that which was denied him.)

Baniyāē kī bat, re Udho!
He has the credit of doing it, Ūdho!

Baniyāē kī faqīrī bhī bhalī.
By practice even the profession of a pauper becomes profitable.

Baniyā jis kā yār, us ko dushman kyā darkār?
Who has a Baniyā for a friend what need has he of an enemy?

Baniyā ke sukh rāj, rajvā ke hīn,
Baidā ke pūt byādh na chinh,
Bhatvā ke chup chup, besvā ke mail,
Kahen Ghāg, pānchon ghar gail.
A prodigal Baniyā, a weak king,
A physician with an ignorant son,
A silent bard, an unclean harlot,
Saith Ghāg, will be ruined.

Baniyā māre jān, thag māre anjān.
The Baniyā cheats his friends, but the swindler cheats strangers.

Baniyā mīt, nā besvā satī.
A Baniyā is no man's friend, nor is a courtezan chaste.

Baniyā rījhe harre de.
When a Baniyā is pleased he gives you a myrabolan.
(His gifts are trifling.)

Baniye kā bahkāyā, aur jogī kā phitkārā.
From the Banyā's guile and the saint's curse (there is no escape).

☛ A countryman happened to possess a gold *mohar*, which he offered for sale. A *baniyā*, hoping to buy it cheap from the simple fellow, offered him five rupees, which the other refused in hopes of getting more. As the *baniyā* gradually raised his offer, the countryman's estimate of the great value of his prize and his reluctance to part with it increased, when the *Baniyā*, finding his offer of 14 Rupees was refused changed his tactics and, assuming the part of a friend, advised him not to part with the gold *mohar* for less than 30 Rupees. The countryman having in vain sought a purchaser at a price which was twice the market value of the coin, finally came back to the *Baniyā* and let him have it for 14 Rupees.

Baniye kā betā kuchh dekh hī ke girtā hai.
The Baniyā's son does not fall without seeing something.

☛ A Banyā's son having fallen down dropped a can of oil which he was carrying on his head. Some people took the sad news to his father, who merely said "he must have seen something on the road." He had picked up a gold *mohar*!)

Baniye kā jī dhaniye barābar.
A Banyā's heart is as small as a coriander seed.
(Very small indeed.)

Baniye kā mūnh grāh, aur pet mom.
The Banyā has the jaws of an alligator, and a stomach of wax.
(He pinches himself to hoard money.)

Baniye kā sāh bharbhūjā.
The grocer's banker is the grain parcher.
(The worthless lending to the worthless.)

Baniye kā salām be garaz nahīn hotā.
A Baniyā does not even salute without an object.

Baniye kā ullū.
The Baniyā's owl.
(Any worthless person or thing that is kept with great care. The phrase originates in the story of a foolish merchant who bought an owl at a great price, supposing it to be a hawk, and used to exhibit it as such.)

Baniye ke peshāb men bichchhū paidā hotā hai.
Scorpions are born from the Baniyā's water.
(*Bichchhū*, a scorpion, means a cunning fellow.)

Baniye kī uchāpat aur ghoṛe kī dauṛ barābar.
A Baniyā's account goes on running with the speed of a horse.

Baniye se syānā, so divānā.
Who is more knowing than a Baniyā is a madman.

Bāṅj achchhī ekaunj burī. Wom.
Better be barren than bear once.
(The barren woman is spared the loss of an only child.)

Bān jal gayā par bal na gaē.
Burn the rope and the twist of it remains.

Bāṅj bajauṭī, Shaitan kī langoṭī. Mah. Wom.
A barren woman is the Devil's breeches.
(The most wretched thing on earth.)

Bāṅj biyānī, sonṭh urānī. Wom.
To expend dry ginger for the delivery of a barren woman.
(Great cry little wool.)

Bāṅj kyā jāne parsūtī kī pīṛā? Wom.
What does a barren woman know of the pains of child-birth?
(He scoffs at pain that never felt a wound.)

Ban ke pāt. ban ke khaṛikā, Kerī karat Bāṛī ke laṛikā. Bhoj.
The woodman's children play with forest leaves and forest stalks.
(*i. e.* with what is most easily procurable.)

Ban men upje sab koī khāē, Ghar men upje ghar hī khāē.
If it grow in the field all eat it, if it grow in the house it eats up the house. Riddle.
(The pun is on the word *phūṭ* which is the answer of the riddle, and means both '*cucumber*' and '*dissension.*' The meaning is 'If it (cucumber) grows in the field every body eats it, if it (dissension) grows in the house, it eats up the house *i. e.* brings the house to ruin.)

Ban par līn bilārī, mūsā kaheli 'je hamrī joē!' E.
When the cat is safe in the forest the rat says 'she's my wife.'
(When the cat's away the mice may play.)

Bāṅs baṛhe jhuk jāē, aranḍ baṛhe ṭūṭ jāē.
The bamboo grows and bends, the castor grows and breaks.

Bāṅs chaṛhī guṛ khāē.
Climbing up the bamboo she eats sweets.
(Said of an acrobat or a dancing girl.)

Bāṅs ḍūben bauṛī thā māṅge.
The fool wants to see how deep the bamboo is in the water.

Bāṅs gun basaur, chamār gun adhaur.
The bamboo is tested in the bamboo yard, and the tanner in the hide-park.

Bāṅs ke bāṅs, mallāhī kī mallāhī.
I had to pay the freight, and had to suffer a beating from the boatman's bamboos as well.
(Double sufferings.)

Bāṅs kī jaṛ men ghamoe jāme hue. Rus.
A prickly shrub grows in the roots of the bamboo.

Bāṅṭal bhāī paṛausī barābar.
A separated brother is merely a neighbour.

Bān-vāle kī bān na jāē, kuttā mūte ṭāng uṭhāē.
A bad habit never leaves, as the dog will ever make water with his leg up.

Bāo ke ghoṛe pe savār hai.
He rides the big horse.
(To draw the long bow).

Bāole kī byāī gāē, sab meṭī le vā ke dhāē. E.
When the fool's cow calves all the neighbours run with their cans for the milk.
(Said of an oppressed people.)

Bāole kutte ne kāṭhā hai.
He has been bitten by a mad dog.
(He talks nonsense; he raves like a madman.)

Bāolī khāṭ ke bāole pāē, bāolī rānḍ ke bāole jāe.
A crooked bed has crooked feet, and a crooked woman has crooked children.
(Like father like son.)

Bāolī ko āg batāī, us ne le ghar men lagāī.
Show a fool fire and he will burn down the house.

Bāo na batās, terā āṅchal kyoṅkar ḍolā?
Pūt na bhatār terā ḍhendā kyoṅkar phūlā?
Wom.
Nor wind nor breeze why does your garment flutter? Nor child nor husband, what are you swaggering about?

Bāp baniyā, pūt navāb.
The father a tradesman, and the son a lord.
(The father to the plough, the son to the bow.)

Bāp beṭon kī laṛāī kyā?
What is a family quarrel?
(Nothing of any consequence.)

Bāp bhalā na bhaiyā, sab se bhalā rupaiyā.
Nor father nor brother is a good thing, the best thing of all is a rupee.

Bāp bhikārī, pūt bhanḍārī.
The father a beggar, the son a large stock owner.
(Each has his own fate.)

Bāp chup chup, pūt lap jhap!
The father so quiet, the son such a chatterbox!

Bāp deotā, pūt rāchchhas.
The father a god, the son a devil.

Bāp dikhā, yā gor batā.
Show your father, or point out his grave.
(Spoken when a thing is lost and one is desired either to produce it, or show how it is gone.)

Bāpe pūt, pitā par ghoṛā, bahut nahīṅ to thoṛā hī thoṛā.
The son resembles his father, the colt his sire; if not exactly yet somewhat.

Bāp kā nām Damṛī, beṭvā kā nām Chhakauṛyā, nātī kā nām Pachkauṛyā, tīn pursā bītī chhadām na pūrā bhayā. E. Wom.
The father Damṛī, the son Chhakauṛī, the grandson Pachkauṛī: three generations passed and a *chhadām* was not complete.
(The point is that even after three generations of labour the family could not earn its expenses: *damṛī* = 12 *kauṛis*, and *chhadām* = 24 *kauṛis*, so the calculation for three generations is 23 *kauṛis* or one *kauṛī* short of the amount required.)

Bāp kā nām Sāg-pāt, beṭe kā nām Paror.
The father Mr. Greens, the son Mr. Vegetable.

Bāp kā nām Ūā Pūā, pūt kā nām Jīte Khāṅ.
The father's name was Mr. So-and-So, the son's name is My Lord Conqueror.

Bāp kanṭak, pūt Hātim.
The father a miser, the son a Hātim.
(Hātim Tāī is the conventional hero of eastern generosity.)

Bāp kare bāp ke āge āē, beṭā kare beṭe ke āge āē.
The father's sin upon the father, the son's upon the son.
(Whoever performs any action he alone shall receive the reward or punishment of it. Make your own bed and lie on it.)

Bāp ke gale meṅ mogre, pūt ke gale meṅ rud-rāchh.
The father wore wooden beads about his neck, the son has a precious necklace.

Bāp kī barāt beṭā jāē !
The son attends his father's wedding.
(Second marriage.)

Bāp kī ṭāṅg tale āī, aur mā kahlāī.
The father's mistress is called mother.
(Undeserved honor.)

Bāp ko āṭā na mile jo īṅdhan ko bheje !
May my father get no flour, that I may be sent to fetch fuel to bake it !
(Put into the mouth of an undutiful son reluctant to do any thing for his parents.)

Bāp kuṅjṛā, beṭā shekh.
The father a green-grocer, and the son a priest.

Bāp marā, ghar beṭā bhayā, is kā ṭoṭā us meṅ gayā.
The father dead, and a son born, the loss of the one is made up by the other.

Bāp mare kā bair lenā.
To take vengeance for a murdered father.
(The *vendetta* : blood feud.)

Bāp mare par bail baṭeṅge.
Upon the death of the father the oxen will be distributed.
(Waiting for the dead man's shoes.)

Bāp marihen tab pūt rāj karihen. E.
When the father dies the son reigns.
(*Le roi est mort : vive le roi !*)

Bāp marle kuṅar, māē marle tuar. E.
Father dies and you are a bachelor, mother dies and you are an orphan.
(Among the poor if the father die the son cannot marry—the mother while alive can always keeps the child.)

Bāp na dāde, Mār Khāṅ zāde.
Nor sire nor grandsire and descended from Mār Khāṅ.
(Spoken of a mean person who shows an un-becoming pride.)

Bāp nā dāde, sāt pu-ht harāmzāde.
Not only sire, and grandsire, but seven generations of bastards.

Bāp na mārī piḍrī, beṭā tīr-andāz.
The father never shot a tomtit and the son is an archer.
(Spoken in contempt of a great boaster.)

Bāp nar-kaṭiyā, pūt bhagatiyā !
The father a cut-throat, the son a saint !

Bāp ojhā, māṅ ḍāyan.
The father a wizard, the mother a witch.

Bāp panḍit, pūt chhinrā.
The father a doctor, the son a rake.

Bāp peṭ meṅ, pūt byāhe chalā !
The father in the stomach, and the son goes to the wedding !

Bāp se bair, pūt se sagāī.
Enmity with the father, friendship with the son. [*chūlhā.*

Bāqī kā mārā gāoṅ, aur chilmoṅ kā mārā
The village is ruined with arrears (of revenue), as the fire is put out by the pipe.
(With frequent demands upon it.)

Bāqī nām Allah kā.
The balance will be the name of God.
(Said to a boaster—after so great a man as you there's nothing but God left.)

Baṛā bol Qāzī kā pyādah. [comes.
He talks big and the Qāzī's messenger
(He boasts of authority he does not possess and is exposed by being carried before the judge.)

Bārah bānī kā hogayā.
He is again restored to youth.

Bārah baras Dillī meṅ rahe bhāṛ hī jhoṅkā.
Twelve years in Dehlī and only a fireman !
(For parching grain. Well bred to evil wed.)

Bārah baras Dillī meṅ rahe, mahsūl nahīṅ diyā 'kyā karte the' ? 'bhāṛ jhokte the' !
He lived twelve years at Dehlī and paid no taxes ; 'what did he do' ? why, he tended the oxen !
(i. e. he did not better his situation in life.)

Bārah baras kā koṛhī ek hī Etwār pāk!
A twelve years' leper cured in one Sunday!

Bārah baras kāṭh men rahe, chaltī dafa pāon se gaë.
Twelve years in the stocks, no sooner free than he broke his leg.
(In his impatience to get out.)

Bārah baras kī kannyā, aur chhaṭī rāt kā bar, man māne so kar.
The bride of twelve years and the bridegroom of six days old may do as they will.
(An allusion to child marriage and its evils.)

Bārah baras kī paṭhiyā, bīs baras kī ṭaṭyā,
At twelve years a maiden and at twenty a rickety screen.
(Allusion to the early maturity of women in India.)

Bārah baras pīchhe kūṛī ke bhī din phirte hain.
After twelve years, even a dung hill begins to prosper.
(Every dog has his day: the notion is that the fortune of every thing changes every twelve years.)

Bārah baras sei Kāshī, marne ko Maggah kī māṭī.
He lived in Kāshī (Benares) for twelve years, but it was his lot to die in Maggadh (Bihār).
(Among the Hindūs it is esteemed good to die within the limits of Benares, as in that case, they conceive they obtain release from future birth; whereas if they die in Maggadh (Bihār), they transmigrate into asses.)

Bārah bāṭ, aṭṭhārah paiṅḍe.
Twelve roads, eighteen foot paths.
(He is puzzled which way to take: *embarras de richesse.*)

Bārah gāon kā chaudhrī, assī gāon kā rāo:
Apne kām na āë, to aisī taisī men jāo.
Squire of 12 villages, and lord of 80:
Let him be: he is of no use to me.

Baṛā hī pāñch hai!
He is very sharp.

Bārah men tīn gaë to rahī khāk.
If out of twelve months three are gone, nothing remains!
(The rain on which fertility depends falls in three months, therefore, if those are gone the remainder is good for nothing. Applied to one disappointed in the object of his labor or his journey.)

Bārah-vafāt kī khichṛī āj hai to kal nahīn. Mah.
The *khichṛī* of the *bārah-vafāt* is only for to-day, not for to-morrow.
(This is the *khichṛī* (rice and peas) of the twelfth of Safar, on which day Mahammad died, and on which the oblation called Fātiha is made by all Musalmāns with this kind of food. To express a present abundance which will not last.)

Baṛā jāne kiyā, bālak jāne hiyā.
The adult looks to deeds, the child to love.

Baṛā nivālā khāiye, baṛā bol na boliye.
Swallow a large mouthful, but speak not harshly.
(Submit to distress yourself rather than give pain to others.)

Baras bhar men sakhī sūm barābar ho jāte hain.
The miser's and the liberal man's accounts balance at the end of year.

Barātī kināre hojāënge, kām dulhā dulhan hī se paṛegā.
All the attendants at the marriage procession will return home, but the business will be continued by the bride and bridegroom.
(In India the bride and bridegroom have many ceremonies to perform after the procession is over.)

Barātiyon ko khāne kī chāh, dulhā ko dulhan kī chāh.
The bridegroom longs for his bride and the guests for the dinner.

Barāt kā chhailā, Sāvan kā khailā.
The joy at a marriage is like grass in the rains.
(Very abundant.)

Barāt kī sobhā bājā, arthī kī sobhā sāṅpā.
Music is becoming at weddings, and wailing at funerals.

Bardhā ek, gāon dui jot; kail baṭiyā lāgal pot? E. Agric.
Only one ox and the whole village lands to plough; how is the turn and turn about to be managed?

Baṛe anpūrnā bane hain.
He sets up to be very charitable.

Baṛe baṛe bahe jāën, gadhā pūchhe kitnā pānī?
The great are drowned and the jackass asks if there is much water.
(He rushes on where angels fear to tread.)

Baṛe baṛe dah gae, baṭai kahe kitnā pānī?
The great are carried away and the traveller asks if there is much water.

Baṛe bartan kī khurchan bhī bahut hai.
Even the scrapings of a large vessel are many.
(Every little counts: many a little makes a muckle.)

Baṛe bikhau bikhdhar ko, chalat sīs nivāë,
Thoṛe bikhau bichchhū ko, chalat dum algāë.
The deadly serpent creeps with bended head, but the milder scorpion walks with his tail up.
(Still waters run deep.)

Baṛe bol kā sir nīchā.
Big words hang the head.
(Pride goes before a fall.)

Baṛe chor kā hissā nahīn!
No share for the master thief!
(He takes what he likes: the lion's share.)

Baṛe ghar paṛiye, patthar ḍho ḍho māriye. Wom.
To marry into a large family is to carry stones.
(If married to a man of many relations the

wife will have to do much work according to Indian custom.)

Bare karhāī men tale jāte hain.

They fry pease-pudding in a frying-pan.

(A pun on the word *barā* which means 'great' or a 'pease-pudding.' Spoken in reply to one who reproves the speaker for disrespect towards a great man.)

Bare kī barāī, na chhote kī chhutāī.

No greatness for the great, no littleness for the little.

(Nor respect for the great, no love for the young; also *liberté, egalité, fraternité.*)

Barelī jāne kā kām karte ho?

Your deeds will take you to Barelī!

(At Bareilly there is a large lunatic asylum; In the Panjāb Lāhor is used in the same way and for the same reason.)

Barelī rūpā relī.

It rains silver at Barelī.

(The land is so rich and productive: London streets are paved with gold.)

Bare miyān so bare miyān, chhote miyān, subhān Allah!

The elder is the elder, but as for the younger, God help us!

(That is, we know the one to be bad enough, but the other is much worse.)

Bare na būran det hain jākī pakren bānh,
Jaise lohā nāo men tirat phire jal mānh.

Great men do not let him sink whose hand they have seized, As the iron fixed to a boat swims in water.

Bare shahr kā barā hī chānd.

Great cities have great moons (dignitaries).

(Ironical: swindlers.)

Bare to the hī the, chhote subhān Allāh!

The elder was but so so, but from the younger God help us!

(Used in a bad sense, to express that the first was a great rogue, but the second goes far beyond him.)

Barhen to amīr, ghaten to faqīr, maren to pīr.

Who thrive are nobles, who fail are holy ascetics, who die are saints.

(The proverb is used by Hindūs to indicate the astute policy of the Mahammadans who have rewards for every condition in life.)

Bār hī jab khet ko khāe, to rakhvālī kaun kare?

If the fence eats up the field, who will keep watch.

(Said of a corrupt Police: setting the wolf to watch the fold.)

Barī bahū, barā bhāg. Hin.

Older the wife, greater the good fortune.

(Allusion to child-marriage, when the bride is older than the bridegroom: this proverb is used to comfort the bridegroom and his parents.)

Barī bahū ko bulāo, jo khīr men nūn dāle. Hin.

Run for the elder brother's wife, she'll put salt in the *khīr.*

(*Khīr* is a mess of milk and rice eaten with sugar: this proverb is applied as a taunt, when a mistake is made by the great or pretentious.)

Barī bhābī, mān ke thānak Hin.

The elder brother's wife ranks with the mother.

(According to custom.)

Barī bhains par mahrāī.

Much butter (comes) from a big buffalo.

Barī fajar, chūlhe par nazar.

His eye on the kitchen in the early morning.

Barī kamāī par non bikvā. E.

Selling salt after great earnings.

(The action of the mean.)

Barī machhlī chhotī machhlī ko khātī hai.

Great fish eat up the small.

(The powerful oppress the weak.)

Bārī men bārah ām, hattī men atthārah ām. E.

Twelve mangoes (for a penny) in the orchard, and eighteen in the market.

(Upside down.)

Barī nāk-vāle.

A man with a great nose.

(Of great honor.)

Barī nanad shaitān kī chharī, jab dekho jab tīr sī kharī. Mah. Wom.

The elder sister-in-law is the devil's wand, when you see her she stands as straight as an arrow.

(The chief disturber of the family peace in India is the elder sister-in-law.)

Barī terhī khīr hai!

This is very crooked pottage!

☞ A man once offered to treat his comrade, who had been blind from his birth, to a mess of milk and rice. His comrade, with the proverbial suspiciousness of the blind, inquired, 'what is it like'? 'It is white,' said the other. 'And what is white like?' 'Like a crane,' 'what is a crane like?' 'Feel this,' said his would be host, bending his forearm and hand from the wrist to imitate the crane's neck, upon which the blindman used the words of the proverb to express his surprise at the idea of *khīr* thus conveyed to him.

Bar ke na mile bhūsā, baryātī mānge chūrā. E.

The bridegroom has not even straw and the guests are asking for sweets!

(Used when a preposterous request is made.)

Bar mare, patvāsī na tūte.

Her husband dead and she continues to dress her hair.

(*Patwāsī* is the dressing of the hair after the fashion of married women and *not* after the fashion of widows: hence proverb means a loose widow.)

Barme kā kām chhidnā nahīn hotā.

The borer is not bored itself.

(You cannot swindle the swindler.)

Baron kā barā hī bhāg. Hin. Wom.

Great men have great good fortune.

Baron kā barā hī munh.

Great men have great mouths (wants).

Baroṅ ke kahe kā, aur āonloṅ ke khāe kā pīchhe savād ātā hai.
The advice of elders and the taste of myrobalans are pleasant after a time.

Baroṅ kī barī bāt.
Great men have great views.

Baroṅ kī bāt bare pahchāne.
Kings only understand kings.

Baroṅ se rakkhe ās, na jāe pās.
Put your hope in princes, but never go near them.

Bar rove barāī ke, chhoṭ roe peṭ ke.
Great men sigh for greatness, small men for food.
(All the world cries for the moon.)

Barsāt, bar ke sāth. Hin. Wom.
The rainy season is best for living with one's husband.

Barsā thorī, bhabhrautī bahut.
Little rain is great drought.
(Is of very little use.)

Barsāt meṅ karhāī ghar ghar.
In the rains there are cakes in every house.
(The rains is the usual season of rejoicing in India.)

Barse Āsauj, ho nāj kī mauj. Agric.
September rain and plenty of grain.

Barsegā, barsāvegā; paise ser lagāvegā.
It will rain and rain, and (corn) will sell for a penny a pound.

Barsegā meṅh, hoṅge ānand,
Tum sāh ke sāh, ham naṅg ke naṅg.
When it rains we all rejoice, But you merchants are still merchants and we beggar still beggars.

Barse Sāḍh to ban jā ṭhāṭ. Agric.
Rain in July and every thing blooms.

Barse Sāvan to hoṅ pānch ke bāvan. Agric.
Rain in August and five becomes fifty two.
(Crops increase tenfold.)

Barso, Rām, karāke se; buṛhyā mar gaī fāqe se.
O Rām, send rain in torrents, for a poor old woman has died of hunger.

Baṛ tale kā bhūt.
A demon of the Banyan tree.
(Demons are said to be attached to particular places, as to the *masāns*, or places where the dead are burned; to various trees, etc.: that attached to Banyan trees is said to be exceedingly obstinate: hence the proverb is applied to a very importunate person, who cannot be got rid of.)

Bārū jaisī bhurbhurī, dhaulī jaise dhūp,
Miṭhī aisī kuchh nahīṅ jaisī miṭhī chup.
Crisp as sand, and white as the sun, (*sugar*),
But not so sweet as silence.

Basant, jāṛe kā ant.
Spring is the end of winter.

Basāo shahr kā, khet nahr kā. Agric.
A house in a city and a field by a canal (are the best of their kind).

Bas ho chukī namāz, musallāh baṛhāiye. Mah.
The prayer is over, so put away the carpet.
(Said when any work is finished.)

Bāsī bache, na kuttā khāe.
Nothing is left for the dog to eat.
(To describe extreme poverty. Living from hand to mouth.)

Bāsī bhāt meṅ Allāh Miyāṅ kā kaun nihorā? E.
Why be grateful to God for stale rice?

Bāsī karhī ko ubāl āyā.
Stale victuals brought for boiling.
(Spoken of a thing brought forward when the time is past: also sudden rage.)

Bāsī muṅh phīkā pānī augan kare hai. Hin. Wom.
Plain water is bad for a stale mouth.

Bāsī phūloṅ meṅ bās nahīṅ, pardesī bālam terī ās nahīṅ. Wom.
As no fragrance in a withered flower, so no hope of aid from a husband in a foreign land.

Bas kar, miyāṅ, bas kar; dekhā terā lashkar! Mah. Wom.
Enough, good sir, enough; I have seen your army.
(Said in derision to a boaster.)

Bāt chhīle rukhṛī, aur kāṭh chhīle chīknā.
Scraped words are rough, scraped wood is smooth.

Bāṭe, ghāṭe kutiyā marī, nāth kahe, merī bāchhā parī. E.
If a bitch die on the road or by the river side, the *jogī* says, my words have taken effect.
(He takes credit to himself for any chance event.)

Bāteṅ aglī kartī haiṅ khuār.
Past times make one sad.
(*Laudator temporis acti.*)

Bāteṅ hāthī pāe, aur bāteṅ hāthī pāe.
Words may bring you an elephant, and words may bring you under his feet!
(An Asiatic punishment: play here on the word *pāe*, 'gets, obtains' and 'foot.')

Bāteṅ kare mainā kī sī, āṅkheṅ badle tote kī sī.
She talks as sweetly as a *mainā*, but shifts her eyes like a parrot.
(A dangerous woman: a prostitute.)

Bāt gaī phir hāth nahīṅ āī.
Honor once gone cannot be recalled.

Bāt insān jab talak kahtā nahīṅ;
Nek o bad uskā kahīṅ khultā nahīṅ.
As long as a man speaks not, His good and evil lie hid within him.
(Speech is silver but silence is gold.)

Baṭiyā āūṅ, baṭiyā jāūṅ; khetak charāūṅ na bālī khāūṅ. Wom.
By the footpath I come, by the footpath I go, on the edge I graze, and destroy not one ear of the corn.
(*i. e.* she grazes her cattle so as not to injure

the fields: figuratively, she is an honest woman.)

Batiyā kī rāh, be-nirbāh.
The narrow pathway leads astray.
(Allusion to the field footpaths in India which may lead anywhere. Exactly the opposite of the Christian notion; See Mat. vii. 3,16.)

Bāt jo chāhe āpnī, to pānī māṅg na pī.
If you would keep up your honor, ask not even for water.
(Scald not your lips in another man's pottage.)

Bāt kā batakkaṛ karnā.
To make a speech of a sentence.
(To make a mountain of a mole-hill.)

Bāt kā chūkā ādmī, aur ḍāl kā chūkā bandar saṅbhaltā nahīṅ.
A man who misses his chance and a monkey who misses his branch cannot be saved.

Bāt kahe kī lāj.
The shame of the spoken word.
(Tell a lie and stick to it.)

Bāt kahī aur parāī huī.
A secret spoken is strangers' property.

Bāt kahīye jag-bhātī, roṭī khāīye man-bhātī.
Speak to please the world, eat to please yourself.

Bāt kī bāt, khurāfāt kī khurāfāt.
It is truth and a jest.
(Many a true thing is said in jest.)

Bāt kī bāt, khurāfāt kī khurāfāt, bakrī ke sīṅghoṅ ko char gaë berī ke pāt.
It is truth and a jest; the plum tree has eaten up the goat's horns.
(i. e. in climbing to eat, her horns have been entangled in the branches and broken off: moral; in hurting others you may injure yourself.)

Bāt kī bāt meṅ.
In the speaking of a word.
(In the twinkling of an eye.)

Bāt lākh kī, karnī khāk kī.
In words a million, in deeds mere dust.
('Words are but sands, 'tis money buys lands.')

Bāt meṅ bāt aib hai.
It is wrong to interrupt.

Bātoṅ būṛhā, kartab khuār.
His words are experienced, but his deeds are worthless.
(An old head on young shoulders:—he never said a foolish thing and never did a wise one.)

Bātoṅ chiknā, kāmoṅ khuār.
Fine words, poor deeds.

Bātoṅ chītoṅ maiṅ baḍī, kartab baṛī jiṭhānī. Hin. Wom.
For talk I'm best, for work my elder brother-in-law's wife.

Bātoṅ se kām nahīṅ chaltā.
Words won't make the work to go.
(Words are but words, it is money that makes the mare to go: empty words buy no barley.)

Bāt pūchhe, bāt kī jaṛ pūchhe.
He wants to know the meaning.
(He is a great critic.)

Bāt rah jātī hai, vaqt nikal jātā hai.
The promise remains, but time flies away.
(This is said by a man who is disappointed in not meeting with that assistance from another which he had reason to expect.)

Battīs dāṅt kī bhākhā khālī nahīṅ jātī. Hin. Wom. Superstition.
The words of thirty-two teeth will never fail.
(The promises of those in the prime of adult life are not lightly made.)

Baṭur hāth dusmanveṅ logo. Bhoj.
Strike your enemy with your clenched fist.
(If you strike at all strike hard.)

Bauhre kī Rām Rām, Jam kā sandesa. Hin.
The traders' salute is a message from the Devil.
(i. e. a dun.)

Baunā jorū kā khilaunā.
The dwarf is the butt of his wife.

Bāvā kamāve, beṭā uṛāve.
The father earns and the son spends.

Bāvan tole paū rattī.
Fifty two ounces and a quarter carat.
(Said of exactness to a small fraction.)

Bāzārī ādmī kā kyā etebār?
What reliance is there on common people's word?

Bāzār kā sattū, bāp bhī khāë, beṭā bhī khāë.
Father and son can both eat market flour.
(Said of prostitutes.)

Bāzār ke bhāo.
At the market rate.

Bāzār ke bhāo bechnā.
To sell at the market rate.

Bāzār kī gālī kis kī? Jo phirke dekhe us kī.
Who gets abused in the town? He that turns and looks.
(To see who did it. Moral; don't take notice of abuse.)

Bāzār kī miṭhāī, jis ne chāhī us ne khāī.
The sweets of the markets who chooses eats.
(Said of prostitutes.)

Bāzār kī miṭhāī se nirbāh nahīṅ hotā.
You cannot live always on the sweets of the town.
(Frequenting prostitutes is a ruinous practice.)

Bāzārū chīz boḍī hotī hai.
Ordinary market goods are always frail.

Bāzār us kā jo le-ke de. Mercantile.
The market is his who pays.

Bazzāz, bad-zāt.
The draper is mischievous.

Bazzāz kī gaṭhrī par jhīṅgar rājā.
The cricket sits king on the draper's bundle.
(i. e. he eats holes in it.)

Be-adab, be-nasīb; bā-adab, bā-nasīb. Pers.
Ill-mannered is unfortunate; well-mannered is fortunate.

Be-aib zāt Khudā kī.
God only is free from flaw.

Be-biyāhī khāë roṭiyāṅ, aur biyāhī khāë boṭiyāṅ.
An unmarried girl eats only bread, a married girl eats flesh.
(You are required to offer rich presents on every occasion to your married daughter.)

Be-būjh nagrī, be-būjh rājā, ṭake ser bhājī, ṭake ser khājā.
Foolish the city, and foolish the king, where greens and sweets are both sold at a penny a pound.
☞ It is said that a priest and his disciple going on a pilgrimage came to a city. The priest gave some coppers to the disciple and wished him to go to market and buy some flour for the evening meal. The disciple went to market and finding every thing selling at one and the same price, he, instead of flour, bought sweetmeats with the money and came back to his priest overflowing with a sense of success. The priest enquired how he came to obtain so many sweetmeats, whereon the disciple explained the matter after much praise of the city and its ruler. His master, however, was greatly shocked, and wished his disciple to leave the city that very night, but in vain. At last seeing that all his remonstrances availed nothing he left him to his enjoyment and started off. The disciple remained behind and day after day feasted on rich food and grew into a robust hulking fellow. Soon afterwards, it happened that a murder was committed in the city, and the murderer was nowhere to be found. The king being much enraged at this, ordered his minister to pick out the fattest man in the city and hang him in place of the undiscovered culprit. The stoutest man was the disciple who had been living all this while upon the fat of the city. He was therefore seized and brought before the king to be hanged. His priest heard the news and came to his rescue. When the fat man was being led to the scaffold the priest cried out and said 'I am the murderer; I have committed this crime; that man who is going to be hanged is quite innocent.' So the hangman let go the disciple and took hold of the priest, and led him on to the gibbet. Just as the rope was about to be pulled the disciple in his turn shouted out that the old man was innocent, and he only was the offender. On this a controversy arose which ended in both being discharged. *Moral:* where everything is sold at one price there can be no real justice.

Bech, bech, merī pakhnī kā biyāh. Mah. Wom.
My tomboy is married off by the sale of all my property.
(Alluding to the great expenses of the girl's father at a wedding.)

Beche ke sāg, kare motiyoṅ kā dām. E.
He sells pot-herbs, and bargains for pearls!

Beche so banjārā, rakkhe so hattiyārā. Hind.
Who sells (grain) is a merchant, who hoards it is a murderer.
(Allusion to the habit of buying grain for the rise commonly practised by Baniyās.)

Be-dard qasāī, kyā jāne pīṛ parāī? Wom.
What knows the merciless butcher of the pain of others?

Be-dharmā bhaī, aur behnā ke sāth meṅ! E. Wom.
I became a pervert to marry a wool-carder!
(These are all low Mahammadans and the speaker is a Hindū.)

Be-dil naukar, dushman barābar.
An unwilling servant is a foe.

Be-fikrī ajab chīz hai.
It is a great thing to be free from care.

Begānā sir kaddū barābar.
Another's head is like a pumpkin.
(Applied to one who swears by the head of another, to imply that no reliance is to be had on such an oath.)

Begānā sir paserī barābar.
Another's head is a lump of iron.
(A thing of no value, or which is not injured by rough handling. Applied to one who uses carelessly, or expends extravagantly the property of others; or who is careless of others' pain.)

Be-gāne kāran lūlī toṛe ṭāng. Wom.
To lose a leg in another's cause.

Begāne kāran lūlī toṛnā.
To make confectionary for another's use.
(Fools build houses for wise men to live in.)

Begāne khatte par jhiṅgar nāche.
A cricket dancing on another's corn-binn.
(Applied to one who is proud of what belongs to others.)

Begānī ās, nit upās.
Dependence on others is perpetual fasting.

Begānī thailī kā muṅh sakrā.
Another's purse has a tight mouth.

Be-gharnī ghar bhūt ke ḍerā.
Without a wife a house is the abode of a devil.

Be-gharnī ghar pādat hai, hai gharnī, ghar gājat hai. E.
Without a wife the house doth howl, with a wife the house doth joy.
(The pleasures of married life.)

Bejrā ke pīsan-hārī gehūṅ kī gīt gāveṅ. E. Wom.
Grinding coarse grains she sings the song of wheat!
(She talks very big: draws the long bow.)

Be-hayāī kā burqa muṅh par ḍāl liyā hai.
He has put over his face the veil of shamelessness.
(Said of a person who is repeatedly punished.)

Be-hayā ke nīche rūkh jamā, us ne jānā kī chhāṅh huī.
A tree sprang up under a shameless man, and he thought it would shade him.
(Applied to one who glories in that which others would be ashamed of.)

Be-kārī, bikārī.
Out of employment, out of health.

Be-kārī se begārī bhalī.
Forced labor is better than idling.
(Doing nothing is more painful than doing something.)

Be-kār mabāsh kuchh kiyā kar.
Kapre hī udher-kar siyā kar.
Don't be idle and do something!
Unstitch your clothes and sew them up.
(If you have nothing better to do.)

Be-kharchī men āṭā gīlā.
The pence are gone and the flour is wet.
(As he had no money to buy fuel to cook it with: used to express the distress of one who is destitute of resource at a time when it becomes necessary to incur expenses.)

Be khār gul nahīn.
No rose without a thorn.

Be-lajjī b ihuryā par ghar nāche. Wom.
A shameless wife dances at others' houses.

Bel, babūl, khāk aur dhūl.
From *bel* (tree) to *babūl* (tree) is dust to ashes.
(Worse and worse:—out of the frying-pan into the fire: both trees are very thorny—the *babūl* being more so than the *bel.*)

Bel baṛhāve, aur jaṛ kāṭe!
He promotes the growth of the creeper, but cuts its root.
(To express one who appears to be friendly, but secretly undermines another.)

Bel ke māre babūl tale, babūl ke māre bel tale.
Hurt by the *bel* he runs to the *babūl*, hurt by the *babūl* he runs to the *bel*.
(Applied to an unfortunate person, whom bad luck pursues wherever he goes. Out of the frying-pan into the fire.)

Bel manḍhe chaṛhtī dikhāī nahīn detī.
I don't think this creeper will grow far.
(I don't think he will succeed.)

Bel pakkā to kavve ke bāp ko kyā?
If the wood-apple ripens, what does it matter to the crow's father?
(The rind of this fruit is too hard to peck through: used by a person who hears advantages described, of which he cannot partake.)

Bel phūṭā rāī rāī ho gayā.
The *bel* fruit is burst, and reduced to mustard seed.
(To describe the ruinous effects of disunion.)

Be Māghe ghī khichṛī khāe, Be mehri sasurāre jāe. Be Bhādon penhai pavva, Kahe Ghāgh, yeh tīnon kavvā.
Eating *ghī* and *khichṛī* except in January; Going to your father-in-law's house without your wife; Swinging except in July: Saith Ghāgh, is to be a crow.
(A crow is the personification of all that is objectionable: *ghī khichṛī* is heating food: when your wife's dead your father-in-law has no particular love for you: the swinging festival is held always in July—August. The moral is obvious.)

Be-menh ke ḍāṅvrī, ghoṛā binā lagām,
Be-māth ke lashkar, tīnon bhail na-kām. Rus.
Ploughing the soil without rain, having a horse without a bridle, and an army without a leader, are three evil things.

Be-mīr, bāzī abtar. Card players.
Without a king it's a false pack.

Ber khānsī kā ghar hai.
Wild plums are the home of cough.

Beron men guṭhliyān milānā.
To mix stones among plums.
(To complicate a matter.)

Be-sirī fauj.
An army without a head.

Besvā satī, na kāgā jatī.
Nor harlot (*satī*) pure, nor crow (*jatī*) pure.
(*Satī*, female chastity: *jatī*, male chastity.)

Beṭā ban-ke sab ne khāyā hai, bāp ban-ke koī nahīn khātā.
Be a son (humble) and you'll get, be a father (proud) and you won't get.

Beṭā beṭī bas kā achchhā.
An obedient son or daughter is the best.

Beṭā huā jab jāniye, jab potā khele bār.
Know that you have posterity, when your grandson plays at the door.
(A son only may die.)

Beṭā khāe, bāp lakhāe, Kaljug apnā bal dikhlāe.
The son feeds well while the father looks on, the iron age shews its might.
(Sons must support fathers in India; the Kaljug is the present degenerate age.)

Beṭā lāegā chamārī, voh bhī bahu kahlāegī hamārī. Mah. Wom.
If my son should marry a low woman, she would still be called my daughter-in-law.
(Make the best of a bad bargain.)

Beṭā mariyo, par tissar na pariyo. Wom. Superstition.
May my son die, rather than I get a third.
(To have three sons (*tissar*) running is held unlucky to the parents.)

Beṭe se nām chaltā hai.
The father lives in the son.

Be-thāng chorī nahīn hotī.
No theft without an informer.

Beṭī kā dhan nimānā hai; āte bhī rulāe, jāte bhī rulāe.
A humiliating portion daughters are, their coming makes you weep and their going also makes you weep.

Beṭī aur kakṛī kī bel barābar hotī hai!
Girls and cucumbers grow fast!

Beṭī ne kiyā kumhār, ammā ne kiyā luhār;
'Na tum chalāo hamār, nā ham chalāen tumhār.'
The daughter attached to a potter, and the mother to a blacksmith; 'You must not speak ill of me, nor I of you.'
(The pot must not call the kettle black: those that live in glass houses must not throw stones.)

Beṭī sasurā na jātī, man man gājatī. E. Wom.
The daughter goes not to her father-in-law's house and frets and fumes to herself.
(A common incident in native life.)

Be-vaqt kī shahnāī, mūë kūṛh ne bajāī. Mah. Wom.
The fool plays the pipe at the wrong time.
(Rājās are accustomed to be awakened by a pipe played at dawn: Sikhs use a drum, and Brāhmans a conch for the same purpose.)

Be-vārsī nāo ḍānvāṅḍol.
The boat without a helmsman is tossed about.
(The fatherless child goes astray.)

Be-sar bishnī bhaṛve barābar.
A penniless paramour is no better than a pimp.
(Used by prostitutes.)

Bhādoṅ dono sākh kā rājā hai. Agric.
August is the king of the two harvests.
(The most profitable crop is that in autumn.)

Bhādoṅ kā ghām, aur sājhe kā kām.
August heat and joint labour are (the most unbearable).

Bhādoṅ kā jhallā, ek sīng gīlā ek sūkhā. Agric.
In August showers one horn is wet and the other dry.
(Allusion to the very partial rains that fall in August.)

Bhādoṅ ke meṅh se dono sākh kī jaṛ bandhtī hai. Agric.
With August rains both harvests thrive.

Bhādoṅ kī chhāchh bhūtoṅ ko, Kātak kī chhāchh pūtoṅ ko. Hin. Wom.
Buttermilk in August for the devil, in October for your children.

Bhādoṅ kī dhūp meṅ hiran kāle hote hain.
In August sunshine the antelope turns black.

Bhādoṅ meṅ barkhā hoë, kāl pachhokaṛ jā-kar roë. Agric.
When the rains fall in August famine steps aside and weeps.

Bhādoṅ se bache to phir mileṅge.
Escaped this August we shall meet again.
(In India August is a bad month.)

Bhāgalpūr ke bhāgaliye, Kahal-gāoṅ ke ṭhag, Paṭne ke divāliye, tīnoṅ nām zad.
A Bhāgalpūr rogue, a foot-pad of Colgong, and a Paṭnā swindler, these three are notorious.

Bhāge hue lashkar kā mard pīchhā nahīṅ kartā.
Brave men don't pursue flying soldiers.
(Don't hit a man when he is down.)

Bhagle chor kaṭharyā hāth. Bhoj.
A flying thief takes away even a wooden cup.
(Any worthless thing.)

Bhāgte bhūt kī langoṭī bhī bahut hai.
Even the loin-cloth from a flying devil is something.
(Better get something out of a runaway thief than nothing: a penny saved is a penny gained.)

Bhāī aisan hit nā, bhāī aisan bairī nā. Hin.
No friend like a brother, no foe like a brother.

Bhaī andhiyārī, phūlī chhātī, chīnh paṛai rānḍ ahibātī.
The widow rejoices in the darkness, as it makes her a married woman.
(Said of a loose widow.)

Bhāī bhāo kā, nahīṅ apne dāo kā.
A brother is he that loves, not he that watches his own interests.

Bhāī bhāo kare, tal māre ūpar chāo kare.
He loves like a brother, but strikes below while he strokes above.
(The double-faced.)

Bhaī chhachhūndarī sarp gatī, uglat bane na khāt.
Like a snake with a mole (in his mouth), that can neither vomit nor swallow.
☞ The legend is that if a snake get a mole into its mouth and swallow it, it becomes leprous, and if it vomit it up it becomes blind: hence proverb means to be on the horns of a dilemma.

Bhāī dūr, paṛausī nere.
Your brother is afar, but your neighbour is near.
(So the latter is of more use to you.)

Bhail biyāh, mor karbā kā? Bhoj.
My marriage is over, what more can they want of me?
(Allusion to the custom of the bridegroom paying for his bride.)

Bhāī na de, bhāo de. Mercantile.
Sell at the market rate, not for friendship's sake.
(Benevolence spells bankruptcy.)

Bhaiṅsā bhaiṅsoṅ meṅ, yā qasāī ke khūṅṭe.
The male buffalo should be among the females, or tied to the butcher's stake.
(To win the horse and lose the saddle.)

Bhaiṅs dūdh jo kaṛhvāṅ pīve,
Hāṅgā ghaṭe na, jab lag jīve. Rus.
Who drinks boiled buffalo's milk will keep his strength through life.

Bhaiṅs kā dūdh, nalī kā gūd.
Buffalo's milk is as marrow from the bone.

Bhaiṅs kā gobar, bhaiṅs ke chūtron ko lag jātā hai.
The dung of a buffalo besmears its buttocks.
(Cannot *all* be put to use—*bhaiṅs kā gobar* is one of the most useful articles of fuel in India: a great man has great expenses is the application of the proverb.)

Bhaiṅs ke āge bīn baje, voh baiṭhī paghurāī. E.
If you play the harp before a buffalo, she will simply chew the cud.
(Pearls before swine.)

Bhaiṅs ko apne sīng bhārī nahīṅ.
The buffalo does not feel the weight of his own horns.
(A man does not find the maintenance of his own children and relations oppressive.)

Bhains pakauṛe hag gaī.
The buffalo has passed sweet-meats.
(Applied contemptuously to one who has met with extraordinary good fortune.)

Bhains pa dūdh kis ne chhoṛā?
Who ever leaves the milk in the buffalo?
(The rich are always fleeced.)

Bhāī sā sāthī, na bhāī sā bairī.
No friend like a brother, no foe like a brother.

Bhāī so bhāī, bāqī chhīnke par.
Brother is brother, the rest are put aside.
(*Chhīnke par rakhnā* is to hang a thing in a net out of the way of cats, etc.: pun on the word *bhāī* which means (1) brother, (2) suited to one's taste.)

Bhaiyā jī bahotere ḍanḍ malvāeṅ, bandā pahalvān nahīṅ banne ke.
My brother often taught me wrestling, but I am no athlete and will never be one.
(The phrase here implies inferiority in any way of the speaker to some of his connections.)

Bhāiyoṅ ke ḍanḍ malo.
Rub your brethren's arms.
(It is a common mode of congratulating a victorious wrestler to rub or squeeze his arms. This phrase is used ironically towards a person who has attempted things above his strength, or boasted greatly of what he would perform, and has failed.)

Bhajan aur bhojan ekānt bhalā.
Prayers and meals in seclusion are best.
(Natives eat and pray alone.)

Bhājī kī bhājī kyā dūsre kī mohtājī? Wom.
A present for a present, what more can one require.
(Short debts long friends.)

Bhakūhā bhīge gāoṅ ke goenṛā. [village.
A fool gets wetted in the outskirts of the
(Has not got sense enough to go inside.)

Bhalā huā dādī gaune gaī, dādī kī pharyā mai kā bhaī. E. Wom.
It is well that my husband's sister is married and gone, for I shall get her gorgeous clothes.
(Allusion to the position occupied by the husband's sister in a native household, in which the man's mother comes first, then his sister and then his wife.)

Bhalāī kar, burāī se ḍar.
Do good and fear evil.

Bhalā kar bhalā ho, saudā kar nafa ho.
Do good and good will come of it, put out to interest and take the profit.
(The mendicant's cry :—lay up for yourselves treasures in heaven, where neither moth nor rust doth corrupt, and where thieves do not break through and steal. Mat. vi 19.)

Bhalā kiyā so Khudā ne, burā kiyā so bande ne.
Good is God's, evil is man's.
(The words of one declining an undertaking, or reproaching another with his being unmindful of favours conferred.)

Bhalā mānas ghar meṅ baṛā, rizāle ne jānā mujh se ḍarā.
The respectable man returned home and the rogue thought he was afraid of him.

Bhal bhail piyā ke bāgh māral, je begārī se bachal. E. Wom.
It is good that my husband has been devoured by a tiger, for I am saved from working for him.

Bhale ādmī kī murgī ṭake ṭake.
A nobleman's hens go for a copper each.
(*Noblesse oblige.*)

Bhale, bābā, band paṛī, gobar chhoṛ kashīde paṛī. Wom.
Father dear, I am a prisoner, and instead of picking up cowdung, I make embroidery.
(Said by a girl who has married above her, while poor and lowly she had freedom, but now that she is rich she is shut up in the house.)

Bhale din āeṅge to, ghar pūchhte chale āeṅge.
When the good time comes it will ask its way to your house.
(Have patience and resignation therefore.)

Bhale ghoṛe ko ek chābuk, bhale ādmī ko ek bāt kāfī hai.
One whip for a good horse, and one word for a good man is sufficient.

Bhale kā bhalā.
Good comes of good.
(Good yields good.)

Bhale kā zamāna hī nahīṅ.
This is not an age of good men.
(There is no humanity in this age.)

Bhale ke bhāī, bure ke jawāī.
Be a brother to the good and a son-in-law to the bad.

Bhale kī bāteṅ ras kī khān, Bure kī bāteṅ dukh nidān.
The words of the good are a pit of delight,
The words of the bad are the home of trouble.

Bhale mānas kī sab tarah kharābī hai.
The patient man is abused by every body.
(Because he will not return abuse.)

Bhale saṅg baiṭhiye, khāiye nāgar pān; bure saṅg baiṭhiye kaṭāiye nāk aur kān.
Association with the good is eating the best betel; Association with the bad is to lose your nose and ears.
(i. e. to be utterly disgraced.)

Bhal janmal, bhal panḍit bhail. E.
Happy his birth who turns out a *panḍit*.
(*Panḍit*, a man learned in the Scriptures.)

Bhal marlās, bhal pillū paṛal. E.
Stone dead and worm eaten.

Bhal māth muraulan, bhal bel girlain! E.
It was well that he shaved his head; it was well that the wood-apple fell on it!
(Great ill-luck.)

Bhalo bhayo, merī maṭukī ṭuṭī, main dahī bechan se chhuṭī. Wom.
It is well, brother, that my pot is broken, for I am saved from selling the tyre.

Bhāṇḍoṅ sang khetī kī, gā bajā-ke apnī kī.
The husbandman went shares in a field with some players, they sang and played, and made it all their own.
(Allusion to the custom of giving grain to bards as a reward for singing.)

Bhang, gāṅjā jan deū gaṅvāran ke,
Haṅṛiyā bhar bhāt sanghāran ke. E.
Don't give *bhang* and *gāṅjā* to the village boor, Or he will eat up a bucket full of your rice.
(*Bhang* and *gāṅjā*, intoxicating preparations of hemp, supposed to be also stomachics.)

Bhang kahe, 'main rangī jangī,'
Post kahe, 'main shah-i-jahāṅ,'
Afīm kahe, 'main chunnī begam,
Mujh ko khā-ke jāë kahāṅ ?'
Says the hemp, I am of gorgeous hue,'
Says the poppy, 'I am king of the world,'
But says the opium, 'I am a lady love!
Who takes me once takes me for ever.'

Bhangī kī zāt kyā ? Jhūṭe kī bāt kyā ?
What caste has the sweeper ? What credit the liar ?

Bhangiyāṅ dar bāg raftand, ber guṭhlī sab ravā. Ped.
The hemp-eaters went into a garden, and swallowed the plums, stones and all.
(Did not know what they were doing.)

Bhang pīnā āsān hai, maujeṅ jān mārtī haiṅ.
Easy is the drinking of hemp, but deadly is the enjoyment thereof.
(Spoken in reproof of those who act without regarding consequences : *facilis descensus Averni.*)

Bhāṅg to aisī pījiye, jaise kunjgalin kī kīch,
Ghar-ke jāne mar gaë aur āp nashe ke bīch.
Swallow your hemp as thick as street mud,
And your friends will think you are dead, but you will only be very drunk.

Bhāo na jāne rāo.
Kings never know the market price.
(Allusion to the uselessness of trying to interfere with trade prices : Asiatic kings do not submit to market rates, they pay what they choose. The proverb is capable of either construction.)

Bhāo rāo Khudā ke hāth.
Market rates and kings are in God's hand.

Bhāo rāo kī khabar nahīṅ.
No one can fortell about kings and market rates.

Bhāṛā, byāj, dakshnā, pīchhe paṛe kuchh nā.
Hire, interest, and gifts should not be kept in arrears.
(*Bis dat qui cito dat.*)

Bharā kahār, khālī kumhār, tez jātā hai.
The laden porter and the empty handed potter move quickly.
(A common observation in native life.)

Bharak bhārī, khīsā khālī.
Great show and an empty pocket.
(Vain show.)

Bharam māre, bharam jiāve.
Opinion slays and opinion keeps alive.
(Moral: earn therefore the good opinion of your neighbours.)

Bharā so dharā.
Full is set down.
(Moral : a man full of worth lives in peace.)

Bhaṛ bhaṛihā achchhā, peṭ pāpī burā.
Better a babbler than a close knave.

Bhaṛ-bhūjan kī laṛkī, kesar kā ṭīkā.
A grain parcher's daughter, and saffron on her forehead !
(*Bhar-bhūṅjās* are a very low caste, whereas the safron *ṭīkā* is only worn by rich and respectable women.)

Bhār ḍāl sab bhāṛ meṅ Samman utre pār.
Samman has thrown all his burdens into the fire, and passed over in safety.
(To express that one has got rid of a difficulty in which he was involved.)

Bhar de, bhar pāve, kāl kanṭak pās na āve !
Fill and you will be filled; death and pain will not near you.
(A cry of mendicants : give and it shall be given you. Luke vi. 38.)

Bhare ko bhartā hai.
(God) fills the full.
(Unto every one that hath shall be given, but from him that hath not shall be taken away even that which he hath. Mat. xxv. 29.)

Bhare samundar ghoṅgā hāth.
You only get shells out of a full ocean.
(Serving the great without benefit.)

Bhare samundar piyāse.
Thirsty amidst oceans of water.

Bhar hāth chuṛī, paṭ sūṅ rāṅṛ. E. Wom.
Bracelets on her arms, and a widow withal!
(A loose widow : bracelets are only worn by a *feme covert.*)

Bharī barsāt meṅ āb-dast na leve, voh bharvā alsetī hai.
Who won't wash after a call of nature in the midst of the rains is lazy rascal indeed.

Bhārī biyāj mūl ko khāe. Mercantile.
High interest means loss of principal.

Bhārī patthar dekhā, chūm-kar chhoṛ diyā.
A heavy stone just touched and let alone.
(He found the task beyond his strength and therefore prudently desisted.)

Bharī thālī meṅ lāt mārnā. Hin. Wom.
To kick over the plate full of food.
(To quarrel with one's bread and butter.)

Bhāṛ līpī jāeṅ, hāth kāle kā kālā. [be black.
Whitewash the oven and your hands will still
(Touch pitch and you will be defiled.)

Bharmā bhūt, sankā ḍāyan. Hin.
Imagination is a devil, and fear a witch.
(Therefore be brave and sensible.)

Bharve ko bhī mūṅh par bharvā nahīṅ kahte.
You don't call a pimp a pimp to his face.

Bhassakkar ke dāmād ko bhāt hī mithāī.
Rice is a sweetmeat to the son-in-law of a glutton.
(He would rather eat a great deal of rice than a small quantity of sweets.)

Bhaṭ, bhaṭiyārī, besvā tīnoṅ jāt kujāt;
Āte kā ādar kareṅ, jāt na pūchheṅ bāt.
Bards, innkeepers, and harlots are an evil lot, When you come they are civil, when you go they care nothing.

Bhāt bin rah jāve, piyā bin rahā na jāve. Wom.
You can go without your dinner, but not without your lover.

Bhāt chhoṛā jātā hai, sāth nahīṅ chhoṛā jātā.
Your dinner may fail you, but not your true friend.

Bhāt hogā, to kavve bahut ā rahenge.
Where there is rice, there will the crows be gathered together.
(For wheresoever the carcase is, there will the eagles be gathered together. Mat. iv, 28.)

Bhāt-khāne bahotere, kām dulhā dulhan se.
The parasites are many, but the business is with the bride and bridegroom.

Bhāt khāte hāth pirāe! Wom.
She can't eat rice because it makes her hand ache!
(She is so delicate.)

Bhaṭ paṛe voh sonā jis se ṭūṭeṅ kān. Wom.
Fire burn the gold that splits the ears!
(Spoken of a son or relation whose conduct renders him a burden or source of vexation to his friends. It is also applied to wealth acquired by much labor, or the acquisition of which produces distress.)

Bhaṭ paṛe voh zamāna, natnī ko ghūre nānā.
A plague on the times when a man ogles his grand-daughter.
(An exclamation on observing anything very absurd; particularly an old man paying amorous addresses to a young girl)

Bhauṅ kā gilā āṅkh ke sāmhne.
Complaining of the eyebrows to the eyes.
(Complaining of a man to his near relatives.)

Bhāvī ke bas sansār hai.
The world is ruled by fate.

Bhejā khāeṅ, sir sahlāeṅ.
He strokes the head and eats the brains.
(Hypocrisy; picking the brains.)

Bhekh se bhīk hai.
Alms are given to the beggar's dress.
(The dress commands respect.)

Bheṛ kī lāt ghuṭnoṅ tak.
A sheep can kick as far as the knee and no further.
(The loss in a petty transaction is trifling.)

Bheṛ pe ūn kis ne chhoṛī?
Who leaves a sheep unshorn?
(They are always fleeced!)

Bheṛ to jahāṅ jāegī muṅḍegī.
A sheep is shorn wherever she may go.
(The rich are always robbed.)

Bheṛyā chāl hai.
Following like sheep.
(All we like sheep have gone astray. Isaiah vii, 21.)

Bheṛyā dhasān.
Blind pursuit.
(See above.)

Bhīgā chūhā.
A wet rat.
(To describe one whose beard only covers the point of his chin, and who is reckoned to be of a bad disposition.)

Bhīgī billī.
A drowned cat.
(A cunning and crafty person.)

Bhīgī billī batānā.
To say that the cat was wet.
☞ This phrase is founded on the story of a lazy servant who once being asked by his master to put out the light in the room replied: 'Better shut your eyes, and all will be dark.' Another time when asked to go out and see whether it was raining, the servant replied that a cat had just passed him, and he had felt her wet; which gave rise to this proverbial phrase, meaning to evade an order through idleness.

Bhīk aur pichhoṛ.
To sift alms.
(Never look a gift horse in the mouth.)

Bhīk ke ṭukṛe, bāzār meṅ ḍakār.
Fed on scraps of alms, he belches in the streets.
(An invariable token of having dined well in India.)

Bhīk māṅge, aur āṅkh dikhāve!
To beg and scowl.
(Said of the *Suthre shāhi faqīrs* and *Mīrāsis*, who beg as a right and abuse those who don't give.)

Bhīk māṅge aur pūchhe gāoṅ kī jamā!
He a beggar, and asking about the revenue of the village!

Bhiṛ kā chhattā.
A bees' nest.
(To describe a family or tribe, who adhere firmly to one another, so that whoever provokes one is attacked by the whole.)

Bhītar kā ghāo, Rānī jāne yā Rāo.
The hidden wound, either the King knows or the Queen.
(Husband and wife only know where the skeleton in the cupboard is.)

Bhīt hogī to leo bahotere chaṛh rahenge. Hin. Wom.
While the wall stands it receives lots of whitewash.
(While the bones last flesh there will be.)

Bhīt ke bhī kān hote hain.
Walls have ears.

Bhīt ṭale, par bān nā ṭale.
A wall may move, but a bad habit won't.

Bhog bhāg, chhattīson rāg.
Fortune and enjoyment are the thirty six [modes.
(Into which Indian Music is conventionally divided.)

Bhog bilās, jab tak sāns.
Enjoy yourself as long as you live.
(Eat, drink, and be merry, for to-morrow we die.)

Bhogī so rogī.
Self indulgence breeds sickness.

Bhojan na bhāt, Ḥar Har gīt.
The hungry calls on God.
(The devil was sick, the devil a saint would be: The devil got well, the devil a saint was he!)

Bhojan na bhāt, naihar kā samād! E. Wom.
Nor bread nor rice at home, or at my father-in-law's.
(The widow who is ill-treated wherever she be.)

Bhojpur men jaihā mat, jaihā to khaihā mat, khaihā to soihā mat, soihā to ṭohihā mat, ṭohihā to roihā mat. Bhoj.
To Bhojpur town go not; or if you go, eat not; or if you eat, sleep not; or if you sleep, (your bag) feel not; or if you feel it, cry not.
(A skit at the thieving propensities of the town.)

Bhondū bhāo na jāne, peṭ bharan se kām.
The fool cares nothing for the market rates, he only wants to fill his stomach.

Bhor bhayā jab jāniye, jab pīle bādal hoen.
Know that it is dawn, when the horizon grows yellow.

Bhore bhulāe, sānjh ghare āve, ū bhulāil nā kahāve. E. Rus.
Who forgets in the morning and remembers in the evening cannot be called forgetful.

Bhor kā murgā bolā, panchhī ne munh kholā.
The morning cock hath crowed and the birds have sung.

Bhūā kī naddī men kaun bahe?
Who would swim in a river of scum?

Bhūbal men roṭī dāb-kar to nahīn āī hai? Wom.
You haven't left your bread on fire, have you?
(Said to a visitor who wants to depart soon.)

Bhūīn bisvā bhar nahīn nām Prithvī-pāl.
Not a plot of land his own and his name Protector-of-the-world.

Bhujā ḍanḍ hī āp ke kahe dete hain.
Your arms speak for you.
(They are weak. Said in derision of an impotent menace.)

Bhūkā Bangālī 'bhāt bhāt' pukāre.
The hungry Bangālī cries out for boiled rice.
(Habits are not easily rooted out.)

Bhūkā gayā jo bechne, aghānā kahe "bandhak rakkho."
A hungry man went to sell off his wife and the surfeited said, "mortgage her."!
(Taking advantage of another's necessities.)

Bhūkā joru beche, rajā kahe 'udhār lūn.'
The hungry man sells his wife, the full stomach says, 'I will take her on tick.'

Bhūkā mare, ki satvā sāne?
Better pulse meal than starvation.
(Something is better than nothing: pulse meal is very poor food.)

Bhūkā martā kyā na kartā?
What will not the famished dare?
(The belly teaches all arts.)

Bhūkā so rūkhā.
The hungry man is an angry man.

Bhūkā Turak na chheṛiye, ho jāe jī kā jhār.
Don't provoke a hungry Turk, for he will prosecute you to death.

Bhūkā uṭhātā hai, bhūkā sulātā nahīn.
(God) wakes the hungry, but never sends hungry to sleep.
(God's providence.)

Bhūke ber, aghāe gānḍe. Rus.
Berries for the hungry, sugarcane for the full.
(To him that hath shall be given.)

Bhūke bhajan na hoë, sādho!
Saints, a hungry person cannot count his [beads!

Bhūke bhale-mānas se ḍariye!
Fear the hungry gentleman!

Bhūke ghar men non nihārī.
Salt is a repast in a hungry house.

Bhūke ho to hare hare rūkh dekho.
If you are hungry look at the green trees.
(Put into the mouth of a miser who never knows anything of persons in distress.)

Bhūke ko an, pyāse ko pānī, jangal jangal avādānī.
With grain for the hungry and water for the thirsty; in every wood and forest there are means of life.

Bhūke ko khilā aur nange ko pahnā!
Feed the hungry and clothe the naked!

Bhūke ko kuchh dījye yathā shakt jo hoë. Hin.
Feed the hungry as much as in you lies.

Bhūke ko kyā rūkhā, aur nīnd ko kyā takiyā.
Hunger needs no sauce, and sleep no pillow.

Bhūke ne bhūke ko mārā, donon ko gash ā gayā.
One starveling dealt another a blow, and both fell down.

Bhūke se kahā do aur do kaë? kahā, "chār roṭiyān."
Ask the hungry man what two and two make, and he will reply "four loaves."

Bhūk gaë bhojan mile, jārā gaë qabāë,
Joban gaë tiryā mile, tīnon deo bahāë.
A dinner when hunger has gone, warm clothes when the cold has gone, and a wife when youth has gone, are three things to be avoided.

Bhūk ko bhojan kyā aur nīnd ko bichhonā kyā ?
Hunger is content with any food, and sleep with any bed.

Bhūk lagī to ghar kī sūjhī.
When hunger gnaws then think of home.

Bhūk men gūlar pakvān.
To the hungry wild figs are delicious.

Bhūk men kivāṛ pāpaṛ.
To the hungry a stale loaf is a crisp cake.
(Hunger makes raw beans relish well.)

Bhūk sab se mīṭhī hai.
Hunger is the best sauce.

Bhūlā jogī dūnī lābh.
The forgetful *jogī* makes double gains.
(He gets alms wherever he goes, if he has been there before or not.)

Bhūlal bhāṛ Divālī gāve. Bhoj.
It is a mad bard that sings at the Divālī.
(He ought to sing at the Holī in spring, whereas the Divālī falls in the autumn.)

Bhūlā phire kisān jo Kātag māṅge meṅh. Agric.
It is a mad peasant that wants rain in November.

Bhūl chūk kā ḍar nahīṅ.
There is no harm in mere mistakes.

Bhūl chūk lenī denī. Mercantile.
All mistakes should be given and taken.
(Errors excepted; the E. E. of English traders.)

Bhūle Bāman gāe khāī, ab khāūṅ, to Rām duhāī. Hin.
The forgetful Brāhman ate beef, (and said) 'I will never eat it again, by God !'
(Burnt child fears the fire : spoken also of one, who having committed an offence, solemnly promises not to repeat it.)

Bhūle bisre Rām sahāī.
God forgive our errors.

Bhūle chūke ḍanḍ nahīṅ.
No fine for unwitting mistakes.
(*De minimis non curat lex.*)

Bhūl gaī din dihāṛā, muṇḍo ne sehrā bāṅdhā.
Forgetting the olden time the widow is wearing a marriage chaplet.
(Making a swell of herself : applied to those who in prosperity have forgotten the meanness of their origin.)

Bhūl gaë rāg rang, bhūl gaë chhakṛī, tīn chīz yād rahīṅ, nūn, tel, lakṛī.
Forgotten his songs, forgotten his dance, he cares for but three things, salt, oil and wood.
(*Res angusta domi* : the gay bachelor turned benedic.)

Bhūl gaī nār, hīṅg ḍāl diyā bhāt meṅ. Wom.
The woman has blundered and put the assafœtida into the rice.
(It should be put into split peas. Used when through mistake one thing has been done instead of another.)

Bhūlī, re Rāghuā, terī lāl pagiyā par. Wom.
I was taken in, Rāghuā, by your gay red turban.
(Imposed upon by outward show, or beguiled by appearance.)

Bhumiyā to bhūmī pe marī, tū kyoṅ marī, baṭer.
Farmers fight for the land, why dost thou fight, thou quail ?
(Said to little men mixing themselves up in the quarrels of the great.)

Bhūn boyā, upaṭ gayā. E. Agric.
The burnt seed came to nothing.
(Said of a child who turns out ill.)

Bhūnī bhāṅg, na karvā tel.
Nor fried hemp nor bitter oil.
(Destitute of every thing.)

Bhūrā bhaiṅsā, chāndlī joë, Pūs mahāvaṭ birle hoë. E. Agric.
A brown buffalo, a bald wife and rain in December are indeed rare.

Bhūṛ ke hūṛ hote haiṅ.
Country bumkins are fools.

Bhus ke mol, malīdā !
Sweets at the price of straw !

Bhus men chingī ḍāl Jamālo dūr khaṛī ! Wom.
Jamālo fired the straw and stood aloof !
(A mischief-maker : a fire-brand : an incendiary.)

Bhus par līpnā.
To plaster over straw.
(To make a ginger-bread work that won't last long.)

Bhūt jān na māre, satā māre.
The evil spirit kills not, but afflicts.

Bhūt kā pakvān.
Ghost's delicacies.
(Unsubstantial things.)

Bhūt ke patthar kī choṭ nahīṅ lagtī.
Stones don't hurt ghosts.
(Being impalpable.)

Bhuṭṭā kā bhagvā, mūnjak ḍorī, bīvī dusoī chhat naihā mor ! E. Wom.
With a gown of sack cloth, and a thick rope for the strings, she thinks none like her !

Bībī Bakrī, nāo men khāk uṛātī ho !
Madam Sheep, you are raising a dust in the boat !
(A groundless accusation, made by the wolf on the strength of which he eats her up : applied to those who pick a quarrel to excuse intended injustice.)

Bībī hain bharmālī, kān pītar kī bālī ! E. Wom.
My lady is very consequential on the strength of a brass ear-ring !

Bībī Khailā, do chiṭṭe, ek mailā. Mah. Wom.
Madam Slut has two white and one dirty (skirt).
(A whited sepulchre.)

Bībī Khailā, do jaṭṭī ek melā. Mah. Wom.
Madam Slut and two farmers' wives make a fair.
(Three women and a goose make a market.)

Bibī ko bāndī kahā, hans dī; bāndī ko bāndī kahā, ro dī. Wom.
Call a lady a slave and she will laugh; call a slave a slave and she will fret.

Bibī Makke na gaīn, lāḍlī ho āīn. Mah. Wom.
My lady did not go to Mecca, yet she became a darling.
(Kissing goes by favor.)

Bibī vāre bāndī khāē, ghar kī balā kahīn na jāē. Wom.
The wife gives alms, the slave girl takes them, and the misfortunes of the family still remain in the house.
(*Vārnā* is the act of passing any article round the head and then presenting it to another with a view to averting *balā*, misfortune. Hence the proverb is used of one who confines his benefactions entirely to his own family.)

Bichchhū kā mantar nā jāne, sāṅp ke bil men hāth ḍāle.
He knows not the charm even for the scorpion's bite, and he thrusts his hand into a snake's hole.
(Applied to one who undertakes a task far above his abilities.)

Bibī nek-bakht, damṛī kī dāl tīn vaqt. Mah. Wom.
A careful housewife makes a penny worth of peas serve for three meals.

Bīch ke chale jāenge kām dulhā dulhan se paṛegā.
When the guests retire the business falls on the bride and bridegroom.
(Spoken of those who busy themselves in promoting a quarrel in which they have no concern, and which must finally be discussed between the parties interested.)

Bī Daulti apne tehe men āp hī khaulti. Mah. Wom.
Madam Purse-proud boils in her own flames.
(Fries in her own fat.)

Biddiyā lohe ke chane hain. Hin.
Learning is as hard as iron (to digest).

Biddyā men bibād base.
Controversy dwells in learning.

Bigāṛ sanvār Khudā ke hāth.
To make and mar is in God's hands.

Bigṛī laṛāī, baktar-poshon ke sir.
The lost battle is laid on the soldier.
(By the commander who loses it!)

Bīj boyā nahīn, khet kā dukh.
The seed not sown and he frets at the field.

Bijlī chamke, mehā barse.
When the lightning flashes it will rain.
(Oriental observation.)

Bijlī kānsī par girtī hai.
Zinc attracts the lightning.
(It is the rich that are liable to misfortune.)

Bijlī mehmān, ghar men nahīn tinkā.
The lightning is a guest and not a straw in the house (to burn)!
(A poor man inviting guests of higher position than himself.)

Bijulik māral, luāṭh dekh bhāge. E.
Singed by lightning he runs from a burning stick.
(Burnt child dreads the fire.)

Bijyā pīve, sejyā sove, tā ke baid pichhāṛī rove.
Who drinks *bhang*, and sleeps on a bed, his doctor weeps.

Bikh kī aukhad kyā?
No remedy for poison.

Bikh sone ke bartan men rakhne se amrit nahīn hotā. Hin.
Putting poison into a golden vessel does not make it nectar.

Billī aur dūdh kī rakhvālī.
To set a cat to watch milk.

Billī bhī dab-kar harbah kartī hai.
Even a cat at bay will turn.
(Even a worm will turn at last.)

Billī bhī laṛtī hai, to mūnh par panjah dhar letī hai.
When a cat fights she covers her face with her paws.

Billī bhī mārtī hai chūhā peṭ ke liye.
Even the cat kills mice for its belly's sake.

Billī chūhā Khudā ke vāste nahīn mārtī.
The cat does not kill mice for the sake of God.
(To express that the person spoken of does good from interested motives.)

Billī ke bhāgon chhīnkā ṭūṭ paṛā. Wom.
It was the cat's luck that the net broke.
☞ *Chhīnkā* is a net for hanging eatables out of the way of ants, cats, and other depredators. It is usually hung from the roof of the house; hence the proverb is spoken of one who meets with some unexpected good fortune, or is promoted far above his merits.

Billī ke khuāb men chhīchhṛe.
The cat dreams of her tit-bits.
(Applied to one who on all occasions brings forward his own wants.)

Billī ke khuāb men chūhe kūden.
The cat dreams of mice running up and [down.
(Moral as in the preceding.)

Billī khāegī nahīn, par phailā tau bhī jāegī.
What the cat can't eat she is sure to scatter.
(The dog in the manger.)

Bīmār kī rāt pahāṛ barābar.
A sick man's night is as long as a hill.

Binā ṭhagāē kām nahīn nikaltā!
Without deceit business can never thrive!

Binaulon kī lūṭ men barchhī kā ghāo!
When plundering cotton seeds he is wounded with a spear.
(Great loss, little gain.)

Binā vastle chakrī, binā buddh ke deh,
Binā gurū kā bālkā, sir men ḍāle kheh.
Employment without interest, body without sense, and a disciple without a teacher are valueless.

Bin bahū prīt nahīṅ.
There is no love without a wife.
(Your father-in-law will love you only while your wife is alive.)

Bin biddiyā nar nār, jaise gadhā kumhār.
A man or a woman without sense is but a potter's ass.
(i. e. made to work hard for another's gain.)

Bin bulāī ahmaq le daṛī sahnak. Mah. Wom.
The fool has come uninvited with a platter.
(Spoken of one who comes without invitation to a feast, or who unasked intermeddles in any affair.)

Bin bulāī ḍomnī laṛke bāle samet āē. Wom.
Uninvited the songstress comes with all her children.

Bin chūchī bārah baras laṛke ko rakhtā hai.
He can keep a child for twelve years without giving it suck.
(Said of one who makes false promises.)

Bin dāmoṅ ke naukar haiṅ.
I am a servant without pay.
(A devoted slave.)

Bin dekhā chor bāp barābar.
An undetected thief is (honoured) as your father.

Bindh gayā so motī, rah gayā so patthar.
Pierced it is a pearl, unpierced it is a stone.
(Said of one who uses his opportunities.)

Bin gāṅṛ kā badhnā.
A pitcher with a round bottom.
(Said of an unsteady feeble character.)

Bin gharnī ghar bhūt ke ḍerā.
Without a wife a house is the abode of the devil.

Bin gharnī ghar pādat hai, Hai gharnī, ghar gājat hai.
Without the wife the house is dull, With the wife the house is lively.

Bin honī hotī nahīṅ, aur honī hovan hār.
If it is not to be, it will not be; if it is to be, it will be.
(*Che sara sara.*)

Bin jane kā thanailā huā hai. E. Wom.
No child brought forth and breasts inflamed.

Bin jāne kaun māne ?
Who believes without knowing ?

Bin julāhe Īd !
No festival without a weaver !
(Because he makes the praying carpet, *musalla.*)

Bin julāhe namāz nahīṅ; biṅ ḍholak tazīr nahīṅ.
There can be no prayer without a weaver, nor public punishment without a drum.

Bin kuṭnāpe chhinālā nahīṅ.
No adultress without a procuress.

Bin lāg khele jūā, āj na mūā kal mūā.
Who plays at dice without skill will lose to-day, at any rate to-morrow.

Bin māṅge mile so dūdh, aur māṅge mile so pānī.
It is milk if obtained without asking, and water if by begging.
(To beg I am ashamed.)

Bin māṅge motī mile, aur māṅgī mile na bhīk.
Without asking you can get pearls, by begging not even alms.

Bin māre kī tobā karnā.
To cry out before you are hurt.

Bin paisā kauṛī ke telī sāhū, ṭūṭī hāṅḍī kāṅdū sāhū.
The oilman trades without capital, the grain parcher on his broken pot.
(Their occupation brings them sustenance.)

Bin parche partīt nahīṅ. Hin.
No belief without proof.

Bin roē to māṅ bhī dūdh nahīṅ pilātī.
Even the mother doesn't give milk unless (the child) cries.
(Spare to speak, spare to speed.)

Bin ruke baid kī ghoṛī na chale.
The doctor's mare never goes without jibbing.
(At the places she is accustomed to stop at.)

Bin tāl pakhāvaj nāche hai.
He dances without a drum or a tune.
(Without music or singing. To dance without a pipe.)

Bipat barābar sukh nahīṅ, jo thoṛe din kī hoē.
No pleasure like misery, when it does not last long.
(The pleasures of melancholy.)

Bipat parī jab bheṭ manāī, mukar gayā jab denī āī.
When the trouble was on him he made a vow, when the trouble passed he denied it.
(When the devil was sick the devil a saint would be, When the devil got well the devil a saint was he.)

Bipat sanghātī tīn jane, jorū, beṭā, āp.
Misery hath companions three, a wife, a son and self.

Biphre risāle aur bhūke bhale mānas se ḍariye.
The angry low and the hungry high are alike to be feared.

Birachh kī chhāyā, aur purush kī māyā. Wom.
The shade of a tree, and the influence of a man (go with them.)

Birādar-i-haqīqī dushman i-mādar-zād hai.
Your greatest enemy is your uterine brother.
(Very true of royal families in the East.)

Birādrī ko na khilāyā, chār kāndhī hī jimā diye. Hin.
The kinsfolk have not been feasted, only the corpse bearers have been fed.

Bisī khisī !
Shrivelled and twenty !
(Allusion to the early maturity of women in India.)

Bismillāh hī galat. Mah.
Wrong at the very *Bi'smi'llah.*
(*Bi'smi'llahi-r-rahmāni-r-rahim*, in the name of God the merciful the compassionate, is the prayer used at all commencements, so the proverb means to be wrong at the very beginning.)

Bi'smi'llāh ke gumbad men baiṭhe hain. Mah.
He resides under the dome of *Bi'smi'llah.*
(*i. e.* he leads a resigned and retired life : in the odour of sanctity. *Bi'smi'llah* means in the name of God.)

Bis pachīs kā andar men jo pūt sapūt huā so huā, Māt o pitā kul tāran ko, jo Gayā na gayā, so kahīn na gayā.
If a son be dutiful between twenty and twenty five it is well, but if he has not gone to Gayā to procure salvation for his parents, he has made no pilgrimage at all.
(Said by Brāhmans to encourage pilgrimages.)

Bisunī bilār ḍabrī men ḍerā. E.
The unexpected cat sits on the dish.
(Cats always wait silently and come on one unawares, so the proverb is applied to an uninvited guest.)

Bisvā bis kī gānṭh hai.
A share in a village is a dangerous thing.
(*Bisvā* is a twentieth part of a village: allusion to a coparcenary community always at feud.)

Bisyar pakar, zahar ko chāt :
Par nārī sang chāl nā bāt.
Better catch a serpent and suck its poison,
Than have dealings with another's wife.

"*Bīvī, bīvī, Id āī,*" "*Chal, haram zādī, tujhe kyā ?*" Mah. Wom.
"My lady, my lady, the feast has come !" "Go, along you wretch, what has it to do with you ?"

"*Bīvī, bīvī, Id āī !*" "*Chal, murdār, tujhe ṭikyā se kām.*" Mah. Wom.
"My lady, my lady, the feast has come !" "Go, you wretch, and mind your loaf of bread !"

Biyāh huā nahīn, gaune kā jhagṛā.
The marriage is not yet over and he is quarreling about taking the bride home.

Biyāhī beṭī kā ghar rakhnā aur hāthī pālnā barābar hai.
To keep a married daughter at home is to keep an elephant.
(*i. e.* great expense.)

Biyāhī beṭī paṛausan dākhil.
A daughter married hath entered into neighbourhood.
(She no longer belongs to the family.)

Biyāhī, na barāt chaṛhī, ḍolī men baiṭhī na chūnchūn huī.
Nor wed, nor gone in marriage procession, she never sat in a palanquin to make it creak.
(Unwed.)

Biyāh kā ashgun mālūm bhae, lahore men āī bhaṭṭā ! E.
It is ill for the marriage, when rubbish is sent for the first present !

Biyāh men bid kā lekhā ?
Pasturage accounts are not settled on a wedding day.
(There is a time for every thing.)

Biyāh men k'hāī būr, phir kyā khāegī dhūr ? Wom.
If you eat saw-dust on a wedding day, you will eat dust afterwards.
(If you live on the alms of the wedding you cannot live long.)

Biyāh nahīn kiyā barāten to dekhī hain.
I have not been married, but I have seen marriage processions.
(That is I have not done this kind of work, but have seen it done by others. In reply to one who asks another tauntingly what he knows of the matter.)

Biyāh na karāo, jhūṭ mūṭ kā chāo.
Nor wedding nor nuptials, but sham love.
(Dishonorable intentions.)

Biyāh pīchhe pattal bhārī. Hin.
When the marriage feast is over, even the leaf plates are a heavy expense.
(Plenty ceases with the feast.)

Biyāj baṛhāve dhan ghanā, rāṛ baṛhāve chho,
Jaise gandak āg men gire to dūnī ho.
Wealth grows greatly on interest and a quarrel on anger, As a fire increases doubly if sulphur fall on it.

Biyāj moṭā, mūl kā ṭoṭā. Mercantile.
High interest loses the capital.

Boē ām phale bhanṭā.
I planted mangoes and got egg-plants.
(To sow the wind and reap the whirlwind.)

Boē peṛ babūl ke to ām kahān se hoen ?
If you sow acacias how will you eat mangoes?
(You shall reap as you sow: as you sow you shall mow.)

Bohnī ṭhonī, rad balā. Mercantile.
Cash for handsell puts away misfortune.

Bole ke na chāle ke, main to sūte ke bhalī. E. Wom.
No good for talk or company, I'm the one for sleep.
(The mother-in-law reproving the idleness of her daughter-in-law.)

Bole to bīvī merī, nahīn to darkār nahīn terī.
If you can talk you are my wife, if not I care not for you.

Bolī bolī to ye bolī "merī jūtī bole." Mah. Wom.
When she did speak all she said was, "May my shoe speak."
(She would not talk at all.)

Bolo to bolo nahīn pinjrā khālī karo.
Either speak or leave the cage.
(Said to a parrot. Do thy work or go thy way.)

Boltā chākar munīb ke āge gūṅgā.
A chattering servant is dumb before his master.
(Nervousness.)

Boltā hai jab talak hai boltā.
While there is life, there is speech.

Bolte ke āshnāī hai.
Attachment ends with life.
(Used in two ways—1. When one evinces a disposition to quarrel, another says, our friendship is only during the short space of our lives, why disturb it prematurely? 2. When any one is inconsolable on the death of a friend, the expression is employed by way of consolation to represent the unavailing nature of his grief.)

Boltī band hogaī.
His speech has left him (for grief.)

Boltī par sadma hai.
A blow hath fallen on his speech.
(He is overwhelmed with sorrow.)

Boṭī de-kar bakrā lete hain.
Giving a piece of meat and getting a goat.
(A great bargain.)

Boṭī nahīṅ to shorba hī sahī.
If not meat it is at any rate broth.
(A penny if not a pound.)

Boyā gehūṅ, upjā jau. Agric.
I sowed wheat and reaped barley.
(I received evil for good.)

Boyā na jotā Allāh Miyāṅ ne diyā potā. Mah. Wom.
Without sowing or ploughing God gave him a grandson.
(Undeserved good fortune: also allusion to the custom of widows' remarriage among Muhammadans and Jāṭs.)

Būcha, sab se ūṅchā.
A man without ears is above all.
(*i. e.* conspicuous.)

Buḍḍhā biyāh kare, parausiyoṅ ko sukh hove.
When an old man takes a wife, the neighbours have a pleasant life.

Buḍḍhā huā ūṅṭ, par mūtnā na āyā.
The camel grew old, but knew not how to make water.

Buḍḍhe kī aulād.
The issues of old age (are weak).

Buḍḍhe kī nā mare jorū, bāle kī nā mare māṅ.
(God) preserve the old man's wife and the infant's mother.

Buḍḍhe kī sīkh kare kām ko ṭhīk.
An old man's teaching sets the work straight.

Buḍḍhī bakrī aur hunḍār se ṭhaṭṭhā.
An old goat should not jest with a wolf.

Buḍḍhī bhaiṅs kā dūdh shakkar kā gholnā,
Buḍḍhe mard kī jorū gale kā ḍholnā.
An old buffaloe's milk is sugar sweet, An old mans' wife is a garland for his neck.

Buḍḍhī ghoṛī, lāl lagām.
An old mare with a red bridle.
(Applied to an old woman who decorates her person sumptuously.)

Buḍḍhī huīṅ nāēkā is hāl ko pahoṅchīṅ,
Sir hilne lagā, chhātiyāṅ pattāl ko pahoṅchīṅ.
The old harlot comes to this—Her head begins to shake, and her breasts to hang down.

Būḍhoṅ ne jo kām sikhāyā, dhokā mūl na vā meṅ āyā.
What an old man teaches has no flaw in it.

Bū gaī, bū-dār gaī, rahī khāl kī khāl.
The fragrance and the perfume are gone, and the skin remains as it was.

Bulāve, na chalāve, "main to dulhan kī chāchī"
Nor called nor invited and 'I am the bride's aunt.'

Bulāve, na chalāve, mor tīn bakhre. E.
Nor called nor invited, she claims three shares for herself.

Bulbul kā sā choṅḍā. Mah. Wom.
Hair-braided like a crested shrike.
(The plaiting of the hair exactly on the crown of the head is considered to be the mark of a prostitute.)

Būṅd būṅd kar-ke tālao bhartā hai.
Drop by drop fills the pond.
(Many a little makes a muckle.)

Būṅd kā chūkā ghaṛe ḍhalkāve.
A cask-full too late won't make up for the loss of one drop.
(A stitch in time saves nine.)

Būṅd se gaī, so phir hauz se nahīṅ ātī.
Lost by a drop can't be recovered by a pond-full.
(A miss is as good as a mile.)

Būṅṭ baṛā hoe to bhansār na phoṛe. E.
One grain, howsoever big, cannot break the oven.

Būṛā bans Kabīr kā, jo upje pūt Kamāl.
A doomed race was Kabīr's whence sprang such a son as Kamāl.
☞ Kamāl (perfection) the son of Kabīr, used to make *dohās* (couplets) in refutation of those pronounced by his father. For example,—*Kahe Kabīr, do nāve chaṛhiye, Ek būṛhe to ekhe rahiye.* Saith Kabir, always get into two boats, for when one goes down, the other will remain for you. *Kahe Kamāl, do nāo na chaṛhiye, Phāṭe gāṅṛ, utān ho paṛiye.* Saith Kamāl, never get into two boats, for your thighs will split and you will turn over.

Burā beṭā, khoṭā paisā, ek vaqt par kām ā jātā hai.
A bad son and a bad coin will serve you some time or other.
(It is an ill wind that blows no one any good.)

Burā hākim Khudā kā gazab.
A bad ruler is a scourge of God.

Burā kahne-vāle par tīn harf. Mah.
For evil speakers three letters.
(Viz. *lam, ain, nūn,* which spell *lān,* meaning a curse in Arabic.)

Burbak barke sāñjhe bichaunā. Bhoj.
A stupid bridegroom goes to sleep in the evening.
(To sleep before dark is considered very unlucky.)

Burbak Dās gaē harvāī, duī bail meṅ eko nāhīṅ. Bhoj.
Mr. Fool went to plough and lost both his oxen.
(By ill treatment and folly.)

Burbak debī ke kulthī kī achchhat. Bhoj.
Linseed is offered to a foolish goddess.
(The ceremony of the *achchhat* consists of putting rice on the idol's forehead.)

Burbak dhanaī kā rahikā bās, koṭhī meṅ chāur, ghar meṅ upās. Bhoj.
Riches don't give pleasure to a fool; rice in his barn, and his house without food.
(He can't learn to spend.)

Burbak ek gaē baṛ gāoṅ, ḍerā pāīṅ ūñche ṭhāoṅ, bahe beār, āṛ nahīṅ pāveṅ, phāṭe gāṅṛ malār gāṅveṅ. Bhoj.
A fool went to a great village, and got a lodging in a high place; the wind blew hard and no shelter could he get; so as miserable as possible he whistled and sang the song of rain.

Burbak gaile, machhlī māre, tāp aile ganvāe Bhoj.
A fool went to fish and lost his rod.

Burbak ke dhan fahīma mār khāē.
The intelligent spend the fool's wealth.
(A fool and his wealth are soon parted.)

Burbak kī jorū sab kī bhaujāī.
A fool's wife is every body's sister-in-law.
(*i. e.* any body may flirt with her.)

Burbhas lagī hai.
Second childhood has come over him.

Bure bhale meṅ chār ungal kā farq hai.
Between the good and the bad there is but a hand breadth.

Bure kā sāth de, so bhī burā.
Who sides with the wicked is wicked.
(Evil communications corrupt good manners.)

Bure kā sāthī koī nahīṅ.
No one befriends the wicked.

Bure kī burāī se ḍarīye.
Fear the wicked man's wickedness.

Bure se deo ḍarāē.
Even the gods fear the wicked.

Bure se Khudā bhī ḍartā hai.
God even fears the bad.

Bure, tujh se ḍarye, yā terī burāī se?
Bad man, why should I fear you or your vicious deeds?

Bure vaqt kā Allāh belī.
God helps us in bad times.
(Man's extremity is God's opportunity.)

Bure vaqt kā kaun hai juz Khudā?
Who helps in bad times but God?

Būṛhā, bālā barābar hotā hai.
An old man and a child are alike.
(Second childhood)

Būṛhā Baniyā aur ber chunne jāē!
The old shop-keeper going for wild plums!
(That is, undertaking more than he can perform.)

Būṛhā chochlā janāze ke sāth. Mah. Wom.
An old woman's wantonness ceases at her funeral.

Būṛhā jāne kīyā, bālā jāne hīyā.
Old age judges deeds, childhood judges the heart.

Būṛhā kuttā, pilvā nāoṅ!
An old cur and called a pup!

Buṛhāpe meṅ aql mārī gaī hai?
Have you turned mad in your old age?

Buṛhāpe meṅ maṭṭī kharāb.
Old age is misery.

Būṛh bhaī guīyāṅ, dimāg mor vaise. E. Wom.
My friend has grown old, but her airs are the same.
(Skittishness in old age.)

Būṛh bhailan, nāk lagle rahlain. Mag.
He has grown old, but doesn't know how to wipe his nose.

Būṛh bhail, buṛh ghaus na chhūṭal. E. Wom.
He has grown old but his childishness has not left him.

Būṛhe kalāṅvat kī kaun sune?
Who would listen to an old man's singing?

Būṛhe muṅh mūhāse, log dē tamāshe.
When pimples break out on an old face people run to see the wonder.
(Applied to one who in old age affects the manners of youth.)

Būṛhe tote bhī kahīṅ paṛhte haiṅ?
Does an old parrot ever learn?

Būṛhī jurvā nām Khatījā!
An old woman and her name Youth and Beauty.

Buṛhiyā dīvānī huī, parāē bartan uṭhāne lagī.
The mad old woman takes away another's plates.
(There is method in her madness.)

Buṛhiyā, gazab kī puṛyā.
An old woman is a packet of evil.

Buṛhiyā ko peṅṭh binā kab sare?
The old woman cannot go without marketing.

Buṛhiyā mar gaī, to kuchh gam nahīṅ, par farishtoṅ ne ghar dekh liyā.
If the old woman is dead no matter, but the angel of death knows the house.
(He may come again.)

Būṛh na savād ghīu khichṛī. E. Wom.
An old man has no taste for dainties.

Burī ghaṛī na āve!
May the evil hour never come!

Būr ke laḍḍū khāe to pachhtāe, na khāe to pachhtāe.
Saw-dust sweetmeats; who eats grieves, who eats not also grieves.
(A siren that allures to destruction.)

Būvad ham-pesha, bā-ham-pesha dushman. Pers.
Two of a trade can never agree.

C

Chabokaṛ so laṛokaṛ. Wom.
Joking leads to fighting.

Chachā banā-kar chhoṛūṅgā.
I'll treat you as an uncle.
(Ironical: I'll give you good beating.)

Chachā chor, bhatījā Qāzī.
The uncle thief, and the nephew Judge.

Chachere mamere, baṛ tale bahutere.
Many cousins collect about a Banian tree.
(A rich man.)

Chahār chīz ast tohfa-i-Multān:
Gard, garmā, gadā o goristān. Pers.
Multan is famous for four things:
Dust, heat, beggars and graves.

Chahār-shambah na dārad. Ped.
He can't keep Wednesday.
(This is a bad pun: the Pers. *chahār-shambah* is the Hindī *Budh*, Wednesday, and *buddh* is wisdom, whence the proverb means he has no sense.)

Chāhat kī chākrī kīje, an-chāhat kā nām na līje.
Serve him that likes you, but mention not him that dislikes you.

Chāh, chamārī, chūhṛī; sab nīchan kī nīch.
Avarice is cobbler, scavenger; the lowest of the low.
(No vice like avarice.)

Chāhe kodoṅ dalāle, chāhe manḍūā pisā le. Wom.
Be it wheat or be it corn, I'll grind and pound it for you.
(*Kodoṅ* and *manḍūā* are names for the same plant *eleusine corocana*.—Stewart, *Panjāb Plants*, 254.)

Chāh kare jā kī chākrī kīje, na kare tā kā nām na līje.
Serve him that desires you, but mention not him that spurns you.
(Spoken by one to whom any thing has been offered with a bad grace, which he in consequence will not accept.)

Chāh karūṅ, pyār karūṅ, chūtar tale aṅgār dharūṅ, jal jāe to maiṅ kyā karūṅ? Wom.
I'll love him, and I'll caress him and I'll put fire under him; if it burn him, what can I do?
(Sham affection.)

Chahle kī bhaiṅs.
A buffalo of the mire.
(A fat slovenly woman.)

Chāhne ke nām gadhī ne bhī khet khānā chhoṛ diyā thā.
Even the she-ass was scared from her pasture when one talked to her of love.
(Follow love and it will fly from thee, fly from love and it will follow thee.)

Chākar hai to nāchā-kar, nā nāche to nā chākar.
If you're a servant you must dance, if you won't dance you're no servant.

Chākar ke āge kūkar, kūkar ke āge pesh-khema.
Before the servant a dog, before the dog a *pesh-khema* (a tent sent on in advance).
(The phrase is used when a servant, who has received an order from his master, sends another instead of going himself.)

Chākar ko uzr nahīṅ, kūkar ko uzr hai.
The servant can make no excuse, but a dog can.

Chākar se kūkar bhalā jo sove apnī nīnd.
Happier than a servant is a dog that hath his fill of sleep.

Chakaryā chākrī kar-ke āp apne hāth biktā hai.
Service is self inflicted slavery.

Chakh ḍāl māl dhan ko, kauṛī na rakh kafan ko,
Jis ne diyā hai tan ko, degā vohī kafan ko.
Eat up all thy wealth, keep not a penny for thy shroud. He that hath nourished thy body will provide thy shroud.
(Eat, drink, and be merry for to-morrow we die.)

Chakkī pherī, huī chūn kī ḍherī. Rus. Wom.
It is the turning of the mill that makes the flour heap.

Chakkī meṅ kaul ḍāloge to chūn pāoge. Wom.
Throw grain into the mill and you 'll get flour.
(You'll get nothing for nothing.)

Chakkī tale ghar terā, nikal, sās, ghar merā. Wom.
Get out, thou mother-in-law, thy house is under the mill-stone; this house is mine.
(Among the poor the mother on her son's marriage leaves the house and lives in the outhouse where the hand-mill is kept.)

Chāk ko Taqdīr ke mumkin nahīṅ karnā rafū:
Sozan-i-tadbīr sārī umr go sītī rahe.
You cannot close up the rent made by Fate, Though the needle of your remedies be plied all your life.
(*L' homme propose et Dieu dispose.*)

Chakmak dīdah, khāe malīdah. Wom.
Wanton eyes are on dainties fed.
(Said of harlot.)

Chākrī meṅ ākrī kyā?
What excuse is there in service?

Chakvā chakvī do jane, in mat māro koī.
Yeh māre Kartār ke, rain bichhoyā hoī.
No one should ever kill the sheldrake, for they are separated at night by the curse of God.
☞ The natives have a legend that two lovers for some indiscretion were turned into two

sheldrake and condemned to pass the night apart from each other on the opposite banks of a river. All night long each asks in its turn if it shall join its mate, and the answer is always in the negative. The peculiar cry of the sheldrake at night no doubt gave rise to this legend.

Chalā chalī kā saudā, pyāre, bhalā bhalī kar leo.
Death is in the market, friend, do good betimes.

Chalā chalī kī rāh meṅ bhalā bhalī kar leo.
Do good in this way of Death.

Chalat phirat dhan pāiye; baiṭhe degā kaun?
By moving and going about you can get money; who will pay you for sitting idle?

Chal base jo log the Islām ke,
Rahgaë bāqī Musalmān nām ke.
The true Musalmāns have gone from us,
The remainder are Musalmāns in name merely.

Chal chakhe! mere mūṅh mat lag. Mah. Wom.
Away! avaunt! don't stick to my mouth.
(Don't talk with me.)

Chal, chhāoṅ, maiṅ āī hūṅ, jumla pīr manāī hūṅ. Mah. Wom.
Go on, shadow; I will follow, for I have invoked all the saints.
(Put into the mouth of a woman who affects extreme delicacy, so as to be unable to walk without great difficulty. She desires her shadow to go on before, and says that with the assistance of the saints she will follow as fast as she can.)

Chale na jāne āṅgan ṭeṛhā. E. Wom.
Can't walk because, forsooth, the yard is crooked.
(A bad workman quarrels with his tools.)

Chale rānḍ kā charkhā, aur bure kā peṭ.
A widow's spinning wheel, and a bad man's belly are always moving.
(The widow earning her livelihood by spinning, and the bad man suffering from the effects of intemperance.)

Chalī chalī āī saut ke pīhar. Wom.
She went for refuge to the family of the co-wife.
(To express one's taking a step that must inevitably lead to his or her ruin.)

Chalī chalī Bī Mākho āīn.
Dame Rumour travelling along has alighted here.

Chālīs baras kā rezah.
A boy of forty years.

Chālīs serā ūt.
A forty *ser* fool.
(A complete fool: see following.)

Chālīs serī bāt kahte haiṅ.
His words are full forty *sers*.
(40 *sers* make a *man*: so that his words are complete, *i. e.* good and valuable.)

Chal marghaṭ ko, lakṛiyāṅ sastī haiṅ.
Come to your funeral pyre, wood is cheap now!
(Said to a niggardly person.)

Chal mere charkhe charrakh chūṅ, kahāṅ kī buṛhiyā? kahāṅ kā tū?
Go along spinning wheel and hum away, whence the old woman and whence thou?
☞ A common variant of the nursery tale of the Lambkin relates how an old woman persuaded a tiger, a leopard, and other beasts of the forest to defer eating her, till her return from her daughter's house after she had grown plump and fat. On her way back she cheated the hungry expectants by concealing herself in a spinning-wheel and repeating from within the above couplet in answer to the anxious enquiries of each beast of prey.

Chalnā bhalā na kos kā, beṭī bhalī na ek,
Denā bhalā na bāp kā, jo Pirbhū rākhe ṭek.
It is not well to walk even a mile, to have even one daughter, To owe to your father: God preserve you from these.

Chalnā hai, rahnā nahīṅ, chalnā bisve bīs.
Aise sahej suhāg par kaun guṅdhāve sīs?
Go we must, we cannot stay, this is very certain: Who would deck her hair for such a short married life?

Chal na sakūṅ merā Kūdan nām.
I cannot walk and my name is Jumper.

Chalnī chammā, ghoṛ lajammā, Kāith gulammā, ye tīnoṅ nahīṅ koī kammā. E.
The strings of a sieve, the bit of a horse, a Kāith as a servant, are three useless things.
(The two first can't be used second-hand, as constant use wears them out.)

Chalnī dūse sūp ko ki jis meṅ bahattar chhed.
The sieve with seventy two holes chides the winnowing fan.
(The pot calls the kettle black.)

Chalnī meṅ gaī dūhne, karam ko kā dosh? E. Wom.
She went to milk with a sieve, so what blame to fate?

Chalo na jāë, yaṭhṛī murauṭho. E. Wom.
He can't walk and a bundle on his head.

Chalo, sakhī, vahāṅ chaleṅ jahāṅ baseṅ Brij Rāj,
Goras bechat Hari mileṅ, ek panth do kāj. Wom.
Come, friend, let us go to the place where the sovereign of Brij lives, To sell our milk and meet with Krishna, and thus kill two birds with one stone.

Chaltā phirtā na marai, baiṭhaā mar jāë. E.
Walking and wandering don't kill, sitting still does kill.

Chalte bail kī chūtaṛ meṅ lakṛī karnā.
To goad the willing ox.

Chalte chor langoṭī lābh.
A loin-cloth is a prize to a passing thief.
(All's fish that comes to his net.)

Chaltī hāth pāoṅ sulūk kar lo.
Do good while you may.

Chalte hāth pāoṅ uṭhāle.
May I die while I am able to stir about.
(May I never be bed-ridden)

Chaltā chākī dekh-kar diyā Kabīrā roē,
Do pāṭan ke bīch meṅ sābit rahā na koē.
Kabīr wept to see the mill go round,
As nothing remained whole betwixt the two stones.
(Allusion to the earth and sky and whatever is between them.)

Chaltī gāṛī meṅ roṛā aṭkānā.
To stop a running cart with a stone.
(To put a spoke in his wheel.)

Chaltī havā se laṛtī hai.
She quarrels with the breeze.
(Quarrelsome beyond endurance.)

Chaltī kā nām gāṛī, gāṛī kā nām ūkhlī.
What moves they call a cart, what is fixed they call a mortar.
(There is a double pun here: *gāṛī* means "a cart" as well as "a fixture:" *ūkhlī* means "a mortar and "uprooted," so that the phrases can be taken in exactly opposite senses.)

Chaltī meṅ kaun kasar kartā hai?
Who fails to do what he can for himself?
(Every one tries his best in his own interest: to put one's best leg forward.)

Chamār chamṛe kā yār.
A cobbler is a friend to leather.
(He can't be kept straight except by shoe-beating.)

Chamār kī chhokrī Chandan nām!
A cobbler's daughter and named Sandal!
(*Sandal* is applied by high caste Brāhmans for the *ṭikā* or sectarial mark on the forehead.)

Chamār ko arash par bhī begār.
Even in Heaven forced labor is the cobbler's lot.
(To describe an unlucky person whose fortune does not change by change of situation.)

Chamār ko Dīvālī meṅ bhī begār.
A Chamār must work even on the Dīvālī.
(*i. e.* on a holiday, he is then employed to light the lamps.)

Chamāroṅ ke kose ḍhoṛ nahīṅ marte. Rus.
Cattle don't die of the currier's curse.
(If the cattle die he will get their skins for leather.)

Chamgiddaroṅ ke ghar mehmān āē: "ham bhī laṭkeṅ, tum bhī laṭko."
The bats entertained some guests and said "we are hanging (from the roof) and so do you hang."
(In Rome do as Rome does.)

Chām kā chamoṭā, kūkar rakhvāl!
A dog set to watch a leather strap!
(He will be sure to walk off with it.)

Chām kā ghar kuttā liye jātā hai.
Dogs will walk off with a house of leather.
(Build your house of durable materials.)

Chām ke chanḍū chalal pahāṛ, pīchhlal ṭaṅgṛī ṭūṭal kapār. E.
A man of leather (weak) went up a hill, he missed his footing and broke his pate.

Chām ke dām.
The price of the skin.
(Said of anything bought cheap: allusion to the debased coinage of Muhammad Tuglaq, who issued in 1330 A. D. copper tokens having ficticious values in gold and silver.)

Champā ke das phūl, chaṅbelī kī ek kalī,
Mūrakh kī sārī rāt, chātūr kī ek ghaṛī.
A bud of jasmine is better than ten flowers of *champā*. An hour with a clever man is better than the whole night with a fool.
(Better fifty years of Europe than a cycle of Cathay.)

Chamṛe kī zibān hai, bhūl chūk ho hī jātī hai.
The tongue is but skin and liable to err.

Chamṛī jāē par damṛī na jāē.
He 'll part with his skin, but not with his cash.
(You will get nothing out of a miser but his skin.)

Chanā aur chugal mūṅh lagā burā.
It is a bad thing to get a taste for pulse and tale-bearing.
(Pulse is a very difficult taste to give up.)

Chanā aur chugal mūṅh lagā chhuṭtā nahīṅ.
The taste for pulse or tale-bearing once acquired never leaves you.

Chanā kahe "merī ūṅchī nāk, Ek ghar dalye, do ghar ṛāṛ. Jo khāve merā ek ṭūk, Pānī pīve sau sau ghūṅṭ."
Saith pulse, "my honor is great, When I am ground in one house the noise is heard in two. Who eats bread made of me Will drink a hundred gulps of water."

Chanā mard nāj hai.
Pulse is a grain for warriors.

Chaṅbelī chāo meṅ āī, Bakhtāvar reoṛiyāṅ bāṅṭe. Mah. Wom.
The jasmine has begun to bloom, for Bakhtāvar is dispensing sweets.
(The phrase is used to express that one who is generally morose is in an uncommonly good humour, or that a miser is beginning to spend his money like a gentleman.)

Chaṅbelī chāo meṅ āī, bakhtyāre sāth lāī. Mah. Wom.
Show my lady Jasmine favor and she 'll bring her whole family.

Chanchal nār chhail se laṛī, Khan andar, khan bāhar khaṛī.
When a mistress quarrels with her lover, She is sometimes in the house and sometimes outside.
(Lover's quarrels.)

Chaṅchal nār kī chāl chhipe nahīṅ, nīch chhipe na baṛappan pāē,
Jogī kā bhek nek dharo, koī karam chhipe nā bhabhūt ramāē.
The wanton's gait betrays her, the low-born though in place betrays himself.
Put on a saintly garb and the ashes will hide no evil deeds.
(Scratch the Russian and you will find the Tartar.)

Chandan kī chuṭkī, nā gāṛī bharā kāṭh.
A pinchful of sandal-powder is better than a cart-load of wood.

Chandan paṛā chamār ke nit uṭh kūṭe chām,
Ro ro chandan mahī phire "paṛā nīch se kām."
A log of sandal wood got into a cobbler's house who beat leather with it,
The log went bewailing to the world that it had fallen into the hands of the mean.

Chānd āsmān chaṛhā sab ne dekhā.
Everybody sees the moon rising.
(Worshipping the rising sun.)

Chānd chaṛhe kul ālam dekhe.
All the world can see the moon in the sky.

Chande āb, chande mahtāb.
Fair as the moon, and bright as the sun.

Chānd gahan men chakki rahē kā kyā kām?
What has the mill-stone dresser to do at an eclipse of the moon?
(He is never employed at that season.)

'*Chanḍī, ghar lipegī?*' '*Nahīn, nigoṛe, khodūngī,*'
'*Chanḍī, ghar khodegī*' '*Nahīn, nigoṛe, līpūngī.*'
Hin. Wom.
'You shrew, will you plaster the floor?' 'No, you wretch! I'll dig it.'
'You shrew, will you dig the floor?' 'No, you wretch! I'll plaster it.'
(Mary, Mary, so contrary.)

Chāndī kā chashmā lagāte hain.
He wears silver spectacles.
(He takes bribes.)

Chāndī kā jūtā sir par.
A silver shoe is tolerated on the head.
(Money can do what force cannot.)

Chānd kā ṭukṛā.
A part of the moon.
(Very bright and shining.)

Chānd ko gahan lag gayā.
The moon is eclipsed.
(Said when a beautiful girl is matched to an ugly fellow; also when the fame of a virtuous man is tarnished.)

Chānd men mail nahīn.
No dirt in the moon.

Chānd ne khet kiyā.
The moon has risen.

Chāndnī mār gai.
The moon has struck him.
(Said especially of a horse that is weak in the back.)

Chāndnī men fasd khulvānī mana hai. Superstition.
It is not advisable to open the veins in the bright fortnight of the month.

Chāndnī men shahd nahīn hotā.
Bees don't make honey in the moonlight.
(Native observation.)

Chānd pe khāk ḍālne se nahīn chhiptā.
You cannot hide the moon by throwing dust on her.
(A good man's reputation is not injured by speaking ill of him. Solid worth is not sullied by slander.)

Chane chabāo yā shahnāī bajāo.
Chew the peas or play the bag-pipe.
(Either dance or hold the candle.)

Chane chiraunjī hogaē, gehūn hogaī dākh,
Ghar men gahne tīn hain, charkhā, pīṛhī, khāṭ.
Wom.
Peas dear as almonds, wheat as raisins, And three ornaments only in the house, a spinning-wheel, a stool and a bed.
(Hard times)

Chane kā mārā martā hai.
A man dies from the stroke of a pea.
(To express the instability of human life.)

Chane ke sāth kahīn ghun na pis jāē!
May the weevil not be ground up with the peas!
(Let not the poor suffer with the rich: let not the innocent suffer with the guilty.)

Chāo ghaṭe nit ke ghar jāē, Bhāo ghaṭe kuchh mukh ke mānge, Rog ghaṭe kuchh aukhad khāē, Giyān ghaṭe kusangat pāē.
Liking lessens by meeting every day,
Respect lessens by making a request,
Sickness lessens by using medicine,
Knowledge lessens in bad company.
(Familiarity breeds contempt.)

Chāplūsī kā mūnh kālā.
Fawning hath a black face.

Chapnī bhar pānī men ḍūb maro.
Drown yourself (for shame) in a saucer-ful of water.

Chapnī likh-kar sir par dharī, nikal paṛā yā nikal pāṛī. Mah. Wom.
The inscribed platter is placed upon her head, a fairy boy or fairy girl will come out.
(This couplet, together with the name of Sheikh Farid, is inscribed on an earthen plate, and placed as a charm on the head of a lying-in woman to facilitate delivery.)

Chaprāsī be satāē nahīn rahte.
The *chaprāsī* won't go without pinching you.
(Without squeezing something out of you.)

Chāq chau band, ṭakā nāl-band.
A fine horse and a penny to the farrier.
(False economy.)

Chār afīmī aur tīn huqqa.
Four opium eaters and three pipes.
(Great inconvenience and serious disputes in consequence.)

Chār Bed aur pānchvān labed.
Four Vedas, the fifth a cudgel.
(He who does not listen to precepts or reason must be compelled to do so. A bridle for the horse, a saddle for the ass, and a rod for the fool's back.)

Charbī chhāī ānkhon men to nāchan lāgī āngan men. Mah.
When there is a film before her eyes, she goes dancing about in her yard.
(*Ānkhon men charbī chhānā*, to be blind and

also to be shameless, so there is a pun in the proverb.)

Chār chor chaurāsī Baniye, ek ek karke lūṭā.
Four thieves plundered eighty four Baniyās one after the other.

☞ The story goes that four thieves met eighty four Baniyās on a road. The thieves began to pick out one man at a time from amongst the Baniyās and to loot him till they had plundered them all; the Baniyās not daring to make common cause against them.

Chār dināṅ kī chāṅdnī pher aṅdherā pākh.
There is moonlight for a few days, and then it is as dark as before.
(Riches have wings. Applied to express the transitory nature of prosperity.)

Chār din kā rang chang: chhor, dahī-jarvā, morā sang! E. Wom.
Your love lasts four days only; none of your company, you mean brute! [Wom.

Chār din kī āiyāṅ, aur soṅth bisāhan jāiyāṅ.
But four days married and she's off to buy dry ginger.
(For her *accouchement*!)

Chār din kī chamār jotish!
Four days ago he was a cobbler and is now an astrologer!

Chār din kī chamār chaudash hai.
The cobbler's feast is for four days in the year.
(A nine days' wonder.)

Chār ghar chau-bhaīyā, tekrā bīch meṅ bhikhan bhaiyā. E. Wom.
Four brothers dwell in four houses, and one of them is a beggar.
(The inequality of men.)

Chār-gorvā bāṅdhā jāē, du-gorvā na bāṅdhā jāē.
You can tie up the four-footed, but not the two-footed.

Chār hāth pāoṅ sab ke hain.
Every man has two hands and two legs.

Charhegā so giregā.
Who climbs falls.

Charhe par na charhāo, sir dikhe na pāoṅ.
He did not mount step by step, nor distinguish the head from the feet.
(To do any thing in a confused manner.)

Charhī karhāī tel na āyā, kab āegā? Wom.
The oil may keep away, if it comes not when the frying-pan is on the fire.

Charh jā, beṭā, sūlī par, Bhagvān bhalī karenge.
Come, my son, and impale yourself, God will help you.
(Said of sinister advice.)

Charh mār, gūlar pakke.
Get up, the fruit is ripe for you.
(The ball is at your feet, or the game is in your hands.)

Charhte barse Ardrā, utrat barse Hast,
Kitnā rājā dand le, rahe anand girhast. Agric.
If rain falls in July and October the peasants will be happy, however much the king may tax them.

Charhtī bār-gāh.
A walking mosque.
(Said of any holy personage.)

Charhtī kalā, jāgtī jot.
May you shine like the waxing moon, brighter and brighter.

Chār jāt gāveṅ har bhong, Ahīr, Dafālī, Dhobī, Dom.
Four castes are always singing, Neatherds, Musicians, Washermen and Bards.
(Common observation in India.)

Chār mahīne hāl kā, bhār mahīne tāl kā, chār mahīne pāl kā.
Four months fresh (water), four months tank (water), and four months kept (water).
(In the rainy season fresh water, in winter tank water and in summer kept water is best.)

Chāroṅ raste mokle.
All four roads are open.

Chārpāē baro kitābe chand. Pers.
A quadruped with some books on it's back.
(Originally from the Gulistāṅ.)

Chār pāoṅ kā ghorā chaunktā hai, do pāoṅ kā ādmī kyā balā hai?
If a horse with four legs stumble, what can the man do who has only two?

Chār sāl, burā havāl.
Four years are full of risk.
(Said of a horse.)

Charsī yār kis ke? dam lagāyā khiske.
The smoker is no one's friend! he smokes and is off.

Chārū so bhārū.
Strong porters are great eaters.

Chashm bad dūr, āṅkheṅ motī-chūr!
May the evil eye never fall on this eye of pearl!

Chashm-i-mā raushan, dil-i-mā khush. Pers.
Light of my eyes and my heart's delight.
(A son.)

Chaskā din das kā; parāyā khasam kis kā? Wom.
Illicit love is but for ten days: who can claim another's spouse?

Chaskā lagā burā.
A bad habit is a bad thing.

Chaṭ maṅgnī paṭ biyāh: ṭūṭ gaī ṭangrī, rah gayā biyāh. Wom.
The betrothal now, and the wedding anon: a leg is broken and the wedding is put off.
(The uncertainty of human affairs.)

Chaṭorā khāve apnā ghar, baṭorā khāve doū ghar.
The glutton eats up his own house, the spongers eat up others.'

Chaṭorā kuttā alonī sil.
A ravenous dog (will eat) a saltless stone.

Chaṭorī zabān daulat kī hān.
An epicure's tongue wastes his wealth.

Chātur kā kām nahīṅ pātar se aṭke.
Pātar kā kām yehī, liyā diyā saṭke.
The wise man's work is not stopped for a harlot. A harlot's work is this—to give and take and be off.

Chātur kā qaraz man meṅ nistār.
The wise man's debts are a pleasure to his heart.
(He borrows money to make more by it.)

Chātur kī cherī bhalī mūrakh kī nār se.
Better be a wise man's slave than a fool's wife.
(Better be an old man's darling than a young man's slave.)

Chātur ko chaugunī, mūrakh ko saugunī.
The wise man's four fold is the fool's hundred fold.
(The wise man's estimate of another's wealth is four fold, whereas a fool's estimate is a hundred fold its real value.)

Chātur nār, nar kūṛh se biyāh hoe pachhtāē,
Jaise rogī nīm ko āṅkh mīch pī jāē.
A clever maid married to a fool sorrows, As a sick man takes his bitter draught with closed eyes.

Chātur to bairī bhalā, mūrakh bhalā na mīt,
Sādh kahe haiṅ, 'mat karo ko mūrakh se pīt.'
Better a wise foe than a foolish friend.
The sages have said 'have no friendship with a fool.'

Chaube gaē Chhabbe hone, Dubbe hī rah gaē.
A Chaube went to be a Chhabbe and remained Dubbe.
(*Dube, Chaube* and *Chhabbe* are 3 castes of Brāhmans, who (God save the mark !) have read respectively 2,4 and 6 *Vedas*.)

Chaube mareṅ to bandar hoṅ, bandar mareṅ to Chaube hoṅ.
Chaubās dead to monkeys turn, and monkeys dead to Chaubās turn.
(They are both so attached to their country that they cannot leave it.)

Chaudah biddyā nidhān.
Learned in the fourteen arts and sciences.
(All that there are in Oriental estimation.)

Chaudhvīn rāt ke chānd ko gahan lagā.
The full moon is eclipsed.
(Said when an ugly man marries a handsome woman.)

Chaukī gāoṅ-vāloṅ ko lūṭ khātī hai.
The police station loots the village.

Chāval, pache ṭāval.
Rice is soon digested.

Chele chīnī ho gaē, gurū gūṛ hī rahe.
The pupil became sugar, and the teacher remained treacle.
(To surpass one's master.)

Chele lāveṅ māṅg-kar, baiṭhā khāē mahant.
Rām bhajan kā nām hai, peṭ bharan kā panth.
The disciples beg and the priest eats at his ease. The name is "Praising God," the sect is "Filling the stomach."

Chenā jī kā lenā : chaudah pānī denā, byār chale to lenā nā denā. Agric.
Millet eats up the heart : give it fourteen floodings, and then comes the hot wind, and there is nothing to give or take.
(*Chenā, panicum miliaceum*, is an uncertain crop requiring much water; hence proverb.)

Chene ke bans meṅ sapūt bhaē māṛhā. E.
Parched maize is the excellent offspring of millet.
(An expression used, but rather contemptuously, when the child of worthless parents turns out good for something: *parvenu, nouveaux riches, novus homo.*)

Cherī sab ke pāoṅ dhove, apne dhotī lajāē.
The maid servant washes other's feet, but feels ashamed to wash her own.
(*i. e,* no one will serve his own relatives.)

Chhabbe hone gaē the, Dubbe bhī na rahe. Hin.
Wanting to become a *Chhabbe* loses even his original rank of *Dubbe*.
(It is used to express the folly of him who, like the dog in the fable, loses what he actually possessed in the vain pursuit of higher attainments: For explanation see above *Chaube gae*, etc.)

Chhab gaṭhṛī meṅ, joban rakābī meṅ. Mah. Wom.
Show in his bundle, and youth in his platter.
(Fine feathers make fine birds.)

Chha chāval aur nau pakhāl pānī.
Six grains of rice and nine bags of water.
(To cook them !)

Chhachhūṅdar chhoṛnā.
To let loose a musk-rat.
(Mischief making.)

Chhachhūṅdar ke sir meṅ chaṅbelī kā tel.
Oil of jasmine on the head of the musk-rat.
(Said of a worthless swaggerer.)

Chhaēdām meṅ laṛāī, paise meṅ sughaṛ bhalāī. E. Wom.
A half-penny will settle a row about a farthing.
(A *chhadām* = 12 *kauṛīs* = a farthing: a *paisā* is a half-penny, hence point of proverb.)

Chhail chhīṅṭ, bagal meṅ īṅṭ.
He is a queer *beau* that has bricks under his armpits.
(To swell out the muscles of his arms and make him look a powerful man.)

Chhājā, bājā, kes, tīn Bangāle des :
Chūnā, chūchī, dahī, tīn Bangāle nahīṅ.
Thatches, music, and long hair: these three are in Bengal : Lime, busts, and tyre : these three are not in Bengal.

Chhāj bole so bole, chhalnī bhī bole, jis meṅ bahattar sau chhed. Wom.
If the winnowing fan speak it is well, but if the sieve full of holes speak, what then?
(The innocent can speak out freely but not the criminal : those that live in glass houses can't throw stones.)

Chajje kī baiṭhak burī, aur par-chhāvan kī chhāṅh, Dhere kā rasiyā burā, jo nit uṭh pakṛe bāṅh.
Sitting on view is bad, the shadow of another is bad, A lover at hand is bad as he is always worrying. [*janā.* Bhoj.

Chhajjū gaile chha janā, Chhajju aile nau
When Chhajjū went there were six of them, when he returned there were nine.
(Don't be too ready to make friends.)

Chhal kā phal burā hotā hai.
The fruits of deceit are always bad.

Chhallo chhalhāī.
Deceive and be deceived.
(Biter bit.)

Chha mahīne mimyānī to ek bachchā biyānī. Rus.
The she-goat was six months pregnant and produced one kid.
(Great boast, little roast.)

Chhānī par phūṅs nahīṅ, deoṛhī par nāch. E.
No straw on his thatch and dances at his door!
(Living for appearances.)

Chhān kā kyā ghar? Aur meṅḍak kā kyā ḍar?
What home under a mere thatch? What fear of a frog?

Chhappar par phūṅs nahīṅ rahā.
Not a straw left of the thatch.
(Said of utter bankruptcy or pillage. *Chhappar par phūns* is an idiom for a competency.)

Chhatar bor kā tavā bāṅdh-ke ānā.
Better come with an iron pan on your head.
(To protect the head from severe beating: intimation of an imminent danger.)

Chhatar-patī, ghaṭe pāp, baṛhe ratī. Hin. Prayer.
O goddess, forgive his sins and increase his fortune.
(Said when a child sneezes.)

Chhātī chhalnī honā.
A heart full of holes.
(To bleed at every pore: be filled with grief.)

Chhaṭī kā dūdh yād āve.
The milk of the sixth day after birth is remembered.
(Maternal affection never diminishes.)

Chhātī kā jam.
A devil on the breast.
(An irksome person who is perpetually persecuting: a bore; an incubus.)

Chhaṭī kā khāyā pīyā sab nikal gayā.
All he had eaten on the sixth day of his birth is gone from him.
(Baffled in his attempts: an utter failure.)

Chhātī kā saudā hai.
It is a bold business.
(Courage is the back-bone of a transaction.)

Chhaṭī ke potṛe ab tak nahīṅ dhule.
He has not yet thrown off his clouts.
(He is still a baby.)

Chhaṭī ke rajjā.
A king installed on the sixth day after his birth.
(Used ironically.)

Chhaṭī na chilla, harām kā pilla.
Nor feast on the sixth day, nor on the fortieth for the bastard pup.
(Those who to treat refuse will always get abuse.)

Chhātī par mūṅg dalte hain.
They grind pulse on my breast.
(To do any thing so as to vex or give another pain.)

Chhātī pe bāl nahīṅ, bhāl se laṛāī. E.
No hair on his breast, and he is going to fight the bear.
(Quite unfit to the task: hair on the breast is the sign of manly vigour.)

Chhātī pe dhar-ke koī nahīṅ le jātā.
None carries (his wealth) on his breast (after his death.)
(Naked came I out of my mother's womb and naked shall I return thither. Job. I, 24.)

Chhātī pe koī nahīṅ dhar degā.
None will lay your wealth on your breast (at your death).

Chhattīs parkār ke bhojan meṅ sattar do bahattar rog bhare haiṅ. Hin.
In thirty six dishes are seventy two complaints.

Chhattrī kā bhagat, na mūsal kā dhanak. Hin.
You can no more make a monk out of a Chhatrī (soldier) than a bow out of a pestle.

Chhattrī kā shohdā, Kāeth kā bodā;
Bāman kā bail, Baniye kā ut.
The Chhatrī for rake, the Kāyath for weakness; The Brāhman for idiot, the Baniyā for fool.
(The characteristics of the four castes.)

Chhāvat maṅḍuā, gāvat gīt, pīyā bin lāgat sab anrīt. E. Wom.
Singing songs and making a bower is all unseemly without a lover.

Chhāyā baṛī māyā hai. Hin.
Shade is a great blessing.
(*Chhāyā* — also 'roof over your head.')

Chhāyā chhūā ghar pāyā aur bāṅdhī pāī ṭaṭṭī.
Dūsre kā janmā laṛkā pāyā chummā leṅ ke chaṭṭī.
He found the house thatched and doors to the walls, He found another's child and began to kiss it.
(The man who marries a widow.)

Chhelī jī se gaī, khāne-vāloṅ ko savād na āyā. Hin. Wom.
The goat lost its life, but the eaters were not pleased.
(Said of unappreciated self-sacrifice.)

Chhīle chār baghāre pāṅch. Wom.
She peeled but four, and brought out five.
(Said tauntingly to a conceited daughter-in-law.)

Chhīlī chhālī ṭaiyā sī.
Clean cut and clipped.

Chhināl kā beṭā 'babuā re babuā.' E. Wom.
A harlot's child is every body's darling.
(Many talk with the children for the sake of the maid.)

Chhināl lugāī, chātar sipāhī.
A loose woman and a gallant soldier.
(Cannot hide their qualities.)

Chhīṅkat nahāiye, chhīṅkat khāiye, chhīṅkat rahiye soë, Chhīṅkat par ghar na jāiye, chahe sarb sone kā hoë. Hin. Superstition.
You may sneeze and wash, eat, and sleep,
But must not sneeze and go to another's house, though all of gold.

Chhīṅke hī pe rakkhī milegī.
What's already in your net you will obtain.
(*Chhīṅkā*, a net suspended from the roof and containing eatables. It is used to keep these safe from cats, dogs, rats, ants, etc.)

Chhīṅkte gaë, jhīṅte āë.
He went sneezing and came back weeping.
(Allusion to the wide-spread notion of the ill-luck of sneezing before starting on a journey.)

Chhīṅkte hī nāk kaṭī.
Cutting off the nose for sneezing.
(Biting the nose to spite the face.)

Chhiṭāṅk chūn chaubāre rasoī! Hin. Wom.
An ounce of meal and a feast on the housetop !

Chhiṭāṅk satvā, Mathurā meṅ bhanḍār. E.
An ounce of pease-meal and a granary in Mathurā.
(Vain show.)

Chhoṛ chale banjāre kī sī āg.
Deserted like a carrier's fire.

Chhoṛe gāoṅ kā nām kyā ?
What name has a deserted village ?

Chhoṛe gāoṅ se nātā kyā ?
Who is connected with a deserted village ?

Chhoṛ, Jāṭ, parāī khāṭ.
Give up, O Jāṭ ! the couch of others.
(Leave off your habits of rapacity and violence.)

Chhoṛ jhāṛ mujhe ḍūban de. Wom.
O bramble ! let me drown.
☞ The story goes that a woman threw herself into a pond but repenting of her determination to commit suicide caught at a bush on the bank and pretended that the bush had caught her: applied to one who perpetually intrudes his company on another, and pretends that the other person will not part with him.

Chhoṛo, Bī Billī, chūhā landūrā hī jīegā. Wom.
Let go the rat, my Lady Cat, he will live, though he has lost his tail.

Chhoṭā ghar, baṛā samdhiyānā. Wom.
A small house and large connections.

Chhoṭā mūnh, baṛā nivālā.
A little mouth and a large morsel.
(For point see preceeding.)

Chhoṭā mūṅh, baṛī bāt.
Small mouth, big words.
(Small wit great brag: said to any low person who presumes to use language incompatible with his situation; old head on young shoulders.)

Chhoṭā, sab se khoṭā.
Small stature, bad nature.

Chhoṭā so moṭā.
Short is stout.

Chhoṭe miyāṅ so chhoṭe miyāṅ; baṛe miyāṅ, subhān Allāh ! Mah.
The young lord is the young lord; God save us from the old lord !

Chhoṭe se Gāzī Miyāṅ, baṛī sī dum !
A short priest with a long beard !

Chhoṭī būnd barsī chaunkāë, ālas sabhī miṭāë.
A few drops of rain startled her and all her drowsiness was gone.
(A trifling accident will often bring a man to his senses.)

Chhoṭī moṭī kāmnī sab hī bis kī bel,
Bairī māre dāoṅ se, yeh māreṅ hańs khel.
All pretty maids, or small or plump are poisonous pests, An enemy kills by hiding; these by smiles and jests.

Chhoṭī nanad, angiyā kā band, baṛī nanad bijlī basant. Wom.
My younger sister-in-law is as my bodice-strings, my elder sister-in-law is as the summer lightning.
(The younger one she loves and the elder she fears.)

Chhoṭī sī bachhyā, baṛī sī hatiyā. Hin.
The calf is small but the sin is great.
(As well be hanged for a sheep as a lamb.)

Chhoṭī sī gauraiyā, bāghoṅ se nazārā. E.
A little sparrow staring at the lion.
(Little roast great boast.)

Chhūā aur mūā.
They die as he touches them.
(Said of a mischievous man.)

Chhūṅchhā kā sang na sāthī, bhalā duāre jhūm le hāthī. Bhoj.
No friends for the empty handed, but elephants at the rich man's gates.

Chhūchhe phaṭke uṛ uṛ jāëṅ.
Winnow hollow grain and it will all fly away.
(Little talent seldom stands test.)

Chhūchhī hāṅḍī bāje ṭan ṭan.
An empty vessel makes a great noise.

Chhūchhī kaṛhāī, majīr kā phoṛan.
Rust breaks up the empty pan.

Chhūoṅ nā chhāoṅ, Algaṭṭe nāoṅ.
Nor spell nor charm and his name Exorcist.

Chhupe Rustam.
An unknown Rustam.
(Rustam is the Eastern Hercules: an angel unawares: ironically said of a coward.)

Chhurī bhalī na kaṭārī. Wom.
The knife is no better than the dagger.

Chhurī kharbūze par girī to kharbūze kā zarar, kharbūzā chhurī par girā to kharbūze kā zarar.
Whether the knife fall on the melon, or the

melon on the knife, either way the melon is cut.
(It cuts both ways.)

Chhurī par kaddū, kaddū par chhurī.
The knife on the cucumber, or the cucumber on the knife.
(It is all the same, the cucumber gets cut either way.)

Chhurī pātā hūn to āp ko nahīn pātā,
Āp ko pātā hūn to chhurī nahīn pātā.
When I've found my knife I can't find you, When I've found you I can't find my knife.
(Vindictive hatred.)

Chhurī tale dam lo.
Take breath under the knife.
(Bear up to the last.)

Chhūṭal ghorā bhusaule ṭhāṛh. E. Rus.
The loose horse makes for his stall.

Chhūṭ bhalāī, sāre gun. Wom.
He has all the qualities except goodness.

Chhuṭe bail bhusaurī men. E. Rus.
The loose ox goes to his stall.

Chih nisbat khāk rā ba-ālam-i-pāk? Pers.
What connection is there between Earth and Heaven?

Chikanyā faqīr, makhmal kā langoṭ! E. Wom.!
A foppish beggar with velvet breeches!

Chiknā dekh phisal pare. Wom.
A fair appearance misleads.

Chiknā gharā būnd paṛī aur ḍhal gaī.
A drop on a greasy jar will roll down.
(A shameless person does not feel the sting of a taunt: water on a duck's back.)

Chiknā gharā ho gayā hai.
He is grown into a greasy jar.
(A shameless person: see preceding.).

Chikne gāl tilinyān ke, aur jare bare bhurjinyān ke. E. Wom.
The oilman's cheeks are smooth and shiny; the grain parcher's burnt brown.

Chikne galvā malvā ke. Rus.
The smooth cheek of a rich man.

Chikne ghare par pānī.
Water on a greasy jar!
(Water down a duck's back slips away like money.)

Chikne mūnh ko sab chāṭte hain.
All kiss the smooth cheek.
(All welcome the great.)

Chiknī bāten jan patyāo.
Trust not an oily tongue.

Chiknī chupṛī bāton se peṭ nahīn bhartā.
Fair words won't fill the belly.
(Soft words butter no parsnips.)

Chīl baiṭhe, to ek khaṛ lehī uṛe.
From wherever the kite sits she takes away a straw.
(Some men will always manage to take away something with them: to feather one's nest.)

Chīl kā mūt.
Kites' urine.
(Something very rare and useless.)

Chīl ke ghar māns kahān?
There is no flesh in a vulture's nest.
(It is all eaten.)

Chīl ke ghar men mās kī dharoṛ!
To deposit flesh in a vulture's nest!

Chīl ke ghar men pāras hotā hai.
The philosopher's stone is in the kite's nest.
☞ Kites sometimes carry off gold ornaments: Muhammadan women allege the reason to be that the young kites won't open their eyes till some gold is placed in the nest.

Chillaṛ, chamokan, chithṛā, ye tīnon bipat kā bakhrā. E.
Lice, slaps, and rags; these three are the lot of adversity.

Chillaṛ chunne se bhagvā halkā hove? E. Wom.
The breeches won't grow lighter for picking out the lice.
(Cheese-paring won't result in large savings.)

Chillaṛ māre, kuttā khāen.
Killing the louse and eating the dog.
(Straining at a gnat and swallowing a camel.)

Chīl sā manḍlāyā, aur kabūtar sā bindtā phirtā hai.
He hovers like a vulture and flutters like a pigeon.
(To pick up what he can.)

Chinḍāl na chhoṛe makkhe, na chhoṛe bāl. Hin.
The low castes leave neither hair nor flies.
(High caste Hindūs will not eat food with either hair or flies in it.)

Chintā juāl, sarīr ban, dāh lage na butāī,
Parghaṭ dhūān na dekhiye, ur andar hī dhundhūāī.
Care is flame and your body the wood, and when it catches fire none can put it out. Others see no smoke, for it burns within your breast.

Chīnṭī chāhe sāgar thā.
The ant wants to fathom the sea.

Chīnṭī dal.
The army of ants.
(Great crowd.)

Chīnṭī kā bil nahīn miltā: kahān chhipūn?
I cannot find an ant's hole: where shall I hide?
(No escape.)

Chīnṭī ke ghar nit mātam.
There is perpetual mourning in an ant's nest.
(They are always being killed.)

Chīnṭī ke par nikle aur maut āī!
When the ant's wings come out his death has come.
(No sooner shown his airs than his doom was sealed.)

Chīnṭī kī āvāz Arsh par.
The cry of the ant (the poor) riseth up to Heaven.

Chīṅṭī ke jo maut ānī hotī hai to par nikalte haiṅ.
When the ants are about to die they get wings.
(A common observation in the rains. *Quem Deus vult perdere prius dementat.*)

Chīṅṭī ko maut hī kī balā bas hai.
The mere misery of dying is enough for the ant.
(A small misfortune is ruin to the poor.)

Chīṅṭī sasarne ko jagah nahīṅ. E.
No room even for an ant to creep in.

Chirāg gul, pagṛī gāyab.
The candle out and the turban lost.
(Said of maladministration.)

Chirāg jalā, dāoṅ galā.
When the lamp is lighted, the chance is gone.
(Said of a thief.)

Chirāg meṅ baṭṭī, aur ānkh pe paṭṭī. Wom.
A wick in the lamp and a bandage over the eyes.
(Said of a sleepy head.)

Chirāg raushan, murād hāsil. Mah.
The lamp is lighted and the wishes are fulfilled.
(Allusion (1) to the practice of lighting lamps at the shrines of holy men, in order to procure the accomplishment of wishes, (ii.) to the practice of the Naqshbandī *faqīrs* who go about begging with a lamp in their hands, whence the alms given to them is called *chirāgā*, as much as to say "My lamp is lighted, you have now an opportunity of obtaining a blessing by giving me alms." (iii.) to the habits of libertines, thieves, and others, who look to the night, when lamps are lighted, as the favorable time for obtaining their wishes.)

Chirāg tale andherā.
Darkness under the lamp.
(Used when crimes are committed near the seat of authority: the nearer the church the farther from God.)

Chiṛā maran, gaṅvār hāṅsī.
Killing birds is villagers' sport.
(It is sport to you but death to us: allusion is to the habit of keeping fighting cocks and other birds.)

Chīre chār, baghāre pānch.
She pares four and fries five.
(Said tauntingly by the mother-in-law to her sharp daughter-in-law.)

Chīrā hai jis ne vohī nīregā. Hin.
Who opened the mouth will feed it.

Chiṛī mār hamesha bhūke nange rahte haiṅ.
The fowler is always a half-starved ragged creature.
(A judgment on him.)

Chiṛī mār ṭolā, bhāṅt bhāṅt kā panchhī bolā.
In a street of bird-catchers the voices of many birds are heard.
(Applied to an assembly where every man gives a different opinion.)

Chīr phāṛ ke Aṅgrez Ḍāktar ustād haiṅ.
The English Surgeons are the best at cutting and sawing.
(*i. e.* dissection.)

Chiṛyā apnī jān se gaī, khānevāle ko savād nā āyā. Wom.
The sparrow lost its life and still the eater was not satisfied.
(Said when the master does not appreciate his servant's work, or the husband his wife's.)

Chiṛyā apnī jān se gaī, laṛkā khush na huā.
The bird perished and the boy was still displeased.
(See preceding.)

Chiṛyā aur dūdh.
A bird and its milk.
(That is, the two are incompatible.)

Chiṛyā kare khoṅchā, chiṛā kare nauchā.
The hen-sparrow collects the stuffing (for the nest) and the cock scratches it to pieces.
(Said of a prudent woman with an extravagant husband.)

Chiṛyā kī choṅch meṅ chauthāī hissah.
The fourth share is in the sparrow's beak.
(A very small share.)

Chiṛyā kī jān gaī, laṛke kā khilaunā.
Birds' destruction is children's sport.

Chiṛyā ko shahīn se kauth?
What has a sparrow to do with a hawk?

Chit bhī merī, paṭ bhī merī.
Heads I win and tails I win.
(Heads I win, tails you lose.)

Chiṭṭhī na parvāna, mār khāeṅ mulk begānā.
A stranger has seized the country without letter or license.

Chīz na rākhe āpnī aur choroṅ gālī de. Wom.
He takes no care of his things and then abuses the thieves.

Cholī dāman kā sāth hai.
Combined together like bodice and skirt.
(One cannot be parted from the other.)

Chor aur moṭ kas ke bāṅdhe ke chāhe. E.
A thief and a bundle should be tied tightly.

Chor aur sāṅp dabe par choṭ kartā hai.
A thief and a serpent hurt when hard-pressed.

Chor aur sāṅp kī baṛī ḍhāk hotī hai.
A thief and a serpent create great fear.

Chor chakār chūke, lekin chugal na chūke.
A thief and a swindler may cease from evil, but a backbiter never.

Chor chorī kar gayā, mūsloṅ ḍhol bajā.
The thief steals and bangs the drum.
(*i. e.* steals openly: said of misgovernment.)

Chor chorī se gayā, to kyā herā pherī se bhī gayā? Wom.
The thief has left off stealing, but has he also left off haunting?
(That is, bad habits though suppressed, will

show themselves occasionally. What is bred in the bone will never wear out of the flesh.)

☞ It is related that a thief having been detected and punished, determined to reform, and took on himself the profession of a *Faqir*. While travelling in company with other *Faqirs*, when his fellow travellers were asleep, his old propensities came strong upon him, and his mode of gratifying them, without being guilty of theft, was to take the bundle of one from under his head and put it under another's.

Chor chor mausere bhāī.
All thieves are cousins to each other.
(Birds of a feather fly together: a thief knows a thief as a wolf knows a wolf.)

Chor churāve, gardan hilāve.
The thief steals and shakes his head.
(Denies the charge.)

Chor ḍhor donoṅ hāzir haiṅ.
The thief and the cattle are both present.
(Full proof.)

Chor gaṭhrī le gayā, begāriyoṅ ko chhuṭṭī huī.
When the thief walks off with the bundle the forced labourer is free.

Chor hathelī pe jān liye phirtā hai.
A thief carries his life on the palm of his hand.
(Careless of his life.)

Chorī aur jārī kabhī band nahīṅ hotī.
Theft and adultery will never be stopped.

Chorī aur mūṅh zorī.
Stealing and shouting!

Chorī aur sīnā-zorī!
Thieving and bullying!

Chorī aur sarhangī?
Are you a thief and a soldier?

Chorī aur sir-zorī!
Theft and boldness together!
(Spoken of one who glories in his crimes.)

Chorī be-surāg nahīṅ nikaltī.
No theft can be traced without a clue.

Chorī be-thāṅg nahīṅ hotī.
No theft without previous knowledge.

Chorī kā guṛ mīṭhā.
Stolen sugar is sweetest.
(Stolen kisses are sweetest.)

Chorī karke sāhūkār bante ho?
Would you be a merchant on stolen property?

Chor jāne chor kī sār.
A thief knows a thief's ways.
(Set a thief to catch a thief.)

Chor jāne mangnī ke bāsan?
Does a thief care if the vessels have been borrowed?

Chor jāte rahe ki andhyārī.
Thieves and darkness are inevitable.
(Every dog hath his day, and every man his hour.)

Chor, juārī, gaṭh-kaṭā, jār aur nār chhinār,
Sau sau saugand khāeṅ jo, mūl na kar itbār.
A thief, a gamester, a pickpocket, a rake and a harlot, Are never to be trusted though they take a thousand oaths.

Chor kā bhāī gaṭh-kaṭā.
The pickpocket is the thief's brother.

Chor kā bhāī gaṭṭhī chor.
The thief's brother is the betrayer of trust.

Chor kā hāl so merā hāl.
May the thief's deserts be mine.
(If I am in fault.)

Chor kā jī kitnā?
What heart has a thief?

Chor kā koī himāetī nahīṅ.
The thief has no friends.

Chor kā māl sab koī khāe, chor kī jān akārat [jāe.
All enjoy the thief's property and his life is thrown away.
(He has to give up so much of his property as hush money.)

Chor kā man buqche meṅ.
The thief's mind is intent on the packet.

Chor kā mūṅh chāṅd sā.
A thief's face is like the moon.
(I) because it wears an aspect of innocence and (II) it is marked with dark patches like the moon, *i. e.* he is betrayed by his looks.)

Chor kā shāhid chirāg.
The witness against the thief is the lamp.

Chor kā sir nīchā.
A thief cannot lift his head (for shame).

Chor ke ghar meṅ chhichor.
A great thief is robbed by petty thieves.

Chor ke ghar mor.
A peacock in the thief's house.
(A thing that betrays itself. The proverb is founded on the story of a peacock who swallowed a gold necklace which a thief had stolen and brought home: the biter bit.)

Chor ke hāth meṅ diyā.
A lamp in the thief's hand.
(May help or betray him.)

Chor ke khuāb meṅ buqche.
A thief dreams of bundles.

Chor ke man meṅ chorī base.
A thief always thinks of theft.

Chor ke pair nahīṅ hote.
A thief has no feet.
(He never stands, but flies.)

Chor ke peṭ meṅ gāe, āp hī āp rambhāe.
A cow lows spontaneously in the thief's stomach.
(He betrays himself.)

Chor kī aur sāṅp kī dhāk baṛī hotī hai.
The fear of a thief and a snake is very great.

Chor kī ḍāṛhī meṅ tinkā.
The straw in the thief's beard.
(By which he was detected.)

☞ The story goes that a Qāzī, when he was hearing a case of theft and was at a loss to find out who was the real offender from among the several suspected persons before him, made use of the sentence "the thief has a straw in his beard," upon which the real thief not suspecting any thing looked to his beard and brushed it thinking that there must be a straw in his beard, which betrayed him. Hence proverb.

Chor kī jorū kone meṅ sir de-kar rotī hai.
The thief's wife goes into a corner and cries.
Chor kī māṅ koṭhī meṅ sir de-kar rotī hai.
The thief's mother shuts the door and cries.
Chor kī nazar gaṭhrī par.
The thief's eye is on the wallet.
Chor kī zamānat nahīṅ hotī.
No one will go surety for a thief.
Chor ko chor hī pahchāne.
A thief knows a thief.
(Set a thief to catch a thief.)
Chor ko angārī miṭh. Bhoj.
Live coals taste sweet to a thief.
(Allusion to the ordeal by fire. The person accused of theft is made to eat live coals in order to prove his innocence.)
Chor ko chaukī-dār karnā!
To set a thief to keep watch!
Chor ko chor hī sūjhe.
A thief takes every body for a thief.
Chor ko chorī hī sūjhe.
A thief thinks only of thieving.
Chor ko pakaṛiye gāṅṭh se, chhināl ko pakaṛiye khāṭ se.
Catch a thief with the purse, and a harlot on the bed.
(Or you will be unable to prove your charge.)
Chor ko panhaī dūr se sūjhe hai. E.
The thief spies the shoe from afar.
(With which he is to be beaten.)
Chor lāṭhī do jane, ham bāp beṭe akele.
The thief with his stick were two, and I with my father were alone.
(What could we do against him?)
Chor le, n ā sādhū pūche.
When a thief steals he does not enquire if (his victim) be a saint.
Chor le, na sāh chhūe.
Nor thief can take nor banker touch it.
(So it is quite safe.)
Chor sab ghar le mare.
When a thief dies he takes the whole household with him.
(He gives information against his accomplices and even accuses the innocent.)
Chor se kahe, 'tū chorī kar,' aur sāh se kahe, 'tū jāgtā rahiyo.'
He tells the thief to steal and the honest man to keep watch.
(Applied to a go-between, who stirs up both parties in a dispute: to hunt with the hounds, and run with the hare.)
Chorvā ke man base kakṛī kā khet. E. Rus.
The petty thief's mind is running on the cucumber field.
Choṭ lagī pahāṛ kī aur toreṅ ghar kī sil. Wom.
Hurt by the hill he goes home to break the grind-stone.
(Said of one who vents his rage on his wife.)
Chhoṭī kuttiyā jalebbiyoṅ kī rakhvālī.
To set a hungry dog to watch sweetmeats.

Chūchiyoṅ meṅ hāṛ ṭaṭolnā.
To look for bones in the breasts!
(To draw blood from a stone.)
Chugal-khor, Khudā kā chor. Mah.
The tale-bearer is God's enemy.
Chuglā baiṭhā nīm pe, de sāle ke tīn saī.
The tale-bearer is up the tree, let us give the blackguard three hundred (blows.)
Chūhā bajāve chapnī, aur zāt jatāve apnī.
The rat rattles the lid and makes his nature known.
Chūhā billī kā shikār hai.
The mouse is the cat's prey.
Chūhā bil meṅ samātā na thā, kānoṅ bāṅdhā chhāj. Wom.
The rat was already unable to enter his hole and he tied a winnowing fan to his ears.
(A sarcasm aimed at those who enter into extravagant marriages.)
Chūhe kā bachchā bil hī khodegā.
The mouse's young set to work to make holes.
(What's bred in the bone will never come out of the flesh.)
Chūhe kā bil ḍhūṅḍhnā.
To look for a rat's hole.
(To creep into.)
Chūhe ke hāth lagī haldī kī girah, pansārī hī ban baiṭhā. Wom.
The mouse got hold of a piece of turmeric and set up a druggist's shop.
Chūkā aur gayā.
Missed and gone.
Chūkā so marā.
To be missed is to be ruined.
Chūlhā chhoṛ, bhaṅsār jāo.
Out of the frying pan into the fire.
Chūlhā jhoke chāvar hāth!
He feeds the oven with a fan in his hand!
Chūlhe āg na ghaṛe pānī, ūpar hī ūpar jā gaibānī! Mah. Wom.
No fire in her grate, no water in her jar, may she fly away above!
Chūlhe, chakkī, sab hī kām pakkī. Wom.
She is quite up to the hearth and the mill.
(She is expert in every art, as grinding, baking, etc: a good housewife.)
Chūlhe kā rāo, lāo hī lāo pukāre. Wom.
The king of the kitchen always cries 'more, more.'
(Said of a gormandiser.)
Chūlhe kī, na chakkī kī. Wom.
Nor fit for the hearth, nor fit for the mill.
(She can neither bake nor grind flour.)
Chūlhe pīchhe soveṅ aur ṭaihrī ko ṭopeṅ. Wom.
He sleeps behind the hearth and feels the empty plate.
(Living from hand to mouth.)

Chullū chullū sādhegā to duāre hāthī bāndhegā.
Save little by little and an elephant will wait at your door.
(Take care of the pence and the pounds will take care of themselves.)

Chullū men ullū, loṭe men gaṛgap.
Drunk on a thimble full, is blind drunk on a cup full.

Chullū pānī, tang zindgānī.
Life goes hard on a drop of water.

Chūm chāṭ ke khā liyā.
He licked him all clean.
(Absolutely ruined him—Jack Sprat could eat no fat, his wife could eat no lean, so 'twixt them both, you see, they licked the platter clean.)

Chūnā aur chamār kuṭe par ṭhīk rahtā hai.
Mortar and cobbler are best when beaten.

Chūnā, chūchī, dahī, ye Bangālā nahīn.
Lime, bosoms, and tyre are never good in the Bengal.

Chungal bhar āṭā Sāīn kā, beṭā jīve māī kā!
A handful of flour in the name of God: may my lady's son live long!
(Street cry of beggars.)

Chūnī kahe, "mujhe ghī se khāo."
The split pea cries, "eat me with butter"
(The coarsest food requires money.)

Chuniye, khudiye poslon dhīyā,
Ail damdā, le gail dhīyā. Mag. Wom.
Bring up a daughter on cakes and tarts,
And a son-in-law comes and takes her away.

Chūn khāē bhusanḍ hove, talā khāē rogī.
Eat bread and you will be robust, eat sweets and you will be sickly.

Chup ādhī marzī.
Silence is half consent.

Chup kī dād Khudā degā.
God will avenge the wrongs in silence borne.
(Virtue is its own reward. He that humbleth himself shall be exalted.)

Chupṛī aur do do!
Buttered cakes and two of them!
(Dainties and plenty. Said usually of offices in which authority is combined with a large salary.)

Chuṛail pe dil ā gayā, to phir parī kiyā hai?
Fallen in love with an ogress, what is fairy then?

Chuṛail pe dil ā jāē, to voh bhī parī hai.
Fall in love with an ogress, and even she is a fairy!

Chūrā jhāṛ khāo, laḍḍū na toṛo.
Eat the crumbs only and not the loaves.
(Don't touch the principal, but live on the interest.)

Churāve nath-vālī, nām lage chīrkuṭhī-vālī kā. E. Wom.
A nose-ringed woman steals, and a ragged wench is charged with it.
(The wealth of the rich covers a multitude of sins.)

Chūtar se kān gānṭhte hain.
He joins the ears to the buttocks.
(Said (i) of the eavesdropper (ii) of those who join the head and tail of a story.)

Chuṭiyā ko tel nahīn, pakauron ko jī chāhe. Wom.
No oil for her locks and she longs for fried cakes.
(*Pakaurās* are fried with oil, and every woman uses oil for her hair—she would rather go without the cakes than without oil for her hair.)

Chūtiyā mar gae, aulād chhoṛ gae.
The fool died and left offspring.
(Said to the stupid survivor of a stupid father, who makes a mess of every thing.)

Chūtiyon ne gāon mārā hai?
Is the village plundered by fools?
(Have all gone mad? Said to one who makes improper demands.)

Chuṭke kā khāiye, ukte kā na khāiye.
Eat at the hands of the niggardly, but not at the hands of the illiberal.
(*Ukta* is a man who reminds of an obligation.)

Chūtṛon se supārī phoṛnā.
To crack betel nuts under the buttocks.
(To lie on a bed of roses: to loll in the lap of luxury.)

D

Dabā baniyā pūrā tole.
The overawed shopman gives full weight.

Dabā hākim mahkūm ke tābe.
A bribe-taking judge is subservient to his subordinates.

Dabak shīre ke maṭke men.
Go and hide yourself in a jar of treacle.
(Take advantage of a good opportunity.)

Dabā paṛī gūjrī, 'gahrā bāsan lāo.'
The milk-maid is in our power, 'go and fetch a large basin.'
(Extortion.)

Dābar ḍūbe jag tire, jag ḍūbe ḍābar tire. Agric.
When the low lands are flooded the world swims (with plenty); when the world is drowned (with drought) the low lands swim (with rich produce.)

Dabe par chīnṭī bhī choṭ kartī hai.
Even an ant will bite when hard pressed.
(Even a worm will turn at last.)

Dabe par sab sher hain.
Every body plays the lion to an humble man.

Dabī billī chūhon se kān kaṭāē.
The cowed cat lets the rat bite her ears.

Dabte ko sab dabāte hain.
Who yields is oppressed.

Dādā jān parāë barde āzād karte the.
My grandsire freed another's slaves.
(To cut a thong out of another's bucket.)

Dādā kahne se banyā gur detā hai.
Call a Baniyā father and he will give you treacle.
(Please and get ease.)

Dādā maregā jab bail batenge.
When the grandfather dies the oxen will be divided.
(The dead man's shoes.)

Dādā marenge jab mīrās bategī.
When the grandfather dies the estate will be divided.

Dādā marenge to potā rāj karenge. Wom.
When the grandsire dies, the grandsons reign.
(*Le roi est mort vive le roi.*)

Dādā marihen to bhoj kari hain. E.
When the grandsire dies we 'll have good feast.

Dādā par-dādā ke rāj kī bāten kartā hai. E.
He talks of the times of grandfathers and great-grandfathers.
(*Laudator temporis acti :* the good old times.)

Dāde rāj na khāë pān, dānt dikhāvat gae pirān
He never tasted betel-leaf even in the time of his grandfather; but fatigued himself to death in showing his teeth.
(It is applied to a person who gives himself airs in showing off any new acquisition.)

Dādū, dunyā bāorī, phir phir mānge dān,
Likkhan-hārā likh gayā, metan-hārā kān.
Saith Dādū, the world's gone mad, again and again it prays, But what is written by fate cannot be effaced.

Dāge ke sānrh, to dāge le lohār. E.
If the bull is to be branded, let the blacksmith do it.
(Every cobbler to his last.)

Dāg lagāë langotiyā yār.
Your childhood's acquaintance will put you to shame.
(If you attempt to injure him.)

Dah dar duniyā, sad dar ākhirat. Mah.
Ten in this world is a hundred in the next.
(Street cry of Muhammadan beggars.)

Dah 'poish' shalitah bhārī.
Ten 'look outs' come from the heavy load.
(Porters carrying heavy weight are always crying "*poish poish*" in the streets.)

Dahī bechan chalīn, pīth pichhārū kamoīyā. E. Rus. Wom.
She goes out to sell her tyre, and hangs the pitcher down her back.
(Ashamed to put it on the head: above her work.)

Dahī bhāt kā mūsal.
A pestle for rice and curds.
(A sledge-hammer to kill a fly.)

Dahī kī gavāhī chūrā. E.
The fried rice proves the curd.
(As it cannot be used without them.)

Dāhnā dhove bāën ko, aur bāyān dhove dāën ko.
The right hand washes the left, the left the right.
(We all have to depend on one another.)

Dāī Chanbelī ke Mirzā Mogrā. [Mogrā.
The son of nurse Chambelī, is called Mirzā
(Applied to one of mean descent who affects greatness. The two names are the names of flowers, but are also applied to persons.)

Dāī, dāī, ūntnī, savā gharā mūtnī.
Nurse, nurse is as tall as a camel, and makes a jar-full and a quarter of water.

Dāī ho mīthī, dādā ho mīthā, to suarg kaun jāe ?
Your nurse is dear and your grandfather is dear, which of the two is to go to heaven ?
(Hobson's choice.)

Dāī ke sir pān phūl. Mah. Wom. [flowers.
On the head of the nurse are betel and
(Taken from the game of blindman's buff, in which one child, under the character of a nurse closes up the eyes of that one who is to search for the thief.)

Dāī jāne apnī hāī.
The midwife knows her own feelings.
(Allusion to their habit of making light of the pains of the lying-in-woman.)

Dāī rī, dāī tere sāt hon bhāī !
Nurse, may you have seven brothers !
(Said by children in blindman's buff.)

Dāī se pet chhipānā. Wom.
To hide the belly from the midwife.
(Applied to one who affects mystery towards the person who is already in his secrets.)

Dāī se pet nahīn chhiptā. Wom.
You can't hide the belly from the mid-wife.

Daiv na māre ḍing se, kumatī det charhāë. Hin.
God does not kill any one with a club, but takes away his understanding.

Dakhl dar māqūlāt karnā.
To interrupt a reasonable proposition.

Dakkhan gaë na bāhore, rahe Chanderī chhā. Wom.
Who went to the Dakkhan never returned, but took up his abode at Chanderī.
(Said of Aurangzeb's army which was before Chanderī for twelve years. Applied to one who has been abroad for a long time and has deserted his own country.)

Dāl bhāt khichrī.
Peas and rice made up into a mess.
(A medley.)

Daliddar ghar men non pakvān. Wom.
Salt is a delicacy in the house of poverty.

Ḍāl kā chūkā bandar aur bāt kā chūkā ādmī phir nahīn sanbhalte.
A monkey missing his branch and a man missing his chance cannot be saved.

Ḍāl kā ṭūṭā.
Just plucked from the stalk.
(Brand new.)

Ḍallū kā dah-serā.
The ten pound weight of Ḍallū.
(Expresses intrusion into a conversation with something entirely foreign to the subject. Popularly, Ḍallū was a grain merchant who used a weight of ten *sers* while all others used only one of five. However, the term is applied to any thing incongruous.)

Dāl meṅ kālā hai.
There is something black in the peas.
(That is, I suspect some latent mischief: to smell a rat.)

Ḍālte der nahīṅ, sir par koṭwāl.
No sooner in than the police were on him.
(Caught in the act.)

Damā dam ke sāth.
Asthma goes with life.

Dām āve kām.
Money is a good servant.

Dam banā rahe!
May you live long!

Dam banā rahe, phūṅk nikal jāē!
May your life remain and your breath pass [away.
(A blessing and a curse.)

Dam bhar kī khabar nahīṅ.
No one knows what will happen at the next breath.

Damdame meṅ dam nahīṅ, khair māṅgo jān kī!
No power in your batteries, so ask for quarter!

Dam darūd na honā.
To be without breath.
(Either dead, or very nearly so; at the last gasp.)

Dām dīje, kām līje.
Give your money and get your work done.

Dam ganīmat hai.
Breath is my prize.
(Said by the old.)

Dam hai, jab tak gam hai.
While there is life, there is grief.

Dam hai to kyā gam hai?
While life remains, what do I fear?

Dam kā damāmā hai.
Breath is the music of life.
(Of very short duration.)

Dam kā kiyā bharosā hai? āyā, nā āyā?
What certainty is there in the breath, that comes and comes not?

Dām kare sab kām.
Money does all the business.
(Money makes the mare to go.)

Dam mārne kī jagah nahīṅ.
There is no room to take breath.
(To criticise the works of God, or of a superior.)

Dam meṅ hazār dam.
In one breath, a thousand breaths.
(While there is life, there is hope.)

Dam nahīṅ badan meṅ nām Zorāvar Khāṅ!
No strength in his body and called Mr. Armstrong.

Dam nāk meṅ ā gayā.
The breath is in my nostrils.
(Weary of life.)

Dāmoṅ ḍherī, yā hāḍoṅ ḍherī.
Either (have) a heap of money, or be a heap of bones.

Dāmoṅ rūṭhā bātoṅ se nahīṅ māntā.
Dissatisfied with his dues is not reconciled [by words.
(Fair words don't fill the stomach.)

Damṛī kā postī.
A farthing doll.
(*Postī*, a paper figure made for the amusement of children, the head shaking or nodding with the wind, like that of one who is drowsy from the use of opium. Applied to signify a contemptible, good-for-nothing, creature: a man of straw.)

Damṛī ke pān Banyāiṅ khāē, kaho "ye ghar rahe ke jāē?"
If the shopman's wife spend a farthing on betel—saith he—"Will the house be ruined or not?"
(Allusion to the niggardly habits of the Baniyā class.)

Damṛī kī arhar, sārī rāt kharar. Wom.
A farthing's worth of peas, and the sound of grinding all night.
(Great cry and little wool.)

Damṛī kī bulbul, ṭakā chhuṭāī.
A penny for plucking a half-penny bird.
(Expending on any thing more that it is worth.)

Damṛī kī buṛhiyā ṭakā sir muṅḍāī.
A penny for shaving a half-penny hag.
(Widows in India shave their heads.)

Damṛī kī chūṅ chūṅ.
A penny whistle.
(*Chūṅ chūṅ* signifies the chattering or chirping of birds, and is also applied to a small bellows made to imitate that sound. The proverb means an idle talker.)

Damṛī kī dāl, āphī kutnī, āphī chhināl. Wom.
With only a farthing's worth of split peas, I must be host and guest myself.
(There is not enough for one person.)

Damṛī kī dāl, "būā, patlī na ho." Mah. Wom.
A farthing's worth of peas, and 'be careful sister, that (the soup) be not thin.'
(To express a miser who exacts impossibilities.)

Damṛī kī ghoṛī, chha paserī dānā.
A farthing mare wants thirty *sers* of corn.
(Which would be worth about a rupee.)

Damṛī kī guṛiyā ṭakā ḍolī kā. Wom.
A penny for fetching a half-penny doll.
(Said of the weddings of the poor.)

Damṛī kī hāṅḍī gaī, to kutte kī zāt pahchānī.
Miss a farthing pitcher and know the dog's nature.
(A petty trap to catch a petty thief.)

Damṛī kī hāṇḍī lete haiṅ, to ṭhok bajāke lete haiṅ.
In buying even a farthing pitcher, we test it and sound it.

Damṛī kī lāī Banyāin khāë, "ye ghar rahe ki jāë ?" E.
The shopman's wife ate a farthing's worth of parched rice, (and quoth she) "the house will be ruined."

Damṛī kī murgī, nau ṭakā nikāī. E.
A farthing for the hen and three half-pence for its plucking.

Damṛī kī nihārī meṅ ṭāṭ ke ṭukṛe. Mah. Wom.
Farthing soup is made of (soaked) canvas.

Damṛī kī pāg, adhelī kā jūtā.
A farthing for the turban, and a shilling for the shoes.
(Topsy turvy; upside down.)

Dānā chhitrānā tahāṅ jānā zarūr hai. E.
Where your grain (food) is scattered there should you go.

Dānā dushman nā-dān dost se behtar.
A wise enemy is better than a foolish friend.

Dānā jald bāzī nahīṅ karte.
Wise men don't hurry.
(Haste makes waste.)

Dānā khāë na pānī pīve, voh ādmī kaise jīve ?
How will he live, who doesn't eat and drink ?

Dānā khā moṭh kā, pānī pī soṅṭh kā.
If you eat millet drink ginger water.
(Millet being very indigestible requires a digestive: look before you leap.)

Dānā na ghās, ghoṛe terī ās.
You trust in the horse that gets nor corn nor grass.

Dānā na ghās "hīṅ hīṅ" kare.
He keeps on neighing for his corn and grass.

Dānā na ghās, khurairā chhae chhae bār.
Nor grass nor corn for him, but curry-combing six times a day.

Dānā na ghās, pānī chhae chhae bār.
Neither corn nor grass for him, but water six times a day.
(Spoken of one who is ready to give any worthless thing, but not what is asked for.)

Dān, bit saman. Hin.
Be charitable according to your means.

Ḍanḍā sī pūṅch, Buṛhāne kā rasta.
The tail like a pole and on the Buṛhānā road.
(Unfit for the task: the road near Buṛhānā is very sandy and hard to travel over; *ḍanḍā sī pūṅchh* implies an old emaciated ox.)

Dāne dāne ko mohtāj hai.
In need of even a grain of corn.

Dāne dāne par mohar hai.
Every grain has its seal.
(Every bullet has its billet.)

Dāne ko ṭāpe, savārī ko pāde.
He stamps for grain, but breaks wind when ridden.
(He is ready to eat, but unwilling to work.)

Dāne pānī ke hāth hai.
He looks to his meat and drink.
(Moral as in preceding.)

Dāne pānī ke ikhtyār hai.
It lies in the power of meat and drink.
(The doctrine of the fatalists.)

Dānī kī bhākhā khālī na jāë.
A charitable person's words don't pass away empty.

Dāṅt gire, aur khur ghise, pīṭh na bojhā le,
Aise būṛhe bail ko kaun bāndh bhus de ? Rus.
Teeth all out, hoofs worn away, back unfit to load: Who would feed up such a decrepit old ox ?

Dāṅt kāṭī roṭī hai.
Bitten bread.
(To express that such great intimacy subsists between two people, that they eat each other's food: hand and glove with each other.)

Dāṅt kuredne ko tinkā nahīṅ bachā.
Not even a straw was saved to pick his teeth with.
(To express extreme distress in consequence of the loss of property by fire, etc.)

Dāṅt par mail nahīṅ.
Not even dirt upon his teeth.
(He is in great poverty.)

Ḍarā so marā.
Be afraid and die.

Dar ba-dar, khāk basar phirā hai.
He roams from door to door with ashes on his head.
(Wretched.)

Dar dar māṅgte phirte haiṅ.
He begs from door to door.

Dard ko voh samjhe jo khud dard-mand ho.
He knows the feelings of others who has felt pain himself.

Ḍareṅ lomṛī se, nām Diler Khāṅ.
Afraid of a fox, and his name Sir Valiant.

Ḍareṅ lomṛī se, nām Sher Khāṅ.
Afraid of a fox, and is named *Coeur-de-lion.*

Ḍāṛhī Khudā kā nūr hai. Mah.
The beard is the light of God.

Ḍaṛhyālā dhan. Mah. Wom.
A treasure of a beard.
(Spoken contemptuously of one with a long beard: male issue.)

Dar-i-taubah bāz hai. Mah.
The door of repentance is open.

Ḍariye, randī, tere dīde se ! Mah. Wom.
We fear your gaze, you wench !
(Abuse: allusion to the evil eye or a wanton look.)

Dar na dahshat, utār phirī khishtak. Mah. Wom.
Nor fear nor awe, she goes about naked.

Darog ba gardan-i-rāvī. Pers.
The sin of the lie is on the head of the teller.

Darog-go ko hāfiza nahīṅ hotā.
A liar has no memory.

Darog ko farog nahin.
A lie does not prosper.

Darshan ke nainā lobhī. Hin.
The eyes long to see.

Darshan moṭā, paiṅḍā khoṭā. Hin.
Great object, but a bad road.
(Such as a pilgrimage to Badri Nath in the hills.)

Darshan thoṛe, nām bahut.
Great name, but little to see.
(Great cry, little wool)

Dārū-i-gazab khāmoshī. Pers.
Silence is the best cure for anger.
(Compare. A soft answer turneth away wrath.)

Darvāze par āī barāt, samdhan ko lagī hagās. Wom.
The marriage procession has arrived at the gate, and the bride's mother feels a call of nature.

Daryā ko kūze meṅ bharnā.
To put the ocean into a goblet.
(To say much in a few words; *multum in parvo*: also to attempt impossibilities.)

Daryā meṅ rahnā, aur magar machh se bair.
Live in the river and fight the crocodiles.
(To be on bad terms with him under whose authority one is placed.)

Daryā pe jānā aur piyāse ānā.
To go to a river and come back thirsty.

Darzī kī sūī kabhī tāsh meṅ, kabhī ṭāṭ meṅ.
A tailor's needle, now in embroidery and now in canvas.

Dāsī karam kahār se nīche. Hin.
To serve is worse than to be a scullion.
(Service is another name for slavery.)

Das nakṭoṅ meṅ nāk-vālā—Nakkū.
Among ten noseless men one with a nose is Swollen-nose.
(In Rome do as Rome does.)

Dason uṅgliyāṅ, dasoṅ chirāg. Mah. Wom.
Her ten fingers are ten lamps.
(She is highly accomplished.)

Dastār, guftār, apnī hī kām ātī hai.
Your own turban and your own speech suit you best.

Dastār, guftār, raftār, judī judī.
Each has his own turban, gait and speech.

Dastar-khān ke bichhāne meṅ sau aib, na bichhāne meṅ ek aib. Mah.
Who spreads his table hath a hundred faults, who spreads it not hath only one.

Dastar-khān kī billī. Mah.
The cat of the banquet.
(One who presents himself uninvited at every feast: sponger; toad-eater.)

Dastar-khān kī makkhī.
The fly of the dinner-table.
(Said contemptuously of a person who goes uninvited to a feast.)

Dātā dātā mar gaē, aur rah gaē makkhī-chūs, Den len ko kuchh nahīn, laṛne ko maujūd.
The liberal are dead, and the fly-eaters (misers) have remained, With nothing to give and ready to fight.

Dātā dātār, suthnī utār. Wom.
(My husband) is so liberal that he would even take off my trousers to give them away.

Dātā de, bhanḍārī kā peṭ phaṭe.
The liberal man gives and his steward breaks his heart.

Dātā de, bhanḍārī peṭ piṭe.
The liberal man gives and his steward beats his belly.

Dātā de, kanjūs jhur jhur mare.
The liberal man gives, and the miser grieves. (to see him give.)

Dātā deve aur sharmāve, bādal barse aur garmāve.
The liberal gives and feels modest, as the clouds rain and it grows hot.
(Hot weather means more rain.)

Dātā ke ghar Lachchhmī ṭhāṛī rahat hasūr, Jaise gārā rāj ko bhar bhar det masūr.
Fortune waits at the gate of liberal and supplies him, As a labourer supplies mortar to the mason.
(Spend and God will send.)

Dātā ke tīn gun, de, dilāve, de-ke chhīn le. Hin.
God has three qualities, to give, to make others give, and to take back what He has given.
(Said also of a king or master.)

Dātā kī nāo pahāṛ chaṛhe.
The boat of the generous goes up hill.
(He is always successful.)

Dātā ko Rām chhappar phāṛ-ke detā hai.
God gives to the liberal through the roof.
(Unexpectedly.)

Dātā pun kare, kanjūs jhur jhur mare.
The generous gives, and the miser frets (to see him give).

Dātā sadā diladrī.
A liberal man is always in want.
(Benevolence spells Bankruptcy.)

Daulat andhī hotī hai.
Wealth is blind.
(A rich man is prone to ignore his poor friend.)

Daulat kā khel hai.
(All things are) the sport of fortune.

Daulat ke pāoṅ lag gaē.
Riches have legs.

Daulat ke par lag gaē.
Riches have wings.

Daulat kharch ke vāste dī gaī hai.
Wealth is given to spend and give.

Daulat-mand kī ḍeoṛhī ko sab sijdah karte hain.
Every body kisses the threshold of the rich.

Dauṛ chale na auṅdhā gire.
Never run fast or you will fall on your face.

Daur chale na chaupaṭ gire.
Who runs fast falls on his back.

Daur-kar chalegā so giregā.
Who runs falls.
(More haste less speed.)

Davā aur duā dono.
Medicine as well as prayer.
(Pray to God, but keep your powder dry.)

Davā ke līye ḍhūṅḍo, to nahīṅ miltī.
Even as medicine it is not procurable.
(Said of a thing which is very scarce and rare.)

Davā kī davā, gizā kī gizā.
It is both food and medicine.

Dāvat nahīṅ, adāvat hai.
It is not a feast, it is enmity.

Davāt qalam.
It is only pen and ink.
(There is no cash behind the paper.)

Dayā bin sant qasāī.
A saint without sympathy is a butcher.

Dayā dharam kā mūl hai, pāp mūl abhimān: Tulsī, dayā na chhāṛiye, jab lag ghaṭ meṅ prān.
Mercy is the root of faith and pride the root of sin: Saith Tulsi Dās, give not up mercy as long as thou dost live.

Ḍāyan bhī das ghar chhoṛ-kar khātī hai. Wom.
Even a witch will pass over ten houses before she fastens on her prey.
(Even the wicked have some regard for their neighbours; witches are supposed to feed on the brains and liver of children.)

Ḍāyan khāē tau mūṅh lāl, na khāē tau mūṅh lāl.
The witch has a bloody mouth—whether she devours human beings or not.
(Give a dog a bad name and hang him.)

Ḍāyan ko bachchā sauṅpnā.
To entrust a child to a witch.
(To risk its life: she will eat its brains and liver.)

Ḍāyan ko bhī dāmād piyārā.
Even a witch loves her son-in-law.
(For the sake of her daughter: one touch of nature makes the whole world kin.)

Debī din kāṭe, log parchā māṅgeṅ. Hin.
Devī (Goddess) spends her days (in care), and man is ever demanding a miracle.

Debī Madār kā kaun sāth?
What connexion is there between *Devī* and *Madār*?
(The former is a Hindū goddess, and the latter a Mahammadan saint: irreconcilable incongruity.)

De dāl meṅ pānī, paigā bah chale chuhānī. E.
Put enough water into the pea-soup to float a log.
(To prevent your neighbours from sponging on you.)

De de bārūd meṅ āg, kis kī rahī? aur kis kī rah jāēgī?
Throw gunpowder into fire and whose will it be? or whose will it remain?

De, dilāve, de de kare, so pirānī bhausāgar tire. Hin.
He that gives, causes to be given, and persuades others to give, passes through the sea of this world.

De duā samdhiyāne ko, nahīṅ phirtī do do dāne ko. Hin. Wom.
Call blessings on the marriage relations, but for whom you would have been a beggar.
(Honour to whom honour is due.)

Deh dhare ke daṇḍ haiṅ. Hin.
The penalty for being created.
(Disease and suffering; no body no pain: Adam's legacy.)

Deh meṅ anek rog bhareṅ haiṅ. Hin.
Innumerable maladies lurk within the body.

Deh meṅ na lattā, lūṭe ke Kalkattā! E.
Without a rag on his body, he intends to plunder Calcutta!

Dekhā bhālā topchī, aur chaprā Sayad hoe.
Known for a gunner he affects the Sayad.
(Affects the rank of a nobleman.)

Dekhā dekhī sādhe jog, chhīje kāyā, bāḍhe rog!
Imitate the ascetic's life to waste in body and increase your ailments.

Dekhā, Mīrdād, terā rambā; Gājroṅ kī rel pel, roṭiyoṅ kā chambā!
Mīrdād, I have seen what your hoe can do: plenty of carrots and no bread!

Dekhā na bhālā, sadqe gaī khālā. Mah. Wom.
The aunt is devoted to the nephew whom she has never seen.
(Applied to one who launches out in praise of that of which he has no knowledge of but by report. Distance lends enchantment to the view.)

Dekhan ke atīt haiṅ, besvā se rahe phaṅs!
Māthe tilak lagāē haiṅ, mālā gal meṅ das.
In appearance a saint, but in love with a prostitute! For all his sectarial marks on his forehead and his ten ascetic's garlands round his neck.

Dekhā shahr Bangālā, dāṅt lāl, mūṅh kālā.
I have seen the land of Bengal, where the teeth are red and the faces black.
(The former from chewing betel leaf, and the latter from excessive heat.)

Dekhā so khāyā, na mūṅh pāoṅ jogā. Wom.
He ate what he saw and nothing saved for his face or feet.
(Living from hand to mouth.)

Dekh bhāl ke pāoṅ rakhnā chāhiye.
Put down your foot with care.
(Pick your way: look before you leap.)

Dekhe bhāle Shekhjī aur chiṛiyeṅ said hoeṅ.
He puts on the face of a saint to catch birds.
(*In fronte nulla fides.*)

Dekhe ke baurahiya, āve pāṅchoṅ pīr. E. Wom.
In appearance she is mad, but she knows how to invoke the five *pīrs*.
(The five great ones: Muhammad, Alī, Fāti-

mā, Hasan and Husain, properly speaking, but any five great saints the speaker may happen to know in practice.)

Dekhe ko buḍḍhī, kām ko āṅdhī. Wom.
An old woman to look at, but a whirl-wind at her work.
(Not much to look at, but a devil to go.)

Dekhe rāhī, bole sipāhī.
The wayfarer looks and the soldier speaks.

Dekhī ṭhok bajā-ke, dunyā tālib zar kī.
I have tested it and know that the world runs after riches.

Dekhī, pīr, terī karāmāt! Mah. Wom.
Your miraculous powers are known, my saint!
(We know the length of your tether.)

Dekhī, Rām! terī kartūt. Hin. Wom.
I know, Rām! thy wondrous works.
(See preceding.)

Dekhī terī Kālpī, aur bāvan purā ujāṛ.
I have seen your Kālpī, and its 52 desolate villages.
(So what are you boasting about?)

Dekhīye dīdār, aur mārīye paizār. Mah. Wom.
Look at them, but don't touch them.
(Advice to a young man with regard to the frail of the fair sex.)

Dekhīye qasāī kī nazar, aur khilāīye sone kā nivālā.
Behave to your child as a butcher, and feed it with tit bits.
(Spare the rod, spoil the child.)

Dekhīye ūṅt, kis kal baiṭhtā hai.!
See on which side the camel sits down.
(Mark the end—Spoken when two persons are contending and the victory is yet uncertain.)

☞ A potter and a green grocer hired a camel between them to carry their pots and greens respectively. On the way the camel made free with the grocer's greens, whereat the potter rejoiced that his pots were safe. But the green grocer, said, "*Dekhīye ūṅt, kis kal baiṭhtā hai!* We shall see on which side the camel squats" and at the journey's end the tables were turned, for the camel sat down on the side the crockery was loaded and crack went all the pots. Hence proverb. Don't count your chickens before they are hatched.

Dekhnā so pekhnā. Hin. Wom.
To see is to desire.

Dekhne aur sunne meṅ baṛā farq hai.
There is a great difference between seeing and hearing.

Dekhne ko bulbul, nigalne ko domaryā baṛ. E.
A nightingale to look at, he can swallow wild figs.
(Applied to one who is weak in appearance, but can perform the work of a strong man: the race is not to the swift, nor the battle to the strong. Ecclesiastes ix, 11.)

Dekhne meṅ na, so chakhne meṅ kyā?
If it is not fit to look at, how will it be to taste?

Dekho re, Ahīrinyāṅ ke ḍīṭhā,
Chhanṭlās chāur, paroslal pīṭhā. E. Wom.
Look at the perversity of the cowherd's wife; She takes out the grains and serves the husk.

Dekho Miyān ke chhand band, phāṭā jāmā, tīn band. Wom.
Look at this gentleman's consequential airs and his tattered robe, with three straps.
(Whereas it ought to have eight or nine.)

Dekh parāī chūpṛī, gir paṛ be-īmān,
Ek gharī kī be-hayāī, din bhar kā ārām.
Pounce upon the buttered bread of others, thou faithless wretch, A moment's shamelessness, and comfort for the day.
(Said to a greedy person.)

Dekh parāī chūpṛī mat lalchāve jī.
Missī kussī khāē-ke, ṭhanḍā pānī pī.
Don't let your mouth water at another's bread and butter, Content yourself with your crust and cold water.

Dekh paṛausan jal marī. Wom.
My neighbour saw and died with envy.

Dekhtā hai so kahtā nahīṅ, kahtā hai so dekhtā nahīṅ.
What sees (eye) doesn't speak, what speaks (tongue) doesn't see.

Dekhtī āṅkhoṅ makkhī nahīṅ niglī jātī.
No one swallows a fly with his eyes open.
(A man apparently bad is avoided: attitude is every thing.)

Dekh tiryā ke chāle, sir munḍā,, muṅh kāle!
"*Dekh mardoṅ kī pherī, mā terī ki merī?*"
"See the wily tricks of women, the head is shaven and the face is black."
"See the superior skill of men, Is she your mother or mine?"

☞ The story goes that a tricksy woman feigned sickness beyond all hopes of recovery, unless *apnī māṅ* (own mother), meaning the mother of her *husband*, were brought before her on an ass with her head shaven and her face blackened. Her ingenious husband, however, went to *her* mother (*apnī māṅ*) and induced her by appealing to her maternal affections to undergo shaving and the other humiliations desired by her daughter; the simple mother hesitated not to submit for the sake of her daughter, and when brought before her daughter, the sick woman exultingly repeated the first line of the proverb, being proud of her tricks having worked so well, when to her great disappointment the tables were turned upon her by her husband instantly retorting with the second line.

Denā aur marnā barābar hai.
Debt is death.

Denā bhalā na bāp kā, beṭī bhalī na ek,
Chalnā bhalā na kos kā, jo Sāīṅ rākhe ṭek.
From a debt to your father, from a single daughter, and from travelling a mile on foot, may God preserve you.

Denā lenā kām ḍom dhāṛiyoṅ kā, mohabbat ajab chīz hai.
Taking presents is the way of pimps and buffoons, love is quite a different thing.
(Cupboard love.)

Denā ṭhoṛā, dilāsā bahut.
Little gift, great promise.
(The land of promise.)

Dene ke nām to darvāze ke kivāṛ bhī nahīṅ dete.
On account of the name of giving he won't even shut (give) the door.
(*Kivāṛ denā, lit.* to give the door, means to shut the door.)

Dene-vāle se dilāne-vāle ko ziyādah savāb hai.
The merit of causing to be given is greater than the merit of giving.

Denī paṛī bunāī, aur ghaṭā batāve sūt.
Now that he has to pay for the weaving he says that the thread is short.

Deotā bāsnā ke bhūke haiṅ. Hin.
The Gods hunger after the smell only.
(Of the offerings, which are the daily meal of the worshipper when made in the house, and the perquisite of the priest when made in the temple.)

Der āē, durust āē.
Come late, come right.
(More haste less speed: slowly does it.)

Ḍeṛh chāval apne jude hī pakāte haiṅ.
He has a grain and a half of rice, and cooks it by itself.
(Eccentricity: going one's own way.)

Ḍeṛh īṅṭ kī masjid judī hī banāte haiṅ. Mah.
They built a separate mosque of their own with a brick and a half.
(Going their own way.)

Ḍeṛh pāo āṭā, pul par rasoī. Hin. Wom.
A pound of flour and a dinner on the bridge.
(In a public place: a vain show.)

Desā desā chāl, kulā kulā beohār.
Every country its fashion, and every family its custom.
(Each to his own taste: *de gustibus non disputandum.*)

Des chorī na, pardes bhīk.
Begging in a foreign land is better than stealing in one's own country.

Des chorī, pardes bhīk.
Begging in a foreign land brings no shame.
(Spoken to one, who, being fallen from better circumstances, is ashamed to beg in his own country, where he is known.)

Desī gadhā, Panjābī reṅgh.
A native ass with the Panjābī bray.
(A hit at the Panjābī language.)

Desī gadhā, Pūrbī chāl.
A native ass with the Eastern gait.
(See above: a counter hit at the people of the N.-W. Provinces.)

Desī ghoṛī, Marāṭhī chāl.
A native mare and Marāṭhī pace.
(Things that don't go together.)

Desī murgī, Valāētī bolī.
A native hen with the English cluck.
(Things that don't go together: the English being the finer of the two birds.)

Des par chaṛhāo, sir dukkhe na pāoṅ.
Nor head nor feet ache on the road home.

Detā bhale, na letā.
It is better to give than to receive.
(It is more blessed to give than to receive.)

Detā bhūle, nā letā. Mercantile.
Neither giver, nor taker can make a mistake about it.
(Said of an easy and plain calculation.)

Devegā so pāvegā, bovegā so kāṭegā.
Who gives will get, who sows will reap.

Dhable meṅ khāk. Wom.
Dust on her skirt.
(An abuse.)

Dhadhāēgā so butāēgā. E. Wom.
A blazing fire is soon out.
(Pride goes before a fall.)

Ḍhāk tale kī phūhaṛ, Mahve tale kī sughaṛ. Wom.
A blockhead under a *Ḍhāk* tree is as good as a clever fellow under a *Mahvā.*
(The former gives no shade and the latter no edible fruit.)

Ḍhāke ke Baṅgāl, kūze ke kaṅgāl. E.
At Dacca in Bengal the paupers have no goblets.
(Although it is famous for their manufacture. The nearer the church the further from God.)

Ḍhāl bāndhūṅ, talvār bāṅdhuṅ, kas-ke bāṅdhūṅ pheṭā, Bīch bazār meṅ ḍākā mārūṅ, tau bāp kā beṭā.
I wear a sword and I wear a shield, and a turban is on my head, I'll rob the market openly, if I be my father's son.
(Straightforwardness: hammer and tongs.)

Ḍhāl talvār sirhāne, aur chūtaṛ bandī-khāne! E.
Sword and shield on the pillow, and his legs in the prison!
(A coward.)

Ḍhaltī phirtī chhāṅ hai.
The shadow is ever shifting.
(The changeableness of the world.)

Dhamdhūsar kā hai moṭā, baṅaj kare, na āve ṭoṭā.
The son of Dhamdhūsar is very fat, doing no trade and suffering no losses.
(Free from cares.)

Dhamkāē pāyā Banyā, dhar dī ḍeṛh serī.
Frighten the shopman and you 'll get a pound and a half (for a pound).

Dhan aur gend khel kī doū ek subhāo,
Kar āvat chhin ek meṅ, chhin meṅ kar se jāē.
Wealth and a child's ball are in nature alike, One moment in your hands, and in another out of them.

Dhān, bichāre bhalle, jo kūṭā, khāyā, challe. E. Wom.

Rice is a very good thing; pound it, eat it, and go your way.
(Pounded rice is very soon cooked.)

Dhan chāhe to dharm kar, mukt chāhe bhaj Rām.
To be rich be charitable, to procure salvation call on God.

Ḍhāṅḍā bālā, jāḍā ṭālā. Rus.
When the log burns the cold goes away.
(Care leads to success.)

Dhan de jī ko rākhiye, aur jī de rākhe lāj.
Sacrifice your wealth to your life, and your life to your honor.

Dhan kā dhan gayā, aur mīt kī mīt gai.
He lost both money and friendship.
(Lend your money and lose your friend: 'Lend your money to your friends, Money lost, so friendship ends.')

Dhān kā gāṅo puāl se jānā jātā hai. Agric.
The rice village is known by the straw (lying about).
(The tree is known by its fruit.)

Dhan ke pandrā, Makar pachchīs, Chille ke yeh din chālīs.
15 days of December and 25 days of January are the 40 days of winter.

Dhan meṅ dhan tīn āṅṭhī san.
His wealth consists of three bundles of hemp.
(Worth very little.)

Dhannā seṭh ban-ke baiṭhe haiṅ!
Look, he is now a merchant prince!
(A petty dealer assuming the airs of a rich merchant.)

Dhan nātī hukkā, posāk nātī juluph. E.
A pipe for property, and hair for clothing.
(Wretchedly poor.)

Dhān, pān, ho rahī hai.
She is as delicate as the rice plant and betel leaf.

Dhān, pān, pānī, Kātak savād jānī. Wom.
Rice, betel and water taste best in October.

Dhān, pān paniyaule, nānh jāt latiyaule. E. Agric.
Rice and betel, must be well watered or. they will not thrive.

Dhān sūkhtā hai, kavvā ṭarṭarātā hai. E. Wom.
As long as the rice is drying the crows will keep on cawing.
(Wheresoever the carcase is, there will the eagles be gathered together. Mat. xxiv, 28.)

Dhanvantā ke kāṅṭā lagā, dauṛe log hazār,
Nirdhan girā pahāṛ se, koī na āyā kār.
A thorn runs into a great man and a thousand run to help; A poor man falls down a mountain and no one comes near him.

Dhāo dhāo, karam likhā so pāo! Hin. Wom.
Work on and get what 's in your fate!
(Said by the lazy: what is the good of working?)

Dhāo, jo Bidh likhā so pāo. Hin.
Rush on, but you 'll only meet your fate.

Dharam hār dhān koī khāē. Hin.
Any body can make money by dishonesty.

Dharam kī jaṛ sadā harī. Hin.
The root of faith is ever green.

Dharam rahe to usar meṅ jure
By faith you can make the desert green.
(Compare Hebrews, Ch. xi.)

Dhar chal sir kolū kī lāṭh,
Mat chal sāth kuchāl ke bāṭ.
Go with the piston of an oil mill on thy head, rather than in the company of a bad man.

Dhaṛī bhar kā sir to hilā diyā, paisā bhar kī zabān na hilāī gaī.
He will shake his heavy head, but won't wag his light tongue.
(Said of one who nods his head in returning a salute, but does not say good morning.)

Dhaṛī dhaṛī kar-ke luṭā.
Robbed of the last penny.

Dhar jā, mar jā.
Deposit and die.
(Used to describe a person of bad faith. It is his wish that whoever commits anything to his care may die, so that he may convert the deposit to his own use.)

Dharnī kī mā sāṅjh. Hin.
Evening is the mother of patience.
(All natives eat in the evening under any circumstances.)

Dharā mātā bojh saṅbhāle!
May mother earth long bear your weight!
(May you live long.)

Dhaṭiṅgar kāhe moṭā? lāhā gine na ṭoṭā.
Why are the worthless fat? They neither care for gain nor loss.

Dhaulā bāl, maut kī nishānī.
Grey hair is the forerunner of death.

Dhāvegā so pāvegā. Hin.
Who runs gets, *or* who worships gets.

Dhelā sir muṇḍaī, ṭakā badlāī.
Pay a half-penny for the shave and two pence for the discount.

Dheṅḍas o kaddū, lānat ba har dū!
A gourd and a pumpkin, a curse on both!
(Applied to a dispute between two persons equally worthless.)

Dhī beṭī apne ghar bhalī. Hin. Wom.
Daughters are best in their own houses.
(*i. e.* their husbands' houses.)

Dhī chhoṛ, dāmād pyārā!
To neglect the daughter and cherish the daughter's husband!
(Usual custom in India, expressing exactly the opposite of the English proverb—My son is my son till he marries a wife, my daughter is my daughter all the days of her life.)

Dhī, janvāī, bhānjā, yeh tīnoṅ nahīṅ āpnā.
A daughter, a son-in-law, and a nephew, these three are never one's own.
(They have always other and nearer ties.)

Dhī mārūṅ, putoh le tarās. Tir. Wom.
I beat my daughter to frighten my daughter-in-law.
(*Pour encourager les autres.*)

Dhī mūī, janvāī chor. Wom.
The daughter dead, the son-in-law is as a thief.
(That is, no more seen.)

Dhī na beṭī, udhal gaī samdheṭī. Wom.
Nor child, nor daughter, and she cries out that her daughter's sister-in-law has gone wrong.
(*Samdhan* is the daughter's mother-in-law: *samdheṭī* is her daughter.)

Dhī na dhiyānā, āp hī kamānā, āp hī khānā. Hin. Wom.
Nor daughter, nor son-in-law, whatever he earns goes into his own stomach.

Dhīn-dhaunkaṛ, Allāh Miyāṅ kā naukar.
A fat man is God's servant.
(*i. e.* a lazy fellow who won't work and resigns himself to God's forbearance.)

Dhīṅg dhīṅgī Ballū kā rāj.
Violence prevails under the government of Ballū.
(Might is right: Ballū was a Jāṭ, whose government was a kind of anarchy, under which every thing belonged to him who had the strongest arm.)

Dhīṅvar ke bas parī.
A fairy under the power of a (black) fisherman!
(Said of an ugly husband.)

Dhī parāī, āṅkh lajāī.
The eyes feel shame for another's daughter.
(When married into the owner's family.)

Dhīraj, dharm, mitr aur nār.
Āpat kāl parakhiye chār.
Patience, virtue, a friend, and a wife, are all tried in the time of misfortune.

Dhīrā kām Rahmānī, shitāb kām Shaitānī.
Deliberation is of God, hastiness of the Devil.

Dhīrā so gambhīrā.
Steady and deep.
(Still waters run deep.)

Dhīyā pūt ke na gātī, bilaīyā ke gātī. E. Wom.
No clothing for his son or daughter, but for his cat (mistress).

"*Dhiyā, to ko kahūṅ. Bahuryā, tū kān dhar!*"
"Daughter, I speak to you. Daughter-in-law, do you listen!"
(And learn better next time.)

Dhobī beṭā chānd sā sīṭī aur paṭāk.
The washerman's son is always clean on a whistle and a bang.
(He is dressed in the clothes of others, which his father washes. The *dhobī* of India whistles at his work and bangs about the clothes to clean them. Applied to one who keeps up a respectable appearance at the expense of others.)

Dhobī chhoṛ saqqa kīyā, rahī Khizar ke ghāt. Mah. Wom.
She left the washerman, and wedded a water-bearer, but still her fate is connected with water.
(*Khwājā Khizar* is the lord of the flood in India.)

Dhobī kā chhailā, ek ujlā ek mailā.
The washerman's son has on one clean and one dirty coat.
(He is rigged out in the clean and foul linen of his father's customers.)

Dhobī kā kuttā ghar kā na ghāṭ kā.
A washerman's dog belongs neither to the house nor to the washing place.
(From pillar to post. Said of any person who has no fixed habitation.)

Dhobī ke biyāh, gadhe ke māthe mauṛ.
At the washerman's wedding, the chaplet goes on to the donkey's head.
(Allusion to the marriage customs of the *Dhobīs*.)

Dhobī ke ghar biyāh, gadhe kā chhuṭṭī bhail. E.
On the wedding of a washerman, the donkeys have a holiday.
(As above.)

Dhobī par bas na chalā gadhaīyā ke kān maroṛe.
He could do nothing to the washerman, so he twisted his ass's ears.
(Spoken of one who is unable to punish the person who offended him, but wreaks his vengeance on those who are unable to resist.)

Dhobī par dhobī, khendhṛe meṅ sāban. [a clout.
Washerman after washerman is as soap to
(Moral: don't change your servants too often.)

Dhobī rove dhulāī ko, miyāṅ roveṅ kapṛoṅ ko.
The washerman cries for his wages, the master for his clothes,
(Very true in India.)

Dhobī dhāī bheṅṛī pāṅke lagī. E.
When the sheep was washed and cleansed she went into the mud again.

Dhoke kī ṭaṭṭī.
A deceitful screen.
(Not so secure as it is supposed. It is applied to a new religious doctrine or teacher.)

Ḍhol bāj dammāme bāje. Hin. Wom.
The large drums followed the small ones.
(Used to express that a man's misconduct was formerly known to few, but is now published to the whole world.)

Ḍhol ke bhītar pol!
Hollowness within the drum!

Ḍhol na ḍaf, Har Har gīt!
No drum nor kettle-drum, and chanting hymns to God!
(In India drums are necessary to the praise of God.)

Dhor mare na kavvā khāē.
The cattle will never die, nor the crow eat (their carcases.)
(Vain hope.)

Dhotī meṅ sab naṅge.
All are naked under the coverings of their loins.

Dhotī thī do pāoṅ, dhone paṛe chār pāoṅ. Wom.
There were but two feet to wash, and there are now four.
(An idle husband who won't even wash his own feet.)

Dhove ke ṭokrī, gāve ke gīt. E.
He works as a labourer and sings songs.
(A light heart.)

Dhūl kī rassī baṭnā. Rus.
To twist a rope of sand.
(To draw blood from a stone.)

Dhūlkoṭ kā kharbūza, jaise misrī kā kūza. Local.
Dhūlkoṭ musk melons are sweet as sugar-candy.
(Dhūlkoṭ is a piece of low-lying land near Dehlī.)

Dhūṅḍ lāo, batā deṅge.
Find him and I'll tell you about him.
(First catch your hare.)

Dhūṅdū-kār meṅh baras rahā hai.
It is raining from black clouds.
(Cats and dogs.)

Dhūnī pānī kā sanjog hai. Hin.
There is some connection between his fire and water.
(Allusion to the common Hindū belief of the transmigration of souls: *dhūnī* is the sacred fire of the *jogī* beside which he sits absorbed in religious meditation; to add wood to his *dhūnī* is supposed to procure a share in his next life, and a partnership in his future bliss and joy resulting from his present asceticism.)

Dhūp meṅ bāl safaid nahīṅ kiye haiṅ.
I have not turned grey (by idling) in the sun.
(I have not spent my life without some experience.)

Dhūp paṛat jo dāeṅ chalāve, rās nāj oh turat uṭhāve. Agric.
Who threshes his corn in the sun, will quickly get a heap of grain.
(Make hay while the sun shines.)

Dīdār bāzī aur Maulā rāzī.
Looking (at pretty women) does not displease God.
(A cat may look at a king.)

Dil dunyā kī dam badam kīje,
Kis kī shādī o kis kā gam kīje?
Enjoy this world every moment of your life,
For whom would you mourn, and for whom would you rejoice?
(Eat, drink, and be merry, for to-morrow we die.)

Dil ḍaul gumbaz, āvāz dar phish.
A dome to look at and his voice in a well.
(A big man with a weak voice.)

Dilerī mardoṅ kā gahnā hai.
Bravery is man's jewel.

Dil kā dil āina hai.
The heart is a mirror for the heart.
(Friendship breeds friendship; love begets love.)

Dil kā mālik Khudā hai.
God is Lord of the heart.

Dil lagā gadhī se, to parī kyā chīz hai?
When the heart is set on a she-ass, what is fairy then?
(Love sees no faults.)

Dil lagā meṅḍkī se to Padmanī kyā chīz hai?
Whose heart is fixed on a frog thinks nothing of a fairy.
(Spoken by way of contempt: love is blind.)

Dillī dūr hai.
Dehlī is a long way off.
(It is a far cry to Loch Awe.)

Dillī gadar pahle chaman banī huī thī.
Before the mutiny Dehlī was a garden.

Dillī ke bāṅke, jin kī jūtī meṅ sau sau ṭāṅke.
A Dehlī fop with shoes of a hundred patches.

Dillī ke dilvālī, muṅh chiknā peṭ khālī.
A Dehlī swell with a smooth face and an empty stomach.

Dillī kī beṭī, Mathurā kī gāē, Karam phūṭeṅ to bāhar jāē.
A Dehlī girl and a Mathurā cow are ruined by going abroad.
(They are each the most delicate of their kind.)

Dillī kī kamāī, Dillī hī meṅ gaṅvāī.
The earnings of Dehlī are consumed at Dehlī.
(Saving nothing from service.)

Dillī se hiṅg āī tab baṛe pakke.
When the asafœtida comes from Dehlī, the savoury will be got ready.

Dillī se maiṅ āūṅ, khabar kahe merā bhāī!
I am come from Dehlī and my brother tells me news of it!
(Stale news! Queen Anne is dead!)

Dil kī thī maiṅ sādī, jis kā pātī us kā khātī. Wom.
So simple was I that I ate from whoever gave me.
(Without reference to caste.)

Dil ko dil se rāh hai.
There is a way from heart to heart.
(Love begets love.)

Dil ko ho qarār, to sab sūjheṅ tehvār.
The heart at rest sees a feast in every thing.

Dil meṅ āī ko rakkhe so bharvā.
Who speaks not his mind is a pander.

Dil meṅ nahīṅ ḍar, to sab kī pagṛī apne sar.
No fear in his heart and every one's turban on his head.

Dil soz, khānā tarāsh.
A fire in the heart and a knife in the house.
(A bad son.)

Dimakā ke khāil penr, soch ke maral deh kavano kām ke na rahe. Bhoj.
A tree eaten by white ants, and a body worn with care are nothing worth.

Din achchhe hote hain, tau kankar javāhar ho jāte hain.
When fortune smiles stones turn into gems.

Din bhale āënge to ghar pūchhte chale āënge.
When good fortune comes she will seek my house.
(I need not seek her, *i. e.* exert myself: A doctrine of the fatalists.)

Din bhar chale arhāī kos.
Travelled all day long, but covered only two and a half miles.
(An idle man.)

Din das ādar pā-ke karnī āp bakhān,
Jo lag, kāg, sarādh pakh, to lag to sanmān.
Having obtained honour for a few days, extol yourself, O crow! As long as the fortnight of the *sarādh* remains, you are respected.
(This proverb is used when a man is guilty of oppression in consequence of the office he holds. The speaker means to say, that you may do as you please now, but these golden days of your's will soon have an end, when you will no longer have it in your power to tyrannize over me. The allusion is to the custom of making presents to crows during *sharādhs* or funeral ceremonies of Hindūs.)

Din Divālī ho gaī.
The day is turned into the Dīvālī.
(Turning day into the night: great rejoicings.)

Din dūnī, rāt chaugunī!
Double by day and four times by night.
(A blessing.)

Dīn Īd aur rāt Shab-barāt. Mah.
Each day was an Īd, and each night a Shab-i-barāt.
(A scene of constant mirth. The Īd is a Muhammadan day feast and the Shab-i-barāt a night feast.)

Din jab bhale āte hain, to maṭṭī pe hāth ḍālo sonā hotā hai.
When good days come, if you take up dust it turns into gold.

Din jab bure āte hain, to sone pe hāth dālo maṭṭī ho jātī hai.
When evil days come, if you take up gold it will turn into dust.

Din jāte der nahīn lagtī.
Time knows no delay.

Din khasā, mazdūr hansā.
When the sun goes down, the labourer laughs.

Din ko sharm, rāt ko bagal garm.
Coy by day and lusty by night.
(Allusion to the Hindū custom of married women covering their faces by day before their own husbands until they have borne a child.)

Din ko ūnī ūnī, rāt ko charkhā pūnī. Wom.
She saunters all day to spin at night.
(Said to those who don't work at the proper time.)

Din men sove, rozī khove. Superstition.
Who sleeps in the day time loses his livelihood.

Din nīke bīte jāte hain, pher nahīn woh āte hain.
The good times are passing away, and they won't come back again.
(O hard times, come again no more.)

Dīn o dunyā men us kā hoë burā, Jo kisī kā koī burā chīte.
May he suffer in this world and the next who meditates injury to any one.

Dīn se dunyā hai.
Faith keeps the world going.

Dīn se dunyā rakhnī mushkil hai.
It is harder to serve the world than God.
(Faith is easier than practical virtue.)

Dīvālī baras men ek din.
Dīvālī comes but once a year.
(Christmas comes but once a year.)

Dīvālī jīt, sāl bhar jīt. Hin. Superstition.
Win at Dīvālī, win all the year round.
(Allusion to the custom of gambling at the Dīvālī festival for luck, common to all the trading classes.)

Dīvālī ke batāse.
Dīvālī sweetmeats.
(During the Dīvālī festival a kind of sugar cake called *batāsā* is interchanged among friends. The proverb is applied to one who wanders here and there without having any fixed abode: a rolling stone.)

Dīvālī ke dīve chāṭ-kar jāënge.
They will lick up your Dīvālī lamp and go.
(They will completely ruin you: at the Dīvālī it is incumbent on every orthodox Hindū to light as many lamps as he can afford: also said of flies which grow less annoying at this season on account of the approaching winter.)

Dīvālī kī kulhiyā.
A Dīvālī dish.
(Very fine, but good for nothing; at this feast small plates of clay are made and painted gaudily.)

Dīvālī kī rāt ko būnṭī būnṭī pukārtī hai. Superstition.
On the night of the Dīvālī every herb and plant finds tongue.

Dīvāliye kī sākh Paṭṭāl men.
The bankrupt's credit is in Hell.

Dīvāl rahegī to leo bahotere charh rahenge. Hin. Wom.
While there is a wall lots of the plaster will adhere.
(While there is life, flesh will grow.)

Dīvānah bakār-i-khud hushyār. Pers.
Mad, but in his interests wise.

Dīvāna hai va lekin bāt kahtā hai ṭhikāne kī.
Mad as he is, his words are full of meaning.
(There is method in his madness.)

Dīvāne ko bāt batāī, us ne le chhappar charhāī.
Disclose a secret to a fool, and he 'll cry it from the housetop.

Dīvāne se āṅkh nahīṅ milāiye.
Don't even catch the eye of a madman.
(It is best to have nothing to say to an unreasonable person.)

Dīvānī ādmī ko dīvānā kar detī hai.
The Civil Courts make men mad.
(Allusion to the length of Civil suits.)

Dīvānoṅ ke kyā sir sīṅgh hote haiṅ?
Have blockheads horns?
(They are like other people to look at.)

Dīvār ke bhī kān hote haiṅ.
Walls have ears.

Dīvār khāī āloṅ ne, ghar khāyā sāloṅ ne.
As nitches weaken walls, brothers-in-law weaken the house.
(Allusion to the love between brothers and sisters in India, which induces the sister to give her husband's food to her brother.)

Dīyā bast anūp hai, dīyā kahe sab koē,
Dharā bast na pāiye, jo pāe dīyā na hoē.
The lamp is precious thing, every body praises it, You cannot find a thing if no lamp be with you.
(There is a pun on the word *dīyā* in the first line which means a lamp and also a gift in charity.)

Dīyā dān māṅge Musalmān. Hin.
Musalmāns will claim bac k the given alms.
(Allusion to the Muhammadan custom of taking back the dowry after the decease of a daughter.)

Dīyā dūr se, lāgī sāth khāne. Wom.
He gave her (food) at a distance and she sat down to eat it on the spot.
(Gifts make beggars bold. Hindūs throw food to beggars and they are supposed to go to a distance before they eat it.)

Dīyā fātehā ko, lage luṭāne. Mah.
He squandered away what was given him as an offering.
(*Fātehā* gifts should be kept: he sold even his wedding presents.)

Dīyā hai to dekh le.
(i) If you have a lamp you can see.
(ii) You may see if you have given.
(See above under *dīyā bast* etc.)

Dīyā hāth, khāne lagā sāth.
I gave him food into his hands, but he began to eat out of my own dish.
(Impudence.)

Dīyā līyā hī āṛī ātā hai.
Charity protects you.
(What you have given in alms will be your safety at the last day.)

Dīyā na bātī, muṇḍo phire itrātī. Wom.
There is neither lamp nor candle, and the widow is strutting about.
(Said of persons attempting to do what they are unable to effect.)

Dīyā to chānd thā, na diyā to mūṅh mānd thā.
If he gives his face is as the moon, if he won't give his face is dull.
(Flattery.)

Dīye kī raushnī mahshar tak. Mah. Wom.
The lamp's light extends to the day of judgment.
(Pun on the word *diyā*, which means also alms.)

Dīye tale andherā.
Darkness under the lamp.
(Said of the police when thefts take place under their noses.)

Do ādmiyoṅ kī gavāhī se to phāṅsī hotī hai.
Two witnesses are enough to hang a man.
(Allusion to the proceedings of courts upon false evidence.)

Do chūn ke bhī bure hote haiṅ.
Even two men of straw are good at a fight.
(Said to a person who challenges two persons at a time.)

Do dil rāzī to kyā karegā Qāzī? Mah.
When two hearts agree what can the Qāzī do?
(That is, when the two parties to a dispute come to a mutual reconciliation there is no longer room for the judge to interfere.)

Doḍo āī bāl thūtrāē.
The old hag came with her hair dishevelled.
(Untidiness.)

Do ghar Musalmānī, tis meṅ bhī āṇā kānī.
Even two families of Musalmāns cannot agree.
(Allusion to the quarrelsome nature of the Indian Musalmāns.)

Do hī chīz haiṅ, beṭā yā beṭī.
There are but two things (of value in the world), a son or a daughter.

Do hī chīz haiṅ, hār yā jīt.
There is a choice of but two things, loss or gain.

Do jorū kā khasam, chausar kā pāsā.
The spouse of two wives is no better than the dice on the backgammon board.
(He is tossed from one side to the other.)

Do khasam kī jorū, chausar kī goṭ.
The wife of two husbands is no better than a draught in backgammon.
(Allusion to the custom of polyandry.)

Do laṛeṅge to ek gire hī gā.
When two fight one must fall.

Ḍolī āī, ḍolī āī, mere man meṅ chāo,
Ḍolī meṅ se nikal paṛā bhoṅkṛā bilāo! Wom.
The *ḍolī* comes, the *ḍolī* comes, and my heart longs (for her), But out of the *ḍolī* has come an ugly old cat.
(Allusion to the custom of never seeing the

bride until she is brought home: the *ḍolī* is the bride's palanquin.)

Ḍolī na kahār, Bīvī bhaī hain taiyār. E. Wom.
Nor palanquin nor bearers, and my lady is ready dressed.
(She is not wanted and no conveyance has been sent for her.)

Ḍom aur chanā mūnh lagā būrā.
A bard and pulse are bad things to take a fancy to.
(It is difficult to part with either.)

Ḍom, baniyā, postī, tīnon be-īmān.
A singer, a shop-keeper, and an opium-eater, are not to be trusted.

Ḍom ḍolī, pāthak piyādah.
The bard in a palanquin, and the priest afoot.
(Society upside down: also used when a bad master has a good servant.)

Do men tīsrā, ānkhon men ṭhīkrā.
A third among two is as grit in the eye.
(Two's company and three's none.)

Ḍom ke ghar byāh, man āve so gā.
When a minstrel has a wedding he may sing what he pleases.
(Allusion to the indecent songs these people are apt to sing and which are not allowed in respectable houses.)

Ḍomnī kā pūt chapnī bajāē, apnī zāt āp hī jatāē.
The Domnī's son drums on an earthen pitcher and shows his caste.
(What's bred in the bone will never come out of the flesh.)

Ḍomnī kī launḍī.
The slave of a Domnī.
(*Domnī*, a woman of a tribe which performs the lowest offices.)

Do Mullā men murgī harām. Mah.
Between two Mullās the fowl remained unlawful meat.
(A Mullā is employed at the slaughter of animals to pronounce over them the name of God, whereby they are rendered lawful food (*halāl*) and for this he has a fee. The proverb supposes two Mullās to be striving for this office and the fowl to die in their hands without receiving the necessary benediction. Too many cooks spoil the broth.)

Donon ber jo ghūme phire, tīn kāl jo khāē.
Sadā nirogī changā rahe, jo prāte uṭh nhāē.
Who walks out morn and eve and eats three times a day, And bathes at early dawn, will always keep good health.

Donon dīn se gaē pānḍe, halvā mīlā na mānḍe.
From both creeds the priest was expelled, (from Muslim's) *halvā* (sweetmeat) and (Hindūs) buttered bread.
(Greed is a loser: applied to one who deserts one employment in quest of another, and loses both.)

Donon hāthon pagṛī sanbhālnī paṛtī hai.
He has to support his turban with both hands.
(He is hard put to support his position.)

Donon hāthon sanbhālī nahīn sanbhaltī.
With difficulty he supports his turban with both hands.
(He is so hard up.)

Donon hāthon tālī bajtī hai.
Both hands beat time together.
(As you salute so you will be saluted: also, it takes two to make a quarrel.)

Donon khoē jogīyā, mudrā aur ādes. Hin.
The *jogī* lost both his ear-ring and his salute.
(*Jogīs* wear ear-rings, (*mudrā*) to mark them and are saluted by all. Proverb refers to a *jogī* giving up his celibacy.)

Donon vaqt mile nahīn sīte, sūraj kī ānkh phūṭ jāēgī. Women's superstition.
One should not sew when day meets night, as it puts out the eye of the day.

Do piyāle pī to len, harām-zadgī to peṭ men hai.
Let us drink two cups (of wine), and all the wickedness will be in the belly.
(*i. e.* be attributed to drunkenness.)

Do qasāiyon men gāē murdār. Mah.
Between two butchers the cow died a natural death.
(And so became unlawful food.)

Do rakābah ghoṛā, bakhshī kā dāmād.
The high horse is the tax collector's son-in-law.
(Under the protection of the great.)

Dost kā dushman dushman, dushman kā dushman dost.
Your friends' foes are your foes, your foe's foes are your friends.
(*Esprit de corps*: clannishness.)

Dost mile khāte, dushman mile rote!
May I find my friend happy and my enemy wretched!

Doston kā hisāb dil men.
Friends' accounts are kept in the heart.

Duā aur davā nit karnī chāhiye.
Use both prayer and medicine.
(Pray to God, but keep your powder dry.)

Duār dhanī ke paṛ rahe, dhakkā dhanī kā khāē.
Lie at the rich man's door and take the rich man's kicks.

Ḍūbā bans Kabīr kā jo upjā pūt Kamāl.
The race of Kabīr became extinct, when his son Kamāl was born.
☞ An expression used in reprobation of those who abandon the religion or manner of life of their ancestors. The origin of the saying is said to be this. Kabīr instructed his son Kamāl from his infancy in the principles of universal benevolence, telling him that all mankind were his brethren and all women were to be considered in the light either of mothers, sisters, or daughters. When the son came to years of puberty and the father proposed to him a connexion in marriage, he asked whether he meant he should marry his mother, his sister or his daughter, for that the world contained no other women. He therefore declined any closer alliance with the other sex, and thus cut off his father's hopes of posterity.

Ḍūbegā bhāṛū kā bhāṛū, rāt same ne de saë jhāṛū. Rus. (Superstition.)
You will be utterly ruined if you sweep out your house at night.

Dubidhā meṅ dono gaë, māyā milī na Rām.
In his doubt he lost both his wealth and his God.
(Hesitate and be lost.)

Ḍūbī, kanth, bharose tere! Wom.
Reliance on you has ruined me, my husband!

Dublā kunbā, sarāp kī ās.
A weak heir hath his hope in curses.
(If kept out of his inheritance by a stranger, he has no means of redress, but by praying for the death of the other.)

Duble kalāvant kī kaun sune?
Who will listen to a poor singer?
(Who ever heeds the voice of the poor!)

Duble māreṅ Shāh-Madār.
Shāh Madār afflicts the weak.
(Applied to one who oppresses and tyrannizes over those who are unable to resist, but dares not attack the strong. Shāh Madār was a Musalmān saint, whose tomb at Makanpūr is frequented by pilgrims. Hitting a man when he is down.)

Ḍūbte ko tinke kā sahārā.
A drowning man will catch at a straw.

Dudhail gāë kī do lāteṅ bhī sahī jātī haiṅ.
Even two kicks may be borne from a milch cow.
(That is, a man will put up with inconvenience or mortification where he has a prospect of advantage.)

Dūdh bhī dhaulā, chhāchh bhī dhaulī.
The milk is white and the butter milk too.
(All is fish that comes into his net.)

Dūdh kā dūdh, pānī kā pānī.
The milk is by itself, and water is by itself.
(He separates the truth from falsehood. A phrase used to express just decision and accurate discrimination.)

Dūdh kā jalā chhāchh phūṅk phūṅk pītā hai.
Scalded with hot milk will blow on butter-milk (to cool it).
(Burnt child fears the fire.)

Dūdh kā sā ubāl hai, āyā chalā gayā.
Boiled up like milk, and as suddenly went down.
(To be very passionate, but soon over it.)

Dūdh ke dāṅt bhī abhī nahīṅ ṭūṭe haiṅ.
You have not yet shed your milk teeth.

Dūdh kī abhī bū ātī hai.
The smell of your mother's milk is still on your mouth.
(You are still a child.)

Dūdh kī sī makhkhī nikāl-kar phek de.
He was thrown away like a fly out of the milk.
(Suddenly and completely.)

Dūdh meṅ kī makkhī kis ne chakkhī?
Who would ever taste the fly in the milk?
(Hindūs throw away any food in which they may find a dead fly.)

Dūdhoṅ nahāo, pūtoṅ phalo. Wom. Benediction.
May you bathe in milk and be fruitful in children.

Dūdh pūt qismat se.
Milk and children depend on fate.
('Milk' stands here for cattle or wealth.)

Dug ḍug bāje, bahut nīkī lāge,
Ṅavvā neg māṅge, uṭhā baiṭhī lāge! E. Wom.
It is pleasant to listen to the music, But how fidgety one gets when the musician wants his fee.

Dukh bhareṅ Bī Fākhtā, Kavvā meve khāë.
The Lady Dove has all the pains, and the Crow eats up the fruit.
(One beats the bush and another catcheth the birds: the cat's paw.)

Dukh meṅ Har ko sab bhajaë, sukh meṅ bhajaë na koë, Jo sukh meṅ Har ko bhajaë, to dukkh kāhe ko hoë?
All remember God in their trouble, none in their joy, But who remembers God in his joy will never be in trouble.
(The devil was sick the devil a monk would be; The devil got well, the devil a monk was he.)

Dukh meṅ sukh kī qadr hotī hai.
Health is best appreciated in sickness.

Dukh sukh bahin bhāī haiṅ.
Pain and pleasure are brother and sister.
(There is no pleasure without pain.)

Dukh sukh nis-din sang hai, meṭ sake na koë,
Jaise chhāyā deh kī niyārī nek na hoë.
Pain and pleasure are with us ever, none can separate them, As the shadow of the body never departs.

Dukh sukh sab ke sāth lagā huā hai.
Pain and pleasure are ever with all of us.

Dukhte chot, kanauṅḍe bheṭ.
Meeting a man you wish to shun is like an injury to a sore place.
(Adding insult to injury.)

Dukhte dāṅt ko ukheṛnā hī chāhiye.
Better have out the aching tooth.

Dukhyā dukh rove, sukhyā jeb ṭove. E. Wom.
While the wretched weep, the happy feel their pockets.
(To see what they can make out of them: said of lawyers.)

Dukhyā rove, sukhyā sove.
The wretched weeps, the happy sleeps.
(Sleeping with a good conscience.)

Dūlah ḍhāī din kā bādshāh hai.
The bridegroom is a king for two and half days.
(Allusion to his being the prime mover in the marriage procession.)

Dūlah dulhan mil gaë, jhūṭī paṛī barāt.
When the bridegroom and bride have come together, the procession has become useless.
(Applied to the case of two people engaged in a dispute with numerous partisans on each

side, when the principals are reconciled, their partisans are thrown over.)

Dulah dulhan pāē, Shāh-bālā lāten khāē.
The bridegroom gets the bride and the best man gets the kicks.
(The *shāh-bālā* is the boy that follows the bridegroom in all the ceremonies and comes in for all the chaff.)

Dūlah gail barāt.
All the marriage guests follow the bridegroom.
(As sheep follow the shepherd.)

Dūlah ke pattal na, bajaniye ke thār! E.
No platter of leaves for the bridegroom, and the musician wants a brass dish!

Dulārī bityā, īnṭe kā laṭkan! E.
A darling daughter, and bricks for her ear-rings.

Dum dabā-ke bhāgnā.
To run with the tail between the legs.
(To show the white feather: to turn tail.)

Dum men namdā bāndh-ke chāndnī ko saunp diyā.
Tie a felt cloth to its tail and give it to the moonlight.
(To make fun of any thing.)

Dunyā ba ummed qāyam hai.
The world is sustained by hope.

Dunyā be-sabāt hai!
This world is frail!

Dunyā chand roza hai!
This world is but for a few days!

Dunyā dhoke kī ṭaṭṭī hai.
The world is a deceitful screen.

Dunyā dhund kā pasārā hai. Hin.
The world is but an expanse of vapour.
(The world is a mirage: all chaos.)

Dunyā do-rangī makārah sarāē,
Kahīn khair khūbī, kahīn hāē hāē.
The world is double-faced, and an abode of treachery, Here mirth and laughter, there weeping and wailing.

Dunyā hai aur kushāmad!
There is the world and flattery!
(So you can still get on.)

Dunyā hai aur matlab.
There is the world and your object.
(So why despair?)

Dunyā jāē ummed hai.
The world is the abode of hope.

Dunyā khāīye makkar se, roṭī khāīye shakkar se.
Gain the world by treachery, and eat your bread with sugar.
(The end justifies the means.)

Dunyā men aise rahiye, jaise sāban men tār.
Live in the world, as wire in soap.
(That is, not of it, as the wire cuts through the soap.)

Dunyā men chār paise baṛī chīz hain.
A penny is a great thing in the world.

Dūnyā men do hī chīz hain, beṭā yā beṭī.
There are only two things in the world, a son or a daughter.
(Said to console the parents to whom a daughter has been born when they would rather have had a son: Hobson's choice.)

Dunyā men sāṛhe tīn dal hain.
There are three and a half sorts of armies in the world.
(Ants, locusts, and clouds are called the three *dals* or armies, the other half are the rest of the world.)

Dunyā murdah pasand hai. Mah.
The world praises the dead.
(*De mortuis nil nisi bonum.*)

Dunyā zāhir parast hai.
The world worships appearances.
(The world is still deceived by ornament.)

Durangī chhoṛ de, ek rang ho jā;
Sarāsar mom ho, yā sang ho jā.
Eschew the double face; be of one face,
Either be a stone or altogether wax.

Dūr ke ḍhol suhāone. Wom.
Drums at a distance sound well.
(Distance lends enchantment to the view. Spoken of any person or thing that does not answer on inspection to the favorable report which had been made of it.)

Dushāle men lapeṭ-kar mārnā.
To strike under a shawl.
(To say biting words indirectly.)

'*Dushman kaun*'? *ki* '*man kā peṭ.*'
'Who is thy foe?' 'He that was within my mother's womb.'
(Brothers fighting over their estates.)

Dushman ke dil men jagah karne ka hunar chāhiye.
It needs skill to make a home in the heart of your foe.

Dushman kī nigāh jūtī par.
Your enemy will always look at your shoes.
(*i. e.* will never look you in the face.)

Dushman ko kam na samajhye.
Never despise your enemy.

Dushmanon ke man kā chetā huā.
The wish of the enemy's heart has been fulfilled. [*men zabān.*

Dushmanon men yūn rahiye, jaise battīs dānton
You must live amongst your foes, like the tongue amongst the thirty two teeth.
(So as not to be wounded.)

Dushman soē, na sone de.
The enemy nor sleeps himself, nor lets you sleep.

Dusht nā chhāḍe dushtā. kaisī sīkhū deo,
Dhoē hūn sau ber ke kājar swet na hoē.
The wicked will not leave his wickedness for all thy teaching. As lamp-black becomes not white for a hundred washings.
(Can the Ethiopian change his skin or the leopard his spots? Then may ye also do good that are accustomed to do evil. Jer. xiii, 23.)

Dūsre kā seṅdur dekh apnā lilār phoṛeṅ. E.
Seeing the vermillion spot on another's forehead, she cuts her own open.
(Pūrbī married women wear a spot of vermillion on their foreheads to mark the state of coverture: to bite the nose to spite the face.)

Dūsrī bāt dūsre kahte haiṅ.
Let others tell a differeut story.
(*i. e.* I speak the truth whatever others may say. I call him George Washington, you may call him what you darned please.)

Dūsroṅ kā aib baṛī jaldī dekh sakte haiṅ.
Another's fault is very quickly seen.

E

Ehsān kar aur daryā meṅ ḍāl,
Do good and throw it into the river.
(*i. e.* Don't remember it, as its memory breeds pride: let not thy left hand know what thy right hand doeth, Matthew vi, 3)

Ehsān lije jahān kā, na ehsān lije Shāh Jahāṅ kā.
Receive a favor from the world, but not from the king of the world.

Ek ahārī sadā bartī, ek nārī sadā jatī.
One meal a day means a constant fast, one wife only means constant chastity.

Ek Ahīr kī ekī gāē, nā lage to chhāchhī khāē.
The Ahīr has but one cow, and goes without milk if she does not give it.

Ekai sādhe sab sadheṅ, sab sādhe sab jāeṅ.
Stick to one thing and all will come: aim at every thing and all will go.
(At all things strain, all will prove vain: Who serves the root will eat the fruit: don't have too many irons in the fire.)

Ek akelā, do kā melā.
One is lonely, two is company.

Ek akelā, do se gyārah.
One is alone, two make eleven.
(Allusion to the Indian method of writing figures, in which, as in the European method, the figure 1, when placed with another 1, makes eleven; thus 11.)

Ek ām kī do phāṅkeṅ.
Two slices of a mangoe.
(As like as two peas.)

Ek anār, sau bīmār.
One pommegranate to a hundred sick.
(One post to a hundred candidates: pommegranates are much used for medicinal purposes.)

Ek anḍā, voh bhī ganḍā.
Only one egg, and that an addled one.
(Said of a bad and only child.)

Ek āṅkh maṭar kā bīyā, woh bhī āṅkh Bhavānī līyā. E.
She had an eye no bigger than a pea, and even that was taken by (the Goddess) Bhavānī.

Ek āṅkh meṅ lahr bahr, ek āṅkh meṅ Khudā kā qahr.
Prosperity in one eye, God's wrath in the [other.
(Said of a man half blind.)

Ek āṅkh phūṭī hai, to dūsrī par hāth rakhte haiṅ.
When one eye gets blind, the other is protected with the hand.

Ek āṅkh se rove, ek se haṅse.
She weeps with one eye and laughs with the other.
(Said of a crafty person.)

Ek aur ek gyārah.
One and one make eleven.
(Taken from the way of writing 11 in figures: used to express the great advantage of acting in concert. See above *Ek akelā*, etc.)

Ek āve ke bartan haiṅ.
Vessels of the same kiln.
(Chips of the same block.)

Ek bakhiyā more palle, kaun pinaute hoke challe. E. Wom.
I have only a quilt upon my back, what care I where I go?

Ek bār jogī, do bār bhogī, tīn bār rogī.
An ascetic once, a glutton twice, and a sick man thrice.
(Allusion to the state of health as judged by going to stool.)

Ek bolī, do bolī, merī nakṭī saṭā-saṭ bolī. Wom.
For a word or two my graceless offspring answers me at once.

Ek bolī tīn kām.
One word and three deeds.
(Killing two birds with one stone.)

Ek chanā bahoterī dāl.
One whole grain is equal to many broken ones.
(To express that the safety of the general is of more consequence than the lives of many soldiers: only the whole pea can be sown.)

Ek chanā do dāl.
A pea has only two parts.
(Two bites at a cherry.)

Ek chhaunī ke āṅchal meṅ non.
Gharī gharī rūṭhe, manāve kaun?
The girl has salt in her skirt. Who will keep down her hourly rage?

Ek chup hazār chup.
One silence is a thousand silences.
(Silence is golden.)

Ek chup, sau ko harāē.
One silence defeats a hundred.
(One man who is silent will defeat a hundred who talk.)

Ek dam, hazār ummed.
A single life, a thousand hopes.

Ek dam meṅ hazār dam.
On one life a thousand lives depend.

Ek ḍar do taraf.
Fear takes both sides.
(Fear in enemies is mutual.)

Ek dar band, hazār dar khule.
One door shut, there are a thousand open.
(There's hope yet.)

Ek din kā pāhonā, dūsre din ann-khāonā. Hin.
One day a guest, the second day a sponge.

Ek din ke sau sāṭh din.
One day has for its turn a hundred and sixty.
(There is time enough to avenge ourself.)

Ek din mehmān, do din mehmān, tīsre din balā-i-jān. Mah.
One day a guest, two days a guest, the third day a nuisance.

Ek din sab ko marnā hai.
All must die some day.

Ek ḍūbe to jag samjhāve, sab jag ḍūbā jāe!
When one goes wrong the world gives him advice, and then the whole world goes wrong itself!

Ek garīb ko mārā thā nau man charbī niklī thī.
Once I killed a poor man like you and got half a ton of fat out of him.
(Said to those who pretend to be poor: especially at the income tax enquiries.)

Ek ghaṛī kī be-hayāī sārī din kā ādhār.
A moment's shame brings a day's food.
(A sarcasm on the shameless: also used towards prostitutes.)

Ek ghaṛī kī 'nā' sāre din kā uddhār.
'No' for an hour, brings peace for a whole day.

Ek gurū ke bālke. Hin.
Disciples of one teacher.
(To express that two people are equally bad: *arcades ambo.*)

Ek hammām meṅ sab naṅge. Mah.
In one bath all are naked.
(We are all in the same boat. We all do the same thing.)

Ek haṅse, ek dukh meṅ.
One man laughs and another groans.

Ek hāth lenā, ek hāth denā. Mercantile.
Take with one hand and pay with the other.
(Ready money.)

Ek hāth tālī nahīn bajtī.
You cannot clap with one hand.
(It takes two to make a quarrel.)

Ek hāth zikr par, dūsrā hāth fikr par.
One hand on his beads, and the other hand on his affairs.

Ek hī lakṛī sab ko hāṅktā hai.
He drives all with one stick.
(Makes no difference in the rank and position of different men: he is no respecter of persons.)

Ek hunar aur ek aib har admī meṅ hotā hai.
In every man you find faults and virtues.

Ek husn ādmī, hazār husn kapṛā.
Lākh husn zevar, karoṛ husn nakhrā.
Man has one beauty, apparel a thousand, jewels a hundred thousand, and love a million.

Ekī dāl, ekī chāur, karai gun aur bāur. E.
The same pea and the same rice agree with one and disagree with another.
(One man's food is another man's poison.)

Ek īnṭ ke vāste masjid ḍhānā.
To pull down a mosque for a brick.
(To use a sledge hammer to kill a fly: used also towards a niggardly man; the story being told that a man building a mosque took a brick from a neighbour, who had the whole mosque pulled down in order to recover it.)

Ek janā ghar murdā bhel, chār janā mil khāṭī lel, Āp āp ke sabhī malūk, jhānṭ ukhāṛe murda halūk! E.
In a certain house a man died and four men went with the bier; they were so delicate that they lightened the body by cutting off the hair!

Ek jān, do qālib.
Two bodies, but one heart.
(Said of thick friends. Siamese twins.)

Ek jān, hazār armān.
One life and a thousand wishes.

Ek jau kī solah roṭī, Bhagat khāē, bhagtānī moṭī.
The saint eats sixteen loaves made of one barley corn, and the saint's wife gets fat.

Ek jorū kī jorū, ek jorū kā khasam,
Ek jorū kā sis-phūl, ek jorū kī pasham.
Some men are their wives' wives, and some are their wives' husbands, some are their wives' chaplets, and some are their wives cast off hair.

Ek jorū sāre kunbe ko bas hai.
One wife is enough for a whole family.
(Allusion to polyandry, and also to the custom of *karāo* among the Jaṭṭs by which a man marries his deceased brother's wife.)

Ek kaho, na das suno.
Nor say one word, nor hear ten.
(Don't abuse and you 'll not get abuse.)

Ek kā mūṅh shakkar se bharā jātā hai, sau kā mūṅh khāk se bhī nahīṅ bharā jātā.
You can fill one mouth with sugar, but you can't a hundred mouths even with dust.
(Applied to a person who is able and willing to support or entertain one or two people, but is unexpectedly called on to relieve a great number.)

Ek kān bahrā karo, ek kān gūṅgā.
Make one ear deaf, and close the other.
(Said to one who is powerless to avenge what he is made to hear.)

Ek kān sunī, dūsre kān uṛādī.
In at one ear and out at the other.

Ek kā tīte, tino tīt. Bhoj.
One bitter, all three bitter.

Ek kauṛī gānṭhi, "chūṛā pahinūṅ ki māṭhi! E. Wom.
One farthing's all she 's got, and "shall I buy bangles or armlets?"
(Foolish extravagance.)

Ek ke dūnā se sau ke savāī bhal. E. Mer.
A hundred and quarter for a hundred is better than the two for one.
(Small profits on large sales aggregate to a greater quantity than large profits on a scanty sale. Also investments at low rates of interest are safer than those at high ones.)

Ek khāē dūdh malīdā, ek khāē bhus.
One feeds on milk and cake, another lives on straw.
(*Telle est la vie.*)

Ek khatā, do khatā, tīsrī khatā mādar bakhatā.
One fault may pass, two faults may pass, the third is of the mother born.

Ek kī dārū do, do kī dārū chār.
The cure for one is two, the cure for two is four.
(However strong a man may be he cannot be a match for two men: there is safety in numbers.)

Ek kī sair, do kā tamāshā, tīn kā piṭnā, chār kā sāṅpā.
One man travels, two enjoy it, three fight over it, four make a funeral procession of it.
(Moral: don't travel with a large party.)

Ek ko de hai rutba-i-ālī, Ek ko de hai khurpā o jālī.
To one is given high honor, to another net and sickle.

Ek ko sāī, ek ko badhāī.
To one promises, to another congratulation.
(To promise a thing to one person and give it to another: welcome to one, and adieu to another: fickleness, vacillation.)

Ek lakh potā, savā lakh nātī, Us Rāvan ke dīyā na bātī. Hin.
With a thousand sons' sons and a million daughters' sons, nor wick nor lamp to such a Rāvan.
(Allusion to the story in the *Rāmāyan* according to which the whole of Rāwan's numerous progeny were killed in battle by Rām and Lakshman. The *diyā* and *bāti* are placed in dead men's hands by his male posterity to light him to the next world. The point of the proverb is that though you may have a large family don't boast, as they may all die.)

Ek lāṭhī sab ko hāṅktā hai.
He drives every body with the same stick.
(He is no respecter of persons.)

Ek machhlī sāre jal ko gandā kartī hai.
One stinking fish spoils the whole tank.
(The dead fly maketh the ointment of the apothecary to stink.)

Ek main aur merā bhāī, tīsrā hajjām nāī.
One is myself, the second is my brother, the third is the barber and shaver.
☞ Applied to a person, who being invited to an entertainment, carries a number of uninvited guests along with him: The story goes that a barber, at a wedding, refused one share of food, but claimed three shares under three pretended names: hence the proverb. It is also applied to any unreasonable demand.

Ek mās ritu āge dhāve. Agric.
The season runs a month ahead.
(Its character is seen a month previously.)

Ek mere ghar annā, dūsre ravannā. Mah. Wom.
A servant girl I keep and eke an errand boy.
(How rich I am!)

Ek miyān men do chhurī!
Two knives in one sheath!
(Said of two men living with one woman. Also applied as the English 'two kings in Brentford.)

Ek muṅh, do bāt!
Out of one mouth two (contradictory) statements!

Ek murgī nau jagah halāl nahīṅ hotī.
One cock cannot be killed in nine (different) places.

Ek mushkil kī hazār hazār āsān rakkhī hain.
For one difficulty there are provided a thousand remedies.

Ek 'nahīṅ' sattar balā ṭaltī hai.
One 'no' averts seventy evils.

Ek 'nā' sau dukh hare.
One refusal prevents a hundred reproaches.

Ek na shud, do shud.
Two ghosts for one.
☞ A certain man having learnt from a magician three charms by which he could bring a dead man to life, extort a secret, and then deprive him of life, on one occasion revived a corpse and learnt the secret, but forgot the 3rd spell for killing him. So the ghost followed him about wherever he went. In order to get rid of his inevitable companion he restored to life his teacher, who had been long since dead. Unfortunately, however for him, this time he forgot the 2nd charm, so that now he was attended by two ghosts for one. One charge not proved, another against me laid.

Ek nīm, sab ghar sītal.
One *nīm* tree cools the whole house.
(Allusion to its thick cooling shade.)

Ek nīm, sau koṛhī.
One *nīm* tree and a hundred lepers.
(*Nīm* leaves are said to be an effective cure for leprosy.)

Ek nūr ādmī, hazār nūr kapṛā.
One beauty in the man and a thousand in his clothes.
(God makes and apparel shapes.)

Ek oṛ chār Bed, ek oṛ chaturāī.
In one scale the four Veds, in the other natural wit.
(Natural wit is more than a match for erudition.)

Ek pān jo barse Suātī, Kurmin pahire sone kā pātī. E. Agric.
When showers fall in September, the farmer's wife wears golden rings.
(Even a small shower of rain in *Kuār* or September is very useful.)

Ek panth, do kāj.
One road, and two objects.
(To kill two birds with one stone.)

Ek peṛ haṛṛe, sagre gāoṅ khāṅsī. E.
There is one myrabolan tree, and the whole village has a cough.
(To express that the demand for anything is great, and the supply scanty. The myrabolan is said to be an effective remedy for a cough.)

Ek phūaṛ phūaṛ ke gaī, jā kuṭhlā sī ṭhāṛī bhaī. Rus.
A ninny to a ninny went and stood before her like a corn-binn.
(And said nothing !)

Ek ratī bin nāheṅ ratī kā.
A man without fortune is not worth a straw.

Ek roṭī ke do ṭukṛe.
Two halves of a loaf.
(Chips of the same block.)

Ek se ek, do se gyārah.
One is one, two make eleven.
(For explanation, see above—*Ek akelā*, etc.)

Ek se le, ek ko de.
God takes from one and gives to another.

Ek sir, hazār saudā.
One head, a thousand jobs.
(Too many irons in the fire.)

Ek suhāgin, nau launḍā.
One woman and nine boys (after her).

Ek sūrmā chanā bhāṛ ko nahīṅ phoṛ saktā.
One pea, however large, cannot break the oven.
(Don't kick against the pricks.)

Ek tandurustī, hazār nemat.
Health is equal to a thousand blessings.
(Health is better than wealth.)

Ek tarkash ke tīr.
Arrows from one quiver.
(Chips of the same block.)

Ek tave kī roṭī, kyā chhoṭī kyā moṭī !
They are cakes of the same girdle, whether small or great.
(Spoken in answer to one who endeavours to make distinctions between persons of one family or common descent.)

Ek to bhāl, dūsre kāṅdhe kudāl.
A bear with a hatchet on his shoulder.
(He is doubly armed.)

Ek to bhīk, dūsre pachhor pachhor.
Begging and sifting (the alms.)
(Never look a gift horse in the mouth.)

Ek to chorī, dūsre sīnā-zorī.
Thieving and bullying as well.

Ek to ḍāin, dūsre hāth luāṭh.
A witch with a torch in her hand.
(A very dangerous person.)

Ek to gaṛeṛan, dūsre lasson khāe. E.
A shepherdess that eats onions.
(Very dirty: a dirty woman eating offensive food.)

Ek to kānī beṭī biyāhī, dūsre pūchhne-vāloṅ ne jān khāī. Wom.
First I married my son to a one-eyed girl and now they worry me with questions.
(As to the looks of the bride.)

Ek to kānī beṭī kī māṅ, dūsre pūchhne-vāloṅ ne jān khāī. Wom.
First I am the mother of a one-eyed girl and then I am worried by questions about her.
(When it comes to arranging her marriage.)

Ek to kānī thī, dūsre paṛ gayā kunak.
Firstly she had only one eye, secondly grit got into it.
(Misfortunes never come singly.)

Ek to karelā karvā, dūsre nīm chaṛhā.
Firstly *karelā* is bitter of itself, and next it has been added to *nīm* leaves.

☞ Both the *karelā* and *nīm* are exceedingly bitter. To express that a man naturally of a bad disposition has become worse by associating with evil companions. 'Then goeth he and taketh to him seven other spirits more wicked than himself........and the last state of that man is worse than the first,' Luke xi, 26.

Ek to mīṭh, dūsre kaṭhaut bhar!
What ! sweets and a plateful of them !
(Asking for too much.)

Ek to Miyāṅ the hī, dūje khāī bhāṅg. Wom.
He was already possessed by (the evil spirit) Mīrāṅ, and then he took to *bhang.*
(And so got worse. For explanation of *Mīrāṅ* see above—*ūt Mīrāṅ* etc.)

Ek to miyāṅ the hī the, dūsre khāī bhāṅg ; tale huā sir, ūpar huī ṭang.
The good man was already stupid enough, and then he took an intoxicant and turned head over heels.

Ek to mūā an-bhāyā thā, dūsre sahī sāṅjh ātā thā. Wom.
In the first place the fellow was disagreeable and in the next he came at night fall.
(Said by a woman in censure of her husband.)

Ek to paṛā loṭtā hai, dūsrā kahe 'zarā chokhī denā.'
One man is already on the floor, and another says 'brew it stronger.'
(Applied to one who is not deterred from an act of folly by seeing the bad effect of it in others.)

'E kūkar, tū dūbar kāhī' ? 'das ghar kī āvā jāī.'
'My dog, what makes you so lean' ? 'I have to go to ten houses for food.'

Ek to sher, dūsre baktar pahne.
A lion clad in armour.

Ek to thā hī dīvānā, tis par āī bahār.
He was already mad, and spring has come upon him.
(Lunacy is supposed to be at its height in spring : greasing the fat sow's tail.)

Ero ke chero, nawvā ke bardhil. E.
Slavery to the slave and shampooing to the barber.
(It is the barber's business to shampoo: every cobbler to his last.)

Ēchan chhoṛ ghasīṭan meṅ paṛe.
From hauling he was hauled himself.
(Caught in its own honey: hoist with his own petard.)

Ewaz mūwaz gilā na dārad. Pers.
One thing for another prevents complaints.
(Exchange is no robbery.)

F.

Fajar fajar kī 'nāṅh' kuchh nahīṅ. Superstition.
'No' in the early morning bodes no good.
(A saying of the shop-keepers; the idea is never to refuse handsell.)

Fajar fajar 'nāṅ hāṅ' mat karo.
Don't say 'yea' and 'nay' in the early morning.

"*Falāne kī māṅ ne khasam kiyā.*" "*Bahut burā kiyā.*" "*Kar-ke chhoṛ diyā.*" "*Aur bhī burā kiyā.*"
"So and So's mother took another husband." "That was bad." "She ran away from that husband." "That was worse."
(Said of any one who attempts to remedy one blunder by committing another.)

Fāl kī kauṛiyāṅ mullah ko halāl. Mah. Wom.
Divination's fee the divine may lawfully take.
(Money earned is money lawfully got.)

Fālūdah khāte dāṅt ṭūṭe to balā se. Mah.
If the teeth be broken by eating pudding it is of no consequence.
(*i. e.* The teeth must be rotten to break by eating *falūdah*: it is vain to grieve for a misfortune that could not have been avoided.)

Fāl zabān, yā fāl Qurān. Mah.
Divination by word of mouth, or divination by the Scripture.

Fāqah-kashī kī naubat pahunchī.
It has come to starvation.

Fāqah-mastī!
What! pranks in poverty!

Faqat tāvīz se hī kām nahīṅ nikaltā, kuchh kamar meṅ bhī būtā chāhiye.
An amulet alone will not produce the effect, a little strength in the loins is also needed.
(Used as a hint to an impotent man, who, desirous of having children, has recourse to amulets and charms)

Faqīr apnī kamlī hī meṅ khush hai.
The beggar is happy in his blanket.

Faqīrī sher kā burqā hai.
Mendicancy is the lion's veil.
(*Faqīrs* are supposed to be able to do anything.)

Faqīr kī jholī meṅ sab kuchh.
A mendicant's bag contains everything.
(He can grant any request.)

Faqīr kī sūrat hī savāl hai.
The very appearance of the *faqīr* is his best appeal (for alms).

Faqīr kī zabān kis ne kīlī hai?
Who can stop the mendicant's tongue?

Faqīr ko jahān rāt ho gaī vahīṅ sarā hai.
The *faqīr's* inn is where the night overtakes him.

Faqīr ko kambal hī dushālah.
A blanket is a shawl to a beggar. [raydz.

Faqīr ko tīn chīz chāhiyeṅ, fāqah, qanāat, aur
Three things are necessary to a mendicant, fasting, content, and devotion.
(*Fāqah, qanāat* and *raydz* by their initials make up *faqr*, the state of being a *faqīr*.)

Faqīr, qarazdār, laṛkā, tīnoṅ nahīṅ samajhte.
A beggar, a borrower, and a child, are all three destitute of understanding.
(There is no satisfying them except by compliance with their wishes.)

Faqīr rā ba-mujādla che kār? Pers.
What has a friar to do with fighting?

Farīd Shakar Ganj!
O thou Farīd Shakar Ganj.
(Used by street boys as a chaff to an old man riding a decrepit old hack. For an explanation of Farīd Shakar Ganj see below.)

Farīd Shakar Ganj, nā rahe dukh nā rahe ranj.
May Farīd Shakar Ganj bless you, and from pain and grief keep you!

Farishtoṅ ke bhī par jalte haiṅ.
Even angels wings would burn.
(An inaccessible place.)

Farishtoṅ ko bhī khabar nahīṅ.
Even the angels have no news of it.
(A dead secret.)

Fārkhatī likhvānā.
To have the acquittance deed written.
☞ The story goes that a debtor, having assembled a band of musicians at his gate, invited his creditor, a Banyā, to come over to his house for a settlement of his account. As soon as he got the Banyā, with his books, inside his house, he ordered the band to strike up and then belaboured his creditor till he wrote out an acquittance in full, the Banyā's cries being drowned in the drumming outside.

Fārsī rā ṭang toram, tāki ū langṛī shavad.
I will break the leg of Persian, that it may become lame.
(Used as a taunt to half educated scholars with a smattering of Persian, the sentence being a barbarous mixture of Urdū and Persian.)

Farzand vohī hai jo khalaf ho.
A dutiful son is indeed a son. [fars jāne.

Farzand woh jo pand māne, Aur bāp kā kahnā
A son is he who takes advice, And obeys his father's word.

Farz se adā ho gae.
The duty is discharged.
(Said by the parents after the marriage of their child.)

Fatah aur shikast Khudā ke hāth hain.
Victory and defeat are in God's hands.

Fatah dād Ilāhī hai.
Victory is the gift of God. [*kiye jāo.*

Fatah to Khudā ke hāth hai, par mār mār to
Victory is from God, but strike out all you can.
(Pray to God, but keep your powder dry.)

Fātehā na darūd, khā gaë mardūd. Mah. Wom.
The reprobate has eaten without saying grace.
(No Muhammadan will eat before repeating the *fātehā* or grace.)

Fātehā na darūd, khāne ko maujūd. Mah.
He is in too great a hurry to eat to say grace.

Fauj be-vakīl, sāhab be-fīl.
An army without an envoy, a leader without an elephant.
(Moral: always go to war with a 'political' and a swaggering general!)

Fauj kī āgāṛī, āndhī kī pichhāṛī.
The invader's force in front, and a storm in rear (are most severe).

Fazal kare tān chhuṭṭiān, adl kare tān luṭṭiān. Panj.
By mercy I may escape, but by justice I should be ruined.
(A confession of guilt and a plea for mercy.)

Fikr aur zikr dono chahīyen. Mah.
Meditation and prayer both are required.
(Of a mendicant.)

Fikr burā, fāqah bhalā; fikr faqīrān khāë.
Better fast than care: 'tis care that kills the beggar.
(Care will kill a cat.)

Fikr kare kyā hotā hai? Honā thā so ho gayā.
What is the good of pining now? What is done is done.
(Why cry over spilt milk?)

Firnī, fālūdah ek bhāo nahīn hotā.
Rice pudding and bread pudding are not of one price.
(*Firnī* is made with milk, rice and sugar boiled together; *fālūdah* with flour, sugar, and water, the former being the most expensive.)

G.

Gāchh men kaṭhal, honṭh men tel. E.
The jack-fruit on the tree, and oil on the lips.
☞ This fruit, (*artocarpus integrifolia*) has a very glutinous juice, on which account those who pluck it, previously rub their hands with oil, and if its adhesive juice remain on the lips after eating, it is removed by the same means. The proverb is used to express premature precautions.

Gādaṛ āni ūn ko, baiṭhī chare kapās. E. Rus.
The sheep came to be shorn, but ate up the cotton field.

Gadhā barsāt men bhūkā mare!
A donkey starving in the rains!
(The ass cannot stand wet weather and does not flourish however plentiful the grass may be.)

Gadhā ghoṛā barābar!
Are horse and donkey alike?
(See for explanation the next.)

Gadhā ghoṛā ek bhāo!
What! the same price for a horse and an ass!
(Said to a customer who appraises a superior article at the same price as the inferior one.)

Gadhā gire pahāṛ se, murgī ke ṭūṭe kān.
The ass will fall down a hill, when a fowl's ear will split.
(An impossibility: allusion to the sure footedness of the ass tribe.)

Gadhā ke khāil khet, na har-loke ke, na par-loke ke. E.
If an ass eats up your field, it is neither good for this world, nor the next.
(But if a *cow* does it will take you to heaven. Such is the Hindū belief.)

Gadhā kharsā men moṭā hotā hai.
Donkeys fatten in dry weather.
☞ The popular belief is that when the donkey looks round and sees the parched plain he persuades himself that he has eaten up all the grass, whereas in wet weather seeing so much grass every where he believes he has eaten none of it. As a physical fact, asses do thrive better in dry weather than in wet.

Gadhā mare kumhār kā, dhoban satti hoë.
The potter's donkey died, and the laundress sacrifices herself.
(Calamity this one assails, another weeps and wails.)

Gadhā pānī pīye ghangol ke.
Even an ass drinking water rejects scum.

Gadhā pīṭe ghoṛā nahīn hotā.
If you pound an ass you will not make a horse of him.
(Bray a fool in the mortar, yet will he not be wise.)

Gadhe kā jīnā thoṛe din bhalā.
It is best for an ass to be short lived.
(Who leads a life of labor might as well be dead.)

Gadhe kā mās, kutte kā dānt.
The flesh of an ass, and the tooth of a dog.
(Are put to no use.)

Gadhe ke khilāë kā pun nā pāp.
To feed a donkey is neither a good work nor a sin.
(But to feed a cow *is* a good work.)

Gadhe kī ānkh men nūn diyā, us ne kahā "meri ānkh phoṛī."
Put salt in a donkey's eyes (to cure them), and he will say "I am blinded."
(Ingratitude.)

Gadhe kī yārī, lāt kī sansanāhaṭ.
Friendship with an ass results in a kick.

Gadhe ko angūrī bāg !
A vineyard for a donkey !
(Pearls before swine.)

Gadhe ko gadhā khujātā hai.
An ass scratches an ass.
(You scratch my back and I will stratch yours.)

Gadhe ko gulqand !
Rose-candy to an ass !
(*Gulqand*—sugar-candy flavoured with rose flowers, a very expensive medicine used by native ladies and their children : pearls before swine.)

Gadhe ko khushka !
What ! boiled rice for asses !
(For point see the preceding.)

Gadhe ko pūrī aur halvā.
Cakes and sugar plums for an ass !
(For point see the preceding.)

Gadhe ko zāfrān.
Safron to an ass !
(Same point as in several preceding proverbs.)

Gadhī bhī javānī men bhalī lagtī hai.
Even a she-ass looks pretty in her youth.

Gadhon se hal chale to bail kāun bisāë ? Agric.
If donkeys could draw ploughs who would buy oxen ?
(Which are of a higher price.)

Gaë bichāre roze, rahe ek kam tīs. Mah.
When one day of the fast is over twenty nine remain.
(The Muhammadan fast of Ramzān lasts 30 days.)

Gaë Dakkhan, vohī karam ke lakkhan. Hin.
He went to the South, and had the same fortune.

Gāë jab dūb se salūk kare, to kyā khāë ?
If a cow spare the grass, what shall she eat ?

Gaï joban, bhatār !
A husband, when my youth is gone !

Gāë kā dūdh, so māë kā dūdh.
Cow's milk is as mother's milk.

Gāë kā lavārā margayā, to khalṛā dekh panhāī.
The cow's calf is dead, but she gives milk to its skin.
☞ Applied to the consolation derived from the sight of that which resembles any person or thing which is lost, as the picture of a deceased friend, etc. If the calf of a milch cow die, she retains her milk till the stuffed skin be presented to her, which she takes for a live calf, and then yields the milk to the milker.

Gaë Kaṭak, rahe aṭak.
Went to Kaṭak (Cuttack) and stuck there.

Gāë ko apne sing bhārī nahīn.
The cow does not feel the burden of her horns.
(A man does not feel the burden of his family.)

Gāë na āve bachve lāj. E.
A cow is not ashamed of her calf.

Gāë na bachchhī, nīnd āve achchhī. Rus.
Nor cow nor calf, and sound sleep.
(Without care.)

Gāë na ho to bail dūho.
If you have no cow, milk an ox.
(Make the best of a bad job.)

Gaë the rozah chhuṛāne, namāz gale paṛī ! Mah.
He went to be freed from the fast, and prayers were added to it !

Gaë voh din jo Khalīl Khān fākhta mārte the.
The good old days are gone when Khalīl Khān used to shoot doves.
(*i. e.* when there was liberty. A sigh for the good old times.)

Gāhak aur maut kā ṭhīk nahīn kab āve ? Mercantile.
Who knows when death or a customer will come ?

Gāhe tolā, gāhe māshā.
Sometimes a pound, sometimes an ounce.
(To describe a person of a very changeable temper. Either all dirt or all honey.)

Gahrī lālī dekh-kar phūl gumān bhaë,
Kele bāg jahān men lag lag sūkh gaë.
The flower sees his beauteous hues and is proud, But how many a garden in the world is dried up !
(Full many a gem of purest ray serene, The dark unfathomed caves of ocean bear. Full many a flower is born to blush unseen And waste its sweetness on the desert air.)

Gaib kā hāl Khudā jāne.
God alone knows what's hid.

Gaī chaudhrāhaṭ phirī hai.
He has got back his lost office.

Gaī javānī phir na bāhore, chāhe lākh malīda khāo.
Youth once gone will ne'er come back, whatever food you eat.
(The tender grace of a day that is gone will never come back to me.)

Gair gair hī hai, apnā apnā hī hai.
Another's is another's, your own is your own.
(Blood is thicker than water.)

Gair kā sir kaddū barābar.
Another's head is a pumpkin.
(To you, and you may knock it about.)

Gair ke liye kūā khodegā. so āp hī giregā.
He that digs a pit for another falls into it himself.
(Do to all men as you would they should do unto you.)

Gājar kī pūngī, bajī bajī, nahīn toṛ khāī.
If the carrot won't make a pipe, I can at least eat it.
(It is best to have two strings to your bow.)

Galat-ul-ām fasīh. Arab.
Universal errors are correct.
(In language : usage beats grammar.)

Gāle hāth Gopālak māë. E.
Gopāl's mother always has her hand to her cheek.
(Native women sing with their hands about

the faces, and hence the proverb means—a happy joyous woman.)

Gale parī, bajāe siddh.

When you have to do it make the best of it.

(To make the best of a bad bargain.)

Gālī aur tarkārī khāne hī ke vāste hai.

Vegetables and abuse are made to be taken.

(A pun on the meaning of *khānā* to eat, and to suffer: reply to an abuse and it will make two.)

Galla chūn arzān shavad, imsāl Sayyid mī-shavam. Pers.

If corn were to grow cheaper I would turn Sayyid.

(The Sayyids are descendents of the Prophet and so great people among Muhammadans.)

Gal-vālā jīte, māl-vālā hāre.

The noisy wins and the owner loses.

(Make noise enough and you will get your way.)

Gam na dārī buz bakhar. Pers.

If you have no cares, buy a goat!

(And cares will soon follow.)

Gam pashm, jhānṭ shādī, yā Hadī! yā Hadī!

O my Lord God, pleasure and pain are as nothing to me.

(Saying of the free thinking *faqīrs* called *āzād* or *rind*.)

Gānā aur ronā kis ko nahīṅ ātā?

Who is there that neither sings nor cries?

Gānā na bajānā, pādpād-ke rijhānā.

She cannot sing nor play, so she tries to please by stupid jokes.

Gānā uttam, bajānā maddham.

Singing is better than playing (a musical instrument).

Gandī boṭī kā gandā shorbā. Mah. Wom.

Stinking meat makes stinking broth.

Gāṅḍū kā himāētī bhī hārā hai.

The coward's friend meets with defeat.

Gandum az gandum biroyad, jau zi jau. Pers.

Wheat grows wheat, and barley barley.

(As you sow you shall reap.)

Gaṅgā bahī jāē, kalvārin chhātī pīṭe.

The river Ganges flows and the bar-maid beats her breast.

(On seeing so much good water flow away uselessly.)

Gaṅgā gaē, muṅḍāē sidh. Hin. Custom.

When gone to the Ganges, shaving is necessary.

Gaṅgā gaē muṅḍāē sir. Hin.

Gone to the Ganges and shaved his head.

Gaṅgā, kar gaur garībān kī! Hin.

O Ganges, hear the prayer of the poor!

Gaṅgā ke mele meṅ chakkī-rāhe ko kāun pūchhe?

At the Ganges' fair who wants a stone-mason?

(*Chakkī-rāhā* is a mason who dresses and prepares the stones for the native women's hand mills. The people at these fairs buy their food from the market and therefore have no need of grinding or cooking utensils.)

Gaṅgā kis kī khudāī hai?

Who dug out the Ganges?

(Foolish questions: 'why is the sky blue?')

Gaṅgā ko ānā thā, Bhāgīrath ko jas. Hin.

Fate made the Ganges flow, but Bhāgīrath got the credit.

(In allusion to the well-known legend.)

Gaṅgā nahāē kyā phal pāē? Mūchh muṅḍāē ghar ko āē!

What good did you get by bathing in the Ganges? Coming home with your face shaved!

(Allusion to the custom of shaving clean on a pilgrimage to the Ganges.)

Gaṅgā nahāē mukt hoē, to meṅḍak, machchhiyāṅ.
Mūṅḍ muṅḍāē sidh hoē, to bher, kapāṭiyāṅ.

Frogs and fishes must be sure of salvation, if it depend on bathing in the Ganges; and so sheep and lambs, if it depend on shaving the head.

(The saying of a free thinker.)

Gaṅg jahāṅ raṅg.

Where the Ganges is there is joy.

(Allusion to the fertile tract irrigated by the sacred waters of the Ganges.)

Gūṅgā, andhā, chug-ḍaṛhiyā aur kānā.
Kahen Kabīr, suno, bhāī sādho! in ko nā patyānā.

The bald, the blind, the scrubby-bearded and the one-eyed; Saith Kabir, hear friend Saints! don't trust them.

Ganjā marā khujāte khujāte.

The bald-headed dies scratching his head.

(He leads a miserable life.)

Gāṅjā pīe gur giyān ghaṭe, aur ghaṭe tan andar kā: Khoṅkhat khoṅkhat gāṅṛ phaṭe, muṅh dekho jaise bandar kā.

From smoking hemp you lose mind and body, Are worried by cough, and transformed into an ape.

Ganj be ranj nahīṅ.

No gains without pains.

Ganje ko Khudā nākhūn na de.

God grant no nails to the bald.

(That he may scratch his head: never give authority to the wicked and low.)

Ganjfe ke tīnoṅ khilāṛī rote haiṅ.

All three card players are weeping.

(Each complains that he has a bad hand.)

Ganjī kabūtrī aur mahil meṅ ḍerā.

A bald pigeon and a dwelling in a palace.

Ganjī panhārī, aur gokhrū kā iṅḍvā.

A bald water-bearer and a pad of thorns.

(*Iṅḍvā* is the pad placed on the head for protecting it from the articles borne on it.)

Ganjī satti, ūt pujārī. Hin.

A bald goddess and a foolish priest.

Gāṅṛ chale, man bakhtoṅ ko!

His bowels are loose and he wants peas.

(Which are injurious.)

Gāṅṛ meṅ gū nahīṅ, aur kavve mihmān.

Nothing to evacuate, and he invites crows.

(Great boast little roast.)

Gāṅṛ meṅ langoṭī, na sir pe ṭopī.
Not a rag to his loins, nor a cap to his head.

Gāṅṛ na dhoē, so ojhā hoē. E.
Who won't wash his loins will be a wizard.

Gāṅṛ na hotī, to auliyā ho jāte.
If he had no fundament he might have been a saint.

Gāṅṭh girah meṅ kauṛī nahīṅ, "miyāṅ gaṭṭe-wāle hot."
Not a farthing in his pocket and he bellows to the sweetmeat seller.

Gāṅṭh-girah se mad pīve, log kaheṅ matwālā.
He spends his money in drink to get the character of a drunkard.

Gāṅṭh kā pūrā, āṅkh kā andhā.
A blind man and full-purse.
(The Baniyā's morning prayer.)

Gāṅṭh kā pūrā, mat kā hīnā.
Full purse and lack sense.
(As above.)

Gāṅṭh khule na, bahuryā dubras! E.
The bride is so delicate that she cannot untie the knot!
(Refers to the marriage ceremony.)

Gāṅṭh meṅ dām na, paturyā dekh ruāṅ āē. E.
With no money in his pocket he weeps to see a woman.
(Being unable to wed her.)

Gāṅṭh meṅ paisā nahīṅ, Bāṅkīpur kī sair. E.
With no money in pocket he goes to Bānkīpur.

Gāṅṭh na muṭṭhī, phar pharāē uṭṭhī. E. Wom.
Her heart is in a flutter (to buy), but she has no money in pocket or hand.

Ganwār gāṅḍā na de, bhelī de.
The stupid countryman won't give you sugarcane, but he will a lump of sugar.
(Penny wise, pound foolish; the sugar being expressed from the cane is of course much more expensive.)

Ganwār, gaun kā yār.
The village boor knows his own interests.

Ganwār kā hāṅsā toṛe pāṅsā. Rus.
The (practical) joke of a clown will break a rib.

Ganwār ko paisā dīje, par aql na dīje.
Better give money than sense to a clown.

Gāo bajāo banne ke lolo hī nahīṅ. Wom.
You may play and sing, but you won't please the bridegroom.
(Work till you sweat, you 'll nothing get.)

Gāo bajāo kauṛī na pāo. Wom.
Sing and play, but you won't get a farthing.
(More kicks than half-pence.)

Gāoṅ basante bhūtle, shahr basante dev.
Villagers are demons, citizens gods.

Gāoṅ bhāge, paghiyā lāge! Rus.
The village is deserted, and the harvest on!

Gāoṅ dahā jāē, sīwāne kī laṛāī.
The whole village rushes out to join in a dispute about the boundary.

Gāoṅ gayā, sūtā jāge.
Gone from the village is a sleeper awaking.
(You cannot tell when he will be back, as you cannot tell when the sleeper will awake.)

Gāoṅ gaē kī bāt.
It is a matter of having gone to the village.
(Seeing is believing.)

Gāoṅ ke ganwere, mūṅh pe khāk, peṭ meṅ ḍhele.
Village boors have dirt on their faces and mud in their stomachs.
(A coarse appearance and coarse food.)

Gāoṅ meṅ dhobī kā chhail.
The washerman's son is the swell of the village.
(He disports the clothes of his father's customers.)

Gāoṅ meṅ ghar, na jangal meṅ khetī.
No house in the village, no field in the land.
(Improvident.)

Gāoṅ meṅ paṛī marī, apnī apnī sab ko paṛī.
The plague came into a village, and each looked after himself.

Gāoṅ, nāoṅ, ṭhāoṅ.
Name, place and situation.
(Address.)

Gāoṅ sadā ganwāran ke.
Villages always belong to villagers.

Gāoṅ tumhārā, nāo hamārā!
Yours the village, mine the name!

Garabh karante Rāvan hāre. Hin.
Rāvan was humbled for his pride.
(Allusion to the story in the *Rāmāyan.*)

Garabh kā sir nīchā. Hin.
Pride goes before a fall.

Garajte haiṅ, voh baraste nahīṅ.
The cloud which thunders seldom rains.
(A barking dog will never bite.)

Garaz bāolī hai.
Need makes mad.

Garaz kā bāolā apnī gāve.
Full of his need sings of himself.

Garaz-mand bāolā hai.
Needy is mad.

Garaz-mand kare, yā darad-mand kare.
The interested or sympathetic helps.

Garaz parlā se ādmī buṛbak holā. E.
His own interests make him mad.

Garebān meṅ mūṅh ḍālo.
Look to your own coat.
(Look to the beam that is in your own eye.)

Gaṛhe ke pānī meṅ mūṅh dho-kar āo.
Go and wash your face in the pool.
(The water of a pool is considered the best of all for washing: point of proverb is, make yourself clean before you talk so big: said to a boaster.)

Gaṛh to Chittaur-gaṛh, aur sab gaṛhaiyāṅ haiṅ.
The Chittaur fort is *the* fort, other forts are but castles.
(Chittaur was the famous Rājpūt fortress destroyed by Akbar in 1568 A. D.)

Garīb kī javānī, garmī kī dhūp, jāṛe kī chāndnī, akārath jāeṅ.
The poor man's youth, the summer's sun, the winter's moon : these three pass unenjoyed.

Garīb kī jorū aur Umdah Khānam nām. Mah.
The wife of a pauper and named my Lady Excellent.

Garīb kī jorū sab kī bhābī.
A poor man's wife is every one's sister-in-law.
(It is customary in India to jest with the wife of an elder brother. Hence the meaning is, that every one jests or makes free with the poor and helpless.)

Garīb ko kauṛī asharfī hai.
A *kauṛī* is a gold *mohar* to a pauper.
(To a poor man a farthing is a pound.)

Garīb ne roze rakhe din baṛe hue. Mah.
When the poor fast, the days lengthen.
(Fasts among Musalmāns are confined to the day time and consequently are most painful when the days are long, as in summer. The meaning is that every thing conspires to distress the poor.)

Gāṛī ko dekh lāṛī ke pāoṅ phūle.
When the slave girl sees a carriage she gets too tired to walk.

Garmī sabzah rangoṅ se, aur ghar meṅ bhūnī bhaṅg nahīṅ.
Hot upon fair women and no parched *bhaṅg* even in the house!
(Parched *bhaṅg* is an article so cheap as to be worthless.)

Garmīyoṅ meṅ Kashmīr jannat hai.
In summer Kashmīr is a paradise.

Gāte gāte Kalāvant ho jātā hai.
Sing long enough and you 'll become a Kalāwant.
(Kalāwant is the Orpheus of the Hindūs.)

Gaṭhiyā khulā, bityā pāras.
When the packet is unbound, the daughter is a precious stone.
(*Gaṭhiyā khulnā*, idiom, to be in the family way: *pāras*, is the philosopher's stone.)

Gaṭhrī bāṅdhī dhūl kī, rahī pavan se phūl: Gāṅṭh jatan kī khul gaī, ant dhūl kī dhūl.
A bag of dust puffed out with wind : When its string is loosened, the end of the dust is dust.
(Common religious saying: the answer is 'man.')

Gāu dhan, gaj dhan, kanak dhan, ratan khān, bahū khān, Jab āyā santokh dhan, sab dhan dhūl samān.
Wealth in cattle and elephants and gold and mines and gems Are all as dust, when wealth in contentment comes.

Gauṅḍe dī barāt, bahū ko lagī hagās! Rus. Wom.
The bridegroom's procession has arrived and the bride has a call of nature.

Gāūṅ na gāūṅ, to birhā gāūṅ. Wom.
I'll sing of the pangs of love, if I am to sing at all.

Gaurā rūṭhegī, to apnā suhāg legī, bhāg to na legī. Hin. Wom.
If Gaurā be angry, she can take away her gifts, but not my fate.
(Spoken by way of asserting independence by one whose master or protector is angry and threatens to discharge him Gaurā is the great goddess (Devi) of the Hindus.)

Gavāh chust, muddaī sust.
The witness is eager and the plaintiff careless.
(Allusion to the false witnesses, who keep constantly hanging about courts in order to give their evidence to the highest bidder.)

Gayā gāoṅ jahāṅ ṭhākur hansā. Gayā rukh jahāṅ baglā basā. Gayā tāl jahāṅ upjī kāī. Gayā kūp jahāṅ bhaī athāī.
Ruined is the village of which the lord plays the fool. Ruined is the tree in which the storks roust. Ruined is the tank which is covered with scum. Ruined is the well which has no bottom.

Gayā guzrā.
Lost and gone.

Gayā mard jin khāī khaṭāī, gaī rāṅḍ jin khāī miṭhāī.
Ruined is the man that eats acids and the woman that eats sweets.
(Acids are said to make men impotent, and 'to eat sweets' is a common idiom for a woman's losing her character.)

Gayā so gayā, rahā so bachā.
What's gone is lost, what's left is saved.

Gayā vaqt phir hāth ātā nahīṅ.
A lost opportunity cannot be recalled.

Gaz bhar kā hansuā, na nigalte bane, na ugalte.
The sickle that is a yard long, can neither be swallowed, nor spat out.

Gāzī Miyāṅ, Dam Madār, khichchaṛ pakkā, ham taiyār. Mah.
By Gāzī Miyāṅ and Shāh Madār, I am ready to eat the cooked dinner.
☞ Gāzī Miyāṅ or Sālār Gāzī, the nephew of Mahmūd of Ghaznī, who died at Bharāich in 1033 A. D., is a very celebrated Saint, and the expression Dam Madār arises out of the popular practise of jumping into a fire in honor of Shāh Madār, the saint of Makanpūr. This last saint died in 1433 A. D., and is often confounded with Ghāzī Miyāṅ.

Geṅḍe kī ḍhāl aur bijlī kī talvār.
A shield of rhinoceros-hide, and a sword of tempered steel.
(Are the best: sword makers allege that they temper their steel by lightning.)

Gehūṅ kī bāl nahīṅ dekhī.
He has not seen even an ear of wheat.
(He is totally inexperienced.)

Gehūṅ kī roṭī ko faulād kā peṭ chāhiye.
A stomach of steel for wheaten bread.
(Wheaten cakes, which poor men can't afford

are a sign of wealth, and it needs a strong mind to possess wealth without pride.)

Genthī sanbhār, madhurī chāl, āj na pahunchab pahunchab kāl. E.
Look to your baggage and go slowly, and if you don't reach to-day you will to-morrow.
(Slowly does it : the tortoise and the hare.)

Ghāen ghāen torā, manhān bāje morā. E. Wom.
In private he is yours, in public he is mine.
(*i. e.* my husband is your paramour : a taunt of one woman to another.)

Ghāī kī merī, tave kī terī. Wom.
What is in the pot is mine, what is on the plate is yours.
(Selfishness: *I* take what is cooked, *you* take what is still raw.)

Ghap ghoṛā, rūṭhā chākar, in kā etibār nahīn.
There is no reliance on an unbroken horse, or an unwilling servant.

Ghar āe bairī ko bhī na māriye.
Never kill an enemy when he is your guest.

Ghar āe kutte ko bhī nahīn nikālte hain.
Men do not drive away even a dog when he is a guest.
(To express the obligation of protecting one who flies to another for refuge.)

Ghar āī Lachhmī ko lāt mārnā achchhā nahīn hotā. Hin.
Never kick good fortune when she comes to you of her own accord.
(Never decline a spontaneous offer of marriage, or of a post.)

Ghar āyā nāg na pūje, bānbī pūjan jāe. Hin.
They do not worship the snake in the house, but they go to worship at his hole.
(Spoken of one who neglects an advantage when it is offered spontaneously, and afterwards searches for it with great labor.)

Ghar baiṭhal ādhā bhalā. E.
Half at home is better (than all abroad).

Ghar-bār tumhārā, koṭhī kuṭhle ke hāth na lagānā. Wom.
The whole house is your's, but do not touch any thing in it.
(Sham love: sham professions of hospitality.)

Ghar bhar hansyā, na nigalne kā, na thūkne kā. E. Wom.
The house is full of sickles, and there is nothing to swallow or throw up.
(The house is full of knick-knacks of no sort of utility.)

Ghar bhāṛe, hāṭ bhāṛe, pūnjī ko lage biyāj,
Munīm baiṭhā roṭiyān jhāṛe, divālā kāṛhe kāhe lāj? Mercantile. Mar.
His house hired, his shop hired, and his capital borrowed, His agent idle and eating up his goods; no shame to him if he become bankrupt.
(Said of the improvident.)

Ghar bhī baiṭho, aur jān bhī khāo! Wom.
You stick at home and eat up our lives!
(*Jān khānā*, to worry to death: said to an idle son.)

Ghar chain to bāhar chain.
Comfort at home is comfort abroad.

Ghar chhoṛ hazīrā qāyam. Mah. Wom.
He has left his house to lodge in a mean [place.
(A foolish fellow.)

Ghaṛe kumhār, bhare sansār.
The potter makes, the world fills.
(Pitchers.)

Ghaṛe se ghaṛā nahīn bharā jātā. Mercantile.
You cannot fill a jar with a jarful.
(*i. e.* on account of wastage.)

Ghar, ghar kā; sāth, nar kā.
For a house your own house, for company a man.
(*Moral:* don't live in rented houses or with women.)

Ghar ghar ke jāle buhārtī phirtī hain.
She wanders about to sweep out the cobwebs of every house.
(Said of one who is always changing houses and of a gadding wife: also of those who flatter every one.)

Ghar ghar pīt na kīje, to gāon gāon to kīje.
If you have not a friend in every house, have one in every village at least.

Ghar ghar shādī, ghar ghar chain.
Comfort and joy in every house.
(Under a happy rule.)

Ghar ghar shādī, ghar ghar gam.
There is joy and sorrow in every house.

Ghar gharvālī se.
A home is where there is a housewife.

Ghar ghar yehī lekhā. Wom.
In every house there is this one regulation.
(Every community has its peculiar customs.)

Ghar ghar yehī maṭyāle chūlhe hain. Wom.
Every house has an earthen kitchen.
(All are alike.)

Ghar, ghoṛā, gāṛī, in tīnon ke dām khaṛā khaṛī.
A house, a horse, and a carriage, are sold best where they stand.
(*i. e.* where they can be seen.)

Ghar ghoṛā, nakhās mol.
The horse in the stable and his price in the market?
(Buying a pig in a poke.)

Ghar hī men baid, mare kaise?
With a physician in the house, how was it he died?

Ghaṛī bhar kī be-sharmī, sāre din kā ādhār.
Shame for an hour is a living for the whole day.
(Said of prostitutes.)

Ghaṛī men auliyā, ghaṛī men bhūt.
One hour a saint, another a devil.
(Said of a changeable disposition.)

Ghaṛī men gāon jale, nau ghaṛī bhaddrā. Hin.
The village burns in an hour, and in nine hours comes the lucky moment.
(For putting it out : a skit at the astrologers.)

Ghaṛī men ghaṛyāl hai. Hin.
The clock strikes differently every hour.
(Uncertainty of the future.)

Ghaṛī men tolā, ghaṛī men māsha.
One hour an ounce, another a drachm.
(Unstable as water he shall not withstand.)

Ghar jale, ghūr batāve!
The house burns and he says it is smoke!

Ghar jale, gunḍā tāpe.
The house burns and the vagabond warms himself.
(Dead to another's loss.)

Ghar jale to jale, chāl na bigṛe.
If the house burn let it burn, but I 'll stick to my customs.
(The conservative feeling.)

Ghar jal gayā, tab chūṛiyān pūchhīn. Wom.
When the house was burnt they admired her bangles.
☞ It is said of a vain woman that in a fit of vexation, she set fire to her own house because nobody noticed her new bangles. As she was pointing, however, to the burning house her bangles attracted attention. 'Ah,' she said, 'if you had admired them sooner my house would not have been burnt.'

Ghar kā āṭā kaun gūṅdhe kare?
Who kneads his own flour?
(There is always some one to do it for the householder.)

Ghar kā aur dil kā bhed har ek ke sāmhne na kahe.
Don't disclose your heart's secrets and your household affairs to every body.

Ghar kā bhedī Lankā ḍhāve. Hin.
A domestic foe would ruin Lankā.
(Allusion to the siding of Bhabīkan, the brother of Rāvan, with Rām Chandar when he invaded Lankā in the legends of the Rāmāyan.)

Ghar kā bhed jabhīn pāyā, chauk pūran ko ḍhaknā āyā. E.
The household resources were found out, when they brought an earthen vessel for the house-warming.
☞ The Hindū ceremony of *chauk pūrnā* corresponds to the English house-warming. Rich people use silver or brass vessels for it, poor people earthen ones.

Ghar kā gharvāhā kar diyā.
He has brought his house to ruin.

Ghar kā jogī jognā, ann gāon kā siddh. Hin.
A *jogī* is a beggar at home and a saint abroad.
(A prophet is not without honor save in his own country and in his own house. Mat. xiii, 5-7.)

Ghar kāj, bahū giddon ko. Wom.
There is work in the house, but the bride is in the court-yard.

Ghar kar, ghar kar, sattar balā sir kar.
Who builds a house and takes a wife, heaps seventy afflictions on his head.
(Pun here on the phrase *ghar karnā* 'to build a house' and 'to take a wife.')

Ghar ke hī mard hain!
He is valiant in his own house!

Ghar ke jale ban gaë, aur ban men lāgī āg,
Ban bichārā kyā kare, jo karmon lāgī āg?
Burnt out of house and home went to the forest, and the forest caught fire: How shall the forest save the unfortunate when fate plays the incendiary?

Ghar ke khīr khāën aur deotā bhalā mānen. Hin.
The housefolk eat the offering of milk and rice and the gods are propitiated all the same.
(They persuade themselves that they have secured the favor of the gods when they have made in name only the offering which they have themselves eaten.)

Ghar ke pīron ko tel kā malīdā. Mah.
For the house priest only cakes of oil.
(Said one who gives dainties to outsiders and coarse food to his relations: cakes of oil are the cheapest and most indigestable of all human food.)

Ghar ke roven, bāhar ke khāën, duā det qalandar jāen.
The housefolk weep, the outsiders eat, and the beggars go away blessing.
(Point as in the preceding.)

Ghar khīr to bāhar bhī khīr.
Dainties at home, dainties abroad.
(Feed well and you 'll be fed well.)

Ghar khode, īndhan bahot.
A house pulled down will supply abundant fuel.

Ghar kī ādhī bhalī, bāhar kī sārī kuchh nahīn.
Better half at home than the whole abroad.
(Natives love to live at home:—there's no place like home.)

Ghar kī balā ghar hī men,
Evils of the house remain in the house.
(Allusion to the custom of the levirate in Jaṭṭ families.)

Ghar kī bībī hāṅḍnī, ghar kutton jogā. Wom.
When the mistress of the house is always gadding, the house becomes fit for the dogs.

Ghar kī billī aur ghar hī men shikār.
Your house cat hunting in your house.
(Domestic disturbances.)

Ghar kī mūchhen hī mūchhen hain.
Not a rap in the house but his moustache.
(Said of one who has no capital of his own.)

Ghar kī murgī dāl barābar.
The house fowls are no dearer than peas.
(You don't feel their expense.)

Ghar kī puṭkī, bāsī sāg.
A pinch of flour of his own and the pot-herbs stale.
(Said to the braggart.)

Ghar meṅ āī joē, ṭeṛhī pagṛī sīdhī hoē. Wom.
When the bride comes home, the crooked turban is soon put straight.
(To wear the turban crooked on one side is the sign of a rake, whereas the respectable wear it straight.)

Ghar meṅ bhūnī bhāṅg nahīṅ, aur bāhar neote sāṭh. Wom.
Not even parched *bhang* in the house and sixty guests invited.
(Parched *bhaṅg* is a worthless article.)

Ghar meṅ bilauṭā bāgh.
A cat is a lion in its own lair.

Ghar meṅ chane kā chūn nahīṅ, 'gehūṅ kī do poḷāiyo'!
Not even pulse flour in the house, and he calls for two wheaten cakes.
(Flour made of pulse, *chanā*, is very cheap.)

Ghar meṅ chirāg nahīṅ, bāhar mashal.
No lights in the house and torches outside.
(Vain show.)

Ghar meṅ davā, 'hāē ham mare!'
The remedy in the house and 'I am dying!'
(For want of it: said of the stupid.)

Ghar meṅ dekho chhalnī na chhāj, bāhar Miyāṅ Tīr-andāz. Wom.
At home nor sieve nor winnowing fan, and abroad my Lord Archer!
(Every body in India has a sieve and a winnowing fan.)

Ghar meṅ dhān na pān, bīvī ko baṛā gumān! Wom.
Nothing to eat or drink in the house, and the lady of it very proud!

Ghar meṅ dīyā na bātī, mundo phire itrātī. Wom.
In the house nor lamp nor wick, but the shaven-head (widow) proudly strutting.

Ghar meṅ dīyā, to masjid meṅ dīyā. Mah. Wom.
Light your lamp first at home and afterwards at the mosque.
(Charity begins at home.)

Ghar meṅ ghar, laṛāī kā ḍar. Wom.
With close neighbours there is a fear of quarrels.

Ghar meṅ hal na baldyā, māṅge īkh haldyā! Rus.
Without a plough or oxen, he demands sugar-cane for his ploughing fee.

Ghar meṅ jo shahad mile, to kāhe ban ko jāē?
If honey could be got in houses, who would search for it in the forest?

Ghar meṅ jorū kā nām Bahu Begam rakh lo!
Every man may call his wife a queen.

Ghar meṅ khāē nahīṅ, aṭārī par dhūāṅ kare. Bhoj.
Nothing to eat in the house, and he raises a smoke on the balcony.
(Vain show.)

Ghar meṅ kharach nā, ḍeoṛhī par nāch. E.
Not a penny in the house and dancing in the porch.

Ghar meṅ kharach nahīṅ, auṅṭhī pahirtī pokhrāj-jaṛal saukh ḍāhaē. E. Rus. Wom.
Not a rap in the house, and sports a topaz ring.

Ghar meṅ nahīṅ būr, beṭā māṅge motī-chūr. Wom.
Not even bran in the house, and the son wants lollypops.

Ghar meṅ nahīṅ dāne, buṛhiyā chalī bhunāne.
No grain in the house and the grand-mother is gone to the grain-parcher's.
(Making a vain show.)

Ghar meṅ nahīṅ tāgā, albelā māṅge pāgā. Rus.
There is not a thread in the house, and the blockhead wants a turban.

Ghar meṅ pakke chūhe aur bāhar kaheṅ paē.
They are stewing rats at home, and say abroad that they are boiling milk.

Ghar meṅ rahe nā tīrath gaē,
Mūṅḍ muṇḍā-kar jogī bhaē.
He neither stayed at home nor went on the pilgrimage, But having shaved his head has become a *Jogī*.
(Spoken of one who deserts one mode of life for another, which he only adopts by halves, thereby losing the advantages of one without gaining those of the other.)

Ghar meṅ rahe nā tīrath gaē,
Mūṅḍ muṇḍā faẓīhat bhaē.
Nor stayed at home nor went on a pilgrimage, But shaved his head and became disgraced.
(To shave the head is a sign of having returned from a pilgrimage.)

Ghar miltā hai to bar nahīṅ miltā, bar miltā hai to ghar nahīṅ miltā. Hin. Wom.
If you can get a good house you cannot get a good husband, if you can get a good husband you cannot get a good house.
(To marry your daughter.)

Ghar na bar. Hin. Wom.
Nor husband nor home.

Ghar na bār, miyāṅ muhalle-dār!
Nor house nor home, a leading householder forsooth!

Ghar phūṅk-kar birrā mārnā. E.
To burn a house in order to kill a wasp.
(In India wasps' nests are usually burnt out, so to burn down one's house in burning out the wasps is the height of carelessness: hence point of proverb.)

Ghar phūṅk tamāsha dekhnā.
To set one's house on fire and look on at the sport.
(Applied to an inconsiderate spendthrift. You must spend judiciously if you would know what enjoyment is.)

Ghar phūṭe, ganvār lūṭe.
When the house is divided strangers rob it.
(Every house divided against itself shall not stand, Mat. xii. 25.)

Ghar rahe, ghar ko khāē, bāhar rahe, bāhar ko khāē.
At home, he eats up his own household, abroad, he eats up another's.
(The idle man.)

Ghar se bāhar bhalā. Wom.
Better abroad than at home.
(Said to an idle or quarrelsome husband.)

Ghar se khoē to āṅkheṅ hoēṅ
A loss at home opens the eyes.
(Buying experience.)

Ghar sukh to bāhar chain.
Happiness at home is pleasure abroad.

Ghar taṅg, bahū zabar jaṅg.
The hut is small and the lady is tall.

Ghar-vāle kā ek ghar, ni-ghare ke sau ghar.
The married person has but one house, the bachelor a hundred.
(He is free to go and lodge anywhere.)

Ghar yār ke, pūt bhatār ke.
His house a friend's, his child a concubine's.
(The loose liver.)

Ghās khāē din kaṭe, to sab koī khāē.
If man could live on grass all would eat it.

Ghās meṅ kyā sāṅp nahīṅ phirtā ?
Do not snakes creep in grass ?

Ghaṭat chhin chhin, baṛhat pal pal, jāt nā lāgat bār ; Kahat Kabīr, suno bhāī sādho, supnā hai sansār.
Momently it decreases, momently it advances and hastes to depart ; Hear brother saints, saith Kabīr, the world is but a dream.

Ghāṭ ghāṭ kā pānī piyā hai.
I have drunk from many springs.
(I have great experience in the world : I have seen the world.)

Ghāyal kī gat ghāyal hī jāne.
The wounded only knows what it is to be wounded.

Ghī bhī khāo aur pagṛī bhī rakkho.
Eat your butter and keep your turban (honor.)

Ghī gir gayā, mujhe rūkhī bhātī hai.
My butter spilt, dry bread doth please me well.
(A plausible excuse.)

Ghī Jāṭ kā, tel hāṭ kā.
(Buy) your *ghī* of the *Jāṭ*, your oil in the market.
(Pure *ghī* (butter) is best procurable in a village, and good oil in the shops after it has had time to settle.)

Ghī kahāṅ gayā ? Khichṛī meṅ. Khichṛī kahāṅ gaī ? Piyāroṅ ke peṭ meṅ ? Wom.
'Where is the butter gone ? Into the *khichṛī*. Where is the *khichṛī* gone ? Into my dear one's stomach.
(Allusion to the joint family in India where the whole family are apt to live on the earnings of one member.)

Ghī kā laḍḍū ṭeṛhā bhī bhalā.
A sweetmeat is good however crooked it be.
(Don't judge by appearances.)

Ghī ke kuppe se jā lagā hai.
He has reached the bucket full of butter.
(To be in clover.)

Ghī khichṛī ho rahe haiṅ.
Mixed up like *khichṛī* and *ghī*.
(Hand and glove.)

Ghī khichṛī meṅ dāva hai.
He makes a claim even on the provisions.
(Applied to one, who having received all he is entitled to, makes further claims.)

Ghī saṅvāre kām, baṛī bahū kā nām. Wom.
The flavor is in the *ghī*, but the eldest daughter-in-law gets the credit.
(Of being a good cook.)

Ghoṅge meṅ pakāyā, sīpī meṅ khāyā.
Boiled in a mussel and eaten in a cockle-shell.
(Living from hand to mouth.)

Ghoṛā aur phoṛā jitnā rolo, vitnā hī baṛhe.
A horse and a boil, the more you rub the more they grow.

Ghoṛā chāhiye bidāēgī ko, zarā phirtā sā āiyo. Hin.
A horse is wanted for the bridegroom, so bring it quickly.

Ghoṛe bech-kar soē haiṅ.
Having sold their horse they enjoy sound sleep.
(Free from care : *post equitem sedet atra cura.*)

Ghoṛe bhaiṅse kī lāg.
The enmity of a horse and a buffalo.
(*i. e.* fierce enmity ; a horse and a buffalo will always fight if put together.)

Ghoṛe ghoṛe laṛeṅ, mochī kā zīn ṭūṭe.
When two horses fight, the saddler's saddle is broken.
(Applied to a quarrel between two persons, when a third is the sufferer.)

Ghoṛe kā girā saṅbhaltā hai, nazroṅ kā girā nahīṅ saṅbhaltā.
Fall from a horse and you can be saved, fall in esteem and you won't be saved.

Ghoṛe kī dum baṛhegī to apnī hī makkhiyāṅ hilāēgā.
If the horse's tail grows longer, he will brush away the flies from his own body.
(On promotion a native will help his own relatives.)

Ghoṛe kī haṅsī aur bālak kā dukh jānā nahīṅ paṛtā.
You can't find out the jokes of a horse or the ills of a baby.
(Because they can't speak.)

Ghoṛe kī savārī chaltā janāza.
(i) Ride a horse at a funeral's pace.
(*i. e.* very slowly!!)
(ii) Mounting a horse is mounting a bier.
(As it is very dangerous! See below *ghoṛe par sir, &c.*)

Ghoṛe ko lāt, ādmī ko bāt.
A word for a man and a spur for a horse.

Ghoṛe mar gaë, gadhoṅ ko rāj āyā.
When the horses are dead, the asses rule.
(The wise are dead and fools flourish.)

Ghoṛe par sir se kafan bāṅdhke baiṭhnā chāhiye.
Ride a horse with a cere-cloth on.
(As it is very dangerous!)

Ghoṛoṅ ko ghar kitnī dūr?
The horse's stable is never far.
(Because he always gallops to it.)

Ghūṅsoṅ meṅ udhār kyā?
Is a blow ever taken on loan?
(A blow should be returned immediately.)

Ghuṭne nīveṅge to peṭ hī ko.
If the knees bow it is towards the belly.
(The native posture of sitting with the knees against the belly is used to express the natural disposition to serve one's own relations first.)

Gīdaṛ-bhabkī.
A jackal's menace.
(Said in contempt. 'There roared the wrathful mouse.')

Gīdaṛ girā jhere meṅ: 'āj yahīṅ raheṅge.'
The jackal falling down a well said, 'Here I'll camp to-day.'
(Making the best of a bad bargain)

Gīdaṛ kī shāmat, āë to gāoṅ kī taraf bhāge.
The jackal's evil fate drives him towards the village.
(Rushing blindly to destruction.)

Gīd gīd gilauṅdā khāë, ber ber mahuë tal āë. E.
Grown tame on the *gilauṅdā* he makes to the *mahuā.*
(The *mahuā* is the flower and *gilauṅdā* the pod of the same tree.)

Gilahrī kā peṛ ṭhikānā.
The squirrel's home is on the tree.

Gīlī lakṛī sīdhī ho saktī hai.
Green wood can be made straight.
(A child may be trained.)

Gīlī sukhī sab jaltī haiṅ.
Both green and dried (wood) burn.
(The innocent suffer with the guilty.)

Ginī boṭī, napā shurvā. Mah.
The bits of meat are counted and the soup is measured.
((1) Rigid economy. (2) income hardly equal to expenditure (3) said when a man gets no more than his bare pay: no perquisites.)

Ginī ḍaliyāṅ haiṅ. Hin.
Each bit is counted.
(See preceding.)

Ginī gāë meṅ chorī nahīṅ ho saktī.
Count your cows and they won't be stolen.

Gine gināve ṭoṭā pāve. Superstition.
Who counts loses.

Gin poīṅ, sanbhāl khāīṅ. Wom.
She counts (her cakes) and bakes them, and then eats them with care.
(Living from hand to mouth.)

Girah kā dīje, par aql na dīje.
Give out of your pocket, but not out of your head.
(Don't let your brains be picked.)

Girah kā dīje, par zāmin na hūje.
Give out of your pocket, but never stand surety.

Girah-kaṭ kā bhāī gaṭh-kaṭ.
The pickpocket is brother to the shop-lifter.

Girah meṅ kauṛī nahīṅ aur bāzār kī sair.
Without a farthing in his purse he visits the market.

Gire kā kyā giregā?
What will fall from the fallen?

Gire khām, palān bhārī.
When a pillar falls on it the packsaddle becomes heavy.

Gire paṛe vaqt kā ṭukṛā.
A crust for declining years.
(Money saved against a rainy day: said also of a dutiful son.)

Girgaṭ ke se raṅg badaltā hai.
His color changes like a chameleon's.
(Not to be trusted.)

Girgaṭ kī dauṛ biṭaure tak.
The lizard runs no further than the heap of cow-dung.
(*i. e.* to his home.)

Girhast-dharm barābar koī dharm nahīṅ.
Family life is the best of religions.
(Moral: never be a bachelor.)

Gir paṛe kī Har Gaṅgā!
When a man falls down he cries out on Hari and Gaṅgā.
(Allusion to the common cry on falling down.)

Gobar Ganesh.
A cowdung Ganesh.
(An effigy of the fat god Ganesh is made of cowdung on commencing any business: said of a corpulent person.)

Gobar kī sāṅjhī bhī pahrī oṛhī achchhī lagtī hai. Hin. Wom.
Even a *sāṅjhī* of cowdung looks well when dressed up.
(A *sāṅjhī* is a small image or doll made of dried cowdung (*gobar*) by Hindu girls in September.)

Godī kā laṛkā mar jāë, peṭ āg bujhāë. Wom.
When the lapling dies, the belly quenches the fires of grief.
(*i. e.*, all sorrow for the child gives way to hunger.)

Godī meṅ baiṭh ke dāṛhī noche.
Sitting in my lap he plucks at my beard.
(Said of an undutiful child or of a rude person.)

Godī meṅ baiṭh-ke āṅkh meṅ uṅglī.
Sitting in my lap he pokes out my eyes.
(See preceding.)

God kā chhoṛ, peṭ ke kī ās? Wom.
Losing the child in her lap she depends on her womb for another.
(A bird in hand is worth two in the bush.)

God kā khilāyā god meṅ nahīṅ rahtā.
Though fed on your lap, he does not remain there.

God meṅ laṛkā, shahr meṅ dhaṅḍorā.
The child is in his arms and he proclaims it (as lost) in the city.
(Applied to one, who searches for a thing which he has by him; like the butcher, who searched for the knife, which he held between his teeth.)

Goëṅṛā khetī, sīkhā sāṅp, māī bhaë-kāran, bādī bāp. Rus.
A field by the village, a man-eating serpent, a terrible mother, and a disagreeable father are bad things.

Goiṭhā jale, gobar haṅse!
When the cowdung cake burns the cowdung laughs!
(Though its turn is coming: said of a fool.)

Gojhe kā ghāo, rānī jāne yā rāo. Wom.
The hidden wounds only the king or the queen can know.
(The skeleton in the cupboard.)

Golā bārūt kahīṅ jāë, talab se kām.
Let the powder and shot go where it chooses, I have to look after my pay.
(Said of the idle servant.)

Goṅd, panjīrī aur hī khāëṅ,
Jachchā rānī paṛī karhāëṅ. Wom.
The strangers eat the caudle and the lying-in-woman simply groans.

Gor chamāin, garbhe mātal. E.
A fair cobbler's wife is proud of her complexion.

Gore chamṛe pe na jā, voh hī chhachhūṅdar se hai badtar.
Don't go upon her fair skin, it is worse than a muskrat's.
(Advice to a lad as to prostitutes.)

Gorī kā joban chutkiyoṅ meṅ.
The beauty of the fair is effaced by pinching.
(Applied to one, whose wealth has been all expended by giving to others: natives have a way of playfully pinching pretty girls and hence the proverb.)

Gorī, mat kar gore raṅg kā gumān; yeh hai koi din kā mehmān.
My fair one, don't be proud of your complexion, it is the guest of but a few days.

Gorī, tere saṅg meṅ gaī umaryā bīt,
Ab chāli saṅg chhoṛ-ke, yeh nā rīt prīt.
My love, my life I have passed with you,
To leave me now is not the way of love.
(Said by the dying man to his soul.)

Gor meṅ chhoṭe baṛe sab barābar.
In the grave great and small are all alike.

Gor meṅ pāoṅ laṭkāë baiṭhā hai.
He sits with one foot hanging in the grave.
(One foot in the grave.)

Gosht khāë, gosht baṛhe, ghī khāë, bal hoë; sāg khāë, ojh baṛhe, to bal kahāṅ se hoë?
Eat flesh and you will grow stout, eat butter and you will grow strong, eat greens and you will grow pot-bellied and have no strength at all.

Gosht khāë, gosht baṛhe; sāg khāë, ojhṛī.
Eat flesh your flesh will grow, eat herbs and your belly will grow.

Gosht khā lete haiṅ, haḍḍiyāṅ pheṅk dete haiṅ. Mah.
Flesh is eaten and bones are thrown away.
(Take what is good for you.)

Gosht nākhūn se kahīṅ judā hotā hai?
Is the flesh ever separate from the nail?
(Relationship cannot be done away with.)

Goz-i-shutar, na zamīn kā, na āsmān kā.
If a camel breaks wind it goes neither to the earth nor to heaven.

Grah apnā phal kar hī jātī hai. Superstition.
Each star yields its fruit.

Guālan apne dahī ko khaṭṭā nahīṅ kahtī.
The cowherd's wife does not call her tyre sour.
(No one cries stinking fish.)

Guāle kā dahī, mahtoṅ kī bheṭ.
The curds are the milkman's, but the present is the steward's.
(Applied to one person having the credit of another's labor.)

Guār khāë gaṅvār.
Coarse meal for village louts.

Gūdaṛ meṅ giṅdaurā. Hin.
A sweet cake in a rag.
(A wealthy person in a shabby dress: also an intelligent child in an illiterate family.)

Gūdaṛ meṅ lāl nahīṅ chhiptā.
You cannot hide a ruby in a rag.
(Murder will out: truth cannot be hidden.)

Gū dar gū, murgī kā gū.
The filth of filth is the filth of a cock.
(The worst thing of all.)

Gudṛī se bībī āīṅ, 'Shekhjī, kināre ho!' Mah. Wom.
The lady comes in from the market and says 'out of the way, Sir!'

Gūgā baṛā, kyā Bhagwān ?
Which is the greater, Gūgā or God ?
(Both are to be feared. Gūgā is worshipped as a saint who has power over snakes.)

Gūjar se ūjaṛ bhalī, ūjaṛ se bhalī uḍāṛ.
Jahāṅ Gūjar dekhiye vahāṅ dīje mār.
Solitude is better than a cowherd, desolation is better than solitude. When you see a cowherd beat him.

Gū kā kīṛā gū hī meṅ khush rahtā hai.
The maggot born of filth enjoys filth.

Gū kā pūt nausādar.
Sal ammoniac is the child of ordure.
(It is used to clear the bowels.)

Gū kā ṭokrā sir par uṭhātā hai.
Bearing a basket of filth on the head.
(Said of mean work or disgrace: said also of the servant of a prostitute.)

Gū kī dārū mūt, aur mūt kī dārū gū.
Urine for the cure of dung and dung for the cure of urine.
(Tit for tat.)

Gulām kī zāt se vafā nahīṅ.
The race of slaves is a faithless brood.

Gulām sāth, tau bhī nāth.
When your slave is with you, even then put a string in his nose.
(To prevent his running away.)

Gūlar kā peṭ kyoṅ phāṛte ho ?
Don't break open a fig.
(Don't disclose a secret: the allusion is to the fruit of the *gūlar* tree, which is full of a substance like worms and so is abominable in the sight of natives.)

Gūlar kā phūl, pīpal kā mad, ghoṛī kī jugālī,
Kabhī na pāve, aur pāve to rain Divālī !
Gūlar blossoms, *pīpal* juice and a mare that chews the cud have never been seen and if seen it was on Divālī night.
(When the seer was drunk.)

Gū meṅ ḍhelā ḍāle na chhīṅṭeṅ paṛeṅ.
If you throw no clods into dirt it won't spatter your clothes.
(To dissuade from altercation or jesting with a mean and worthless person: touch no pitch and you will not be defiled.)

Gū meṅ kauṛī gire, to dāṅtoṅ se uṭhā le.
If a farthing should fall into ordure, he would pick it out with his teeth.
(Said of a great miser.)

Gū nahīṅ, chhīchhī.
Not dirt, but filth.
(Distinction without a difference: six of one and half a dozen of the other.)

Gunḍe chale bazār, binaulā ḍhāṅk rakhiyo !
The vagabonds are going to market, hide your cotton seeds !

Gūṅge kā guṛ khaṭṭā na mīṭhā.
A dumb man's sugar is neither sour nor sweet.
(Because he cannot talk about it.)

Gūṅge kā guṛ khāyā hai ?
Have you eaten the treacle of dumbness ?
(Said to one who won't speak.)

Gūṅge ne supnā dekhā, man hī man pachhtāe.
When a dumb man has dreams he keeps his regrets to himself.
(That he cannot impart them.)

Gūṅgī jorū bhalī, gūṅgā nārgal na bhalā.
A dumb wife is better than a dumb pipe.
(Natives say that unless the hubble-hubble makes a noise it is not worth smoking.)

Gun sīkh-ke augun sīkhtā hai.
He learns the vices after learning the virtues.

Gunyā to gun kahe, nir-gunyā dekh ghināe.
While the good man praises goodness the wicked man looks on with disgust.

Guṛ bharā haṅsyā, khāte bane na ugalte. E.
A sickle covered with treacle cannot be swallowed nor vomited up.

Gur bin biākul chelvā, kanṭh bin bāur gīt.
The disciple is out of place without the master, like a song sung without a voice.

Gur bin mile na gyān, bhāg bin mile na sampat.
You can get no knowledge without a teacher, nor riches without luck.

Guṛ churāve to pāp, tel churāve to pāp.
It is sin, whether you steal oil or sugar.

Guṛ dīye mare, tau zahr kyoṅ dīje ?
If sugar will kill why give poison ?
(Why have recourse to harsh measures with him that yields to gentle persuasion.)

Gur gur biddyā, sir sir gyān.
Every teacher has his own science, and every head its own wisdom.
(Many men have many minds.)

Guṛ khāegī to āegī andhere meṅ.
If she would eat sweets, she must meet (a lover) in the dark.
(Said of a loose character.)

Guṛ khāeṅ, gulguloṅ se parhez !
Sugar he eats, sweet cakes he shuns !
(Inconsistency. To abstain only from certain modes of transgression: to strain at a gnat and swallow a camel.)

Guṛ khāeṅ, pūā meṅ chhed kareṅ.
He eats the sugar and destroys the cake.
(See above.)

Guṛ na de to guṛ kī sī bāt to kahe.
If you can't give sugar talk sugar.

Guṛ se baigan ho gae.
The egg-fruit is become as dear as sugar.
(Said when any cheap article has risen to a high price.)

Gur se kapaṭ, mitr se chorī, yā ho nir-dhan yā ho koṛhī.
To deceive a master, or deceive a friend, is to be a pauper or a leper.
(Lepers are altogether shunned in India.)

Gur to aisā chāhiye, jūn siqlī-gar hoë,
Janam janam kā morchā, chhin men ḍāre khoë.
A teacher should be like a polisher, and rub away the rust of ages in a moment.

Gurū, baid aur jotshī, deo, mantrī aur rāj,
Inhen bhet bin jo mile, hoe na pūran kāj.
A priest, a doctor, a soothsayer, a god, a minister, and a king, will never do your business unless you pay them.
(Palm-oil is all powerful in India.)

Gurū baṛā ke chelā?
Is the teacher greater, or the disciple?

Gurū guṛ hī rahe, chele chīnī ho gaë.
The teacher remained treacle, the pupil became refined sugar.
(The pupil surpassing his master.)

'*Gurū jī, chele bahut ho gae.*' '*Bachchā, bhūke mareṅge to āp chale jāeṅge.*'
'My master you have many disciples!' 'When they starve, my son, they will go away of their own accord.'

Gurū kīje jān ke, pānī pīje chhān ke.
Test a priest before you appoint him, and strain water before you drink it.
(Choose carefully your household priest.)

Gurū se pahle chelā mār khāë.
The disciple gets beaten before the priest.
(Allusion to the Hindu custom of *faqīrs* sending their disciples to beg.)

Guru, Shukr kī bādrī rahe Sanīchar chhāë,
Kahe Ghāg, sun Ghāgnī, "be barse nahīn jāë."
When Thursday's and Friday's clouds extend to Saturday, says Ghāg to Ghāghnī, "this will never pass without raining."
(It is very common to see cloudy days sometime before rain in India.)

Guṛyon ke biyāh men chīyon kī bel. Wom.
At a doll's marriage the gifts are tamarind seeds.
(Said of the very poor: tamarind seeds are very small.)

Gū se ghināonā kar dūngā.
I will make you worse than filth.

Gussā bahut, zor thoṛā, mār khāne kī nishānī.
A short temper and little strength are the precursors of many a pummelling.

Gussā harām hai.
Anger is unlawful.
(Leads to many sins.)

Gussā kamzor par ātā hai.
Wrath is visited on the weak.

Gusse men aql jātī rahtī hai.
Anger is an enemy to reason.

Gusse men burāī bhalāī nahīn sūjhtī,
Anger knows not good from bad.

Guzar gaī guzrān, kyā jhopṛī? kyā maidān?
Transitory things pass away, what is the difference between a house or the open air?
(It is all one a hundred years hence.)

Guzashta rā salvāt! Pers.
Blessings on what is past!
(Let by-gones be by-gones.)

Guzasht unche guzasht. Pers.
Past is past.

Gyān baṛhe soch se, rog baṛhe bhog se.
Thinking promotes reason; intemperance, diseases.

H.

Haḍḍī khānā āsān, par pachānā mushkil.
It is easy enough to swallow a bone, but it is difficult to digest it.

Hāë re būṛhāpe!
Alas, old age!
☛ "*Hāë re buṛhāpe! Javānī men kiyā patthar parte the!*" 'Alas! I am old now! well, but what great feats did I perform in my youth!" The first portion is supposed to have been uttered in the hearing of listeners. On turning round the vain old man saw nobody, his conscience then asserted itself and he owned to himself humiliating fact mentioned in the last portion of his speech.

Hāë, rī javānī!
Alas! (the folly of) youth!

Hagā, na ghar rakkhā.
He neither stooled, nor kept his house.
☛ The story is told of a Jāṭ having refuted a king in an argument and being promised what he would in return. He asked for leave to soil the royal cushion. The king would not break his word, so the ministers made the proviso that he might soil the cushion but must not make water. If he did so he was to lose his house. The Jāṭ could not manage this so he lost his house. Hence the proverb, which is a variant of the pound of flesh and Shylock.

Hagāse laṛke ke nathne pahchāne jāte hain. Wom.
The child's nostrils show when it wants to [go to stool.

Hag na saken, peṭ ko pīṭen.
They cannot stool, but beat their bellies.

Hā hā khāë būṛhe nahīn byāhe jāte.
The old are not married for begging.

Hai ādmī hai kām: nahīn ādmī, nahīn kām.
If you are a man, there is work for you: If you are no man, there is no work for you.

Hai gharnī ghar gājat hai, nahīn gharnī ghar pādat hai. E.
With the housewife the house is lively, without the housewife the house is dull,

Hai ghaṭ men, sūjhe nahīn, kar se gahā nā jāë:
Milā rahe, aur nā mile, tā se kāhā basāë?
He dwells in the heart, but is never seen, nor touched by hand: What can be done with him who is ever with us but never found? [hain.

Hain mard wohī pūre jo har hāl men khush
They are men indeed who are happy in adversity.

Hajāmat ho gaī.
Clean shaved.
(Cheated.)

Hājit-i-mashshātah nest rūē dil-ārām rā, Pers.
A fair face needs no paint.
(Beauty unadorned is adorned the most.)

Hajjām kā laṛkā pahle ustād hī kā sir mūṅḍtā hai.
The barber's apprentice first practises on his master's head.

Hajjām kā ṭakā,
The barber's penny.
(Any profits for which there is no risk. The barber is employed in negociating marriages and gets his fee however the marriage turns out.)

Hajjām kā ustrā, mere sir par bhī phirtā hai, tumhāre sir par bhī.
The barber's razor shaves your head and my head.
(I am as good as you :—One man is as good as another and a great deal better !)

Hajjām ke āge sab kā sir jhuktā hai.
Every one must bow his head to the barber.

Haj kā haj, nij kā nij. Mah.
Pilgrimage is pilgrimage, and trade is trade.
(The pilgrims to Makkā and other holy shrines in the East, are said to be in the habit of combining profit with piety and while professing to undertake the journey from motives of devotion to purpose in truth a commercial adventure.)

Hākim do jānne-vālon meṅ ek anjān.
The judge is an ignorant man between two knowing ones.
(Plaintiff and defendant.)

Hākim hāre, mūṅh kī mūṅh māre.
If you confute the ruler, he knocks you down.
(It is vain to dispute with him who has the power in his hands.)

Hākim kī agāṛī aur ghoṛe kī pichhāṛī na khaṛā ho.
Never stand before a judge or behind a horse.
(As in both situations you are apt to be injured.)

Hākim ke āṅkh nahīṅ hotī, kān hote haiṅ.
Rulers have no eyes, but only ears.

Hākim ke māre aur kīchaṛ ke phisle kā kis ne burā mānā hai ?
Never fret at the blows of a ruler or a slip into the mud.

Hākim ke tīn, shahnā ke nau.
Nine shares for the minister and three for the king.
(Allusion to the cheating supposed to go on in Native States.)

Hākim mahkūm kī laṛāī kyā ?
Can a subordinate fight his superior ?

Hakīm ko qārūre se lāj !
A physician, and ashamed to see his patient's urine !

Halāl meṅ harkat, harām meṅ barkat.
Sorrows to the upright and blessings to the wicked.
(I have seen the wicked in great power and spreading himself like a green bay tree, yet he passed, and lo, he was not. *Psalms* xxxvii, 55. 56.)

Halaq kā na tālū kā, yeh māl Miyāṅ Lālū kā.
The wealth of Mr. Lālū, is neither for the throat nor the palate.
(Said of a thing which is too bad or unlawful to eat.)

Halaq ke kotvāl.
The guard on the throat.
(Said of children who do not allow their parents to eat any thing without taking it from them.)

Halaq na tālū, khāeṅ Miyāṅ Lālū.
Mr. Lālū eats without palate or throat.
(Miyān Lālū means a boor, clodhopper.)

Halaq rove, jīb tove.
The throat weeps and the tongue gropes.
(Said of a very subtle or small thing in the mouth.)

Halaq se niklī, khalaq meṅ paṛī.
Once out of the throat it spreads over the world.
(Said of a secret.)

Haldī kī gāṅṭh hāth lagī chūhā pansārī hī ban baiṭhā.
A mouse got a piece of turmeric and set up a druggist's shop.
(A little learning is a dangerous thing.)

Haldī lage na phiṭkarī, raṅg chokhā hī āve.
Without turmeric and alum he wants a good dye.
(A preposterous request : *haldī* and *phiṭkarī* make a fine golden hue.)

Haldī lagī na phiṭkarī, paṭāk bahū ān paṛī.
Neither turmeric nor alum was expended, for the bride came all of a sudden.
(To express any thing done gratuitously. Turmeric and alum are used in dying the bride's clothes.)

Haldī zardī nā taje, khaṭras taje na ām;
Jo haldī zardī taje, to augun taje gulām.
Turmeric will never change its yellowness, nor a mango its acidity; when turmeric gives up its yellowness, the vicious will give up vice.
(Shall the leopard change his spots or the Ethiopian his skin ?)

Hāl gayā, ahvāl gayā, dil kā khayāl na gayā.
Health gone, wealth gone, but the bad habit not gone.

Hālī kā peṭ suhālī se nahīṅ bhartā. Agric.
The ploughman's stomach is not filled with crisp cakes.
(His labours require coarser and more substantial food.)

Hāl kā, na qāl kā, ṭukṛā roṭī, chamcha dāl kā. Mah. Wom.
Nor enthusiasm nor doctrine; a bit of bread and a spoonful of peas is all he is fit for.

Hāl kā na rozgār kā.
Not fit for service nor for employment.
(Said of a good-for-nothing fellow.)

Halke pichhoṛe, uṛ uṛ jāen. Wom.
Winnow hollow grain and it will all fly away.

Hāl men fāl, dahī men mūsal.
An oracle in prosperity is a pestle in curds.

Hal na sakūn mere sau bakhre. Wom.
I can't move, but I claim a hundred shares.
(Applied to one who is lazy and greedy.)

Halvāhī charvāhe ko!
What has a shepherd to do with ploughing?
(Every cobbler to his last.)

Halvāī kī dūkān aur dādā jī kī fātihā. Mah.
To celebrate a grand-father's obsequies at a confectioner's shop.
(*i. e.* to distribute the confections necessary to the occasion at the confectioner's expense. To describe one who supplies his own wants at the expense of others. Cocks make free with the horse's corn.)

Halvāī kī jāī aur sove sāth qasāī!
A confectioner's daughter, and mistress to a butcher.
(*Halvāis* are usually Hindūs, and butchers always Muhammadans.)

Halvā khāne ko mūnh chāhiye. Or,
Halvā-khurdan rā rūe bāyad. Pers.
It wants a proud face to eat *halwā*.
(*Halvā* is an expensive luxury.)

Halvā pūrī bāndī khāe, potā pherne bībī jāe!
The slave girl eats dainties, and her mistress has to perform the menial offices of the house!

Halvā pūrī bībī khāe, puṛā piṭāvan bāndī jāe.
It is the mistress that eats the dainties and it is the slave girl that gets the blows.

Hamārā dam to tum par nikaltā hai, aur tum aur par martī ho!
I am dying for you, and you are dying for another!
(Unrequited love.)

Hamārā kām ho bītā: jahān se main chalā rītā
My work is done and over: with empty hands I leave this world.

Hamāre baṛe parāe barde āzād karte the.
My ancestors always emancipated other men's slaves.
(Lived at others' expense.)

Hamāre dādā ne ghī khāyā, aur hamārā hāth sūngho.
My grandfather has eaten *ghī*; smell my hands.
(Applied to one who without any merit of his own, boasts of that of his ancestors.)

Hamāre donon mīṭhe.
Both of mine are sweet.
(Good and plentiful.)

Hamāre ghar āoge, kyā lāoge? tumhāre ghar āvenge, kyā khilāoge?
When you come to my house, what will you bring for me? and when I go to your house, what will you give me to eat?
(Heads I win and tails you lose.)

Hamāre hān se āg lāī, nām rakhā basandar. Hin. Wom.
She brought fire from my house, and called it *basandar*.
(The sacred fire used in religious ceremonies, which fire no Hindū gives to any one. Applied to one, who gives himself consequential airs towards his benefactor.)

Hamārī billī, aur ham hī se miyāūn.
My own cat mewing at me.

Hamārī bismillah aur ham se hī chhal. Mah. Wom.
My own charm practised on me.

Hamārī ham se pūchho, Kohkan kī Kohkan jāne.
Ask me about my affairs, Kohkan knows of his.
(Don't trouble me with what does not concern me: Kohkan or Farhād is the hero of the well known Persian romance *Farhād-o-Shirīn*.)

Ham chauṛe, bāzār sakṛā.
I am broad and the *bāzār* narrow.
(Put into the mouth of a great boaster.)

Hamesha rote hī janam guzrā.
My life has passed in lamentation.

Ham hī ko karnā sikhāne āyā hai.
He has come to teach me my work.
(Teach your grandmother to suck duck eggs.)

Ham-khurmā o ham-savāb. Pers.
Both the palm fruit and its virtues.
(Muhammadans look on the palm fruit as sacred, hence proverb means an action in which you find "earth's joys and heaven's combined.")

Ham kyā rānḍ ke janvāī hain?
Do you take me for a widow's son-in-law?
(*i. e.* a person whom no one looks after.)

Hammām kī lungī, jis ne chāhā us ne bāndh lī.
The washing towel in a bath is free to all who may use it.
(Easy as a barber's chair.)

Ham ne bhī tumhārī ānkhen dekhī hain.
I have seen your eyes.
(I am on the same footing as yourself.)

Ham ne kyā gadhe charāe hain?
Have I been leading asses to graze?
(See the following: do you see any green in my eye?)

Ham ne kyā ghās khodī hai?
Have I been plucking grass?
(Said in asserting a character of experience.)

Ham ne liyā, tum lījyo, rāh rāh jāne dījyo.
I have taken, do you take and let it go way.

Ham pardesī pāhune, aur ān kyā bisrām,
Bhor bhaē uṭh jāēṅge, baso tihārā gām!
A guest from a foreign land am I, and have sojourned here for a while, To-morrow morn I will start away; may your country ever thrive!

Ham-piyāla o ham-nivāla. Pers.
Eating and drinking together.
(Bosom friends.)

Ham roṭī nahīṅ khāte, roṭī ham ko khātī hai.
I don't eat my bread, but my bread eats me.
(The cark and care of earning one's livelihood.)

Ham sāṅp nahīṅ haiṅ, ki jīyeṅ chāṭ ke miṭṭī.
I am not a snake, that I can lick the dust and live.

Ham se aur chausar!
Backgammon and with me!

Ham se bahū baṛī siyānī, paiṅchā māṅge pānī! E. Wom.
The bride is cleverer than me, she asks for water on loan!

Hāṅḍe se dāṅḍā bhalā.
It is better to be confined than to wander uselessly.

Hāṅḍī kā bhāt chhupe, mūṅh kī bāt na chhupe.
You can hide the rice in the pot, but you cannot conceal the words of your mouth.

Hāṅḍī meṅ achchhat nā, 'chalā samdhī jenve.' E.
Not a pinch of rice in the pot and he says 'come, friend, feast with me.'

Hāṅḍī meṅ hogā, so ḍoī meṅ āp hī āvegā.
Whatever is in the pot will of course come into the ladle.
(What there is in the heart the tongue reveals: out of the fullness of the heart the mouth speaketh.)

Hāṅḍī na ḍoī, sab pat khoī. Wom.
Nor pot nor spoon, and all my credit gone.

Hānī ko haniye, pāp dosh na giniye.
Killing an assassin is no sin.

'Hāṅjī hāṅjī' sab se kīje, karye apne man kī.
Chime in with every body, but act in your own interests.

Hāṅ karo yā nā karo!
Say yes or no!

Hān, lābh, jīvan, maran, jas, apjas Bidh hāth.
Gain and loss, life and death, honour and disgrace are in the hands of Fate.

Hanoz Dillī dūr hai.
Dehlī is still far off.
(The object of an incompetent or ignorant person's labours is not speedily attained. It is a far cry to Loch Awe.)

Hanoz roz avval.
It is still the first day.
(There is room for improvement.)

Hansā chalal bhāg, keo na sangae lāg. E.
When the swan (soul) flies, none goes with it.

Hansā the so uṛ gaē, aur kāgā bhaē divān;
Jā, Bamman, ghar āpne, singh kā ke jijmān?
The swan hath fled and the crow hath filled his place; Go, Brāhman, home, what canst thou expect from lions?
☞ The story is that the cupidity of a Brāhman led him into a lion's cave in the hope of bringing away the ornaments of the bodies he had devoured, and that he was saved by his minister, the swan, who introduced the Brāhman as the lion's spiritual preceptor. The new prime minister the crow, however, was partial to carrion and the lion generously warned the grasping Brāhman against the sinister advice which the crow would be likely to give him.

Hanse to auroṅ ko, rove to apnoṅ ko.
If a man laughs, it is at others; if he weeps, it is for himself.

Hanse to hansye, are to ariye.
Laugh with those who laugh, war with those who war.
(A smile for a smile, a blow for a blow.)

Hans gun pāve, tevar lāge. E.
What is given with smiles he receives with frowns.
(Ingratitude.)

Hans hans khāiye phūhaṛ kā māl. Wom.
Enjoy the ninny's wealth and laugh at her.
(A fool and his money are soon parted.)

Hansī aur phansī.
Smile and be entangled.
(A woman that laughs is half won.)

Hāṅsī bairī baīyar kī, khāṅsī bairī chor kī.
A smile is the enemy of woman, and a cough of a thief.

Hansī meṅ bikhelī bhail. E.
Jest leads to earnest.

Hansī meṅ khansī.
Laughing leads to coughing.

Hansnā Bāman, khansnā chor, kupaḍh Kāyath, kul kā bor.
Laughing Brāhmans, coughing thieves, and illiterate Kāyaths are destroyers of their race.

Hansiye dūr, paṛausī se nā.
Flirt with a stranger, but never with your neighbour.

Hanste hī ghar bastā hai.
Flirting leads to wedding.

Hanste ho, kuchh paṛā pāyā hai?
Why do you laugh? have you found anything?

Hanste ṭhākur, khanste chor, in donoṅ kā āyā or.
A laughing king and a coughing thief are near their end.

Hansvā chokh, na khurpā bhotar. E.
Nor sickle sharp, nor axe blunt.
(Fairly matched: when Greek meets Greek then comes the tug of war.)

Hansvā dūr, ki paṛausan kī nāk? E. Wom.
Which is farthest off, the sickle or the neighbour's nose?
(Neighbours never can agree.)

Hansvā ke biyāh, khurpā ke gīt. E.
The sickle is to be wedded, and the song is of the axe.
(Irrelevancy.)

'Hańsvā re! tūń ṭeṛh kāhe'? 'a to apnā gauń se'! E. Rus. Wom.
'Sickle, why are you crooked?' 'Because it suits me!'

Hap hap, jhap jhap khāte hāń, dhandā karte taje pirān.
Quick to eat and slow to work.

Haq Allah, pāk zāt Allah. Mah. Wom.
God is truth and God is pure.

Haq-dār tarseń, ańgār barseń.
When the rightful owners are deprived of their rights it rains live coals.
(On those who deprive them.)

Haq, haq hai; aur nā-haq, nā-haq.
Right is right and wrong is wrong.

Haq kahe so dārī jār. E. Wom.
Tell the truth and be abused.
(The candid friend.)

Haq kahe so mārā jāë!
Tell the truth and be hanged!
(*Moral*:—tell a lie and save yourself!)

Haq kahne se ahmaq be-zār.
He is a fool that is offended at the truth.

Haq kā razī Khudā hai. Mah
The guardian of truth is God.

Haq kar, halāl kar, din meń sau bār kar. Mah.
Do the right and lawful, and do it a hundred times a day.

Haq karvā hai.
Truth is bitter.

Haq kā sāthī Khudā. Mah.
God sides with the truth.

Haq nām Allāh kā. Mah.
The true name is God.

Haq na pāve, inām! E.
He cannot get his rights and wants a present!

Haq sab ko pyārā hai.
Truth is loved by all.

Harām chālīs ghar le-kar ḍūbtā hai.
The adulterer sinks with forty neighbours.
(Involves many others in his disgrace.)

Harām kā bol uṭhtā hai, halāl kā jhuk jātā hai.
The bastard will speak out boldly where the true born hangs his head.

Harām khānā aur shalgam! Mah.
Unlawful food and a turnip at that!
(As well be hanged for a sheep as a lamb.)

Harām-khorī mushkil se chhūṭtī hai.
Bribe-taking (or laziness) is hard to shake off.

Harām kī kamāī, harām meń gańvāī.
Ill got, ill spent.

Harām koṭhe chaṛh-ke pukārtā hai.
Adultery cries out from the housetop.
(Murder will out.)

Harām meń baṛā mazā hai.
Sin is sweet.
(Sweet and naughty.)

Harām-zāde kī rassī darāz hai.
The wicked man has a long rope.

Harām-zāde se Khudā bhī ḍartā hai.
Even God fears the wicked man.

Har bār guṛ mīṭhā?
Treacle is not always sweet.
☞ The story is told of a boy employed at a Baniyā's shop, who was in the habit of eating secretly from a jar full of treacle. One day the Baniyā happening to find the jar half empty and wishing to fathom the mystery, removed it to another corner and placed another jar full of *birozah* (resin) in its place. The next day the boy as usual came up to the place and not suspecting any change put a lump of the resin into his mouth, which clogged it and enabled the Baniyā to discover the thief and chastise him. Hence the proverb.

Harbhūm kā rāj.
The government of Harbhūm.
(The name of a village near Allahabad, whose Rājā was famed for injustice. The whole Proverb is elaborately explained in Elliot's *Glossary*, Beames' edition, *s. v.*)

Har degī chamchā. Mah. Wom.
A spoon for every pot.
(A jack of all trades: also a faithless husband.)

Hāre bhī harāve, jīte bhī harāve.
Win and suffer, lose and suffer.
(Heads you lose and tails I win.)

Hāre juārī ko kab kal paṛtī hai?
What rest has the ruined gambler?

Har ek bāt kī kuchh intehā bhī hai.
There is a final end to every matter.
(Every thing must have an end.)

Hāre ke Harnām.
When a man is ruined he remembers God.

Har ek ke kān meń Shaitān ne phūk mār dī hai, 'tere barābar koī nahīń.'
The Devil whispers in every one's ear, 'there is none like you.'

Hare rūkh par sab parand baiṭhte haiń, ṭhuṇṭh par koī nahīń baiṭhtā.
Birds perch on every green tree, but not on a blasted trunk.

Hāṛ hoṅge to mās bahoterā ho rahegā.
Where the bones are, there the flesh will come.
(If he only live he will grow strong again.)

Hari-gun gāve dhakkā pāve, chūtaṛ ḍulāve ṭakkā pāve. E. Wom.
Sing psalms and you will be pushed aside, have a wanton gait and you will get money.

Har kase maslahat-i-khesh niko midānad. Pers.
Every one knows his own interests best.

Harī khetī, gyābhan gāë, mūńh paṛe tab jānī jāë. Agric.
The standing crop and the pregnant cow are only your own when they yield.
(The uncertainty of the future.)

Hari kī māyā, chhin meń dhūp, chhin meń chhāyā. Hin.
God's wondrous deeds, one moment sunshine, and another moment shade.

Hariyā hāthī, hākim chor, donon ke bigre or na chhor.
A wild elephant and an extortionate ruler know no bounds.

Har jaise ko taisā.
To every one according to his merits.

Hār jīt qismat ke hāth.
Loss and gain are in the hands of fate.

Hār jīt sab men rahe, hāre nāh datār.
Loss and gain come to all, but the liberal man never loses.

Har kamāle rā zavāle. Pers.
All maturity is destined to decay.

Har kā māne, par kā na māne. E
A disappointed man can be appeased, a snubbed one never.

Hār kā niyāo kyā?
What redress for a lost cause?

Har kāre o har marde. Pers.
Every man to his own business.

Harkāyā bhalā, parkāyā na bhalā. E.
Better disappoint than snub.

Harkāyā ban gayā.
Become a man-eater.
(Said of an utterly abandoned man who raves like a madman.)

Harkāyā kuttā.
A mad dog.

Har khāen, uglen baherā.
Eat myrabolans and vomit myrabolans.
(You will mow as you sow.)

Harkhe pitar tilanjal pāve.
The shades of the dead are pleased by the *til anjalī.*
(A funeral ceremony in which a libation of sesamum seeds and water is made in the name of the dead.)

Har ko bhaje so Har kā hoē; Jāt pāt pūchhe nahīn koe.
Who remembers God will go to God: No matter his caste and clan.

Hār mānī, jhagrā jītā.
Own defeat and you will win the battle.

Hār men hār, na ghar men khetī.
Loss upon loss, and no harvest in the house.
(Misfortunes never come singly: it never rains but it pours.)

Har nivāle bi'smi'llah. Mah.
Every mouthful in the name of God.
(Said to one who is always ready to take all he can get, but very unwilling to work: to be "unco guid:" perpetually saying "D. V.")

Hāron bhī hār, jīton bhī hār.
Lose and lose, win and lose.
(Said of suits in civil courts owing to delays, costs, and damages.)

Hāron dherī, yā dāmon dherī.
Either a heap of money, or a heap of bones.

Hāron thakā, beohāron thakā.
Weary of his bones and weary of his toil.
(An old man.)

Har roz Īd nest, ki halvā khurad kase. Pers.
Every day is not Īd, that one may eat cakes.
(There is a time for every thing.)

Har roz kūā khodnā aur nayā pānī pīnā.
To dig a well every day in order to drink its water.
(To live from hand to mouth: to live by the sweat of the brow.)

Hari sevā solah baras, gur sevā pal chār,
Tau bhī nahīn barābarī; Bedon kiyā bichār!
Serving God for sixteen years is not equal to serving the priests for four minutes; according to the Scriptures!
(A skit at the extravagant pretensions of the Brāhmans.)

Har shab Shab-i-barāt hai, har roz roz-i-Īd.
Every night is merry night, and every day a festive day.
(Living like a prince: to be in clover: happy as a Queen.)

Hārūn to hūrūn, jītūn to thūrūn.
If I lose I'll hammer you, if I win I'll hammer you.
(A man compelled against his will is of the same opinion still.)

Hāsid kā mūnh kālā.
Jealousy hath a black face.
(*Kālā mūnh*, idiom, disgraceful.)

Hastī kā kyā bharosā?
What reliance on life?

Hast o nest barābar hai!
His existance or non-existance is all one (to me)!

Hātam kī gor par lāt mārī. Mah.
He has kicked the tomb of Hātam.
(*i. e.* outstripped Hātam in charity: ironically said of a miser: Hātam is the conventional Eastern hero of liberality.)

Hāt hāt pukāre Baisā, 'jaisā kare so pāve taisā.'
Baisā proclaimed from market to market, 'to every one according to his deeds.'
(Baisā was a *faqīr*.)

Hāth bechā hai, kuchh zāt nahīn bechī. Hin.
I have sold you my limbs, not my caste.
(Said by a servant to his master when he abuses him or orders him to perform what it is not meet for the servant to do.)

Hāth dekhan ko ārsī kyā? Hin. Wom.
Why (keep) a glass to look at the hand?
(*Ārsī*, a small mirror worn in a ring by women on the thumb.)

Hathelī kā phapholā.
A pustule on the hand.
(Said of a troublesome fellow. *Compare* the 'wart' of a Regiment.)

Hathelī par jān līye phirtā hai.
He goes about with his head on the palm of his hand.
(Careless of his life: said of a desperate character.)

Hathelī par sirsoṅ jamāte haiṅ.
He is sowing mustard in the palms of his hands.
(Said of a person professing to undertake extraordinary feats: also of saints.)

Hathelī par zahar rakkhā raho; khāegā so maregā.
If poison be put on the palm of the hand there is no fear; *he* will die who eats it.

Hāth, goṛ lakṛī, peṭ bakrī!
Sticks for arms and legs and a goat's stomach!

Hāth, goṛ sirkī, peṭ nadkolā!
Reeds for arms and legs and a swollen stomach!

Hāthī āeṅ, ghoṛe jāeṅ, ūṅt bechāre gote khāeṅ.
Elephants come and horses go (by swimming), but the poor camels are drowned.
(Said of very deep water.)

Hāthī apnī hathiyāī par ā jāe, to ādmī bhungā hai.
If the elephant put forth his strength, man is but a fly.

Hathī chaṛhe kuttā kāṭe.
A dog may bite the rider of an elephant.
(When ill-luck overtakes him.)

Hāthī ghoṛā bahā jāe, gadhā kahe 'kitnā pānī?'
The elephant and horse are carried away, and the jackass asks if there is much water.

Hāthī hazār latā, tau bhī savā lākh ṭake kā.
An elephant, however lean, is valuable.
(Even the wrecks of a large fortune are considerable: natives value the elephant alive or dead; alive for itself and dead for its ivory and bones for ornaments.)

Hāthī kā bojh hāthī hī uṭhātā hai.
An elephant's load only an elephant can bear.
(A difficult task is only to be performed by men of ability.)

Hāthī kā dāṅt, ghoṛe kī lāt, mūṅī kā chungal.
The elephant's teeth, the horse's heels, and the tormentor's claws (be upon you).
(A curse.)

Hāthī kā dāṅt, niklā jahāṅ niklā.
When the elephant's tusk is out, it's out.

Hāthī kā jag sāthī, kīṛī pāhan pīṛī. Rus.
The world befriends the elephant and tramples on the ant.

Hāthī kā kandhā khālī nahīṅ rahtā.
The elephant's shoulder (neck) is never unemployed.
(Oriental observation.)

Hāthī kā pīr ankas.
The goad is the elephant's master.

Hāthī ke dāṅt khāne ke aur, dikhāne ke aur.
Like elephant's teeth, some to eat with and some for show.
(The elephant in popular belief has four teeth, two for eating and two tusks for show. Said of a double-faced person.)

Hāthī ke pāoṅ meṅ sab kā pāoṅ.
All others' feet in the elephant's feet.
(The great man has numerous attendants.)

Hāthī nikal gayā, dum rah gaī.
The elephant is over, only his tail remains.
(1. Said when very little remains to be done of a great work. 2. To express that a work is left imperfect, when nearly brought to a conclusion. To swallow a cow and be choked with the tail.)

Hāthī phire gāoṅ gāoṅ, jis kā hāthī us kā nāoṅ.
The elephant goes from town to town, but always bears the name of his owner.
(Borrowed plumes.)

Hathiyā barse, Chitrā manḍrāe, ghar baiṭhe kisān ririyāe. Agric.
Rain in October and clouds in November, and the peasant sits at home and weeps.

Hathīyā barse tīn hot haiṅ, shakkar, shālī, māsh;
Hathiyā barse tīn jāt haiṅ, tillī, kodo, kapās. Agric.
Rain in October and three things prosper, sugarcane, rice and pulse; Rain in October and three things die, sesamum, millet and cotton.

Hathiyā chale nā paiyā, baiṭhe 'de Gusaīṅyā!' E.
He cannot stir his hands or feet, (and says) "God give me as I sit!"
(Said of a lazy fellow.)

Hāthiyoṅ se ganne khāne.
To snatch sugar-cane from elephants.
(To provoke the wrath of a strong person.)

Hāth kā chūhā bil meṅ paiṭhā.
The rat in his hand escaped to his hole.
(There's many a slip betwixt cup and lip.)

Hāth kā denā, aur bair bisānā. Mercantile.
Lend your money and make an enemy.

Hāth kā diyā āṛī āe!
What thou givest shall be thy shield.
(Charity averts calamity: beggar's cry.)

Hāth kā diyā sāth chalegā.
What thy hand giveth shall go with thee.
(To the next world at the Judgment Day: beggar's cry.)

Hāth kā diyā sāth khāne lagā.
Given by the hand and eaten before me.
(It is an insult for a servant (or a beggar) to eat food with his master.)

Hāth kā hatiyār, peṭ kā ādhār.
A weapon in hand is food for the stomach.
(Might is right.)

Hāth kangan ko ārsī kyā hai? Wom.
To see the bracelet on your arm needs no mirror.
(In answer to one who puts a question, the reply to which is self evident: the *ārsī* is a small mirror worn in a ring on the thumb by women.)

Hāth kashīdah, āsmān dīdah. Wom.
Needle-work in her hands and her eyes towards the sky.
(Want of proper attention: in the clouds.)

Hāth kauṛī na bāzār lekhā.
Not a farthing in his hand, nor credit in the town.

Hāth ke sankal muṅh ke piyār. E. Wom.
Handcuffs on his hands and loving words upon his lips.
(Sham affection.)

Hāth kī lakīreṅ kahīṅ miṭtī haiṅ?
Can the lines in the palm of the hand be ever blotted out?
(Said by hereditary menials when demanding their customary fees.)

Hāth ko hāth nahīṅ sūjhtā.
One hand cannot see the other.
(A darkness that may be felt.)

Hāth ko hāth pahchāne.
One hand knows another.
(In answer to a person who goes to demand the payment of money lent by another: The meaning is I will pay only him to whom I owe.)

Hāth liyā kāṅsā, to roṭīon kā kyā sāṅsā?
Once you take to begging have you any fear of a livelihood?
(Mendicancy is the last and unfailing resource of getting a living.)

Hāth meṅ lānā, pāt meṅ khānā. H. Wom.
Brings it in his hands and eats it from a leaf.
(To live from hand to mouth)

Hāth meṅ, na gāt meṅ, "maiṅ dhanvantī jāt meṅ!" Rus. Wom.
Nothing in her hands, and nothing on her body, "and I am of a great caste!"

Hāth na gale, nāk meṅ piyāz ke ḍale! Wom.
Nothing on hands and neck, and pieces of onion in her nose.
(To describe a strange and incongruous set of ornaments.)

Hāth na muṭṭhī halbalātī uṭhī. Wom.
With nothing in her fist she gets up in a hurry to buy.
(Said of a person, who is very desirous to obtain a thing which he has not the means to purchase.)

Hāthoṅ hāth bik gayā. Mercantile.
Sold from hand to hand.
(A rapid sale.)

Hāthoṅ meṅhdī, pāvan meṅhdī, āpne lachchhan aurāṅ deṅdī. Panj. Wom.
She has stained her own hands and feet with *hinā* and recommends the same practice to others.
☞ *Meṅhdī* or *hinā*, *lawsonia alba*, is used by native *feme covert* only: the point here is that an unmarried girl or widow is using it, in which case it would mean that she is of easy virtue.

Hāth, pāoṅ bachāiye mūzī ko tarkāiye.
Save thyself and keep clear of thy foe.

Hāth pāoṅ diyā-salāī, bāt karne ko fazal Ilāhī!
Hands and feet are matches, but God save us from his words!
(A venomous tongue.)

Hāth pāoṅ hilā, Bhagwān degā. Hin. Wom.
Labor, and God will give.
(God helps those that help themselves.)

Hāth pāon ke langṛe, nām Salāmat Khāṅ!
A cripple and named Mr. Sound.

Hāth pāon kī kāhelī aur muṅh meṅ mūchheṅ jātī. Mah.
His moustaches go into his mouth for very laziness.
(Musalmāns cannot allow their moustaches to go into the mouth and usually cut them so as to prevent it.)

Hāth sūkhā, faqīr bhūkā.
When his hand is dried up, the beggar starves.
(Because he can't hold out the begging bowl.)

Hāth sumarnī, bagal katarnī, paṛhe Bhāgwat Gītā re,
Auroṅ ko tū gyān batāve, āp phire tū rītā re.
Beads in hand, and knife in pocket, you repeat the Bhāgwat Gītā,
To others you learning preach, and yourself are wanting.
(*Bhagavad Gītā* is the name of a celebrated Hindū religious book: practise what you preach.)

Hāth sumarnī, peṭ katarnī.
Beads in his hand, but scissors in his belly.
(To describe one who looks like a gentleman, but is a common rogue: a swell mobsman.)

Hāth uṭhānā achchhā nahīṅ.
It is not good to lift one's hand.
(To strike.)

Hauṅs se ris bhalī.
Emulation is better than envy.

Hauz bhare to favvāre chhūṭeṅ.
When the tank is full, the fountain spouts.
(Expenditure follows income.)

Havāī dīdah.
Aerial eyes.
(Applied to a wanton person.)

Havā ke ghoṛe par savār haiṅ.
He rides a steed of air.
(To build castles in the air.)

Hazār āfateṅ haiṅ ek dil lagāne meṅ.
There are a thousand miseries in one love.

Hazār baras kā rezah aur Nannhī nāoṅ. Wom.
A damsel of a thousand years and called Miss Trot.

Hazār bhaṛve mareṅ, to ek khidmat-gār hoe.
It takes a thousand pimps to make a *khidmatgār*.
(*Khidmatgārs*,—*vulgo kits*,—are the table servants of Europeans: they are notorious rascals.)

Hazār davā aur ek duā.
A thousand medicines and one prayer.

Hazār ilāj aur ek parhez.
A thousand remedies and one regimen.

Hazār jūtiyāṅ lagīṅ aur izzat nahīṅ gaī.
Though beaten with a thousand shoes, his honor is not yet gone.
(Said of a truly shameless person.)

Hazār jūtiyāṅ mārūṅ aur ek na ginūṅ.
I will give him with my slipper a thousand blows, a .. not count it one.
(I am .. of him, though I treat him like a dog.)

Hazār kaho is ke kān par ek jūṅ nahīṅ chaltī.
You may speak to him a thousand times, it has no more effect on him than a louse on his ear.

Hazār lāṭhī ṭūṭī, tau bhī ghar bār ke bāsan toṛne ko bahut hai.
Though the club be broken into a thousand pieces, it is still strong enough to break crockery.
(There is life in the old dog yet.)

Hazār nemat aur ek tandurustī.
Health is equal to a thousand other gifts.
(Health is better than wealth.)

Hazāroṅ ghaṛe pānī ke paṛ gaë.
A thousand water pots have fallen.
(With shame at this proceeding.)

Hazār randiyāṅ mareṅ to ek āyā ho.
It takes a thousand harlots to make an *āyā*.
(*Āyās* are the nurses and maids of Europeans; they are commonly of easy virtue.)

Hāzir ko luqma, gāyab ko takbīr.
Sustenance to the living and offerings to the dead.
(A good man.)

Hāzir māre, gāfil roä.
The present receives and the absent deplores.
(*Moral*: always be on the spot. *Les absents ont toujours tort.*)

Hāzir meṅ hujjat nahīṅ, gair kī talāsh nahīṅ.
No objections (to giving) to those present and no search for the absent.
(See preceding.)

Hāzrī ke mele meṅ koī ho. Mah.
Any one may be present at the breakfast-meeting.
(*Hāzrī kā melā*, a feast held by Shias after the mourning for Hasan and Husain, to which all sects are invited.)

Her pher āve to kākṛī maṭkāve. Rus.
If I can get it again, I'll again enjoy cucumber.
☞ The story is told of a village boor who had found a gold *mohar*, but not knowing its real worth, he parted with it to a petty money changer who promised him a farthing a day to buy cucumbers with. At last when the villager had acquired a taste for cucumbers, the money changer refused to pay him any longer. Hence the proverb.

Hijre ke ghar beṭā huā.
There is a son in the eunuch's house.
(Applied to one who professes to have done what he cannot possibly have effected.)

Hijre kī kamāī, muṅraunī meṅ gaī.
The eunuch's earnings go to the barber.
(He has to shave so often to look feminine and attractive.)

Hikmat-i-Chīn, hujjat-i-Bangālā. Rus.
China for art, Bengal for litigation.

Hilāo na jhulāo, mujhe baiṭhe hī khilāo.
Neither shake me nor swing me, but feed me sitting.
(Give me some sinecure.)

Hīle risaq, bahāne maut.
Livelihood by some means and death from some cause.
☞ The point is that God gives livelihood and causes death, not the apparent labor or the apparent disease.

Himāīt kī ghoṛī Irāqī ke lāt māre.
The protected mare will kick the Arab horse.
(The tyranny of the *protegés* of men high in office.)

Himmat-i-mardāṅ, madad-i-Khudā. Pers.
Endeavour is man's, help is God's.
(God helps those that help themselves.)

Hindī na Fārsī, lālā jī Banārsī. Hin.
With neither Hindī nor Persian, he is a scholar from Banāras.
(Banāras is noted for its Sanskrit scholars.)

Hindū, Musalmān kā cholī dāman kā sāth hai.
Hindūs and Muhammadans are as close knit as skirt and boddice.

Hiṅg hagte phiroge.
You shall pass dirty stools.
(I will beat you till you get diarrhœa.)

Hīnī puṛyā, chhattīs rog.
Cheap drugs, and thirty six diseases.
(Cheap and nasty.)

Hīre kī qadar jauhrī jāne.
A jeweller only knows the value of a diamond.

Hire phire, khet meṅ ko rāh.
He looks every where and then goes through the field.
(Instead of by the road: a downright fool.)

Hirī phirī bal gaī, jalve ke vaqt ṭal gaī. Mah.
She is always at hand for the benediction, but steals away when she should make a present (to the bride).
(Applies to any one who after a shew of zeal and activity is found wanting when the decisive moment arrives.)

Hīr kā kyā jijmān? aur lapsī kā kyā pakvān? Rus.
Can an Ahīr have a (religious) client? and can a crust be a dainty?
(*Jijmān* is a client to a Brāhman priest.)

Hirsī ṭaṭṭū!
The spawn of emulation!

Hisāb-i-dostāṅ dar dil. Pers.
Friend's accounts are kept in the head.

Hisāb jau jau, bakhshish sau sau.
In accounts to a barley corn, in gifts hundreds.

Hisāb jyoṅ kā tyoṅ, kunbā ḍūbā kyoṅ?
The account is correct, and why is the family drowned?
☞ The story is told of a Kāyath who was travelling with his family in a cart. On their way

they had to cross a river and the Kāyath himself, as head of the family, went ahead, took measurements of the depth of the water at different places in the river, and then struck an average, which showed that the river was not deeper than the wheels of the cart. Being thus sure of his calculation and apprehending no danger in fording the river, he ordered the cart to be driven into it. But when to his great disappointment and embarrassment the cart came to a deep place, the Kāyath looked over his calculation and exclaimed in the words of the proverb. *Moral* : a little learning is a dangerous thing.

Hisāb leb, ki Banyā ḍāṅrab? Bhoj.
Are you taking an account, or fining the Baniyā?
(Are you dealing fair or cheating?)

Hisāb nit nayā.
Let an account be always new.
(It should never be allowed to lie by and be forgotten.)

Hoē bhale ke an-bhale, hoē dānī ke sūm,
Hoē kapūt sapūt ke, jūṅ pāvak meṅ dhūm.
The good beget evil, the liberal beget misers:
Good fathers beget bad sons, as fire begets smoke.

Ho gaī ḍhaḍḍo, ṭhumak chāl kaisī?
What is the use of mincing when you are grown old?

Holā khāē, mūṅh hāth dono kāle.
Eat parched peas and your hands and mouth will both be black.
(Touch pitch and you will be defiled.)

Holī kā bhaṛvā hai!
A pimp of the *Holī!*
(Holī, a sort of Saturnalia, is held in the beginning of spring.)

Hom karat hāth jare. Hin.
Burning the hand in making a sacrifice.
(To be injured by a good action.)

Honā na honā Khudā ke hāth hai, mār mār to kīye jāīye.
To succeed or not to succeed is with God, but do your best.
(Try, try, try again, if at first you don't succeed.)

Honhār birvā ke chikne chikne pāt.
A thriving plant has tender leaves.
(Applied to a promising child that gives indications of genius and a good disposition.)

Honhār hirde base, bisar jāē sab budh.
What is to be will fill the heart and destroy your sense.
(You can't fight against fate.)

Honhār ho-ke ṭale.
What is to be will happen and be off.

Honhār miṭtī nahīṅ, hove bisve bīs.
What is to be will not be blotted out, but will surely be.

Honī balvān hai!
The inevitable is invincible.

Hoṅṭ chāṭne se piyās nahīṅ bujhtī.
Thirst can't be quenched by licking the lips.

Hoṅṭ hile na jibbhyā kholī, phir bhī sāe kahe baḍ bolī. Rus. Wom.
Nor opened her lips, nor moved her tongue, and still the old woman scolded her.

Hoṅṭoṅ niklī, koṭhoṅ chaṛhī.
Out of the lips is up on the house-top.

Hoṅṭoṅ se abhī dūdh kī bū nahīṅ gaī.
The smell of his mother's milk has not yet left his lips.
(The cradle straws are not yet out of his breeches.)

Hoṅṭ se niklī huī parāī bāt.
Out of the lips is another's property.

Hoṛ kā kār, jī kā bhār.
Competitive business is heavy on the heart.

Hosh kī banvāo!
Collect your senses!

Hosnāk buṛhiyā chaṭāī kā laṅhgā. E.
A gay old woman with a mat petticoat.
(A person with more inclination than means.)

Hote hī nā mar gaē, jo kafan bhī thoṛā lagtā.
Had you died just after your birth, so much cere-cloth would have been spared.
(Said to a worthless or good-for-nothing person.)

Hotī āī hai!
It is a continuous custom.
(A custom from time immemorial.)

Hotī āī hai, ki achchhoṅ ke bure hote haiṅ.
It is an old custom that good men beget bad sons.

Hotī āī hai, ki achchhoṅ ko burā kahte haiṅ.
It is an old custom for men to speak ill of the good.

Hot kā bāp, an-hot kī mā.
In prosperity a father, in adversity a mother.
(Mothers are more valued than fathers in India.)

Hot kī jot hai.
To have is to be bright.
(While the oil lasts the wick burns.)

Hujjatī lā ummatī. Mah. Wom.
Argument is scepticism.
(To doubt is to go to hell.)

Hukmī bandah jannat meṅ. Mah. Wom.
Obedience on Earth (leads to) a place in Heaven.

Hukm-i-hākim marg-i-mafājāt. Pers.
The ruler's order is sudden death.

Hukm ke sāth sab kuchh maujūd hai.
All things wait on authority.

Hukm nishānī bahisht kī, jo māṅge so pāē.
Authority is Heaven, for then to desire is to get.

Hukūmat kī ghoṛī aur chhai paserī dānā. [corn.
The Governor's mare eats thirty *sers* of
(*i. e.* The animal eats four or five and the remainder goes into the pockets of the hangers on.)

Hunar-mand bhūkā nahīṅ rahtā.
A master of his trade never starves.

Hunḍār chīnhe Bāmhan kā pūt? E.
A wolf won't spare a Brāhman's son.
(For his piety.)

Hunḍrā re, bakrī charāībe paṭhru samet. E.
O wolf, graze this goat and its kid!

Hūn sajnī, jānat nahīn, pīyā bichhṛan kī sār,
Jīyā bichhṛan se kaṭhan hai, pīyā bichhṛan kī bār.
My friend, I did not know what it was to part from my love,
It is easier to part with life than to part with my love.

Huqqā afīmī kā.
No pipe like the opium-eater's.

Huqqā bhar baroṅ ko dīje, jab sulge tab āp hī līje.
Fill the pipe and place it before your superior (as etiquette requires,) when it is lighted, then enjoy it yourself.

Huqqā chār vaqt achchhā—soke, muṅh dho-ke, khāke, nahā-ke; aur chār vaqt burā—āndhī meṅ, andhere meṅ, bhūk meṅ, aur dhūp meṅ.
At four times is a pipe pleasant: after a sleep, after a wash, after a meal, and after a bathe. At four times it is unpleasant: in a storm, in the dark, in hunger and in the sun.

Huqqā Har kā lāḍlā, rakkhe sab kā mān,
Bharī sabhā meṅ yūṅ phire, jūṅ gopin meṅ Kānh.
The pipe is beloved of God, it maintaineth the repute of all, and moveth in the assembly, as Krishna among the neatherdesses.

Huqqā hukm Khudā kā: chilam bahisht kā phūl: Pīveṅ mard Khudā ke: ghūreṅ nā-māqūl.
(We smoke) the pipe by the order of God. Its bowl is a flower of heaven. It is the men of God that smoke it, and it is rogues that jeer at it.

Huqqā pair daurī kā, roṭī qismat kī.
Livelihood depends on fate, but smoking on one's own exertion.
(In going about in search of fire.)

Huqqā, sukkā, hurkanī, Gūjar aur Jāṭ.
In meṅ aṭak kahā, Bāvā Jagan Nāth kā bhāt.
Pipe, tobacco, courtesan, the Gūjar and the Jāṭ.
All are one, as is the rice from Father Jagan Nāth.
(At the feast of Jagan Nāth (Juggernaut) there is no distinction of caste.)

Huqqā yak dam, do dam, sih dam bāshad,
Na ki mīrās-i-jadd o am bāshad. Pers.
Take one, two or three puffs at a pipe, but don't use it as an heirloom.
(When smoking in company etiquette in India requires people to smoke by turns.)

Huqqe aur bātoṅ meṅ bair hai.
Smoking and talking are enemies.

Huqqe kā mazā jis ne zamāne meṅ na jānā,
Woh mard mukhannas hai, na aurat, na zanānā.
Who knows not the taste of a pipe in this world, is a eunuch; nor man nor woman.

Huqqe pānī kā sukh.
The delights of smoking and drinking.

Huqqe se hurmat gaī, nem gayā sab chhūṭ!
Pagṛī bech tamākū līyā, gaī hīye kī phūṭ!
Lose your honour and virtue for a pipe! Sell your turban for tobacco and lose your wits!

Hūr bhī saukan ko ḍāyan se burī hai. Wom.
To a co-wife a fairy is uglier than a goblin.

Huzūrī kī mazdūrī bhalī.
It is well to work under the eye of the master.
(For he can see the value of it.)

I.

Ibtidā-i-ishq hai, rotā hai kyā? Āge āge dekhiye, hotā hai kyā!
Love hath but begun, why weepest thou? Look before thee to what will happen!
(Faint heart never won fair lady.)

Ibtidā se intehā tak.
From beginning to end.
(From top to toe.)

Īd, Baqrīd, Shabrāt kuṭnī; Dāhā kare hāē hāē, Phagvā bisnī. E.
At the Īd, Baqrīd and Shabrāt they have procuresses; at the Dāhā they mourn and at the Holī they have prostitutes.
(A slap at the Musalmāns and their feasts.)

Idhar girūṅ kūāṅ, udhar girūṅ khāī.
Here I fall into a well, there into a ditch.
(Scylla and Charybdis.)

Idhar kāṭā, udhar palaṭ gayā.
He bites and turns (as a snake).
(Said of the crafty.)

Idhar na udhar, yeh balā kidhar?
This misfortune is neither here nor there, where is it?
(Neither die nor get well.)

Idhar Qiblah Quṭab, udhar Khatījah, mūtūṅ kidhar? Mah.
This side Mecca, the other Khatījah, where I am to make water?
(Muhammadans don't make water to the side of Mecca and Khatījah: to be put on the horns of a dilemma.)

Īd ke chāṅd ho gaë. Mah.
He is become the moon of the Īd.
(Said of a person highly prized and rarely seen. The Ramzān or fast of the Musalmāns ends with the Īd at the new moon, which is accordingly anxiously looked for.)

Īd pīchhe chāṅd mubārak! Wom.
Congratulations after the Īd.
(Compliments of the season after the season; a day too late.)

Īd pīchhe ṭar.
Rejoicings after the Īd.
(See preceding.)

Īd pīchhe ṭar, barāt pīchhe dhaunsā.
Rejoicings after the Īd, and music after the wedding.
(See preceding.)

Ijārah, ujāṛah.
Farming is famishing.
(Farming the revenue of an estate to a contractor or middleman is ruin.)

Ikkā, vakīl, gadhā, Paṭnā shahar meṅ sadhā. E.
Ikkās, pleaders, and donkeys abound in Paṭnā.
(An *ikkā* is a conveyance drawn by one pony.)

Ikke chaṛh-ke jahāṅ jāē, Paise de-ke dhakke khāē.
Wherever you go in an *ikkā* you get jolted for your money.
(Very true!)

Illat jāē dhoē dhāē, ādat kahāṅ jāē?
Filth is got rid of by washing, but not an habit.

Ilm dar sīnah, na dar safīnah. Pers.
Knowledge is in the heart, not in books.

Ilm kā paṛhnā lohe ke chane chabāne haiṅ.
Learning is like chewing iron.

Imān hai, to sab kuchh.
Where there is faith there is every thing.

Imān kā saudā hai.
Dealings on good faith.
(Fair and square.)

Ināyat-i-shāhī kisī kī mīrās nahīṅ.
The king's favour is no inheritance.

In bechāroṅ ne hīṅg kahāṅ pāī, jo bagal meṅ lagāī?
Whence could such poor men get assafœtida to rub under their armpits?
(*Moral:* how could such men have committed such a crime?)

Inchā khiṅchā voh phire, jo parāē bīch meṅ paṛe.
He gets into trouble who interferes with others.
(Of little meddling comes great ease. They who in quarrels interpose, will often wipe a bloody nose.)

Indar rājā garjā, mhārā jīā larjā. Hin.
My heart trembles when the clouds thunder.
(The sign of rain and therefore a terrible sound to the Baniyā, who has been hoarding up corn for the rise.)

In ke chāṭe, rūkh nahīṅ rahe.
The tree they lick remains not.
(Metaphor from the attacks of locusts, applied to prostitutes and bad characters.)

In ke hāṅ to chamṛe kā jahāz chaltā hai. Slang.
They commerce by a ship of flesh.
(They earn by prostitution.)

In kī nāk par gussa rakkhā hī rahtā hai.
He always keeps anger on the tip of his nose.

In ko bhī likkho.
Put him down also.
☞ Akbar once asked Birbal whether there were more men in the world with eyes than with no eyes. Birbal replied that the blind were most numerous, and to prove his assertion he set out, accompanied by a writer, and began collecting stones on the road. Seeing this every one who passed him asked what he was doing? Every time he was so addressed he said to the writer, '*Inheṅ bhī likho*' 'Enter him too (as a blind man')

In ko to patthar māre maut nahīṅ.
Though he were stoned he would not die.
(An iron constitution.)

Insān hī to hai.
Man is but human.
(And so prone to err.)

Insān meṅ kyā rakkhā hai?
What then is in a man?
(He very easily dies.)

Insān pānī kā bulbulā hai.
Man is but a water bubble.

Inshā Allah-tāla billī kā muṅh kālā.
May God grant that the cat's face be black.
(Said to ridicule earnestness about trifles.)

In tiloṅ tel nahīṅ.
There is no oil in these sesamums.
(You cannot draw blood from a stone.)

Īṅṭ kā ghar, maṭṭī kā dar.
A brick house with a door of earth.
(The strength of a chain is its weakest link.)

Īṅṭ kā ghar maṭṭī kar diyā! Wom.
She has brought his brick house to dust.
(A bad manager.)

Īṅṭ kī devī, jhamkayā kā parshād.
A goddess of brick, and brick dust for offerings.

Īṅṭ kī leni, patthar kī denī.
To receive bricks and return stones.
(Retaliation: tit for tat.)

Īṅṭ kī pānt, dam Madār.
A row of bricks and the power of Madār.
☞ A stone is said to be suspended by some unknown means over the tomb of Shekh Badru'd-din surnamed Madār at Makanpur. The phrase is applied to one who undertakes any thing extraordinay without recollecting his inability to perform it.

Īṅṭ se īṅṭ baj gaī.
When brick strikes brick.
(Then is the time to make something out of the quarrel. When two dogs fight it is a third that gets the bone.)

Iqrār-i-jurm, islāh-i-jurm. Pers.
A fault confessed is half redressed.

Irāqī par zor na chalā, gadhī ke kān amṭhe.
Force will do little with the Arab steed, but you may pull the ass's ears.

Īsā ba dīn-i-khud, Mūsā ba dīn-i-khud. Pers.
Let Jesus stick to his faith and Moses to his.
(Religious toleration.)

Is ghar kā Bāvā Ādam hī nirālā hai.
The Ādam of this house is a strange person.
(Strange custom, or practice, or eccentricity.)

Is hāth lenā, us hāth denā. Mercantile.
Give with one hand and receive with the other.
(Cash dealings.)

Ishq chhupāne se nahīṅ chhuptā.
Love cannot be hid by hiding.

Ishq-i-majāzī se ishq-i-haqīqī hāsil hotā hai.
Love of man leads to love of God.
(Doing your duty towards your neighbour leads you to your duty towards God.)

Ishq ke kūche meṅ āshiq kī hajāmat hotī hai.
The lover is shaved clean in the lane of his love.
(He gives away everything where his heart is.)

Ishq meṅ ādmī ke ṭāṅke udharte haiṅ.
Love rips open every joint of the body.

Ishq meṅ shāh o gadā barābar.
In love beggars and kings are equal.
(Love levels all.)

Ishq, mushk, khāṅsī khushk, khūn kharābā chhuptā nahīṅ.
Love, musk, a dry cough, and murder cannot be hid.

Ishq yā kare amīr, yā kare faqīr.
Love befits both the rich man and the beggar.

Is kā dukh dikhāve mukh.
His face betrays his sorrows.

Is kān sunī, us kān uṛā dī.
In at one ear, and out at the other.

Is ke peṭ meṅ ḍāṛhī hai.
He has a beard on his stomach.
(Old head on young shoulders.)

Is meṅ bhī kuchh bhed hai.
There is some mystery in this too.

Issar āë, dāliddar bhāge, Hin.
When good fortune comes poverty runs away.

Issar se bheṭā nahīṅ, daliddar se bigāṛ. Hin.
Good fortune he has not and quarrels with misfortune.
(Making the matter worse.)

Is tarah kāṅptā hai jaise qasāī se gāë. Hin.
He is trembling like a cow before a butcher.

Ītar ke ghar tītar, 'bāhar bāṅdhūṅ ki bhītar.'?
A partridge has walked into the house of a vain man and it is, 'shall I tie it up inside or outside?'

Ītar ke ghar tītar, ghaṛī bāhar, ghaṛī bhītar.
A partridge in the house of a vain man is one hour out of it and one hour in it.
(Applied to any acquisition of a vain, light-minded person.)

Itnā jhūṭ bolo, jitnā āṭe meṅ namak.
Tell as much of a lie as there is salt in flour.
(i. e. as much as will go down.!)

Itnā khāe jitnā pache.
Eat no more than you can digest.

Itnā nafa khāo, jitnā āṭe meṅ non. Mercantile.
Make as much profit as there is salt in flour.
(Don't exceed safe limits in speculating.)

Itnā pakkā kī bāsī thikkā.
So much cooked as to leave heaps of stale food.

Itne kī kamāī nahīṅ, jitne kā laṅhgā phaṭ gayā.
Wom.
The earnings will hardly cover the rents of the petticoat.

Itnī bhī aqal ajīran hotī hai.
There is flatulence even in so much wisdom.
(You are too sharp, you may cut yourself.)

Itnī sī jān, gaz bhar kī zabān!
Such a small thing and a yard of tongue.

Itnī to rāī hogī, jo rāëte meṅ paṛe,
There is mustard enough to put in the pickles.
(I have enough to serve my turn.)

Ittifāq baṛī chīz hai.
Union is a great thing.

Ittifāq hī meṅ quvvat hai.
Union is strength.
(The bundle of sticks.)

Izzat ke āge māl kyā chīz hai?
Wealth is nothing in comparison with honor.

Izzat kī ādhī bhalī, be-izzatī kī sārī kuchh nahīṅ.
Better the half with honor than the whole with disgrace.

Izzat-wāle kī kambakhtī hai!
A man of honor generally gets into a difficulty!

J

Jab aise ho, tab aise ho.
If such you are, such you are.

Jab āṅkheṅ chār hotī haiṅ, muhabbat āhī jātī hai.
When eyes meet eyes love slips out of them.

Jab apnī utār lī, to dūsre kī utārte kyā lagtā hai?
Who disgraces himself, will not be slow to disgrace others.

Jabar kī joë mahtārī hoë, nibal kī joë merī sārī. E.
The strong man's wife is treated as a mother and the weak man's wife as a sister-in-law,
(i. e. chaffed and jested with.)

Jab āve barsan kā chāo, pachhvā gine, na purvā bāo. Agric.
When it means to rain it will rain whether east or west wind blows.

Jab āyā dehī kā ant, jaisā gadhā vaisā sant.
When the body perishes the saint is no better than an ass.
(Better a living dog than a dead lion.)

Jab bhaē sau, tab bhāg gayā bhau. Mercantile.
(i) When it (debt) reaches to a hundred he no longer fears it.
(Owe a man £10,000 and you are his master.)
(ii) When a hundred join together fear flies from them.
(The bundle of sticks: union is strength.)

Jab bhājan ko hoē lugāī, toṛe koṭ aur phānde khāī. Rus.
When a woman wills to run away she will break the fort and leap over the ditch.
(Neither bolt nor bar shall keep my own true love from me.)

Jab bhī tīn, aur ab bhī tīn, jab pāē tab tīn kī tīn.
It was three, it is three, and whenever I look I find but three.

Jab bhūk lagī bharve ko tandūr kī sūjhī, aur peṭ bharā us kā, to phir dūr kī sūjhī. Mah, Wom.
When he was hungry the rascal had his eyes on the kitchen, but when he was satisfied his eyes began to wander.
(Cupboard love.)

Jab bigṛe jab sughaṛ nar, kyā bigṛegā kūḍh ?
Matthe kā kyā bigṛe, jab bigṛe jab dūdh ?
A wise man can be spoilt, but not a fool;
As milk can be spoilt, but not tyre.

Jab chane the, tab dānt na the, Jab dānt hue, tab chane nahīn.
When I had peas, I had no teeth, And now that I have teeth, I have no peas.
(Spoken when the means and capacity for enjoyment come at different times.)

Jab dānt na the, tab dūdh diyo, Jab dānt bhaē kā ann na dego ?
When I had no teeth, He gave me milk, And now that I have teeth will He not give me bread?

Jab dekho, tab nāzir Miyān Natthū kā ṭālā.
Wherever you look it is Mr. Natthū that is about.
(A hanger on ; parasite, sponger.)

Jab denā hotā hai, to chhappar phāṛ-kar detā hai.
When (God) gives, He gives through the [roof.
(Unexpectedly.)

Jab din āē bhale, tab laḍḍū mārai, chale. E. Rus.
When good times come you enjoy sweets.

Jab diyā dil, to phir andesha-i-ruswāī kyā ?
Why fear disgrace when you have given your heart ?
(In India love is necessarily illicit.)

Jā bidh rākhe Rām, tā hī bidh rahiye.
Live with contentment in that state of life to which God calls you.

Jab jaisā, tab taisā.
When it was so, it was so.
(Change befalleth all things.)

Jab karī ās, tab āē tere pās.
When I have an object I come to you.

Jab lagī chāṭ, to sūjhī halvāī kī hāṭ.
When he has a desire he goes to the sweet-meat shop.

Jab lag paisā gānṭh men, tab lag us ke yār.
Sāīn, is sansār men suārath kā beohār.
As long as there is a copper in your pocket, so long does he befriend you. O God ! the business of this world is to one's own ends.

Jab lag sāqī, tab lag ās.
As long as there is a cup-bearer there is hope.

Jab lau kuṭhlā men nāj, tab lau julahṭū ko rāj. E.
As long as there is corn in the bin, the weaver's son is a king.

Jab le sakhā ke bhāo āī, tab le pūt ke ānkhe jāī. E. Wom.
The son will lose his eyes before the brother comes to believe.

Jab nāchne niklī, to ghunghaṭ kīyā ?
When come out to dance what need of a veil ?
(All dancing girls in India are of easy virtue.)

Jab naṭnī bāns par chaṛhī, to ghūnghaṭ kyā ?
A girl acrobat performing in public needs no veil.
(Same as preceding.)

Jab prajā nahīn, to rājā kahān ! Hin.
When there are no subjects where is the king ?

Jab phenko, tab pānche tīn.
When the dice are thrown it is always a five and a three.
(These are unlucky throws at *chausar*. Compare the English 'he always throws deuce ace.')

Jab sab pan hārī to panhārī kahāī.
When all trades fail she becomes a water-bearer.
(They are of easy virtue as a rule.)

Jab satī sat par chaṛhe, to pān khānā rasm hai:
Ābrū jag men rahe, to jān jānā pashm hai.
When a chaste wife prepares for her funeral pyre a betel leaf she eats; To keep her honor in the world her life is sacrificed.
(Extolling the custom of *sati* or burning of widows: Ābrū, and Jān Jānā are also the names of two famous players, hence there is a pun in the second line.)

Jab se uge bāl, tab se yehī ahavāl. Wom.
He has been like this ever since his hair began to grow.
(Since his infancy; always used in a bad sense; ever since he began to acquire power his conduct has been thus evil and oppressive.)

Jab tak bahū kuārī, tab tak sās vārī.
Bahū āī god men, lāḍ gayā hauḍ men. Wom.
As long as a maid is not wed the would-be

mother-in-law is devoted to her. No sooner is she brought to her arms, than all her love goes down into the pit.
(Observation of Indian domestic life.)

Jab tak chāṅd sūraj haiṅ!
While the sun and the moon shall last!

Jab tak dam hai, tab tak gam hai.
While there is life there is sorrow.

Jab tak Gangā Jamnā bahe.
While the Ganges and the Jamnā flow.
(While the Thames flows.)

Jab tak jīnā, tab tak sīnā. Wom.
While we live we must sew.
(Work while we live.)

Jab tak karūṅ bābū bābū, tab tak karūṅ apne qābū. E. Wom.
While I call him "my lord, my lord" I can keep him under my thumb.

Jab tak pahiyā luṛhaktā hai, jab hī tak gāṛī hai.
It is a carriage as long as the wheels go round.
(The business thrives when business drives.)

Jab tak pahiyā luṛhke luṛhkāē jāo.
As long as the wheel goes let it go.
(Make hay while the sun shines.)

Jab tak rakābī meṅ bhāt, merā terā sāth.
While there is rice in your dish I am your friend.
(Cupboard love.)

Jab tak sāṅs, tab tak ās.
While there is life there is hope.

Jab tak tang-dastī hai, parhezgārī hai.
While there is poverty there is abstinence.
(Superfluity is the root of many evils: *effodiuntur opes irritamenta malorum.*)

Jab tak ūṅṭ pahāṛ ke nīche nahīṅ ātā, tab tak voh jāntā hai 'mujh se ūṅchā koī nahīṅ.'
As long as a camel does not come to a hill he thinks that there is nothing taller than himself.

Jab tere peṭ meṅ khuddiyā lage, mīṭhā aur salonā kyā re?
When hunger gnaws at the stomach, sweet and salt are both alike.

Jab tīr chhuṭ gayā, to phir kamān meṅ nahīṅ ā saktā.
When the arrow has flown it cannot return to the bow.
(Once out, always out.)

Jab tū niyāē kī gaddī par baiṭhe, to apne man se tarafdārī, lālach aur kirodh ko dūr kar.
When you sit on the judgment seat give up avarice and anger and partiality.

Jachchā aur bachchā donoṅ jīeṅ! Wom.
May the lying-in woman and her child both live!
(A benediction used by the hangers on who profit by a birth.)

Jāegā sāhū kā, rahegā sāhū kā.
The loss or gain is my master's.
(So what can I do?)

Jāē īmān, rahe sab kuchh.
(i.) Let faith go if all else remains.
(ii.) Your faith will go with you, all else will remain behind.
(The proverb is capable of either interpretation.)

Jāē jān, rahe īmān.
Let life go if honor remains.

Jāē lākh, rahe sākh.
Sacrifice thousands, but keep up your credit.

Jāē ustād khālī.
The master misses nothing.
(He is sure to find a blot somewhere to criticise.)

Jafā kafā rājaoṅ par paṛtī āī hai.
From troubles and hardships not even kings are free.

Jagan Nāth kā bhāt, jis meṅ jhagṛā nā jhāṭā.
Like food at Jagan Nāth, without strife or question.
(There is no 'caste' allowed at the festival of Jagan Nāth.)

Jagan Nāth ke bhāt ko kin ne na pasāro hāth!
Who would not open his hand for the rice of Jagan Nāth?
(See preceding.)

Jag darshan kā melā hai.
The world is a fair to look on at.

Jāgegā so pāvegā, sovegā so khovegā.
Who wakes gets, who sleeps loses.
(It is the early bird that gets the worm.)

Jāgiyo! jāgnā bhalā haigā!
Wake! for waking is good!

Jāg jagante pahrvā, lāg lagante aur.
Let watchmen keep awake, and others do their own business.

Jag jalā to jalne de, maiṅ āp hī jaltī hūṅ. Wom.
If the world suffer, let it suffer, for I am suffering.

Jag-jānī, des-bakhānī.
Known to the world and familiar in the land.
(World wide reputation.)

'Jag jītā morī kānī.' 'Bar ṭhāṛ hoe jab jānī!'
'Thou hast won, my one-eyed bride.' 'Thou shalt know when thy husband stands up.'
☞ The story goes that the friends of the bride who had palmed off a one-eyed girl for a wife were outwitted by the imposition on them of a lame husband for her.

Jag meṅ dekhat hī kā nātā.
Relations in this world are but relations to the view.

Jāgte kī kaṭiyā, aur sote kā kaṭrā.
A female buffalo calf for him that keeps awake, and a male one for him that sleeps.
(A female buffalo calf, *kaṭiyā*, is more valuable than the male, *kaṭrā*.)

Jahāṅ bahū kā pīsnā, vahīṅ susar kī khāṭ.
Near to the grind-stone of the daughter-in-law the father-in-law has his bed.
(Immodesty: the daughter-in-law cannot

speak to her father-in-law in an Indian house.)

Jahāṅ bālak tahāṅ pekhnā ; jahāṅ goras, tahāṅ ghor ; jahāṅ rājā mīṭh-bolnā, baseṅ ghanere log.

Where there are children, there are toys; where there is milk, there is cowdung; where there is an affable king, there reside many people.

Jahāṅ bāloṅ kā baiṭhnā, vahāṅ bhūtoṅ kā bās. Superstition.

Where the children are, there dwell the ghosts.

(Children are the special victim of *bhūts* or malignant ghosts.)

Jahāṅ baṛī sevā, tahāṅ ochhā phal.

Hard service means little fruit.

(Much service, little reward.)

Jahāṅ dal, tahāṅ bādal.

Where there's a crowd there's a cloud (of dust).

Jahāṅ ḍar vahāṅ hamārā ghar.

My abode is at the post of danger.

Jahāṅ dekheṅ gunnā pūrī, tahāṅ jāeṅ luṛhī luṛhī. E. Wom.

Wherever the cakes and sweets are she soon slips in.

Jahāṅ dekhī roṭī, vahāṅ munḍāī choṭī. Wom.

She would shave her head for the sake of the bread.

(*i. e.* ready to humiliate herself for the sake of food : *choṭī munḍānā*, is a disgrace to any woman but a widow.)

Jahāṅ dekhe tavā parāt, vahāṅ gāve sārī rāt. Hin. Wom.

Wherever she sees plate and dish she sings the whole night.

(Said of a greedy person.)

Jahāṅ ḍhāk, vahāṅ ḍākū.

In *Ḍhāk* woods do robbers lurk.

(*Ḍhāk, butea frondosa*, has a very thick foliage.)

Jahāṅ Gang, vahāṅ rang. Hin.

Where Ganges flows are gala shows.

Jahāṅ ganj, vahāṅ ranj.

No gains without pains.

Jahāṅ gaṛhā hogā, vahāṅ pānī maregā.

Wherever there's a hole water will run into it.

(No smoke without fire.)

Jahāṅ guṛ hogā, vahāṅ makkhiyāṅ āeṅgī.

Where there are sweets there are flies.

(For wheresoever the carcase is, there shall the eagles be gathered together.)

Jahāṅ jāeṅ Bāle Miyāṅ, tahāṅ jāe pūṅchh.

Where the rich man goes, there follows his tail.

(The retinue that follows the rich.)

Jahāṅ jāe bhūkā, vahāṅ paṛe sūkhā.

Where goes the hungry, there goes famine.

(To describe a person who is very unlucky.)

Jahāṅ jis ke sīṅg samāeṅ, vahāṅ nikal jāeṅ.

Let a man go where his horns are safe.

Jahāṅ kā murdā, tahāṅ hī gor.

Where the dead man is, there is his grave.

(Fight out a quarrel on the spot.)

Jahāṅ ke murde, tahāṅ hī gaṛte haiṅ.

The dead are buried where they die.

(To express that a dispute is best settled where it arose; or that in every place matters must be determined according to the customs of that place.)

Jahāṅ khānā, vahāṅ sab kā ṭhikānā.

Where the dinner is, there is the resting place of all.

Jahāṅ kharch nahīṅ, vahāṅ har ek gāṅṭh kā pūrā.

Where there are no expenses there are full pockets.

(Offers of money are plentiful when it is not wanted, but when it is wanted every pocket is empty.)

Jahāṅ kuttā hotā hai, vahāṅ nekī kā farishtā nahīṅ ātā. Mah. Superstition.

Where the dogs are no good angels will [come.

Jahāṅ murgā nahīṅ hotā, vahāṅ kyā saverā nahīṅ hotā ?

Will it never be dawn because there is no cock to crow ?

Jahāṅ na jāe sūī, vahāṅ bhālā ghuseṛte haiṅ.

No room for a needle and he puts in a lance !

(Drawing the long bow.)

Jahāṅ na jā ko gun lahe, tahāṅ na tā ko ṭhāoṅ.
Dhobī bas-kar kyā kare Digambar ke gāoṅ ?

Let not a man go where his qualities are not appreciated. What occasion has a washerman to live in a village of Digambars ?

(The Digambars are a sect of Jains who go naked.)

Jahāṅ paṛe mūsal, vahāṅ khem kūsal !

It is safe and sound, where pestles pound !

Jahāṅ rūkh nahīṅ, tahāṅ aranḍ rūkh.

Where there are no trees, even the castor is a tree.

(A man with very little wisdom, science, wealth, &c., is highly esteemed where no body has any : the *aranḍ* is a small straggling shrub with large leaves.)

Jahāṅ sau, vahāṅ savā sau.

When it is a hundred it is a hundred and a quarter.

(In for a penny, in for a pound.)

Jahāṅ ser, vahāṅ savaiyā.

Where there is a pound there is a pound and a quarter.

(See preceding.)

Jahāṅ tumhārā pasīnā gire, vahāṅ ham khūn girāeṅ.

For every drop of your sweat I am ready to spill my blood.

(Said by a devoted friend.)

Jahāz kā kauvā.

The crow of a vessel.

(Which finding no land returns ever and anon

to the masts and yards. Said of a man whom there is no getting rid of.)

Jāhil faqīr, Shaitān kā ṭaṭṭū.
An ignorant monk is a nag for the devil.

Jāhī teṅ kuchh pāiye, karye tā kī ās. E.
Expect where you get.
(Blessed are they that expect nothing, for they shall never be disappointed.)

Jaisā bo, vaisā kāṭ. Agric.
As you sow, so you mow.

Jaisā deotā, vaisī pūjā. Hin.
As the God, so the worship.

Jaisā des, vaisā bhes.
As the country, so the fashion.
(In Rome do as Rome does.)

Jaisā deve, vaisā pāve : Pūt bhatār ke āge āve. E. Wom.
As you give you shall get, Even to your sons and husband.
(For I the Lord thy God, am a jealous God, visiting the iniquity of the fathers upon the children unto the third and fourth generation of them that hate me. Exodus, xx, 5.)
☛ It is related that in order to test this saying, a woman once gave a *faqīr* (beggar) two poisoned cakes, which were unfortunately eaten, however, by her two sons, to whom the *faqīr* had hospitably offered them, while they stopped at the *faqīr's* hut for a drink of water.

Jaisā duddh, vaisā buddh.
Your sense is as your mother's milk.
(*i. e.* according to your inheritance.)

Jaisā dūdh dhaula, vaisī chhāchh dhaulī.
As the milk is white, so the butter-milk is white.
(To be deceived by appearances)

Jaisā kāchh kāchhe, vaisā nāch nāche.
As your dress, so dance.
(Cut your coat according to your cloth.)

Jaisā kan bhar, vaisā man bhar.
As the piece, so the whole.
(Judging by the sample.)

Jaisā karoge, vaisā bharoge.
As you do, so will it be done to you.
(As you brew, so you must drink. Do unto others as you would that they should do unto you.)

Jaisā karoge, vaisā pāoge.
As you act, so will you be rewarded.
(As you make your bed, so you must lie.)

Jaisā kiyā, vaisā pāyā.
As you did, so have you received.

Jaisā līkṛā bhar, vaisā ṭhīkrā bhar.
A little of a bad thing is as bad as much of it.

Jaisā man harām meṅ, taisā Hari meṅ hoë,
Chalā jāë Baikunṭh meṅ rok sake nā koë.
Fix thy mind on God, as thou hast fixed it on evil and thou shalt go to Heaven, and there shall be none to stay thee.
(When the wicked man turneth away from the wickedness that he hath committed and doeth that which is lawful and right he shall save his soul alive. Ezek. xviii, 27.)

Jaisā mān, vaisā dān.
As the respect, so the alms.

Jaisā muṅh, vaisā thappaṛ.
As the face, so the blow.
(As the burden, so the bearer; that is, the punishment of every crime will be in proportion to its magnitude.)

Jaisan dekhe gāoṅ kī rīt, taisan kare log se prīt. E. Wom.
Be friendly with the people in the fashion of the village.

Jaisan ko taisan, suktī ko baigan.
Well matched, like the egg-plant and dried fish.
(To signify that things are not well matched: used in a satirical sense.)

Jaisā pīve pānī, vaisī bole bānī.
As he drinks the water, so he speaks the language.
(The man is like his country.)

Jaisā rājā, vaisī parjā.
As the king, so his subjects.

Jaisā sotā, vaisī dhārā.
As the spring, so the stream.

Jaisā suī chor, vaisā bajjar chor.
Steal a pin, steal an anvil.

Jaisā sūt, vaisī pheṭī; jaisī mā, vaisī beṭī. Wom.
As the thread, so the skein; as the mother so the daughter.

Jaisā terā denā lenā, vaisā merā gānā bajānā.
As you pay, so will I sing.
(No supper, no song.)

Jaisā terā ghuṅghar, piyā, taisī hīṅg hamārī.
As your empty pods, my friend, so my assafœtida.
(Tit for tat: two rogues having made an exchange, one gave earth smeared over with assafœtida instead of the drug, and the other paid him with pulse, that had been blighted and the pods of which were empty.)

Jaisā terā khoṭ rupayā, taisā merā khokhar paisā.
As your bad silver, so my bad copper.

Jaisā terā non-pānī, taisā merā kām jānī.
As your wages, so my work.

Jaisā ūṅṭ lambā, taisā gadhā khavās.
Tall as a camel with an ass for servant.
(Tall men are generally considered to be simpletons.)

Jaise chiṛyoṅ meṅ ḍhel.
As a hawk among sparrows.

Jaise dām, vaisā kām.
As the pay, so the work.

Jaise ek bār, vaise hazār bār.
As it is once, so will it be a thousand times.

Jaise Har gun gāë, taise gāl bajāë.
As he worships God, so he makes a noise.
(Spoken of one who does not discriminate between those who serve him well or ill, allusion to the articulations made in worshipping Shiva only.)

Jaise Hasan, vaise Husain. Mah.
As is Hasan, so is Husain.
(Both are alike; chips of the old block: six of

one and half a dozen of the other: Hasan and Husain the sons of Ali, are always worshipped together.)

Jaise kanthā ghar rahe, vaise rahe bides:
Jaise oṛhī kāmlī, vaisā oṛhā khes. Wom.
It is all one to me whether my husband stay at home or live abroad, As I would as soon wear a blanket as a shawl.
(Contentment.)

Jaise kī sevā kare, taisī āsā pūr. E.
As the master you serve, so the fulfilment of your hopes.

Jaise ko taisā.
Such for so.
(Paid in his own coin.)

Jaise ko taisā, Bābū ko bhainsā.
To each according to his quality; to the Rājā's son a buffalo.
(Honor to whom honor is due: a buffalo is more expensive than a cow.)

Jaise ko taisā mile, jūn Bāman ko Nāī;
Is ne kahī āshīrbād, un ārsī kāṛh dikhāī.
Met his match, as when Brāhman meets Barber: says the one 'God be with you' and the other shows his glass.
☞ When the Brāhman says *āshīrbād* (God be with you), it is customary to make him a present, and similarly when the barber shows his looking-glass his customer is expected to fee him.

Jaise ko taisā mile, suno Rājā Bhīl!
Lohe ko chūhā khā gayā, laṛkā le gaī chīl.
One turn deserves another, listen Rājā Bhīl! If rats can eat iron, a kite may carry off a child.
☞ This proverb is founded on the following story. A man having occasion to travel abroad left a quantity of iron in charge of a friend. On his return after several years, his friend told him the rats had eaten up the iron. He said nothing, but waiting an opportunity seized the other's child, concealed him, and told his father he had seen a kite carry him off. On the other's alledging the impossibility of the thing, his friend made the above reply.

Jaise ko taisā: parakhne ko paisā!
Tit for tat: coins are tested!

Jaise miyāṅ kāṭh, vaise san kī ḍāṛhī.
As the gentleman is made of wood, so is his beard of tow.
(Spoken in contempt of any one.)

Jaise murde pe sau man miṭṭī, vaisī hazār man. Mah.
One ton of earth on a corpse is as good as a hundred tons.

Jaise nāg nātha, taise sāṅp nātha.
To slay a snake is as good as slaying a serpent.
(Six of one and half a dozen of the other.)

Jaise Nīm Nāth, taise Bakāeṅ Nāth.
Bakāyan Nāth is no better than Nīm Nāth.
(Nīm Nāth and Bakāyan Nāth are personifications of the *Nīm* and *Bakāyan* trees, which are both very bitter and useful and belong to the same family.)

Jaise sājan āe, taiso bichhaunā bichhāe.
As the guest, so the seat.

Jaise Ūdho, vaise Bhān; na in ke choṭī, na un ke kān.
Like Ūdho like Bhān; one has no locks and the other no ears.

Jaisī bandagī, vaisā inām.
As the service, so the reward.

Jaisī bahe biār, pīṭh tab taisī dīje.
From whatever quarter the wind blows you must turn your back towards it.
(Sail before the wind, or swim with the tide. It also means that you must conform to or act according to circumstances. Pull down your hat on the windy side.)

Jaisī gaīṅ thīṅ vaisī āīṅ, haq mahar kā boriyā lāīṅ. Mah. Wom.
She came back as she had gone, and brought a mat for her marriage portion.
(Ill luck.)

Jaisī dāī āp chhināl, vaisī jāne sab sansār. Wom.
As a wet-nurse is wanton, so she thinks every woman a wanton.

Jaise Gangā nahāe, vaisā phal pāe.
As you bathe in the Ganges, so will you reap your reward.

Jaisī hot hotabbitā, vaisī upje buddh;
Honahār hirde base, bisar jāt sab suddh.
As it is fated, so will he have sense; As it is fated his heart will dictate, and deprive him of his sense.

Jaisī māī, vaisī jāī. Wom.
As the mother, so the daughter.

Jaisī karnī, vaisī bharnī.
As you do, so will you receive. [*dekh,*

Jaisī karnī, vaisī bharnī; hove na hove karke
As you do, so will you receive; try and see if it is not so.
(As you measure so shall it be meted out to you again.)

Jaisī nīyat, vaisī barakat.
As the intent, so the blessing.

Jaisī phūaṛ āp chhināl, taisī lagāve kul brohār.
As the harlot is herself wanton, so will she corrupt her family.
(Evil communications corrupt good manners.)

Jaisī rūh, vaise farishte. Mah.
As the soul, so the angels.
(Which come to receive it at the time of death. To express that every one will be rewarded according to his deeds; it is generally used in a bad sense. It also means that people or things are well matched in a satirical sense.)

Jaisī terī bhagat, vaisī merī āshīrbād.
As your reception, so my benediction.

Jaisī terī phāphaṛ kodo, vaisī merī hing. Mah.
As your millet, so my assafœtida.
(Assafœtida is used to season millet and similar grains.)

Jaisī terī tānī, Baniye, vaisā merā bunnā.
As your thread, Baniyā, so my weaving.
Jaisī terī tānī, vaisī merī bharnī.
Like warp, like woof.
(Tit for tat.)
Jaisī terī til-chaulī, vaisā merā gīt. E. Wom.
As your fee, my song shall be.
Jā ke kāran pahrī sārī, vohī ṭāng rahī ughāṛī. Wom.
The same leg is exposed for which I had put on the skirt.
(Position not improved by marriage.)
Jā ke pās rahiye, tā hī kī sī kahiye.
Espouse the cause of him with whom you live.
Jā kī āchhī sās, vā kā hī ghar vās;
Jā kī sās nakārā, vā kā nahīn guzārā. Rus. Wom.
Who has a good mother-in-law has the whole house; Who has a bad mother-in-law cannot live long in the house.
Jā ko ḍanḍā, jā ko gāē, mat karo koī hāē hāē.
As he has the stick, so he'll have the cow, and don't you howl over it.
(Don't cry over spilt milk: what can't be cured must be endured.)
Jā ko jaiso subhāo, jāegā jīū se:
Nīm na mīṭhā hoē, sīch guṛ ghīū se.
As your nature, so will it be all your life:
The bitter *nīm* becomes not sweet though nourished with sugar and butter.
Jā ko jāṅ suārath sadhe, soī tāhi suhāt,
Chor na pyārī chāndnī jaise kārī rāt.
What promoteth one's own end is sweet, as the thief loveth not the moonlight as he doth a dark night.
Jā ko loh, tā ko soh.
All is his, whose is the iron.
(Might is right.)
Jā ko rākhe sāīyāṅ, mār na sakke koē.
Whom God protects none can slay.
(What God will, no frost can kill.)
Jā ko Rām rachchhak, tā kā kaun bhachchhak. Hin.
Whom Rām protects none can slay.
Jalāne ko phūns nahīn, aur tāpne ko koelā.
No straw for burning and she wants charcoal to warm herself.
Jalebiyoṅ kī rakhvālī aur choṭṭī kutiyā!
A hungry dog set to watch the sweets!
Jale ghar kī baleṅḍī.
The ridge of a burnt house.
(A man who survives his family.)
Jale hue to patthar mārā karte haiṅ.
The offended throw stones.
Jale hue yūṅhī kahā karte haiṅ.
Just as the offended talk.
(*i. e.* they abuse him who has offended them.)
Jale ko jalānā, namak mirach lagānā.
To burn the wound and rub in salt and pepper.
(To add injury to insult.)

Jale pāoṅ kī billī. Mah. Wom.
A cat with a burnt paw.
(Said of a wily woman who is continually eaves-dropping and pumping secrets.)
Jale parāī dhī aur hanse baṭāū log.
A man's daughter is burnt alive (*satī*) and the spectators laugh.
Jale phaphole phoṛte haiṅ.
He breaks burnt blisters.
(From the hatred in the heart, ill words come into the mouth: to vent one's rage on any one.)
Jal mai Bhagwān hai.
Water is godlike.
(Cleanliness is next to godliness.)
Jal meṅ base kamodnī, aur chandā base akās;
Jo jan jā ke man base, so jan tā ke pās.
The *nymphæa* dwells in water, and the moon in the sky; but he that resides in the heart of a man, is always with him.
(This species of *nymphæa* expands its flowers at night and is hence supposed to be in love with the moon.)
Jal meṅ khaṛī piyāsoṅ mare. Wom.
Standing in water, she dies of thirst.
Jal meṅ machhlī, nau nau kuṭyā bakhrā.
The fish is in the water, and the people are dividing it into nine shares.
(Don't count your chickens before they are hatched.)
Jal sūr Bāman, ran sūr Chhattrī,
Kalam sūr Kāeth, ganḍ sūr Khattrī.
Brāhman is lord of the water, Chhatrī is lord of the field, Kāyath is the lord of the pen, Khatrī is lord of the back (coward).
(The peculiarities of the four castes.)
Jalte kī jāī, garīb ke gale lagāī.
The daughter of misfortune married to poverty.
Jamāat, karāmāt,
A following commands respect.
(See under *akele dukele kā Allāh belī.*)
Jama lage Sarkār kī, aur Mirzā kheleṅ phāg.
The revenue is the Government's and Mirzā is enjoying himself.
(On the proceeds thereof.)
Jamnā kināre ghar kiyā, qarz kāṛh ke khān,
Jab āve koī māṅgne, gaṛap Jamnā meṅ jān.
He builds his house on the Jamnā bank with borrowed money, And when his creditor comes to ask after his loan he is ready throw himself into the river.
Jam se burī janet. Hin.
Better Hell than the plagues of a marriage procession.
Jānā apne bas, ānā parāē bas.
To go is at one's own option, but to return depends on another's.
Jānā hai, rahnā nahīn; jānā bisve bīs:
Aise sahaj suhāg par kaun gundhāve sīs?
Go we must, we cannot remain; of this there is no doubt: Who would deck her hair for such a short married life?
(The above couplet is said to have been delivered by Amīr Khusro on his death-bed.)

Jānā hai, rahnā nahīn, mohe andesa aur,
Jagah banāī hai nahīn, baiṭhoge kis ṭhaur?
Depart I must, I cannot stay, I am full of anxious care; no place (my soul) have you prepared, what seat can you have there?

Janam janam ko chhuṭ gaī.
Released from birth after birth.
(The *summum bonum* of believers in metempsychosis, as all Hindūs are.)

Janam ke dukhiyā, karam ke hīn; tin kā Deo tilangvā kīn. E.
Wretched from birth and unfortunate are those of whom God hath made soldiers.
(*Tilangā*, properly Telugu, a soldier in Northern parlance.)

Janam ke dukhiyā, nām Sadāsukh.
Wretched from birth and called Fortunate.
(Said when penury at home affects the appearance of wealth abroad.)

Janam ke kambakht, nām Bakhtāvar Singh.
Unfortunate from birth and named Mr. Luck.

Janam ke mangtā, nām Dātā Rām.
Born of a beggar and called My Lord Bountiful.

Janam ke sāthī hain, karam ke sāthī nahīn.
Companions of your birth, but not of your fate.

Janam na dekhā boriyā, supne ā khāṭ.
He never saw a mat in all his life and he dreams of a bed!

Janam-patrī kī bidh to milā lo!
Compare the details of the horoscopes!
(Never be in a hurry. Point of the proverb lies in the custom of ascertaining if the horoscopes of the parties 'agree' in the astrological sense before a marriage can be entered into.)

Janam-patr sab dekhte hain, karam-patr koī nahīn dekhtā.
All consult the horoscope, but none the Book of Fate.

Jānan-vāle jāniye, mūrakh man pachhtāë,
Karnī bhūlī āpnī, auron dosh lagāë.
The wise know, though the fool grieves for the duties he himself forgot, while he laid the blame on others.

Jān bachī, lākhon pāë.
Save life, save millions.

Jane jane kā man rakhte, besvā rah gaī bānjh.
By pleasing every one the harlot has grown barren.
(Allusion to the well known fact that harlots do not as a rule bear children.)

Jānetī chilam jin kā par charhela angārī. E.
The pipe knows what it is to bear the fire.

Jānevāle ke hazār raste, dhūnḍnevāle kā ek.
The run-away has a thousand roads, the pursuer but one.

Jānevāle sipāhiyā ke ke rokelā? E. Wom.
Who can ever stop a soldier on his way?

Jangal Jaṭ na chheṛiye, haṭṭī bīch kirāṛ,
Bhūkā Turak na chheṛiye, ho jāë jī kā jhāṛ.
Insult not the Jāṭ in the wilds, nor the shopman in his shop, nor a hungry Turk, or they will take your life.

Jangal men khetī nahīn, bastī men nahīn ghar.
No field in the wilds, no house in village.

Jangal men mangal, bastī men virān:
Jā ghar bhang na sānchare, vā ghar bhūt samān.
Revelry in the jungle and a wilderness in the town: where is no *bhang*, it is the haunt of ghosts.
(A saying of *bhang* takers.)

Jangal men mangal bastī men kaṛākā.
A feast in the forest and a fast in the town.

Jangal men mor nāchā kis ne jānā?
Who ever heard of a peacock dancing in the forest?
(Applied to one who has displayed wealth, abilities, splendor, &c., among strangers, or those who cannot judge of his excellence, and not in the place where he is known. Wasting his sweetness on the desert air.)

Jangal men motī kī qadr nahīn.
Pearls are of no value in a desert.
(A man of talents and learning is of no estimation among ignorant people. Full many a gem of purest ray serene The dark unfathomed caves of ocean bear. No man is a hero to his valet.)

Jān hai to jahān hai.
While life is yours, the world is yours.

Jān jāë, māl na jāë.
Life may go, but not my money.
(Said of a miser.)

Jān kā mūnh nahīn karte, rupaë kā mūnh karte hain.
No regard for his life, great regard for his cash.
(Said of a miser.)

Jān kā sadqā māl, izzat kā sadqā jān.
Wealth is sacrificed for life, and life for honor.

Jān ke sāth dushman lagā huā hai.
He has a mortal enemy.

Jān ke sāth jeoṛā.
This rope will last as long as my life.
(*Jeoṛā*, a thick rope; hence any entanglement or encumbrance, especially a disagreeable wife or husband.)

Jān kī jān gaī, īmān kā īmān.
Lost is life and lost is honor.

Jān māre Bāniyā, pahchān māre chor.
The Baniyā cheats his dearest friend, and the thief all he knows.

Jān men jān ā gaī.
Life restored to life.
(Refreshed and revived.)

Jannā aur marnā barābar. Wom.
The throes of child-birth are as the agonies of death.

Jān na pahchān, "khālā barī, salām." Mah. Wom.
Nor known nor recognized, and "good morrow, aunt."

Jān sab ko piyārī hai.
Life is dear to all.

Jān sab men barābar hai.
The life is the same in all living things.

Jān se hāth dho baiṭhe hain.
He has washed his hands of his life.

Jāntā chor gāon ujāṛe.
A familiar thief depredates the village.

Jānte kā dil, an-jānte kā kalejā. Wom.
The soul of the wise and the heart of the foolish.
(Ignorance is responsible for most of the cruelty in the world.)

Jantī na ḍhol bajtā.
Had you not been born no drum would have been beaten.
(Said of a fool whose existence is looked upon as a disgrace to his family. Drums are beaten always on the birth of a son, not on the birth of a daughter.)

Jāo Naipāl, sāth jāë kapāl. E.
Go to Naipāl and your fate will follow you.

Jāo, pūt, Dakkhan, vohī karam ke lakkhan. Wom.
My son, if you go to Deccan, your fate will still be the same.

Jare jāin, sūjhe Sūkar. E. Wom.
Going to the burning place and thinking of (the Planet) Venus.
(*Shukr*, Venus, is an unlucky star—the point is "thinking of the omen when she is going to be sati or burn with her husband.")

Jāṛe men rūī yā dūī.
In the winter cotton (clothes), or a concubine!

Jaṛ kāṭte jāen, pānī dete jāen!
He first cuts its roots and then waters it!

Jaṛ ko pakṛo, shākhon ko kyon pakaṛte ho?
Hold on to the roots; why hang on to the branches?
(Look to the chief, not to the subordinates; also, worship God only and not the idols.)

Jas dūlah, tas banī barāt. Hin.
As the bridegroom, so the wedding party.

Jā se jā ko kām, soī tā ko Rām. Hin.
He is thy God, whom thou hast to serve.

Jas kele ke pāt men, pāt pāt men pāt.
Tas gyānī kī bāt men, bāt bāt men bāt.
As the plantain's leaves are leaves within leaves, So the wise man's words are words within words.

Jas kiyā, tas pāyā.
As you did, so have you received.

Jas mukund tas pāval ghoṛī: Bidhnā ās milāval joṛī!
The horse is fitted to the rider: God hath made a good match!

Jāṭ kahe, 'sun, Jāṭnī, yā hī gāon men rahnā:
Ūnṭ bilaiyā le gaī, to "hān jī, hān jī" kahnā.'
Saith the Jāṭ, 'Listen, wife, we must live in this village; (when they say) a cat walked off with a camel, we must chime in.'

Jatne ke tīn roṭī, talne ke ṭikṛī, alag karo tīn roṭī ene lāvā ṭikṛī. E. Wom.
One loaf is equal to three cakes, so let go the three cakes and bring the one loaf.

'Jāṭ, re Jāṭ, tere sir par khāṭ' 'Telī, re telī, tere sir par kolhū.' 'Tuk to milā hī nahīn.' 'Tuk nahīn milā to kiyā hai? bojhon to maregā.'
'O friend Jāṭ, there is a bed on your head. 'O friend oilman, on your head there is an oil-press!' 'But that doesn't rhyme?' 'Rhyme, or no rhyme, the weight's enough for you.'
(A skit at the horse-play these people are fond of indulging in.)

Jau-farosh, gandum-numā. Pers.
He shows you wheat and sells you barley.
(A swindler.)

Jauhar ko jauharī pahchāne.
Only jewellers can test gems.

Jau ke khet kanduā upje!
Millet growing in a field of barley!
(A black sheep.)

Jau ko gaë, satuānī ko āë. E.
Started for barley comes for barley flour.
(Unfair demand: a shilling's worth for six pence.)

Jaule Daliddar Dādā chhīpā lāvat, table hamrā bhuiën men do. Mag.
While Father Poverty is bringing me a plate, give me some food on the ground.

Javāb-i-jāhilān bāshad khamoshī. Pers.
Answer the ignorant with silence.

Javāb Turkī ba Turkī.
Retort Turkish for Turkish.
(A Roland for an Oliver.)

Javān ḍarāve bhāgne se, būṛhā ḍarāve marne se.
Youth threatens to run away, and old age threatens to die.
(Observation of native habits.)

Javānī aur us par sharāb, dūnī āg lagtī hai.
A youth in his cups is as fire upon fire.

Javānī divānī.
Youth is mad.

Javānī men gadhe par bhī joban hotā hai.
Even she-ass in her youth is fair to look upon.

Javān jāë Pattāl, buṛhiyā mānge bhatār. E.
The maidens are dying and the grandmothers demanding husbands.
(Upside down: topsyturvy; incongruity.)

Javānoṅ ko chalā chalī, buṛhiyā ko byāh kī paṛī.
The young men are dying and the old women thinking of marrying.
(See preceding.)

Javān rāṅḍ, buṛhe sāṅḍ!
The young women are widows and the old men lusty.
(*Tempora mutantur.*)

Je bahut dhadhalā, so āg meṅ paṛelā. Bhoj.
Who makes a bonfire will fall into the fire.
(Playing with edged tools)

Jeb meṅ nahīṅ khīlī kī ḍalī, chhailā phire galī galī. E. Wom.
Without a farthing in his pocket the blockhead strays from shop to shop.
(*Khīlī kī ḍalī, lit*, a piece of betel nut.)

Jekar maiyā pūā pakāve, tekar dhīyā lilke! Bhoj.
The girl whose mother makes cakes must cry for them.
(The cobbler's wife is worst shod, and the tailor's worst clothed.)

Jekar purkhā na dekhal poē, tekā ghar khur bandī hoē? Bhoj.
Shall the man who never saw a potherb have a horse shod in his stable?
(Said of a self-made man, or an upstart, who gives himself airs.)

Jekrā bīghā bhar kapās, tekrā ḍāṅre ḍarā nā. Bhoj.
You can fine him who has a cotton field.
(Because he can pay.)

Jekrā horī aisan Ṭhākur, tekrā Jam ke ḍar? E.
Why should he fear the Angel of Death who has such a (merciful) God?

Jekre ghuṛvā baiṭhīṅ, tekre āṅṛ dāgīṅ. Bhoj.
He injures him whose horse he rides.
(Ingratitude.)

Jekrī joe tekre pās, dekhan-hārā tā ke ās. Bhoj.
The wife is his who has her, the looker on can only hope.

Je morā lāl ke na, se kauna kām ke? Bhoj. Wom.
If he be not my son, what has he to do with me?

Je mūṅh chīrelā, se to āhār dele chāhe? Bhoj.
Shall He not give the mouth food that opened it?

Jeoṛe se nāṛā ghisnā hai. Wom.
It is a thick rope that I have to rub my neck with.
(What can't be cured must be endured. Cattle and wives must rub along in their tethers.)

Je pūt pardesī bhaile, deo pittar sab se gaile. E. Wom.
The sons who have gone to foreign lands, have gone from the worship of Gods and ancestors.

Je Pāṅṛe ke patrā meṅ, se Paṅṛiāiṅ ke aṅchrā meṅ. E. Wom.
What is writ in the Paṇḍit's book, his wife hath in her wrapper.

Jeṭhe laṛke laṛkī kī shādī Jeṭh meṅ nahīṅ karte. Hin. Superstition.
The first born is never wed in the month of Jeṭh (May and June.)

Jeṭh Jeṭhe, Āsāṛ heṭe. Hin.
(The weather is) best in Jeṭh and worst in Asāṛh.
(*Jeṭh* is May-June, *Asāṛh* July-August.)

Jeṭh ke bharose peṭ. Hin.
Pregnant on expectations from her husband's elder brother.
(Said of the pregnant wife of a younger brother that earns nothing in the Hindū joint family.)

Jhagṛā jhūṭā, qabzā sachchā.
Litigation is wrong, possession is right.
(Possession is nine points of the law.)

Jhagṛe kī tīn jaṛ; zan, zamīn, zar.
Contention's roots are three: women, land and gold.

Jhāṅṭ upāṛe se murda halkā nahīṅ hotā.
A corpse is not made lighter by plucking off the hair.

Jhaṛ berī kā kāṅṭā.
The thorns of a bramble.
(To describe one who sticks fast and from whom it is hard to disengage one's self: a leech.)

Jhaṛ berī ke jangal meṅ billī sher.
In a forest of brambles a cat is a tiger.
(She has it all her own way owing to the closeness of the thorns.)

Jhāṛ bhī Baniye kā bairī hai.
Even a bush is an enemy to a Baniyā.
(Because it can hide a thief. In India every man's hand is against the Baniyā.)

Jhāṛ bichhāī kāmlī, aur rahe nimāne soē.
He dusted and spread his blanket, and lay on it without.
(Said of *faqīrs*: contentment.)

Jhaṭ paṭ kī ghānī, ādhā tel ādhā pānī.
Half water and half oil comes out of a hurried squeeze.
(*Ghānī* is one out-turn of the oil-mill and if the work be done hurriedly, the oil is bad: haste makes waste.)

Jhīṅgar baiṭhe bakucha par kahas, ki 'ham hīṅ mālik haiṅ.' E.
The cricket sitting on a bundle of clothes says, "I am the owner."
(Crickets are very destructive to cotton goods in India.)

Jhopṛī meṅ rahe, mahloṅ kā khuāb dekhe.
He lives in a hut and dreams of palaces.

Jhoṭe jhoṭe ṭakkareṅ laṛeṅ, jhuṇḍiyoṅ kā nās ho.
When buffaloes fight the plantation is ruined.

Jhuke jo koī us se jhuk jāiye, ruke āp se us se ruk jāiye.

If any one bow to you, bow to him; if he hesitate, do you hesitate.
(You scratch my back and I'll scratch yours.)

Jhūṭā jūṭh se burā jo sone kā hoē.
A lie is worse than leavings, though they be [of gold.
(*i. e.* To the purpose.)

Jhūṭhā khāiye mīṭhe ke lālach.
Leavings are eaten only when they are [sweet.

Jhūṭā mare na shahr pāk hoē.
Neither does the liar die, nor is the city [purified.

Jhūṭ barābar pāp nahīṅ hai.
There is no sin like a lie.

Jhūṭ bolnā aur khe khānā barābar hai.
To tell a lie is to eat dirt.

Jhūṭ bolne meṅ rakkhā kiyā hai?
What is gained by telling a lie?

Jhūṭ bolne meṅ sarfā kyā?
What occasion is there for economy in tell- [ing lies?
(When a man has once transgressed the bounds of truth, there is nothing to restrain him within any bounds.)

Jhūṭ-bolne-vāloṅ ko pahle maut ātī thī, ab bukhār bhī nahīṅ ātā.
In former days liars died, now they don't [even get fever.
(*O tempora, o mores!*)

Jhūṭ bolūṅ tere mūṅh par.
I will tell a lie before your face.
(To be brazen faced.)

Jhūṭe ghar ko ghar kaheṅ, aur sāṅche ghar ko gor: Ham chale ghar āpne, aur log machāven shor.
It is a false home they call a home, the true home is the grave: I go to my home and yet the people weep.

Jhūṭe hāth se kuttā bhī nahīṅ mārtā.
He does not even beat a dog till he has wiped his hands.
(Said of a miser. *Jhūṭhā hāth* is a hand from which the food eaten with it is not yet wiped off, so the point is that the miser is afraid of losing even the food sticking to his hand after eating.)

Jhūṭe jag patiyāē.
Liars obtain credit in this world. *Or* we believe in a deceitful world.
(A saying taken from the Vedantic philosophy which denies the reality of external objects. Applied when an impostor obtains credit.)

Jhūṭe kā mūṅh kālā, sachche kā bol bālā.
The liar's face is black, and the true man's prosperous.
(Tell the truth and shame the Devil. *Kālā mūṅh* black faced is idiomatic for disgraced.)

Jhūṭe ke āge sachchā ro mare.
Truth weeps before a lie.

Jhūṭe ke mūṅh meṅ bū ātī hai.
The liar's mouth stinks.

Jhūṭe kī kuchh pat nahīṅ, sajjan; jhūṭ na bol; Lakh-patī kā jhūṭh se do kuṇḍī ho mol.
The liar has no credit; speak no lies, my friend; Lies will reduce the lord of thousands to a farthing's worth.

Jhūṭe kī nahīṅ bāhvartī.
The liar has no success.

Jhūṭe ko ghar tak pahoṅchānā chāhiye.
The liar should be escorted home.
(By questioning and cross-questioning you pump out the truth.)

Jhūṭī bāt banā le, pānī meṅ āg lagā le.
To tell a lie is to set water on fire.

Jhūṭ kahe so laḍḍū khāē, sāṅch kahe so mārā jāē.
Tell a lie and get sweets; tell the truth and lose your life.

Jhūṭ ke pāoṅ nahīṅ hote.
Falsehood has no feet.
(Won't stand examination.)

Jhūṭ kī nāo manj-dhār ḍūbtī hai.
Falsehood's boat sinks in midstream.

Jhūṭ na bole to peṭ āphar jāē.
Lie he must or burst.

Jhūṭ na bole to peṭ phaṭ jāē.
Lie he must or burst.

Jhūṭoṅ kā bādshah.
The king of liars.

Jhūṭoṅ kā ghar nahīṅ bastā.
The house of the liar never prospers.
(Cheating play never thrives.)

Jhūṭ se kām nahīṅ chaltā. Mercantile.
Business can't thrive on lies.

Jīat pitā kī pūchhī na bāt, mare pitā ko dūdh aur bhāt.
He cared nothing for his father while he lived, but now that he is dead he offers milk and rice.
(Ungrateful offspring: it benefits the living to offer to the dead in Hindū ideas.)

Jī bahut chaltā hai, magar ṭaṭṭū nahīṅ chaltā.
His fancy soars high, but his pony won't go.
(Great hankerings in a low state of life.)

Jībh jalī, na savād āyā.
Nor the tongue touched, nor the taste known.
(Said of a very small quantity of food.)

Jībh jane ek bār, māṅ jane bār bār.
The tongue brings forth but once, the bearing woman oft.
(What is once said cannot be unsaid.)

Jī chāhe bairāg ko aur kunbā phāṛe gōṅṛ.
His heart longs to be a monk, and his family worries him to death.
(To stick to his worldly affairs)

Jidhar jalnā dekheṅ, tidhar tāpeṅ.
Where they see the fire burning, there they go to warm themselves.

Jidhar Maulā, udhar Āsafu'd-daula.
Where God is there is Asafu'd-daula.

☞ Āsafu'd-daula was a Nawāb of Lucknow, who was greatly famed for his charity. The story goes that once a beggar came to him and asked him for a thousand rupees. The Nawāb gave him ten rupees saying that only that much was in his fate. The beggar refused to take it, upon which the Nawāb asked him to come over next day. When the beggar came to him the next day, the Nawāb placed before him two bags previously filled, one with rupees and the other with coppers and told the beggar to take one of them. Unfortunately he took the one filled with coppers. Hence proverb.

Jidhar Rab, udhar sab.
Where God is, there is every thing.

Jigar jigar hai, digar digar hai.
Liver is liver, and gall is gall.
(The skin is nearer than the coat: blood is thicker than water.)

Jī hai, to jahān hai.
While life is yours the world is yours.

Jī jāē, ghī na jāē.
Life may go, but not my butter (money).

Jījā ke māl par sālī matvālī. Wom.
The sister-in-law vain of her brother-in-law's wealth.
(It is nothing to her: folly.)

Jijmān chāhe suarg ko jāē, chāhe nark ko, mujhe dahī pūrī se kām.
Let the client go to heaven or hell, I only care for my cake and sweets.
(*Jijmān* is the client of a priest.)

Jī kā bairī jī.
Life is an enemy to life.
(Animal eats animal.)

Jī kahīn lagtā nahīn, jab dil kahīn lag jāē hai.
Life is no longer one's own, when the heart is fixed on another.

'Jī' kaho, 'jī' kahlāo.
Say 'Sir' and you will be called 'Sir.'

Jī ke badle jī.
Life for life.
(Eye for eye and tooth for tooth.)

Jīnā thoṛā, āsā bahut.
Life is short, but hope is long.
(Hope sustains the world.)

Jin barhā har charo, so kaise charen puār. Agric.
How should the animal that has lived on green grass eat straw.
(Accustomed to luxury, reduced to misery.)

Jin ḍhūnḍhā tin pāīyān gahre pānī paiṭh,
Bak bichārā kyā kare rahā kināre baiṭh?
He that searcheth in deep water shall find,
But what shall the crane obtain that sitteth on the shore?
(In order to make profits you must run some risk.)

Jin din dekhe ve kusam, gaī so bīt bahār; Ab, alī, rahī gulāb men apat kaṭīlī ḍār.
That spring, in which we saw the blossoms, is gone; Now, oh bee, only the thorns remain upon the rose.
(Make hay while the sun shines.)

Jīne se dūr, marne ke nazdīk.
Away from life and near to death.
(With one leg in the grave.)

Jin jāē unhīn lajāē.
The shame is his who begot them.
(Unworthy sons.)

Jin kā muṅh nahīn dekhte, unkā pāon chhūnā paṛtā hai.
We have to kiss the feet of him whose face we cannot see.

Jin kī bolī men 'dagā,' un ke dil men kyā dagā na hogī?
How full of guile their hearts must be when their speech is filled with it!
(A bad pun; said of Kābulīs in India who usually say '*dagā dagā*' 'of this, of this, but in Hindustānī "guile, deceit," when they want to know the price of anything.)

Jin kī yahān chāh, un kī vahān bhī chāh. Hin Wom.
Who are loved in this world are loved of heaven.
(*i. e.* They die early whom the gods love.)

Jin ko chāo ghanerā, un ko dukh bahoterā.
Who are loved most are troubled most.
(Spoilt children.)

Jin pāēn panthī nahīn, tinhen det gajrāj, bikh dete bikhā mile Sāhab garīb-navāj.
The All-bountiful gives a stately elephant to him who is shoeless, and instead of poison he finds a bride.
☞ A merchant importuned by a beggar for *bhik* (alms), gave him an order on his correspondent for *bikh* (poison), in order to get rid of him; the correspondent's daughter, however, being named Bikhā, he misread the order, and treating the mendicant with great respect, mounting him on an elephant, etc., made him his son-in-law. The proverb is partly a sarcasm on the merchant's script, called Mahājanī, which is singularly indistinct and the use of which leads to many ridiculous and perplexing mistakes.

Jis ban sūā na sāmrā, vān kāgā khāēn kapūr.
In the wood where there is no parrot nor cuckoo, the black crow eats camphor.
(A one-eyed man among the blind: alludes to the native notion that parrots and cuckoos live on camphor.)

Jis bartan men khānā, usī men chhed karnā.
To make a hole in the vessel out of which one has eaten.
(To prove ungrateful, or injure one's benefactor.)

Jis darakht ke sāē men baiṭhe, usī kī jaṛ kāṭe.
He cuts the roots of the tree which shelters him.
(He bites the hand that feeds him.)

Jise hayā nahīn, use īmān nahīn.
Lack shame, lack faith.

Jise khāne ko mile yon, voh kamāne ko jāē kyon?
Who gets food without working, why should he work?

Jise Khudā rakkhe, use kaun chakkhe?
Whom God guards none can injure.
(Whom God will no frost can kill.)

Jise piyā chāhe, vohī suhāgan, kyā sāṅvrī, kyā gorī?
Who hath her husband's love a husband hath indeed, be she fair or be she dark.

Jis ghar būṛhā na baṛā, voh ghar ḍiggam ḍiggā.
The house without an elder is tottering to its fall.

Jis ghar hoe kuchalyā nārī ; sāñjh bhor ho us kī khuārī. Rus.
The house that has a bad wife is on the eve of ruin.

Jis ghar hoe pūrakh kuchalyā, us ghar hove khīr kā dalyā. Rus.
The house that has a bad husband gets gruel for its milk and rice.
(*Dalyā* is coarse food in India and of course very inferior to *khīr*.)

Jis ghar meṅ sampat nahīṅ, tā sūṅ bhalā bides.
It is better to go abroad, than to remain at home in poverty.

Jis ghar nārī phūṛī, oh ghar jāno kūṛī. Rus.
The house of a slut is no better than a dunghill.

Jis hāṅḍī meṅ khāeṅ, usī meṅ chhed kareṅ.
He makes a hole in the dish he fed from.
(See above, *jis bartan meṅ*, etc,)

Jis kā āṅḍū bike, voh badhiyā kyoṅ kare. Mercantile.
If the entire bull will sell, why castrate him?

Jis kā Banyā yār, us ko dushman kyā darkār?
Who has a *Banyā* for his friend needs no enemy.

Jis kā chiknā dekhā phisal paṛe.
Wherever he sees a sleek countenance he slides upon it.
(Spoken of a time-server, who courts the favor of the great and prosperous, and suits his conversation to their inclinations.)

Jis kā chūegā, so chhavā legā.
Whose house leaks will repair it.

Jis kā chun, us kā pun.
The merit is his from whom the alms proceed.

Jis kā ḍar, vohī nahīṅ ghar. Wom.
Whom most I fear is not at home.
(*i. e.* my husband, so now I can do as I like.)

Jis kā fikr, us kā sikr.
What 's in the heart is on the tongue.
(Out of the fullness of the heart the mouth speaketh.)

Jis kā guīyāṅ nahīṅ, us kā kūkar guīyāṅ. Wom.
Who has no friend has a dog for her friend.

Jis kā jāve, vohī chor kahāve.
Who has lost the property is called the thief.
(A skit at the practice of the Police, who are apt to accuse the loser when they cannot trace the real offender.)

Jis kā kām, usī ko sāje; aur kare to ṭheṅgā bāje.
Do your own work and it will suit you; do another's and you will be laughed at.
(Every cobbler to his last.)

Jis kā khāiye an pānī, us kī kīje avādānī. Wom.
Bless him whose food you eat.

Jis kā khāiye, us kā gāiye.
Sing his praises who feeds you.

Jis kā khūn, usī kī gardan par.
The guilt of the murder is on the murderer's neck.

Jis kā marvā, us kā gīt. Wom.
The songs are in his praise whose is the marriage bower.
(Who pays the fees hears the song.)

Jis kā pallā bhārī, vohī jhuke.
If your pocket is full you can give.

Jis kā pāp, us kā bāp.
A man's sin is his father (master).

Jis kāran mūṅḍ muṅḍāyā, so dukh āge āyā.
The ill for which he shaved his head still gives him trouble.
☞ A silly fellow who complained of having to work for his bread was recommended to shave his head and become a mendicant; but he found begging much harder work than earning his livelihood.

Jis kāran pahnī sāṛī, wohī ṭāṅg rahī ughāṛī. Hin. Wom.
The leg is exposed for which I put on a gown.
(My marriage has not improved my condition.)

Jis kā tej, us kā bhej. Agric.
Who has the power has the rent.

Jis kā yār Kotvāl, use ḍar kāhe kā?
He need not fear who has the *Kotwāl* for a friend.
(*Kotwāl* is the native name still in use for the chief local police authority.)

Jis ke chār bhaiyā, māreṅ dhaul, chhīn leṅ rupayā.
He who has four brethren may knock you down and take your money.

Jis ke chār paise lo, unheṅ halāl karke khāo.
Whose pence you take, work faithfully for him.
(Be true to your salt.)

Jis ke dhī nahīṅ, us kī dehlī dhī. Hin. Wom.
Who has no daughter, looks upon his threshold as his daughter.
(Usually it is the daughter that gets the gifts of the native household, so while there is a daughter the beggars at the threshold get little. Hence the proverb.)

Jis ke dil meṅ rahm nahīṅ, voh qasāī hai.
Who feels no pity is a butcher.

Jis ke ghar bhoj, us ko bhāt nahīṅ.
Who gives a feast gets no rice himself.

Jis ke hāth ḍoī, us kā sab koī.
Who holds the ladle has the love.
(Cupboard love : who holds the purse has the power.)

Jis ke hoveṅ assī, voh kare khassī. Mah.
Who has eighty rupees must sacrifice a goat.
(Muhammadans are bound to give in alms (*zakāt*) one tenth of their money.)

Jis ke kāran jogan bhaī, voh saiyāṅ pardes. Wom.

For whom I am turned a *Jogan* (female ascetic) is gone abroad.
(Unrequited love.)

Jis ke liye chorī kī, vohī kahe chor.
For whom I have stolen calls me a thief.
(To describe ingratitude.)

Jis ke māṅ bāp jīte haiṅ, voh harām kā nahīṅ kahlātā.
Whose father and mother are alive is never called a bastard.
(As long as proof to the contrary is obviously forthcoming it is useless to make a false accusation.)

Jis ke nahīṅ pūt, voh kyā jāne māyā. Wom.
Who has no son knows no motherly feelings.

Jis ke paisā nahīṅ ho pās, us ko melā lage udās.
Who has no money in his pocket, finds the fair dull.
(Every one speaks of the fair, as things went with him there.)

Jis ke pās ḍhibuā, vohī hamārā babūā. E. Wom.
Who has the pence is 'your honour.'

Jis ke pās nahīṅ paisā, woh bhalā-mānas kaisā ?
If he has no money, can he be a gentleman?
(Money makes the gentleman. When Adam delved and Eve span, where was then the gentleman? Upstart a churl and gathered good, and thence did spring his gentle blood.)

"*Jis ke peshe meṅ bān, us kā gurū Shaitān.*" "*Hāṅ mehrbān.*"
"Whose trade ends in a *bān* has the devil for a priest." "True, kind sir."
(This is badinage: many trade names end in *bān*, as *fīl-bān*, *gāṛī-bān*, *shutur-bān*, &c., and so does *mehrbān*, 'kind sir,'—hence the wit of the retort.)

Jis ke sabab laṛāī ho, voh ādmī nahīṅ ;
Kāṅṭā hai ghar meṅ sī kā, yā gul kaner kā.
Who causes quarrels is not a man,
But is like a porcupine quill or an oleander flower in the house.
(There is a superstition that a porcupine quill or an oleander flower will breed strife in the house.)

Jis ke sir par jūtā rakh diyā, vohī bādshāh ho gayā.
On whose head I place my feet becomes a king.
(The boast of a saint.)

Jis ke sir par paṛtī hai, vohī jāntā hai.
He knows who feels.

Jis ke vāste roē, us kī āṅkh meṅ āṅsū bhī nahīṅ.
He has no tears for him for whom he weeps.
(Crocodile's tears.)

Jis kī āṅkh meṅ til, voh baṛā be-sil. Superstition.
Who has a flaw in his eye has a bad heart.

Jis kī bīvī se kām, us kī launḍī se kyā kām ?
Whose business is with the mistress, what has he to do with the maid?
(Go to the fountain head.)

Jis kī deg, us kī teg.
Who has the pot, has the sword.
(Who feeds his soldiers best is best served.)

Jis kī god meṅ baiṭhe, usī kī ḍāṛhī noche.
To pull the beard of him who carries you in his arms.

Jis kī jībh chaltī hai, us ke nau hal chalte haiṅ.
The power of the tongue is as the power of nine ploughs.
(Said of a braggart.)

Jis kī jorū andar, us kā nasībā Sikandar.
Whose wife has the run of the house is as lucky as Sikandar.
☞ This proverb is used by *mehtars* or sweepers in the service of the English to express the influence and emoluments of one whose wife serves in the house as an ayah to a lady: Sikandar is the native name for Alexander the Great.

Jis kī jūtī, usī kā sir.
To strike the head of a man with his own shoe.
(To refute a man out of his own mouth; to draw arrows out of a man's quiver: to feast a man at his own expense.)

Jis kī khāiye chandiyā, us kī hūjiye bandyā. Wom.
Be the slave of him whose bread you eat.

Jis kī lāṭhī, us kī bhaiṅs.
Who has the cudgel has the buffalo.
(Might is right. Club law. The good old rule, the honoured plan, that he should take who has the power and he should keep who can.)

Jis kī mahal meṅ maiyā, māṅge paisā mile rupaiyā.
Whose mother is in the palace, if he asks for a penny he gets a shilling.

Jis kī na phaṭī bivāī, voh kyā jāne pīr parāī ?
Who never had a sore heel, what can he know of another's pain?

Jis kī sīrat achchhī, us kī sūrat bhī achchhī.
Who is good natured has a good face.

Jis kī sīrat achchhī nahīṅ, us kī sūrat ko kiyā dekhnā ?
Who is not good natured, heed not her beautiful face.

Jis kī teg, us kī deg.
Who has the sword has the pot.
(Might is right.)

Jis ke bārah bīgah bāṅgā, us kī kamar meṅ ḍorā nahīṅ. Rus.
Who has twelve acres of cotton field, has not a rag to his back.

Jis kī deg, us kī teg.
Who has the pot, has the sword.
(Who feeds his soldiers best is best served.)

Jis ko Khudā bachāē, us par kabhī na āfat āē.
Whom God befriends know no troubles.

Jis ko rakhe Sāīyāṅ mār na sakke koē : bār na bīkā kar sake, jo jag bairī hoe.
Whom God protects none can injure and none can trouble, though the whole world be his foe.

Jis mūṅh se pān khāiye, tis mūṅh se koële na chabāiye.
Eat not charcoal with the same mouth that you eat betel.
(1st. Do not abuse him whom you have once commended. 2nd. Do not submit to indignity where you have formerly been treated with respect.)

Jis ne beṭī dī, us ne kiyā rakkhā?
Who has given his daughter has kept back [nothing.

Jis ne beṭī dī, us ne sab kuchh diyā.
Who gives his daughter gives his all.

Jis ne chīrā, vohī niregā.
Who opened the mouth will feed it.
(Take no thought for the morrow, for the morrow shall take thought for the things of itself: sufficient unto the day is the evil thereof. Mat. xi, 34.)

Jis ne dīyā, us ne pāyā.
Who gave hath now received.
(Allusion to the doctrine of the transmigration of souls, according to which it is believed that men are wealthy now in proportion to their charity in former lives.)

Jis ne kī be-hayāī, us ne khāī dūdh malāī.
Who loses all sense of shame eats milk and cream.
(Said of prostitutes.)

Jis ne kī sharm us ke phūṭe karm.
Modesty means misfortune.
(Said by prostitutes.)

Jis ne koṛā diyā voh ghoṛā bhī degā.
Who gave you a whip, will give you a horse also.
(Trust in God.)

Jis ne lagāī, vohī bujhāvegā.
Who has set it on fire will quench it.
(1st. A commotion is easily appeased by him that excited it. 2nd. The afflictions sent by God can only be alleviated by him. 3rd. A beggar's cry: God will appease my hunger by making people give me alms.)

Jis ne na dekhā ho bāgh, voh dekhe bilāī, Jis ne na dekhā ho ṭhag, voh dekhe qasāī.
Whoever has not seen a tiger let him look at a cat, and whoever has not seen a robber let him look at a butcher.

Jis ne na dekhī ho kannyā, voh dekhe kannyā kā bhāī.
Who has not seen the bride let him look at her brother.
(Judge by the family likeness.)

Jis ne randī ko chāhā, use bhī zavāl; aur jis ko randī ne chāhā, us kī bhī tabāhī!
Love a harlot and be ruined; be loved by a harlot and be ruined!

Jis rāh hī nahīṅ chalnā, us ke kos ginne se kyā kām?
What is the use of counting the miles on a road you have not to travel?

Jis shahr meṅ phūl bechīye, vahāṅ dhūl na uṛāīye.
Do not kick up the dust of the city where you once sold flowers.
(That is, if disgrace befall you where you were once respected, do not remain there.)

Jis ṭahnī par baiṭhe, usī ko kāṭe.
He cuts away the branch which supports him.
(1st. Extreme folly. 2nd. Ingratitude. It is an ill bird that befouls its own nest.)

Jis tan lāge, vohī jāne.
Who feels knows.
(It is the wearer that knows where the shoe pinches.)

Jītā so hārā, aur hārā so mūā.
Who wins loses, who loses dies.
(Said of a law-suit.)

Jīte āsā, mūë nirāsā.
Life is hopeful, death hopeless.

Jīte chāb chāb, mūë dāb dāb.
While he lived he chewed them, now he is dead they are buried.
(Said of a miser: *chabānā* is to chew whole grain: the point is that the miser ate pulse and other cheap grain whole, to save the cost of grinding and buried the savings thus made.)

Jīte haiṅ, nā marte haiṅ, sisak sisak dam bharte haiṅ.
I neither live, nor die, I breathe in agony.

Jīte jī kā melā hai.
While there is life there is company.

Jīte jī kā nātā hai.
Relationship lasts only for life.
(Used by way of expostulation to those who lament extravagantly over the dead.)

Jīte kā ghar aur mūë kā gor batā.
Point out a living man's house and a dead man's grave.

Jīte ke khūn meṅ hīrā dhundlā hotā hai.
Superstition.
In a living man's blood the diamond grows dull.

Jīte na pūchhe, mūë dhaṛ dhaṛ pīṭe.
Alive they cared nothing for them, dead they mourn them bitterly.
((i.) Ungrateful offspring. (ii.) A man's worth is known when he is dead.)

Jīte rahe to lānat kahnā!
Curse me if you live any longer!
(A *faqīr's* curse when offended: it means that the victim will die soon.)

Jīte to hāth kālā, hāre to mūṅh kālā.
Win and your hands will be black; lose and your face will be black.
(In gambling: a black face means disgrace in India.)

Jiṭhānī kā bhaiṅsā agaṛ dhaundhauṅ.
The elder brother's wife's buffalo (son) is always a fat one.
(The *jiṭhānī* has a great voice in native household matters.)

Jītī makkhī nahīṅ nigli jātī.
You cannot swallow a live fly.
(1st. One does not take poison or do wrong consciously. 2nd. No one willingly involves himself in ruin. 3rd. An evident truth cannot be denied.)

Jit ki havā bhī achchhī.
Even the name of success is worth having.
(Nothing succeeds like success.)

Jitnā chhāno, utnā hī kirkirā.
The more you strain, the more grit you get.
(The closer you examine, the more faults you find.)

Jitnā chhoṭā, utnā hī khoṭā.
As vicious as he is little.

Jitnā degā, utnā pāegā.
You will get as much as you give.

Jitnā garmāegā, utnā hī barsegā.
The hotter it grows the more it rains.
(Indian observation.)

Jitnā guṛ ḍāloge, utnā hī mīṭhā hogā.
The more sugar you put in the sweeter it will be.
(Good material, good work.)

Jitnā karam meṅ likkhā hai, utnā milegā.
You will get as much as is written in your fate.
(So why work hard!)

Jitnā maṛve meṅ āvelā, otnā kohbar meṅ na āve. E.
All that sit at the marriage feast cannot enter the marriage chamber.

Jitnā ralā hai, so chuglo. Panj.
Whatever your share is take it.
(And be thankful.)

Jitnā sāṅp lambā, utnī hī goh chauṛī.
The lizard is as wide as the snake is long.
(One matches the other.)

Jitnā sastā, utnā kharāb.
Cheap and nasty.

Jitnā syānā, utnā dīvānā.
Wiser is more scrupulous.

Jitnā tapegā, utnā barsegā.
As the heat, so the rains.
(Indian observation.)

Jitnā ūpar, utnā nīche.
As much above, so much below.
(Said of a crafty fellow.)

Jitne ghane, utne bhale.
The more (sons) the merrier.

Jitne kāle, utne mere bāp ke sāle.
So many black men, so many blackguards.
(*Sālā*, and *bāp kā sālā* are strong terms of abuse in India.)

Jitne munḍ, utne pinḍ. Hin.
As many heads (sons), so many offerings to your manes.
(Every Hindū son offers sacrifices to the manes of his parents, so the more sons a man has the more offerings he is sure of. Lo, children are an heritage of the Lord. Happy is the man that hath his quiver full of them. Psalms cxxvii, 3-5.)

Jitne muṅh, utnī hī bāteṅ.
As many men, so many minds.
(*Quot homines tot sententiae.*)

Jitnī āmad, utnā lobh.
Avarice increaseth according to the income.

Jitnī āmdanī, utnā kharch.
As the income, so the expenses.
(Paying for a name.)

Jitnī chādar dekho, utne hī pāoṅ pasāro.
Stretch your legs according to your coverlet.
(Cut your coat according to your cloth.)

Jitnī daulat, utnī hī musībat.
So much wealth, so much trouble.

Jitnī lābh, utnā lobh.
Avarice increaseth according to the gains.

Jitnī miyāṅ kī lambī ḍāṛhī, utne gāoṅ gulzār.
Superstition.
The village prospers according to the length of my lord's beard.

Jīvan maran Bidhnā ke hāth hai.
Life and death are in the hands of fate.

Jīve merā bhāī, galī galī bhaujāī. Wom.
While my brother lives there's a wife for him in every lane.
(Never mind about a wife for him, the main thing is that he live.)

Jiye na māne pitr aur mūe kare sirādh.
He disregards his father whilst alive and mourns for him when dead.
(An unworthy son.)

Jo āṅkh se dūr, voh dil se dūr.
Out of sight, out of mind,

Jo apne kām na āe, so chūlhe bhāṛ meṅ jāe.
Who is of no service to me may go into the fire.

Jo bahut qarīb, so syādah raqīb.
The nearest are the greatest rivals.
(A man's foes are those of his own household.)

Jo Bāman kī jībh par, so Bāman kī pothī meṅ.
What is on the Brāhman's tongue is in the Brāhman's books.
(The devil can cite Scripture for his purposes.)

Jo Bāman kī pothī meṅ, so yāroṅ kī zabān par.
What's in the Brāhman's book is on my tongue.
(See preceding.)

Jo bandah-navāzī kare, jān us pe fidā hai;
Be-faiz agar Yūsuf-i-sānī hai to kyā hai?
Who shows me kindness, I'll give my life for him; Without bounty a second Joseph is of no use to me.

Joban thā jab rūp thā, gāhak thā sab koī:
Joban ratan gaṅvāe-ke, bāt na pūchhe koe.
When youth I had, beauty I had, and every body wooed me: My gem of beauty lost, none cares a jot for me.

Jo bar dekh tap mujhe āve, soī bar mujhe biyāhan āve! E. Wom.
Such a bridegroom is come to marry me, as I cannot look on without fever!

Jo bāt hai so khūb hai, kyā bāt hai āp kī!
What is said is well said, and how well you have said it!
(Spoken ironically.)

Jo Bhādoṅ meṅ barkhā hoe kāl pachhohaṛ jā-kar roē. Agric.
When rain falls in August famine goes behind a wall and weeps.

Jo bhūke ko det hai, jathā shakt jo hoe,
Tā ūpar sītal bachan, lakhe ātmā soē.
Who feeds the hungry as far as in his power lies, And speaks kind words, is a truly sympathetic man.

Jo bin sahāre khele jūā āj na mūā, kal mūā.
Who gambles without experience will be ruined to-day or to-morrow.

Jo bole so ghī ko jāē.
He that speaks first shall go for butter.
☞ It alludes to a story of four blockheads, who having agreed to provide a meal jointly, quarrelled about who should bring the *ghi*, and not being able to decide the matter in any other way, agreed that he who should first break silence should go. As they sat silent, they were seen by the watch, and giving no account of themselves, were carried before the Magistrate, who, as they still refused to speak flogged them all, and when one cried out with the pain, the others exclaimed, "you are to go for the *ghī*." Hence proverb means persistence in a foolish matter.
Another story is that four men provided a joint meal. When the meal was cooked one of them exclaimed 'you have forgotten to put in the *ghī*' and the others said 'yes, you go and bring some:' hence the proverb. He who recommends a cure has to provide it.

Jo bole, so kunḍā khole. Hin.
Who speaks first must open the door.
(Allusion to a native custom of calling out to the inmates to open the door.)

Jo bovegā, so kāṭegā.
Who sows will reap.

Jo chap chap-kar āṅkh jhapāve, voh ke ran māṅ sel chalāve?
Who blinks and turns away his eyes will never use his spear in battle.

Jo chaṛhegā, so giregā.
Who climbs will fall.
(Vaulting ambition.)

Jo chhāve, so pāve.
Who thatches gets.
(Who works gets.)

Jo chorī kartā hai, so morī bhī rakhtā hai.
Who is bent on theft provides himself with a loophole for escape.

Jo dam guzre, so ganīmat hai.
Best is the time that is enjoyed.

Jo dhan jātā dekhiye, to ādhā dīje bāṅṭ.
When you are going to lose your money better give away half of it.
(Make settlements and then go bankrupt!)

Jo dhartī pe āyā, use dhartī ne khāyā.
Who is born on the earth will be devoured by the earth.
(The earth is the womb and grave of all.)

Jo dhāve so pāve, jo sove so khove.
Who runs gets, who sleeps loses.
(Who works gets.)

Jo dekhā, so pekhā.
Seeing is beholding.
(Applied to two people who tell the same story but in different words: six of one and half a dozen of the other.)

Jo gadhe jīteṅ saṅgrām, to kāhe ko tāzī ko kharcheṅ dām?
If by asses battles could be won, who would spend to keep Arabs?

Jo gaṅvār pingal paṛhe, tin bastū ke hīn,
Bolī, chālī, baiṭhkī, līnh Bidhātā chhīn.
If a village boor be a poet, he still lack three things; Speech, gait and manners, which Fate has taken from him.
(You cannot make a silk purse out of a sow's ear.)

Jo garajte haiṅ, voh baraste nahīṅ.
The cloud that thunders much rains little.
(The greatest barkers bite not sorest. Dogs that bark at a distance bite not at hand. Great promisers are small performers. Great cry little wool.)

Jogī jogī laṛeṅ, khoproṅ kā khaur.
When *jogis* fight their begging cups are smashed.
(Because they possess nothing else: poor men are ruined in the quarrels of the great.)

Jogī jugat jānī nahīṅ, kapṛe raṅge to kyā huā?
If the *jogī* does not know his business what is the use of his dyeing his clothes?
(A *jogi* is a religious mendicant and *jugat* is the knowledge or teaching of a *jogi*. They wear clothes dyed with ochre.)

Jogī kā laṛkā khelegā to sāṅp se. [a snake.
If a snake charmer's son play, he plays with
(What is bred in the bone will never be out of the flesh.)

Jogī keh ke mīt, kalandar kehi ke sāth? Bhoj.
The *jogī* is no one's friend, and the *qalandar* no one's companion.
(*Jogi* is a Hindū mendicant and *Qalandar* a Muhammadan mendicant; neither of them has any fixed abode.)

Jogī kī pīt kyā?
What friendship can there be with a *jogī*?
(He is always wandering about.)

Jogī kī sī pherī.
Like mendicant's visits.
(Said to one who pays short visits and seldom.)

Jogī kis ke mīt?
Whose friends the *jogis* are?
(Friendless—See preceding proverbs.)

Jogī ko bail balā. [to a devotee.
Even the care of an ox is an encumbrance
(As he is always wandering.)

Jogī māre chhār hāth.
Who beats a *jogī* soils his hands with ashes.
(To express that it is unprofitable to oppress the poor: *jogis* cover their bodies with dust and ashes as a rule.)

Jo girā khāī ke andar, so paṛā pherī meṅ.
He that tumbles into a ditch has wandered out of his way.

Jogī thā so uṭh gayā, āsan rahī bhabhūt.
The devotee is gone and nothing but ashes remain at his abode.
(The soul is fled and nothing but dust is left: the vacant chair.)

Jo guṛ khāe, so kān chhidāe.
He that eats treacle must have his ears pierced.
(Allusion to the custom of giving treacle to a child whose ears are about to be bored.)

Jo hāṅḍī meṅ hogā, so rakābī meṅ āegā.
What is in the pot will be served in the dish.
(Out of the fullness of the heart the mouth speaketh.)

Johīṅ kahā, vohīṅ kiyā.
No sooner said than done.

Jo jāe Kalkatte, voh khe khāe albatte.
(i.) Who goes to Calcutta will certainly eat dirt.
(Allusion to the nasty and dirty water of the river impregnated with the filth of the city, before the water-works were constructed.)
(ii.) Who goes to Calcutta can live by rowing at any rate.
(Calcutta being a great port.)

Jo jīve so khele Phāg, mūā so lekhe lāg.
Who lives will play at the Holī, who dies is done for.
(Life is for the living.)

Jo Kabīr Kāshī meṅ marikeṅ Rām heṅ kaun nihorā? E.
If Kabīr die at Benares, what obligation is he under to God?
☞ The allusion is to the Hindū belief that the mere fact of dying at Benares brings salvation, so that if a man thus obtains salvation he is not under obligation to God. The proverb is used by a man who has been paying court to another with a view to personal benefit and has had after all to gain his object by his own exertions.

Jo kahte haiṅ, voh karte nahīṅ.
Great promisers are small performers.

Jo kām hikmat se nikaltā hai, voh hukūmat se nahīṅ nikaltā.
Skill succeeds where authority fails.

Jo Khudā sir par sing de, to voh bhī sahne paṛte haiṅ.
If God were pleased to give me two horns, even then would I bear them patiently.
(Contentment and resignation.)

Jo kisī kā burā chītegā, us kā pahle burā hogā.
Evil be to him that evil thinks.
(*Honi soit qui mal y pense.*)

Jo koī kalpāe hai, so kaise kal pāe hai?
How shall he that gives pain to others enjoy tranquility?

Jo koī khāe chane kā ṭūk pānī pīve sau sau ghūṅṭ. Rus.
Who eats pease-pudding will drink a hundred gulps of water.
(*Chane kā ṭūk* is very thirst giving.)

Jo koī khāe nibāh ke jūār, Mūl bane voh mūṅḍh gaṅvār. Rus.
Who hath eaten millet from his birth, Hath been a clodhopper from the beginning.
(Millet (*juār*) is very coarse food.)

Jo man meṅ base, so supne ḍase.
What fills the heart appears in the dreams.

Jo māṅ se sivā chāhe, so ḍāyan.
Who fondles a child more than a mother is a witch.
(Over-acting a part.)

Jo mere hai, so rājā ke nahīṅ.
Even the king has not what I possess.
(Said of a vain person.)

Jo mere so tere, kāhe dāṅt nipoṛe?
What I have you have, so why do you grin?
(Nakedness is no shame.)
☞ An Englishman is said to have expostulated with some Assamese womem for bathing naked in the open whereon they replied, 'What have we that your mother and sister have not?'

Jo nikle, so bhāg dhanī ke.
Whatever happens is my master's luck.
(What do I care? said of a bad servant.)

Jo pahle māre, so mīre.
Who strikes first wins.

Jo pāras se kanchan upje, so pāras hai kāṅch;
Jo pāras se pāras upje, so pāras hai sāṅch.
The touchstone that breeds gold is a false stone; The touchstone that breeds a touchstone is a true stone.
(Like begets like: *pāras*, the philosopher's stone, which can turn the baser metals into gold.)

Jo phal chakkhā nahīṅ, vohī mīṭhā hai.
Untasted fruit is sweetest.
(The joy in prospect is sweeter than the joy possessed.)

Jo piyāz kāṭegā, so āp roegā.
Who cuts onions shall shed tears.
(Who sows mischief will suffer the consequences; allusion to the pungent juice of the onion bringing tears into the eyes.)

Jo pūt Darbārī bhae, deo pittar sab se gae. Hin.
Those who enter the service of Government give up the service of gods and ancestors.
(*i. e.* contact with Europeans has a tendency to destroy superstition.)

Joṛ joṛ mar jāeṅge, māl jaṅvāiṅ khāeṅge:
Jaṅvāī bhī na hogā, to khālse lag jāeṅge.
Collect wealth and die, that thy son-in-law may squander it: And if thou have no son-in-law, that it may escheat to the king.

Jorū kā dhablā bech-kar tandūrī roṭī khāī hai. Mah.
He has enjoyed a loaf on the proceeds of his wife's gown.
(Downright selfishness.)

Jorū kā marnā, aur jūtī kā ṭūṭnā barābar hai.
A dead wife is like a torn shoe.
(Both are replaced by new ones in India!)

Jorū kā marnā, ghar kā kharābā.
The death of the wife is ruin to the house.

Jorū kā murīd.
His own wife's pupil.
(A henpecked husband.)

Jorū khasam kī laṛāī, dūdh kī malāī.
A quarrel between husband and wife is like the cream of milk.
(There is nothing serious in it.)

Jorū khasam kī laṛāī kyā?
What is a quarrel between husband and wife?
(Nothing of any consequence.)

Jorū na jātā, Allāh miyāṅ se nātā.
Nor wife nor daughter and God his only relative (friend).
(Said of a bachelor.)

Jorū ṭaṭole gaṭhrī, aur māṅ ṭaṭole antṛī.
The wife feels the purse, the mother feels the stomach.
(The wife wants money and the mother likes to see her son well-fed.)

Jo sādhū kī māne bāt, rahe anand voh din rāt.
Who follows out the teaching of the saints is happy night and day.

Jo sādī chāl chaltā hai, voh hamesha khush-hāl rahtā hai.
Who leads a simple life is always happy.

Jo sevā kare, so mevā pāve.
He that does the service will receive the fruits of it.

Jo sir uṭhā-kar chalegā, so ṭhokar khāegā.
Walk with your nose in the air and you will trip.

Jo sove, us kā paṛvāyā ; jo jāge, us kī paṛyā.
The sleeper's is the bull calf, the waker's the cow.
(The cow-calf being more valuable than the bull. The early bird gets the worm.)

Jo tairegā, so ḍūbegā.
Who swims will (sometimes) drown.

Jo ṭakā degā, us kā laṛkā khelegā.
His child will play who pays.
(*i. e.* for its toys.)

Jo til had se ziyādah huā, so massā huā.
When a mole grows beyond bounds it becomes a wart.
(A virtue in excess may become a vice: moles on the face are much admired by orientals.)

Juā baṛā beohār, jo is meṅ hār na hotī.
Gambling would be a capital trade, if there were no such thing as losing.

Juārī hamesha muflis.
A gambler is always poor.

Juārī ko apnā hī dāo sujhtā hai.
The gambler flatters himself that his own throw is the best.

Jūē meṅ bail bhī hāre haiṅ.
The ox sinks under the weight of his yoke.
(Pun on the word *jūā* which means (1) yoke (2) gambling.)

Jug ṭūṭā, nard marī.
When the pair (at *chausar*) are separated one man is lost.
(*Chausar* is a game played with dice according to the throws of which the men (*nard*) are moved. The men must be moved in pairs according to the throws, and when it happens that a player cannot move both his men he loses one, hence the proverb means "union is strength.")

Julāhā chūrāve nalī nalī, Khudā churāve ekke berī. E.
The weaver steals a reel at a time; but God makes lose him all at once.
(Of all his ill-gotten gains: poetical justice.)

Julāha jāne jau kāṭe?
Can a weaver cut barley?
☞ The story goes that a weaver, unable to pay his debts, was set to cut ripe barley by his agriculturist creditor, who thought to repay himself in this way. Instead of reaping he employed himself in untwisting the tangled barley stems as he would skeins of thread. The saying is a hit at the proverbial stupidity of the weaver caste.

Julāhe kā begārī Paṭhān!
A Paṭhān working gratis for a weaver!
(Society upside down: *begārī* is a forced laborer and the point is that the turbulent and pugnacious Paṭhān would be the last man in the world to do forced labour for such a wretched menial as the *Julāhā* usually is.)

Julāhe kā tīr na ho?
May it not be the weaver's arrow!
☞ Alluding to a story of a weaver who went to fight and being wounded with an arrow, prayed that it might not prove that he was hit. The proverb implies a hope that a misfortune may be prevented before it is too late.

Julāhe kī jūtī, sipāhī kī joē, dharī dharī purānī hoē.
A weaver's shoe, and a soldier's wife grow old without being used.
(A weaver sits at his work barefooted and a soldier lives abroad.)

Julāhe kī maskharī māṅ bahan se!
The weaver will crack indecent jokes with his mother and sister!
(Allusion to the stupidity of the weaver caste.)

Julāhe kī tarah, Īd, Bakrīd ko pān khā lete haiṅ. Mah.
He enjoys the luxury of betel leaf like a weaver at the *Īd* and *Bakrīd*.
(These feasts occur once each in the year: hence proverb means luxury rarely enjoyed.)

Juma chhoṛ sanīchar nahāē, us kā sanīchar kabhī na jāē. Superstition.
Who omits Friday and bathes on Saturday misfortune will never leave him.

Jūṅ jūṅ bāo bahe Purvāī, tūṅ tūṅ aū dukh ghāil pāī. E.
When the wind is in the East, the pains of wounds are much increased.

Jūṅ jūṅ bhīje kāmlī tūṅ tūṅ bhārī hoë.
The wetter a blanket gets, the heavier it becomes.
(Used as an expostulation with one, who, having run in debt, does not even take care to pay the interest, whereby the load accumulates daily.)

Jūṅ jūṅ liyā terā nām, voṅ voṅ mārā sārā gāon.
The more I used your name the more the villagers beat me.
(Said of a tyrannical ruler.)

Jūṅ jūṅ murgī moṭī ho, tūṅ tūṅ dum sukṛe.
As a fowl gets fat its tail shrinks.
(The richer a miser becomes, the closer fisted he grows.)

Jūṅ ke ḍar se gudṛī nahīṅ phekī jātī.
A blanket is not thrown away on account of the lice in it.
(A great advantage is not given up for a slight inconvenience which attends it.)

Jūṛī balvān hai.
Mating is beyond control.
(Marriages are made in heaven and we next.)

Jūṛī ke hāth hai.
Marriage is in the hands of fate.

Jūṛiyā sanjog hai.
Marriage depends on (fated) union.
(See preceding.)

Juṛtī nahīṅ Dhūr kī ṭūṭī, dharī rahe sab dārū būṭī.
What Heaven breaks cannot be joined, so put aside your medicines and herbs.

Jūtā pahne sāī kā, baṛā bharosā byāhī kā,
Jūtā pahne narī kā, kyā bharosā karī kā!
Shoes made to order last as a wedded wife,
But shoes made to sell as a mistress only.

Jut jut maren bailvā, baiṭhe khāeṅ turang.
Agric. [their stalls.
The oxen work to death, the horses feed in
(The poor work that the rich may thrive.)

K

Kabāṛī ke chhappar par phūns nahīṅ.
The old clothes-man has no straw on his thatch.

Kab dādā mareṅge aur kab bel baṭegī?
When will the grandsire die, and when will the funeral gifts be made?
(Waiting for the dead man's shoes.)

Kabhī ghan ghanā, kabhī muṭṭhī bhar chanā.
Sometimes plenty, sometimes only a handful of corn.

Kabhī ghī ghanā, kabhī muṭṭhī bhar chanā, kabhī voh bhī nahīṅ!
Sometimes butter in plenty, sometimes but a handful of corn and sometimes not even that!

Kabhī ke din baṛe, kabhī kī rāt baṛī.
Sometimes the days are long and sometimes the nights.

Kabhī kūṅḍe ke is pār, kabhī kūṅḍe ke us pār.
Sometimes on this side, sometimes on that side of the *bhang* mortar.
(To express excessive laziness and sottishness.)

Kabhī na dekhā boryā aur supne āī khāṭ.
He never even saw a mat and dreamed of a bed.
(Said of an upstart.)

Kabhī na dekhī chaddar chadrī!
She never saw a shawl or a wrapper!
(A taunt to a boastful woman.)

Kabhī na gāṅḍū ran chaṛhe, aur kabhī na bājī bam.
The coward never went to field and never heard the battle drum.
(Abuse by *bhāṭs* (bards) when refused their demands.)

Kabhī nāo gāṛī par, kabhī gāṛī nāo par.
Sometimes the boat is on the waggon, and sometimes the waggon on the boat.
(Individuals of different rank and qualities have it in their power to help each other. Boats are carried on waggons to be launched and waggons are ferried over on boats.)

Kabhī na soī sāṅthre, supne āī khāṭ!
She never even slept on straw and dreamed of a bed.
(Chateau en Espagne.)

Kabhī ranj, kabhī ganj.
Sometimes gains and sometimes pains.

Kabhū na kabhū ṭesū phūlā.
The *palās* tree sometimes blossoms.
(Spoken of one who seldom does a good act and based on common observation.)

Kabīr Dās kī ulṭī bānī; āṅgan sūkhā, ghar meṅ pānī.
A dark saying of Kabīr: the yard is dry and water is in the house.
(Reference to the obscure sayings attributed to Kabīr, which have an obvious and an allegorical meaning: *e. g.* this means that good men do not enjoy this world, but have joys in store for the next.)

Kabīr Dās kī ulṭī bānī; barse kammal, bhīje pānī.
A dark saying of Kabīr: the blanket rains and the water is wetted.
(See preceding. It means that bad men flourish and the good suffer frequently in this world.)

Kabit sohe Bhāṭ ne, aur khetī sohe Jāṭ ne. Rus.
Verses befit a bard, and husbandry befits a Jat.
(Every cobbler to his last.)

Kab ke banyā, kab ke seṭh?
Yesterday a grocer, to-day a merchant prince!
(Said of an upstart.)

Kab mare aur kab kīṛe paṛe?
When he will die and when the worms will eat him?
(I care not.)

Kab muā aur kab rāchchhas huā ?
When did he die and become a demon ?
(Applied to an upstart, who assumes airs of consequence.)

Kab se rājā īsar bhaë, kodoṅ ke din bisar gaë ?
Since when have you become a mighty king, and forgotten the days of plain porridge ?

Kābul gae, Mugal ban āë bolanlāge bānī,
'Āb āb' kar mar gaë sirhāne rahā pānī.
He went to Kābul, became a Mugal, and so began to speak their language.
The water was by his side and he died, crying *'l'eau l'eau.'*
☞ The proverb is founded on the following story. A man, who had visited Kābul and had learnt Persian there at the sacrifice of his own mother-tongue, used to flaunt Persian phrases when he returned home to his native land, and consequently died of thirst, crying in vain for water in Persian "*āb āb,*" instead of the common Hindustāni *pānī*, which none of his servants and relations could understand

Kābul meṅ kyā gadhe nahīṅ hote ?
Are there not donkeys in Kābul ?

Kābul meṅ mevā bhaī, Brij meṅ bhaī karīl.
Kābul for fruits and Brij for *karīl*.
(The *karīl* is a thorny bush, and the point is that in Kābul, which the Hindūs look on as a barbarous place, good things are found, whereas their holy land of Brij produces only what is of little worth.)

Kabūtar khāne kā sā hāl hai, ek ātā hai ek jātā hai.
Like a pigeon house, one goes out and another comes in.
(Said of an establishment in which a large number of servants is kept up.)

Kachahrī kā darvāza khulā hai.
The doors of the Courts are open.
(So why fight among yourselves !)

Kachaurī kī bū ab tak nahīṅ gaī.
The smell of the cakes is not yet gone.
(*Kachaurī* is a cake made of flour and pulse, generally eaten by children. The proverb is applied to a mean person elevated suddenly to consequence and who still shews traces of his base origin.)

Kachchā dūdh sab ne piyā hai.
Every one has drunk fresh milk.
(Every body is apt to err: the point of the proverb lies in the native idea that boiled milk is more nourishing than fresh.)

Kachchā to kachaurī māṅge, pūrī maṅge pūrā,
Non mirach to Kāëth māṅge, Bāman māṅge būrā.
Raw youth likes crisp cakes, ripe age soft sponge-cakes,
Kāëths like pepper and salt, and Brāhmans sugar.
(*Pūrīs* are more wholesome than *kachauris*, and the rest of the proverb is a skit at the Kāëths and Brāhmans.)

Kachche bāṅs ko jidhar nivāo niv jāë, aur pakkā kabhī na ṭeṛhā hoë.
The young bamboo can be bent as you please, but the old one never.
(Teach a child betimes in the way it should go.)

Kachchī kalī kachnāl kī toṛat man pachhtāë.
Pluck the unripe buds of the *kachnāl* tree and sorrow for it.
(Because you can do nothing with them.)

Kachchī khānā, dānt na lagānā, sābit hī ṭhūṅs jānā. Superstition.
Don't put the herb between your teeth, swallow it whole.
(A common saying of the native *hakīms* or medical practitioners : *kachchī khānā* is any concoction of medicinal herbs.)

Kachchī peṅḍī dastar-khuān kā zarar. Mah.
The under-baked pot will soil the cloth.
(Because it will not hold liquids properly : with raw youth deal, you'll get no weal.)

Kachchī reṅḍī dastar-khuān ka zarar. Mah.
An unripe melon is a disgrace to the table.
(To describe an unprofitable servant as above.)

Kachchī shīshī mat bharo, jis meṅ paṛī lakīr,
Bāle-pan kī āshqī, gale paṛī zanjīr.
Fill not a flimsy, nor a flawed glass;
Love in early youth is a chain round the neck.

Kachrī khāë din bahlāë, kapṛe phāṭe ghar ko āë.
I ate unripe melons, and wasted my time, and when my clothes became in tatters I returned home.
(I was employed unprofitably.)

Kadhī na dekhā boriyā, supne āī khāṭ.
He never saw a mat and dreamed of a bed.
(Castles in the air.)

Kad kad Manglū bove dhān, sūkhā ḍālā, he Bhagwān !
Whenever Manglū sowed his rice; God caused a drought !

Kad ke kad āë, mere man nahīṅ bhāë.
You have come so late that you are not welcome.

Kāgā bole, paṛ gaë raule.
When the crows caw all nature wakes.
(The crows in India play the part of chanticleer.)

Kāgā raul.
The cawing of crows.
(The chattering of noisy persons when they meet together.)

Kāgā, kavvā aur khargosh, yeh tīnoṅ nahīṅ māne pos.
The crow, the jackdaw and the hare ; these three can never be tamed.

Kāgaz ke ghoṛe dauṛāte haiṅ.
Galloping a paper horse.
(Castles in the air: used also of the rapid postal arrangements of the English.)

Kāgaz kī nāo āj na ḍubbī, kal ḍubbī ; or
Kāgaz kī pan-guḍḍī āj na ḍubbī, kal ḍubbī.
A paper boat will sink to-day or at any rate to-morrow.
(Spoken of things which cannot last.)

Kāgaz kī nāo nahīṅ chaltī.
A paper boat won't float long.

Kāge kāg na bhikārī bhīk!
No bread for the crows, and no alms for the beggars.
(Said of a miser: it is obligatory on Hindūs to feed cows at funerals and to give alms to mendicants.)

Kahā na ablā kar sake? Kahā na sindhu samāë? Kahā na pāvak men jare? Kahā kāl na khāë?
What cannot a woman do? What cannot the ocean contain? What cannot the fire burn? What cannot death destroy?

Kahān bībī, kahān bāndī?
What equality between maid and mistress?

Kahān burhyā? kahān rāj-kannyā?
There is a vast difference between an old woman and a young princess!
(Applied to one without merit making high pretensions.)

Kahānī jaisī jhūṭī nahīn, bāt jaisī mīṭhī nahīn.
Nothing so false as fiction, nothing so sweet as a tale.

Kahān jāūn chūhe kā bil nahīn miltā.
Wherever I may go I cannot even find a rat's hole.
(To creep into.)

Kahān Rājā Bhoj, kahān kānglā telī?
There is a vast difference between Rājā Bhoj and a poor oilman.

Kahān Rām Rām? kahān ten ten?
What connection is there between the worship of God and idle talk?
(Allusion here to the talking of *mainās* which are taught to say "*Rām Rām*" (God, God) and parrots which are taught to say "*ten ten*.")

Kāhe ko gūlar kā peṭ pharvātë hai.
Why do you try to break open a fig?
(To disclose a secret: the fruit of the *gūlar* is full of a substance like worms and so is very disgusting to a Hindū.)

Kahen khet kī, sune khaliyān kī.
They are talking of the fields and he hears about the barn.
(A dull-head.)

Kahen zamīn kī, sune āsmān kī.
He talks of Earth and hears of Heaven.
(He talks of chalk and I of cheese: cross purposes.)

Kahe se koī kūë men nahīn girtā.
No one will fall into a well if you tell him to do so.

Kahe se kumhār gadhe par nahīn charhtā.
The potter won't mount his ass if you tell him to do so.
(Unreasonable obstinacy.)

Kahīn ḍūbe bhī tīre hain?
Will the drowned ever swim again?

Kahīn kī īnṭ kahīn kā roṛā, bhānmatī ne kunbā joṛā.
With bricks from here and stones from there, the juggler doth a family rear.

Kahīn nākhūn bhī gosht se judā huā hai?
The flesh and the bones cannot be separated.
(Blood is thicker than water.)

Kahīn sūkhe darakht bhī hare hue hai?
Can the withered tree put forth green leaves?
(Can these dry bones live?)

Kahīn to sūhā chunrī, aur kahīn ḍhele lāt!
Sometimes a red kerchief, and sometimes kick and knocks.
(The chances of a woman's married life.)

Kāhnā āsān, karnā mushkil.
It is easy to promise, but hard to perform.

Kahūn to mā mārī jāë, na kahūn to bāp kuttā khāë.
If I tell, my mother will be beaten; if don't tell, my father will eat dog's flesh.
(The speech is supposed to be uttered by a son who discovers that his mother by mistake has dressed dog's flesh instead of mutton for his father's dinner. It is used to express being in a dilemma.)

Kājal gayā Bihār, bahoṛyā naṛcre hī hai. E. Wom.
They have gone to Bihār for the lamp-black and the bride is on the tip-toe of expectation.
(To express expectation of a thing of which there is no hope. *Kājal* or lamp-black is necessary for the adornment of the bride's eyes before the marriage.)

Kājal kī koṭhrī.
A room full of lamp-black.
(To express a place from frequenting which you will only obtain disgrace: used towards the houses of prostitutes.)

Kājal kī koṭhrī men jāëgā, to dhabbā lage hī gā.
Go to the house full of lamp-black and you will be surely stained.
(Touch pitch and you will be defiled.)

Kājal to sab lagāte hain, par chitvan bhānt bhānt. Wom.
They all apply lamp-black, but their glances differ.
(Beauty unadorned is adorned the most.)

Kākā kāhū ke na bhaë.
An uncle is no body's friend.

Kākā kī bhainsī, bhatīje kī tond.
The buffalo is the uncle's, the pot belly the nephew's.
(*i. e.* the uncle gets the good things of the world.)

Kākā na kare sākā.
An uncle won't make a row.
(Men in India are apt to be very fond of their brother's children, and frequently adopt them.)

Kakṛī ke chor ko gardan nahīn mārte.
A man is not hanged for stealing a cucumber.
(*De minimus non curat lex.*)

Kālā koelā!
Black as charcoal!

Kalāl kī beṭī ḍūbne chalī, logoṅ ne kahā, 'mat vālī hai.'
The publican's daughter went to drown herself and the people said 'she's drunk.'
(To express enjoyment at other's troubles.)

Kalāl kī dūkan par pānī bhī piyo, to sharāb kā gumān hotā hai.
Drink even water at a tavern and you are suspected of having drunk spirits.

Kālā mūṅh karīl ke dāṅt.
A black face and teeth like the *karīl.*
(The *karīl* is a kind of gourd of a dirty brown colour.)

Kālā mūṅh, nīle hāth pāoṅ.
A black face, with blue hands and feet.
(To express abhorrence of any thing.)

Kālejā ṭūk ṭūk, āṅsū ek bhī nahīṅ.
His heart broken, but never a tear.
(Crocodile's tears: sham grief.)

Kāle kā kāṭā pānī nahīṅ māṅgtā.
Bitten by a black snake does not even ask for water.
(Because he dies before he can do so: black snakes are deemed to be very deadly by natives.)

Kāle ke āge chirāg nahīṅ jaltā. Superstition.
No lamp will burn before a black snake.
(Because it is supposed to carry a bright jewel in its head: proverb means that nothing avails before a powerful tyrant.)

Kāle ke kāṭe kā jantar na mantar.
The black snake's bite no spell nor charm can cure.
(There is no cure for tyranny.)

Kāle kī sī ek lahr ā jātī hai.
Caprice has laid hold of him like a black snake's bite.
(The whims and caprices of a tyrant.)

Kāle kosoṅ.
Black miles.
(Descriptive of a distant journey, which may be said to terminate in darkness: he is gone to the world's end.)

Kāle sir kā be-ḍhab hotā hai.
Man is the lord (of creation).

Kāle sir kā ek na chhoṛā.
He left not a man (alive).

Kalhārī kal kal kare, chhohārī chho hoā.
Apnī apnī bān se kabhī na chūke koē.
The quarrelsome will quarrel, the waspish will be so:
As her nature is, each will always show.

Kālī bhalī na set: donoṅ ko māro ek hī khet!
Nor black is good, nor white: at one blow kill them both!
☞ The story goes that a certain woman transformed herself into a white kite in order to avenge herself on her faithless husband. Her rival thereupon assumed the form of a black kite. The husband killed them both as dangerous witches.

Kālī gāē Bāman ko dān. Hin.
A black cow given in alms to a Brāhman.
(A black cow is the best in the Hindūs' eyes for a free gift.)

Kālī ghaṭā ḍarāonī aur dhaulī barsan-hār.
The black cloud threatens, but the white cloud gives the rain.
(Barking dogs seldom bite.)

Kālī hāṅḍī pīchhe.
Old pitchers are set aside.
(To be broken on the owner's death or departure, and upon the removal of an unpopular chief or governor, as indicative of the hope of a new era.)

Kālī Jumerāt kā vādā karnā. Mah.
To promise on Black Thursday.
(To make a long promise: *Kālī Jumerāt* is the second (or last) Thursday of the dark fortnight of the moon.)

Kāl juārī.
A gambler to the death.

Kal kā līpā deo bahāē, āj kā līpā dekho dē. Wom.
Wash off yesterday's plaster and look to to-day's.
(Let by-gones be by-gones.)

Kāl, kaṛhāū, kisān kā khāū. Agric.
Famine and dearth are the death of farmers.

Kāl kā sāg garīb kā bhāg.
In famine time herbs are the lot of the poor.

Kāl ke āge kisī kā bas nahīn chaltā.
There is no resisting death.

Kāl ke āge sab lāchār haiṅ.
All are helpless in the presence of death.

Kāl ke hāth kamān, būṛhā bache na javān.
When his bow is in the hand of death nor old nor young escape.

Kāl ke mūṅh meṅ sab haiṅ.
All are in the mouth of death.

Kal kis ne dekhī hai.
Who has seen to-morrow.
(Who knows the future: also don't delay.)

Kāl koṭhṛī.
A black house.
(A dangerous place.)

Kallahr kā khet jaise kapṭī kā heth. Agric.
A traitor's friendship is a barren field.

Kallah chale sattar balā ṭale.
When the jaws grind they keep seventy hardships away.

Kāl na chhoṛe rājā, na chhoṛe rank.
Death leaves nor beggar nor king.
(Death is no respecter of persons.)

Kāl sab ko khāē baiṭhā hai.
Death eats up every one.

Kāl ṭale, kalāl na ṭale.
Death may be put off, but the bottle never.

Kalvārī kī agāṛī, aur qasāī kī pichhāṛī.
To the wine-merchant early, to the butcher late.
(In India the best wine is exposed first for sale and the best meat last.)

Kamāī na dhamāī, mo ke bhūj bhūj khāī. E. Wom.

He neither earns nor gets, but feeds on me.

(A lazy husband or son.)

Kamānī na pahiyā, "gāṛī jot, mere bhaīyā." Rus.

Nor spring nor wheels, and says he, "bring up the cart, friend."

Kamān se niklā tīr aur mūṅh se niklī bāt, phir nahīṅ ātī.

An arrow out of the bow and a word out of the mouth return no more.

Kām apnā hī kām hai.

Self done is well done.

(If you want a thing done well do it yourself.)

Kamar meṅ toshā, baṛā bharosā.

To have your food with you is a great comfort.

Kamar na būtā, sāṅjhe sūtā! E. Wom.

No strength in his loins and early to bed!

Kamāū āve ḍartā, nikhaṭṭū āve laṛtā. Wom.

The bread-winner comes home quietly, and the earn-nothing quarrelsome.

Kamāū khasam kis ne na chāhe? Wom.

Who would not wish for a hard-working husband?

Kamāū pūt kaleje sūt. E. Wom.

The son who earns lies on his mother's breast.

(He is the darling of his mother.)

Kamāū pūt kī dūr balā.

A son who earns keeps off calamity.

Kamāve dhotī-vālā, uṛāve ṭopī-vālā.

The Hindū earns and the European dissipates it.

(*Dhotī* is a cloth worn by Hindūs round the waist, passing between the legs and fastened behind: the *ṭopī* or hat is the peculiar dress of the European in India.)

Kamāveṅ Khāṅ-khānāṅ, uṛāveṅ Miyāṅ Fahīm.

The master earns the money, and his slave dissipates it.

☞ It is said that Bairām Khāṅ, better known by his title of Khāṅ-khānāṅ, the celebrated friend and minister of the Emperor Akbar, had a slave named Fahīm, who was liberal to extravagance with his master's money.

Kam-bakht gae hāṭ, na milī tarāzū, na mile bāṭ.

If an unlucky man go to market, he finds neither scales nor weights.

(So that he can be easily cheated by the traders.)

Kam-bakhtī kī nishānī, jo sūkh gayā kūē kā pānī.

Misfortune is nigh, when wells run dry.

Kām chor, nivāle hāzir.

Shirking his work, but ready for his meals.

Kām isrā, dukh bisrā, chhāchh na det Ahīr.

The Ahīr's business is done and the trouble forgotten, and he will not give even a draught of butter-milk (to the workman.)

(When a man's turn is served, he is apt to forget those to whose aid he owed his success: after you have mounted, you kick away the ladder.)

Kām kā, na kāj kā, dushman anāj kā.

Nor for work, nor for toil, is an enemy to his food.

(It is waste of money to feed an idle workman or servant.)

Kām kā, na kāj kā, ser bhar anāj kā.

Nor for work, nor for toil, but for a pound of corn.

(See preceding.)

Kām kare nath-vālī, pakṛī jāē chirkut-vālī. E. Wom.

The bejewelled woman did it and the ragged woman was taken up.

(Riches hide thousands of our crimes: wealth covers a multitude of sins.)

Kam kharch, bālā nashīn. Pers.

Small cost and great show.

Kām kī biryāṅ ṭhosā dikhāē.

When it is time to work she shows her thumbs.

(*Ṭhosā dikhānā*: idiom, to refuse point blank.)

Kām, kirodh, mad, lobh kī jolo man meṅ khān,
Kā panḍit, kā mūrkhā, doū ek samān. Bhoj.

As long as passion, anger, pride and avarice fill the mind,
The learned and the ignorant are one and the same.

Kām ko aṅhāṅ! khāne ko hāṅ!

For work, O no; for dinner, O yes!

Kām ko kām sikhātā hai.

Work teaches work.

(We learn by experience.)

Kām korhī, mūṅh bajjar.

To work a leper, to eat a stone-mouth.

(Lepers of course can do no work: *mūṅh bajjar*, idiom, to be able to eat anything.)

Kamlī oṛhne se faqīr nahīṅ hotā.

The habit does not make the priest.

Kām lo, dām do.

Get your work done and pay me.

Kām pyārā hai, chām pyārā nahīṅ hai.

Work is sweet, not good looks.

(Handsome is that handsome does.)

Kānā kavvā.

A one-eyed crow.

(A taunt: any ugly man.)

Kānā kuttā pich hī se āsūda.

The one-eyed dog is pleased with rice-water.

☞ The prize goes with merit: any thing one-eyed is unlucky to the natives and a one-eyed dog the most of all, so these are habitually ill-treated; rice-water is of no value and is thrown away, hence point of proverb.)

Kānā mujh ko bhāē nahīṅ, kāne bin suhāē nahīṅ. Wom.

I dislike the one-eyed rogue and yet I cannot do without him.

(Said by a woman of a husband she dislikes.)

Kānā ṭaṭṭū, buddhū nafar.
A wall-eyed pony and a stupid groom.
(To describe a miserable equipage.)

Kanaunḍī billī chūhoṅ se kān kaṭāē.
A cowed cat will let rats bite her ears.
(A superior is obliged to put up with insolence from an inferior, who knows some of his secret faults.)

"*Kāṅdhe dhanush, hāth meṅ bānā, kahāṅ chale Dillī Sultānā?*"
"*Ban ke rāo, bikaṭ ke rānā, baṛan kī bāt baṛe pahchānā.*"
"With bow on shoulder, and arrows in thy hand, where art thou going, O Emperor of Dehlī?"
"O king of the forest, and lord of the wilds, the great only know the great!"
☞ The story goes that a wool-carder (*dhunyā*) travelling in a forest with the implements of his trade met a jackal, which had just come out of an indigo vat. The jackal took him for an archer, and being frightened accosted him with the first line. And the carder taking the jackal for a tiger (!) replied to him with the second line. *Moral:* mutual fear makes men wondrous civil.

Kāne ke ek rag sivā hotī hai.
The one-eyed have always one extra sense.
(They are generally believed to be very wicked.)

Kānī āṅkh, maṭar kā bīyā, voh bhī āṅkh Bhavānī līyā. E.
Even my one eye, small as a pea, hath the Goddess of small-pox taken.

Kānī apnā ṭeṅṭ na nihāre aur kī phullī nihāre.
The one-eyed perceives not the film on her own eye, but sees the speck in another's.
(Thou hypocrite, cast out first the beam out of thine own eye and then shalt thou see clearly to pull out the mote that is in thy brother's eye. Luke, vi. 42.)

Kānī gāē Bāman ke dān! E.
A one-eyed cow for the Brāhman's alms!
(When a thing is useless give it away in charity.)

Kānī gāē ke alge bathān? E.
Has the one-eyed cow a separate stall?
(Must I be put out of the society of the most worthy because I am less worthy than they?)

Kānī ke bīyāh ko sau jokhoṅ.
In marrying off a one-eyed girl there are a hundred risks.
(That the husband elect may find it out and refuse to marry her.)

Kānī ko kānā pyārā, rānī ko rānā pyārā.
The one-eyed wife loves her one-eyed husband and the lady loves her lord.
(Each happy with her lot.)

Kānī ko kaun sarāhe? kānī kā mīyāṅ!
Who would extol a one-eyed wife but her husband?

Kanjā bhāgvān hotā hai. Superstition.
Blue-eyed is fortunate.

Kanjūs makkhī-chūs.
The miser will eat flies.
(*Every* Hindū will throw away any food containing a dead fly, hence the sting of the proverb.)

Kāṅ kahat nahīṅ bain, jūṅ jibbhyā sunat nahīṅ baiṅ!
The ears can't speak, as the tongue can't hear!

Kankhajūre ke kaē pāoṅ ṭuṭeṅge?
Can all the feet of a centipede be broken?
(Spoken of one who is well able to bear a loss.)

Kān meṅ tel ḍāle baiṭhe haiṅ.
They have poured oil into their ears.
(To turn a deaf ear to advice.)

Kān meṅ ṭheṅṭiyāṅ delī haiṅ.
He has stuffed his ears with wax.
(See preceding.)

Kān par ek jūṅ nahīṅ chaltī. Rus.
Even a louse does not venture on his ears.
(Spoken of one who does not yield to advice.)

Kān pyāre to bāliyāṅ, jorū pyārī to sāliyāṅ.
Love my ears, love my earrings: love my wife, love her sisters.
(Love me, love my dog)

Kāṅrā raggī.
A haughty one-eyed man.
(The height of incongruity to the native's mind.)

Kāṅṭā burā karīl kā, aur badlī kā ghām.
Saukan burī hai chūn kī, aur sājhe kā kām.
Sharp are the thorns of the *karīl*, great the heat of a cloudy day. Hateful even the image of a co-wife and a business in partnership.
☞ The *chūn kī saukan*, or co-wife of flour, of the proverb is founded on the story of a man, who set up a *chūn* (flour) model of an ideal co-wife, which he covered with a rich dress and jewels and caressed and worshipped every day in order to vex his living wife.

Kanth na pūchhe bāt, merā dhanā suhāgan nām. Wom.
My husband never speaks to me, yet I am called a happy married woman.
(Applied to one who falsely pretends to be in the confidence of his master, or of a great man.)

Kā par karūṅ singār, pyā mor āṅdhar? E. Wom.
For whom should I deck myself, when my husband is blind?
(The blind man's wife needs no paint.)

Kapṛā kahe, "tū mujhe kar tah, maiṅ tujhe karūṅ shah."
Say your clothes, "you keep me carefully and I will make a king of you."
(The tailor makes the man.)

Kapṛā pahnīye jag bhātā: khānā khāīye man bhātā.
Dress to please the world: eat to please yourself.

Kapre phaṭe garībī āī.
When the clothes are torn poverty has arrived.

Kapṭī kī prīt, maran kī rīt.
Friendship with a knave will lead you to your grave.

Kapūt beṭā marā bhalā.
An undutiful son is best dead.

Karā, aur kar na jānā, main hotī to kar dikhātī. Wom.
She did it, but didn't know how to do it; if I had been there I would have shewn her.
(Said of a woman who gets into trouble for a lover in allusion to a well-known tale in the *Alaf Lailā.*)

Karain Kallū, bharain Lallū. E.
Kallū does the deed, and Lallū pays for it.
(The cat's paw.)

Karākar bājen thothe bāns.
Hollow bamboos break with a crack.
(Empty vessels give the loudest sound.)

Karam hīn jab hot hain, sabhī hot hain bām,
Chhānh jān ke baiṭhat hain, tahān hot hain ghām.
When misfortune comes, every thing is upside down; When the unfortunate expects cool shade he finds a burning sun.

Karam-hīn khetī kare, bail mare, sūkhā paṛe. Agric.
If an unlucky man become a cultivator, his oxen die or there comes a drought.

Karam-hīn sāgar gaē, jahān ratan kā ḍher,
Kar chhūat ghongā bhaē: yehī karam kā pher!
An unlucky man goes to a sea where gems abound, And whenever he touches one it turns into a shell: such is the caprice of fate!

Karam ke baliyā pakāī khīr, ho gayā dalyā.
If an unfortunate man cook a dish of milk and rice it turns out to be gruel.
(*Khīr* is a dish of milk and rice; and *dalyā* a gruel much inferior to *khīr.*)

Karam rekh amiṭ hai.
The lines of fate are immutable.

Karam rekh na miṭe, karo koī lākhon chatrāī.
The lines of fate you can't efface, though a hundred thousand arts you try.

Kār ba kasrat hai.
Practice makes perfect.

Kar bhalā, ho bhalā, ant bhale kā bhalā.
Do good and find good, for the fruit of good is good.

Karchhī hāth sailāne hī ko karte hain.
Ladles are made to save the hands.
(I don't keep dogs and bark myself: fingers were made before spoons.)

Kardanī khesh, āmdanī pesh; na kī ho, to kar dekh.
As you do, you will receive; if you have not tried it, try now.

Kare ḍāṛhī-vālā, pakṛā jāē mūchhon-vālā.
The long-beard did it and the moustache suffered.
(A man with a long beard in India is respected, whereas one with a moustache only is distrusted; the cat's paw.)

Kare ek, bharen sab.
One does and all suffer.
(Want of justice: allusion to the old native method of punishing the whole family of a criminal for the crimes he only had committed.)

Karegā so bharegā.
Who does will suffer.

Karen par-panch, kahlāen panch!
Who does injustice calls himself a judge!

Kargah bīch julāhā sohe, hal par sohe hālī,
Phaujan bīch sipāhī sohe, bāgan sohe mālī.
The weaver looks well at his loom, the ploughman by his plough, The soldier in his army, the gardener among his beds.

Kargah chhoṛ julāhā jāē, nā-haq choṭ bichārā khāē.
If a weaver leaves his loom and takes to roaming he is certain to be knocked about.
(Applied to one who suffers mischief by intermeddling with what does not concern him.)

Kaṛhāī chāṭegā, to tere byāh men menh barsegā.
Children's superstition.
Lick the platter and it will rain on your wedding day.
(As great a misfortune in the East as in the West.)

Kaṛhī kā sā ubāl.
Hot as curry.
(A bad temper.)

Kaṛhī men koelā.
Coals amongst curds.
(*Kaṛhī* is a dish of sour milk and pulse. It implies that two things or persons are ill associated together.)

Kāṛh men yā ḍāṛh men.
Lust or feeding.
(The world, the flesh and the devil: the pleasures of sensuality.)

Kaṛī kāṭ belan banānā!
To cut a beam to make a rolling-pin!

Kariye apne man kī, aur suniye sab kī.
Do as you desire, but listen to all men.
(Take advice, but decide yourself as to how you should act.)

Karkā sohe pālī ne, bārāh sohe mālī ne. Rus.
Pastorals suit the shepherd, and the song of the well the gardener.
(*Bārāh*, the song sung by gardeners when drawing water from their wells.)

Kar-ke khānā, aur magan rahnā.
Earn your living and be merry.

Kar khetī, pardes ko jāē, tā ko janam akārath jāē. Agric.
Who tills the soil and goes abroad wastes his life.

Kār ko kār sikhātā hai.
Working teaches you your work.
(Practice makes perfect.)

Kar le, so kām: bhaj lo, so Rām!
If you work, work at your business; if you sing hymns sing of God!

Karnā chāhe āshqī, aur māmā jī kā ḍar!
A lover and afraid of your uncle!
(Faint heart never won fair lady.)

Karne ko chākrī, sone ko ghar. E.
Service is for work, the house for sleep.
(A taunt to a person who is loth to go abroad on service.)

Karnī kare to kyoṅ ḍare, aur kar-ke kyoṅ pachhtāē? Peṛ boe babūl ke, to ām kahāṅ se khāē?
Why fear to do thy duty, and having done it why repent? If thou sowest acacias, can'st thou eat of mangoes?
(*Babūl*, the *acacia arabica*, a thorny tree.)

Karnī khāk kī, bāt lākh kī.
His deeds as dust; his speech of thousands.
(Words without deeds are like a garden full of weeds.)

Karnī na dharnī, nām Gulabyā!
Nor management, nor arrangement in her, and her name Rosa!
(*Gulabyā*, being a name of good import, is applied to sensible women only.)

Karnī nā kartūt, 'chaliyo mere pūt.'
Nor deeds nor action, and (he cries) 'come along my son.'
(Jack is doing nothing and Jim is helping him.)

Karnī nā kartūt, kahlāeṅ pūt sa-pūt.
Nor acts nor deeds, and he is called a good son.

Karnī nā kartūt, laṛne ko maujūd.
Fit for nothing, but ready to quarrel.

Karnī nā kartūt, laṛne ko mazbūt.
Fit for nothing, but strong in battle.
(Said to a boaster.)

Karo khetī aur bharo ḍanḍ. Agric.
Raise a crop and pay a fine.
(Allusion to cases of over assessment of land revenue.)

Karo khetī aur boö bail. Agric.
Plough a field and sow oxen.
(A good breed of oxen is becoming extinct.)

Karo to savāb nahīṅ, na karo to azāb nahīṅ.
Do it and gain not, don't do it and lose not.
(A transaction from which neither gain nor loss accrues.)

Kar pānī, na mūṅh pānī!
Nor water on the hands, nor on the face!
(Said of a dirty man.)

Kar sevā, khā mevā.
Do your duty and reap the fruits.
(Serve and be served.)

Kartab kī biddiyā hai.
Art depends on practice.
(See next.)

Kartā ustād, na kartā shāgird.
Who works is master, who works not is pupil.
(Plod beats genius.)

Kar to ḍar, na kar to Khudā ke gazab se ḍar.
Do it and fear, do it not and fear God's vengeance.

☞ There were two mendicants (*sādhū*) one of whom said "do it and fear": said the other "If I don't do it why should I fear!" The first said nothing and went away. Shortly afterwards some thieves went to rob the king's palace and gave, according to their custom a necklace to the *sādhū*, which they put on his neck without his knowledge, while he was meditating: next morning when it was found on him he was led to execution. His friend the first mendicant saw him and used the second part of the proverb. *Moral:* Always fear God.

Karūṅgā, par ṭalūṅgā nahīṅ.
I won't move until I have done it.
(A headstrong man.)

Kaṛvā subhāo, ḍubantī nāo.
A bad temper is like a sinking boat.
(As it is always in trouble.)

Kaṛvā thū thū, mīṭhā hap hap.
He spits out the bitter, and gulps down the sweet.

Kaṛvā zahar.
Bitter as poison.
(Bitter as gall.)

Kaṛve se milye, mīṭhe se ḍarye.
The bitter greet, but fear the sweet.
(All is not gold that glisters.)

Karyā bāman, gor chamār, tekrā sang na utre pār. E.
A black Brāhman, and a fair Chamār won't do you any good.
(Pure Brāhmans are usually fair, and pure Chamārs, a very low caste, usually black.)

Kāsā bhar khānā, āsā bhar chalnā.
A pot full of meal and a walk the length of the staff.
(An easy life.)

Kāsā dīje, bāsā na dīje.
Give food, but never give lodging.
(To a stranger: be cautious in your dealings with strangers.)

Kashmīrī be-pīrī, lazzat na shīrīṅ.
The faithless Kashmīrī hath nor flavour nor sweetness.

Kashmīrī se gorā so koṛhī.
Who is fairer than a Kashmīrī is a leper.
(The natives hold Kashmīris to be the fairest of all orientals.)

Kātā aur le dauṛī. Wom.
Off to the market as soon as she has spun.
(To be in a needless hurry.)

Kāṭā aur ulaṭ gayā.
The snake bit and turned round.
(By which the poison is said to be more completely infused and its effect rendered more certain.)

Kātak, bāt kahā tak.
October is over before you can speak.
(The pleasant cold weather is soon over.)

Kātak jo āṅore tare khāē, Kuṭumbh sahit baikunṭhe jāē. Supestition.
Who eats beneath the *āṅlā* tree in October will go to Heaven with all his family.
(Allusion to the feast of *āṅlā ekādashī* held on the 11th of Kātak (October.) The *āṅlā* is the *emblica officinalis.*)

Kātak kutyā, Māh bilāī, Chait meṅ chiṛyā, sadā lugāī.
Bitches in October, cats in January, sparrows in April, women always.

Kātā sūt paretan ko, pakkī roṭī juṛyāve ko. E. Wom.
She can reel off the spun thread, and manage the baken cakes.
(Said of a malingerer who avoids really hard work.)

Kāṭe bār, nām ho talvār kā ; laṛe sipāhī, nām ho sardār kā.
The sharp edge slays and the credit is the sword's; the soldier fights and the credit is the general's.

Kaṭegā baṭāū kā, sīkhegā nāū kā.
The wayfarer is cut, while the barber's son learns.
(A barber learns by shaving fools.)

Kāṭe kaṭe, na māre mare.
It can't be cut by cutting, nor killed by killing.
(The cat's nine lives.)

Kaṭe par non mirach lagānā.
To put salt on the wound.
(To add insult to injury.)

Kāṭh chhīlo to chiknā, bāt chhīlo to rukhī.
Scratch wood and it grows smooth, scratch a word and it grows rough.

Kāṭh kā ghoṛā, lohe kā zīn, jis par baiṭhe Langaṛ Dīn.
A wooden horse and an iron saddle, on which sits Lame Jack.
(A crutch.)

Kāṭh kā ghoṛā nahīṅ chaltā.
A wooden horse will never walk.

Kāṭh kā ullū.
A wooden owl.
(A blockhead.)

Kāṭh ke ghoṛe dauṛate haiṅ.
To set the wooden horse galloping.
(To raise the wind : to fly a kite.)

Kāṭh kī hāṅḍī bār bār nahīṅ chaṛhtī.
You can't put a wooden vessel on the fire twice.
(I am not to be cheated twice : deceit cannot be repeated with impunity and effect.)

Kāṭne-vāle ko thoṛā, baṭorne-vāle ko bahut. Agric.
Little to the reapers and much to the sheaf-makers.
(Because the latter get the gleanings.)

Kāṭo to khūn nahīṅ.
If he were cut, no blood would flow.
(Describes a man pale with fright.)

Kaunā kamāī par tel bukvā ? E. Wom.
On what income do you expect oil and cosmetics ?

Kaune rūp par etnā siṅgār ? E. Wom.
On the strength of what beauty do you deck yourself thus ?

Kaun har roz atāliq ho samjhāne ko ?
Who will teach day after day ?
(*i. e.* without payment : workmen won't work without payment.)

Kaun kahe Rājā jī naṅge haiṅ ?
Who would say that the Rājā is in rags ?
(Nor one ever cavils at the rich or powerful.

Kaun kisī ke āve jāve ? dāna pānī lātā hai. Superstition.
No one visits another; it is the prospect of food that takes him there.

Kaun sā darakht hai jise havā nahīṅ lagī.
What tree is there that the wind does not reach ?
(All are subject to the troubles of life.)

Kaunsī chakkī kā pisā khāyā hai ?
At what flour-mill have you eaten ?
(That you have grown so plump.)

Kauṛī gāṅṭh kī, jorū sāth kī.
Keep your penny in your pocket and your wife with you.

Kauṛī kauṛī māyā joṛī, kar bāteṅ chhal kī;
Bhārī bojh dharā sir ūpar ; kis bidh ho halkī ?
Money and wealth gathered by deceit are a heavy load upon the head; how will you get rid of it ?

Kauṛī kauṛī pe jān detā hai !
For the sake of a penny he would risk his life !

Kauṛī ke tīn tīn ho gaë.
Three for a farthing.
(Dirt cheap)

Kauṛī ke vāste masjid dhāte haiṅ. Mah-
He would let the mosque go to ruin to save a penny.

Kauṛī nahīṅ gāṅṭh meṅ chale bāg kī sair !
He has not a penny in his purse and goes to visit the gardens !
(Where the gardeners will expect a present. Applied to one, who sets about any undertaking without possessing the necessary means to accomplish it.)

Kauṛī na ho, to phir kauṛī ke tīn tīn haiṅ.
If you have not a penny you are dirt cheap.
(See above *kauṛī ke tīn tīn*, etc.)

Kauṛī na rakh kafan ko, bijjū kī shakl ban rah.
Don't keep enough to buy a winding sheet, but be like a hyena.
(Who lives upon dead bodies and has no occasion for a shroud. The spend-thrift. Eat, drink, and be merry for to-morrow we die.)

Kauṛī pās nahīṅ, parī afīm kī chāṭ.
Without a penny about him he has acquired a taste for opium!
(Opium is a very costly drug.)

Kauṛī pe khūn nahīṅ hotā!
Blood is not shed for a penny!

Kavvā chalā hans kī chāl, apnī chāl bhī bhūl gayā.
The crow in imitating the swan's gait forgot his own.
(Imitate the ways of the wealthy and you will lose your own.)

Kavvā kān le gayā.
The crow has carried off his ears.
☞ Spoken of a fool, who believes whatever is said without examination. The saying is taken from the story of a silly fellow, who being told that a crow had taken away his ears, began to pursue the crow, without waiting to examine if it was so.

Kavvā ṭar-ṭarātā hī hai, dhān sūkhte hī haiṅ. E. Wom.
The crows keep on cawing, but the corn dries all the same.
(The business in hand goes on well, notwithstanding the opposition of cavillers.)

Kavve kī dum meṅ anār kī kalī.
Pommegranate blossoms on a crow's tail.
(To describe a black ugly person finely dressed.)

Kavvoṅ ke kose se kahīṅ ḍhor marte haiṅ?
Do cattle ever die for a crow's curse?
(If one person wish ill to another from interested motives, it has no effect.)

Kavvoṅ ko angūrī bāg.
A vineyard for crows.
(Pearls before swine.)

Kāyā kashṭ hai, jān jokhoṅ nahīṅ.
It is pain to the body, but not a danger to life.
(A common consolation in sickness in the mouths of physicians and priests.)

Kāyā māyā kī kyā bharosā hai?
No reliance on wealth and life.

Kāyā pāpī achchhā, man pāpī kuchh nahīṅ.
Better be a leper than a knave.

Kāyā rākhe dharam, aur pūṅjī rākhe beohār.
Your religious observances preserve your body, and your capital your trade.

Kāyath kā beṭā paṛhā bhalā, yā marā bhalā.
A Kāyath's son should be either learned or dead.
(All occupations are hereditary in India: that of a Kāyath is to read and write; hence point of proverb.)

Kāyath kā hathyār qalam hai.
The pen is the Kāyath's weapon.
(See preceding.)

Kāyathoṅ meṅ sab se chhoṭe, aur bhāṅḍoṅ meṅ sab se baṛe kī kambakhtī hai.
The youngest among the Kāyaths and the chief among players are the most unfortunate.
(The youngest in a Kāyath family is made to do all the household work and of course the best player is most in requisition.)

Kehū ke jeṭh pūt, kehū ke lekhe kanwā. E.
To some he is an elder son, to others only a boy.
(His relatives are proud of him and strangers merely know him as a boy.)

Kekar kekar dharo nāoṅ, kamrā orhle sāre gāoṅ. E.
The whole village wears a blanket, whatever you choose to call it.
(A rose by any other name would smell as sweet.)

Ke karnī kare, kekrā sire bīte. E.
One does the act, and another is called to account for it.

Khāē kāsā bhar, chale āsā bhar.
He eats a bowlful and walks the length of a stick.
(Applied to a lazy gluttonous fellow.)

Khāē ke gāl, nhāē ke bāl nahīṅ chhipte.
The face of the well-fed and the hair of the bathed cannot be hid.
(Spoken of one who denies something that he has done, but whose countenance betrays him: thy speech doth betray thee.)

Khāē kī baṛiāṅ, ṭāṅg raheṅ khaṛiāṅ! Panj.
Fed on balls of pulse and strong on his legs!
(*Baṛiāṅ* is very nutritious food.)

Khāē na khilāē, khālā dīdoṅ āge pāē! Mah. Wom.
My aunt neither eats nor gives me to eat, may she lose her eyes and legs!
(A curse.)

Khāē nānā kā, kahlāve dādā kā.
He lives on his mother's father and is called the grandson of his father's father.

Khāeṅ to ghī se, nahīṅ jāēṅ jī se.
If he cannot eat with butter he'll die.
(A *gourmet*.)

Khāe to pachhtāē, na khāē to pachhtāē.
Eat and repent, eat not and still repent.
(Said of nasty food not easily procurable: proverb usually refers to *būr ke laḍḍū*, sweetmeats made of sawdust and covered with sugar, distributed as a joke at the Holi festival.)

Khag jāne khag hī kī bhāshā.
Only a crow understands crows' language.

Khāī bhalī, ki māī bhalī?
Feeding is dearer than a mother!

Khāī kare kamāī, kappaṛ kare siṅgār.
Eat to earn and dress to adorn.

Khāī Mugal kī tāērī, kahāṅ jāēgī bāhrī ?
She has tasted the Mugal's food, and will never leave him.
(Said of a mistress: Mugals are popularly supposed to be the best livers in India.)

Khairāt ke ṭukṛe aur bāzār meṅ ḍakār.
He lives upon alms, and belches in the market.
(Applied to any one who boasts of acquirements, which in fact are borrowed: to eructate is in India a sign of having dined well!)

Khair ! jo hūā so huā !
Well ! let bygones be bygones !

Khair kā beṛā pār hai.
The boat of the upright goes across.
(Virtue succeeds: *beṛā pār honā*, idiom, to succeed.)

Khair kī jūtī, khairāt kā nāṛā, paṛh de, Mullā, aqd udhārā. Mah. Wom.
My shoes and breeches were got as alms, so Mullah, marry me on credit.
(*Mullahs* or priests always receive a fee for the marriage ceremony.)

Khāiye man bhātā, pahniye jag bhātā.
Eat to please yourself, dress to please the world.

Khāk chāṭ-ke kahtā hūṅ.
I lick the dust before I speak.
(To imply extreme humility.)

Khāk chhānte, ber bīnte.
Winnowing dust and picking up wild plums.
(To be unprofitably employed: *ber*, or the fruit of the *zyziphus jujuba*, is of no value.)

Khāk ḍāle chānd nahīṅ chhiptā.
The moon is not hid by throwing dust on it.
(Solid worth is not sullied by slander.)

Khāk dhūl bakān ke phūl.
The dust of the ground, and the flower of the *bakāyan*.
(They are equally worthless: proverb used to typify a person of worthless character, or one who makes worthless assertions.)

Khā-ke jaldī chalīye kos, marīye āp, Daib ke dos!
Walk a mile quickly after your food and die and blame Fate!

Khā-ke pachhtātā hai, nahā-ke nahīṅ pachhtātā.
You may eat and regret, but not bathe and regret.

Khākī anḍe kī paidāyash.
The brood of an addled egg.

Khākī anḍon meṅ bachche nahīṅ hote.
Addled eggs bring forth no chicks.

Khālā jī kā ghar nahīṅ hai. Mah.
It is not your aunt's house.
(Not an easy matter: in India a man can do much as he pleases in his aunt's house.)

Khālā kā dam aur kivāṛ kī joṛī. Mah.
Only an aunt alive and a pair of door flaps.
(Said to a boaster.)

Khālā kā rutba māṅ ke barābar. Mah.
An aunt is as a mother.
(Allusion to the affection entertained in India by women for their sisters' children.)

Khālā kī mehmānī, hāth ḍāl pachhtānī. Mah. Wom.
To accept the invitation of an aunt and repent of it.
(Visit your aunt, but not every day in the year: don't outstay your welcome.)

Khā le, pahan le, so apnā.
Only what you eat and wear is yours.
(Said of the childless, as what he would save would go to strangers.)

Khal guṛ ek hī bhāo !
Treacle and oil cakes at the same price!
(A bad government: *guṛ* is much more expensive than *khal*.)

Khālī banyā kyā kare? Is koṭhī ke dhān us koṭhī meṅ dhare.
The unemployed shopkeeper will move his grain from one room to another.
(He cannot bear to be idle and will do a useless thing rather than nothing.)

Khālī ghar meṅ qalandar baiṭhe.
The *qalandar* will reside in an empty house.
(The *qalandar* is a Mahammadan ascetic: moral is, lock up your house when you leave it.)

Khālī hāth kyā jāūṅ? Ek sandesa letā jāūṅ.
How can I go empty handed? Let me at least take some message!
(Allusion to the natives' trick of never saying straight out what they want: to beat about the bush.)

Khālī hāth muṅh tak nahīṅ jātā.
Empty hands don't go to the mouth.

Khālī kharītī, pūrī fazīhatī. Wom.
An empty purse is a great curse.

Khalīl Khān fākhtā mārte haiṅ.
Khalīl Khāṅ is shooting doves.
(Idiomatic phrase: to make a happy hit.)

Khālī mabāsh, kuchh kiyā kar !
Never be idle, do something!

Khālī se begār bhalī.
Forced labor is better than idleness.

Khalq kā halq kis ne band kiyā?
Who can stop the people's voice?

Khalq Khudā kī, mulk bādshāh kā.
The people are God's and the land the king's.

Khalq kī zabān Khudā kā naqqāra.
The voice of the people is the drum of God.
(*Vox populi vox Dei.*)

Khalyā sās kin sāsoṅ meṅ? Kodoṅ kā bhāt kin bhātoṅ meṅ? E.
The wife's aunt is no mother-in-law, as millet is no rice.

Khām ko kām sikhātā hai.
Work teaches the unskilled.
(Practice makes perfect.)

Khānā aur aiṅḍnā.
Eating and lounging.
(Said of an idle lad.)

Khānā aur aghānā!
(1.) Overeat and be drowsy!
(2.) Overeat and swell!

Khānā aur gurrānā.
Feed and growl.
(Ingratitude.)

Khānā na kapṛā, saiṅt kā bhatrā. E. Wom.
Nor food nor raiment, a husband but in name.
(See next.)

Khānā na kapṛā, sent kā karnā.
No food nor raiment, and to keep her on nothing.
(Said of an improvident marriage.)

Khānā parāyā hai, to peṭ to parāya nahīṅ hai.
The food is another's, but the belly is your own.
(Said to one who gormandises at a feast.)

Khānā pīnā gāṅṭh kā, nirī salām alek.
My food and drink at my own expense, and my salutation returned.
(The point is that the speaker hoped by making friends with a great man to get something out of him: hence proverb describes fruitless court paid to a great man.)

Khānā sharākat, rahnā farāgat!
Eat in company, and live at ease!

Khānā vahāṅ khāo, to pānī yahāṅ pīnā.
Take your food there, and your drink here.
(Used in summoning a man in an emergency.)

Khāṅḍā bāje ran paṛe, dāṅtā bāje ghar paṛe.
The clatter of swords portends war and domestic jars a ruined house.

Khāṅḍ aur rāṅḍ kā joban rāt ko.
Sweets and harlots are best at night.
(Sweets are usually eaten by natives at the evening meal.)

Khāṅḍ binā sab rāṅḍ rasoī. Hin.
Without sugar a dinner is like a widow.
(For whom no one in India has any regard.)

Khāṅḍ khūṅdegā, so khāṅḍ khāegā.
Who treads out sugar will eat sugar.

Khāṅḍ kī roṭī, jahāṅ toṛo, tahāṅ mīṭhī.
A sweet cake is always sweet, wherever you may break it.

Khāne ke dāṅt aur, dikhāne ke aur.
Some teeth to eat with and some for show.
(Said of elephants' teeth and tusks and applied to hypocrites.)

Khāne ko bi'smi'llah, kām ko istagfiru'llah. Mah.
Ready for the grace before meat, but for work "God forbid."

Khāne ko mawwā, pahnne ko amawwā.
He eats *mawwā* flowers and wears *amawwā.*
(He starves the belly and feeds the back: *mawwā* flowers contain no nutrition in them, and *amawwā* means gaudy clothing.)

Khāne ko na mile; khair, par nashe ko mile.
It is of no use for food; well, it will do for strong drink.
(*Nashā* is a wider term than any in English and includes anything intoxicating, as *bhang*, opium, liquor, etc.)

Khāne ko pīchhe, nahāne ko pahle. Hin.
Bathe before eating.

Khāne ko sher, kamāne ko bakrī.
He feeds like a lion, but works like a goat.

Khāne ko ūd, kamāne ko majnūṅ.
Ready to eat, useless for work.
(*Majnūṅ*, properly a madman, used for any emaciated or weakly person.)

Khāne meṅ chatnī, palang par naṭnī.
Take sauce to your meat and a harlot to your bed.

Khāne meṅ sharm kyā? aur ghūṅsoṅ meṅ udhār kyā?
Who is ashamed to eat? and who takes a blow on loan?
(An eye for an eye and a tooth for a tooth.)

Khanjar tale ṭuk dam liyā, to phir kyā?
A moment's respite under a sword is of no consequence.

Khān khānā, jin ke khāne meṅ batānā.
Khānkhānā's dinner was served on gold.
(Bahrām Khāṅ, Khān Khānān, the friend and adviser of the emperor Akbar, is the person here alluded to.)

Khaṛā bahist meṅ gayā.
Anchored in heaven.
(Died in the odour of sanctity.)

Kharab arab lauṅ Lakshmī, ude ast lauṅ rāj,
Tulsī, Hari kī bhagt bin yeh āve keh kāj?
Millions of money and dominion from East to West avail
Nothing, saith Tulsī, without devotion to God.
(Tulsī Dās was the celebrated author of the Hindī *Rāmāyan.*)

Kharāb khasta, nāj sastā.
Forlorn as cheap corn.
(A man reduced to very low circumstances.)

Kharā khel Farrukhābādī.
The fair play of Farrukhābād.
(Allusion to the purity of Farrukhābād rupees.)

Kharbūzā chāhe dhūp ko, aur ām chāhe menh,
Nārī chāhe zor ko, aur bālak chāhe neh.
Melons want the sun, and mangoes want the rain, Women want a strong hand, and children want love.

Kharbūze ko dekh-kar kharbūzā rang pakaṛtā hai.
Melons mixed with melons change colour.
(*i. e.* ripen; society moulds men.)

Kharch ghanā, aur paidā thoṛī, kis par bāndhūṅ ghoṛā ghoṛī?
With great expenses, and small income, on what shall I keep horses?

Khaṛe pīr kā roza rakkhā hai kyā?
Are you keeping a fast for the standing priest?
(Said to one who doesn't take a seat on paying a visit.)

Khaṛe rassī, baiṭhe kos, khāte pīte tīn kos.
Stand still and it will be a chain, sit a-

while and it will be a mile, eat and drink and it will be three miles.
(Said of time lost on a journey. *Moral*, don't waste your time.)

Kharī mazdūrī, chokhā kām.
Cash payment means good work.

Khārishtī kuttyā aur makhmal kī jhūl!
A mangy bitch in a velvet dress!
(An ugly woman in a handsome dress.)

Kharsā piyārā bijnā, siyāle piyārī āg,
Barkhā piyārī tīn chīz, kambal, chhāvā, rāg. Rus.
In summer I like a fan, in winter a fire,
In the rains a blanket, a roof and a song.

Khasam, devar donoṅ ek sās ke pūt; yeh huā, yā voh huā. Rus. Wom.
Your husband and his younger brother are sons of one mother; if it is not the former, then it is the latter.
(That you can live with: allusion to the *kareo* marriage, or levirate, among the Jāṭs.)

Khasam kā khāeṅ, bhāī kā gāeṅ. Wom.
She is supported by her husband, but gives her brother the credit of it.
(A habit among native women.)

Khasam kīyā sukh sone ko, ki pāṭī lag-ke rone ko. Wom.
I took a husband to live with and have only a wall to weep against.
(Allusion to the misfortunes attending to the marriage of a young girl with an old husband, by which the father of the bride for mercenary interests renders the poor girl the victim of life-long misery.)

Khasam se chhūṭe, to yāroṅ ke jāe.
Free from the husband, off to the lover.
(Be off with the old love before you're on with the new.)

Khas kam, jahāṅ pāk.
The less the filth the purer the earth.
(Said of the death of a bad man: These three years I came seeking fruit on this fig tree and found none: cut it down: why cumbereth it the ground? Luke, xiii. 7.)

Khātā bhī jāe, baṛṛātā bhī jāe.
He goes on eating and grumbling over it.

Khātā kare bīvī, pakṛī jāe bāndī.
The mistress sins and the slave girl pays for it.

Khāte kamāte raho!
May you earn and eat!
(A benediction.)

Khāte pīte jog mile, ausar mile na koe.
In prosperity all are your friends, in adversity no one.
(A friend in need is friend indeed.)

Khāt paṛe to khet, nahīṅ, bhūṛ kā ret. Agric.
Manure it and it is a field, otherwise it is sandy desert.

Khatrī se gorā, so piṅḍrogī.
Who is fairer than a Khatrī is a leper.
(Applied to one who endeavours to deceive a person wiser than himself: Khatrīs are famous for their fair skins and good complexions.)

Khāūṅ to gehūṅ, na to rahūṅ ehūṅ.
If I eat, it shall be wheat, else I 'll remain as I am.
(*i. e.* hungry: said of the dainty.)

Khāve bakrī kī tarah, sūkhe lakṛī kī tarah.
He eats like a goat, yet is dry as a stick.
(Spoken of a lean person with a great appetite.)

Khāve chanā, rahe banā. Agric.
Eat pulse and keep your health.
(Pulse is considered to be very wholesome food by natives.)

Khāve ghoṛā, yā khāe roṛā.
To feed a horse and build a house.
(Is ruin: building is sweet impoverishment.)

Khāve moṭ, toṛe koṭ.
Who eats vetches can storm a fort.
(See *khāve chanā, rahe banā.*)

Khāve mūṅg, rahe ūṅg.
He that eats *mūṅg* is drowsy.
(The *phaseolus mungo* is considered weakening food: see preceding.)

Khāve pān, ṭukṛe ko hairān.
No bread for his stomach and a taste for betel leaves.
(Which are a luxury only for the wealthy.)

Khave se khavā chhiltā hai.
Shoulder rubs shoulder.
(A great crowd: a crush.)

Khāvind rāj buland rāj, pūt rāj dūt rāj. Hin. Wom.
The husband's reign is a great reign, the son's reign is the devil's reign.
(A woman is better off while her husband is alive than when she is a widow dependent on her son.)

Khāyā pīyā aṅg lagā.
Food and drink nourishes the body.

Khedī gillo ant ko peṛ hī nīche ātī hai.
The hunted squirrel runs to the tree.
(The wanderer returns home at last.)

Khel khilāṛī kā, bhagat bhaiyā jī kī.
Good play comes from practice, devotion comes from the heart.

Khel khilāṛī kā, paisā madārī kā.
The player has the game, but the money goes to the conjuror.
(*Madārī* is a man who makes money by playing conjuring tricks.)

Khel meṅ rove so kavvā. Children.
Who cries in a game is a crow.
(*i. e.* a spoil-sport.)

Khel na jāne murgī kā, uṛāne lagā bāz.
He does not understand cock-fighting and has taken to hawking.
(Spoken of a man incapable of even an easy matter who attempts one more difficult.)

Khep hārī, janam nahīṅ hārā.
I have lost this trip, but not my life.
(While there is life there is hope.)

Khet baranī, jaise niām rājānī. Agric.
An unirrigated field is like the gift of a king.
(Who is generally a capricious tyrant and his gifts uncertain: allusion to the uncertain character of the cultivation in India that depends only on rainfall.)

Khet bigāṛe khartuā, aur sabhā bigāṛe dūt. Agric.
Backbiters ruin society, as weeds ruin the field.

Khet gae kisān. Agric.
He is a husbandman that goes to the field.
(A man's qualifications can only be known by trial: a tree is known by its fruit.)

Khetī kar-kar ham mare, bahore ke koṭhe bhare. Agric.
I worked myself to death in the fields, and it was the banker that filled his granary.
(Allusion to the indebtedness of the cultivating class of India.)

Khetī khasam setī.
Husbandry depends on the master.
(The master's eye makes the mare fat.)

Khetī, pātī, bintī, aur ghoṛe kā tang,
Apne hāth sañvāriye, chāhe lākhoṅ hoṅ sang.
Your fields, your letters, your wants, and your horse's girths Look to yourself, even if you have a thousand servants.
(If you want a thing done well do it yourself.)

Khetī rāj rajāë, khetī bhīk mangāë. Agric.
Husbandry makes kings and beggars both.
(A good harvest means wealth and a bad one ruin.)

Khichṛī chalī pakāvan ko charkhā toṛ jalā;
Āyā kuttā khā gayā, baiṭhī ḍhol bajā.
To cook her dinner she burnt her spinning wheel; Then came a dog and ate it, and now she grieves.
(Spoken of one who gives up a thing in possession to obtain another and loses both: *ḍhol bajānā*, to do an unprofitable thing: a bird in hand is worth two in the bush.)

Khichṛī khāte pahoṅchā utar gayā.
His wrist is dislocated by eating *khichṛī*.
(By a very slight exertion. To express great affected delicacy: *khichṛī* is merely rice and pulse.)

Khidmat se azmat hai.
Advancement depends on service.
(Those can best command who can best obey.)

Khilāë kā nām nahīṅ, rulāë kā nām.
You will get no name by feeding (a child), but you will by making him cry.

Khīl batāshoṅ kā mel hai.
It is a fair of *khīl* and *batāshā*.
(*Khīl*, parched rice, and *batāshā*, a sweet, are always distributed together at the *Dīvālī*. Proverb expresses things well paired.)

Khīl batāsoṅ kā meṅh.
It is raining *khīl* and *batāsās*.
☞ It is related of a noted Shekh Chillī (typical fool) that he once brought home some stolen property which his mother hid away. She, however, fearing lest his stupidity should lead to discovery, contrived to let fall unseen a shower of *khīl* and *batāshā* (parched rice grains and lumps of sugar) which the fool was made to believe had dropped from the sky. In due course enquiries were set on foot and the fool confessed to the theft. But his mother pleaded that he was an idiot, and by way of proof suggested the question, "when was the theft committed"! The fool promptly replied, "Don't I know! it was the day it rained *khīl* and *batāsās*."

Khiñchā khiñchā voh phire jo ṛarāë bīch meṅ paṛe.
Who interferes in other's affairs are dragged here and there.
(To give evidence, etc: of little meddling comes great ease.)

Khirādī kā gāṅṭh kāhe hī kaṭe. E.
The turner's tool cuts through every thing.

Khisyānī billī khambā noche.
An angry cat scratches the pillar.
(Applied to one who shews impotent rage.)

Khizar mile, jī, Khizar mile! Mah.
I have found Khizar.
(*Eureka!* Said by a person who succeeds according to his wish. Agreeably to oriental story, Khizar is the name of a prophet, who is said to have found out the fountain of life, and having drunk thereof to have become immortal. In Hindustāni he is generally called Khwājā Khizar, and is considered as the great guide to those who have lost their road in the wilds, and is *par excellence* the god of the flood.)

Khizrī khabar sachchī hotī hai.
The words of Khizar are true.

Khogīr kī bhartī.
The stuffing of a pack saddle.
(Applied to any worthless thing, which is only required to fill up space.)

Khol ghaṛā, kar be dhaṛā. Mercantile.
Open the jar, and get ready the scales.
(The phrase is applied to one who, without having the means of payment, is extremely urgent in his demand to be expeditiously served.)

Khol kīsah, khā harīsah.
Open your purse and eat your pottage.
(Prate is but prate, it's money buys land.)

Khon baṛā, khon-posh baṛā; khol-ke dekho, to ādhā baṛā. Mah Wom.
The tray is large and so is the cover; take it off and you will find only half a cake in it.
(A pun on the word *baṛā*, great, and also a cake.)

Khon pāk, khon-posh pāk; khol-ke dekho, to khāk hī khāk. Mah. Wom.
The tray is clean and so is the cover; take it off, you will see nothing but dust.

Khoṭā paisā, khoṭā beṭā, vaqt par kām ātā hai.
A bad penny and a bad son will serve some turn or other.
(*Moral*: cast aside nothing as useless: waste not want not.)

Khūb dunyā ko āzmā dekhā; Jisko dekhā, so bevafā dekhā.
I have tried the world well; And all in it are untrustworthy.

Khūb guzregī, jo mil baiṭheṅge dīvāne do.
When madman meets madman they spend a jolly time.
(Birds of a feather flock together.)

Khūb hī dāṅt khaṭṭe huē.
His teeth were completely set on edge.
(He was rendered entirely helpless : used of a man completely worsted in argument or very severely reprimanded : he had not a word to say for himself.)

Khudā bhare ko bhartā hai.
God fills the full.
(To him that hath shall be given.)

Khudā bhūkā uṭhātā hai, bhūkā sulātā nahīṅ.
God wakes the hungry, but does not send the hungry to sleep.
(*i. e.* men wake up hungry and go to bed full : in India the very poorest have an evening meal.)

Khudā dekhā nahīṅ, to aqal se to pahchānā hai.
You have not seen God, but you may comprehend Him with your understanding.
(Applied to any fact which is ascertained by presumptive evidence.)

Khudā detā hai, to chhappar phāṛ-ke detā hai.
When God gives He gives through the roof.
(*i. e.* unexpectedly.)

Khudā detā hai, to nahīṅ pūchhtā, " tū kaun hai. ? "
When God gives He does not enquire, " who art thou. ? "

Khudā do sīṅg de, to voh bhī sahe jāte haiṅ.
If God were to give me two horns, even with them would I be content.
(To express resignation.)

Khudā ganje ko nākhūn na de!
May God never give the bald-head nails !
(A prayer that a mean man may *not* be put in a position of authority : Jack in office.)

Khudā hāzir o nāzir hai.
God is omnipresent and omniscient.

Khudāī khuār gadhe savār !
May you be deserted of the world and ride on an ass !
(A curse : to be set on ass with the face to its tail was a favorite degrading punishment before the English occupation.)

Khudā kā darvāzah hamesh khulā hai.
God's gate is ever open.

Khudā kā dīyā kandhe par, panchoṅ kā dīyā sir par.
God's judgment is on the shoulder, but the judge's on the head.
(Men pay more attention to the opinion of the world than to their consciences.)

Khudā kā dīyā sir par.
God's decree is on my head.
(Resignation : this proverb is also a riddle, the answer being 'the moon,' based on a pun on the word *dīyā*, which means 'decree, gift' or 'lamp' ; so the riddle is " God's lamp is overhead.")

Khudā kā mārā harām, apnā mārā halāl ! Hin.
Killed by God is unlawful, killed by yourself is lawful food !

Khudā ke gazab se ḍarte rahiye.
Fear the wrath of God.
(Said to one who is about to commit any bad action.)

Khudā ke ghar meṅ chor kā kyā kām ? Mah.
What business has a thief in the house of God ?

Khudā ke ghar meṅ sab kuchh. Mah.
In the house of God there is every thing.
(With God all things are possible.)

Khudā ke ghar se phire haiṅ. Mah.
They have returned from the house of God.
(Said of a person who has just escaped death : also in derision of a person who affects to foretell events.)

Khudā khafā ho, to paidal chalāē ; ziyādah khafā ho, to sir par bojhā rakhāē ; jo khush ho, to meṅh barsāē; ziyādah khush ho, to beṭā de.
When God is angry He makes you travel on foot, and when He is more angry He puts a load on your head ; but when God is pleased He sends rain, and when He is best pleased He gives a son.

Khudā kī bāteṅ Khudā hī jāne.
God only knows the things that pertain to God.
(The mysteries of God, God only knows : the proverb is a part of a line in a well known poem by Nazir " *jo khūb dekhā to, yaroṅ, ākhir Khudā kī bāteṅ,*" etc.)

Khudā kī chorī nahīṅ, to bande kā kyā ḍar ?
When you cannot hide from God, why fear man ?

Khudā kī lāṭhī meṅ āvāz nahīṅ.
God's club makes no noise.
(Spoken by one enduring oppression which he can't avoid.)

Khudā kisī ko kisī kā mohtāj nā kare !
May God never make one man dependent on another !

Khudā kisī ko lāṭhī le-kar nahīṅ mārtā.
God never strikes with a stick.

Khudā ko yād karo.
Remember God.

Khudā lagtī koī nahīṅ kahtā, mūṅh dekhī sab kahte haiṅ.
No one says what is pleasing to God, but every one says what is pleasing to man.
(*i. e.* mankind prefers flattery to truth.)

Khudā laṛne kī rāt de, bichhaṛne kā din na de ! Wom.
God grant us the night of fighting, but never the day of separation !

Khudā mahfūz rakkhe har balā se !
God keep us from every calamity !

Khudā mehrbān, to jag mehrbān.
When God is kind the world is kind.

Khudā mehrbān, to kul mehrbān.
If God is kind, then all are kind.

Khudā ne to javāb de diyā hai, be-hayāī se jīte haiṅ !
God has long done with him, but the shameless fellow won't die !
Khudā razzāq hai, bandah qazzāq hai.
It is God that provides, man that robs.
(*Qazzāq*, robber, a word derived from the plundering Turkish tribe of the Qāzzāqs (Cossacks.)
Khudā sab kī mehnat suārath kartā hai, akārath nahīṅ kartā.
God makes the labour of all successful, never unsuccessful.
Khudā se khair māṅgo !
Pray to God to keep thee safe !
(Said to boasters, liars, evil prognosticators, etc.)
Khudā shakkar-khore ko shakkar hī detā hai.
God gives sugar to the sugar-eater.
(God tempers the wind to the shorn lamb.)
Khudā ke vāste billī bhī chūhā nahīṅ mārtī.
The cat does not catch mice for the sake of God.
(People are generally moved by selfish motives.)
Khudā vāste kī dushmanī hai.
Enmity for the sake of God.
(*i. e.* without reason.)
Khudā zālim se pālā na ḍāle !
God save me from the tyrant's clutches !
Khudī aur khudāī meṅ bair hai.
There is enmity between self-love and holiness.
Khud kardah rā ilāje nest. Pers.
There is no remedy for one's own actions.
Khud rā fazīhat, digare rā nasīhat. Pers.
A scoundrel himself he preaches to others.
Khufta rā khufta kai kunad bedār ? Pers.
How shall a sleeping man awake a sleeping man ?
Khunḍā hathyār, aur kīyā bhatār, kisī ke kām nahīṅ ātā. Wom.
A blunt tool and a paramour are of no use.
(*Kīyā bhatār*, is used towards a man not formally married to the woman he lives with.)
Khūn voh jo sir chaṛh-ke bole.
Murder speaks of itself.
(Murder will out.)
Khurchan Mathrā kī, aur sab naqal.
Real cream comes from Mathurā, all others are copies.
Khurdā na burdā, muft dard gurdā. Pers.
Nothing for eating and drinking, but a stomach-ache all the same.
Khuṛkā huā, chor ubhṛā.
No sooner there is a sound than the thief is off.
Khur khāṅsī, terī dāī ke gāle meṅ phāṅsī !
Coughing and coughing, the nurse is throttled !
(Said to children.)

Khush-āmdī kā muṅh kālā.
The flatterer's face is black.
(He is disgraced.)
Khush-āmad se āmad hai.
Flattery brings income.
(You must learn to please, if you want to live at ease.)
Khushkā khāo.
Eat rice.
(Idiomatic phrase: hold your tongue.)
Khush rah, Paṭhānī, nikal gayā pānī !
Thanks, Paṭhān, my work is done !
(Used when an employer is satisfied with work done for him.)
Khutke par sonā.
There is gold on his stick.
(Born with a silver spoon in his mouth.)
Kiryā aur tarkārī khāne hī ke bā. Bhoj.
Greens and oaths are made to be taken.
Kis bāg kī mūlī hai ?
What garden is this radish from ?
(An expression of contempt,)
Kis birte pe tattā pānī ? Wom.
On what account do you want warm water ?
(Used towards a worthless husband : warm water for washing is a luxury in India.)
Kisī kā āvā bigṛe, in kā khadāne kā khadānā bigaṛ gayā.
The kilns of some go wrong, of others the very clay.
(Of some families but one is led to take to evil ways, in others all are.)
Kisī kā ghar jale, koī tāpe.
One man's house burns and another warms himself.
(Applied to those who are pleased with great misfortunes befalling others, if they bring a small advantage to themselves.)
Kisī kā hāth chale, kisī kī zabān chale.
Some use their fists, some their tongues.
Kisī kā laṛkā, koī mannat māne.
One man prays for another's son.
(Applied to sons-in-law and to adopted children,)
Kisī kā muṅh chale, kisī kā hāth.
Some bite and some strike.
(He that strikes with the sword, will be beaten with the scabbard.)
Kisī ke kyā dabail baste haiṅ ?
Why should I care for any one ?
(I care for nobody and nobody cares for me!)
Kisī ke nuqsān kā ravā-dār na ho !
Wish not loss to any one !
Kisī kī mehnat zāyā nahīṅ hotī.
No one's labor goes for nothing.
Kisī ko apnā kar lo, yā kisī ke ho raho.
Make some one your friend or some one your patron.
Kisī ko baigan bāē, kisī ko baigan path.
Aubergines agree with some and disagree with others.
(One man's meat is another's poison.)

Kisī ko sāī, kisī ko badhāī.
Earnest to one man and performance to another.
(Breach of contract.)

Kisī ko tave meṅ dikhāī detā hai, kisī ko ārsī meṅ.
Some persons see themselves in an iron plate, others in a mirror.
(The point is that some have to use a ready-made mirror, others are sharp enough to polish an iron plate into a mirror for themselves: hence proverb refers to the superior intelligence of some people over others.)

Kisī ne yeh bhī nahīṅ pūchhā, ki tere muṅh meṅ kaë dāṅt haiṅ?
No one even asks now how many teeth you have in your mouth?
(The roads are safe: said of the English Government. *Pax Brittanica.*)

Kis khet kā bathvā hai?
What field is this weed from?
(See above *kis bāg kī mūlī hai?*)

Kis kī māṅ ne dhauṅsā khāyā hai?
What ill-fated mother bore thee?

Kiyā, par kar na jānā; maiṅ hotī, to kar dikhātī. Wom.
She did it, but did not know how to do it; had I been there I would have shown her how.
(Based on a story in the *Alif Laila.*)

Kodoṅ de-ke paṛhen haiṅ.
He studied on a present of millet.
(He did not give a proper fee to his master, who consequently did not attend to him with care.)

Kodoṅ kā bhāt kin bhātoṅ meṅ? mamiyā sās kin sāsoṅ meṅ? E.
What's millet among the kinds of grain or a wife's aunt among mothers-in-law?
(In India when the wife's mother is dead her uncle's wife takes her mother's place, but indifferently.)

Koelā hoë na ūjlā sajjī sābān lāë.
You can't make charcoal white by washing it with soap and soda.
(Proving white's black.)

Koeloṅ kī dallālī meṅ hāth kāle.
Coal brokers have black hands.
(Touch pitch and you will be defiled.)

Koh kandan o kāh bar āvudan. Pers.
To dig up a hill to find a straw.
(To look for a needle in a bundle of hay.)

Koī aine meṅ dekhe, koī ārsī meṅ.
Some look at themselves in a mirror, and some in a tiny looking glass.
(*Ārsī* is the mirror worn in a ring on the thumb by women: the point is that the face is the same wherever seen. A rose by any other name would smell as sweet.)

Koī āṅkh kā andhā, koī hiye kā aṅdhā.
Some are blind of the eyes and some of the heart.
(None are so blind as those that won't see.)

Koī bhī mā ke peṭ se to lekar nahīṅ niklā hai. Wom.
No one was taught in his mother's womb.

Koī dam kā damāmā hai.
It is a show of but a few moments.
(Said of human life.)

Koī dam kā mehmān hai.
He is but a moment's guest.
(Said of a dying person, or of a very old man.)

Koī dam meṅ sarsoṅ phūltī hai.
The mustard will blossom by and bye.
(He will soon be intoxicated.)

Koī ilm ko dost rakhtā hai, koī rupaë ko.
Some love learning, and some money.

Koī kah-ke sunāë, ham kar-ke dikhāëṅ.
Some talk, but I act.
(Deeds not words.)

Koī kām kare dām se, ham dām kareṅ kām se.
Some get work by money, I get money by work.
(Some occupations require capital.)

Koī khīṅche lāṅg langoṭī, koī khīṅche mūchhar-yāṅ; Koṭhe chaṛh-ke dī duhāī, 'koī mat kāri-yo do janyāṅ.'
One wife strips off his breeches and the other pulls off his moustaches, So he cries from the housetop, 'let no man marry two wives.'

Koī kisī kā kuchh nahīṅ kar saktā.
No one can do any thing to any body.
(Said of a good government or full liberty.)

Koī kisī kī qabr meṅ nahīṅ jātā.
No one goes into another's grave.
(We are all accountable for our own actions.)

Koī māl meṅ mast, koī khyāl meṅ mast.
Some love their wealth, and some their tastes.

Koī mare, koī malhār gāve.
One dies and another sings songs.
(*Malhār*, a song of joy for the rains.)

Koī mol meṅ bhārī, koī tol meṅ bhārī.
Some are heavy in price and some in mere weight.

Koī mujh ko na māre, to maiṅ sāre jahān ko mārūṅ!
If no one would beat me, I should beat the [whole world!
(Spoken in reproach to a coward.)

Koirī kā gāoṅ meṅ dhobī paṭvārī.
In the village of *Koirīs* the washerman is an accountant.
(Washermen in India carry their accounts of clothing very correctly in their heads, and so are good mental accountants, but they are wholly illiterate: *Koirīs* are an agricultural class in the east of Hindustān.)

Koī sune na sune, maiṅ kahtā hūṅ.
I'll have my say, let any body hear or not.
(Said of an idle talker.)

Koī toloṅ kam, koī moloṅ kam?
Some are light in weight, some in price.

Kokh kī āṅch sahī jātī hai, peṛū kī āṅch nahīṅ sahī jātī. Wom.
The pain of the womb can be borne, but not the pain of the pelvis.
(A woman can console herself at the death of her child, but not at the death of her husband.)

Kokh māṅg se ṭhanḍī rahe! Wom. Benediction.
May you ever be happy both in womb and head!
(Here *kokh*, womb, stands for offspring, and *māṅg*, crown of the head, for coverture.)

Kolhū kāṭ mogrā banānā.
To cut a pestle out of an oil-mill.
(To spoil a large and costly thing in order to make a small thing of little value.)

Kolhū kā bail ho gayā.
He has become the ox of an oil-mill.
(To work as a galley slave: the oxen of oil-mills are proverbially overworked.)

Kolhū ke bail kī tarah rāt din phirtā hai.
He works night and day like the ox of an oil-mill.
(See preceding.)

Kolhū ke bail ko ghar hī kos pachās.
The mill-ox is always fifty miles from his stall.
(Allusion to his continuous work.)

Kolhū se khal utrī bhaī bailoṅ jog.
When the oil-cake is removed from the mill, it is fit for the oxen.
(Spoken of one worn out with age, or out of place, so as to have lost the estimation in which he was formerly held: *khal* is the cake from which the oil has been expressed, and so is the refuse of the seeds.)

Kolī kā ghar jale, qalandar gānḍā māṅge.
The grazier's house is on fire, and the mendicant begs for sugarcane.
(To do a thing out of season: also expresses that all people think only of their own interests.)

Koṛhī ḍarāe thūk se.
The leper will frighten you by spitting at you.
(His spittle is greatly shunned, the disease being supposed to be contagious.)

Koṛhī kalanyāṅ, mungrā san āṅṭī, Ār pār baiṭhe girast ḍāṅṭī. Tir. Agric.
For idle reapers heavy sheaves, For those that work from end to end but fallen straws.
(I have seen the wicked flourishing as the green bay tree.)

Koṛhī ke jūṅ nahīṅ paṛtī.
The leper has no lice.
(Native observation.)

Koṛhī ko dāl bhāt, kamāsut ko phuṭhā. E.
The lazy lives on rice and pulse, the hard-working only on peas.
(Which are very cheap. See above *koṛhī kalanyāṅ*, etc.)

Koṛhī mare sangātī chāhe!
When the leper dies he wants a companion!

Koṛh meṅ khāj.
Itch on top of leprosy.
(Misfortunes never come singly.)

Kos chalī na, 'bābā, pyāsī.' Wom.
Not a mile travelled and "father, I am athirst."
(Applied to a person, who has hardly commenced a work and complains of fatigue.)

Kose jīeṅ, asīse mareṅ.
The accursed live and the blessed die.
(Threatened men live long: whom the gods love die early.)

Kotah gardan dum darāz.
A short neck and a long tail.
(Said of a wicked person.)

Kotah gardan, tang peshānī, harām-zāde kī yehī nishānī.
A short neck and a narrow forehead are the signs of a wicked man.

Koṭhe se girā saṅbhaltā hai, nazar se girā nahīṅ saṅbhaltā.
Fall from the housetop, and you can be saved; fall under the evil eye and you will never be saved.

Koṭhe-vālā rove, chhappar-vālā sove.
The dweller in brick weeps, while he of the hut sleeps.
(Uneasy lies the head that wears a crown.)

Koṭhī dhoe kīch hāth lage.
In washing the house the plaster sticks to the fingers.
(Touch pitch and you will be defiled.)

Koṭhī kuṭhle ko hāth na lagāo, ghar bār sab tumhārā. Wom.
Except the cupboard and the wardrobe the whole house is yours.
(Sham love: said of women who ill-treat their son's wives.)

Koṭhī meṅ chāur, ghar meṅ upās. E. Wom.
Grain in the barn, hunger in the house.
(Said of a fool or a miser.)

Koṭhī meṅ se moṭhī nahīṅ niklī.
One grain has not been taken from the store.
(Said 1st, of a man's estate that is unimpaired and of which no part is spent or lost. 2nd, of a young man come to years of maturity and yet uncorrupted by intercourse with the world, especially with regard to women.)

Koū ko kalpāē ke, koū kaise kal pāē?
Who troubles others, how shall he get repose?
(Admonition to children: when you trouble us like this remember that your children will trouble you.)

Koyal bolī aur seh-bandī ḍūbī.
The cuckoo sings and the tax collector has disappeared.
(The engagement for the revenues was formerly made with reference to the period of harvest, when the money was collected by persons appointed temporarily for that purpose. The *koyal*, or Indian cuckoo, sings at the *Rabī* or spring harvest, and the proverb

implies that a person is absent precisely when he should be engaged in his duty.)

Koyal kāle kavve kī jorū.
The cuckoo is the black crow's wife.
(One matches the other: both birds being black in India.)

Kūān bechā hai, kūēn kā pānī nahīn bechā.
I have sold the well, not its water!
(A quarrel on ridiculous grounds.)

Kuārī khāē roṭiyān, biyāhī khāē boṭiyān. Wom.
The virgin daughter eats bread, but the married eats the (parents') bones.
(In India any thing does for the unmarried daughter living with her parents, but as soon as she is married, presents must be made to her at every one of the numerous Hindū festivals.)

Kuārī ko sadā basant.
Maidenhood is perennial spring.

Kuār jāṛe kā duār.
September is the door of winter.

Kuār kā sā jhallā, āyā, barsā, challā.
Like September clouds, they came and rained and passed away.

Kuchāl sang hānsī, jīū jān kī phānsī. Wom.
To joke with the vicious is to hang yourself.

Kuchāl sang phirnā, āp mūt men girnā.
To associate with a wicked man is to fall into a sewer.

Kuchh ānsū se ponchhte hain.
They wipe their eyes as if they were full of tears.
(Sham affection.)

Kuchh basant kī bhī khabar hai?
Do you know that the spring has come?
(Said to one who does not rejoice when it is spring, and ironically to one who laughs when he should weep.)

Kuchh dāl men kālā kālā hai.
There is something black in the pulse.
(There is something wrong: to smell a rat.)

Kuchh ham samjhe, kuchh tum samjhe.
You thought one thing and I thought another.
(Cross purposes: to be at sixes and sevens. See story under *kuchh tum samjhe, etc.*)

Kuchh kho hī ke sīkhte hain.
Lose and learn.
(To buy experience.)

"*Kuchh lete ho?*" *kahā*, "*apnā kām kyā hai?*"
"*Kuchh dete ho?*" *kahā*, "*yeh sharārat bande ko nahīn ātī!*"
To, "Will you take any thing?" he replies, "what other business have I?" To, "Will you give any thing?" he answers, "so villainous a practice is unknown to your humble servant!"

Kuchh lohā khoṭā, kuchh luhār khoṭā.
The iron somewhat bad, the smith somewhat of a bad workman.
(Faults on both sides.)

Kuchh suārthī, kuchh parmārthī.
Somewhat for self and somewhat for Heaven.
(Serving God and Mammon.)

Kuchh to bāolī, kuchh bhūton khaderī. Wom.
Somewhat mad and somewhat possessed by evil spirits.
(Said of a silly and foolish woman.)

Kuchh to gehūn gīlī, kuchh jindrī ḍhīlī.
The wheat is somewhat damp and the pin (of the hand mill) is rather loose.
(Faults on both sides.)

Kuchh to khalal hai, ki jis se yeh khalal hai.
There must be defect to cause this fault.
(There is a screw loose somewhere.)

Kuchh to kharbūza mīṭhā, aur kuchh ūpar se qand!
The melon's something sweet, and on it there's some sugar.
(Doubly sweet.)

Kuchh tum samjhe, kuchh ham samjhe.
You think one way, and I another.
☞ A foot passenger, carrying some treasure, asked a horseman to relieve him of his load as far as the next stage. The horseman declined to burden himself, and went on. Soon after the horseman regretted that he had missed such a rare opportunity of making off with so much money, while the foot passenger, on his part, congratulated himself on the other's refusal, but for which he might have lost his money. The two met again and on the horseman offering to take charge of the treasure the other replied in the words of the proverb.

Kūde, phānde, toṛe tān, tākā dunyā rākhe mān.
Who dances and sings commands the world's regard.

Kūd kūd machhlī, bagule ko khāē!
The fishes jump up to eat the heron!
(The world upside down.)

Kūd, mue, kūd; terī nalyon men gūd.
Nikal gayā gūd, to rah gayā murdūd. Mah. Wom.
Jump, you rascal, jump, while marrow is in your bones.
When that marrow is gone, you will be no better than a corpse.

Kūdte kūdte nachanyā ho jātā hai.
By skipping and skipping one becomes a dancer at last.
(Practice makes perfect.)

Kūēn jhakāte hain.
They are bawling in a well.
(To try its echo; said of any unprofitable diversion.)

Kūen kā biyāh, gīt gāven masīt kā!
At the marriage of a well, she sings the song of the mosque!
(Applied to a person who does any thing out of place. It is an agricultural custom in Hindustān to marry two wells together for luck and to sing an appropriate song on the occasion.)

Kūen kī maṭṭī, kūen hī ko lag jātī hai.
The clay of the well is expended on the well.
(Said of the profit of any thing being laid out on that whence it was derived.)

Kūen men bhang paṛī hai.
Bhang (hemp) has fallen into the well.
(The water is as green and deleterious as the color of *bhang*, said when a whole community seems foolish or intoxicated.)

Kufr toṛā Khudā Khudā kar-ke.
By the grace of God I broke his wicked spirit.
(*Kufr*, properly unbelief in Islām, but here a wicked disposition: said of a turbulent man when subdued.)

Kulel men gulel.
A shot in a merry time.
(To fall like a bomb shell: a sudden interruption of happiness: to throw cold water upon.)

Kulhyā men guṛ nahīn phūṭtā hai.
You cannot break sugar into a little pot.
(A great event cannot be kept a secret: *guṛ* is always kept in large and strong pots owing to the weight of the balls into which it is made up.)

Kumhārī kā gussa utre gadhe par.
The wrath of the potter's wife falls upon her ass.

Kumhār kā gadhā, jahīn ke chūtaṛ maṭṭī dekhe, tahīn ke pīchhe dauṛe. E.
The potter's ass runs after any one whose breeches are muddy.
(He takes him for his master.)

Kumhār kahe se gadhe par nahīn chaṛhtā.
The potter won't ride his ass if you tell him to do so.
(Said of an unreasonably obstinate person.)

Kumhār ke ghar bāsan kā kāl !
A scarcity of pots in the potter's house !

Kumhār ke ghar chukke kā dukh !
A want of saucers in the potter's house !

Kumhār se pār na basāī, gadhe ke kān amethe.
Unable to settle with the potter he wreaks his vengeance on his ass.
(Said of one who, unable to retaliate himself on him who has offended him, bullies others.

Kunbe-vāle ke chāron palle kīchaṛ men hain.
The man with a family is dragged into the mire on all sides.

Kunda-i-nā-tarāsh. Pers.
An unlopped trunk.
(A block-head.)

Kūnḍe ke is pār, yā us pār.
On this or that side of the platter.
(To migrate from the blue bed to the brown: a lazy man.)

Kunjṛan kī agāṛī, aur qasāī kī pichhāṛī.
To the green-grocer early, and to the butcher late.
(If you want to get good things: in India the best vegetables go early in the day and the best meat is sold late.)

Kūnth ke zor kīyā, tau bhī na ṭūṭā pāpaṛ;
"In bhujā ḍanḍon pe," kahte the, "sipar chīrenge."
With all your strength you could not break a wafer, and yet you cry, "with these arms I could tear a shield."

Kūṛh aur ḍhīt !
Ignorant and confident !
(Ignorance is the mother of conceit.)

Kūṛī par phulel ḍālnā,
To pour oil of roses on a dunghill.
(To throw pearls before swine.)

Kursī kā ahmaq.
A consequential fool.
(*Kursī* means a chair, used only by the rich and persons of consequence; it is also the name of a town in Oudh noted for the folly of its inhabitants.)

Kuryāl men gulelā lagā.
The pellet hits the perch.
(A sudden misfortune upon a person when he feels himself secure and happy: *kuryāl* is properly a bird sitting at its ease and preening its wings.)

Kushtah kushtah mīkunad. Per.
I. Alchemy kills.
II. Alchemy strengthens.
(*Kushtah* in India is a medicine made of metals treated alchemically and used by *hakīms* in cases of impotence.)

Kusum kā rang tīn din, phir bad rang.
The safflower keeps its gaudy hues for three days only, and after that it gets pale.
(The temporary nature of beauty.)

Kuṭnī se to Rām bachāve ! pyārī ho-kar pat utrāve. Wom.
God protect you from a procuress ! She will gain your heart and betray your honor.

Kūṭo to chūnā; nahīn, khāk se dūnā.
Well-beaten it is plaster; unbeaten it is worse than dust.
(*Chūnā*, a plaster made of lime and hardened by being beaten while wet.)

Kuttā bhaunkā hī kartā hai; hāthī chalā hī jātā hai.
The dog may bark, but the elephant goes on.

Kuttā bhaunke, qāfila sidhāre.
The caravan proceeds in spite of the yelping [dog.

Kuttā bhī baiṭhtā hai, to dum hilā-kar baiṭhtā hai.
Even when a dog sits down, he brushes the spot with his tail.
(Said in recommendation of neatness.)

Kuttā chauk chaṛhāē, chapnī chāṭan jāē.
Make a dog into a bridegroom, and he will still lick the pot-lids.
(With whatever respect a mean person may be treated, he will not relinquish his beggarly habits.)

Kuttā dekhegā na bhaunkegā.
If the dog does not see it, he will not bark.
(Keep it out of sight, or somebody will want it.)

Kuttā ghās khāē, to sabhī pāl leṅ.
If dogs could live on grass, every body could keep one.

Kuttā ke āṭā hoē, to liṭṭī lagā-ke khāē. E.
If the dog had flour he would have baked bread for himself.

Kuttā mare apnī pīṛ, mīyāṅ māṅge shikār.
The dog is dying in agony, and his master wants him to go hunting.

Kuttā mūṅh lagāne se sir chaṛhe.
Indulge the familiarity of a dog, and he will jump on to your head.
(Keep the mean in their own place.)

Kuttā pāē, to savā man khāē; nahīṅ, to dīyā hī chāṭ-kar rah jāē.
A dog will eat a hundred-weight and a quarter, if he can get it; if not, he is content to lick the lamp.

Kuttā pāle voh kuttā, sāsre janvāī kuttā, bahan ke ghar bhāī kuttā; sab kutton kā voh sardār, jo rahve beṭī ke bār.
Who keeps a dog is a dog, the son-in-law living on his father-in-law is a dog, the brother living on his sister is a dog; but the father who lives on his daughter is a dog of dogs.

Kutte kā magz khāyā hai.
He has eaten dogs' brains.
(Said of a great talker.)

Kutte ke bhauṅkne se hāthī nahīṅ ḍartā.
An elephant is not frightened at the barking of a dog.

Kutte ke pāoṅ jā, aur billī ke pāoṅ ā.
Go at the dog's pace and come back at the cat's.
(Post haste: both animals travel rapidly.)

Kutte kī dum bārah baras nalve meṅ rakkho, tau bhī ṭeṛhī kī ṭeṛhī.
Put a dog's tail into a straight pipe for twelve years, and it will still be as crooked as ever.
(Said of a man incorrigibly bad.)

Kutte kī maut marnā.
To die a dog's death.

Kutte kī nīnd.
A dog's sleep.
(Said of a light sleeper: dogs awake at the slightest noise.)

Kutte kī sī paslī phaṛke. Superstition.
My heart beats like a dog's.
(The sensation of a throbbing over the ribs is supposed to indicate the approach of an absent lover or friend.)

Kutte ko ghī nahīṅ pachtā!
Dogs can't digest butter!
((i.) A worthless person cannot keep a secret. (ii.) he cannot possess wealth without feeling proud of it.)

Kutte ko haḍḍī bhalī lagtī hai. Hin.
Dogs best love a bone.
(Hindū skit at the Muhammadans.)

Kutte ko masjid se kyā kām? Mah.
What business has a dog in the mosque?

Kutte ko maut āve, to masjid meṅ mūt jāve. Mah.
Death approaches the dog, when he makes water in the mosque.
(As he will be severely punished.)

Kutte! terā mūṅh nahīṅ, tere saiṅ kā mūṅh hai.
Not your mouth, dog, but your master's, (barks.)
(He presumes on his master's protection.)

Kuttoṅ ko dūṅ, par tujhe na dūṅ.
I'd rather throw it to the dogs than give it to you.
(Bitter hatred.)

Kutyā choroṅ mil gaī, to pahrā kaun de?
If the dog befriend the thief, who then is to keep watch?
(Said of dishonest servants.)

Kutyā ke chhināle meṅ phaṅse haiṅ.
Entangled in the meshes of a lustful bitch.
(Overwhelmed in undeserved misery.)

Kūze ḍhaleṅ ki māṭ?
Will the cup upset first or the jar?
(To express that no one knows whether an old man or a child will die first.)

Kyā āg lene āē the?
Did you only come for fire?
(Ulterior objects.)

Kyā bālū kī bhīt? Kyā ochhe kī prīt?
Pīt kare gambhīr se, janam janam jā bīt.
What is a wall of sand? What is the friendship of the vile? Make friends with the weighty and keep it up all your life.

Kyā bharosā hai zindgānī kā?
Ādmī bulbulā hai pānī kā!
What reliance is there on life?
Man is but a bubble of water!

Kyā chūṛyāṅ phūṭ jāeṅgī?
Will you let your armlets be broken?
(An assignation.)

Kyā dam kā bharosā hai?
What reliance is there on life?

Kyā darzī kā kūchh, kyā muqām?
What matters it to a tailor whether he march or halt?
(He has only his needle, etc., to carry.)

Kyā din jāte dekhe?
Don't you see that the world is passing away?

Kyā ghās meṅ sāṅp nahīṅ chaltā?
Does not a serpent creep in grass?

Kyā Gomtī kā pānī pīyā hai?
Have you drunk of the Gomatī?
(The Gomatī is the river of Lucknow, the people of which are noted for effeminacy.)

Kyā hījṛoṅ ne rāh mārī hai?
Will eunuchs rob you on the high way?
(A reproof to one, who pleads frivolous difficulties about going any where.)

Kyā hī muṭṭhī pakṛī hai!
What a grasp he has of his wrist!

Kyā jāne ganvār ghungaṭvā kā yār?
What does a village boor know of the art of making love?

Kyā Kābul meṅ gadhe nahīṅ hote?
Are there not donkeys in Kābul?

Kyā karegā Daulā? Jise de tise Maulā.
What can Daulā do? God gives to whom he [wills.
(The speech of a celebrated *faqir* of the 17th century A. D. named Shāh Daulā, to whom people used to go to request the accomplishment of their wishes. Shāh Daulā's tomb is in the Gujrāt District of the Panjāb.)

Kyā khāk terī arvāh? Chūlhe meṅ se nikal bhāṛ meṅ jā.
Dust on your wishes; go out of the stove into the oven!
(Out of the frying pan into the fire.)

Kyā khūb saudā naqd hai? is hāth de, us hāth le.
What splendid business cash transactions are! given with one hand and taken with the other.

Kyā koeloṅ kī nāo ḍūb jāegī?
What if the charcoal boat be upset?
(It will bring no great loss.)

Kyā laṛe sūrmā? kyā laṛe anjān?
It wants a warrior or an ignorant man to make a good fight.

Kyā legayā Sher Shāh? Kyā legayā Salīm Shāh?
What have Sher Shāh or Salīm Shāh carried to the tomb?
(Said when any one boasts of his wealth or possessions: Sher Shāh Sūr and his son Salīm Shāh Sūr were two celebrated emperors of Dehli between 1542 and 1554 A. D.)

Kyā main terī paṭṭī ke nīche paidā huī hūṅ? Wom.
Was I born under your bed?
(Am I inferior to you?)

Kyā makkhī ne chhīṅk dīyā?
Did a fly sneeze?
(That you have dropped your work: Hindūs will not begin anything if any one sneeze, but will wait a while.)

Kyā mūṅh aur kyā masālah?
What a mouth and what spices!
(Spoken of one who undertakes anything for which he is unfit, or which does not become him.)

Kyā mūṅh meṅ ghungniyāṅ haiṅ?
Have you got a pellet in your mouth?
(*Ghungniyāṅ* are pellets of pulse boiled and seasoned with pepper and salt.)

Kyā mūṅh meṅ panjīrī bharī hai?
Have you crumbs in your mouth?
(*Panjīrī* is pounded bread made with *ghī* and sugar into crumbs.)

Kyā mūṅh par phiṭkār barastī hai?
Curses are raining down on your face!
(The result of a very disgraceful act.)

Kyā mūṅh se phūl jhaṛte haiṅ?
Flowers are falling from his mouth!
(Said of a person who deals in scandal or abuse: ironical.)

Kyā nangī nahāegī aur kyā nichoṛegī?
Can a naked bather wring out his clothes?
(Said of a man of small possessions.)

Kyā pānī mathne se bhī ghī nikaltā hai?
Can you get butter by churning water?
(Drawing blood from a stone: also sticking to a futile argument.)

Kyā pāoṅ meṅ meṅhdī lagī hai?
Have you *hinā* on your feet.
(Said to one who won't walk quickly: *hinā lawsonia alba*, is put on the feet to beautify them and also medicinally to cool them. When it is on the wearer he naturally walks carefully to keep it there.)

Kyā pardesī kī pīt? Aur kyā phūs kā tāpnā? Diyā kalejā kāṛh, huā nahīṅ āpnā. Wom.
What is a fire of straw, and what is a stranger's love? Give him your heart and he is never your own.

Kyā pidṛī? Aur kyā pidṛī kā shorbā?
What's in a tom-tit and what's in tom-tit soup?
(I am but a poor creature; hit a man of your own size.)

Kyā qāzī kī gadhī churāī hai?
Have I stolen the judge's ass?
(Said when a man is unjustly threatened or punished.)

Kyā sāṅp kā pāoṅ dekhā hai?
Have you seen a serpent's legs?
(Spoken in reproach of an impossible statement.)

Kyā sāṅp sūṅg gayā?
Has a serpent smelt you?
(*Sūng jānā*, idiom here for bitten: the notion is that after a snake has bitten a man, he is unable to speak; hence proverb asks "why are you so silent?")

Kyā sau rupaē kī pūṅjī? aur kyā ek beṭe kī aulād?
What's hundred rupees for capital, and what is one son for posterity?
(So small a sum is soon spent and an only son may die.)

Kyā shān meṅ baṭṭā lag jāegā?
Will it stain you character?
(It never injures a man to work with his own hands, or to do a kind office for an inferior.)

Kyā shān meṅ jufte paṛ jāeṅge.
Will the threads of your dignity be unravelled?
(This and the one preceding are also said in reproof of frivolous and indolent reluctance to do any thing.)

Kyā sove rājā kā pūt, kyā sove jogī abdhūt?
Either a royal child or an ascetic enjoys a sound sleep.

Kyā tamāshe kī bāt hai? Jis kā jāē vohī chor kahlāē!
What a wonderful thing! the person robbed is called the thief!
(It is a common practice of the Indian Police to make out that there is some trick on the part of the complainant, when they are unable to trace a theft.)

Kyā ṭoṭkā karne āī thī? Wom.
Have you come to cast a spell?
(Said of a short visit.)

Kyā udhār kī māṅ marī hai? Mercantile.
Is the race of credit extinct?
(Credit can always be had somewhere or other: usually said by the disappointed applicant for a loan.)

Kyoṅ andhā nautā aur kyoṅ do bulāē?
Why invite a blind man and feast two?
(If you invite a blind man to a feast, he is sure to bring with him another man for his assistance; why run a risk and bear a loss?)

Kyoṅ āṅkhoṅ meṅ khāk ḍālte ho?
Why do you throw dust in my eyes?

Kyoṅ bahisht meṅ lāteṅ mārte ho?
Why do you spurn paradise?
(Said in reproof of wordly enjoyment.)

Kyoṅ chabā chabā-kar bāteṅ karte ho?
Why do you speak as if you were chewing something?
(Why do you hesitate?)

Kyoṅ kahī aur kyoṅ kahāī?
Why speak so as to be spoken against?
(Think before you speak: look before you leap.)

Kyoṅ kāṅṭoṅ meṅ ghasīṭte ho?
Why do you drag me amongst thorns?
(Said to an old man who shews too much respect towards a young man.)

Kyoṅkar, rī, tū utrī pār? kyoṅkar, rī, tū chālī bāṭ? kyoṅkar, rī, tu ne yeh ghar jānā? kyoṅkar, rī, tū ne mujhe pahchānā?
How did you cross the river? how did you fare on the way? how did you find this house? and how did you recognize me?
(It is said that a woman being disgusted of *karhī*, which, being considered a luxury among natives, was presented day after day for her food, went to one of her relations on the other side of the river to avoid it. On her arrival the hospitable relative placed the same dish before her: *moral*, one man's meat is another man's poison.)

L.

Lābhe lohā ḍhoīye, bin lābh na ḍhoīye rūī.
A person will carry iron for gain, and not even cotton without it.

Lachārī parbat se bhārī.
No hill so heavy as (the weight of) helplessness.

Lachār meṅ bichār nahīṅ.
Necessity lacks judgment.
(Necessity knows no law.)

Lachchhmī bin ādar kaun kare?
No money, no respect.

Lachchhmī se bheṭ na, daridr se bair! Bhoj.
He cannot get prosperity, and quarrels with adversity!

Lād de, ladā de, hāṅkne-vālā sāth de.
Give me a load for my beast and give me a driver too.
(Used in reproof of an unreasonable request.)

"Laḍḍū" kahe, mūṅh mīṭhā nahīṅ hotā.
The mouth is not sweetened by saying "sweets."
(Fine words butter no parsnips.)

Laḍḍū laṛe, chūrā jhaṛe.
When sweetmeats quarrel crumbs fall off them.
(When rich men fight counsel looks bright.)

Laḍḍū na toṛo, chūrā jhār khāo!
Break not the sweetmeat, but live on the crumbs that fall from it.
(Don't touch the principal, but live on the interest.)

Lāḍ kā nāoṅ Bhanbhār Khātūn!
The darling's name is My Lady Meddlesome!

Lāḍlā laṛkā juārī, laḍlī laṛkī chhinālī.
A spoilt son becomes a gambler, and a spoilt girl a harlot.

Lāḍ meṅ āve kukṛī, bal bal jāve kavvā.
When he falls in love with a hen a crow sacrifices himself on her.

Lāē dām, bane kām.
Money ensures success.
(Money makes the mare to go.)

Lāēgā dārā to khāegī dārī, na lāēgā dārā to paṛegī khuārī.
If the husband earns the wife eats it; if he does not earn there is a quarrel.
(Marriage is an insane desire to keep another man's daughter.)

Lagā so bhagā.
Begun and over.
(Said of the shortness of life, etc.)

Lagā to tīr; nahīṅ, tukkā hī sahī.
If it hits it is an arrow; if not, it is at any rate a reed.
(Advice to keep on trying till success is insured.)

Lage āg to bujhe jal se, jal meṅ lage to bujhe kaho kaise?
Water can quench fire, but how shall the fire be quenched if the water takes fire?

Lage dam, miṭe gam!
Smoke and drive dull care away!
(Opium eaters' proverb: said when they begin to smoke.)

Lage ko biḍāriye nā, bin-lage ko hilāīye nā.
Don't desert a friend, and don't make a friend of a stranger.

Lage ragṛā, miṭe jhagṛā.
When the grinding begins the talking ceases.
(*Bhang*-drinkers' proverb: *bhang* is hemp leaves

ground to a fine powder and mixed with water. *Bhangis*, or *bhang*-drinkers, always grind their own *bhang*: hence proverb.)

Lage tote bhiton belne.
The parrot is out with the secrets.
(The cat's out of the bag.)

Lagī men aur lagtī hai.
A sore place is always being hurt.
(Misfortunes never come singly.)

Lag gaī jūtī, ur gaī kheh, phūl pān sī ho gaī deh.
The shoe struck me and blew away the dust, so my body is now as light as a flower.
(*i. e.* I don't care for the shoe-beating: said of a shameless person.)

Lāg lagī, tab lāj kahān?
When one is in love, what shame remains?
(All "love" in India is illegitimate.)

Lahū lagā sahīdon men mile!
He sprinkles himself with blood and thinks himself martyr.
(Said of the vain-glorious.)

Lajādhur bahoryā, sarāē men ḍerā! Bhoj.
A shameful wife, and an abode in an inn!

Lajāēl larikā dhonṛhī tohve. Bhoj.
A boy ashamed looks at his own stomach.

Lajālū mare, dhiṭhāū jīe; Gangā-jal Chamāron piye!
The worthy are dying and the unworthy living, for Chamārs are drinking Ganges water.
(According to high caste Hindūs the low caste Chamār is not entitled to the holy Ganges water.)

Lajānā bolū mūnh biḍore. E.
The shame-faced goat shows his teeth.
(Said of one who covers his shame with a forced laugh.)

Lāj kī ānkh, jahāz se bhārī.
A good reputation is heavier than a ship.
(Obliges people to keep it up: *noblesse oblige.*)

Lākh kā ghar khāk men milā diyā!
The mansion is levelled to the dust.
(By a bad house-wife.)

Lākh tadbīr ek taraf, aur ek taqdīr ek taraf!
A hundred thousand plans on one side, and one fate on the other!

Lakīr par faqīr.
Devoted to an old track.
(A slave to old customs or manners.)

Lakṛī ke bal bandrī nāche.
A monkey dancing to a stick.
(A rod for a fool's back.)

Lakṛī par faqīr!
It is his staff that makes him a *faqīr!*
(Outward show.)

Lālach bas parlok nasāē.
Avarice leads to hell.

Lālach burī balā hai.
Avarice is a truly bad thing.
(No vice like avarice.)

Lālach gun ghar bināē.
Avarice is the root of all evil.
(*Effodiuntur opes irritamenta malorum.*)

Lālach pashemān hai.
Avarice leads to shame.

Lālā kā ghoṛā, khāē bahot chale thoṛā.
The tradesman's horse eats much, and goes little.
(Because he does not understand how to keep it.)

Lāl Bujhakkaṛ būjhiyān, aur na būjhā ko:
'Karī baṛangā tār-ke ūpar hī ko lo.'
Lāl Bujhakkar understood, but no one else: "Take off the beams and pull him up."
(Said of a foolish expedient.)
☞ The story goes that while a boy had his two arms round a pillar his father gave him some peas into his two hands. Thereupon a difficulty arose among the people of the town as to how he could be extricated from his uncomfortable position without sacrificing the peas. So they summoned their wisest man, Lāl Bujhakkaṛ, who advised that an opening should be made in the roof and the boy drawn up through it!

Lāl Bujhakkaṛ būjhiyān, aur na būjhā koe:
"Pair men chakkī bāndh ke koī hirnā kūdā hoe."
This Lāl Bujhakkaṛ understands and no one else: "A deer with a mill-stone fastened to his leg must have jumped here!"
(The wise observation of the wise-acre on seeing the foot mark of an elephant. For Lāl Bujhakkaṛ see preceding.)

Lālchī ko jahān tang.
The world is too small for the avaricious.

Lāl Khān kī chādar baṛī hogī, to apnā badan ḍhānkegā: ham ko kyā?
If Lāl Khān's sheet be large, it will cover his body, but what does that concern me?
(In reply to one, who describes the riches of another.)

Lāl-kitāb uṭh bolī yon, "Telī bail laṛāyā kyon?
Khal khilā-ke kiyā musanḍ; bail kā bail aur ḍanḍ kā ḍanḍ."
The Red-book (Qāzī) up and spake, "Oil-man, what made the ox to fight? The cakes you gave it made it strong, so I must have the ox and a fine as well."
☞ The story goes that a Qāzī passed the verdict above quoted on an oilman who was charged with allowing his ox to kill the Qāzī's. But when it was finally proved that it was the Qāzī's ox who killed the oilman's, the Qāzī made light of the offence by saying, "*Jānvar hī to thā:* he was only an animal, (knows no better.)"

Lāl, nīch nir-bachan kah, bānh det sau bār.
Bher pūnchh Bhādon nadī ko gah utre pār?
My friend, the worthless promise, and give their hands a hundred times. Can you cross a river swollen by the rains by holding on to a ram's tail?
(Natives give the hand to clench a bargain.)

Lālon ke lāl ban rahe hain.
They have become the sons of the worthy.
(To be in clover.)

Lāl pyārā, to us kā khayāl bhī pyārā hai.
If you love your love, you love his thoughts.
(Love me love my dog.)

Lambe ghūnghaṭ-wālī se ḍarye!
Fear the long-veiled woman!

Langaṭ parle ughār ke pāle. Bhoj.
The shameless has fallen into the power of the naked!

Langoṭī men phāg khelte hain!
He plays the Holī without even clothes!
(Applied to one, who without the means sets up for luxury and elegance: it is necessary to have money to perform the ceremonies at the Holī festival satisfactorily.)

Langre lūlhe gaë barāt, bhāt ke biryā khailan lāt.
When the crippled go in a marriage procession, they get kicks instead of food.
(More kicks than half-pence.)

Langṛe lūlhe gaë barāt, do do jūte, do do lāt.
When the crippled go in a marriage procession, they get two shoes and two kicks.
(*Jūtā* means here a blow with a shoe, considered most ignominious in India.)

Langre ne chor pakṛā, " dauṛyo, Mīyān Andhe "!
The cripple seized a thief, and said, " Blind man, come and help !"

Langrī ghoṛī, masūr kā dānā!
A lame mare and *masūr* for food.
(Pearls before swine: *masūr* is an expensive kind of pulse.)

Langrī kaṭṭo, āsmān pe ghonslā!
A lame squirrel with a nest in the sky!

Lankā men se jo nikle so bāvan gaz kā.
All who come from Lankā are 52 yards high.
(The people of Lankā (Ceylon) are supposed in their ignorance by the Hindūs to be still *rākshashas*, or ogres. The proverb is used to describe a very wicked person.)

Lāo kūā, main ḍūbūn!
Bring me a well, that I may drown myself!
(Put in the mouth of a shameless person, when reproached with his faults and told that he ought to drown himself.)

Lāo sīpī, khakhor bhītī, mere saiyān par itnī bītī! E. Wom.
Bring me a shell to scrape the wall, my husband's substance must not be wasted thus!
☞ The story goes that a young wife entering her husband's house, to show off her anxiety to assume her duties scraped off the pat of rice placed by custom on the wall as part of the marriage rite, so that nothing of his might be wasted. A new broom sweeps clean.

Laṛāī aur āg kā baṛhānā kyā?
It is not difficult to fan a quarrel or a fire.

Laṛāī kā ghar hānsī, aur rog kā ghar khānsī.
Laughter is the source of quarrels, and coughing of disease.

Laṛāī men laḍḍū nahīn baṭte hain.
Sweetmeats are not distributed during a battle.

Laṛāke ke chār kān.
The quarrelsome have four ears.
(They have twice as many things to quarrel over as the peaceable.)

Lārā līrī kā yār, kabhī na utre pār.
Procrastination's friend never gains his end.
(Procrastination is the thief of time.)

Laṛen na bhiṛen, tarkash pahne phiren.
They neither fight nor combat, but flourish their quivers.
(Barking dogs seldom bite.)

Laṛen na bhiṛen, zirā pahne phiren.
Neither fights nor combats, but struts about in his mail.
(A carpet knight.)

Laṛen sānḍ, bārī kā bhurkas.
When bulls fight the fields are spoilt.

Laṛe sipāhī nām ho Sardār kā.
The soldier fights, but the general gets the credit.

Laṛkā jane Bīvī, aur paṭṭī bāndhe Mīyān.
My Lady is brought to bed, and my Lord girds his belly!
(*Paṭṭī bāndhnā*, is to tie on a bandage to alleviate pain.)

Laṛkan ke bhagvā nā, bilāī ke gātī. E. Wom.
Not a strip for the child, but a coat for the cat.
(Not a penny for my own, and help for the stranger.)

Laṛkā parkāve ke na chāhīn, harkāve ke chāhīn. E.
Rather snub than encourage a child.

Laṛkā rove bālon ko, nāī rove munḍāī ko.
The child cries over its shaven poll, the barber for his fee.
(All mind their own interests.)

Laṛkā rove, khasam chillāë, laṛkauṛī mehariyā fazīhat hoë. E. Wom.
The child cries, the husband roars, and the mother gets abuse.
(A family quarrel.)

Laṛke ke pāon pālne men pahchāne jāte hain.
You can tell what a child is like in his very cradle.
(Said of a promising child.)

Laṛke ko jab bheṛiyā legayā, tab ṭaṭṭī bāndhī.
When the wolf has run off with the child the door is made fast.
(Shutting the stable door after the horse is stolen.)

Laṛke ko mūnh lagāo to dāṛhī khasoṭe, kutte ko mūnh lagāo to mūnh chāṭe.
Pet a child and he'll pull your beard; pet a dog and he'll lick your face.

" Laṛkī, terā biyāh kar den "? kahā, " main kaise kahūn?"
" My girl, must we get you married?" Said she, " how can I say?"

Laṛkoṅ kā khel, chiṛyā kā marnā.
Boys' play is death to the birds.
(What's fun to you is death to me.)

Laṛkoṅ meṅ laṛkā, būṛhoṅ meṅ būṛhā.
A child among children and a man among men.
(All things to all men.)

Laṛte to nahīṅ, mūë mārte haiṅ. Wom.
They fight not, but speak ill of the dead.
(Said of backbiters.)

Laṛtoṅ ke pīchhe aur bhāgtoṅ ke āge.
In the rear of the warriors and in the van of the fugitives.
(Said of a coward: he who fights and runs away will live to fight another day.)

Lashkar kī agāṛī aur āndhī kī pichhāṛī.
The front of an army and the rear of a storm.
(Are the most fearful to see.)

Lashkar meṅ ūṅṭ badnām.
The camel gets abuse in the army.

Laṭā hāthī biṭauṛe barābar.
A lean elephant is equal to a stack of cow-dung.
(Even the wreck of a large fortune is considerable: in India the elephant is valuable for his ivory however weak he may be and cow-dung is a very valuable article in domestic use. Also the meaning may be taken that a lean elephant looks as large as a village stack of cow-dung.)

Laṭe kī joë, sāre gāoṅ kī sarhaj. E.
The wife of a poor man is the sister-in-law of the whole village.
(*i. e.* Every body is free to flirt with her: in India it is customary to jest with a sister in-law.)

Laṭe paṭe din kāṭiye.
To pass the day reeling about.
(To be in difficulties.)

Lāṭhī hāth kī, bhāī sāth kā.
A stick is best in the hand and a brother on the spot.

Lāṭhī ke hāth mālguzārī be-bāq.
With a stick in your hand your rent is paid up.

Lāṭhī līye pāoṅ par khāk.
The feet will only get dusty from the use of a staff.

Lāṭhī māre pānī nahīṅ judā hotā.
There is no separating water by beating it with a stick.
(Relations cannot be divided, however they may quarrel: blood is thicker than water.)

Laṭh mūṅh phaṭ.
Breaking the mouth with a club.
(Said of those who speak without thinking.)

Lāt mārī jhopṛī; "chūlhe-miyāṅ salām."
He kicks his hut and bids adieu to his hearth.
(Said of nomads who have no fixed abode.)

Lātoṅ kā deo bātoṅ se nahīṅ māntā.
A devil only fit for kicks won't heed words.
(Bad men must be beaten: a rod for the fool's back.)

Lauṅḍī ban-kar kamānā, aur bībī bankar khānā.
Work as a slave and live as a lady.
(Work and you will get.)

Lauṅḍī kī zāt kyā? raṅḍī kā sāth kyā?
Bheṛ kī lāt kyā? aurat kī bāt kyā?
What is a slave-girl's dignity? What is a harlot's friendship?
What is a sheep's kick? What is a woman's word?

Lauṅḍī ko lauṅḍī kahā, ro dī; bībī ko lauṅḍī kahā, haṅs dī.
Call a slave a slave and she will weep; call a lady a slave and she will laugh.

Le de āṭā kaṭhautī meṅ.
Put the flour into my platter.
(Said of a person who thinks only of his own wants.)

Le-ke dīyā, kamā-ke khāyā, aisī taisī jagat meṅ āyā.
Who pays his debts and earns his living, came for nothing into the world.
(Put into the mouth of a bad man.)

Le liyā pallā, aur bīnan lagī sillā. Agric.
The gleaner brings her basket and begins.
(Said to one who acts without previous permission.)

Le lugṛī, chal gudṛī! Wom.
Take the old clothes and go to the market!

Lenā denā kām ḍom ḍhāṛiyoṅ kā; muhabbat ajab chīz hai.
Taking gifts is for pimps and harlots; love is quite another thing.

Lenā denā sāṛhe bāīs!
No business at twenty-two and a half!
(Said of those who bargain but don't buy; *Sāṛhe bāīs* being an incomplete number here represents an incomplete bargain.)

Lenā ek, na denā do.
Don't take one and pay two.
(See that you get your money's worth.)

Lenā na denā, bātoṅ kā jamā-kharch!
No business, but a mere bargain of words!

Lenā na denā; "gāṛī bhare chanā."
Nor give nor take, and "fill the cart with pulse."
(Empty words buy no barley.)

Lenā na denā jhūṭhoṅ mūṅh chhuṭavval.
No business, but plenty of jabber.

Lenā na denā; kāre na masle!
Nor give nor take; nor business nor bargain!

Lene dene ke mūṅh meṅ khāk; muhabbat baṛī chīz hai.
Giving and taking are as dust in the mouth; there's nothing like pure friendship!
(The miser's maxim.)

Lene ke dene paṛ gaë.
It is come to giving instead of taking.
(A bad speculation.)

Letā mare ki detā?
The taker or the giver must die.
(Before I pay the debt: put into the mouth of a man who does not mean to pay his debt.)

Lihāz kī ānkh jahāz se bhārī. Wom.
No ship so heavy as a good reputation.
(See *lāj kī ānkh, etc.*)

Likhe Īsā, parhe Mūsā. Mah.
Moses only can read the writings of Jesus.
(Said of an illegible hand.)

Likhe Mūsā parhe Khudā. Mah.
i. God only can read the writings of Moses.
ii. His writing is so scratchy that only he himself can read it.
(Said of a bad hand: bad puns on the words *Mūsā*, Moses, and *Khudā*, God, by dividing them thus *mū sā*, like a hair, and *khud ā*, having come himself.)

Likhe na parhe, dūdh māre karhe.
He can neither read nor write and has plenty of milk (to drink.)!

Likhe na parhe, nām Muhammad Fāzil.
He neither reads nor writes, but is named Muhammad the Doctor!

Likhnā āve nahīn, mitāven donon hāth.
He cannot write, but blots with both hands.

Likhtam ke āge baktam nahīn chaltī. [written.
Oral (evidence) is valueless in the face of

Līk līk gārī chale, līk chale kapūt:
Līk chhor tīn chalen, shāir, singh, sapūt.
On the old beaten track a cart and a foolish son will go, But a poet, a lion, and a clever son will leave it.
(These three will shew their inventive genius and skill and valour.)

"*Līp, bahū, dīvālī, āī! pot, bahū, Dīvālī āī.*"
"*Chhed chhidālī māthe mārī! kyon, sāsū, yehī Dīvālī thī?*"
"Plaster, my girl, the Dīvālī has come! White-wash my girl, the Dīvālī has come!"
"What! the leavings thrown at my head! Why, mother-in-law, is this the Dīvāli?"
(A skit at the bad treatment of young brides at the hands of their husbands' mothers in India. All houses are plastered and whitewashed at the Divāli festival.)

Līpūn otā, mare motā!
I will plaster thee, *otā*, if a rich man die!
(The prayer of the Achāraj Brāhman, who gets the rich covering in which the corpse is wrapped, besides other presents. The *otā* is a small image kept in a corner of these Brahmans' houses as a household god, and is now supposed to be thus addressed.)

Lohā jāne, luhār jāne: dhaunkne-vāle kī balā jāne!
Let the iron care and the smith care; why should the bellows-blower care?
(Smiths in India keep a man on fixed wages to blow their bellows, and the point of the proverb is, that the business is between the iron and the smith, and the bellows-man has merely to do his own work.)

Lohā kare apnī barāī, ham bhī hain Mahādeo ke bhāī.
The iron to extoll himself becomes the brother of Mahādeo.
(Said when mean people claim a right to relationship with some great man: allusion to the iron *tirsūl*, or trident of Mahādeo (Siva), now itself regarded as a god.)

Lohe kī mandī men mār hī mār.
In the iron mart, it's hammer, hammer, hammer.

Lomrī ke shikār ko jāë, to sher kā sāmān kar lījiye.
If you go a fox-hunting, prepare to meet a lion.
(Even a small work needs large appliances: make sure of your object.)

Lugāī rahe to āp se; nahīn, jāë sage bāp se.
(1.) If a woman will stay in the house, stay she will: if not, her own father can't keep her.
(2.) If a woman is chaste, chaste she will be; if unchaste, she will go with her own father.

Luhār kī kūnchī, kabhī āg men, kabhī pānī men.
An iron-smith's brush, sometimes in the fire and sometimes in water.

Lūr na ūr, chalā miyān Jāgdīspūr. E.
Nor sense nor skill and he goes to Jagdīspūr.

Lutāyā bigānā māl: bandī kā dil daryāo. Mah. Wom.
It is another's property that is plundered; pitiless is the slave's heart.
(She cares nothing as to what happens to her master's wealth.)

Lūt kā mūsal bhī bahut.
Even a pestle is something to plunder.

Lūt koelon kī, mār barchhī kī.
In plundering charcoal to get a wound from a spear.
(Much loss, little gain.)

Lūt lāe, kūt khāyā.
Got by plunder and eaten in comfort.
(A successful thief or cheat.)

Lūt men charkha nafa.
In plunder even a spinning wheel is a gain.

M

Mā bāp jīte harām kā nahīn kahlātā.
Whose parents are alive, is not called a bastard.
(Used by those who assert that they can prove their claims.)

Mā betī gāne-vālī, bāp pūt barātī! Wom.
Mother and daughter for singers, and father and son for wedding procession!
(A poor man's marriage.)

Mā betiyon men larāī huī, logon ne jānā bair parā! Wom.
Mother and daughter quarrel and people think them enemies!
(Lover's quarrels: kiss and make up.)

Mā bhatyārī, pūt Fateh Khān. Wom.
The mother an innkeeper and the son my Lord General.
(See preceding.)

Mā bhatyārī, beṭā tīr-andāz. Wom.
The mother an inn-keeper and the son an archer.
(All trades and occupations in India are hereditary and hence the sting of the proverb.)

Mā chāhe beṭī ko aur beṭī chāhe moṭe ḍhīṅg ko. Wom.
The mother on her daughter doats and the daughter on her stout lover.

Machhlī ke bachchoṅ ko tairnā kaun sikhāē?
Who shall teach young fish to swim?
(That is, one descended from virtuous parents will naturally be virtuous: innate good quality: instinct: allusion also to the hereditary nature of all occupations in India.)

Machhlī to nahīṅ, ki saṛ jāegī. Wom.
It is not fish, that it should putrify.
(Said in deprecation of undue haste.)

Mā chhoṛ, mausī se mazāq. Mah.
You can flirt with your aunt, but not with your mother.

Mā ḍāyan ho, to kyā bachchoṅ hī ko khāegī? Wom.
Even an ogress will not devour her own child.

Mā dhoban, pūt bazāz.
The mother a laundress, the son a draper.

Madhure āṅche, roṭī mīṭh. Bhoj.
A slow fire makes the bread sweet.
(Slow and sure.)

Mā elī, bāp telī, beṭā shākh-i-zāfrān.
The mother a daily laborer and the father an oilman and the son a bunch of saffron.
(The metaphorical epithet of the son means a person who gives himself airs.)

Maggah des kanchan purī, des achchhā, bhākā burī.
Maggah is a land of gold with a vile speech!
(A skit at the rough dialects of Behār.)

Maggah meṅ marnā, agle janam meṅ gadhā bannā. Hin. Superstition.
Who dies in Maggah will be an ass in his next life.
(Superstition based on the doctrine of the transmigration of souls.)

Māghe jāṛ na Pūse jāṛ, batāse jāṛ. Agric.
December and January make no winter, but the wind does.

Māgh kā jāṛā, Jeṭh kī dhūp,
Baṛe kashṭ se upje ūkh. Agric.
With frost in February and heat in June,
The sugar-cane grows with difficulty.

Māgh nange, Baisākhe bhūke.
Naked in January and hungry in May.
(Downright misery.)

Māgh talātal bāṛhe, Phāgun goṛe kāṛhe.
We draw up our knees in January and straighten them in February.
(The weather is getting warm, and people no longer sleep huddled up.)

Mahad se lahad tak.
From the cradle to the grave.

Mahalle meṅ āī barāt, paṛausan ko lagī ghabrāṭ.
When the procession came into the street the neighbours got excited.
(Although it did not concern them.)

Mahāvaṭ barsī aur sādhī sarsī. Agric.
With winter rains the spring crop thrives.

Mahīnā purāyā aur kamerā aghāyā.
When the month is over the workman wants his pay.
(Wages are paid by the month in India.)

Māī bāp ke lātan māre, mehrī dekh jurāē;
Chāroṅ dhām jo phiri āve, tabhūṅ pāp na jāē.
Hindu.
Who kicks his parents to please his wife,
His sin will cleave to him though he makes all the pilgrimages.
(It is a great sin for a Hindū to neglect his parents in favor of his wife.)

Maide aur shahāb kī sī loī.
A red and white loaf.
(A pink and white face.)

Mailā kapṛā, pātar deh, kuttā kāṭe kaun sandeh?
It is no wonder if a dog bite a man with dirty clothes and a weak body.
(A hit at the exactions of native subordinates from the weak and defenceless.)

Mail kā bail banāte haiṅ.
To make a bullock out of a speck of dirt.
(To make a mountain of a molehill.)

Mainā jo "maiṅ-nā" kahe dūdh bhāt nit khāē: Bakrī jo "maiṅ maiṅ" kare ulṭī khāl khichāē.
The *mainā* cries "not I" and eats milk and rice for ever. The goat cries "I, I" and loses his skin.
(Said to a boaster: There are puns upon the words *mainā* and *maiṅ nā* "not I" and upon *maiṅ* "I" and also the bleating of a goat. The point is that the humble *mainā* is well treated and the boastful goat is killed.)

Maiṅ aur merā mānas; tīsre kā mūṅh bhulas. Hin. Wom.
I and my husband; let every one else's face [burn!
(Selfishness.)

Maiṅ bhalī, tū shābāsh! Wom.
I am all right and hurrah for you!
(Mutual praising.)

Maiṅ bhī hūṅ pāṅchveṅ savāroṅ meṅ.
I, too, am one of the five horsemen.
☞ This proverb is founded on the following story. Four horsemen were going to the Dakhan and were joined by a man riding a very miserable hack, who replied in the words of the proverb to any one that enquired who he was.

Maiṅ bhalī ki paneṭhā? Wom.
Which is the simpleton, I or the peddlar?

Maiṅ hī pāl karā mustaṇḍā, moē hī māre le-ke ḍaṇḍā! Wom.
I brought him up to be a strong man and he beats me with his stick!
(A woman to her undutiful son.)

Maiṅ kab kahūṅ, 'tere bete ko mirgī āve hai'? Wom.
When did I ever say that your son has epileptic fits?
(She purposely makes known what she denies having said.)

Maiṅ karūṅ terī bhalāī, tū kare merī āṅkh meṅ salāī. Wom.
I seek to do you good, and you would run a needle into my eye.
(Returning evil for good.)

"Maiṅ" ke gale par chhurī.
"I" (egotism) gets its throat cut.
(Allusion to the bleating of goats (*maiṅ*) and their slaughter for food, with a pun upon the word *maiṅ* which means also I (egotism.)

Maiṅ kī gardan par chhurī.
A knife is at my throat.
(Supposed to be said by a kid. The sword of Damocles.)

Maiṅ kyā terī paṭṭī tale kī hūṅ. Wom.
Am I in any way your inferior?

Māīṅ māīṅ sab milāṅ, bābū koī nahīṅ milā.
You have met mothers in plenty, but not a master.
(Beggars get most from the women of the houses where they beg as the men see through them better. They usually call women "mother" and men "master," hence point of proverb.)

Maiṅ marūṅ tere līye, tū mare vā ke līye!
I am dying for you, and you for another.
(Unrequited love.)

Maiṅ ne kyā us kī khīr khāī hai?
Have I eaten any of his rice and milk?
(Am I under any obligation to him?)

Maiṅ to terī lāl pagiyā pe bhūlī re, Raghuā! Wom.
It was your red turban, Raghūa, that misled me.

Maiṅ tujhe chāhūṅ, aur tū kāle dhīṅg ko. Wom.
I love you and you a black paramour.
(Spoken by one, who from regard admonishes another, but is not attended to.)

Majnū ko Lailī kā kuttā bhī pyārā.
Even Laili's dog is dear to Majnūṅ.
(Majnūṅ and Lailā are the Romeo and Juliet of the East: love me love my dog.)

Mālūm hogā Hashr ko pīnā sharāb kā.
You will know on the Day of Judgment what it is to drink wine.

Mā kā mān bhalā!
A mother's esteem is the best!

Mā kā peṭ kumhār kā āvā; koī gorā, koī kālā.
A mother's womb is a potter's kiln, some come black (from it) and some fair.
(Said of children of the same mother having different complexions.)

Makar-chakar kī ghānī, ādhā tel aur ādhā pānī.
The press is of deceit and fraud, half oil and half water.
(Said of the double-dealer.)

Mā ke peṭ se koī sīkh-kar nahīṅ niklā hai.
No one comes learned out of his mother's womb.

Mā khet meṅ, pūt janet meṅ. Riddle.
The mother in the field, the son at the wedding.
(Answer—the *kusumbhā* flower, or safflower used for dying the marriage turbans.)

Mā kī sauk, na bāp se yārī,
Kis nāte kī tavṅh mahtārī? Rus. Wom.
Nor my mother's co-wife, nor my father's mistress, How come you then to be my mother?
(Natives call the mother's co-wife or father's mistress "mother.")

Makke gaë na Madīne gaë, bīch hī bīch meṅ hājī bhae. Mah.
He went to neither Makkā nor Madīna, but became a pilgrim half way.
(Said to one who gets what he wants easily.)

Makke meṅ rahte haiṅ, par haj nahīṅ karte. Mah.
Living in Makkā he never made the pilgrimage.
(The nearer the church, the farther from God.)

Makkhī baiṭhī shahad par pankh gae lipṭāë,
Hāth male, aur sir dhune, "lālach burī balāë."
A fly alights in honey and entangles her wings; struggling in vain she laments her fate: (saying) "avarice is a great misfortune."

Mālī chāhe barsnā, dhobī chāhe dhūp,
Sāhū chāhe bolnā, chor chāhe chūp.
The gardener wants rain, the washerman sunshine, A banker a talk, and a thief quietude.

Makkhī chhoṛnā, aur hāthī nigalnā.
To pass by the fly and swallow an elephant.
(To strain at a gnat and swallow a camel.)

Makkhī mār, baṛā chamār.
A killer of flies, is a real Chamār.
(Applied to misers as an expression of contempt: the Chamārs are a very low class.)

Māl-i-muft, dil-i-be-rahm. Pers.
The heart has no pity on another's wealth.

Mallāhī kī mallāhī dī, bāṅs ke bāṅs khāë.
I paid my fare in full and got beaten with a bamboo.
(Passengers by boat are liable to be struck by the long bamboos used as barge poles.)

Mallāh kā laṅgoṭā hī bhīgtā hai.
The very breeches of a boatman get wet.

Māl kā mūṅh karte haiṅ, jān kā mūṅh nahīṅ karte.
They care for their property not for their lives.
(Said of misers.)

Māl ke nuqsān meṅ jān kī khair.
In the loss of wealth life's safety lives.
(A friendly consolation on any loss.)

Māl par zakāt hai.
Charity is for the wealthy.

Māl-vālā hāre, gāl-vālā jīte.
The real owner loses while the loquacious wins.
(Allusion to the practice of special pleading before the British Courts.)

Mā māre, aur 'mā hī mā' pukāre.
His mother beats him and still he calls out "mother."
(The dog licks the hand that beats him.)

Mā mare, mausī jīve!
Let my mother die, my aunt is alive!
(In India an aunt bears great affection for her sister's children.)

Māmū ke kān meṅ bāliyāṅ, bhānjā aiṅḍā aiṅḍā phire.
The uncle wears the ear-rings, and the nephew struts proudly.
(Proud of another's wealth: reflected glory.)

Mā, na mā kā jāyā: sabhī lok parāyā.
Nor mother here, nor any of my mother born: all the land is strange to me.
(Said of a strange country.)

Mā nārangī, bāp kolā, beṭā Raushanu-d-daula,
The mother an orange, the father a lemon, and the son Mr. Light-of-fortune.
(Said of a half breed.)

Mānas kasne ko muāmla kasauṭī hai.
Business is the touch-stone for men.

Man bhāē to ḍhelā supārī.
If you like it, a clod is a betel-nut.
(Love is blind: the proverb is based on the fact that women and children will some times eat small lumps of earth.)

Man bhar kā sir hilāte hain, paisā bhar kī zabān nahīṅ hilāte!
The ton-weight head waggles, but the ounce weight tongue won't waggle.
(Said of a person who in answer to a salutation nods his head, but does not say "good morning.")

Man bhoīg, karam diladdrī.
Desirous of pleasures, but doomed to poverty.

Man chāhe, mundyā hilāē.
The heart desires, but she refuses.
(A woman's 'nay' is 'yea.')

Man chaltā hai, par ṭaṭṭū nahīṅ chaltā.
His mind goes, but his hack won't.
(Want of means.)

Man chanchal, karam diladdrī.
Desirous of pleasures, but doomed to poverty.

Man changā, to kaṭhautī meṅ Gangā.
If your mind be pure, then Gangā is in your *kaṭhautī*.
(Gangā is the holy water of the Ganges and *kaṭhautī* the vessel used by a leather-worker for tanning hides and so a thing much despised by Hindūs.)

☞ The following story is told about Rāē Dās, the Chamār Bhagat, or saint. Rāē Dās was at his work when a company of pilgrims to the Ganges passed by him and he asked them to offer a few *kauṛis* to the Ganges for him, on the condition that the goddess Gangā appeared and held out her hand for the *kauṛis*. Gangā duly appeared and took the *kauṛis* and gave them in return a golden *kaṛā* (wristlet) to be given back to Rāē Dās. The pilgrims however took the *kaṛā* to the Rājā of Rāē Dās's country, who gave it to his Rānī and she desired to have it matched. In their extremity the pilgrims again went to Rāē Dās and told him what had happened, and he having pity on them showed them the pair to it in his *kaṭhautī*, and hence proverb.

Maṅḍve ke āṭe meṅ shart kyā?
What conditions are made on buying *maṅḍvā* flour?
☞ It is customary in buying things of value to stipulate a certain price on condition that on examination the article proves of good quality; but the flour of *maṅḍvā* (a millet,) being of little value, no such condition is required.

Māne na jāne, 'maiṅ bhī naushā kī khālā.' Mah. Wom.
Nor known nor recognized and "I am the bridegroom's aunt."
(Unreasonable interference: having a finger in the pie on any pretext.)

Māne to deo, nahīṅ bhīt kā leo! Hin. Wom.
Believe and he is a god, otherwise he is only plaster!
(Faith can move mountains.)

Mangāī chhīnt, lāyā īṅt.
He called for chintz, and they brought him bricks.
(To ask for bread and get a stone.)

Mangāī hīng, lāyā adrak.
The one asked for asafœtida and the other brought ginger.
(Cross purposes.)

Māṅgan gaē so mar gaē aur mareṅ jo māṅgan jāēṅ; Woh nar pahle hī mare, jo hote karde nāṅh.
Those that begged were disgraced and those that will beg will be disgraced; But he is most disgraced, that can but won't give!
(A saying of the Brāhmans to encourage alms-giving.)

Māṅge bhīk, pūchhe gāoṅ kī jama!
A beggar! and he wants to know the rental of the village!

Māṅge haṛ, de baheṛā.
He asks for *haṛ* and he gives *baheṛā*.
(*Haṛ* and *baheṛā* are two kinds of myrabolans: Cross purposes.)

Māṅge ke mangnī, guṛyā kā singār.
A doll dressed up in borrowed clothes.
(Borrowed plumes.)

Māṅge meṅ tāṅgā.
A gift of a borrowed thing!

Māṅge par tāṅgā, buṛhiyā kī barāt.
Begging from a beggar, is like marrying an old woman!

Māṅge tāṅge kām chale, to byāh kyoṅ kare?
If a man could do with borrowing (a wife), why should he marry?

Mān ghaṭe nīt ke ghar jāē.
Gyān ghaṭe ku-sangat pāē,
Bhāo ghaṭe kuchh mukh ke māṅge,
Rog ghaṭe kuchh aukhad khāē.
Every day visits lessen esteem, Bad company lessens holiness, Asking favors lessens self-respect, Using a remedy lessens illness. Respect is lessened by constant visiting.
(Familiarity breeds contempt.)

Māṅg jāṅch-ke gae jhāṅjhā: māṅg leṅ to lāge lājā.
If he give he is angry over it: if he take back he is put to shame.
(Unwilling charity.)

Mangnī ke bail ke dānt nahīṅ dekhte haiṅ.
Never look at the teeth of a gift ox.
(Never look a gift horse in the mouth.)

Mangnī ke satvā, sās ke pindā. E. Wom.
Borrowed meal is offered to the mother-in-law.
(Expresses the dislike young brides have in India to their mothers-in-law, who are apt to treat them as slaves.)

Mangnī kī chādar, tā par pachās kā ādar! Wom.
A borrowed sheet, and she offers it to fifty different people!

Man hamrā pās, dhan ān kā pās. E. Wom.
My mind is mine, his wealth is his.
(Contentment: my mind to me a kingdom is.)

Man hulāsa, gāve gīt.
A merry heart sings songs.

Man jāne pāp; māī jāne na bāp.
The heart knows its own sin; not mother, nor father.

Man kā aṅkus gyān.
Conscience is the goad of the mind.

Mān kā māhur, aur apmān kā laḍḍū.
Rather poison with respect than dainties with contempt.
(Better is a dinner of herbs where love is, than a stalled ox and hatred therewith. Proverbs xv. 17.)

Mān kā pān bhī bahut hotā hai.
A betel-leaf presented with respect is a great gift.

Mān kā pān, hīrā samān.
A betel-leaf presented with respect is as good as a diamond.

Mankā pherat janam gayā, aur gayā na man kā pher. Kar kā mankā chhoṛ-ke, tū man kā mankā pher.
In counting your beads you have spent your life, but the crookedness of your mind has not gone; Give up the rosary in your hand, and devote yourself to the rosary of the heart.
(There is an elaborate play on the words *man, mankā, pher,* and *phernā* in this saying. Servants be obedient to them that are your masters; not with eyeservice as men-pleasers, but doing the will of God from the heart. Ephesians vi. 6.)

Man karbe moṭā, khaiben soṅṭā; man karben meṅhīṅ, sagre lehīṅ. Bhoj.
Be niggardly and get blows, be generous and get everything.

Man kare pahiran chautār, karam likhe bheṛī ke bār. Wom.
Her heart on satins, but her fate on sheep's wool.

Man ke hāre hār hai, man ke jīte jīt,
Pār-Brahm ko pāiye, man hī ke partīt.
Lose heart and lose all; brace up your mind and win, Almighty God can only be found through faith in the heart.
(Ask and it shall be given you: seek and ye shall find; knock and it shall be opened unto you. Luke xi. 9.)

Man ke laḍḍū phoṛnā.
To break imaginary sweets.
(To build castles in the air.)

Man ke laḍḍuoṅ se bhūk nahīṅ miṭtī.
Hunger is not appeased by imaginary sweets.
(The belly is not filled with fair words.)

Man kī mārī kā se kahūṅ? Peṭ masosā de de rahūṅ. Wom.
To whom shall I tell my grief? I can but press my belly!
(To show very extreme hunger, said by beggar-women.)

Man malīn, sundar tan kaise?
Bikh ras bharā kanak ghaṭ jaise!
With a foul mind shall the body be fair?
It is a golden vessel filled with poison!

Man māne, ghar jāne.
Going home when so inclined.
(Independence.)

Man mānī, an-jānī.
My heart knows though I don't.
(Pretended ignorance.)

Man maujī jorū ko kaheṅ "bhaujī."
A jolly fellow calls his wife a sister-in-law.
(In order to crack jokes with her: allusion to the custom often mentioned above of cracking jokes with the elder brother's wife in India.)

Man-maujī, karam diladdrī.
The heart would indulge, but fate is adverse.

Man meṅ base, so supne dase.
What is in the mind will be seen in dreams.

Man meṅ gātī, ṭas ṭas rove!
Chūhā khasam kar sukh se sove.
Happy in her heart she sheds tears!
For married to a rat she sleeps in comfort.
(Allusion to marrying grown girls to small children, encouraged by the Brāhmans.)

Man meṅ mūrakh, jūn meṅ dukhī koī nahīṅ hai.
No one thinks himself a fool, and no one is tired of his life.

Man meṅ Shekh Farīd, bagal meṅ īṅṭ.

A Shekh Farīd at heart, a brick under his arm!

(A saint in intention, but prepared for mischief. Hell is paved with good intentions.)

☞ Also to describe a hypocrite. The saying is said to have originated with the act of a thief, who became the disciple of Shekh Farīd, the saint of Papkaṭṭan, and professed repentance for his evil deeds, but was unable to resist the temptation of an ingot of gold, which he found on the road, and concealed under his arm.

Man mile kā melā, chit mile kā chelā.

When hearts agree there's a company; when minds agree there's a following.

Man motiyoṅ byāh: man chāoloṅ byāh. Hin. Wom.

A *man* of pearls and it is a marriage: a *man* of rice and it is a marriage!

(A *man* is ℔s. 80. The point is that a marriage is valid whatever be spent on the ceremonies.)

Mān na mān, maiṅ dulhā kī chāchī! Wom.

Believe me or not, I am the aunt of the bridegroom.

(Said of a stranger who claims a near relationship from interested motives.)

Mān na mān, maiṅ terā mehmān!

Recognized or not, I am still your guest!

(Addressed by way of reproof to an impertinent intruder.)

Mantrī binā rāj sūnā.

A kingdom is empty without a minister.

Man umrāo, karam diladdrī.

His heart bent on riches, but poverty in his fate.

Manvā mar gayā, khel bigaṛ gayā.

Lose heart and you will lose the game.

(Faint heart never won fair lady.)

Mā Panhārī, bāp Kanjar, beṭā Mīrzā Sanjar! Mah. Wom.

The mother a chamber-wench, the father a basket maker, and the son my noble Lord!

(Said of an upstart.)

Mā pe pūt, pitā par ghoṛā: bahut nahīṅ, to thoṛā hī thoṛā. Wom.

The son is as the mother, the colt is as the sire: if not altogether, at least somewhat.

(The child is father to the man; a chip of the old block.)

Mā pisanhārī achchhī, aur bāp haft-hazārī kuchh nahīṅ. Wom.

A mother that grinds corn is better than a father that is captain of seven thousand men.

(The love of a mother is of more value than the love of a father.)

Mā pisan-hārī, pūt chhailā, chūtaṛ par bāṅdhe būr kā thailā!

The mother a grinder of corn and the son a fop, swaggering with a bag of chaff on his buttocks!

Maqdūr kī māṅ kauṛī hī ragaṛtī hai.

The scowering of *kauṛīs* is the mother of opulence.

(Take care of the pence and the pounds will take care of themselves.)

Mā rā che aṅīṅ qissa, ki gāo āmad o khar raft? Per.

What is it to me, that a cow hath come and a donkey gone?

(Expresses a feeling of no desire to intermeddle with what does not concern one.)

Maral bachhiyā Bāman ke dān? E.

The dead cow is given to the Brāhman.

(Said of a useless gift.)

Mārā mūṅh tabāq āge dharā na khāe.

A beaten man is afraid to eat, though the platter is before him.

Maran chalī aur Sūkh sāmhne! Wom.

Going to her death and (the planet) Venus in front of her!

☞ It is a rule among Hindūs not to go upon any business, particularly a religious ceremony, if the planet Venus be in front. Hindū married girls will not go to their father-in-law's houses if Venus be in front of them on the road. The meaning of the proverb is, when she goes to die of what consequence are good or evil omens?

Marā Rāvan faẓīhat ho!

A dead Rāvan is disgraced.

(Allusion to the story in the *Rāmāyan*: Rāvan is a typical tyrant and his fate in the legend is here likened to that of ordinary oppressors in power who come to destruction.)

Mard aurat rāzī to kyā karegā Qāzī!

When man and woman are agreed, what shall the Qāzī do?

(The Qāzī or Muhammadan priest performs marriages and has usually a considerable voice in settling the engagement.)

Mard jekrā gāṅth rupaiyā! E. Wom.

A man with silver in his pocket.

(Born with a silver spoon in his mouth.)

Mard kā dikhāyā na khāiye, mard kā lāyā khāiye. Wom.

Eat not before your husband; but eat what he brings you!

(Indian custom: one of those which must make their homes so happy!)

Mard kā hāth phirā aur aurat ubhṛī.

Toyed with by a man the woman develops.

Mard kā kyā hai? ek jūtī pahnī, ek jūtī utārī. Wom.

It's nothing to the man: he puts on the new shoe and throws off the old one.

(He gets a new wife as soon as the old one is dead or misbehaves herself. High caste women cannot of course marry again at all.)

Mard kā nahānā, aurat kā khānā barābar hai.

A man's bath and a woman's dinner are soon over.

(Men spend very little time in beautifying themselves, and women in India usually eat quickly.)

Mard kā naukar mare baras bhar meṅ : ranḍi kā naukar mare chhae mahīne meṅ.
The servant of a man may live a year, the slave of a prostitute will die in six months.
(Because her many visitors will over-work him.)

Mard ke chār nikāh durust haiṅ. Hin.
It is lawful for a man to have four wives.
(Hindū chaff of the Muhammadans.)

Mard kī bāt, aur gāṛī kā pahiyā āge ko chaltā hai.
A true man's word and a carriage wheel always go forwards.

Mard ko gard zarūr hai.
Labor is the lot of man.

Mard mare nām ko, nā-mard mare nān ko.
The hero dies for a name and the wretched for mere bread.

Mardoṅ kā ek qaul hotā hai.
A true man has but one word.
(He will never go back from it.)

Mare kā koī nahīṅ, jīte jī ke sab lāgū haiṅ.
None cares for the dead, all follow the living.
(Worshipping the rising sun.)

Mare ko mar jāne de, halvā pūrī khāne de.
Let the dead be counted with the dead, and let me eat the sweets.
(Allusion to the custom of holding a feast at the death of an old man among the Hindūs.)

Māre na chūhī, nām Fateh Khāṅ!
He never killed a rat and they call him my Lord Conqueror.

Mare na jīye, hukur hukur kare.
He neither dies nor lives, but only gasps.
(Which is very painful to his relatives: said of a very old man.)

Mare na māṅjhā le.
Nor dead nor taken off the bed.
(We wish him dead. Among Hindūs a dying man is taken down from his bed to the floor as it is believed to be irreligious to die on a bed.)

Mare na pīchhā chhoṛe.
He neither dies nor relieves us.
(Of his presence: see preceding.)

Māreṅ mehar, aur bhāge paṛausin. E.
The wife is beaten, and the neighbour flies through fear.
(Of being beaten too if she were mixed up with the quarrel: selfishness.)

Mare pe baid.
After death the doctor.
(After meat mustard.)

Māre sipāhī nām Sardār kā; Kāṭe bār, nām talwār kā.
The soldier fights and the credit is the General's; The edge cuts and the credit is the Sword's.

Mare to shahīd, māre to gāzī. Mah.
A martyr if killed, a *gāzī* if he kills.
(A *gāzī* is a man who fights for the faith. The saying is to encourage Musalmāns to fight and alludes to the doctrine of the *jihād* or war to the death against all unbelievers.)

Mar gaë mardūd, jin kī fāteha na darūd. Mah.
The wretch has died without ceremony or burial.
(Without extreme unction.)

Mār, gusaīyāṅ, terī ās.
Master, you may beat me, yet I still depend on you.
(Addressed to a master or patron and commonly by an aggrieved wife to her husband.)

Marihoṅ par ṭarihoṅ nāhīṅ! E.
I'll die before I budge from here!

Marī kyoṅ? sāṅs na āyā? Wom.
Why did she die? For want of breath!

Mār ke āge bhūt nāche.
A devil will dance to a beating.
(Spare the rod and spoil the child.)

Mār khānā, masjid meṅ so rahnā.
To live by robbery and sleep in a *masjid.*
(To live in a very disorderly way; sleeping in a *masjid* implies having no home, like sleeping under the arches of a bridge in London.)

Mār khātā jāë, aur kahe "zarā māro to sahī."
He gets a beating and still says "beat me if you dare."
(Said of cowards: of the Banyās especially.)

Mār mār ke satī karnā.
To beat a woman until she becomes *satī.*
(*Satī* is burning at the husband's pyre, and the custom is dissuade a woman from becoming *satī*, at any rate, as far as show goes; so the proverb means downright bullying.)

Mār mār kīye jāë, fateh dād Ilāhī hai.
Fight your battle, for the victory is with God.

Mar mar na jāte, to bhar ghar hote. E. Wom.
Had none of us had died the house would have been full.

Mār, muë, mār, terī hatṛiyāṅ piṛāeṅ; merī ādat na jāë! Mah. Wom.
Beat me, you wretch, beat me till your hands ache: but my habits will not leave me.
(An obstinate wife to her husband.)

Marnā bhalā bides kā, jahāṅ na apnā koī.
Better die abroad where you have no friends.
(A saying of the Bhagats: die where your death will be a grief to no one.)

Marnā jīnā sab ke sāth lagā huā hai.
To be born and die is the fate of all men.

Māṭ na jure, māṅge tāṛī! E.
He has no right even to butter-milk and demands *tāṛī.*
(*Tāṛī* is a brew from the juice of palm trees and is expensive, whereas every peasant can command butter-milk.)

Marne jāeṅ, malhār gāeṅ.
He goes singing to his death.
(*Malhār* is a song of rejoicing sung especially to bring on rain.)

Marne ko jī chāhe, kafan kā ṭoṭā.
He wishes to die, but is at a loss for a shroud.
(If wishes were horses beggars would ride.)

Marne ko kyā hāthī ghoṛe juṛte haiṅ?
Do you want horses and elephants on the road to death?

Marne pe Ḍom rājā.
The Ḍom is the lord of death.
(*Ḍoms* are employed to perform the funeral ceremonies.)

Mārne-vāle se jilāne-vālā baṛā dātā hai.
The life-giver (God) is greater than the life-taker (man.)

Mā rove talvār ke ghāo se, bāp rove tīr ke ghāo se.
The mother mourns a sword wound and the father an arrow wound.
(They appreciate a son's demerits or blemishes differently.)

Mār pīchhe saṅvār.
To strike and apologize.
(To kiss and make up.)

Martā kyā na kartā?
What will not the dying man do?
(The desperate man all things can.)

Mārte kā hāth pakṛā jātā hai, kahte kī zabān nahīṅ pakṛī jātī.
You can hold the hand of the striker, but not the tongue of the reviler.

Mārte ke pīchhe, bhāgte ke agāṛī.
Behind the fighters and ahead of the flying.
(Said of a coward.)

Marte ke sāth marā nahīṅ jātā.
No one dies with the dead.
(Why weep to death for one that's dead?)

Mārte Khāṅ se sab ḍarte haiṅ. Mah.
Every one fears my lord Tyrant.

Marte ko māre Shāh Madār.
Shāh Madār is beating the dying.
(Shāh Madār the famous saint of Makanpūr who died in 1433 A.D: the words are here a corruption of *shāmat-zadah*: see next. Hit a man when he is down.)

Marte ko māre shāmat-zadah.
The truly shamless beats the dying.
(See preceding.)

Marīz-ishq ko dīdār kāfī hai.
For the love-sick the pleasure of the eyes is enough.

Marzī-i-Maulā az hamah aulā. Pers.
God's will before all things.
(Thy will be done!)

Mās binā sab sāg rasoī. Mah.
Without meat a dinner is but greens.

Māse bhār kī chār kachaurī, khurmā māse ḍhāī kā,
Ghar meṅ roveṅ bahan, bhānjī, bāhar rove nāī kā,
Dhīre dhīre jīmoṅ panchon: dekho gajab Khudāī kā,
Lālā-jī ne byāh rachāyā lahṅgā bech lugāī kā!
Cakes of one grain weight, sweets of two and a half:
Sister and niece weeping in the house, the barber weeping outside:
Little eat the wedding guests: see the wrath of God:
The gentleman is celebrating the wedding on the proceeds of his wife's petticoat!
(Used as a skit at the extravagant weddings indulged in by the poor in India.)

Mashālchī mare to paṭbījnā ho, yahāṅ bhī chamke, wahāṅ bhī chamke!
When a torch-bearer dies he turns to a glow-worm, that he may shine there as he shines here!

Mashālchī andhā hotā hai.
The torch-bearer cannot see his own way.
(Darkness under the lamp.)

Masjid ḍhah gaī, mihrāb rah gaī.
The mosque is destroyed, but the arches remain.

Mās khāe mās baṛhe, ghī khāe bal hoe,
Sāg khāe ojh baṛhe, būtā kahāṅ se hoe?
Eat flesh, and you will make flesh, eat butter and you will get strength,
Eat pot-herbs and your belly will swell and no strength will you find.

Maskharī ke chūṛā bhar bhar gāl. E.
Filling his cheeks with flattery's cakes.
(Said of a toady.)

Mastāī bakrī bok kā muṅh chūmtī hai. E.
The she-goat on heat kisses the buck-goat's mouth.

Māshūq kī zāt be-vafā hai!
Mistresses are a faithless brood!

Mātā bargī māmtā, saukan bargā bair;
Dūjā ko rākhe nahīṅ, dekhā sāṅjh saver. Rus. Wom
A mother's love, a co-wife's hate;
There is nothing like them, though thou search from morn to eve.

Mātā kā hāth, bhāī kā sāth.
A mother's love and a brother's company.
(Are most worth having.)

Mātā ke parse, Bhādoṅ ke barse se peṭ bhartā hai. Agric.
The meal served by a mother, like August rains, fills the stomach.

Mat bo chāpaṛ, ujṛe ṭābar. Agric.
Sow not on a stony soil, or you will ruin your family!

Mā telī, bāp Paṭhān, beṭā Shākh-i-zāfrān.
The mother an oil woman, the father a Paṭhān, and the son is a Bunch-of-saffron.
(Said of a low-born man. Saffron is a most expensive thing.)

Mā ṭenī, bāp kulang, bachche nikleṅ rang ba rang.
A short mother and tall father produce children of all sizes.
(Said of a mixed breed.)

Māthe gaṭhrī, madhurī chāl; "āj na pahuṅchab pahuṅchab kāl." E.
A bundle on his head, and easy his gait; and, "I'll reach to-day or at any rate to-morrow."
(An easy-going man.)

Māthe kā muraunā, bel kā khisnā. E.
No sooner was his head shaved, than a *bel* fruit fell on it.
(The *bel* fruit or wood-apple is a fruit with a very hard rind: proverb expresses great misfortune.)

Māth murā-ke phajīhat bhaē, jāt pāṅt donoṅ se gaē.
He shaved himself to his own disgrace, and lost both caste and clan.
☞ The story goes that an idle man shaved his head to become a *faqir* under the impression that begging meant an easy life, but he soon found that it was very hard work; in former times if a man became a *faqir* he could not be received back into his caste.

Māth par moṭrī, Basant ke gīt. E.
With a bundle on his head, he sings the songs of spring.
(Vanity: the idea is of a man who is so unlucky as to be a common labourer pretending to be perfectly happy and careless.)

Mathrā de bundā, lubhāve das gunḍā. E. Wom.
With spangles on her forehead she lures ten lecherous men.

Mathvā, Madārī kā kyā sāth? Rus.
What has a Hindū to do with a Muhammadan?

Māṭī meṅ māṭī milī, milī paun meṅ paun,
Maiṅ toe pūchhūṅ, ē sakhī, donoṅ meṅ muā kaun?
Earth mixed with earth, and air with air:
Which of them dies, I ask you, dear?
(The soul never dies.)

Māṭ kā māṭ hī bigrā hai.
The entire vat is spoiled.
(The whole family are tainted.)

Mat kar sās burāī: tere bhī āge jāī. Wom.
Mother-in-law, don't ill-treat me: you too have a daughter to come after you.
(Said by a young bride to her mother-in-law when she ill-treats her, as is often the case in India.)

Matlā sāf huā.
The sky is clear.
(All obstacles are removed; my wishes are accomplished. The coast is clear.)

Maṭṭhā māṅgan chalīṅ, aur malaīyā pīchhe lukāī! E. Wom.
She asked for butter-milk with butter behind her back!

Maṭṭī kā gharā bhī ṭhoṅk bajā-kar lete haiṅ.
Mercantile.
Even an earthen pot is rung before it is bought.
(Look before you leap: earthen-pots are of hardly any value.)

Maṭṭī meṅ hāth ḍāle sonā hoe hai.
If he touch earth, it will turn to gold.
(A lucky man.)

Maullā hāth baṛhāiyāṅ; jis chāheṅ tis deṅ Mah.
Greatness rests with God; He gives to whom He pleases.

Maullā yār, to beṛā pār. Mah.
If God be kind you will succeed.

Mauqe kā ghūṅsā talvār se baṛh kar.
A box on the ear in time is better than a sword-cut.
(A stitch in time saves nine.)

Maut aur gāhak kā etebār nahīṅ, jāne kis vaqt ā-jāē. Mercantile.
None can tell when death or a customer will come.

Maut bhalī ki jān-kandan?
Is death best or the agonies of death?
(Better a sudden death than a lingering one.)

Maut ke āge kisī kā bas nahīṅ chaltā.
No one's might avails against death.

Maut ke āge sab hāre haiṅ.
Every body is baffled by death.
(See preceeding.)

Maut kī dārū nahīṅ.
There is no remedy for death.
(Death shames the doctor.)

Maut sir par kheltī hai.
Death hovers over our heads.
(The sword of Damocles.)

Māyā ganṭh, aur biddyā kanṭh.
Let your money be in your pocket and your knowledge in your head.

Māyā huī to kyā huā, hirdā huā kaṭhor?
Nau neze pānī chaṛhā, taū bhī na bhīgī kor.
What boots his wealth if his heart be hard?
Put him into nine fathoms of water and he won't be wetted.
(*i. e.* nothing has any effect on him; said of misers.)

Māyā kā kyā joṛnā, khal khānā kambal oṛhnā?
What is the use of wealth heaped up by living on oil cakes and wearing a blanket?
(Said of a miser who mortifies himself to hoard money.)

Māyā ke bhī pāoṅ hote haiṅ; āj mere, kal tere.
Riches have legs; to-day they are mine, to-morrow thine.

Māyā marī na man mare, mar mar gaē sarīr,
Āsā trishnā nā marī: kah gaē Dās Kabīr.
Nature hath never died, nor hath mind died; only men's bodies have died:
And desire and hope have never died: saith Kabīr.

Māyā mere Rām kī Dharnī-dhar kī deh,
Pūñjī Sāhūkār kī, jas koī kar le.
Money is God's lent by the Lord of the Earth,
The wealth is of (God) the Banker, and any one can take the credit.
(Of being generous with it: said to encourage charitable gifts.)

Māyā se māyā mile kar-ke lambe hāth:
Tulsī Dās, garīb kī koī na pūchhe bāt.
The rich salute the rich with out-streched hands: Saith Tulsī Dās, it is the poor that none regards.
(Tulsī Dās; the author of the Hindī *Rāmāyan.*)

Māyā se māyā mile, mile nīch se nīch:
Pānī se pānī mile, mile kīch se kīch.
The rich join with the rich, the low with the low: Water mingles with water, and mire with mire.
(Birds of a feather flock together.)

Māyā tere tīn nām: Parsū, Parsā, Paras Rām.
Wealth hath three names; Parsū, Parsā, and Paras Rām.
(A man is respected according to his means: when poor he is nicknamed Parsū, a diminutive form; when he gets on in the world he becomes Parsā, still a familiar form of address: when he becomes wealthy he is Paras Rām the full form of his name.)

Mazā mā mazā. Arab.
What is past is past.
(Let bygones be bygones.)

Mehariyā ke āge sugan asgun.
With women good omens are bad omens.
(Women in India are generally very superstitious and given to believing in omens, of which they know an extraordinary number.)

Mehmā ghaṭī samudr kī jo Rāvan basā paṛaus.
The greatness of the sea diminished when Rāvan was its neighbour.
(The proverb is based on the story in the *Rāmāyan*: evil communications corrupt good manners. Rāvan is typical of everything that is bad.)

Mehnat ārām kī kunjī hai.
Labor is the key to rest.

Mehr gaī, muhabbat gaī, gaī nān aur pān,
Huqqe se muñh jhulas, ke bidā kiyā mehmān.
Neither hospitality nor civility, neither bread nor betel-leaves, the guest got a whiff of a pipe, and his leave.
(Said of niggardly host.)

Mehr hai, par dūdh nahīñ.
There is kindness, but no milk.
(Fair words won't fill empty bellies: sham affection.)

Mehrī kī rok, jān ke sok.
Check your wife and she 'll make you suffer.

Mehr kare, to meñh barsāve.
When (God) is pleased he sends rain.

Mele meñ jhamelā huā hī kartā hai.
A quarrel is sure to occur at a fair.

Meñdkī ko bhī zukām huā!
The very frog has caught cold!
(A sailor and afraid of the sea! Said of an insignificant person, who gives himself airs of importance. A poor man falling in love with a rich man's daughter.)

Meñh, aur laṛkā, aur naukrī, ghaṛī ghaṛī nahīñ huā kartī.
Rain, posterity and service are not to be had at command.

Meñh barsegā to bauchār ā hī jāegī.
If it rain heavily some of the spray will come over me.
(Spoken by one who expresses a hope that he will come in for a share in the bounty of a liberal person.)

Meo beṭī jab de, jab okhlī bhar rupayā rakh-vāle.
When the Meo gives his daughter in marriage he receives from the bridegroom a mortar full of silver.
(The Meos are low Musalman fishermen and the proverb alludes to their marriage customs.)

Meo kā pūt bārah baras meñ badlā letā hai.
The Meo's lad can take his revenge at twelve years old!
(The Meos are popularly a well-grown and powerfully made race.)

Meo marā jab jāniye, jab tījā ho jāe.
Know that the Meo is really dead when the *tījā* has been performed.
☞ It is related that a Mevātī who was indebted to a Banyā caused a report of his death to be spread abroad. His creditor, to assure himself of the fact, followed the body to the grave where he saw it interred. The friends of the reputed dead man, however, as soon as he had gone away returned and rescued their friend from his living grave. The Banyā seeing him alive again gave utterance to the proverb above quoted. The *tījā* is one of the funeral obsequies performed by Muhammadans on the third day after death.

Merā bail manṭiq nahīñ paṛhā hai.
My ox doesn't know logic.
☞ The story goes that a logician enquired of an oilman the use of the bell which he had hung from the neck of his ox. The oilman replied that when he was away from the mill, he could tell that the ox was working by the tinkling of the bell. Whereupon the logician said, "suppose the ox were to stand still and shake his head and ring the bell, how could you tell whether the ox was working the mill or not?" Upon which the oilman replied in the words of the proverb.

Merā dil be-dil huā dekh jagat kī rīt.
My mind is ill at rest from watching the ways of the world.

Merā māthā usī vaqt ṭhinkā thā. Wom.
It was hammered into my forehead at that very time.
(Said on hearing that any thing distressing has happened.)

Merā thā, so terā huā; barāë Khudā ṭuk dekhne de! Mah. Wom.

He was mine and is yours: for God's sake let me see him sometimes.

(The proverb is put in the mouth of an old mother remonstrating with her daughter-in-law, who has acquired great power over her son.)

Mere byāh, jījī ke ṭhik ṭhik. Wom.

The wedding is in my house, and my sister has the music.

(*Jījī* is the wife of a sister's husband, who can have no concern in the matter: hence proverb means a stupid waste of money.)

Mere gāoṅ kā kūryā, nām rakhā indarjau.

In my village it is *kūryā*, but here it is called *indarjau.*

(Both words are names for the same plant, *nerium antidysentericum.* Proverb is applied to a man who in his native place is in a low station and assumes airs of consequence abroad: cheap swagger.)

Mere hai, so Rājā ke nahīṅ, aur Rājā merā māngtā. Wom.

I have what the Rājā has not, so he must come begging to me.

(Applied to one who boasts of his own comforts or possessions.)

Mere hī se āg lāī nām dharā basandar. Wom.

She got the fire from me, and now she calls it sacred fire.

(*Basandar* is the sacred fire which no *Hindū* can give away, hence the point of the proverb is that, having borrowed the fire the woman calls it sacred fire, when asked to return the favor: unmindful of an obligation.)

Mere lālā kī ulṭī rīt! Sāvan mās chunāven bhīt! Wom.

The eccentricities of my husband! He builds his wall in August!

(Walls in India are made usually of mud and hence it is folly to build one in August, the wettest month in the year.)

Mere lāl ke sau sau yār, dhuniā, julāhe, aur manihār! Wom.

My son has hundreds of friends; wool-carders, weavers and bangle-sellers.

(A man is known by the society he keeps: all the trades mentioned are followed by the lowest people only.)

Mere, mere mūṅh kī sī; tere, tere mūṅh kī sī kartā phirtā hai.

He tells the story my way to me and your way to you.

(A flatterer.)

Mere miyāṅ ke do kapṛe, suttan, nāṛā, bas. Wom.

A pair of trowsers and a string compose my husband's apparel!

(Great poverty.)

Mere yahāṅ āj gurrah hai.

It is a fast with me to-day.

(I have nothing to eat.)

Merī ek bolī, do bolī, merī nakṭī saṭā saṭ bolī. Wom.

I speak once or twice, that impudent wretch speaks a hundred times.

(By 'speak' understand 'abuse.')

Merī hī billī aur mujh se hī miyoṅ!

My own cat mewing at me!

Merī tere āge, terī mere āge kahnā achchhā nahīṅ.

Speaking of me to you, and of you to me is not good.

(Never tell tales out of school.)

Mil gaë kī salām alek hai.

When he meets he salutes.

(Said of a false friend.)

Milkī kyā jāne parāë dil kī?

What do the wealthy know of what's in others' minds?

(One half the world never knows how the half lives.)

Milkī na kahe dil kī; paiṭheṅ darvāze, nikleṅ khiṛkī. E.

The wealthy keep their own counsel, going in by the front door and out by the back.

(Under native rule to expose your wealth meant losing it.)

Mintar voh mar jāë, jo aṛī meṅ kām na āë.

Perish that friend who serves not in distress.

(A friend in need is friend indeed.)

Mīrāṅ gor barābar.

Mīrāṅ and his grave fit each other.

(Expenditure as the income: cutting your coat according to your cloth.)

Mīrāṅ kī boṭī hai. Mah.

A dish of offerings to Mīrāṅ.

(A thing to be let alone. The *mujāvirs* and attendants at the shrine of any saint are in the habit of putting aside a large portion of the offerings and dedicating it to the 'saint,' the rest they distibute among the worshippers. They warn them that if they touch the dedicated portion they will have to pay a heavy fine in kind.)

Mirg, bāndrā, tītar, mor; ye chāroṅ khetī ke chor. Agric.

The deer, the monkey, the partridge, and the peacock; these four are the thieves of the field.

Mirg kī sī āṅkheṅ, chīte kī sī kamar.

Eyes as the gazelle's and waist as the leopard's.

(A beautiful woman.)

Mīr Sāhib kī zāt ālī hai, mūṅh chīknā aur peṭ khālī hai!

Mīr Sāhib is truly of a high family, with his smooth cheeks and his empty stomach!

Mīr Sāhib, zamāna nāzuk hai; donoṅ hāthoṅ se thāmīye dastār.

Mīr Sāhib, times are difficult; put both your hands to your turban.

(The last paragraph is an idiom meaning "take the greatest care." The proverb is used as a warning against a strict superior.)

Mirzā phoyā!
Prince fool!

Missī, kājal kis ko? Miyāṅ chale bhus ko! Mah. Wom.
For whom shall I stain my teeth or blacken my eyelashes? My husband gathers straw!
(To express scanty means: *res angusta domi.*)

Mīṭhā aur kaṭhautī bhar!
What, sweet and a platter-full!
(Good things are scarce.)

Mīṭhā mīṭhā hap hap; karvā karvā thū thū.
Sweet is gobbled up; bitter is spat out.

Mīṭhe se mare, to māhur kyoṅ dīje?
Why give poison, if he can be killed with sweets?

Mīṭhī bātoṅ meṅ din rāt kaṭte mālūm nahīṅ hote.
Pleasant conversation makes the time pass without your knowing it.

Mīṭhī chhurī.
A sugared sword.
(A gilt pill: temporary suffering or inconvenience leading to future advantage. Also a velvet glove: a man pleasant in conversation, but dangerous to deal with.)

Miṭṭī pakṛe sonā ho.
If he takes up dust it turns into gold.
(A lucky man.)

Miyāṅ bīvī rāzī, to kyā karegā Qāzī?
When husband and wife agree, the judge has no cause to interfere.

Miyāṅ gaë raund, bīvī gaīṅ paṭ raunḍ.
When the husband goes abroad the wife also goes abroad.
(When the cat's away the mice may play.)

Miyāṅ hāth angūṭhī, bīvī ke kan pāt,
Launḍī ke dāṅt missī, tīnoṅ kī ek bāt. E.
The ring on a husband's hand, the ring in a wife's ear, the black on a slave-girl's teeth, are all alike.
(All three are of a foppish kind: as the master so the servant.)

Miyāṅ kā dam aur kivāṛ kī joṛī!
My Lord's life and a pair of doors!
(Are all my Lord possesses; to express genteel poverty: shabby genteel.)

Miyāṅ ke Miyāṅ gaë, bure bure supne āë! Mah. Wom.
My husband gone and bad dreams as well!
(Misfortune never comes singly.)

Miyāṅ kī dāṛhī vāh vāhī meṅ gaī!
My Lord's beard is pulled off in flattery!
(See story under *mulla kī*, etc.)

Miyāṅ meṅ se niklā hī paṛe hai!
He is all too ready to draw his sword.
(A fire-eater.)

Miyāṅ nāk kāṭne ko phireṅ, bīvī kaheṅ, "nath gaṛhā do! Wom.
The husband comes to cut off her nose and the wife says, "buy me a nose-ring!"
(Cross purposes.)

Miyāṅ ne ṭohī, sab kām se khoī. Mah. Wom.
Her master toyed with her and she ran away.
(Losing a good servant by a foolish act.)

Miyāṅ phire lāl gulāl, bīvī ke haiṅ bure havāl! Mah. Wom.
My Lord enjoying himself and my Lady in distress!

Miyaūṅ ko kaun pakṛegā?
Who will stop the cat's mewing?
(Belling the cat.)
☞ The story goes that a company of rats agreed to kill a cat, and agreed also which part of each would take for himself, but when the chief rat said, "who will stop her mewing?" they all ran away from fear?

Mizāj kyā hai? ki ek tamāshā!
Ghaṛī meṅ tolā, ghaṛī meṅ māshā!
What is his temper like? As good as a play! One moment a pound and the next an ounce!

Mīzān jūṅ kī tūṅ, kunbā ḍūbā kyuṅ.
The account is correct and why is the family drowned?
(See story under *Hisāb jūṅ kā tūṅ*, etc.)

Mohareṅ luṭī jāëṅ, koeloṅ par mohar.
His gold is squandered, and his charcoal marked with care.
(Penny wise and pound foolish: pun on the word *mohar*, a gold coin and also a seal.)

Mo ko na to ko, le chūlhe meṅ jhoko. Wom.
Not for you, nor for me; take it, and throw it into the fire.

Mom ho to pigle, kahīṅ patthar bhī piglā hai?
Were he wax he would melt, but can you melt a stone?
(Said of the miserly and hard-hearted.)

Mom kī nāk.
A nose of wax.
(A credulous man.)

More bāp ke upjal kapās, more lekhe paṛal tusār. E. Wom.
My father's cotton crop has come up, but for me there's only hail (misfortune.)
(She cannot expect any thing out of it: according to orthodox Hindū law a daughter is not entitled to a share in her father's property while he has male issue to succeed him.)

Morī kī īṅṭ chaubāre chaṛhī. Wom.
The brick of the drain is raised to the terrace.
(Said of an upstart or of a worthless man raised to high position: also of a *mesalliance* by which a girl of low birth is married above her.)

Mor saīyāṅ chikanyā, pachās bīṛā khāë;
Āge pichhe rinihā; dīvānā bane jāë. E. Wom.
My husband is a fop eating 50 betel leaves (a day); and when his creditors surround him he feigns madness.
(Betel leaves are expensive luxuries.)

Moze kā ghāo mīyāṅ jāneṅ yā pāoṅ.
The owner of his foot knows where the shoe rubs.
(Every one knows where his own shoe pinches.)

Muā ghoṛā bhī kahīṅ ghās khātā hai?
Does a dead horse ever eat grass?
(1. An objection made against offerings made to the dead. 2. A reproof to those who in old age seek the pleasures of youth.)

Mūchh-maroṛā, roṭī toṛā!
Twirling his moustache and eating his bread!
(An idler.)

Muddai, muddāēlah nāo meṅ; shāhid tairte jāēṅ.
The plaintiff and defendant go in a boat, while the witnesses are obliged to swim.
(The proof of the transaction resting with the witnesses, they have more occasion to exert themselves in court than the parties. *Moral,*—never be a witness.)

Muddaī sust, gavāh chust.
The plaintiff careless and the witness eager.
(Allusion to the false witnesses who keep constantly hanging about courts to give their evidence to the highest bidder.)

Mūe bail kī baṛī baṛī āṅkheṅ.
The eyes of a dead ox are always large.
(Said when praises are bestowed upon a deceased person. *De mortuis nil nisi bonum.*)

Mūṅge aur so raheṅge!
When we die we sleep well!
(The long sleep.)

Mūē par sau durreh. Mah.
A hundred stripes on the dead.
(Hitting a man when he is down. Dead men tell no tales.)

Mūē sher se jītī billī bhalī.
A live cat is better than a dead tiger.

Muflis hameshah khuār.
The poor are always in disgrace.
(No crime like poverty.)

Muflisī aur fālse kā sharbat.
Indigence and *fālsā sharbat.*
(Incompatibility of circumstances and pretensions: *fālsā* is a small plum, and a very costly article.)

Muflisī aur hāṭ kī sair.
Indigence parading in the market.

Muflisī meṅ āṭā gīlā.
In poverty the flour is sodden.
(Misfortunes never come singly.)

Muflisī sab bahār khotī hai, Mard kā etebār khotī hai.
Poverty spoils all pleasures and ruins a man's credit.

Muflis kā chirāg raushan nahīṅ hotā.
The poor man's lamp is never lit.

Muflis kī jorū sadā naṅgī.
The poor man's wife is always under-clad.

Muflis se savāl harām hai. Mah.
It is wicked to beg from the poor.

Muft kā chandan ghise jā, bilallī! Wom.
Thou fool, thou art grinding the sandal wood for nothing!
(Sandal wood ground to powder is used only by the wealthy; the point here is that the poor woman addressed has no business to be grinding it.)

Muft kā karnā aur dūr lejānā?
To do it for nothing and carry it a long way.
(To take needless trouble.)

Muft kā māl kis ko burā lagtā hai?
No one objects to taking a gift.

Muft kā sirkā shahad se mīṭhā.
Vinegar for nothing is sweeter than honey.

Muft ke chirvā bhar bhar phanke. E.
Parched rice for nothing is swallowed by mouthfuls.

Muft ke khāne-vāle, ham aur hamārā bhāī. Wom.
We two eat for nothing, I and my brother.
(Allusion to the affection between brother and sister in India, which makes the sister spend her husband's goods on her brother.)

Muft kī dāvat meṅ faqat roṭī hī gosht hai. Mah.
A feast of bread which costs nothing is as (good as) meat.
(Never look a gift horse in the mouth.)

Muft kī sharāb Qāẓī ko bhī halāl! Mah.
Even the Qāẓī may drink of a present of wine!
(Wine is of course unlawful to the orthodox Muhammadan.)

Muft meṅ nikle kām, to kāhe-ko dīje dām?
Why pay for work that can be got for nothing?

Muft rā che guft? Pers.
Why cavil at a gift?

Muharram kī paidāyash. Mah.
Born at the Muharram.
(Said of a sulky fellow because of the mourning observed by Muhammadans of the Shia sect in memory of Hasan and Husain who fell martyrs in battle with Yazid.)

Muī bachhiyā bāman ke dān. Hin.
A starving heifer given in alms to a Brāhman.
(A useless gift.)

Muī kyoṅ? Sāṅs na āyā. Wom.
Why did she die? For want of breath!
(A misfortune that cannot be avoided.)

Muā tolo āṅḍoṅ par.
The dead penis falls on the testicles.
(The ire of the weak falls on the innocent.)

Muī māī, ṭūṭī sagāī.
When a mother dies, the relationship is sundered.
(Death spares not any worldly ties. Death is no respecter of persons.)

Mujarrad sab se ālā, jis ke laṛkā na bālā.
The bachelor is happiest of all, that hath nor chick nor child.

Mujhe aur, na tujhe ṭhaur.
For me no other, for you no whither.
(The wife to her husband after a quarrel: "I may not take another husband and you could not be happy elsewhere.")

Mujhe de sūp, tū hāthoṅ phūṅk!
Give me the winnowing fan and winnow in your own hands!

Mujh ko na māre, to sāre jahān ko mār āūṅ!
If no one would whip me I should whip creation!

Mukhādim Khān ke sāle.
My Lord's brother-in-law.
(Said of a poor man who gives himself airs. Also of the *protégé* of a rich man who bullies under the protection of his patron.)

Mukh meṅ "Rām Rām," bagal meṅ chhurī.
"God" on his tongue, and a knife under his arm!
(Said of a scoundrel.)

Muktā māl bānar līye, Bed līye aggyān,
Param sundar jogī līye, kāyar hāth kamān.
A pearl for a monkey's share, the *Vēdas* for a fool, A beautiful wife for a *jogī*, a bow for a coward's hand.
(Are pearls before swine.)

Mulāzim-i-nau tez-rau. Pers.
A new servant is very active.
(A new broom sweeps clean.)

Mūlī apne hī pātoṅ bhārī.
The weight of its own leaves is too much for the radish.
(Applied to one, who labors under difficulties of his own and is thereby unable to relieve others.)

Mūlī aur mūlī ke patvāloṅ par lon kī ḍalī! E.
Radishes and radish-leaves with a pinch of salt!
(Applied to one who in a pompous manner enumerates possessions of no value.)

Mūlī hāth parāīyāṅ; jis chāhe tis de.
The radish is in others' hands: they may give it to whom they please.

Mullā-jī kyā kaheṅ, ākhūn-jī āge hī samjhe hue haiṅ? Mah.
What can the priest teach, that the high priest has not learnt before?

Mullā kī ḍāṛhī tabarruk meṅ gaī. Mah.
The Mulla's beard goes in relics.
☞ It is related of a Mulla who was distributing sacred tokens among his disciples, that a wag taking a fancy to his beard, plucked a hair which he desired to keep as a sacred relic. Thereupon another and another did the same till at last, in spite of the poor man's protestatious he was left without a beard. The proverb is used when any one gives away his whole substance in alms or in presents to his friends.

Mullā na hogā, to kyā, masjid meṅ azāṅ na hogī? Mah.
If there be no priest, will there be no call to prayer in the mosque?

Mulk-i-Khudā taṅg nest, pāë marā laṅg nest. Pers.
God's universe is wide enough, no helpless cripple am I.
(I can shake another oak. "Are ye able to drink of the cup that I shall drink of?" They say unto him, "We are able." Matthew, xx, 22.)

Mūl se byāj pyārā hotā hai. Mercantile.
The interest is dearer than the principal.
(The love of making money will induce a trader to risk his capital in order to secure a high interest on it. The more you get the more you want.)

Munḍā jogī, aur pisī davā, pahchānī nahīṅ jātī.
A shaven *jogī* and a powdered drug cannot be recognized.
(You cannot tell his caste, or what it is made of.)

Muṅḍe sir par pānī paṛā ḍhal gayā.
Water runs off a shaven head.
(No good counsel produces any effect on a shameless or headstrong person: water off a duck's back.)

Mūṅḍ muṅḍāë, jaṭā dharāë, nagan phireṅ jūṅ bhaiṅsā,
Khalṛī upar rākh lagāë; man jaise kā taisā.
Some shave their heads, some let their hair grow, some go naked as a buffalo, Some rub themselves with ashes; but their minds remain as before.
(A skit at the *sādhūs* or *faqīrs*.)

Mūṅḍ muṅḍāë tīn gun: gaī ṭāṅṭ kī khāj,
Bābā ho jag meṅ phire, peṭ bhar khāyā nāj.
The three benefits of a shaven poll: the disappearance of itching, The reverence of the world and a belly-full of corn.
(A shaven poll denotes the mendicant who is highly respected and who is a successful beggar.)

Mūṅḍ dīā, māṅg khāo.
I have shaven you, go and beg for yourself.
(A *jogī* to his novice.)

Mūṅg, moṭh meṅ baṛā kaun?
'Twixt pea and pea, which is larger?
(Caste brethren are all equal: like as two peas. *Mūṅg* and *moṭh* are varieties of pulse.)

Mūṅh chiknā, peṭ khālī.
Smooth face and an empty belly.
(Said of a dandy or swaggerer.)

Mūṅh dekhe kī muhabbat hai.
Friendship before one's face.
(Cupboard love.)

Mūṅh dekhī sab kahte haiṅ, Khudā lagtī koī nahīṅ kahtā.
All say to please the countenance, and none [to please God.
(Men prefer to say what is pleasing to what is the truth. *Mūṅh dekhnā* is to watch another's face while speaking to him.)

Mūṅh dekh-ke bīṛā aur chūtaṛ dekh-ke pīṛhā.
Look at the face and offer betel-leaf, look at the buttocks and offer a seat.
(*i. e.* be civil when you see a man and be friendly when you know him.)

Mūṅh dho rakkho.
Go and wash your face.
(Addressed to a person who asks any thing of another, which he does not intend to give him. Go to school. Said in reply to a preposterous request.)

Mūṅh gail tamāche haiṅ.
As the face so the slap.
(As the person so the respect.)

Mūṅh hāle, sattar balā ṭāle.
Grind the jaws and keep off seventy evils.
(Said to a sick man.)

Mūṅh hī mūṅh māre aur tobah tobah pukāre.
When boxed on the ears he promises amendment.
(Spare the rod spoil the child.)

Mūṅh kahe "khāyā khāyā," halaq kahe "savād na āyā."
The mouth says, "I have eaten," and the throat says, "I felt no taste."
(Said of a very small quantity of food.)

Mūṅh kālā, bakht ujlā.
Foul face, fair fortune.

Mūṅh kā nivālā to nahīṅ hai.
It is not a morsel of food.
(That can easily be gulped down. Said of a difficult task. Rome was not built in a day.)

Mūṅh ke āge khandaq nahīṅ.
No ditch before his face.
(Nothing prevents tall talk.)

Mūṅh khāē, āṅkh lajāē,
The mouth eats, and the eyes are kept down.
(To place oneself under an obligation.)

Mūṅh kī mīṭhī, hāth kī jhūṭī. Wom.
A sweet tongue and a false hand.
(To excite false hopes.)

Mūṅh ko kālak lag gaī.
The face is blackened.
(A badge of infamy : allusion to the favorite oriental punishment.)

Mūṅh lagāī Ḍomnī, bāl bachche samet āē.
Encourage a songstress and she will bring her whole family.
(Give him an inch and he'll take an ell. Applied to one, who having been encouraged to expect patronage and protection, presumes to recommend several others. The Ḍoms are a very low class of singers.)

Mūṅh lagāī Ḍomnī gāve tāl be-tāl.
Favor a songstress and she will sing out of time.
(Three years a good servant, three years a pleasant companion, three years a hard master. *Moral,* don't favour a servant too much.)

Mūṅh lagī aur fel mere peṭ meṅ.
The vice was in my stomach before I put it to my lips.
(A villain sober is a villain drunk.)

Mūṅh māṅge dām nahīṅ milte. Mercantile.
The price asked for cannot be had.
(Allusion to the haggling that is habitual in Indian Markets.)

Mūṅh māṅgī maut to miltī hī nahīṅ.
Not even death will come when called.
(Death shuns the wretch.)

Mūṅh māṅgī murād mile!
May you get your heart's desire!
(A beggar's cry.)

Mūṅh meṅ āyā so bak diyā.
To blurt out what comes into the mouth.
(Speaking without thinking.)

Mūṅh meṅ dāṅt, na peṭ meṅ āṅt.
No teeth in his head, and no guts in his belly.
(Said of a very old man.)

Mūṅh na tūh, nām Chāṅd Khāṅ.
Neither face nor countenance and his name Mr. Moon.
(*Chāṅd* (Moon) means a beautiful face in India, hence the sting of this saying.)

Mūṅh nūr, na peṭ sabūr.
Nor light on the face, nor patience in the belly.
(To have neither fortune nor philosophy.)

Mūṅh par havāīyāṅ uṛne lagīṅ.
The air is playing upon his face.
(His looks betray him. To turn pale with fear.)

Mūṅh par kahe so mūchh kā bāl; pīchhe kahe so jhāṅṭ kā bāl.
Who speaks to your face is as a moustache; who speaks behind your back is as cast off hair.

Mūṅh par kahnā khushāmad hai.
To praise before the face is flattery.

Mūṅh par mumānī, pīṭ pichhe sūar khānī. Mah Wom.
Relations to their faces, pigs behind the backs.
(Said of a treacherous woman.)

Mūṅh par pūt, pīchhe harāmī mūt. Mah. Wom.
A son to his face, and a bastard behind his back.
(See preceding.)

Mūṅh pe phiṭkār barasne lagī.
Curses rain upon his head.
(Said of a bad character.)

Mūṅh rahte, nāk se pānī pīye.
He drinks water with his nose, while he has a mouth.

Mūṅh se bolo, sir se khelo!
Speak with your lips, or shake your head!
(Said to one who assumes taciturnity.)

Mūṅh se hazār chāur khāī, nāke se eko nā. E. Wom.
With your mouth you may eat a thousand grains of rice, with your nose not one.
(You may do as you like, as long as you do it properly.)

Mūṅh se lām kāf mat nikālo. Ped.
Let not *lām kāf* out of your mouth.
(This is one of the bad puns the *literati* are so fond of; *lām* and *kāf* are the first letters of the words *lāf* and *kazāf* which mean jabber and be silent.)

Mũṅh se mahāba.
The face creates fear.
(The master's eye keeps the horse fat.)

Mũṅh se niklī huī parāī bāt.
Out of the lips is another's property.

Mũṅh se rāl ṭapkī partī hai.
Saliva drops from his mouth.
(To water at the mouth: an unmannerly man.)

Mũṅh sūī, peṭ kūā.
His mouth like the eye of a needle, and his belly like a well.
(1. One who eats in small quantities, but consumes a great deal. 2. One mild in appearance, but mischievous in reality.)

Mūṅj kī ṭaṭṭī, aur Gujrātī tālā.
A shutter of grass, with a Gujrātī lock.
(Gujrāt in the Panjāb is noted for its locksmiths: the strength of a chain is in its weakest link.)

Murabbī biyār o murabba bikhur. Pers.
Get a patron and eat dainties.

Mūrakh ke samjhāēte gyān gāṅṭh ko jāē.
In teaching an idiot knowledge gets knotted.
(It is thrown away on him.)

Mūrakh kī sārī rain, chātar kī ek gharī.
Better an hour with a clever man, than a whole night with a lout.
(Better fifty years of Europe than a cycle of Cathay.)

Mūrakh ko samjhāonā saras bīj chalī jāē,
Jaiṅ patthar ke mārne chokho tīr nasāē.
In teaching a fool the whole principle is lost, as in hitting a stone the best arrow is broken.

Mūrakh se kyā kahiye, jā se kyā bausāē?
Why speak to a fool whom nothing avails?

Murdah ba dast-i-zindah. Pers.
The dead are at the mercy of the living.

Murdah bahisht meṅ jāē yā dozakh meṅ, yahāṅ to halve māṇḍe se kām. Mah.
The dead may go to heaven or hell, my concern is with the sweets and cakes.
(Put into the mouth of a Mulla who reads prayers over the dead, and receives a present of sweetmeats.)

Murde ko baiṭh-kar rote haiṅ, aur rozgār ko khaṛe ho-kar.
They mourn for the dead sitting and for food [standing.
(They take their ease over mourning for the dead, but are active enough in mourning over loss of means.)

Murde par sau man miṭṭī, to ek man aur bhī sahī.
There are a hundred tons of earth on the body, so a ton more makes no odds.

Murdoṅ se shart bāṅdh-ke sotā hai.
He will challenge a dead man in sleeping.
(Said of one who sleeps long and is not easily awakened.)

Murgā bāṅg na degā; to kyā subah na hogī?
If the cock should not crow, will there be no dawn?

Murgā hazam, bakrī par dam. Mah.
He has gobbled up a fowl, and is waiting for a goat.
(A greedy man.)

Murgā pasham, bheṛ bhasam! Mah.
What's a fowl to one who has swallowed a sheep?

Murge kī ek hī ṭāṅg hotī hai.
Fowls have only one leg.
(A transparent excuse. Tell a lie and stick to it.)

☞ The story goes that a great man once had a roast fowl with only one leg set before him, his cook protesting that the fowl belonged to a breed that had but one leg. Next day, he drew his master's attention to a fowl standing on a dunghill on one leg, saying "there's another!" But the master cried "shu," and the fowl flew away displaying both legs. "Well" said the servant, "if you had said 'shu' to the other fowl he would have shown another leg too."

Murgī apnī jān se gaī, khāne-vāle ko mazā na āyā. Mah. Wom.
The fowl lost its life, and the eater was not satisfied.
(Said of a service performed with toil, and accepted with indifference. To take kindness as a right.)

Murgī ke khvāb meṅ dānā hī dānā.
Fowls dream but of grain.

Murgī kī azān kaun suntā hai? Mah.
Who minds the crowing of a hen?
(No one relies on a woman's word. See next.)

Murgī kī bāṅg kā kyā etbār? Mah.
What trust is there in a crowing hen?
(A woman's word is not to be depended on. A whistling woman and a crowing hen are neither good for God nor men.)

Murgī ko takle hī kā ghāo bas hai. Wom.
A wound from a needle is enough for a fowl.

Musāfir chale hī jāte haiṅ, kutte bhauṅkte hī rahte haiṅ.
The travellers go on, while the dogs keep barking.

Musalla pasār, bagal meṅ yār. Mah.
Kissing a girl over the praying carpet.
(Said of a hypocrite.)

Musalmānān dar gor, va Musalmānī dar kitāb. Pers. Mah.
The Musalmāns are in their graves, and their faith in their books.
(No true Muhammadans are left.)

Musalmānī, ābādānī. Mah.
Where there are Musalmāns, there is population.
(Allusion to their habit of herding together.)

Musalmānī meṅ ānā kānī kyā? Mah.
There should be no reserve among Musalmāns?
(Addressed to one who declines partaking of a meal to which he is invited.)

Mushk ān ast ki khud boyad, na ki attār goyad. Pers.
Musk is known by its smell, not by the praises of the perfumer.
(The best wine has a bush.)

Mushkil-i-nest ki āsān na shovad:
Mard bāyad ki hirāsān na shavad. Pers.
No difficulty so great but it may be overcome: A true man never sinks under it.

Mūt kā chullū hāth men.
To throw dirty water.
(To cast in the teeth.)

Mūzī kā chungal.
The clutches of a miser (tyrant.)

Mūzī kā māl, nikle phūṭ ke khāl. Superstition.
The miser's wealth breaks out in sores.
(It is unlucky and brings evil on his heir.)

Mūzī ko namāz chhoṛ-ke māre. Mah.
You may leave your prayers to kill an obnoxious beast.

N.

Nāche Bāman, dekhe dhobī.
The Brahman dances and the washerman looks on.
(Society upside down.)

Nāchegā so pāvegā.
Who dances (works) gets.

Nāche, kūde, toṛe tān, vā kā dunyā rākhe mān.
Who dances, skips and plays, is loved by the world.

Nāch kūd bāndrā, mere māl madārī khāē.
The monkey dances and skips, and the acrobat gets the present.
(The cat's paw.)

Nāch na sakūn āngan ṭeṛhā! Wom.
I can't dance because the floor is uneven.
(When the devil couldn't swim he laid the fault on the water. Bad workmen quarrel with their tools.)

Nāchne niklī to ghūngaṭ kyā? Wom.
When you come out to dance, why be veiled?
(Dancing women in India are of course unveiled. *Moral*: don't be above your work.)

Nāchnā ān yeī nā, "āngan bānkre,"
Rāndhnā yeī nā, "oli lōnkre." E.
Not knowing how to dance (he says), "the floor is uneven!" Not knowing how to cook (he says), "the greens are tough!"
(A bad workman quarrels with his tools.)

Nādān bāt kare, dānā qayās kare.
The fool speaks, but the wise man thinks.
(Think before you speak.)

Nādān dost se dānā dushman bhalā.
Better a wise foe than a foolish friend.

Nādān kī dostī, jī kā ziyān.
The friendship of a fool is the plague of one's life.

Na dauṛī chalainge, na ṭhas lagegī. E.
Who runs not, stumbles not.
(Look before you leap.)

Nadī kināre rūkhṛā jab tab hoe binās.
Trees on the river bank are apt to fall.
(Applied to those who follow a dangerous profession.)

Nadī men jānā aur piyāse ānā!
To go to a river and come back thirsty!

Nadī nāo sanjog.
The union of boat and river.
(A chance union.)

Nadī, tū ghurrātī kyon hai? Main pāon hī nahīn rakhtā.
Pray, Mr. River, what are you clattering about? I will not deign to wet my feet in you.
(Addressed to one who evinces much pride and ostentation. I wouldn't touch you with the end of a barge pole.)

Nadiyā, nāo, ghāṭ bahoterā, kahen Kabīr, "nām ke pherā."
There are many rivers, boats and ferries, but, says Kabir, "they all have different names."

Naē bāvarchī, sāg men shorbā!
An untrained cook and a soup of greens!
(*Shorba* is made of meat.)

Naē naē hākim, naī naī bāten!
New rulers, new laws!

Naē namāzī, aur boriye kā tahmad! Mah.
A new Musalmān and a mat for aprou!
(Muhammadans usually wrap a cloth round their legs reaching down to the knees while engaged in prayer.)

Naē navāb, āsmān par dimāg!
A new lord and his pride in the sky!

Naē sipāhī, mūchh men ḍanḍā!
A new soldier and a stick in his moustache!
(To keep it erect, as a sign of youth and boldness.)

Nafrī men nakhrā kyā?
There is no disputing daily wages.

Na gāē ke than, na kisān ke bhānḍe.
The cow has no udder, nor the milkman a can.
(Spoken of any thing useless.)

Na gāṛī bhar āshnāī, na jau bhar nātā.
Nor a cart-load of friendship, nor a barley-corn of relationship.
(He is nothing at all to me.)

Na gūh men ḍhelā ḍālo, na chhīnṭen uṛen.
Throw no clods into mire, and you will not be spattered.

Nahā-kar khāve, khā-kar sove, Us ko ausak kabhī na hove.
Who bathes before his meals and sleeps after them will never get ill.

Nāhaq ḍanḍ, putr kā sog, Nit uṭh panth chalen jo log, Jinī birdhā men mar gaī nārī, Bin āgī yeh jar gaī chārī.
Who is wrongly fined, Who mourns a son, Who is ever on the tramp, Who loses a wife in old age: These four are burnt without fire.

Naī bahū, ṭāṭ kā lahṅgā.
A new wife and a gown of canvass !

Naī bastī aur aranḍī kā phulel.
A new village, and castor-oil for hair-wash.
(Said of any thing of no value. Castor oil is not a substance proper for use as hair oil.)

Nāī, dāī, baid, qasāī ; in kā sūtak kadhī na jāī. Hin.
Barber, mid-wife, leech and butcher; these four are always defiled.

Naī faujdārī aur murgī par naqqārah.
A new government and its drum on a hen's back.
(Expresses the speaker's disapprobation and contempt of some new rules or regulations: *naqqārās* are used by Rājās and here represent the insignia of royalty.)

Naī ghosan aur uploṅ kā takyā !
A new milkmaid and a pillow of cowpats.

Naī javānī, mānjhā ḍhīlā.
Youth and a shabby bed.
(Indolence in the young: too idle to make it up properly.)

Nāī kī barāt meṅ sab hī ṭhākur.
Every body is a lord at a barber's wedding.
(*Ṭhākur*, a nobleman, a lord ; but used also as an honorific title towards barbers (*nāī*): hence the joke.)

Nainā det batāē sab hiye ko het ahet,
Jaise nirmal ārsī bhalī burī kah det. E.
The eyes show the love and hatred of all hearts, As a clear glass showeth both fair and foul.

"*Nāī nāī, bāl kitne ?*" "*Jijmān, āge hī āte haiṅ.*"
Pray, Mr. Barber, how much hair is there on my head ? "Sir, it will presently be laid before you."
(In reply to one, who inquires after the result of something which will soon become evident of itself. In India the Hindū head is usually shaven.)

Nainan ko neh na ṭūṭe, jaise bel birachh ko lipṭe, sūkh jāē na chhūṭe.
Love leaves not the eyes, as a creeper clasps a tree, and clings to it till it die.

Naī nāgan, ṭange par phan !
A young snake, with its hood on its tail !
(Applied to one who foolishly engages in a business which he does not understand: the allusion is to the cobra which has a hood on its head.)

Nainā, tohe paṭak dūṅ, ṭūk ṭūk ho jāē !
Pahle neh lagāē-ke, pāchhe alag ho jāē.
Eyes, I could cast you down and break you in pieces ! You entangled me in love and then took yourselves off !

Naī nau dām, purānī chha dām !
A penny for a new thing, and a farthing for an old one !

Naī nāyan aur bāṅs kī naharnī !
A new barber with bamboo nail-scissors !
(These should be of steel or iron. Applied to those who introduce dangerous innovations. A leap in the dark.)

Nain chhupāe nā chhupeṅ, paṭ ghūngaṭ kī oṭ :
Chatar nār aur sūrmā kareṅ lākh meṅ choṭ.
Veils do not hide their eyes : Clever women like warriors slay their thousands.

Nāī sab ke pāoṅ dhoē, apne dhote lajāē !
The barber washes every one's feet, but is ashamed to wash his own !

Na īṅṭ ḍālo, na chhīṅṭoṅ bharo.
Nor throw a stone, nor get splashed.

Na jīne kī shādī, na marne kā gam.
Nor delight in life, nor dread of death.

Nāk chane chabvānā.
To make one eat peas through the nose.
(*i. e.* to torment one.)

Nāk de, yā naharnī de.
Give me your nose or your nail-cutter.
(To put one on the horns of a dilemma.)

Nākhalaf beṭe se beṭī bhalī.
Better a daughter than an undutiful son.
(Sons are valued in India, daughters not; hence point of proverb.)

Nāk ho to nathiyā sobhe. Hin. Wom.
The nose-ring becomes a nose.

Nakh se sikh tak.
From top to toe.
(Said in praise of personal charms.)

Na Khudā hī milā, na visāle sanam :
Na idhar ke hue, na udhar ke huē.
I met neither God nor my love; So I am fit neither for this nor for the next world.
(Said by a disappointed *faqīr*.)

Nāk kaṭī balā se, dushman kī bad shugnī to huī.
If my nose is cut it is well, because it is then a bad omen to my enemy.
(It is a bad omen to meet a noseless man when starting on a journey, hence the proverb is put into the mouth of a shameless man, who thus consoles himself for having no nose (honor).)

Nāk kaṭī mubārak, kān kaṭe salāmat. Mah. Wom.
If her nose be off it is lucky, if her ear be off it is blessed.
(To describe a very impudent person.)

Nāk ke bāl ho rahe haiṅ.
He is the hair of his nose.
(Said of a favorite.)

Nāk pakṛe dam nikaltā hai.
He will die if you pluck him by the nose.
(Very weak.)

Nāk par diyā bāl-kar āē haiṅ.
He is come with a light on his nose.
(*i. e.* by candle-light: too late.)

Nāk par supārī toṛtī haiṅ. Wom.
He cracks betel-nuts on his nose.
(He is very irascible.)

Nakṭā, būchā, sab se ūṅchā !
No nose, no ears, and yet the highest of the high !
(Both conditions implying personal shame in India.)

Naktā jīve bure havāl!
Noseless he lives in a miserable state!
(Spoken of one who has fallen from a prosperous state into distress.)

Na-koī ātā thā ghar meṅ, Na-koī jātā thā, Na-koī god meṅ le-kar mujhe sulātā thā.
No-body came into the house and No-body left it, No-body took me into his lap and put me to sleep.
☞ The story goes that a husband left his wife at home and went on a journey. During his absence a stranger was in the habit of visiting her, and her child asked her who he was. She replied "nobody (na-koī) came and went," and henceforth the stranger's name to the child was Na-koī (No-body.) When the husband returned he petted the child and put the child to sleep, and when he remarked that in his absence there was no one to do this for the child, it replied in the words of the proverb; the meaning to it and the father being of course quite different. Cross purposes.

Nakṭe kā khāīye, ukṭe kā na khāīye. Wom.
Better be fed by the noseless than by the disagreeable.
(*Ukṭā* is a man who reminds of an obligation.)

Nakṭe kī nāk kaṭī, savā gaz aur baṛhī.
The nose of the noseless grows an ell and quarter.
(A person who has suffered public disgrace becomes callous to the loss of reputation and is more likely than ever to sin.)

"*Nakṭī maiyā, pānī pilā!*" "*Pūtā, inhīn gunvan se!*" E. Wom.
"My nose-less mother, give me some water!"
"What upon such language, my son!"

Nāk to kaṭī, par voh khūb hī meṅ marī!
Her nose is cut off, but she will still die a beauty!

Nālain, tahatu'l-ain. Arab.
Keep your shoes under your own eyes.
(Or they will be stolen.)

Nāle mūṅj bagaṛ, nāle Delī dā darshan. Punj.
Both *mūṅj* and *bagaṛ* and also the worship of *Debī*.
(To kill two birds with one stone: *Mūṅj* and *bagaṛ* are kinds of coarse grass used in making ropes for beds and grow by river sides, where the shrines to Devī are usually located. The point is that the pilgrims go to worship Devī and take the opportunity of bringing back *mūṅj* and *bagaṛ* to turn an honest penny.)

Nal kā mārā nalvā ṭūṭe.
A blow with a reed may break the shins.
(*i. e.* can open a vein.)

Na maiṅ jalāūṅ terī; na tū jalā merī. Wom.
I will not burn yours, and don't you burn mine.
(I'll throw no dirt at you, don't you throw it at me.)

Na maiṅ kahūṅ terī; na tū kaho merī. Wom.
I speak not ill of you; don't you speak ill of me.
(Said after a quarrel is made up.)

Na māre mare, na kāṭe kaṭe.
He neither dies from a blow, nor is cut by a gash.
(Invulnerable.)

Namāzī kā ṭakā. Mah.
The holy man's penny.
☞ The story goes that a mischievous boy was in the habit of pulling back the legs of the worshippers at prayer in a *masjid*. He did so to an old man who gave him a *ṭakā* (penny). This encouraged the boy, who next chanced on a Paṭhān, who turned round and killed him.

Namāz chhuṛāne gaë the, roze gale paṛe! Mah.
They went to get rid of their prayers and were obliged to fast as well!
☞ The story goes that the people begged Moses (*Mūsā*) to pray to God to relieve them of their five obligatory prayers, the result was that God added fasts to the prayers owing to the wickedness of mankind.

Nām Basantī, mūṅh kūkur as. E. Wom.
Her name Beauty and a dog's her face.

Nām baṛā, aur darshan thoṛe.
A great name, and little to see.
(Great cry, little wool.)

Nām baṛā ūṅchā, kān donoṅ būchā. E.
A great name, and both ears cut off.
(A stain on the family escutcheon.)

Nām baṛā yā dām?
A good name is better than wealth.

Nām Hīrā Mal, damak kankar sī bhī nahīn.
His name is Mr. Diamond, but he has not even the lustre of a pebble.

Nām Imrit, pilāë bis.
His name Elixir and he gives poison to drink.

Nāmī shāh kamā khāë, nāmī chor mārā jāë.
A famous banker makes much profit and a famous thief is hanged.
(Give a dog a bad name and hang him.)

Nām ke Bābājī, karnī chhāvar.
Reverend his name and dust his deeds.

Nām kī Nannī, uṭhā le jāë dhannī!
Her name Trot and she can lift a beam!

"*Nām kyā?*" "*Shakar-pārā.*" "*Roṭī kitnī khāë?*" "*Das bārah.*" "*Pānī kitnā pīye?*" "*Maṭkā sārā.*" "*Kām karne ko?*" "*Laṛkā bichārā!*" Wom.
"Your name?" "I'm Lollypop." "You eat?" "Loaves ten or twelve." "You drink?" "A large jar full." "You work?" "I am but a lad, you know!"

Nām levā, na pānī-devā.
None to take his name or perform his funeral.
(Destitute of issue: in Hindū law the *pānī-devā*, or the one who performs the obsequies of the dead, is a son or male issue of a daughter.)

Nām merā, gām terā.
The name mine, and the village yours.
(*i. e.* I get the benefit of your property.)

Namūd, be-būd. Pers.
Show without substance.

Nanad kā nandoī, gale lāg lāg roī. Hin. Wom.
She embraces and weeps over her husband's sister's husband.
(Applied to one, who pretends great affection for another with whom he has none or a very remote connexion.)

Nānā ke tukre khāve, dādā kā potā kahlāve.
He eats the bread of his mother's father and is called the grandson of his father's father.
(One does the work, another gets the credit.)

Nānā kī daulat par navāsā aiṇḍā phire.
The grandson consequential on his grandfather's wealth.

Nānak, nannhā ho raho, jaisī nannhī dūb,
Per bare gir jāeṅge, dūb khūb kī khūb.
Saith Nānak, be humble as the lowly *dūb* grass, Tall trees fall, but the *dūb* is ever well.
(Bābā Nānak was the founder of the Sikh religion and flourished 1469—1538 A. D. The sacred *dūb* (*kusā*) grass is a fresh low growth much valued in India.)

Na nau man tel hogā, na Rādhā nāchegī.
No nine *mans* of oil, no dance from Rādhā.
(Applied to one, who conceals his ignorance of any art by offering to exercise it on impracticable conditions.)
☞ The story goes that a dancing girl called Rādhā, conscious of her inability to dance well, would only do so on the condition that her employers should burn nine *mans* of oil while she was dancing, knowing very well that they could not afford it.

Nān chuk deotā, tilak urāele. E.
The *tilak* destroyed the wretched little god.
(Ironical honors. The *tilak* is a mark made by rubbing sandal wood on the forehead of an idol: hence the point is that rubbing it on destroyed the god.)

Naṅgā kharā ujār meṅ, "hai koī kapre le?"
Stark naked in the wilds he cries, "Who dare strip me?"
(A beggar dances before a thief.)

Naṅgā Khudā se barā!
A bad man is greater than God!
(He is more feared.)

Naṅgā mādar-zād.
Naked as on the day he was born.

Naṅgā nāche phate kyā?
A naked dancer tears no clothes.

Naṅgā sāth rupae kamāē, tīn paise khāē.
A single man earns sixty rupees and spends only three pence.
(Said of a man who has no family and hoards money.)

Naṅg dharaṅg.
Stark naked.
(Shameless or bare-faced.)

Naṅgī bhalī ki chhīṅke pāoṅ? Wom.
Is it best to go naked, or be hung up by the heels?
(Of two evils choose the least.)

Naṅgī bhalī ki tetak machwā.
Is it best to be naked or to create a row? Wom.
(See above.)

Naṅgī ho-ke kātā sūt, buḍḍhī ho-ke jāyā pūt. Wom.
She spins when she is naked, and bears when she is old.
(If she had spun sooner she would not have been in want of clothes; if she had borne a son when she was young he would have supported her in her old age. Shutting the stable door after the horse is stolen.)

Naṅgī kyā nhāegī, aur kyā nichoregī?
With what shall a naked woman bathe herself, or how shall she wring out (a cloth)?

Nangī ne ghāt rokā, nahāve na nahāne de.
A naked woman has stopped the bath, and neither bathes, nor allows others to bathe.
(The dog in the manger.)

Naṅgoṅ ko bhūkhoṅ ne lūṭ liyā.
The hungry have rifled the naked.

Nānī ke āge nansār kī bāteṅ! Wom.
She speaks ill of her grandmother's relations before her grandmother.
(Want of tact.)

Nānī khasam kare, navāsā chaṭṭī bhare. Wom.
The grandmother goes astray, and the grandson pays the fine.
(One person is punished for the crime of another: allusion to the custom of fining a family by the caste *panchāyat* when one of its female members goes astray.)

Nānī marī, nātā ṭūṭā.
When the grandmother is dead the relationship with her family is broken off.
(The Hindū custom is for the relations of a man's mother or grandmother to cease communication with him as regards family ceremonies on the death of either of them.)

Nānī to kuārī hī mar gaī, aur navāse ke sāṛhe satreh bān.
The grandmother died a virgin and 17½ baths for the grandson!
(Said of an upstart: a man without a grandfather! *Bān* is an ablution which the bride and bridegroom perform before marriage: the proverb means that the grandson goes through all these ceremonies when none were performed at his grandmother's wedding.)

Nannhe ho-kar rahiye, jaisī nannhī dūb.
Be lowly as the *dūb* grass is lowly.
(The *dūb* or sacred *kusa* grass is a low growth and of course much valued.)

"*Nāo kis ne ḍaboī?*" "*Khuāja Khizar ne.*"
"Who upset the boat?" "Khwāja Khizar."
(Khwāja Khizar is the god of the flood in modern days. This superstition is of extra-Indian origin and was brought in by the Musalmāns, who often confound Khwāja Khizar with the Prophet Elias.)

Nāps sau gas, phāṛe na ek gas.
He would measure a hundred yards, but would never give even one.
(Said of one who always promises but never fulfils.)

Nāp na tol, bhar de jhol!
Never mind weight and measurement—fill my wallet!

Napūtī kā ghar sūnā, mūrakh kā hirdā sūnā, dilāddrī kā sab kuchh sūnā.
The sonless house is empty, a fool's heart is empty, and the unfortunate's all is empty.

Naqad ko chhoṛ nase ko na dauṛiye.
Don't part with your ready cash for profits in the future.
(A bird in hand is worth two in the bush.)

Naqal rā che aql? Pers.
Imitation is not intelligence.

Naqd hū hurmat hū. Arab.
Pay cash and keep up your credit.

Naql-i-kufr, kufr nabāshad. Pers.
To copy an infidel is not to be an infidel.
(Allusion to the habits of the *naqqāls* or mimics, who personate all kinds of people for public amusement.)

Naqqāre bāj dammāme bāj gae!
The kettle drums have sounded, great and small!
(Birth's shrill trumpet and the muffled drum of death! *Naqqārā* is a kettle drum used at the births of sons and at the deaths of old people.)

Naqqār-khāne men ṭūṭī kī āvāz kaun suntā hai?
Who minds the voice of a parrot in the midst of drums?
(A poor man's voice is not heard against the rich.)

Na rahegā bāns, na bajegī bānslī.
When there are no reeds there will be no flutes.

Na rahe mān, na rahe manī, ākhir dunyā fanā fanī. Mah.
Nor respect nor pride can last for ever, for all the world will die at last.

Nārī ke bas bhae gusāīn, nāchat hain markaṭ kī nāīn.
A man in the power of a woman dances to her like a monkey.
(A hen-pecked husband)

Narm chob rā kirm mī-khurad. Pers.
Weevils eat soft wood.

Nāṛī kī kuchh surat nahīn hai, davā sabhan kī karte hain!
Baidon kā kyā jātā hai, bīmār bechāre marte hain!
He has no knowledge of the pulse and doctors all! What matter it to the doctor if the helpless patients die?

Nār ne nikālā dant, mard ne tārā ant!
When the woman shows her teeth, the man knows the end.
(The woman who laughs is half won.)

Nār sulakkhnī kuṭumb chhikāve, āp tale kī khurchan khāve. Wom.
A good housewife feeds the household well and is content with the leavings for herself!

Nāryal men pānī nahīn jāntā, khaṭṭā ki mīṭhā.
No one knows whether the water in the cocoa-nut is sweet or sour.
(Used to express that what is spoken of is doubtful.)

Na sānp mare, na lāṭhī ṭūṭe.
Nor let the snake die, nor the stick break.
(An amicable settlement.)

Nasha us ne piyā; khumār tumhen chaṛhā!
He drank the wine; why are *you* drunk?
(Said to a great man's relatives when they give themselves airs.)

Na sūp dūse jog, na chalnī sarāhe jog. Wom.
The winnowing-fan is not worth abusing, nor the sieve worth praising.
(*Arcades ambo.*)

Nātā na gotā, kharā ho-kar rotā! Wom.
Neither kith nor kin, so what are you howling at?
(Said when people make a fuss about what does not concern them.)

Nāṭā sab se ṭānṭā.
The shortest men are strongest.

Naṭbiddyā pāī jāē, Jaṭbiddyā na pāī jāē.
You may fathom the acrobat's art, but not the wit of the Jāṭ.

☞ The story goes that a king having promised his kingdom to a female acrobat if no one were found to surpass her, a simple *Jāṭ* to the astonishment of all, took up the gauntlet she had thrown down and forthwith scrambled up the pole. On reaching the top he discharged a stream of water from his person all round the place! So the woman was beaten and the kingdom restored.

Naṭ kā bachchā to kalā-bāzī hī karegā.
The rope-dancer's son is always turning summersaults.
(What is bred in the bone will come out of the flesh.)

Nāt kā na got kā, bāntā mānge poth kā. Rus.
Nor relative nor clansman, and he has the assurance to ask for a share.
(In the hereditary property.)

Na tel talī, na ūpar palī. Wom.
Nor oil at the bottom, nor in the ladle.
(Said of a very small dole.)

Nātin sikhāve ājī ko, ki bārā ḍeoṛhe āṭh! E. Wom.
She is teaching her grandmother that twelve times one and a half makes eight!
(Go and teach your grandmother to suck eggs.)

Nauā dekh le, kānkhe bār. Bhoj.
On seeing a barber he finds hair under his [armpit.

Nauā ke ghar chorī bhel, tīn changā bār gel. E.
There was a theft in the barber's house and three cups full of hair stolen.

Nau din chale arhāī kos !
In nine days he walked five miles !
(A very lazy man.)

Nau Kannaujī, aur nabbe chūlhe.
Nine Kanaujīs and ninety hearths.
☞ The Kanauji Brāhmans are noted for their religious scruples, and the proverb is a skit purporting to say that nine Kanaujīs had to build ninety hearths to prevent pollution by eating with each other.

Naukar āge chākar, chākar āge kūkar.
A servant's servant is a servant's dog.

Naukar ko chākar, manṛai ko usārā ! E.
A servant to a servant is a shed to a hut !
(The one is as absurd as the other.)

Naukar Lāṭkapūr ke honṭh malen aur haq len.
The servants of Lāṭkapur take their rights forcibly.
☞ Applied to idle and insolent servants. Lāṭkapūr was a famous singer in Akbar's time and the noblemen at whose houses he performed, used, in the usual complimentary style, in giving him a present to say it was for his servants. These are said to have been so insolent as upon this to claim it from their master.

Nau kī lakṛī, nabbe ḍhulāī.
The wood is worth nine, and the freight ninety.

Nāū kī sī ārsī har kāhū ke pās.
Like a barber's looking glass, now in one hand, now in the other.
(Easy as a barber's chair.)

Naukrī aranḍ kī jaṛ hai.
Service is like the root of the castor tree.
(Which has no roots to speak of : service is no inheritance.)

Naukrī hai yā bhāī-bandī ?
Is it service or brotherhood ?
(That is our mutual relation: said when a servant makes excuses.)

Naukrī kī jaṛ zabān par.
The root of service is on the tongue.
(Of the employer : he can discharge any time.)

Naukrī nit naī.
Servitude is ever new.
(There is always fresh work to be done. Said also of an uncertain master.)

Naukrī peshe kā ghar kyā ? kabhī yahāṅ, kabhī vahāṅ.
Who serves another has no home; (and lives) now here, now there.

Naukrī tāṛ kī chhāṅ.
Service is the shadow of a palm tree.
(Very transient: there is no telling how long it will last.)

Nau kūṅḍe aur das negī. E.
Nine platters, and ten to receive them.
(The *neg* is a present made to relations and servants at weddings.)

Nau mahīne mā ke peṭ meṅ kaise rahā hogā ?
How came you to live in your mother's womb for nine months ?
(Said to a mischievous boy.)

Nau man tel khāe, phir tiler kā tiler.
He has consumed nine tons of oil and is still as thin as a starling.

Naumī Gūgā Pīr manāūṅ, nā charkhe ke hāth lagāūṅ. Wom.
At Gūgā Pīr's *naumī* I cannot spin my wheel.
(The feast in honor of Gūgā Pīr, who died in 1024 A. D., is held on the ninth *(naumī)* of Bhādoṅ (August): to shrink from working on a lame excuse.)

Nau naqad na terah udhār. [credit.
Nine in cash is better than thirteen on
(A bird in hand is worth two in the bush.)

Nau sau chūhe khā-ke billī haj ko chalī. Mah.
After eating nine hundred rats the cat went on a pilgrimage.
(A death-bed repentance : at the eleventh hour.)

Nau terah bāīs na batāiye !
Don't tell me nine and thirteen make twenty two !
(Said to a person who will not be convinced. A man compelled against his will, is of the same opinion still.)

Nayā atīt, peṛū par alāo. Hin.
The unversed ascetic squats on his haunches.
(Which will soon tire him out : the *atīts* sit with their hands on a *bairāgan*, a kind of wooden support, which enables them to remain in one position for a very long time.)

Nayā chikanyā, reṅḍī ke phulel ! E. Wom.
A raw youth with castor oil for cosmetic !

Nayā dānā, nayā pānī.
New grain and fresh water.
(Used to imply a change of masters or situation.)

Nayā hakīm, de afīm.
A quack gives poison.
(Doctors kill more than they cure.)

Nayā jogī aur gājar kā saṅkh.
A novice with a conch of a carrot-root.
(*Saṅkh* is the shell-horn used by *jogīs* when begging to attract attention : it should be a sea-shell, or failing this of brass, copper or deer-horn.)

Nayā Musalmān "Allāh hī Allāh" pukāre. Mah.
A Musalmān convert cries "Allah Allah" all day long.
(Allusion to the proverbial zeal of all converts.)

Nayā nau din, purānā sau din.
The new is for nine days, the old for a hundred.
(The conservative feeling: distrust of what is new.)

Nayā nau ganḍā, purānā chha ganḍā. E.
For the new nine, for the old six.

Nayā naukar māre hiran.
A new servant will catch a deer.
(A new broom sweeps clean.)

Nayā naukar sher māre.
A new servant will kill a tiger.
(See preceding.)

Nayā nayā rāj bhail, gagrin anāj bhail. E.
Changes of government fill the pitchers with grain.
(*i. e.* they create many posts.)

Nayā nayā Rāj, ḍhab ḍhab bāj.
A new Government makes a great noise.

Nek andar bad, bad andar nek. Mah.
Good out of evil, evil out of good.
(Used to express that good parents sometimes have unworthy sons and *vice versa.*)

Nek bāt kā pūchhnā kyā?
Why take counsel about the right thing to be done?

Nekī aur pūchh pūchh!
Charity after enquiry!
(Charity should be freely given to all: in opposition to the teaching of Brāhmans, who maintain that only themselves should be objects of charity.)

Nekī barbād, gunah lāzim. Mah.
The good is forgotten, and evil returned for it.
(Evil for good.)

Nekī hī rah jātī hai.
The good you do will last.

Nekī kā badlā badī.
Evil returned for good.

Nekī kar aur daryā men ḍāl.
Do good and throw it into the river.
(Let not the left hand know what the right hand doeth.)

Nekī karne-vāle ko nekī kā masā, aur mūsī ko ṭakkar kā.
The doer of good has a taste for goodness, and the doer of evil for blows.

Nekī karo Khudā se pāo.
Do good and God will reward you.
(Beggar's cry.)

Nekī kī jaṛ Pattāl men.
The root of good is in Pātāl.
(*i. e.* very deep. Pātāl is popularly the infernal regions below the earth.)

Nek-nām banyā, bad-nām chor.
The trader has credit and the thief none.

Nemī pānḍe kamar men jaṭā.
A scrupulous Brāhman has his locks down to the waist.
(*i. e.* only for show: the Pharisee.)

Neotal Brahman shatrū barābar. E.
To invite a Brāhman is to call an enemy.
(A skit at the greediness of the class.)

Nestī men barkhurdārī.
Children in poverty.
(Are a burden to their parents.)

Nīchān kūṭān, devān pūjān. [ped.
The low are crushed, the gods are worship-
(One man may take away a horse while another may not look over a hedge. The king can do no wrong.)

Nichant sove Herū, jis ke gāe na gerū.
Herū sleeps sound, because he has neither cow nor calf.

Nīche se jaṛ kāṭnā, ūpar se pānī denā.
To cut the root from beneath and to water from above.
(Said of hypocrites.)

Nīch hanse hulse rahen, līye gend ko pot,
Jūn jūn māthe māriye, tiyūn tiyūn ūnchī hot.
The mean live happy and joyous, for like a ball, The more you hit them the higher they rise.
(The more you beat them the better they go.)

Nīch na chhoṛe nichāī, nīm na chhoṛe titāī. E.
The base will not give up his baseness, nor the *nīm* (tree) its bitterness.

Nīch zāt chhachhūndrī, nāk dhare pastāī.
The low man is like a muskrat, if you smell him you repent.

Nīch zāt ek na ek udmād!
The base-born have some vice or other!

Nīch zāton men ab bhī baṛā ekā hai.
Among the low castes still the bond of union doth survive.
(Said in reproof to a man who quarrels with his relatives. The low castes, such as *Chamārs*, are apt to settle their family quarrels by the decision of caste *panchāyats* or assemblies. It is a fact that no case between the *Khaṭbunās* or cot-weavers has been instituted as yet in the courts: cases between *Kahārs* are rare.

Nihang lāḍlā sadā sukhī.
The free and easy are ever happy.

Nikāhī na byāhī; munḍo bahū kahān se āī. Mah.
There was no marriage ceremony; so whence came this scald-head to be a wife.
(The *byāh* is the formal marriage of a virgin; the *nikāh* is a marriage without public ceremonies: *munḍo*, scald-head, also a widow, as applied to women, is a term of great reproach.)

Nikāh kī shart karnā.
A marriage settlement.
(*i. e.* a bargain made with difficulty, as marriage settlements in India are always attended with squabbles.)

Nikauṛyā gāe hāṭ, kakrī dekh jīrā phāṭ. E.
Without a farthing he went to the mart, saw a cucumber and broke his heart.

Nikhaṭṭū āve laṛtā, kamāū āve ḍartā. Hin. Wom.
The ne'er-do-weel comes home noisy, the bread-winner quietly.

Niklī halaq se, chalī khalaq men.
Out of the mouth is throughout the world.
(The cat out of the bag.)

Niklī honṭon chaṛhī koṭhon.
Out of the lips is upon the housetop.
(See preceding.)

Nīk nīk more bhāg, ek ek machhalyā kī ḍo do machhalyā! E. Wom.
How fortunate am I, for every fish I have two!
(Little Jack Horner, sat in a corner, eating a Christmas pie: he put in his thumb and pulled out a plum, and said, "what a good boy am I.")

Nikso chandā to andher bhayo mandā.
When the moon appears, the darkness flies.
(Falsehood fails before the truth.)

Nīl kā māṭ bigṛā hai.
The indigo vat is spoiled.
(Said when the whole of any goods is spoilt.)

Nīl-kanṭh kīṛā bhake, mukh meṅ birājeṅ Rām!
Khoṭ kapaṭ kyā dekhiye, darshan se haiṅ kām.
The king-fisher eats worms and calls on Rām! Why should you note its defects? Your business is to look on it.
(The *nīlkanṭh* is the vehicle of Rāma Chandra and is therefore very sacred. It is a good work for the faithful to behold it at the Dasahrā festival.)

Nīl kā ṭīkā, koṛh kā dāg.
A mark of tattooing and a stain of leprosy.
(Can never be effaced: applied to an indelible stain on the character.)

Nīl-ṭāṅs jis sir manḍlāve, mukaṭ-patī sūṅ lābhā pāve. Superstition.
The head round which a blue jay flies is marked for royal gifts.

Nīm hakīm khatra-i-jān!
Nīm mullā khatra-i-īmān! Pers.
Half a doctor and danger to life!
Half a priest and danger to the faith!
(A little knowledge is a dangerous thing.)

Nīm na mīṭhā hoe sīṅch gūṛ ghīv se;
Jā ko jo subhāo, jāegā jīv se.
The *nīm* is not sweetened by sprinkling sugar and butter; As the nature is, so it will be for life.
(The *nīm* leaf is very bitter.)

Ninnānve ke pher meṅ paṛ gaë.
She fell into the toils of ninety-nine.
☞ Two sisters married, the one a rich and the other a poor man. The poor sister asked for help, whereon the rich one gave her ninety nine rupees. Up to this time she had been contented though poor, but now she was always striving to make the ninety-nine into hundred, and so became wretched. *Moral:* contentment is better than wealth. Another story is that the content of a poor man and his wife who lived on four *paisās* a day, having excited the envy of his brother's wife, who was very rich, by way of destroying their happiness, she placed in their house a bag of 99 rupees. The delight of the poor couple at the sight of the bag was, however, turned to mortification, when, on counting the money it was found to be one rupee short of a hundred. They resolved to make up this rupee by living on one *paisā* less per day. When the rupee was thus made up, it occurred to them that by spending only two *paisās* a day they could secure twice that sum. Thus their greed growing with what it fed on, brought with it only an increase of care and suffering.

Nipūtī ke mūṅh dekhle sāt upās. E. Wom.
To see a barren woman's face is to go seven days without food. (Superstition.)
(Allusion to the belief in the "unfortunate face" very prevalent in India. To meet a barren woman early in the morning is to be sure of disaster during the day.)

Nirdhan ke dhan Girdhārī.
The poor man's wealth is God.

Nis din khānā, kām ko askatānā.
He eats night and day, and dawdles over his work.

Niṭhallā banyā patthar tole.
An unemployed Banyā will weigh stones.
(Rather than do nothing.)

Nit khodnā, nit pānī pīnā.
Ever digging and ever drinking.
(Living from hand to mouth.)

Niyāre chūlhe bal bal jāūṅ, Sārā khātī ādhā khāūṅ! Wom.
I shall be so delighted to have a separate hearth, That half a meal will be a whole one to me!
(A young wife to her mother-in-law.)

Nīyat sābit, manzil āsān. Mah.
Honesty makes the journey easy.
(Honesty is the best policy.)

Noh bhar khāyā to khāyā, mūṅh bhar khāyā to khāyā.
You have eaten all the same, whether it be a pinch or a mouthful.
(Steal a pin, steal a gridiron.)

Nūn-vāle kā nūn girā, us ne uṭhā liyā; tel-vāle kā tel giregā, to kyā uṭhā legā?
When the salt dealer's salt falls he can pick it up again; but if the oil man's oil is dropped, how is *that* to be recovered?

Nūn-vāle kā nūn girā, dūnā huā, telī kā tel girā, ūnā huā.
When a salt dealer's salt falls it becomes double; but when an oilman's oil spills it becomes less.
(Because the former can then mix earth with it, and the latter can only save what has not been spilt.)

O.

Ochhā pātr ubaltā hai.
A shallow vessel bubbles up.
(They are still waters that run deep.)

Ochhe ke bail gire.
The mean man's oxen have fallen.
(Which is a matter of no consequence to any one: said in ridicule of an exaggerated account of a loss.)

Ochhe ke ghar khānā, janam janam kā tānā. Wom.
Dine with the mean, and be reminded of it all your life.

Ochhe ke sāth ehsān karnā aisā hai, jaise bālū meṅ mūtnā.
Favor shewn to the base person is as water made in sand.

Ochhe kī pīt jaise bālū kī bhīt.
The friendship of the base is a wall of sand.

Ochhe sang na baiṭhiye!, ochhā burī balā;
Pal māṅ ho ghī khichṛī, pal māṅ bisyar ḍhāl.
Sit not with the mean, for the mean are a

great evil: One moment thick friends, and the next moment venomous serpents.
(Blessed is the man that hath not walked in the counsel of the ungodly, nor stood in the way of sinners. Psalms; I, 1.)

Ochhe se Khudā kām na ḍāle.
God preserve me from any concern with the worthless.

Ochhī ke hāth lagī kaṭorī, pānī pī pī marī padoṛī. Wom.
A mean woman got a cup, and drank till she burst.
(Set a begger on horse-back and he'll ride to the Devil.)

Ochhī lakṛī pharrās kī, be-biyāre pharrāe:
Ochhe ke sang baiṭh-ke, sughṛoṅ kī pat jāe.
The brittle branches of the fir break without a wind: Good men lose their character by mixing with the base.
(Evil communications corrupt good manners.)

Ochhī pūṅjī khasmoṅ khāe. Mercantile.
A small capital ruins its master.
(A small stock swallows up the owner. The aggregated profits are insufficient to cover the expenses.)

Ojh bhare, na rog jhaṛe.
Nor stomach filled, nor illness cured.
(Unfulfilled desires.)

Oltī kā pānī balaiṅḍī nahīṅ jātā.
The water of the eaves does not run up to the ridge pole.
(Water does not run up hill.)

Oltī tale kā bhūt, sattar purkhoṅ kā nām jāne. E. Wom. Superstition.
The ghost under the eaves has known the names of seventy ancestors.

Onā-māsī na āve, "maiyā, pothī lā de!" Hin. Wom.
He knows not the alphabet and asks his mother to get him a book.

Oṛhī chādar huī barābar, "maiṅ bhī shāh kī khālā hūṅ." Mah. Wom.
She puts on a veil like a lady, and says, "I, too, am the king's aunt."
(Said to one who claims relationship with some great man.)

Oṛhnī kī batās lagī.
Affected by the wind of a woman's cloak.
(He is a slave to his wife: a henpecked husband.)

Osoṅ pyās nahīṅ bujhtī.
Thirst is not quenched with dew.
(Spoken by one to whom any thing greatly short of his wants is offered.)

P.

Pāband phaṅse, āzād haṅse.
The free man laughs at the prisoner's chains.
(What's fun to you is death to me.)

Pachhvā chale, khetī phule. Agric.
When the west wind blows, the harvest [thrives.
(When the wind's in the west, the weather's at its best.)

Padmanī Chamāroṅ meṅ hotī hai.
Beauty will occur even amongst the Chamārs.
(*Padmanī* is the most beautiful of the four classes into which womankind is divided according to features and complexion. Chamārs are a low caste of black complexion and ugly features as a rule, so a *padmanī* amongst them is a *rara avis*.)

Padnī āil na peṭhyā lāgal. E.
It is no market without the shameless wench.
(Prostitutes are always to be found at markets in India.)

Pādshāhoṅ aur daryāoṅ kā pher kis ne pāyā hai?
Who knows what course the ocean or the king will take?

Pāejāme meṅ se kyoṅ nikle paṛte ho?
Why do you come out of your breeches?
(*i. e.* why do you fret and fume so much?)

Pag bin kaṭe na panth.
You cannot complete your journey without feet.
(No effort, no goal.)

Pag pavitr tīrath gavan, kar pavitr kuchh dān,
Mukh pavitr jab hot hai bhaj le Srī Bhagvān.
Feet are made pure by pilgrimage, the hands by charity, And lips by calling on Bhagwān (God).

Pagṛī aṭkī hai.
There is something catching at his turban.
(Said when a man's honor is at stake: *pagṛī*, turban, is constantly used metaphorically for honor.)

Pagṛī bhītar rakkh!
Keep your turban inside!
(Keep your honor.)

Pagṛī donoṅ hāthoṅ se thāmbī jātī hai.
Hold on to your turban with your both hands.
(Sustain your honor and fame: said when matters require delicate handling, especially when under the eye of a strict master.)

Pagṛī rakh, ghī chakh!
Keep your turban, and eat butter!
(Honesty is the best policy.)

Pāhan meṅ ke mārbe chokhā tīr nasāe! E.
If you shoot at a stone, you will spoil a good arrow.
(Don't kick against the pricks.)

Pahāṛī gadhā, Pūrbī reṅk.
A hill donkey with an Eastern bray.
(Said of natives who affect European manners and aimed especially at the Bengālī Bābūs.)

Pahāṛ ke aṭhgan silūt. E.
The support of the hill is a stone.

Pahāṛ kī utrāī chaṛhāī donoṅ par lānat.
Cursing both up and down hill.
(An ill-tempered man.)

Pahle apnī hī ḍāṛhī kī āg bujhāī jātī hai.
Every body puts out the flames in his own beard first.
(Charity begins at home.)

Pahle bhittar, tab deotā pittar.
First fill your own inside then the gods' and ancestors.'
(See preceding.)

Pahle bo, pahle kāṭ. Agric.
Early sow, early mow.
(The early bird gets the worms.)

Pahle chūme gāl gāṭhā.
He bit the cheek at the first kiss.
(Applied to him who behaves ill in the first employment given to him.)

Pahle ghar meṅ to pīchhe masjid meṅ. MahWom.
First at home, and afterwards at the mosque.
(Charity begins at home.)

Pahle hī bi'smi'llah galat. Mah.
Wrong from the very beginning.
(For explanation see under *avval hī b'ismi'l-lah* etc.)

Pahle hī gasse meṅ bāl āyā. Hin.
Hair in the very first morsel of food.
(Bad omen: no good Hindū can eat food with a hair in it.)

Pahle khānā, pīchhe bāt karnā.
Eat first and talk afterwards.
(Attend to the business in hand.)

Pahle māre so mīrī.
Who hits first conquers.

Pahle pahre sab koī jāge, dūje pahre bhogī,
Tīsre pahre chor jāge, chauthe pahre jogī.
In the first watch all are awake, in the second pleasure-seekers, in the third thieves, in the fourth ascetics.

Pahle pīve bhakvā, phir pīve tamakhvā, pīchhe pīve chilam-chaṭ. E.
The first puff is smoke, the second is tobacco, and the third is clearing the pipe.
(The tobacco in a *huqqā* lights slowly and (runs short quickly.)

Pahle pīve jogī, bīch meṅ pīve bhogī, pīchhe pīve rogī.
The ascetic smokes first, the wordly man next, and the sick man last.
(See preceding: this proverb also alludes to the drinking of water while taking food, in which case read "drink" for "smoke.")

Pahle soch bichār, pīchhe kīje kār.
First think and then act.
(Look before you leap.)

Pahlī bohnī Allāh Miyāṅ kī ās. Mah. Mercantile.
After handsell my hope is in God.
(Native traders never refuse handsell, as it would bring ill luck for the rest of the day.)

Pāhonā pyārā, par ek do din.
A guest is welcome, but for a day or so.
(Don't outstay your welcome.)

Paidā huā nā paid ke vāste.
What is born is but to die.

Paidal aur savār kā kyā sāth?
Footmen and horsemen are not company.
(Drunk and sober can't agree.)

Paisā gāṅṭh kā, jorū sāth kī. [wife with you.
Keep your money in your pocket, and your

Paisā kabhī nahīṅ ṭiktā.
Money abideth not.
(The fickleness of fortune.)

Paisā nahīn hāth, chale Navāb kī sāth!
No money in his hand, and he accompanies my Lord!

Paisā nahīṅ pās, to kaise sūṅgheṅ bās?
Without pence how shall you smell perfumes?
(The penniless are turned away from the cook-shop.)

Paisā na kauṛī, Bāṅkīpūr kī sair!
Without a penny to his name and rambling with the swells!
(*Bāṅkā* is a fop, swell, and hence point of Bāṅkīpūr, the city of *bāṅkās*. Bāṅkīpūr is also a well-known place near Paṭnā.)

Paisā na kauṛī, bāzār meṅ dauṛī. Wom.
Without a penny to her name, and off to the market.

Paisā pās kā, ghoṛī rān kī.
(Keep) your money in your pocket, and your horse under you.

Paise par dhar-ke boṭiyāṅ uṛāūṅ, tau bhī dard na āve. Mah. Wom.
I could break your bones on the grind-stones and feel no remorse.
(Parents to their children.)

Pājī to pājī, voh baṛā pajauṛā hai. [scoundrel.
A rogue is a rogue, but *he* is a great

Pakāē so khāē, nahīn khāē koī aur; dauṛe so pāē nahīṅ pāē koī aur.
Who cooks will eat, or somebody else will eat; who runs will get, or some body else will get.
(All work is of use.)

Pakhāl kā lādnā aur ḍāṅk chalānā ek sā.
To carry a water-bag and to carry the post is the same thing.
(Both are quickly carried in India.)

Pakkā honā chāhe, to pakke ke sang khel:
Kachchī sarsoṅ pel-ke kharī hoē na tel.
If you would be an expert keep company with experts: You can't get oil out of unripe mustard.
(There is a play upon *pakkā* ripe, complete, and *kachchā* unripe, incomplete, in this proverb.)

Pakkā pān khāṅsī na sukām.
In a ripe betel-leaf there is neither cold nor cough.
(An unripe betel-leaf is said to cause cough and a ripe betel to cure it.)

Pakkā phoṛā ho rahā hai.
It is like a ripe boil.
(Smarting and aching.)

Pakke ām ke ṭapakne kā ḍar hai.
A ripe mango is on the point of dropping.
(An old man is at the point of death.)

Pakkī phalī nahīn phoṛtā hai.
He won't even open a ripe pod.
(To describe extreme laziness.)

Pakle gūlar kawwe ke nīnd āvā le? Bhoj.
How can a crow sleep soundly when the figs are ripe?
(Crows are very fond of this fruit.)

Pāk nām Allāh kā. Mah.
Only God is pure.

Pāk rah, be-bāk rah. Mah.
Be innocent and fear not.
(Innocent actions carry their warrant with them.)

Palās ke tīn pāt.
The *palās* tree has but three leaves to a stalk.
(*i. e.* not enough for shade: used when expectations are not adequately fulfilled.)

Pal, pakhwārā, ghaṛī, mahīnā, chau ghaṛye kā sāl;
Jis ko Lālā "kal" kahen, us kā kyā ahvāl?
A minute, a fortnight, an hour, a month, a watch, and a year;
Which does he mean when Lālā says "to-morrow?"
(Procrastination: putting off from day to day.)

Pāl pāl tere jī kā hogā kāl.
Your fosterling will be your ruin.
(To nourish a serpent in your bosom.)

Pān aur īmān phere hī se achchhā rahtā hai.
A betel-leaf and conscience are best when they are turned.

Pāñche ām, pachāse imlī.
Five mango trees are better than fifty tamarind.
(With reference to their relative value.)

Pāñche mīt, pachāse ṭhākur.
For five your friend and for fifty your ruler.
(For five rupees do not quarrel with your friend, nor for fifty with your ruler.)

Pañch jahāñ Parmeshuar. Hin.
Where is the jury, there is God.
(In council truth comes out: by *pañch* in this and the succeeding similar proverbs must be understood the tribal or caste gathering or syndicate that controls the morals, etc., of most Hindūs by immemorial custom.)

Pāñch jūtiyāñ aur ḥuqqe kā pānī.
Five strokes with a shoe, and the water of a *ḥuqqā.*
(Are enough for you! said in reply to an extravagant demand: a shoe-beating is very ignominious in India and the water of a *ḥuqqā* is of course filthy.)

Pañch kahen billī to billī hī sahī.
If the jury say it's a cat it is a cat.
(Speaking against the majority has no weight: in a multitude of counsellors they are established.)
☞ There is also a story of a Banyā who caught a thief in the dark. The thief began to mew like a cat, whereon the Banyā said to him in the words of the proverb, "If in the morning the Court says you are a cat you shall be a cat, meanwhile I lock you up."

Pāñch mahīne byāh ko bīte, peṭ kahāñ se lāī? Wom.
How is it that she has a child after five months' marriage?

Pañch māne Khudā, Khudā māne pañch. Mah.
The jury believes in God, and God believes in the jury.

Pañch mil Khudā, aur Khudā mil pañch. Mah.
God is with the jury, and the jury with God.

Pañch mukh Parmeshuar.
The jury's mouth is God's.
(*Vox populi vox Dei.*)

Pañchoñ kā jūtā aur merā sir.
The jury's shoes are upon my head.
(I am ready to do their bidding.)

Pañchoñ kā kahnā sir āñkhoñ par, magar parnālā yahīñ rahegā.
I bow to the decision of the jury, but the drain shall remain where it is.
(Said of stubbornness: quarrels over *parnālās* or water drains from the tops of houses are very frequent among natives.)

Pāñchoñ Pāṇḍe, chhaṭe Narāyan.
Nārāyan makes the sixth among the five Pāṇḍās.
(Spoken when a person unexpectedly joins a company in which he is very welcome and wished for: allusion to the stories in the *Mahābhārata* and the *Purāṇas*, which mix up the legends of the five Pāṇḍavas or heroes of the *Mahabhārata* and those of Nārāyaṇa or Krishṇa.)

Pāñchoñ savāroñ meñ milnā.
To mix with the five horsemen.
(Applied to one who ranks himself among those who are greatly his superiors.)
☞ It is said that four horsemen, well mounted and armed, were followed by an unarmed clown on a sorry pony, who on being asked where he was going, said, "we five horsemen are come from Dehli."

Panchoñ shāmil mar gaē, jāno, gaē barāt.
Suffering in company is as good as going to a wedding.
(We don't feel what is suffered along with our friends. All in the same boat.)

Pāñchoñ ungliyāñ barābar nahīñ hotī haiñ.
The five fingers are not all of the same length.
(All men are not alike.)

Pāñchoñ ungliyāñ ghī meñ, chhaṭā sir kaṛhāē meñ.
His five fingers in the butter, and his head in the pot.
(Metaphor from a cat, or other animal, head and shoulders in a butter pot. Expresses having great abundance: to be in clover.)

Pāñch panch mil kīje kāj, hāre jīte na āve lāj.
When a company does business no one is blamed if it succeed or fail.
(Division of responsibility: the difficulty of fastening blame on the individuals composing a corporate body.)

Panch-phūlā Rānī banī haiṅ. Wom.
She sets up to be a Panchphūlā Rānī.
(Panchphūlā Rānī or Five-flower Princess is the heroine of many a fairy tale in India, and is always of course very beautiful.)

Pāṅḍe doū dīn se gaë.
The Brāhman lost both faiths.
☞ The story goes that a Brāhman wishing to better his condition left his original creed and became a Muhammadan. But after a while he, being disgusted at his new faith, desired to rejoin his former one, which, by Hindu custom, was impossible. Between two stools he fell to the ground.

Pāṅḍe, jī pachhtāēṅge, aur vohī chane kī khāēṅge.
You will repent, Brāhman, and eat the same pulse after all.
(Addressed to one who rejects a proposal made him, and used to express that he will afterwards gladly accept it. You may go further and fare worse.)

Panḍit bhaë to kyā bhaë, gale lapeṭe sūt ;
Bhāo bhagat jānī nahīṅ, bhaë jangal ke bhūt.
To be a Panḍit naught avails, nor (sacred) threads about the neck; If he knows not true religion he is merely a demon of the wilds.

Panḍit Pothī bāṅchte, Mulla paṛhe Qurān :
Log dikhāvo lakh karo, nāṅh milye Bhagvān.
The Panḍit reads his Scriptures, and the Mullā his Qurān : Men make a thousand shows, but meet not God.
(The *Panḍit* represents the Hindūs here and the *Mullā* the Musalmāns.)

Panḍiyāin kī mīṭhī mīṭhī batyāṅ.
The Brāhman's wife speaks sweetly.
(A cajoling woman.)

Pānī bāḍhā nāo meṅ, ghar meṅ bāḍhe dām :
Donoṅ hāth ulīchye, yehī suhānā kām !
Like much water in a boat is much wealth in a house : To bale out with both hands, is a pleasant business !

Pānī deṅ aur jaṛ kāṭeṅ !
Cut its roots and water it !
(Stroke with one hand and slay with the other.)

Pānī kā hagā ūpar ātā hai.
Throw filth into the water and it will come up again.
(Concealed enmity or wickedness comes to light at last. Murder will out.)

Pānī kā sā bulbulā hai.
Like a water-bubble.
(Said of a thing very transient or feeble.)

Pānī meṅ machhlī, nau nau ṭukṛā hissa. E.
The fish is in the water, and is being divided into nine shares.
(Count not your chickens before they be hatched.)

Pānī meṅ pakhān, bhīge par chhīje nahīṅ :
Mūrakh ke āge gyān rījhe, par būjhe nahīṅ.
Throw a stone into water and it is wetted and nothing more ; So a fool mocks at knowledge which he does not understand.

Pānī meṅ patthar nahīṅ saṛtā.
Stones don't rot in water.
(A claim, though suspended, is not lost.)

Pānī pīje chhān-ke, gurū kīje jān-ke. Hin.
Strain your water before you drink it, and test your priest before you retain him.

Pānī pī ghar pūchhnā.
First drink their water, and then ask about the house.
(*i. e.* what caste the inhabitants are: see next.)

Pānī pī-kar zāt pūchhte ho ?
First drink his water and then ask his caste !
(In India the rules of caste do not allow a man of one caste to drink water from the hand of a man of another caste.)

Pānī pīveṅ chhān-ke, jīv māreṅ jān-ke.
Who drinks water after straining kills life knowingly.
(Said of Jains, who are prohibited by the tenets of their religion from drinking unstrained water for fear of killing insects. The proverb is a skit at their excessive show of doing nothing which will destroy life.)

Pānī se pahle pul bāṅdhte ho.
You throw a bridge before there is any water.
(Excessive caution.)

Pānī se patlā kar ḍālā.
I have made him thinner than water.
(Reduced him to extremes.)

Panj aib sharaī haiṅ.
He is addicted to the five deadly sins.

Pān purānā, ghrit nayā aur kulvantī nār;
Yeh tīnoṅ tab pāīye, jab pirsan hoeṅ Murār.
Old betel, new *ghī*, and a chaste wife ; these three you may obtain when Krishṇa (God) is propitious.

Pān sā patlā, chānd sā chaklā.
Thin as a betel leaf, and round as the moon.

Pāoṅ gor meṅ laṭkāë baiṭhe haiṅ.
His feet hang over his grave.
(To have one foot in the grave.)

Pāoṅ lo bintī, sau lo gintī. Hin.
Prostration is the end of bowing, as a hundred is of reckoning.

Pāoṅ meṅ jūtī, na sir pe chapoṭī.
Nor shoes for his feet nor cap for his head.

Pāoṅ tale kī zamīn sarkī jātī hai.
The very ground trembles under my feet.
(An expression of disgust or horror at hearing any thing very false or wicked.)

Pāp bhī kabhī chhipāë se chhiptā hai ?
Can a sin be concealed by hiding ?

Pāp chhipāë nā chhipe, jas lahsun kī bās.
Like the smell of garlic, a sin cannot be hid.

Pāpī kā māl akārath jāë.
The wealth of the wicked runs to waste.
(Ill got ill spent.)

Pāpī kā māl pirāchat jāē, ḍanḍ bhare, yā chor le jāē!
The wealth of the wicked is expended in expiation, is paid in fines, or taken by a thief!

Pāpī ke man men pāp hī base.
Only sin dwelleth in the sinner's mind.

Pāpī kī nāo bhar-ke ḍūbe.
The sinner's boat fills and sinks.
(*i. e.* first he is successful and then ruined.)

Pāpī kī nāo ḍūbe par ḍūbe.
The sinner's boat must necessarily sink.
(See preceding.)

Pāpiyon ke mārne ko pāp mahā balī.
It is their own sin that chiefly slays sinners.
(He is his own greatest enemy.)

Pāp kā ghaṛā bhar-kar ḍūbtā hai.
The vessel of sin sinks when it is full.
(A sinner first flourishes and is then ruined.)

Pāp ubhre par ubhre.
Sin will out.
(Murder will out.)

Par-ādhīn supne sukh nāhīn.
Who serves has no pleasure even in his dreams

Parāē barde āzād karte hain.
To emancipate another's slaves.
(To cut thongs from another's leather.)

Parāē bharose khelā jūā, āj na mūā, kal mūā.
Who gambles on expectations will sink sooner or later.

Parāē dhan par Lachchhmī Narāyan. Hin.
He is the Lord of Wealth on others' property.
(*i. e.* he wastes it.)

Parāē dhan par jhingar nāche.
The cricket dances on another's property.
(Reflected glory.)

Parā-gandah rozī, parā-gandah dil. Pers.
An uncertain living makes an uncertain mind.
(The miseries of a hand to mouth life.)

Parāē ganḍon ke bharose na rahna!
Put not your trust in another's charms.
(Use your own strength.)

Parāē hāth pe shikrā pālte ho?
You train your hawk upon another's hand.
(You live at another's expense.)

Parāī dhī, aur hansen batāū log.
Wayfarers flirt with other men's daughters.

Parāī jeb se apnī jeb men dharnā mushkil hai.
It's not easy to transfer money from another's pocket into your own.

Parāē māl pe, yā Husain! Mah.
Invoking Husain with another's property.

Parāī naukrī karnī aur sānp kā khilānā barābar hai!
Serving another is (as dangerous) as feeding a snake!

Parāī sarāē men kaun dhūān kartā hai?
No one raises a smoke in another's house.
(*i. e.* helps him by lighting his fire.)

Parāī thailī kā munh sakṛā.
Other people's purses have a narrow neck.
(All are slow to give.)

Parāī tond kā ghūnsā!
A blow in another's stomach!
(Does not teach me!)

Par āsā nit upās.
Who relies on others always fasts.

Pāras Nāth se chukkī bhalī, jo āṭā deve pīs.
Kūṛh nar se murgī bhalī jo, anḍe deve bīs.
A mill-stone is better than Pāras Nāth, because it grinds flour. A hen is better than a fool, because she lays twenty eggs.
(A skit at the Jains. Pārasnāth is one of their Tīrthankars or special objects of worship.)

Paraus chhoṛ pīt kare.
To leave out your neighbours in making friends.
(Said of a bad man: too well known at home.)

Paraus ke menh barsegā, to bauchhāṛ yahān bhī āvegī.
If rain falls in my neighbour's house, some drops may extend to mine.
(Implies that some advantage may be derived from living near a man of property.)

Parāyā dil pardes barābar.
Another's mind is like a foreign country.
(Strangers yet.)

Parāyā dil samandar ke pār.
Another's mind is across the sea.

Parāyā māl, jhānṭ kā bāl.
Another's property is refuse hair.

Parāyā sir kaddū barābar.
Another's head is like a pumpkin.
(You may beat it without mercy.)

Parāyā sir lāl dekh, apnā sir phoṛ ḍālenge? Wom.
Shall I break my own head because I see the red spot on another's?
(Hindū women who live happy with their husbands, paint a red spot on their foreheads. Shall I bite my nose to spite my face?)

Parāyā sir panserī barābar.
Another's head is a lump of iron.
(See *parāyā sir kaddū barābar.*)

Parāyā sir Qurān kī jageh. Mah.
Another's head is instead of the *Qurān.*
(Oaths are usually sworn on the *Qurān* and on the head of another person.)

Par-bas men sukh hai nahīn, nij-bas hī sukh bhog. Yā te par-bas tyāg-ke, rahen su-bas budh log.
In servitude is no pleasure, in freedom pleasure is. 'Tis hence the wise shun servitude, and dwell in liberty.

Parbat ko rāī kare, rāī parbat mān.
(God) can reduce a mountain to a mustard seed. and can raise a mustard seed into a mountain.

Parche partīt hai.
Testing is believing.
(Seeing is believing: not trusting further than you can see.)

Parde kī bībī aur chaṭāī kā lahṅgā !
A lady in a mat petticoat.
(*Pardā nashīn*, or secluded woman, means a woman of respectability and a lady.)

Parde meṅ sardā lagāī haiṅ. Mah. Wom.
She has thrown a stain on the curtain.
(For *pardāh* see preceding: she has cast a stain on her own character.)

Pardesī balam, terī ās nahīṅ, bāsī phūloṅ meṅ bās nahīṅ. Wom.
There is no hope of a lover gone abroad, nor scent in stale flowers.

Pardesī kā jī ādhā hotā hai.
The stranger has but half a heart.
(He is very sensitive. Natives inculcate tenderness towards the stranger, because away from home and friends, his feelings are easily wounded.)

Pardesī kī pīt ko sab kā man lalchāë;
Doī bāt kā khoṭ hai:] rahe na saṅg le jāë. Wom.
All hanker after a stranger's love: But there are two drawbacks: he'll neither stay, nor take you with him.

Pardes kales nareshan ko. Hin.
Even kings suffer in strange land.

Pār gaë, mor ho āë.
Gone abroad and come home a peacock.
(Travellers' tales.)

Par ghar kūdeṅ Mūsal Chand.
Squire Pestle jumps for joy in stranger's houses.
(The name of *Mūsal*, or Pestle, is here applied to a busy-body, who goes uninvited to other people's houses, and officiously intermeddles in their affairs, because that instrument is very commonly borrowed, and goes the round of a whole village: Paul Pry.)

Par ghar nācheṅ tīn janeṅ: kāith, baid, dalāl.
Three people (thrive by) dancing attendance at other's houses: scribes, doctors, touts.

Parghaṭ ān pīchhe kah ānā:
Adham na ek jag tā hī samānā.
Who says one thing before (your face) and another behind your back; The world holds no baser man than he.

Paṛhā na likkhā, nām Biddyā-dhar. Hin.
He can neither read nor write, and named Mr. Doctor.
(Applied to one who lays claim to qualities to which he has not the smallest pretension.)

Paṛhā na likkhā, nām Mahammad Fāzil. Mah.
He can neither read nor write, and is named Mr. Doctor.
(See preceding.)

Paṛhe Fārsī beche tel; yeh dekho qudrat ke khel!
He knows Persian and sells oil! Behold the caprice of fortune!

Paṛhe ghar kī paṛhī billī!
A learned house has a learned cat!
(Learning attracts learning.)

Paṛhe ke āge ṭokrā ḍālā; us ne kahā, "mujhe uploṅ ko bhejā."
Throw a basket before a learned man, and he will understand that he is meant to bring cow-dung cakes!

Paṛhe ke pās baiṭhiye dūnā lābh.
Keep company with the learned and enjoy double benefits.

Paṛhe to haiṅ, par gune nahīṅ.
He has learnt, but not digested it.
(Read, mark, learn and inwardly digest it: parrot learning.)

Paṛhe totā, paṛhe mainā, kahīṅ sipāhī kā pūt bhī paṛhā hai.
Parrots and *mainās* may read, but the soldier's son never.
(The military classes are very illiterate in India, as they were formerly in Scotland.)

Parhez baṛī davā hai.
Regularity is the best medicine.

Parhez bhī ādhā ilāj hai.
Regularity is half a cure.

Paṛhā na, qazā kī. Mah.
Who does not know, cannot fail to pray.
(*Qazā karnā* is the sin of failing to pray at the stated times.)

Paṛhiye, bhaiyā, soī, jā meṅ hanḍyā khudbud hoī. E.
My son, learn those things that will keep the pot boiling.

Paṛhoṅ meṅ an-paṛhā, jaise hansoṅ meṅ kavvā.
The unlettered among the learned are as crows among swans.
(Crows are typical of what is objectionable in India; *hansās* or swan of what is honorable.)

Paṛho to paṛho; nahīṅ piṅjrā khālī karo.
Learn or leave the cage.
(Metaphor drawn from talking parrots: used to a lazy servant.)

Parjā maran, rājā kī hāṅsī.
The people die for the king's pleasures.
(Allusion to the oriental custom of forced loans to pay for royal pleasures.)

Parkā dhan gauraiyā mār. E.
Sparrows may eat up another's wealth.
(For all I care.)

Pār kaheṅ so vār hai, vār kaheṅ so pār:
Pakaṛ kinārah baiṭh rah, yehī pār, yehī vār.
This side is called that side, and that side this: Stick to one side and it is both this and that.

Parkal ghoṛ bhusaule ṭhāṛh. E. Rus.
The tame horse runs to its stall.

Par ke dhan par chor rove.
The thief weeps over another's property.
(When recovered from him.)

Par kī khetī par kī gāë, voh pāpī jo māran jāë. Hin.
The field is another's and so is the cow: he is a sinner who drives it away.
(Don't meddle with what does not concern you.)

Par ko kuāṅ khodiye aur āp hī ḍūb ḍūb mariye.
Who diggeth a pit for another shall fall into it himself.

Parlī, piyā, tore bas ; jinne chāhā tinne ghas. E. Wom.
I am fallen, husband, under your power; use me as you like.
(Said by an obedient wife to express meekness and contentment.)

Par mūī sāsū, eson āī āṅsū. E. Wom.
Last year her mother-in-law died, and now she is weeping.
(Crocodile's tears.)

Par nārī painī chhurī, koī mat lāo aṅg.
Dasoṅ sīs Rāvan ke ḍhae gae is nārī ke saṅg.
Another's wife is a sharp knife, have no dealings with her. Rāvan lost his ten heads for such a woman.
(Allusion to the story in the *Rāmāyana*: *Rāvana* the ten-headed king of Lankā carried off Sītā, wife of Rāma Chandra, and was slain in the war that ensued.)

Par tiryā, par dhan ke ūpar jo koī sutā dhare hai,
Jab chhūṭe hain pirān, piyāre, jāke Narak paṛe hai.
Who looks with eager eye on another's wife or property, Will go to Hell when he dies.

Parvā gaman na kījiye, jo sarb sone kī hoī.
Commence no journey on *parvā*, even though it be all for gold.
(*Parvā* is the first of the lunar fortnight.)

Pār-vāle kaheṅ vār-vāle achchhe, vār-vāle kaheṅ pār-vāle.
This side calls that side good and that side this side.
(No one is satisfied with his lot: every body would like to be somebody else.)

Par upkārī, dharam dhārī.
Philanthropy is true religion.

Pār utrūṅ, to bakrā dūṅ.
If I get to the other side, I will offer up a goat.
(A vow in time of danger, which is forgotten when it is over. The devil was sick, the devil a saint would be; the devil got well, the devil a saint was he.)

☞ The story is that a Meo crossing a river made a vow to kill a goat if he could get to the other side safely. When he had got into the middle of the stream the danger from the water grew less and his love for his goat grew stronger, so he altered his vow from a goat to a hen. But when he got to the opposite shore all safe and sound, being loth to kill even a hen, he picked a louse out of his coat and killed it as a fulfilment of his vow, saying, "a life for a life!"

Pāsang kā chor tīn jagah ḍanḍāe;
Jhuktā tole, rūkan de, pāsang dikhāe. Mercantile.
The thief with false weights gets punished in three ways; Giving over weight, making a bad bargain, and showing the difference in his scales.
(*Pāsang* is the weight put into scales to balance any difference their may be in the natural weights of the pans. The point here is that the rogue who keeps a false *pāsang* has to give overweight in order to prevent detection.)

Pāsā paṛe, anāṛī jīte.
Even a fool can win with dice.
(The cards will beat their makers.)

Pāsā paṛe so dāo, hākim kare so niyāo!
What the dice does is chance, what the king does is justice!

Pās kā kuttā na dūr kā bhāī.
A dog at hand is better than a brother at a distance.

Pās kauṛī na bāzār lekhā.
Nothing with him and no credit in the town.
(Tom Bowling was a citizen and though of some renown, Of not much credit in his own or any other town.)

Pasū kā satānā, nirā pāp kamānā. Hin.
To torture an animal is a great sin.

Pathān kā pūt, gharī meṅ auliyā, gharī meṅ bhūt.
A Paṭhān is now a saint, and now a devil.
(Observation of the race, very superstitious and very cruel.)

Paṭhān laṛāī māreṅ, aur bahneṅ ḍāṛhī phaṭkāreṅ.
The Paṭhāns fight and their sisters stroke their beards.
(*i. e.* the whole race are pugnacious.)

Paṭhānoṅ ne gāoṅ mārā, julāhoṅ kī chaṛh banī.
The Paṭhāns conquer the town and the weavers get the benefit.
(By serving them, the better classes of course holding aloof from their conquerors.)

Pator sā ko gaṭī nahīṅ, besvā oṛhe khāsā!
The virtuous woman cannot get sack-cloth, and the prostitute is clothed in fine linen!

Pāt pāt ko āp luṭāve, kālā muṅh kar jag dikhlāve, tab lāloṅ meṅ lālī pāve. Riddle.
First it dissipates every rag of its clothing and shews its black face (disgrace) to the world, and is then distinguished among the honorable (red.)
(Answer, the *palās* tree: which first sheds its leaves, then puts out flower-buds of a dark color, and afterwards displays its beautiful scarlet blossoms, with which the whole forest appears in a blaze. There are puns on the words *kālā muṅh* black face and disgrace, and *lālī*, redness and honor.)

Patthar ko jonk nahīṅ lagtī.
Leeches cannot stick to a stone.
(Stories of distress make no impression on a hard and avaricious heart, or instruction has no effect on a blockhead. The heart of a wheel-barrow.)

Patthar māre maut nahīṅ āṭī.
A blow from a stone is not death.
(A person cannot die until the appointed time.)

Patthar mom nahīṅ hotā.
Stones will not melt.
(You cannot draw blood from a stone.)

Paturyā kā ḍerā jaise ṭhagoṅ kā gherā.
The harlot's home is a robber's den.

Paturyā rūṭhī, dharam bachā.
When the harlot gets angry your righteousness is safe.
(Because you will not then go to her.)

Pau bārah ho gaë.
It is the ace and twelve.
(A fortunate chance: the ace and twelve is the best throw at the games of *chausar* and *pachisi*.)

Peṛ boe babūl ke, to ām kahāṅ se khāë?
If you sow acacias, whence shall you eat mangoes?
(Do men gather grapes of thorns, or figs of thistles? To express that evil deeds have evil consequences.)

Peṛ chaṛhe yoṅ hī dikhāī detā hai.
It appeared so from the top of the tree.
(If you were I you would do as I do.)

Pesha habību'llāh, jo na kare so lānatu'llāh. Mah.
The love of God on those who work, and the curse of God on those who won't.
(The devil finds some mischief still for idle hands to do.)

Pesh-i-tabīb marau, pesh-i-kār-āzmūdah bisau. Pers.
Don't go to the doctor, go to the experienced.
(Experience beats learning.)

Petāhā chākar, ghasāhā ghoṛ, khāë bahut kām kare thoṛ. E.
A pot-bellied servant and a fat horse eat much and work little.

Peṭ bhar aur pīṭh lād.
Fill the belly and you may load the back.

Peṭ bhare ke gun.
The result of a full stomach.
(Used to servants when they grumble at work, and towards persons who are hard to please.)

Peṭ bhare ke khoṭe chāle.
The evil habits of a full stomach.
(Sinful pleasures are the portion of the rich.)

Peṭ bhare kī bāteṅ.
The words of a full stomach.
(To express indifference about employment and demand of exorbitant terms for the performance of work.)

Peṭ bhare rizāle aur bhūke bhale-mānas se ḍariye.
Fear the well-fed clown, and the hungry gentleman.
(A low man raised to fortune is likely to be mischievous, and so is a man of means reduced to poverty.)

Peṭ bhī khālī, god bhī khālī. Wom.
Womb and lap are both empty.
(Nor chick nor child.)

Peṭ bich paṛī roṭiāṅ, tāṅ sabhī galāṅ moṭiāṅ. Panj.
Now that his belly is filled, he talks big.
(Said of one who was humble whilst in low circumstances, but gives himself airs upon acquiring affluence.)

Peṭ burī balā hai.
The stomach is a dreadful plague.
(The belly teaches all arts.)

Peṭ chale man bakhtoṅ ko.
He is purged and yet longs for pulse.
(Applied to one who is already involved in misfortune, and yet follows courses which are calculated to increase it.)

Peṭ hai yā be-īmān kī qabar?
Is it a belly or an infidel's tomb?
(Said of a pot-belly.)

Peṭ hai yā kuṭhār?
Is it a belly or a corn-binn?
(Said of a great eater.)

Peṭ jo chāhe so karāë.
The belly makes you do what it chooses.

Peṭ ke āge "na" hai.
The full stomach says "nay."
(Satiety.)

Peṭ ke vāste pardes jāte haiṅ.
For the stomach's sake men go abroad.
(Needs must when necessity drives.)

Peṭ kūā, mūṅh sūī.
His belly a well and mouth a pin-hole.
(Said of a great-eater.)

Peṭ meṅ āṅt, na mūṅh meṅ dāṅt.
No guts in his belly and no teeth in his head.
(Said of an old man.)

Peṭ meṅ chūhe qalābāziyāṅ khā rahe haiṅ.
Rats are racing up and down his belly.
(He has a wolf in his belly.)

Peṭ meṅ ghuse to bhed mile.
You'll know him when you can get into his inside.
(Pumping secrets.)

Peṭ meṅ pāoṅ haiṅ.
The feet grow from the stomach.
(No food no work.)

Peṭ meṅ paṛā chārā, kūdne lagā bichārā. Wom.
When he had filled his belly, he began to show his pranks.

Peṭ meṅ paṛī būṅd, nām rakhā Mahmūd. Mah·Wom.
No sooner she conceives than she calls the child Mahmūd.
(*i. e.* a son: to count one's chicken before they be hatched.)

Peṭ meṭ, kār sameṭ.
Forget your stomach to do your work.
(Said when work is exacted on insufficient wages.)

Peṭ pālnā kuttā bhī jāntā hai.
A dog, too, knows how to fill his own stomach.
(Said of extreme selfishness.)

Peṭ piṭārī, mūṅh supārī.
His stomach a big basket, and his mouth a betel-nut.
(Betel nuts are very small. See above *Peṭ kūī, mūṅh suī.*)

Peṭ sab rakhte haiṅ.
Every body has a stomach.
(No food no service.)

Peṭ se pāon kāṛhe haiṅ.
They take their feet from out of their bellies.
(Applied to those that are insolent under cover of humility.)

Peṭū mare peṭ ko, nāmī mare nām ko.
The glutton dies for food, the ambitious for a name.

Phalsā ṭūṭā, gāoṅ lūṭā.
When the gate is broken open the village can be robbed.

Phal khānā āsān nahīṅ.
It is not easy to eat fruit.
(The plant must be first grown.)

Phāoṛā na kudār, baṛā khet hamār. E. Agric.
Nor hoe, nor spade, and a big field is mine.
(Undertaking what is beyond one's power.)

Phāoṛe kā nām gul-saffā.
The word for a hoe is *gul-saffā*.
(To express that one has long danced attendance on another in vain, and has no longer any hopes of deriving advantage.)
☞ Taken from the story of a *faqīr* whose pretensions to sanctity and wisdom induced a man to attach himself to him as a disciple. After twelve years' attendance, during which he had never got any instruction, he asked his preceptor the word for hoe and got the foregoing answer. *Gul-saffā* has no meaning.

Phar na pharī, bagīchā ke nāoṅ! E.
Nor fruit, nor vegetables, and called a garden!

Pharyā na sārī, baṛī sobhā hamārī! E. Wom.
No gown and no petticoat, and great credit is mine.

Phaṭāhā tilak aur madhurī bānī, Dagā-bāz kī yehī nishānī.
A wide *tilak* and sweet words are the signs of a cheat.
(The *tilak* is the sectarial mark on the forehead borne by the higer castes of Hindūs.)

Phāṭak ṭūṭā, gaṛh lūṭā.
When the gate is broken, the fort can be plundered.

Phaṭe ko na siye, aur rūṭhe ko na manāē to kyoṅ-kar guzārā hoe? Wom.
If you don't repair rents and conciliate the offended how can you get on?

Phaṭe meṅ pāoṅ, daftar meṅ nāoṅ.
Mixed up with a quarrel, he gets on to the court rolls!
(He is, forsooth, an officer of the court, for his name is on the rolls—as a witness!)

Phaṭe na phūṭe, jiu jān na chhūṭe.
It neither rends nor breaks, and nor gives up its life.
(The cat's nine lives.)

Phāṭe se juṛte nahīṅ; koṭan karo upāī
Man motī aur dūdh ras inkā yehī subhāo.
If parted once they'll never join again; however much you try: This is the quality of the heart and pearls and milk.
(Nothing really puts those who have quarrelled on the old footing.)

Pheroṅ kī gunahgār hai. Hin
The marriage tie is her only sin.
(Said of a child-widow, who by orthodox Hindu custom is never allowed to marry again.)

Phir, be ghoṛe, yahīṅ se!
Back, horse, back out of this!
(Get thee behind me, Satan.)

Phir bhī mochī ke mochī rahe.
A cobbler he is still.
(Said to those that won't improve.)

Phir, muṛlī, bel tale. E.
Again, you shaven-head, have you come under the *bel* tree.
(The *bel* fruit or wood-apple is a hard fruit which falling on a bald head would much hurt it, *i. e.* again exposing yourself to danger.)

Phiṭ, vā kā jīnā, to take parāī ās!
Alas, for his life, who is dependant on another!

Phūaṛ chāle, nau ghar hāle. Wom.
When the ninny walks abroad, nine houses tremble.
(*i. e.* because her foolish tongue will do so much mischief.)

Phūaṛ jurvā, sāg meṅ shurvā. Mah. Wom.
The silly house-wife makes gravy of pot herbs.

Phūaṛ kā māl haṅs haṅs khāiye.
The fool's property you can freely take.
(A fool and his money are soon parted.)

Phūaṛ kā māl sarāh sarāh khāiye.
The fool's property you may enjoy by flattering him.

Phūaṛ kare siṅgār, māṅg īṅṭoṅ se phoṛe. Wom.
The ninny decks her forehead by rubbing brick-bats into it.
(Native women deck their foreheads with vermillion paint, made of red lead (*sendūr*) and the point is that the fool rubs red brick-bats into hers and so of course hurts herself.)

Phūaṛ ke ghar khiṛkī lagī,
Sab kuttoṅ ka chintā paṛī:
Bāṅḍā kuttā bānche saun,
"*Lagī to hai, par degā kaun?*"
A window was made to the ninny's house,
And all the dogs felt anxious:
Till up got a tailless cur and said,
"A window there is, but who will shut it?"
(*i. e.* we can get in as easily as ever. A fool does not make use of his advantages.)

Phūaṛ ke ghar ugī chanberī,
Gobar māṅḍ usī par gerī. Wom.
A jesamine grew in a ninny's house,
And she put her cow-dung cakes on it.
(*i. e.* she knew not the use if it.)

Phūaṛ sīne baiṭhe, tab sūī toṛe. Wom.
When a ninny sews she breaks her needle.
(A bad workman quarrels with his tools.)

Phūṅ phūṅ kar-ke tālāb bhartā hai.
Drop by drop fills a tank.
(To express that small savings, long continued, amount to a great sum; or that trifling efforts, long and often repeated, produce great effects: many littles make a mickle.)

Phūlā badan meṅ nahīṅ samātā.
He has grown till his body can't hold him.
(The world can't hold him.)

Phūl āe haiṅ, to phal bhī āeṅge. Wom.
When you see the blossom, you may expect the fruit.
(*Phūl* here means the menses of women and *phal* means issue: when her menses have commenced a woman begins to conceive.)

Phūle phūle phirat haiṅ, "āj hamāro byāh."
Tulsī, "gāe bajāe-ke dīyo kāṭh meṅ pā."
He goes rejoicing: "to-day is my wedding day." Saith Tulsī Dās, "your singing and dancing will put you in the stocks."
(A hit at the expenses of married life.)

Phūlī phūlī gaune ko; ṭhasak nikal gai raune ko. Wom.
Full of pride comes the bride to her husband; crest-fallen returns she from her father's house.
(A Hindū bride visits her parents soon after her marriage and it is when she finally settles in her husband's house that her life of trouble begins.)

Phūl jhaṛe to phal lage.
When the flower falls, the fruit comes.

Phūl kī bairan dhūp, ghī kā bairī kūp.
The flower's enemy is the sun, and the butter's the bag.
(*i. e.* flowers wither in the sun, and *ghī* spoils in the leather bags in which it is kept.)

Phūl kī ḍāl nīche ko jhuke.
A flower stalk hangs down.
(The true gentleman is never proud or stuck up.)

Phūl nahīṅ pankhṛī hī sahī.
A leaflet if not a flower.
(A penny if not a pound.)

Phūl phūl kar-ke changer bhartī hai.
Heaping flower on flower fills the basket.
(Many a littles make a mickle.)

Phūl sūṅgh-kar rahte ho?
Do you live on the scent of flowers?
(Said to a small eater.)

Phūl ṭahnī hī meṅ achchhā lagtā hai.
A flower is best on its stalk.
(*i. e.* it does not droop there. Every thing is best in its own proper place.)

Phūṅke ke na phāṅke ke, ṭāṅg uṭhā-ke tāpe ke. E. Wom.
She'll neither blow nor stir the fire, but she'll warm her legs at it.
(Said of the selfish and idle.)

Phūṅk mashāl, uṭhā chaupālā.
Light the torch, and take up the palanquin.
(To describe great haste.)

Phūṅk phūṅk-ke qadam rakhte haiṅ.
To walk carefully at every step.
(Look before you leap: take heed is a good read.)

Phūphī mis lenā, bhatīje mis denā.
Be an aunt and get, be a nephew and give.
(In India nephews (*bhatījā*) make presents to their fathers' sisters (*phūphī*.)

Phūṭī āṅkh kā tārā.
The apple of a blind eye.
(Said of a child whose mother is dead.)

Phūṭī degchī, qalaī kī bharak.
White-washing a broken pot.
(A painted face: a whited sepulchre.)

Phūṭī sahī, āṅjī na sahī.
He would rather lose his eye than apply a salve to save it.
(Applied to that species of avarice which will not expend a trifle to preserve or improve a valuable property.)

Pīchhā pīchhā hī hai.
Last is really last.
(No time like the present.)

Pichhlī roṭī khāe, pichhlī mat āe. Wom. Superstition.
Who eats the last cake will be a fool.
(It is unlucky among women to eat the last cake, which is accordingly always thrown to dogs.)

Pīch pī, nemat khāī.
I have swallowed your rice-water like sumptuous fare.
(Spoken by a person, who having put up with many inconveniences in the service or society of another, declares his patience to be exhausted *i. e.*, I have put up with these things as if it had been a state of enjoyment: I have heard enough of it.)

Pī kāran pīrī bhai, log kaheṅ piṇḍ rog:
Chhip chhip laṅghan maiṅ kīye, pī milan ke jog.
Silently I kept my fasts to meet my love:
For my love's sake have I become pale, and the people say I have jaundice.
(Unmerited blame.)

Pī ke pātan sir dharo, dharo charan par sīs,
Bāsā ho baikunṭh meṅ phir to bisve bīs. Wom.
Lay on your head your husband's shoes, and on his feet your head, and you will be sure of your place in heaven.
(A woman's advice to her daughter on her marriage.)

Pīne ko pānī nahīṅ, chhiṛakne ko gulāb.
He has no water to drink, and he sprinkles rose-water.

Pīpal kāṭe, pāl bināse, bhagwān bhes satāve,
Kāyā gaṛhī meṅ dayā na byāpe, jaṛā mūl se jāve. Superstition.
Who cuts down *pīpal* trees, pulls down houses, and distresses saints, and has no compassion in his heart, will be ruined root and branch.

Pīpal pūjan main chalī Nigam-bod ke ghāṭ,
Pīpal pūjat pī mile, ek panth do kāj.
I went to worship at the *pīpal* tree, on the banks of Nigam-bod,
I met my love at the *pīpal* tree, and performed two objects at one time.

Pī pyālā, mār bhālā.
Quaff the cup and thrust your spear.
(*Moral* : get drunk before you go to battle !)

Pīrāṅ na-mīparand, murīdāṅ mī-parānand. Pers.
The holy man can't fly, but his disciples can make him.
(The fame of his miracles depends on the praises of his disciples: used in the sense of "union is strength")

Pīr āp hī darmāndah; shafāat kis kī karenge ?
The saint is himself in distress, for whom shall he make intercession ?
(He saved others, himself he cannot save. Mathew xvii, 42.)

Pīr, bāvarchī, bhishtī, khar.
Priest, cook, water-bearer and ass.
(*i. e.* the capacities of the above are all combined in one Brāhman, who is commonly employed by the richer natives as cook, priest and messenger (hence called *khar*), and also for giving water.)

Pīrī aur hazār aib.
Old age means a hundred vices.
(*i. e.* old men are not liked in India, because they have to be supported and bring no grist to the mill.)

Pīrjī kī sagāī, mīrjī ke yahāṅ. Mah. Wom.
The *Pīrs* are betrothed to *Mīrs.*
(Birds of a feather fly together. Mīr is a title of the Sayyids, and both Sayyids and Pīrs lay claim to sanctity.)

Pīr ko na shahīd ko, pahle nakṭe deo ko ! Mah. Wom.
Not to priest, nor to saint, but to the worthless devil first !
(Used when a worthless fellow demands what has been prepared for his betters. "Useless" in India means "worthless.")

Pīr shav, biāmoz. Pers.
Be old and learn.
(Never too late to mend.)

Pisanhārī ke pūt ko chabenā hī lābh.
To the son of a wheat-grinder parched grain is a delicacy.
(The women that grind corn in India are of the very poorest classes.)

Pis lūṅ to piṭūṅ. Wom.
When I have done griding I will thrash you.
(Said to children. Don't think you'll be let off.)

Pīs mūī, pakā mūī, āë lauṭhe khā gae. Wom.
I ground and cooked, and the louts came and ate it.
(A mother to her idle sons.)

Pīsne-vāliyāṅ pīs le jāeṅgī, kuchh hattā thoṛāī ukheṛ le jāeṅgī. Wom.
When the corn-grinders have ground the corn, they don't take away the handle of the (hand) mill.
(So why don't you lend them yours ? the dog in the manger.)

Pītam basen pahāṛ par, aur ham Jamnā ke tīr !
Ab kā milnā kaṭhan hai, ki pāon paṛī sanjīr.
My love dwells on the hill, and I near Jamnā's banks ; And now it is hard to meet him, for fetters are on my feet.
(She is too carefully watched and the distance is great.)

Pītam, terī prīt ko jhuk jhuk karūṅ salām ;
Jab se to sang nehā karo suno, na sukh ko nām.
I bow to your affections my husband ; Since I have been attached to you I have never felt rest.

Pītam, tum mat jānyo, bhayo dūr kā bās.
Deh, geh kitahu rahe, prān tihāre pās.
Think not, my love, that I am far from thee. Be body and country where they may, my soul doth dwell with thee.

Piṭārī men band-kar rakhne ke lāyaq hain.
It is fit to be shut up in a basket and put by.
(Laid on the shelf.)

Pīṭh pīchhe bādshāh ko bhī burā kahte hain.
They can abuse even the king behind his back.

Pīṭh pīchhe Ḍom rājā.
Behind my back the Ḍom is a king.
(The Ḍoms are the lowest of the low.)

Pīṭh pīchhe kuchh hī ho.
After me let it be as it will.
(*Apres moi le deluge.*)

Pīt karī thī nīch se, palle lāgī kīch.
Sis kāṭ āge dharā, ant nīch kā nīch.
I loved a man that was base and he dragged me through the mire. I offered him my head, and still was he base.

Pīt kī rīt nirālī hai.
The ways of love are peculiar to itself.

Pīt to aisī kījiye, jaise rūī kapās ;
Jīte jī to sang rahe, mūë pe hove sāth !
Let your love be as a cotton robe ; Round you in life and round you in death !

Pīt to aisī kījiye ; jūn Hindū kī joë,
Jīte jī to sang rahe, mare pe satī hoë.
Let your love be as a Hindū wife ; With you in life and with you at death !
(By committing *satī* and burning at the husband's pyre.)

Piyā jise chāhe, vohī suhāgan.
She is a wife, whom her husband loves.

Piyā kī kamāī, mohe nahīn lahnā :
Mo pe bāzū-band nahīn, aur sab gahnā. Wom.
My husband's earnings are of no benefit to me : I have no armlets, though all other jewelry.
(Unreasonable discontent.)

Piyāsā kūe ke pās jātā hai, kūā nahīn ātā.
The thirsty goes to the well, not the well to the thirsty.
(What is not worth asking is not worth having. The mountain to Muhammad.)

Postī kī ānch ūpar ko nahīn jāne kī.
The smoke of opium does not evaporate.
(The smoke of opium lies heavy about the room. The point is that the cry of the distressed is not in vain.)

Pothī to thothī bhaī, Pandit bhayā na koē.
Ḍhāī anchhar prem ke paṛhe, so Paṇḍit hoē.
All the scriptures are vain; there is no such thing as a *Paṇḍit*. Who reads two and a half words of love is a true *Paṇḍit*.
(A *Paṇḍit* is a doctor in Hindu divinity. My only books were women's looks and folly all they taught me.)

Prātah kāl karo asnānā, rog dokh tum ko nahīn ānā.
Bathe early every day and sickness will [avoid you.
(Cleanliness is next to godliness.)

Prem kahānī kahat hūn, suno, sakhī rī, āē.
Pī ḍhūnḍan ko ham gaīn, āīn āp harāē! Hin.
I tell thee a tale of love, come near, my love, to hear. I went in search of my love, and lost myself!
(A skit at the Sūfī sect of the Muhammadans, who use the terms of erotic poetry to express their love for God.)

Prem pīt kī rīt men yeh anrit suhāē;
Barsen ānkhen, sūkhe kīyā, āg lage jīyā mānh.
In the course of love this is not meet; That eyes shed tears, hearts pine, and bosoms burn.

Prem piyālā woh piye, jo sīs dachhnā de.
Lobhī sīs na de sake, nām prem kā le!
He can drink of the cup of love, who will offer his head. The coward that will not give his head, how shall he take the name of love?
(Faint heart never won fair lady.)

Prītam, har se neh kar, jaise khet kisān;
Ghāṭā de, aur ḍanḍ bhare, phir khet se dhiyān.
My friend, love God as the husbandman loves his fields; He suffers losses and pays tribute and still he loves his fields.

"Prītam prītam" sab kahen, prītam jāne na koē.
Ek bār jo prītam mile, sadā ānand phir hoē.
All say "my love, my love," but no one knows his love. If once his love be seen, he will ever happy be.
(A skit at the Sūfis. See *prem kahānī kahat hūn*, etc. above.)

Prīt ḍagar jab pag rak'hā, honī hoe so ho;
Neh nagar kī rīt haē, tan man dīno khoē.
When once you tread on love's true path; let it happen as it may; In the region of love you lose both body and soul.

Prīt jo kīje īkh se, jā men ras kī khān;
Gānṭh gānṭh men ras nahīn: yehī prīt kī hān.
Love is made like sugar-cane full of nectar sweet; but where there is a knot no nectar lies: this is the lot of love.
(The thorn within the rose.)

Prīt haren se bāore, kar-ke toṛen chhail.
Gal men rasā ḍāl-ke or nibāhven bail.
Who love are fools, who love and break are fine fellows. Who but an ox will live on with a rope around his neck?

Prīt na jāne jāt ku-jāt, nīnd na jāne ṭūṭī khāt,
Bhūk na jāne bāsī bhāt, piyās na jāne dhobī ghāt.
Love heeds not caste, nor sleep a broken bed, Hunger heeds not stale food, nor thirst soapy water.

Prīt na ṭūṭe an-mile, uttam man kī lāg;
Sau jug pānī men rahe, chakmak taje na āg.
No absence can break love, where virtuous hearts are set; As flint can lose no fire, though a hundred years in water.

Pūchhte pūchhte to Dillī chale jāte hain.
Ask your way often and you will get to Dehlī.
(Seek and ye shall find: you'll lose nothing by asking.)

Pūjle deotā, chhoṛle bhūt. E.
Worship the gods and give up the devils.

Pul bāndhal jāē, bahū kajrī khele. E. Wom.
The bride plays in the boat, while the bridge is being thrown across.
(The mother-in-law works, while the bride plays: upside down altogether in an Indian home.)

Pūle pūle ānch hai.
Every bundle of hay is liable to be burnt.
(To express that every one has his portion of suffering.)

Pūle tale guzrān karte hain.
To live under a thatch.
(Great poverty.)

Pun kī jaṛ sadā harī.
Charity's a plant whose roots are ever green.

Pūrab jāo yā Pachchham, wohī karam ke lakkhan.
Go East or West, and get what is written in your fate.
(The doctrine of the fatalist.)

Pūrā tol, chāhe mahngā bech. Mercantile.
Let the weight be right, whatever the cost.

Purukh kī māyā, birachh kī chhāyā. Hin. Wom.
The reputation of a man is the shadow of a tree.
(As long as he lasts his reputation lasts.)

Purakh sā pakherū koī nahīn.
No bird like man.
(Allusion to the wandering habits of the human race.)

Purakh sāṭhā so pāṭhā, istrī bīsī so khīsī.
A man at sixty is a young elephant, a woman at twenty is on the decline.
(Allusion to the rapid development and decline of women in India.)

Purānā ṭhīkrā aur qalaī kī bhaṛak!
An old potsherd well white-washed!
(An old woman decked out as a young one.)

Purāne chāvalon men mazā hotā hai.
Old rice has a superior flavor.
(To express the advantage of conversing with men of age and experience.)

Purāne gumbad par qalaī karnā.
To gild an old dome.
(To decorate an old worn-out carcase.)

Purāne ṭhikre par naī qalaī.
Fresh whitewash on an old potsherd.
(New wine in an old bottle.)

Purānon ko jhiṛkī, nāyon ko pyār.
Ill treating the old and favouring the new.
(Be kind to an old and faithful servant.)

Pūre gurū ghanṭāl hain. Hin.
An old priest is only a bell-ringer.
(Allusion to the services in Hindū temples.)

Pūrī lapsī ghar men khāē,
Jhūṭī Debī se ās lagāē!
She eats up the offerings at home, and puts false hopes in Devī!

Pūrī paṛe to sapūt kahāven.
If a son supply all wants, he is called a good son.

Pūrī se pūrī paṛe, to sabhī na pūrī khāen? Hin
If *pūris* could fill, would not all live on them?
(*Pūris* are small light cakes of flour, considered delicacies, but are of course not sufficient of themselves to support life.)

Purvā bahal sūkhal ghāo phaphandal. Bhoj.
When the east wind blows healed sores break out.
(When the wind is in the east, 'tis neither good for man nor beast.)

Pūs, kohnī ghūs.
In December men go into corners.
(To avoid the cold.)

Pūt bhāē syāṇe, dukh bhae birāne. Hin. Wom.
When the son grows up, discomforts depart.
(*i. e.* he is then able to support his parents.)

Pūt faqīrnī kā, chāl ahdiyon kī sī.
A beggar woman's son and strutting like an *ahdī*.
(The *ahdis* were pensioners under the Emperor Akbar, liable to service on an emergency, and in their own opinion persons of great consideration.)

Pūt kare bhatār ke āge āve.
The deeds of the son are on the father.

Pūt ke pāon pālne men pahchāne jāte hain.
The child's future is read in the cradle.
(From astrological predictions and their own experience, native women profess to read the child's future even in the womb.)

Pūt kī sāt ko sau jokhon.
There are a hundred risks in a son.

Pūt kupūt ho jāē to ho, par māṅ kumān nahīn hotī. Wom.
A son may be a bad son, but a mother a bad mother never.

Pūt māṅge gaīn, bhatār letī āīn. E. Wom.
She went to get a son and found a husband.
(A skit at women going to *faqirs* to procure sons, as is very commonly done.)

Pūt mīṭh, bhatār mīṭh, kiryā keh kar khāūn? E. Wom.
My child is dear and my husband dear, which shall I swear by?
(The horns of a dilemma.)

Pūt na bhatār, pīchhohī ṭāēn ṭāēn. E. Wom.
Neither her son, nor her husband, yet she howls at his absence.
(Spoken of a person who affects to sympathise with a sufferer, with whom he has no concern and about whose fate he is in reality indifferent.)

Pūton rāt dulambhnī. Hin. Wom.
The begetting of a son is uncommon.

Pūt supūt to kyon sanche? pūt kupūt to kyon sanche? Hin.
If your son is a good son you need not collect money; If your son is a bad son you need not gather wealth.
(In the first instance he will earn it for himself, and in the latter he will soon dissipate all you hoard.)

Q

Qabr kā munh jhānk-kar āē hain. Mah.
I have just peeped into my grave.
(Snatched from the jaws of death.)

Qabr men bhī tīn din bhārī hote hain. Mah.
There's three days' misery even in the grave.
(Muhammadans believe that during the three days after burial they have to render an account of all their doings in life.)

Qabr men pāon laṭkāe baiṭhā hai. Mah.
He has one foot in the grave.

Qabr men rakh-ke khabar ko na āyā koī.
Mūē kā koī nahīn jīte jī kā sab koī. Mah.
When I am laid in the grave, no one will come to see me. None is for the dead; all are for the living.

Qabr par qabr nahīn hotī. Mah.
Grave upon grave is not proper.
(No one ever raises a tomb over a tomb. Two in a house can never agree. This is said in reproof of a widow's marrying again. Also of extravagance; one debt on another.)

Qābū sachchā, jhagṛā jhūṭā.
Possession is right, litigation wrong.
(Possession is nine points of the law.)

Qadam-i-darveshān radd-i-balā. Pers.
The feet of the holy scare away evil.

Qadr-i-āfiyat kase dānad, ki ba musībat-i-girift āyad. Pers.
He knows the value of ease who once falls into difficulty.

Qadr-dān ke Khudā pāēnte biṭhāē, be-qadr ke sirhāne bhī na biṭhāē.
May God rather place us under the foot of

one who appreciates us, than at the head of one who does not.
(Mankind loves appreciation under any circumstances.)

Qadr-dān kī jūtiyāṅ uṭhāiye, nā-qadre ke pāposh mārne na jāiye.
Hold the shoes of the just, but deign not even to kick the unjust.

Qadr-i-āfiyat mālūm hogī.
The value of comfort is known (when it is lost).

Qadr khodetā hai har bār kā ānā jānā.
Visiting every day makes one cheap.
(Familiarity breeds contempt.)

Qadr ullū kī ullū jāntā hai;
Humā ko kab chugad pahchāntā hai? Mah.
Owls know the value of owls, But how shall the owl know the value of the phœnix?
(The *humā* is an imaginary bird about which the Muhammadans believe, that if it sits on any one's head that person will become a king.)

Qahr-i-darvesh bar jān-i-darvesh. Pers.
The poor man's rage only hurts himself.

Qamar dar Aqrab hai.
The moon is in Scorpio.
(An unlucky omen or time.)

Qanāat baṛī daulat hai.
Contentment is the best of riches.

Qand luṭeṅ aur koēloṅ par mohar.
The sugar is squandered and a seal is set upon the charcoal.
(Penny wise pound foolish.)

Qaraz-dār chhātī par savār.
The creditor sits upon the debtor's breast.
(When he refuses him his money.)

Qaraz kāṛh kare beohār, mehrī se jo rūṭhe bhatār, be-bolāval bole Darbār; yeh tīnoṅ pasham ke bār. E.
Who trades on borrowed money, who quarrels with his wife, who speaks at Court without being spoken to; these three are as cast off hair.

Qaraz kāṛh mehmānī kī, launḍoṅ mār dīvānī kī! Mah. Wom.
The feast is on credit and the boys are driving me wild!
(By asking for dainties: a poor man's feast.)

Qaraz kī kyā mā marī hai?
Is the mother of debt dead?
(*i. e.* debts can still be begotten: used when a request for a loan is refused: if you won't lend I'll borrow elsewhere.)

Qasāī bachchā kabhī na sachchā, jo sachchā to harāmī bachchā.
A butcher's boy is always a liar, if he speaks the truth he is a bastard.
(*i. e.* not a butcher's son.)

Qasāī ke bharose shikrā pālnā.
To rear a hawk on butcher's meat.
(Spoken of one who undertakes any thing for the accomplishment of which he must depend upon others. A hawk of course should be taught to catch its own prey.)

Qasāī kī beṭī das baras kī umr meṅ bachchā jantī hai.
The butcher's daughter bears a child when she is ten.
(*i. e.* much before the usual time: used to denote the alacrity with which people carry out the orders of a person in authority.)

Qasāī kī ghās ko kaṭrā khā jāē?
Will the buffalo calf graze the butcher's field?
(Said by the strong.)

Qasam khāne hī ke liye hai.
Oaths are made to be taken.

Qatal-mūzī qabl azīzā! Wom. Mah.
Slay the serpent before he bites you.

Qaul-i-mardāṅ jān dārad, Pers.
An honest man's words carry weight.

Qayāmat ṭūṭī hai.
The Day of Judgment is arrived.

Qāyam mizājī sab vasfoṅ kī bādshāh hai.
Firmness of purpose is the best of all virtues.

Qazā ke āge hakīm ahmaq.
In the face of death the physician is a fool.

Qazā ke tīr ko ḍhāl kī hājit nahīṅ.
Against death's arrows there is no shield.

Qazā se chārā nahīṅ.
There is no cure for death.

Qāzī bahoterā harā rahe, par bandah na hārā!
The judge has given it against me, but I have not lost my point!
(Stubbornness.)

Qāzī-i-dallāl.
A broker of quarrels.
(A mischief-maker.)

"*Qāzī jī, duble kyoṅ*"? "*Shahr ke andeshe se.*"
"Qāzī, why are you thin?" "On the cares of the city."

'*Qāzī jī khānā āyā.*' '*Hameṅ kyā?*'
'*Tumhāre hī liye hai.*' '*Phir tumheṅ kyā?*'
"Qāzī! the dinner waits." "What's that to me?" "It is for you!" "What's that to you then?"
(Said to a busy body.)

Qāzī kā piyādah, ghoṛe savār.
The Qāzī's footman is a horseman.
(A skit at the high-handed ways of the subordinates of officials in India.)

Qāzī ke ghar ke chūhe bhī syāne.
In the Qāzī's house the very rats are knowing.

Qāzī ke mūsal meṅ nārā. Mah.
The Qāzī's pestle has a string (for drawers).
(*i. e.*, he can make others do as he likes however improper his orders may be; native view of all government.)

Qāzī kī launḍī marī, sārā shahr āyā: Qāzī mare, koī na āyā.
If the Qāzī's slave girl die, all the city attends the funeral; if the Qāzī die, not a soul will be present.
(*i. e.* because the Qāzī is alive in the first

case and the people attend to please him, but when he is dead there is no one to please.)

Qāzī kī mūnj.

The Qāzī's rope of straw.

☞ It is said that a new governor on arriving in a district, had occasion for a straw rope, and requested one from the Qāzī, who sent it. The charge was inserted in the revenue books and afterwards became a standing one every year. Hence the proverb signifies the demand of a thing on the grounds that it has once been given.

Qāzī niyāo na karegā, to ghar to āne degā.

If the judge will not do justice, he will let you go home again.

(*i. e.*, there is no harm in trying to get what you want, because if you don't succeed you are no worse off than you were before.)

Qismat de yārī, to kyoṅ ko khuārī ?

If fortune favoured where would then be misery ?

Qismat ke likhe ko koī nahīṅ meṭ saktā.

No one can erase what destiny has written.

Qismat na de yārī, to kyoṅkar kare faujdārī ?

If fortune do not favour, how will you be a great man ?

(The *faujdār* in the old days was the chief military, criminal and general administrator of a province or state, and was therefore a very great man.)

Qormā aisā bhī dāl se behtar hai.

Even spoiled dainties are better than plain pulse.

Qurān par Qurān rakhne kā kyā muzāiqa hai ? Mah.

What harm is there if you put one *Qurān* upon another ?

(But it would be irreverent to put any thing else upon a *Qurān*.)

Qūt thoṛā manzil baṛī.

Scanty provender and a long stage.

(Said of a person who undertakes anything beyond his strength.)

R.

Rāb na rābṛī, le uṭhe khāṅḍā ! Rus.

(I never said a word) sweet or sour, and he drew his sword !

Rāchegā pān, birāchegī mehṅdī.

If with love it is betel : with hate it is henna.

(Better a dinner of herbs where love is than a stalled ox and hatred therewith. *Pān* is a valuable and *mehṅdī* a very cheap article.)

Rādhe Rādhe raṭat haiṅ āk, ḍhāk aru kair ;
Tulsī, yā Brij-bhūm meṅ kahā Rām se bair ?

The *āk*, *ḍhāk* and *kair* repeat the name of Rādhā ; Saith Tulsī, in this land of Brij what enmity is there to Rām ?

☞ A saying of Tulsī Dās, the author of the *Rāmāyan* and so a stout votary of Rāma Chandra. In Brij—the country about Mathurā, the worship is chiefly of Krishṇa whose mistress was Rādhā. The *āk*, *ḍhāk* and *kair* are the special products of Brij and hence the point of the saying.

Rahab bhukhle, chalab ṭukle. E.

I may starve, but I will not stoop.

Rahā Karīmnā, tau ghar gayā ; gayā Karīmnā, tau ghar gayā. Wom.

If the wretched Karīm remain at home, the house is ruined : if he go abroad the house is ruined.

(Observe the contempt thrown into the diminutive form Karīmnā.)

Rāh chhoṛ, kurāh chale.

Who leaves a beaten track goes astray.

Rahe ant mochī ke mochī.

He is a cobbler to the very last.

Rahe jhopṛī meṅ khuāb dekhe mahloṅ kā.

He lives in a hut, and dreams of palaces.

(Castles in the air: *chateaux en Espagne*.)

Rahe ke bhusahul, nāoṅ leve ke dharohar ! E.

He lives in a straw hut, and calls himself a banker !

Rahe Mahmūd ke, anḍe deve Masūd ke.

She lives with Mahmūd and lays eggs for Masūd.

(Kissing goes by favour.)

Rahe nām Allāh kā.

The name of God only will remain.

(*i. e.* all else will die.)

Rahe to ṭek se, jāe to jaṛ bekh se.

Live with honor, or go altogether.

Rahī bāt thoṛī ; jīn, lagām, ghoṛī !

Very little is left : only saddle, reins, and mare !

Rāh kī bāt hai.

It is a matter of course.

Rahmān joṛe palī palī, Shaitān luṛhāve kuppe.

Rahmān stores by ladle-fulls and the devil spills by can-fulls.

(Whatever a good wife saves, the cat eats. He heapeth up riches and cannot tell who shall gather them. Mathew xxxix, 6.)

Rahmān ko Rahmān, Shaitān ko Shaitān.

A Rahmān for a Rahmān and a Devil for a Devil.

(Good mind good find.)

Rahm-dilī baṛāī kī nishānī hai.

Compassion is the sign of magnanimity.

Rahnā bhalā bides kā, jahāṅ apnā nahīṅ koī.

It is best to live in a strange land where you have no friends.

(A saying of the *atīts* or free-thinkers, and attributed to *Kabīr*.)

Raho, rī kutyā, merī ās, maiṅ āūṅ Kātak māṅ ! Wom.

Wait for me, you bitch, I'll be back in October !

Rāh paṛe jāniye, yā bāh paṛe jāniye. Panj.

We know him when we travel or deal with him.

Rah, rah, beṅgnā, hone de bihān; tujh par sājeṅge tīr kamān. E.
Stay, stay, you frog, until it is dawn, that I may shoot you with an arrow.

Rāī bhar nātā, na gāṛī bhar āshnāī.
A mustard seed of relationship is worth a cart load of friendship.
(Blood is thicker than water.)

Rāī bhar sagāī, na peṭhā bhar pirīt.
A mustard seed of kinship is better than a gourd-full of love.

Rāī ko parbat kare, aur parbat ko kare rāī.
He (God) can turn a mustard seed into a mountain, and a mountain into a mustard seed.

Rājā āge rāj; pīchhe chhalnī nā chhāj. Wom.
While there is a king there is a kingdom; after him there is not even a sieve and a basket.
(Said by a widow.)

Rājā Bhīm kī qazā, Rām kī razā!
By God's will Rājā Bhīm died!
(Bhīma, a Pāṇḍava, was an Indian Hercules.)

Rājā bulāve ṭhāṛe āve.
When the king calls, he comes quickly.

Rājā chhoṛe nagrī, jo bhāve so leve.
When the king leaves his city, any body that wants can take it.
(Might is right.)

Rājā chhūē aur rānī hoē.
Whom the Rājā takes up becomes a Queen.
(Whoever enjoys the favor of the prince, rises to power and eminence.)

Rājā, jogī, agan, jal, in kī ulṭī rīt:
Ḍarte rahiye Paras Rām, yeh thoṛī pāleṅ pirīt.
Kings, mendicants, fire, and water have awkward ways; Fear them, Paras Rām, they love but for a short time.
(Put not your trust in princes.)

Rājā, jogī kis ke mīt.
Kings and mendicants are friends to no one.

Rājā kā dān parjā kā ashnān.
The Rājā's alms and the subject's ablutions.
(Are equally efficacious: each is to perform acts of piety as he is able.)

Rājā kā parchānā aur sāṅp kā khilānā barābar hai.
To meddle with kings is to cherish serpents.

Rājā kare so niyāo, pāsā paṛe so dāo.
What the prince declares is justice, what the dice turn up is luck.
(The king can do no wrong.)

Rājā ke ghar gaī, aur Rānī kahlāī. Wom.
When she enters a king's house, she becomes a queen.
(Whatever she might have been before. Instances are not rare in India in which Rājās and others have married very undesirable women.)

Rājā ke ghar kāj, hamāre ghar ṭhak ṭhak.
In the king's palace feasting, and in my house thwack, thwack.
(Native rulers levy forced contributions to pay for the festivities on grand occasions, as marriages, etc.)

Rājā ke ghar motiyoṅ kā kāl!
A Rājā's house and a scarcity of pearls!
(Said on not finding what might be expected.)

Rājā kī beṭī, karmoṅ kī heṭī!
A princess born, her fate forlorn!
(Said of a *mesalliance*.)

Rājā kī sabhā Narak ko jāī.
The king's council go to Hell.
(For saying what they should not, *i. e.* falsehood to please their lord.)

Rājā kis ke pāhone, aur jogī kis ke mīt?
Who hath a king for guest? Who hath a mendicant for friend?

Rājā ko motī kā dukh!
A king feeling the want of pearls!
(An impossibility in India, for there he would take by force all he could lay his hands on.)

Rājā Nal par biptā paṛī, bhūnī machhlī jal meṅ tirī.
When misfortunes befel Rājā Nal, a broiled fish jumped into the water.
(Misfortunes never come singly.)
☞ It is commonly related of the ancient hero Nala, who was deprived by a series of misfortunes of all his possessions and obliged to retire with his wife Damayanti into the forests, where they lived on whatever they could pick up, that once having caught a fish, they broiled it, and the Rānī finding it all covered with ashes went to wash it in the stream, when it recovered itself and swam away. Properly speaking however this legend should be told of the divinely afflicted Harischandra, better known as Rājā Harichand.

Rājā niyāo na karegā, to ghar to jāne degā.
If the king will not do me justice he will at least let me go home.
(There is nothing like having a try.)

Rājā rāj, parjā chain.
When the king rules (with justice) his subjects prosper.

Rājā rakkhe, rānī khāve.
The king saves and the queen spends.
(Common observation in India.)

Rājā rūṭhegā apnā suhāg legā, kyā kisī kā bhāg legā? Hin. Wom.
If the king be displeased he can take back his gifts, but he cannot deprive me of my fate.

Rājā rūṭhegā apnī nagrī legā.
If the king be displeased he can but turn me out of his city.
(Spoken in a spirit of independence. Prepared for the worst. See preceding.)

Rāj kā dūjā, bakrī kā tījā, dono kharāb.
For the king a second son, and for the goat a third kid are both bad.
(The princes fight for the throne, and the

third kid would starve for want of milk, a goat having but two teats.)

Rāj kā rāj meṅ, byāj kā byāj meṅ, nāj kā nāj meṅ.

The king's wealth goes in his state, the money-lender's in his loans, the grain-dealer's in his grain.

Rājpūt, Jāṭ mūsal ke dhanuhī :
Ṭūṭ jāt, neve nahīṅ kabhī.

Rājpūts and Jāṭs are like bows made of pestles : They will break, but never bend.

Rakat le gailoṅ sautin ke naihar. E. Wom.

Go for blood to a co-wife's mother's house.

(Deep hatred.)

Rākhan-hār bhae bhuj chār, to kyā bigṛe bhuj do ke bigāṛe. Hin.

When he that has four hands (Vishṇū) is my protector, what harm can his enmity do me that has only two ?

Rakho is maqūle pe dār o madār,
Ki nau naqd achchhe, na terah udhār. Mercantile.

Depend upon this motto : That nine in cash are better than thirteen on credit.

(A bird in hand is worth two in the bush.)

Rakh pachhtāvā kuchh nahīṅ, bech pachhtāvā achchhā. Mercantile.

It is useless to repent that you have kept, and well to repent that you have sold.

(Better repent you sold too soon, than repent you did not sell in time.)

Rakh pat, rakhā pat.

Pay respect and respect will be paid you.

(Honor pay, honor get : as thou givest so shall thou receive : honor to whom honor is due.)

Rakkhā to chashmoṅ se, uṛā-diyā to pashmoṅ se.

If he keep me I am indebted to him, if he turn me out I don't care.

(Said by an independent servant.)

Rakkhe to pīt ; nahīṅ, to palīt.

If kept up it is love; if not, it is dirt.

Rale mile paṅchoṅ rahiye ; jān jāë, par sach na kahiye !

Keep in with the majority, and risk your life rather than tell the truth.

(Swim with the tide: time-server.)

Rām baṛhāë so baṛhe ; bal-kar baṛhā na koī.
Bal kar-ke Rāvan baṛhā, chhin meṅ ḍāre khoī.

Whom Rām (God) favours, prospers; none prospers of his own strength. Rāvan prospered of his own strength, and was ruined in a trice.

(Allusion to the well known war between Rāma Chandra and Rāvaṇa in the *Rāmāyaṇa.* I returned and saw under the sun that the race is not to the swift, nor the battle to the strong, neither yet bread to the wise, nor yet riches to men of understanding, nor yet favor to men of skill; but time and chance happeneth to them all. Ecclesiastes, ix, 11.)

Rām bharosā bhārī hai !

Reliance on God is a great thing !

Rām bharose jo raheṅ parbat pe hariyāëṅ.
Tulsī birvā bāg ke sīṅchat hī kumhlāëṅ.

Who rely on God can thrive on a mountain. (I have seen) saith Tulsī Dās, that garden plants will die while being watered.

Rām binā dukh kaun hare ?
Barkhā bin sāgar kaun bhare ?
Lachhmī bin ādar kaun kare ?
Mātā bin bhojan kaun dhare ?

Who can take away my pain, but God ?
What can fill the ocean, but the rain ?
Who will show respect, where is no money ?
Who will feed, but a mother ?

Rām chhoṛī Ajudhyā, man bhāve so le.

Rām has left Ajudhyā, who pleases can take it.

(Ayodhyā (Oudh) was the kingdom of Dasaratha, the father of Rāma Chandra, who was banished through the machinations of his step-mother Kaikeyi in favor of her son Bharata. The point is, as Rāma had to go it did not matter who got it.)

Rām hī Rām sat hai.

God alone is true.

Rām jharoke baiṭh-ke, sab kā mujrā le;
Jaisī jā kī chākrī, vaisā vā ko de.

God sitting on his judgment seat hath mercy upon all ; As each man's service, so reward doth unto him befall.

Rāmjī kā āsrā hai !

My hope is in God !

(Said by the childless.)

Rām ke bhakt, kāṭh ke guriyā :
Din bhar ṭhak ṭhak, rāt ke ghuskuriyā. Bhoj.

The worshipper of Rām is a wooden doll : Praying all day and resting at night.

(A skit at the Vaishnava *pujāris* or priests.)

Rām kī māyā : kahīṅ dhūp kahīṅ chhāyā !

Behold the mystery of God : here sunshine, there shade.

Rām milāī joṛī ; ek andhā, ek koṛhī !

God hath well-matched them : the one is blind and the other leprous.

(To describe two rogues, who are closely connected.)

Rām na māre, āpai marai de ku-mati chaṛhāë. E.

God did not kill him, but his own folly did.

(His own worst enemy.)

Rām nām ko āskatī, bhojan ko taiyār.

Slow to call on God, but very ready to eat.

(Said to an idle relative.)

Rām nām laḍvā, Gopāl nām ghī,
Har kā nām misrī, to ghol ghol pī.

Rām's name is as sweetmeats, Gopal's as butter, Har's as sugar, mingle them all and drink.

(A hymn or prayer contantly used at temples. Rāma, Gopāla or Krishṇa, Hari or Vishṇu, are all synonyms for God.)

Rām nām le so dhakkā pāve, chhātar hilāve so ṭakā pāve. Wom.
Call on God and be pushed about, skip and dance and make money.

(The harlot thrives where the honest woman starves.)

Rām nām shamsher pakaṛ lī, Krishn katārā bāndh liyā, Dayā dharam kī ḍhāl banā le, Jam kā duārā jīt liyā.
Make a sword of Rāma's name and a dagger of Krishṇa's; Make a shield of faith and mercy, and conquer the gate of Hell.

Rām nām sumran karo; yehī nām hai tant.
Tīn lok, chaudah bhavan, chhāē rahe Bhagvant.
Call on the name of God; his is the powerful name. In the three worlds and fourteen quarters the power of the Holy one dwells.

Rām, Rām japnā, parāyā māl apnā.
Calling on God, he makes others' property his own.

(A hypocrite.)

Rām Rām kahte raho, jab lag ghaṭ meṅ prān!
Kabhū to Dīn-dayāl ke bhanak paṛegī kān.
Keep on calling on God as long as life lasts; Some day or other the cry will reach the ears of the Merciful God.

Rām Rām ke kārne sab dhan ḍāro khoē.
Mūrakh jāne gir paṛā, din din dūnā hoē.
Spend all thy wealth on God. He is a fool that thinks it lost, for it doubles day by day.

(A saying of the Brāhmans to encourage alms to themselves!)

Rām Rām kī luṭ hai; lūṭī jāē so lūṭ:
Ant kāl pachhtāēgā, jab prān jāēṅge chhūṭ.
It is plunder of the name of God; plunder it as much as you can: Otherwise you will repent, when your soul departs.

Rām Rām likh de, silā tir jāēgī;
Bhajle Sītā Rām, mukt ho jāēgī.
Write the name of Rām, and stones will float: Repeat the names of Sītā and Rām, and you will get salvation.

(The allusion here is to the bridge across the sea made by Rāma Chandra while invading Lankā to recover Sītā, the stones of which did not sink because the name of Rāma was written on them)

Rām Rām sab koī kahe, Jasrath kahe na koe;
Ek bār Jasrath kahe koṭ yag phal hoē.
Every body calls on Rām, and none on Jasrath; Who takes the name of Jasrath once will reap the reward of a million sacrifices.

(Jasrath or Daṣaratha was the father of Rāma Chandra and is now completely neglected in Hindū ritual. The point is that, as the father of Rāma, he is greater than Rāma.)

Rām Rām tū kaho, man mere,
Pāp kaṭeṅge chhin meṅ tere.
Call on God, my heart; And thy sins will be forgiven in a moment.

Rām sahāē kare, to koī kyā kar sake?
While God protects none can hurt you.

Ramzān ke namāzī, Muharram ke sipāhī. Mah.
In Ramzān a worshipper, in Muharram a soldier.

(For the rest of the year he is neither: Said of a hypocrite. The Ramazān is the month's fast prescribed to Musalmāns, and the Muharram is the feast in honor of the martyrdom of Hasan and Hussain, prescribed to the Shia sect, at which the tāziās or biers of the saints are preceded by men representing an army.)

Raṅḍā gayā sagāī ko, āp ko lāē yā bhāī ko?
If a widower negociate a marriage, will it be for himself or his brother?

(He will be sure to do it for himself, so don't send him.)

Rāṅḍ aur khāṅḍ kā joban rāt ko.
Women and candy white shine best at night.

Rāṅḍ, Bhāṅḍ, sāṅḍ bigṛe bure.
The rage of a woman, a player, and a bull is something dreadful.

(Bhāṭs or professional bards are apt to be shockingly abusive when offended.)

Rāṅḍeṅ to bahoterī raheṅ, jo ranḍve rahne deṅ.
Widows would be chaste, if the widowers would let them be so.

(There would be no thieves if there were no receivers of stolen goods.)

Rāṅdho na sijhāo, mujhe baiṭhe khilāo.
Nor boil nor fry it, but give me my food at my ease!

(If there is no bread in the house, give me some toast!)

Raṅḍī faqīr karde dam meṅ shāh-i-zamān ko:
Badfan kare palak meṅ insān nek fan ko.
A harlot will make a king of the world a pauper in a moment: She will make a wicked man of good man in a moment.

Raṅḍī kā joban rakābī meṅ.
A harlot's charms are in the dish.

(She goes to him who can pay her.)

Raṅḍī ke ghar māṅḍe, aur bhaṅḍoṅ ke ghar kaṛāke.
Delicacies for the harlots means starvation for their lovers.

Raṅḍī ke nāk na hotī, to gūh khātī phirtī.
Had a woman no nose she would eat dirt.

(Cutting off the nose for inconstancy was a favorite punishment. Every woman is at heart a rake.)

Raṅḍī ke saikṛoṅ yār.
A harlot's lovers may be reckoned by the hundred. [lagtī.

Raṅḍī kī gālī aur bhūt ke patthar kī choṭ nahīṅ
A woman's threats and goblins' stones break no bones.

Randī kī kamāī, yā khāē ḍhāṛhī, yā khāē gāṛī.
The prostitute's earnings go to the musicians or to the cabmen.
(Dancing girls, who belong to the professional prostitute classes in India, are entirely in the hands of the men who accompany their songs, and are also fond of being driven about in showy vehicles.)

Randī kis kī jorū? aur bharve kis ke sāle?
A harlot is no body's wife, and a pimp no body's brother-in-law.

Randī mom kī nāk hotī hai.
A harlot has a waxen nose.
(By "waxen nose" understand "easy virtue.")

Randī māṅge rupaiyā—"Le le, merī maiyā."
Phakkar māṅge paisā—"Chal be sāle, kaisā?"
If a harlot wants rupees it is—"Take, my dear."
If a beggar wants coppers it is—"Go, you blackguard, how (can I give them?")."

Randī paise kī āshnā hai.
Money is the harlot's love.

"*Randī! terā yār mar gayā.*" *Kahā,* "*kaun sī galī kā?*"
"Harlot, your lover is dead." "Which one?" said she.

Randiyoṅ kī kharchī, vakīloṅ kā kharchā, peshgī hī diyā jātā hai.
A lawyer's fee and a harlot's wages are paid in advance.

Rāṅḍ kā sāṅḍ, chhināl kā chhinṛā.
The widow's son a wandering bull; the adultress' son a rake.
(The hit in the proverb is in the word *sāṅḍ*, which is a "Brāhminī" bull let loose from religious notions to wander at will, and the main use of which is to cover the cows of the neighbourhood.)

Rāṅḍ kā sāṅḍ, saudāgar kā ghoṛā, khāē bahut chale thoṛā.
A widow's son and a dealer's horse eat much and work little.
(*Saudāgar* here means professional horse-dealer, a class to be no more trusted in India than elsewhere in the civilized world.)

"*Rāṅḍ*" *ke āge gālī kyā?* Hin. Wom.
The height of abuse is "widow."
(Among women generally, and especially among high caste Hindū women, to call a married woman, "a widow" is the height of abuse, and will keenly effect her, owing to the ill-omen contained in the expression.)

Rāṅḍ ke charkhe kī tarah chalā hī jātā hai.
Always in motion, like a widow's spinning wheel.
(Indian observation.)

Rāṅḍ kī gāṅṭh meṅ māl kā ṭūk!
There is very little in the widow's pocket!

Rāṅḍ ko beṭī kā bal; raṅḍve ko rupaē kā bal.
A widow's strength is in her daughter; a widower's in his money.

Rāṅḍ muī, ghar sampat nāsī; mūṅḍ muṅḍāe bhaē sannyāsī.
His wife dead and his riches gone; he shaved his head and become an ascetic.
(*i. e.*, owing to circumstances and not from any religious feelings. A skit at the *faqīr* or mendicant classes.)

Rāṅḍ rove, kuārī rove, sāth lagī sat khasmī rove!
Widows weep, and virgins weep, and women with seven husbands weep with them!
(The force of sympathy.)

Rāṅḍ, sāṅḍ, sīṛī, sannyāsī, in se bache to seve Kāshī.
Be on your guard against the women, the sacred bulls, the stairs, and the devotees, and you may worship at Kāshī (Benares.)

"*Rāṅḍ*" *se baṛh ke kosnā nahīṅ.*
No curse so great as calling a woman "a widow."
(See above "*Rāṅḍ*" *ke āge gālī kyā?*)

Ran fateh ho gayā.
He has conquered in the field.

Rang hai usī ko, jo kahe na kisī ko!
Blessed is he that calls no body names!

Rāṅghaṛ, Gūjar do; kuttā billī do; yeh chāroṅ na hoṅ, to khule kivāṛoṅ so.
If there were no Rāṅghaṛs, Gūjars, dogs and cats we could sleep with open doors.
(Rāṅghaṛs, low Musalmāns of corrupt Rājpūt descent, and Gūjars, the cowherd class, are notorious for their thieving propensities.)

Rang kavvā sā aur Mahtāb nām!
As black as a crow, and named Mr. Moon!

Rang kī khushī, man kā saudā.
The choice of colours depends upon the taste.

Rang meṅ bhang paṛ gaī.
All the enjoyment is spoilt.

Rangrez hote, to apnī ḍāṛhī rangte.
Were I a dyer I would dye my own beard first.
(Charity begins at home.)

Rang rūp dekh-kar na bhūliye!
Let not gaudy hues beguile thy heart!
(All that glisters is not gold.)

Rānī dīvānī huī; auroṅ ko patthar, apnoṅ ko laḍḍū mār-ke!
The princess is quite mad; she pelts her own relatives with sweets, and others with stones!
(There is method in her madness.)

Rānī gaīṅ hāṭ, lāīṅ rījh-kar chakkī ke pāṭ.
When the Queen went to the market, it was the handmill that took her fancy.
(She had never known before how the corn was ground!)

Rānī ko kaun kahe "āgā ḍhak?" Wom.
Who will tell a queen to cover her breasts?
(Who can counsel a great man?)

Rānī ko rānā piyārā, kānī ko kānā piyārā.
The lady loves her lord, and the one-eyed wife her one-eyed husband.
(Like clings to like: birds of a feather flock together.)

Rānī rūṭhegī apnā suhāg legī: kyā kisī kā bhāg legī?
When the Queen is angry she can take back her ornaments, but she cannot take away any one's fate.
(The ornaments worn by the women at a native Court belong to the Rājā and of course are worn only during his pleasure.)

Rāṅṛ bhailā ke sukh kaun, jo nichint sūtal nā? E. Wom.
What is the use of being a widow, if one cannot sleep soundly?

Rapaṭ paṛe kī "Har Gangā!"
Slipped into the water he cries on God!
(This involuntary ejaculation is attributed to one who has never bathed in the Ganges and so done a religious duty.)

Ras dīye māre, to bis kyoṅ dīje?
If sweets will kill him, why give poison?

Ras māre rasāin ho.
Mercury dodged up turns to silver.
(*Rasāini* is an alchemist, and one of the commonest tricks of these people is to turn mercury into silver or gold; the generic term for the precious metals treated alchemically is *rasāin*.)

Ras meṅ bis.
Poison in nectar.
(Evil in good.)

Rasoī aur rasāin barābar.
Cooking and alchemy are equally difficult.

Rassī jal gaī par bal nahīṅ gae.
The rope is burnt, but the twist of it remains.
(Applied to one who is ruined, but yet retains his pride.)

Rassī kā sāṅp ban gayā.
A rope turned into a snake.
(A mountain out of a mole hill.)

Rassoṅ jakṛe ab nahīṅ ṭhairte.
Though bound with cords, he will not be restrained.

Rāst-go muflis, Majlis meṅ jhūṭā!
A truthful pauper is a liar in Court!
(A skit at the propensity of rich native suitors for procuring false evidence.)

Rāt bhar gāī bajāī, bachche ke nūnī hī nahīṅ.
All night they played and sang, but the child yet lacked the organ.
(Lacking the very thing for which so much rejoicings and festivities were kept.—In India great rejoicings are made at the birth of a son.)

Rāt gaī, bāt gaī.
The night was lost and so was the object.
(The meaning is that the night was passed in fruitless consultation: applied to ill success in any matter.)

Rāt haṭāī, taṛke hī āī:
Bhūk bednā burī, re bhāī.
Driven away at night, it appears in the morning: Truly hunger is a dreadful thing, my friend.
(Always turning—up like a bad penny.)

Rāt kī mālzādī, din kī khuzādī.
A harlot by night, and a lady by day.

Rāt kī nīyat harām! Mah. Superstition.
Plans made at night are wicked!

Rāt ko jhāṛū denī manhūs hai. Wom. Superstition.
It is unlucky to sweep the house at night.

Rāt ko sāṅp kā nām nahīṅ lete haiṅ. Superstition.
Don't mention a serpent at night.
(Women at night won't say the word *sāṅp*, serpent, but through fear say *rassī*, a rope, instead.)

Rāt mā kā peṭ.
The night is as the mother's womb.
(It covers a multitude of sins.)

Rāt Narbadā utrī, subah kūā dekh ḍarī! Wom
She crossed the Narbadā at night and was frightened next morning at a well!

Rātoṅ kātā kātnā, sir par nahīṅ nātnā. Wom.
All night long she spins and still has nothing to cover her head.

Rātoṅ roī, ek hī mūā! Wom.
Long nights she cursed and only one man died!
(Much labour, little profit: *ronā* here means to call down curses.)

Rāt paṛe upāsī, din ko khoje bāsī. E. Wom.
He passes the night hungry, and in the morning looks for the stale rice.

Rāt paṛī būnd, nām rakhā Mahmūd. Mah. Wom.
She conceived last night and has already named the issue Mahmūd.
(*i. e.*, a son, which is what every woman in India looks for most: to sell the bear's skin before catching the bear: to count one's chickens before they be hatched: first catch your hare.)

Rāt rāt kā paṛ rahnā, bhor bhae chal denā.
It is a sojourn for the night, and a march next morning.

Rāt ṭhoṛī, kahānī baṛī.
The night is short and the tale long.
(The tune the old cow died of.)

Rāt thoṛī, sāṅg bahut.
The night is short and the play is long.
(*i. e.* the time is insufficient for the work.)

Rattī bhar dhan sāth na jāve,
Jab tauṅh mar-kar jīv gaṅvāve.
Not a mite of thy hoards goeth with thee,
When thou diest and givest up the ghost.

Rattī bhar kī tīn chapātī,
Khāne-vāle sāt sangātī. Wom.
Three cakes of a pennyweight each,
And all her friends to eat them.

Rattī bhar sagāī, na gāṛī bhar āshnāī.
Better a dram of kinship than a cart-load of friendship.
(Blood is thicker than water.)

Rattī dān na dhī ko dīyā; dekho, rī, samdhan kā hīyā! Wom.

Look at the liberality of the bride's mother; she has not given her a farthing!
(For dowry.)

Ratti de-kar mānge tolā, vāko kaun batāve bholā.
Who gives a carat and takes an ounce can never be called a simpleton.

Rattiyoṅ jore toloṅ khove, vā ko lābh kahāṅ se hove?
Who spares the pence and dissipates the pound can never gain.
(Penny wise, pound foolish.)

Rau, bandeh, kharīdār Khudā!
Go along, slave, God is thy purchaser!
(A saying of the old.)

Rau meṅ sab ravā hai.
What comes with the stream is a lawful prize.
(All is fish that comes into his net.)

Rāvan kā sālā.
The brother-in-law of Rāvan.
(Spoken of one who exercises oppression under the protection of a powerful person. Rāvaṇa, the opponent of Rāma Chandrā, is the typical tyrant of the Hindūs.)

Rāvan ne jab janam liyā, thī bīs bhujā, das sīs: Māē achambe ho rahī, kis mūṅh meṅ dūṅ khīs?
When Rāvan was born with twenty arms and ten heads, His mother was puzzled at which mouth to feed him!
(Rāvaṇa is represented as having 20 arms and 10 heads at the Dasahrā festival.)

Razā ba qazā.
Satisfied with (God's) decree.

Rāzī haiṅ ham bhī us meṅ, jis meṅ terī razā hai; Yahāṅ yūṅ bhī wāh wāh hai, aur wūṅ bhī wāh wāh hai!
I am pleased with what pleases thee (O God); I am content with this, and with that!

Razīl kī do, na ashrāf kī sau.
The blackguard's two to the nobleman's hundred.
(Foul language.)

Reorī ke pher meṅ ā gaē.
To get into the twist of sugar candy.
(To be entangled in difficulties.)

Richh kā ek bāl bhī bahut hai. Superstition.
One hair of a bear is enough.
(A bear's hair is worn as a charm against the evil eye by little children.)

Rījhenge, to patthar hī mārenge.
He throws stones at you, even when he is pleased.
(Evil for good. Spoken of a mean, avaricious person, from whom, even in his best humour, no good is expected.)

Rikāb par pāoṅ rakhe hue ho.
Your foot is in the stirrup.
(Ready to start: spoken to one who is too eager.)

Ris bhalī, hauns burī.
Emulation is good, envy bad.

Rishvat-khor jahannumī hai.
Who takes bribes is doomed to Hell.

Ris na kar dhan-vant kī, nir-dhan ho-kar, yār. Ris karante saiṅkroṅ dekhe hote khuār.
Never vie with the rich when you are poor, my friend. Look at the misery of hundreds that comes of vying with the rich.

Rītā hāth mūṅh tak nahīṅ pahuṅchtā.
Empty hands don't go to the mouth.

Rīte bhare, bhare ḍhalkāve; Mehr kare to phir bhar jāve.
(God) filleth the empty, and the full he overturneth; And in his compassion he filleth again.

Rīt kī kauṛī na ūt-bilāo kī ḍherī.
An honest penny is better than a hoard of fools.

Rīt na satvāṅsā, merā lāḍlā navāṅsā! Wom.
Nor seventh month rite nor feast, and yet he is her darling grandson!
(The *satvāṅsā* is a ceremony performed by women in the seventh month after the birth of a first-born son, especially if long wished for.)

Riyāsat bagair siyāsat nahīṅ hotī.
There is no government without awe.
(For king and rule, rod and ferule!)

Rizālā mast huā, Khudā ko bhūl gayā. Mah.
When a blackguard is puffed up he forgets that there is a God.

Rizāle kā lath.
A blackguard's cudgel.
(Used to describe one who is very uncouth in his appearance and behaviour.)

Rizāle ke nākhūn hue.
A blackguard's talons.
(The instruments of oppression.)

Rizāle kī jorū ko sadā talāq.
A blackguard's wife is always being divorced.

Rizāloṅ kī dostī pānī kī lakīr; Sharīfoṅ kī dostī patthar kī lakīr.
The friendship of the base is a writing on the water; The friendship of the noble is a writing on stone.

Rizaq hai na maut.
(There is) neither food nor death for him.
(An unfortunate wretch.)

Rizaq na palle bāṅdhte panchhī aur darvesh; Jin kā takyā Rab hai, un ko rizaq hamesh.
Birds and mendicants do not keep their food with them; Those who rely on God shall ever have food.
(Take therefore no thought for the morrow for the morrow shall take thought for the things of itself.)

Rode banyā guṛ degā!
Roar and the shopman will give you sweets!
(Women's advice to children.)

Roe se dān nahīṅ miltā.
Begging is not getting.

Rogī ko rogī milā, kahā "nīm pī."

A sick man met a sick man and said "drink *nim* water."
(The leaves of the *nim* tree are believed to be very efficacious in skin diseases.)

Rogiyā bhāve, so baid batāve.
The doctor prescribes what pleases the sick man.
(*i. e.* when he is rich: valetudenarians make the fortunes of doctors in India just as much as in England.)

Rog kā ghar khānsī, aur laṛāī kā ghar hānsī.
Coughing is the root of disease and chaff the root of a quarrel.
(Native notion.)

Ro-ke pūchh le, hans-ke uṛāde.
He will weep to ask your grievances of you, and will smilingly cast them to the four winds.
(Said of a treacherous friend who evinces sympathy in order to fathom your secrets and then publishes them abroad as a joke.)

Rone ko to thī hī, inte men ā gaē bhaiyā. Hin. Wom.
Just as she was about to cry, her brother came to see her.
(It is customary for women to set up loud cries on the departure or return of a relative. The point here is that she intended to cry anyhow and her brother's arrival gave her the excuse she wanted: to make an excuse.)

Rone se rozī nahīn baṛhtī!
You won't get more to eat by howling for it!
(*Moral*: if you want more, work for it.)

Ro-ro-ke dān māngte ho?
Would you weep to get alms?
(See *Roī se dān nahīn miltā.*)

Rote gaē, mūë kī khabar lāë!
He went whining and brought news of a death!
(Said to an unwilling servant. The point is that he went reluctantly and brought news that the friend was dead, with a view to not being sent on such an errand again.)

"*Rote kyon ho*"? *Kahā* "*shakal hī aisī hai!*"
"Why do you weep?" Said he, "I always look like this!"
(Said of a sulky looking fellow.)

Rote rizaq hai.
By crying you get a living.

Roṭī bin bhonḍe lagen sagar kutum ke log:
Roṭī hī ko jān lo ṭheṭh milan kā jog.
Want of bread will divide the whole family:
It is bread that is the real uniter.

Roṭī gaī mūnh men, zāt gaī gūh men. Mah. Wom.
The bread went down his throat, and his caste into the filth.
(Said of a *mesalliance*, or of a conversion entered into from interested motives: used often of the native Christian converts.)

Roṭī hī kā byāh hai, roṭī hī kā kāj. Sānch baḍon ne hai kahā, 'sab se bhalā anāj.'
Marriages are made for bread, and so are feasts. The ancients have truly said that 'corn is the best of all things'

Roṭī hī ke kārne dar dar māngen bhīk. Roṭī hī ke vāste karen kār sab ṭhīk.
For bread men go about begging from door to door. For bread, too, men do their business well.

Roṭī kāran chhoṛ-kar kuṭum des ghar bār. Lākh kos jā-kar baseṅ roṭī ḍhūnḍan-hār.
For bread do men leave household, home and country. A thousand miles away do the bread-seekers dwell.

Roṭī kāran jāl men phanse pakherū ās. Roṭī kāran ādmī lākhan pāp kamāë.
For bread do birds fall into snares. For bread do men commit a thousand sins.

Roṭī kāran lashkarī ran men sis kaṭāë. Roṭī kāran rain din gīt gavesar gāë.
For bread do soldiers lose their heads in the battle-field. For bread doth the musician sing night and day.

Roṭī kāran sīkhte biddyā hain sab log. Jis ghar māṅ roṭī nahīṅ, us ghar purā sog.
For bread do men learn science and art. That house is full of sorrow, where is no bread.

Roṭī karo, sattū karo, bhāt barobar nāhīn. Mausī karo, phuppī karo, māë barobar nāhīn.
You may make bread and you may mix meal, but it is not rice. You may make an aunt and a father's sister, but she is not a mother.

Roṭī khāiye sakkar se, dunyā khāiye makkar se.
Flatter the world if you would eat sugar with your bread.

Roṭī kī jagah uplā khānā.
To eat cow-dung instead of bread.
(To act absurdly.)

Roṭī kī khāk jhāṛnā.
To butter bread.
(To flatter, to offer officious services; or to live well.)

Roṭī ko rove, chūhle pīchhe sove. Wom.
Weeping for want of bread and sleeping behind the hearth.
(A description of extreme poverty.)

Roṭī ko rove, khapṛī ko ṭohve. Wom.
Weeping for the bread, she caresses the platter. [Wom.

Roṭī ko ṭoṭī, pānī ko billā, khasam ko dādā.
She calls her bread crumbs, her water bubbles, and her husband a grandfather.
(Said of a silly woman.)

Roṭī na kapṛā; sent kā bhatrā. E. Wom.
Nor food nor raiment (from him); a husband in name only.

Roṭī par kā ghī gir paṛā, "mujhe rūkhī hī bhātī hai."
When the butter falls off the bread, (he says) "I prefer it dry."
(Putting a good face on it: making the best

of a bad bargain: *couleur de rose*: putting the best foot forward.)

Roṭī paṛī jo peṭ māñ, to ho gayā mast sarīr; Sujhan lāge jīv ko lākh jatan tadbīr.

When bread goes into the belly the body becomes strong; And all sorts of plans and schemes are framed.

Roṭī pe roṭī rakh-kar khā!

Pile cakes on cakes and eat!

(May plenty be your lot!)

Roṭī qismat kī, huqqā pāoñ-dauṛī kā!

Your bread depends on fate and a smoke on your own exertion.

(The point lies in the custom of offering a pipe to a visitor.)

Roṭī vahāñ khāo, to pānī yahāñ pīo.

Eat there and drink here.

(*i. e.* come back soon: commonly written to persons abroad and said to servants sent on urgent messages. Natives always drink *during* a meal and hence the point of the saying.)

Roṭiyā chākar, ghasīā ghoṛ; khāe bahut, chale thor. E.

An ill-paid servant and a badly fed horse eat much and work little.

(It is not an uncommon custom in India to keep a servant for his board only (*roṭiyā*) without pay: *ghasīā ghoṛā* means a horse fed only on grass.)

Royā so mūñh dhoyā.

Weeping washes the face.

Roze-khor, Khudā kā chor. Mah.

Who eats during a fast pilfers from God.

Roze ko gaē, namāz gale paṛī. Mah.

We went to be relieved of fasting and prayers were added to it.

(We got more than we bargained for.)

☞ The story is related that the people asked Moses (*Mūsā*) to ask God to relieve them of the obligation to fast, but God added prayer to the fasting owing to the wickedness of mankind.

Rozgār aur dushman bār bār nahīñ miltā.

Occupation and enemies are not found at command.

Roz kūāñ khodnā, aur roz pānī pīnā. [daily.

By digging a well daily I can drink water

(Said by a penniless man who has to spend all he earns: living from hand to mouth.)

Rozī kā mārā dar dar rove: pūt kā mārā baiṭh-ke rove.

Deprived of livelihood wanders from door to door: deprived of a son weeps at his ease.

Roz roz kī davā bhī gizā ho jātī hai. Mah.

Medicines taken daily become a part of your diet.

(A skit at drinking strong drinks under the pretence of taking them medicinally.)

Rūkhā khānā, dharti sonā:
Nāñh sukhā phakkar honā.

Eating dry bread and sleeping on the ground:
It is no easy matter to be a mendicant.

(A saying of *faqīrs*! It is no bed of roses.)

Rūkhā so bhūkā.

To eat dry bread is to be hungry.

(Bread without butter or relish.)

Rūkh bina nā nagrī sohe, bin bargan nā kaṛyāñ:
Pūt binā nā mātā sohe, lākh sone meñ jaṛyāñ.

A town without trees is incomplete, so are beams without rafters: A mother without a son is incomplete, though clad in gold.

Rupaē kā kām rupaē se chaltā hai. Mercantile.

Money carries on the business that requires money.

(Money makes the mare to go.)

Rupaē kī khīr hai!

Money makes *khīr*.

(*Khīr* is a dish made of milk and rice and considered a dainty by natives, especially Hindūs.)

Rupaē ko rupayā kamātā hai. Mercantile.

Money begets money.

Rupaē-vāle kā hamesha pūchh hai.

The moneyed man always has a tail.

(A pun here on *pūchh*, a tail, and *pūchhnā*, to ask: the proverb should therefore be read to mean that the moneyed man is always in request.)

Rupayā ānī jānī shaē hai.

Money is a thing that comes and goes.

(That's the way the money goes—pop goes the weasel!)

Rupayā hāth kā mail hai.

Money is but dirt from the hand.

(Sordid gold; trash. Said by beggars.)

Rupayā to Shekh; nahīñ to julāhā. Mah.

If you've wealth you are a Shekh; if not you are a weaver.

(Shekh is here the highest class of Musalmāns: the *julāhā* or weaver is the lowest.)

Rupayā-vāle ko rupaē kī ās, mo ko Rām kī ās. Hin.

The rich man trusts in his wealth, and I in God.

(The self-consolation of the poor.)

Rūp na singār, Khatrānī kī sādh. E. Wom.

Without beauty or ornaments, she would be a Khatrānī.

(The beauty and gorgeous clothing of the wives of Khatris or Panjābi traders is proverbial.)

Rūp nirūp jāe nahīñ bolī. Ha'ukā, garū jāe nahīñ tolī.

Has he beauty or not, who can say? Is He light or heavy, who can say?

(Said of the attributes of God.)

Rūp roe, bhāg khāe.

Beauty weeps while fortune rejoices.

(Spoken when merit is neglected, or unfortunate, and demerit is exalted.)

Rūsal bahuṛya, udgārat āg; Donoñ ṭhaireñ, baṛe haiñ bhāg!

An offended wife and a blazing fire: You are lucky if they remain with you.

Rūṭhe bābā ḍāṛhī hāth.
An old man angry plucks at his own beard.
(He is too feeble to hurt any one but himself. Biting the nose to spite the face.)

Rūṭhe ko manāē nahīṅ, phaṭe ko silāē nahīṅ, to kām kyoṅ-kar chale? Hin. Wom.
If you don't appease the offended or mend your rents, how will you get along?

S

Sāban dīye mail kaṭe, Gangā nahāe pāp. Hin.
Soap cleans from dirt and bathing in the Ganges from sin.

Sāban kāṭe mail ko, jas tan ko kāṭe teg.
Soap washes off dirt, as sword cuts the body.

Sāban thoṛā, pānī gadlā, kyā mal mal-ke dhotā hai? Andar dāg lagā qudrat kā, jab dekho jab rotā hai,
With little soap and dirty water why scrub and wash? When within thee the stain of evil nature is such as makes thee weep.

Sabaq aur ṭabaq donoṅ maujūd haiṅ. Mah.
Learning and food are both before you.
(Allusion to the habit that Mullās have of keeping a boy as a servant whom they also teach: it also alludes to stipends in schools.)

Sabar kā ajar Khudā degā. Mah.
God will requite the patient heart.
(Every thing is his who knows how to wait.)

Sābas, tere saūr ko! survā pakā līyā!
Sakkar ko ghol-ghāl-ke, sarbat banā līyā!
Hurrah for your skill! you have made a soup! And made sherbet by melting sugar!
(A skit at a common mispronunciation: the *s* in all the above words should be *sh*.)

Sab bātoṅ meṅ hai, yāro, yehī sakhun durust. "Allāh ābrū se rakhe aur tandurust."
Of all sayings this is the best. "God keep you in honor and health!"

Sab dhān bāīs paserī. Mercantile.
All the sorts of rice are sold at 110 *sers* (the rupee).
(*i. e.* very cheap; fine and coarse at the same rate. To express a place, where no distinction is made between good and bad, wise and foolish, learned or unlearned. All tarred with the same brush.)

Sab din chaṅge, tihvār ke din naṅge. Wom.
Gay dresses every day and ill clad on holidays.
(Every day is a festival, but a festival is a fast: used to express bad management.)

Sab ek hī māthe.
Every thing goes to (decorate) one head.
(To him that hath shall be given.)

Sab ek hī thailī ke baṭṭe haiṅ.
They are all balls out of one bag.
(Chips of the same block.)

Sab gahnoṅ meṅ chandan-hār.
The necklace is the best of all ornaments.

Sab ghar maṭyāle chūlhe.
Every house hath an earthen hearth.
(All are in the same boat.)

Sab ghaṭā dete haiṅ, muflis ke garaz māl kā mol.
Every body underrates the price of a poor man's goods.

Sab gun bharī bail-rā soṅṭh.
Every good quality is found in ginger.
(Allusion to its great usefulness in India.)

Sab gun kī āgar, dhīyā, nāk binā be-hāl. E. Wom.
You would be perfect, my child, if you had a nose.
(Great braggers, little doers.)

Sab gun kī āgar, phūṭal gāgar. E.
Full of every virtue, but only a broken goblet in the house.

Sab gun pūrī; kaun kahe adhūrī? Wom.
Filled with good qualities, who shall call you imperfect?
(Spoken ironically, to describe one without any good qualities.)

Sab guṛ maṭṭī huā.
All the sugar is turned to dust.
(Much labor has been employed in vain.)

Sabhā bigāreṅ tīn jane; chugul, chūtyā, chor.
Three persons ruin an assembly; a tell-tale, a fool, and a thief.

Sabhā kī chūkī Ḍomnī, aur ḍāl kā chūkā bandar barābar.
A singer that fails in public is like a monkey missing his branch.

Sab hī bāt khoṭī, sire dāl roṭī. Hin.
Best is pulse and bread; all else is bad.
(Pulse and bread are wholesome and cheap.)

Sab hī bhūm Gopāl kī, tā meṅ aṭak kahā?
Jā ke man meṅ aṭak hai, sohī aṭak rahā.
The whole earth is God's, is there any stoppage in it? In whose mind is a stoppage he is stopped.
(Pun on *aṭak* a stoppage and Aṭak on the Indus.)

☞ Orthodox Hindūs had a religious objection to cross the Indus, and it is said that Rājā Mān Singh in 1585 A.D., when he wanted his Hindū troops to cross it, induced them to do so by using the above verse. The story is also attributed to Ranjit Singh on a similar occasion in 1823 A.D.

Sabhī jāt Chamār kī, binā chām nahīṅ koē. Binā chām voh āp hai, jis ko lakhe na koē.
All the world are Chamārs, for none lacketh a skin. He alone is without a skin that none can see.
(*Chamārs* are the low-caste dealers and workers in leather.)

Sab-hī kūkar jo Kāshī jāeṅ, to pātar chāṭan kaun āeṅ? E. Wom.
If all the dogs were to go to Kāshī (Benares), who would there be to lick the platters!
(Dogs in India are the public scavengers.)

Sabhī misrī kī haiṅ ḍalyāṅ.
They are all lumps of sugar.
(They are all good people.)

Sabhī padārath pān hai, ek hī augun āh! Jā ke kar pe dharat hain, bidā karat hain tāh.

The betel is the type of all good things with only one defect! He parts from you to whom you give it.

(*Pān* is given to the parting guest.)

Sabhī sahāyak sabal ke, keū na nibal sahāē. Pavan jagāvat āg ko, dīpak det bujhāē.

All men support the strong, and none the weak. The wind fans the fire and puts out the lamp.

Sābir o shākir, donon jannatī hain. Mah.

Patient and grateful are both for Heaven.

(Blessed are the meek, for they shall inherit the earth.)

Sābit qadam ko sab jagah ṭhāon.

The firm of foot finds a footing every where.

Sābit nahīn kān, bāliyon kā armān. Wom.

She hasn't a whole ear, and yet she wants ear-rings.

Sab jag rūṭhā rūṭhan de, ek Voh na rūṭhā chāhiye.

If all the world be wroth, let it be wroth; as long as (God) is not wroth.

Sab jīte jī ke jhagṛe hain, yeh terā hai yeh merā hai. Jab chal base is dunyā se, nā terā hai nā merā hai.

It is a life-long quarrel about thine and mine. And when we leave this world nothing is thine or mine.

Sab kāmon men pūrī; koī na kahe adhūrī. Wom.

You are perfect in all arts; no one can call you imperfect.

(Said as a snub to a boastful woman.)

Sab kām thakkā, to burā kām takkā.

When all (honest) trades fail he tries a mean one.

(*Burā kām* means here occupation beneath one's dignity.)

Sab ke dāon anḍe bachche; hamāre dāon kuṛak.

The lot of others is eggs and chickens; my lot is a clucking.

(Failure.)

Sab ke dātā Rām.

God gives to all.

Sab kī maīyā sānjh.

The evening is the mother of all.

(The evening crowns the day.)

Sab kehu bole to nīk lāgalā, kapūr bahū bole tihāk barelā. E. Wom.

When others speak it is pleasant, but when my daughter-in-law speaks it pricks me.

(We look to you to give us heirs, madame, but not advice.)

Sab koī jhūmar paire, langṛī kahe 'hamhūn.' E. Wom.

As all wear anklets, the lame girl wants one too.

Sab koī miliyo, langoṭiyā na miliyo.

All may visit me, but the bosom friends of my childhood.

(They know us too well.)

Sab ko ṭhel; main akel!

All others flung aside I am alone!

(Selfishness.)

Sab kuchh gaī, miyān, terī chulbul na gaī. Mah. Wom.

Every thing is gone, husband, but your childishness.

Sab kuchh gayā, miyān kī ṭakh ṭakh na gaī. Mah. Wom.

Every thing is gone but my husband's ill humour.

Sab mad madai hain, biddyā mad udmād.

Spirits intoxicate, but learning most of all.

(A little learning makes men mad.)

Sab peron men baṛā jo baṛ! Ākās vā kī choṭī, pātāl vā kī jaṛ: Hare hare patte, lāl lāl phar. Akbar Bādshāh gīdī khar!

The banian tree is the greatest of all! In heaven its head, in hell its root; Green its leaves, and red its fruit. King Akbar is a stupid ass!

☞ This saying is founded on a story related of four countrymen, who, having heard of the generosity of Akbar towards poets and men of learning, aspired one day to compose a poem worthy of the king. Three of the men succeeded in making one each of the first three lines of the above, but the fourth man was at a loss how to make one for himself. A buffoon passed by them and finding them deeply engaged in completing their poem he suggested to them the fourth line. The four country men being well pleased with this went to the king's palace and having obtained an audience, they were requested to repeat their verses. Each one in turn repeated his line, and when the fourth man had given out his, the whole palace echoed with hisses and the king rebuked him. The countryman, thinking that there was something wrong about it, instantly pointed out the man who had suggested it. The king perceiving that he was the regular country bumpkin put aside the insult with a smile.

Sab pīr chhūṭe, pakṛī gaīn Bībī Nūr. Mah.

All the other saints have escaped and only Lady Nūr is caught.

(Ironical: the great scoundrels have escaped and only a wretched scrape-goat captured.)

Sabr kar man men, tā sukh lahe tan men.

Be patient in your mind, that you may find ease for your body.

Sabr kī dād Khudā degā.

God will reward your patience.

(Said as a consolation to one suffering under oppression.)

Sabr kī dād Khudā ke hāth hai.

The reward of patience is in the hands of God.

Sabr kī ḍāl men mevā lagtā hai.

The branch of patience bears sweet fruit.

Sabr talkh ast, va lekin bar-i-shīrīn dārad. Per.
Patience is bitter, but its fruit is sweet.

Sab sadqe, main alag. Wom.
I sacrifice all to you except myself.

Sab sanse miṭ jāegā, jab hogā Rām sahāë;
Rānī, us Bhagvān se līje dhyān lagāë.
When God helps all anxiety is removed;
So, my queen, meditate on the Blessed One.
(Don't lose heart. This saying is attributed to Nala and also to Harischandra, both well known Hindū heroes, who underwent great troubles in this life.)

Sab se baṛī bhūk, jo pāve so chūkh.
Hunger is the greatest of all things, for it swallows up all it reaches.
(Hunger is the best sauce.)

Sab se behtar hai, miyān, sāhib salāmat dūrkī.
Distant acquaintanceship is the best, my friend.
(Familiarity breeds contempt.)

Sab se bhalā kisān, khetī kare aur ghar rahe.
The husbandman is happiest of all, for he tills his field and lives at home.
(Natives are loth to leave their homes and go abroad. Uneasy lies the head that wears a crown.)

Sab se bhale Mūsal; Chand; karen na khetī, bharen na ḍand.
Mr. Pestle is happiest of all; he cultivates no field, and pays no revenue.
(Said of a plunderer or brigand.)

Sab se bhalī chup.
Silence is best.
(The least said, the soonest mended.)

Sab se hilye, sab se miliye, sab se kīje chāo, Hānjī hānjī sab se kahiye, basiye apne gāon.
Meet all, and play with all, and love all,
And chime in with all, if you would live (peacefully) in your own village.

Sab se mīṭhī bhūk!
No sweets like hunger.
(Hunger is the best sauce.)

Sab se ral mil chāliye, jab lag pār basāë. Mīshṭ bachan mukh boliye, jo nekī hī rah jāë.
Live amicably with all men, as long as you can. Have honey on your tongue, that you may leave a good name behind.
(Be all things to all men.)

Sab shakal langūr kī, ek dum kī kasar hai.
He has all the appearance of an ape but the tail.

Sab toṛen, merā ek Rab na toṛe! Wom.
All may break with me, but God!

Sab ustāre bāndho, koī talvār na bāndhe. Kar do ye manādī, koī dastār na bāndho.
Keep razors, but keep no sword. Proclaim it by the drum, that none should wear a turban.
(A complete subversion of the Indian notions of propriety: oppression.)

Sabzī mat deo gavāran ko, hanḍyā bhar bhāt bigāran ko. E.
Don't give *bhang* to village boors, they will simply spoil a pot-ful of rice.
(*Subzī* or *bhang*, an intoxicant made from hemp, is believed to be a strong appetiser: hence the point here is—don't give *bhang* to a boor, as he won't appreciate it and will eat the more afterwards: caviare to the vulgar.)

Sabzī men surkhī, khabar lāë dhur kī.
(Behold) the glory of *bhang*: it takes you to heaven.
(A saying of *bhang* drinkers in allusion to the delights of intoxication.)

Sachāī men Khudā kī sūrat hai. Mah.
Truth is in the image of God.

Sach aur jhūṭ men chār ungal kā faraq hai.
Between truth and falsehood there is four fingers' breadth.
☞ This proverb is thus explaned: truth is seen but falsehood heard—and the distance between the eye and ear is four fingers.

Sach barābar pun nahīn, aur jhūṭ barābar pāp.
There is no virtue like speaking the truth, and no sin like telling a lie.

Sach bāt ādhī laṛāī hotī hai.
The truth is half a quarrel.
(The candid friend.)

Sach bāt kaṛvī lagtī hai.
The truth tastes bitter.

Sach bolnā aur laṛāī mol lenā barābar hai.
To speak the truth and buy a quarrel is the same thing.

Sach bolnā, sukhī rahnā.
To speak the truth is to live happily.

Sach bol, pūrā tol. Mercantile.
Speak the truth, and give full weight.

Sachchā jāë rotā āë, jhūṭā jāë hanstā āë.
The truthful goes and comes back weeping; the liar goes and comes back laughing.
(Allusion to the complicated procedure of the English Courts in India, which tends to help the adroit liar.)

Sachche ke āge jhūṭā ro mare.
Falsehood weeps before the truth.

Sachche kī bāoṛe, jhūṭe kī na bāoṛe.
Truth's turn will come, the liar's never.

Sachche log qasam nahīn khāte.
A true man never swears.

Sachche Rām ko chhoṛ-ke pūjen Debī bhūt! Āp bichāre mar gaë, un se māngen pūt.
Setting aside the true God they worship idols and ghosts! They themselves are dead and people ask sons from them.
(A saying of the *Āzāds* or free-thinkers.)

Sach hai, harām-zāde kī rassī darāz hai.
True it is that the villain has a long rope.
(*i. e.* ample means for his ends.)

Sach kahe, so mārā jāë!
Tell the truth and be killed!

Sach kahnā ādhī laṛāī mol lenā hai.
To speak the truth is to purchase half a quarrel.

Sach kī sansī burī hotī hai.
The pincers of truth are the severest of their kind.

Sach sab ko karvā lagtā hai.
The truth is bitter to all.

Sadā Bhavānī dāhne, sanmukh rahe Ganesh. Pānch Deo rakshā karen, Birhmā, Vishn, Mahesh!
May Bhavānī be on your right, and Ganesa in front. May all the five Gods, Brahmā, Vishnū and Mahesa defend you!
(This verse is used to head a hymn or religious song.)

Sadā daur daurā, yeh rahtā nahīn; Gayā vaqt phir hāth ātā nahīn.
Happy days never last long; Opportunity once lost is never regained.

Sadā din ek se nahīn rahte.
Your days are not all alike.

Sadā Dīvālī sant ke, jo ghar gehūn hoë.
The virtuous man has a perpetual feast, if he have but wheat in his house.
(The Divālī is the great autumnal festival of the Hindūs.)

Sadā Īd nahīn, jo halvā khāë. Mah.
Every day is not a holiday in which to eat [sweets.
(The *Īd* is the chief Musalmān festival.)

Sadā ke dukhyā, nām Change Khān.
Ill from his birth and called Mr. Health.

Sadā ke ujre, nām Bastī Rām.
Ruined from the first and called Mr. Full.

Sadā ke dānī, mūsal ke nau ṭake.
The ever liberal gives nine pence for a pestle.
(Which is worth only a penny or so: spoken ironically of a miser.)

Sadā kī padnī, urdon dosh! Wom.
Always breaking wind she lays the fault on [the peas.
(To describe one who assigns frivolous excuses for faults which are habitual.)

Sadā kisī kī nahīn rahtī.
Nothing lasts for ever.

Sadā miyān ghore hī to rakhte the!
My lord always kept horses!
(Ironically.)

Sadā na kāhū kī rahī gal pītam ke bānh; Ḍhalte ḍhalte ḍhal gaī, tarvar kī sī chhānh.
No one always keeps her arms round her husband's neck; They drop and drop, till they drop off, like the shadow of a tree.

Sadā nām Sāīn kā.
God's name is everlasting.

Sadā nāo kāgaz kī bahtī nahīn.
A paper-boat will not float long.
(Deceit will not succeed long.)

Sadā na phūle ketgī, sadā na Sāvan hoë; Sadā na joban thir rahe, sadā na jīve koë.
It will not always rain for us, nor flowers blossoms give; Youth will not always be with us, nor shall we always live.

Sadā phūlī phūlī chunī hai.
He has always picked up full-blown flowers.
(A lucky man.)

Sadā rahe nām Allāh kā.
The name of God lives on for ever.
(Used upon occasions of regret for the loss of any person or thing; meaning everything must perish, except God.)

Sadā suhāgan.
A perpetual bride.
(A *faqīr* who wears such ornaments as are worn by married women.)

Sāḍhā ḍhiḍh garbarāiā, haggan dā velā āiā. Panj.
When the stomach is out of order it is time to evacuate.

Sādhan pī, santan pī, pī Kuanr Kanhāī. Jo bijyā kī ninda karen, use khāë Kālikā māī.
Saints drink thee, sages drink thee, the Prince Kanhayyā (Krishna) drank thee. Who speaks ill of the hemp-plant, him will mother Kālkā (Durgā) destroy.
(Said in honor of the intoxicant *bhang*.)

Sādh bhaë to kyā huā, gat mat jānen nāhīn? Tulsī, peṭ ke kārne sādh bhae jag mānhīn.
What boots it to be a saint without true religion? Saith Tulsī (Dās), many turn saints for their stomach's sake.

Sādh bhagat den jinhān asīs, Sukhī rahen ve bisve bīs. Rus.
Whom saints and prophets bless, Will surely happy be.

Sādh bhagat kon jis par chho, Mūl bhalā nā us kā ho.
Whom saints and prophets curse, Will never prosper.

Sādh bhagat kī kare jo sevā, Pār turat ho vā kā khevā.
Who serves saints and prophets, His boat will quickly cross.
(*Berā* (or *khevā*) *pār honā* is a common idiom for success.)

Sādh chale Baikunṭh ko baiṭh pālkī mānh; Raste men se āe phir, bhāng tamakū nānh.
A saint started for Heaven in a carriage; but turned back on the road, because there was no *bhang* and tobacco there.
(A skit at the Indian mendicants' liking for the intoxicant *bhang* and tobacco.)

Sāḍhī kī sākh aur pīpal kī lākh. Agric.
The spring crop and the lac on *pīpal* trees.
(Are the best.)

Sādh khuṭāī nā karen, nā mūrakh se pīt: Chātur to bairī bhalā, mūrakh bhalā na mīt.
Saints do no evil nor have friendship with fools: A wise enemy is better than a foolish friend.

Sādh sant, kī ṭahalkar, līje kuchhu dharm. Tulsī, pher na milegā bār bār yeh janm.
Serve saints and monks, of whatever creed thou be. O Tulsī, this human life thou shalt not get again and again.
(In the doctrine of the transmigration of souls human life comes but once to a being.)

Sādh sant kī ṭahal ko uṭho na baiṭho jāë : Tulsī, lālach len ko dauṛā dauṛā jāë.

In the service of saints and monks he is idle: But, Tulsī, for the love of lucre man will running go.

Sādhoṅ ko kyā savād? Guṛ nahīṅ batāshe hī sahī. Hin.

What cares a saint for relishes? If there be no sugar then give him sugar-candy.

(A skit at the pretended self-denial of the Indian mendicants: if there is no bread in the house let me have some toast.)

Sādhoṅ ne kām sadhā-pan se, kuttan ne kām kutā-pan se.

Saints have the ways of saints, and dogs the ways of dogs.

(A man is known by his deeds.)

Sādhū-bachche, bahute jhūṭe, thoṛe sachche.

Among pedlars many are liars and few truthful.

Sādhū, dukhiyā sab sansārā. Jo sukhiyā so Rām adhārā.

O saint, the whole world is troubled. He is happy that depends on God.

Sādhū ho-kar deve buttā, us ko jāno peṭ ka kuttā.

Hold him to be but a greedy hound, that deceiveth under the garb of holiness.

Sādhū ho-kar kapaṭ jo rākhe, Voh to maza Narak kā chākhe.

Who is a double-dealer in the garb of a saint, Will taste the miseries of hell.

Sādhū ho-kar kare jo chorī, Us kā ghar hai Narak kī morī.

Who steals in the guise of holiness, Lives in the dirtiest lane in Hell.

Sādhū ho-kar kare jo jārī, Us kī ho do jag meṅ khuārī.

Who runneth after women in the garb of a saint, Will be dragged through the mire in both worlds.

Sādhū jan ramte bhale, dāg na lāge koe.

It is best for a mendicant to roam, that there be no stain upon him.

(To keep thyself unspotted from the world.)

Sādhū kahiye sūp ko, pāyā phenke halor: Ochhī kahiye chhālnī, bhūsī rākhe baṭor.

The winnowing fan is a saint that throws away the chaff: The sieve is an evil man that keeps the straw.

Sādhū kī jin sangat kīnī, unhāṅ kamāī pūrī kīnī. Rus.

Who dwell with the holy reap a full reward.

Sādhū milan aur Hari bhajan, dayā, dharam, upkār, Tulsī yā sansār meṅ pāṅch ratan haiṅ sār.

Communion with saints, hymns to God, compassion, faith and kindliness, O Tulsī, are the five jewels of this world.

Sādhū sat kar baiṭh jā, vohī sādh hai ṭhīk: Vā ko sādhū mat kaho, jo ghar ghar māṅge bhīk.

He is a true saint who sits content: Not he that begs from door to door.

Sādhū vohī jo sādhan kare: krodh, lobh, aur moh ko māre.

He is a devotee that practises devotion, and eschews anger, greed and lust.

Sādhū to vohī bhalā, jo bhar sādhū kā bhes; Pūjā kartā Rabb kī, hāṅḍe des bides.

He is perfect saint who in his saint's garb Worshippeth his God and wandereth from place to place.

Sādhū vohī sarāhiye, jā ke hirde gāṅṭh; Laḍḍū le bhītar dhare, charnāmat de bāṅṭ!

Praise ye that saint that hath a kink in his mind; Keepeth the sweets, and distributeth the holy water!

(*Charnāmat* is the water with which idols have been washed: the sweets here are those offered to the idol. The saying is a skit at the *pujāris* or priests at temples.)

Sādhū vohī sarāhiye, jo dukheṅ dukhāveṅ nāṅh; Phal phūl chheṛeṅ nahīṅ, raheṅ bagīche māṅh.

Praise him for a saint who nor frets nor annoys; That plucks nor fruit nor flower, though he dwell in a garden.

Sadqā dīye rad balā. Superstition.

To give alms is to avert evil.

Safar aur Saqar barābar.

Going on a journey is as bad as going to Hell.

(See following.)

Safar aur Saqar meṅ ek nuqte kā faraq hai.

Between Hell and a journey there is but the difference of a dot.

(In the Persian character *f* which has one dot over it becomes *q* if another be added: hence point of proverb.)

Safar kardah bisyār goyad darog. Pers.

Travellers tell many a lie.

(Travellers' tales.)

Safar, vasīla-i-zafar.

You must travel to gain.

(Nothing venture, nothing have.)

Sāg meṅ shurvā; anḍe meṅ pānī! Kyoṅ, Bībī Paṭhānī? Mah. Wom.

Soup out of grass: water out of eggs. How can it be, my Lady Paṭhānī?

(*Shorbā* is made of meat only. Paṭhānī is here a fanciful name.)

Sagoṅ bin sagāī kaisī? Bhaloṅ bin bhalāī kaisī?

Shall there be kinship without kin, Or goodness without the good?

Sagre gāoṅ ghur aili, kahīṅ na dekhī labdā. Patnā shahar aisan dekhlīn, kāṅkh tar labdā. E.

I roamed the whole country and found no profit anywhere; But in Paṭnā city I found it close beside me.

Sagre ghar meṅ reng ke, musrī sir paṭak-ke mar jā.

Better crawl all over the house and dash your head against the pestle and die.

Sagrī rain ban ban phirī, bhor bhae kueṅ se ḍarī. Wom.

She roamed the whole night in the wilds,

And was frightened at a well in the morning.

(Sham modesty.)

Sagrī umar main pāp kamāī; janam na kīnā pun. Levan-hārā ā gayā, to tan man ho gayā sun.

The whole of my life I spent in sin; no good work I have done. The Taker hath come to take me, and lo! my heart and soul are still with fear.

(A saying of the *bhagats* or reformers.)

Sāhib merā bāniyā, banaj kare beopār; Bin dandī, bin pālre, tole jag sansār.

The Lord is a merchant and transacts business; Without a beam or scales he weighs out to all the world.

Sahansar dupkī main laī, motī lagā na hāth. Sāgar kā kyā dosh hai? Hīn hamāre bhāg.

A thousand dips I took, no pearl I found. The fault was not in the ocean, but in my unhappy lot.

Sahansar gopī, ek Kanhaiyā.

A thousand milkmaids and one Kanhayyā.

(A thousand applicants for one appointment. Allusion to the legend of Krishna (Kanhayya) and his *amours* with the milkmaids.)

Sahīh gaē, salāmat āē. Mah. Wom.

Sound he went and safe he returned.

(Ironical: used when a man comes home without earning any thing: gone on a fool's errand.)

Sāh ke savāē; kambakht ke dūne! Mercantile.

The banker's interest is twenty-five per cent; the usurer's is cent per cent!

Sahrī bhī na khāūn, to kāfir na ho jāūn. Mah.

If I were not even to eat breakfast I should be an infidel.

(*Sahri* is the morning meal eaten before a fast.)

☞ The story goes that a Muhammadan, who never kept a fast proposed to join a friend in a *sahri*, whereon the other objected, because he never fasted. He replied in the words of the proverb, the implication being that if he did not take even *sahri*, he would be an infidel.

Sahrī khāē so roza rakkhe. Mah.

Who eats the morning meal, must keep the [fast.

☞ The story goes that a dog ate up the *sahri*, or early morning meal of his master, with which all good Muhammadans fortify themselves for a day's fast. His master thereupon tied him up, declaring that the dog must keep the fast instead of himself, because he had taken the preparatory meal.

Sahtā sahe; na sahtā chhātī dahe.

What can be borne is borne; what can't be borne breaks the heart.

(All do what is pleasing to themselves.)

Sāhū bahe na jāēn, gaun se jāēn. Hin.

The banker is not being carried away, he is going down for some object of his own.

☞ It is said that a money lender was once being carried away by a stream. He shouted for help, and a wag that was standing on the shore said, "You are not being carried away, but you are going down the stream to suit your own ends."

Sāhū batte voh bhī sāh. Mercantile.

Who sells at cost price is still a merchant.

(Selling off an article is better than keeping it unprofitably.)

Sāhūkār ko kisān, bālak ko masān. Mercantile.

A farmer is to a banker, what wasting is to a child.

(The Indian cultivator exists on the money lender, to whom he gives infinite trouble in recovering his claims: *masān* or *sāyā* is an imaginary wasting sickness caused by witchcraft, the practice being to take ashes from a burning-place (*masān*) and sprinkle them on a child, which is then supposed to waste away till it dies.)

Sāīn akkhīān pherīān, bairī mulak jahān. Ṭuk ek jhānkī mihr dī, lakkhān karen salām. Panj.

If the Lord turn away his eyes, the whole world is enemy. If he glance kindly for a moment, then thousands bow.

Sāīn, apne chit kī bhūl na kahiye koē; Tab lag man men rākhiye, jab lag kāraj hoē.

My friend, let not thy secrets escape thee even by mistake; Keep them in thy heart till they prosper.

Sāīn ghore mar gae, gaddhan āyo raj. Kāgā hāth pe let hain, dūr kīye hain bāj.

O God, the horses are dead and asses reign. Crows are perched on the hand and hawks are spurned.

(The times are out of joint.)

Sāīn is sansār men bhānt bhānt ke log! Sab se mil ke baithye, nadī nāo sanjog.

My friend, in this world are men of many kinds! Associate with all men, because the meeting is as that in a ferry-boat.

(I am made all things to all men; I, *Corinthians*, ix. 22)

Sāīn jis ke sāth ho, us ko sānsā kyā? Chhin men us ke kār sab de Bhagwān banā!

What need for anxiety hath he that hath God with him? God in a moment can prosper all his work!

Sāīn jis ko rākh le māran-hārā kaun? Bhūt, deo, kyā āg ho, kyā pānī kyā paun?

Whom God keeps nought can harm. Nor devil, nor demon, nor fire, nor wind nor water.

Sāīn kā ghar dūr hai, jaise lambī khajūr: Charhe to chākhe prem ras; gire to chaknā chūr.

God's house is lofty as a tall date tree: If thou reach it there is sweet fruit; if thou fall thou art destroyed.

Sāīn kā rakh āsrā aur vāhī kā le nām; Do jag men bharpūr hon, jo tere sagre kām.

Trust in God and take his name alone, That thy works may prosper in both worlds.

Sāīn kā sumran karo, jo hoēn sampūran kār; Sāīn bhī sanmukh mile, aur bhagat kare sansār.

Call on God that all thy wishes be fulfilled; That God meet with thee and the world revere thee.

Sāīn ke Darbār men bare bare hain dher: Apnā dānā bīn le; jis men her na pher.

In the Court of God are many great heaps,

Look to thy own (heap of) corn; while there is no mistaking.

(Be content with thy own lot and envy not that of others.)

Sāīn ke sau khel hain.
God hath a hundred whims.

Sāīn ko sānch piyārā : Jhūṭe kā Mālik niyārā !
God loves the true man : The liar has a different Lord !

Sainkṛon ke vāre niyāre ho gaë. Mercantile.
It is a gain of hundreds.

(Said of large and lucrative contracts.)

Sāīn mor āp birūjhal, log dihal pochārā. Lāt mūkā ham sahlauń, aur sahlaon du-gārā, Bhoj. Wom.
My husband was already vexed with me, and the people egged him on. I bore kicks and blows, and a shower of abuse.

(Adding insult to injury.)

Sāīn rāj buland rāj, pūt rāj dūt rāj.
The husband's reign is a good reign, and the son's reign a bad reign.

(Said by a widow lamenting over her late husband, with whom she had everything at her command, in deprecation of the unsatisfactory support rendered by her son, whom she expects to provide for all her wants.)

'Sāīn Sāīn' jībh par aur gabar kopaṭ man bīch, Voh na ḍāle jāënge pakar Narak men khīnch.
With 'Lord Lord' on his tongue and pride and deceit in his heart He shall be dragged through the mire in Hell.

Sāīn sānsā meṭ de aur na meṭe koë. Vā ko sānsā kyā rahā, jā sir Sāīn ho ?
God removeth doubt and none else. But he shall have no doubts that hath God on his side.

Sāīn te sachchā raho, bande te sat bhāo; Bhāven lambe kes rakh, bhāven ghoṭ munḍāo. Panj.
Be sincere with God, and loving to his creatures, Whether you keep your hair long or shave it clean.

(*i. e.* whether you be a Sikh or a Hindū : Sikhs never cut the hair and the Hindūs shave: thou shalt love thy neighbour as thyself.)

Sāīn se jo phir gayā, us ko lābh na hoe; Voh to yūnhī jāëgā janam akārat khoe.
Who hath rebelled against God shall never prosper, For thus he loseth his life for nothing.

Sāīn se sānchī rahūn; bāj bāj, re ḍhol; Panchan men merī pat rahe; sakhiyan men rahe bol.
Beat, beat, o drum, that I may be true to my lord, My honor live among my friends, and my credit among my companions.

Sāīn, Terā āsrā chhoḍe jo an-jān, Dar dar hānḍe māngtā, kauḍī mile na dān.
O God, he that is so foolish as to give up his trust in Thee, Shall beg from door to door and get never a penny.

Sāīn, Tere āsre ān pare jo log, Un ke pūre bhāg hain, un ke pūre jog.
O God, who cometh to Thee for protection, Is a man of good fortune and true religion.

Sāīn, Tere kārne chhoṛā Balakh, Bukhār, Nau lakh ghoṛe, pālkī, aur nau lakh asvār.
O God, for Thee I have left Balkh and Bukhārā, Nine million horses, palanquins, and horsemen.

Sāīn, Tere kārne jin taj diyā jahān, Theṭh kyā Baikunṭh men us ne jahān makān.
O God, he that hath given up this world for Thee, Shall surely find an abode in Heaven.

Sāīn, Tere neh kā jis tan lāgā tīr, Vohī pūrā sādh hai, vohī pīr faqīr.
Who hath been struck with the arrow of Thy love, O God, Is a perfect saint and monk and mendicant.

Sāīn, terī sohlī aur ādar kare na koë: Dur dur kareń saheliyān, main muṛ muṛ dekhūn toë. Wom.
My Lord, I am thy slave, and none respecteth me : My friends keep me at a distance, and I can but look to thee.

(The supplication of a slighted woman to her husband : the point is that if he shows her no respect nobody else will.)

Sāīn, Terī yād men jin tan kīnā khāk, Sonā us ke rūbrū, hai chūlhe kī rākh.
Who hath made his body into dust for Thy sake, O God, Gold is to him as the ashes of a fire.

Sāīn, To bin kaun hai, jo kare navaryā pār ? Tū hī āvat hai nazar chahūn or, Kartār.
God, who is there but Thou to ferry my boat across ? I look on all sides and see but Thee, O God.

('To ferry the boat across' is a very common idiom for 'to grant salvation.')

Sāīsī ilm dariyāo hai.
The groom's knowledge is as deep as the sea.

(There are mysteries in every trade.)

Sāīson kā kāl, munshiyon kī bohtāt.
Grooms are scarce and clerks are plenty.

Saiyān bhae kotvāl, ab ḍar kāhe kā ? Wom.
My husband's now *kotvāl*, so what have I to fear ?

(The *kotwāl* under oriental rule is the chief police officer of a town; under British rule in India he is a petty officer of police. To the native mind he is the embodiment of petty oppression and power.)

Saiyān gae bides, main to kāt kāt muī : Āgre kā charkhā, Burhānpur kī rūī. Wom.
My husband gone abroad, I'm worn to death with spinning, With the wheel from Āgrā and the cotton from Burhānpūr.

Saiyān gae ladnī, lādain jhaṛā jhar : Sau ke pachās kiye, chale āë ghar ! E. Wom.
My husband went a trading and collected

goods no end: But when he had made a hundred into fifty he came back home.

Saiyāṅ, jā mat bides ko, kanthā, hāṭ mat khol! Hunar dekh mere hāth kā, kātūṅ sūt an-mol. Hin. Wom.

Go not, my spouse, to foreign lands, nor open a shop, my husband! Behold my dexterous hands, I 'll spin a priceless thread.

Saiyāṅ ke arjan, bhaiyā ke nāuṅ; Pahan oṛh, maiṅ sāsaṛ jāuṅ! Wom.

The earnings are my husband's, and the credit my brother's: I will dress myself and go to my husband's house!

(In Indian households the bride gets her wearing apparel and customary ornaments and her household utensils from her parents and relatives and these she takes with her to her husband. The point here is that her husband has had to supply these, and this has made the bride feel ashamed.)

Saiyāṅ ne is dunyā meṅ lākhoṅ rupaiye baṭṭe; Kadhī na lāē laḍḍū peṛe, ber khilāē khaṭṭe.

In this world my husband has made a fortune of millions; But he brought no sweets for me, only plums wild and sour.

(A wife complaining of her niggardly and rich husband.)

Saiyāṅ, tere kārne jal bal ho gaī rākh; Pat se maiṅ be-pat bhaī, panchan meṅ gaī sākh.

For thy sake, my love, am I burnt to ashes, and have lost my honor and been disgraced among my kind.

Sājan āvat hūṅ suno, kuchh neṛe, kuchh dūr: Palkan hī se jhāṛ lūṅ un pāvan kī dhūr!

I hear my love approaching nearer and nearer: And I'll brush the dust from off his feet with my eye-lashes.

Sajan bin īd kaisī? Mah. Wom.

It is no festival without a husband!

Sajan chale par-des ko, dhar ghoṛe pe zīn: Jo maiṅ aisā jāntī chābuk letī chhīn.

My husband is going abroad and saddles his horse! Had I known this before I would have taken away the whip.

Sājan dukhiyā kar gaē, aur sukh ko legae sāth; Ab dukh de niyāre bhaē, merī baur nā pūchhī bāt. Wom.

My husband has made me wretched, and taken my joys with him: He has made me wretched by leaving me and has sent me never a word.

(A woman's lament over an absent husband.)

Sājan ham tum ek haiṅ, dekhat ke haiṅ do. Man se man ko tol le, do man kadhī na ho.

I and you my love are one, though seemingly we are two. *Man* weighed against *man* will never make two *man*.

(There is a pun here on the word *man* which means both the heart and a weight of 80lbs; similarly *tolnā*, to weigh, is commonly used both in the abstract and concrete.)

Sājan prīt lagāeke dūr des jin jāo: Baso hamārī nagrī, ham māṅgeṅ tum khāo.

My love, once having loved, go not to foreign lands: Live you in my city and I will beg that you may eat.

Sājan sājan mil gaē, jhūṭe paṛe basīṭh. Wom.

When friend meets friend, the meddler is disgraced.

Sajan sakāre jāeṅge aur nain mareṅge roē, Bidhunā, aisī rain kar, ki bhor kabhī na hoē. Wom.

My love starts to-morrow and my eyes fade with weeping. O God, make such a night that there shall be no morn.

Sajan, tum jhūṭ mat bolo! Khudā ko sāṅch pyārā hai. Kahāvat hai baḍoṅ kī yūṅ, 'kadhī sāṅchā na hārā hai.'

My husband, do not tell a lie! For God loves the truth. It hath been said of old that 'truth injureth not'!

Sājan! voh din kaun the, jo sukh se lāē prīt? Ab dukh de niyāre bhaē:—kaun gāoṅ kī rīt? Hin. Wom.

My love, where are the days when you loved me with gladness? To go and leave me in sorrow now:—what manners are these?

Sājan! yoṅ mat jāniyo, toē bichhrat moē chain; Āle ban kī lākṛī sulgat hūṅ din rain.

Don't believe, my love, that I have pleasure in your absence; Like a green-wood tree, I smoulder night and day.

Sājhā bhalā na bāp kā, Aur tāo bhalā nā tāp kā. Mercantile.

Partnership even with a father is not good, Nor is a burning fever.

Sājhā jorū khasam hī kā bhalā.

The best partnership is that between man and wife.

(Natives have a notion that all partnership in trade is bad!)

Sājhā sadhe na bāp kā. Mercantile.

Partnership even with a father is not lasting.

(See preceding. An acknowledgment of the habitual dishonesty of native traders even towards each other. He would cheat even his own father.)

Sājhā sadhe na bāp kā; saē rāse kī khān: Ghar niyārā kar, bālmā; bāt merī tū mān. Hin. Wom.

Partnership will not last even with one's father; it is the root of strife: Keep a separate house, my spouse; please listen to my words.

(A wife's advice to her husband to secure a house for her apart from his parents, whom she looks upon as a great bore.)

Sājhe kā kām ukhāṛe chām.

A joint concern will tear off the skin.

Sājhe kī hāṇḍī chaurāhe meṅ phūṭe.

The partnership pot breaks where four roads meet.

(Partnership is the source of many disputes.)

Sājhe kī Holī sab se bhalī. Hin.
Partnership at the Holī is a good thing.
(One person of course being unable to perform the festival.)

Sājhe kī mā Gangā na pāve. Hin.
The mother of several sons will never reach the Ganges.
☞ Among the Hindūs, it is the duty of the son to convey his parent to the Ganges before or after death, a ceremony which is attended with some expense. Hence, if there are several sons, one leaves this duty to another, and it is not performed at all. Between two stools the breech comes to the ground. What is every one's business is no one's. Too many cooks spoil the broth.

Sājhe kī sūī sāṅj meṅ chale.
A partnership needle is carried on a pole.
(It is not easy for partners to agree.)

Sajjan chit kabhū na dhareṅ, durjan jan ke bol; Pāhan māre ām ko, tau jhal det amol.
A good man takes no heed of a bad man's words; Throw a stone at a mango tree and it will drop sweet fruit.

Sākh gaē, phir hāth na āē.
Credit lost cannot be regained.

Sakhī deve aur sharmāve, bādal barse aur garmāve.
The liberal gives with diffidence, as clouds when hot drop rain.

Sakhī ho, ham hūṅ rāj-kumār!
My dear, I, too, am a princess!
(A reproof.)

Sakhī kā berā pār, aur sūm kī maṭṭī khuār.
The generous succeed and the miser starves.
(Mendicant's cry.)

Sakhī kā berā pār hai.
The liberal man's boat gets across.
(*Berā pār honā* is an idiom to succeed, and also to obtain salvation.)

Sakhī kā khazānā kabhī khālī nahīṅ hotā.
A liberal man's treasury is never empty.

Sakhī, karīm paṛe eṛiyāṅ ragaṛte haiṅ; Bakhīl mūsloṅ se motiyoṅ ko chhaṛte haiṅ.
The generous and liberal drag on a miserable life: While misers grind pearls with pestles.
(The wicked flourishing like a green bay tree.)

Sakhī kā sar buland, mūzī kī gor tang. Mah.
The head of the bountiful shall be exalted, and the miser's grave shall be narrow.
(Beggar's cry.)

Sakhī ke māl par paṛe, sūm kī jān par paṛe.
A liberal man's wealth suffers, and a miser's life suffers.

Sakhī kī kamāī meṅ sab kā sājhā!
In the generous man's earnings all have a share.
(Beggars' cry.)

Sakhī kī nāo pahāṛ chaṛhe.
A liberal man's boat goes up hill.
(Success attends the liberal.)

Sakhī nā sahelī, Bhalī akelī. Wom.
Neither friend nor companion; It is well that I am alone.

Sakhī sakhāvat se phaltā hai, Adū adāvat se jaltā hai
The liberal thrive on liberality, And the envious burn with envy.

Sakhī se bhetā nahīṅ, to sūm se kyoṅ bigāṛye?
If you can't find a liberal man, why throw up the service of a miser?
(A bird in hand is worth two in the bush.)

Sakhī se sūm bhalā, jo turat de javāb.
Better is the miser who refuses at once than the giver.
(Who keeps you waiting)

Sakhī sūm kā lekhā baras din meṅ barābar ho jātā hai.
The account of the liberal and the miser is balanced at the end of the year.
(*i. e.* the liberal man does not lose by his liberality, nor the miser gain by his greed.)

Sākh lākh se achchhī. Mercantile.
Credit is better than a fortune.

Salah na shud balā shud. Per.
It was not an invitation but a misfortune,

Shāh Khānum kī āṅkheṅ dukhtī haiṅ, shahar ke dive gul kar do. Mah. Wom.
Shāh Khānum has sore eyes, so put out all the lights in the town.
(Throwing the burden of her own misfortune on the head of others.)

Singh chaṛhī Devī mile, garuṛ chaṛhe Bhagvān, Bail chaṛhe Shivjī mileṅ, aṛe saṅvāre kām.
When you meet Devī riding her tiger, or Bhagvān on the wings of his eagle, Or Sivā riding his bull, all difficulties will be removed.
(The above are the vehicles of the gods mentioned, and at religious performances are represented by actors, to meet whom is lucky.)

Salāmat rahe bahū, jis kā baṛā bharosā. Wom.
Long life to my daughter-in-law, in whom I have great hopes.
(Of posterity : a consolation at the loss of a son.)

Salām bisar miyāṅ jī kyoṅ rusāē?
Why offend my lord by not saluting him?
(Politeness costs nothing)

Sāle ke susre aur susre ke labaṛ-dhauṅ-dhauṅ!
A distant connexion of my wife's brother's father-in-law!
(Said of one who claims relationship.)

Salemo bin Īd kaise? Mah. Wom.
It is no festival without Salemo.
(Salemo is a fancy name for a showy woman.)

Sālī ādhī nihālī, salhaj pūrī joē. Mah.
A wife's sister is half a wife, a brother-in-law's wife is a full wife.
(If a wife die it is not uncommon for a man to marry her sister; the brother-in-law's sister is the wife and *his* wife is in many respects on the same footing as the wife in a native household.)

Sālī nihālī, chahiye orhī, chahiye bichhālī !
Your wife's sister is your bedding—to be worn or used !

Samaë chūk phir kā pachhtānī ? Bhoj.
Why regret a lost opportunity ?
(Why weep over spilt milk ?)

Samaë samaë ke dātā Rām. Hin.
God gives in every clime and time.

Samaë na bāram bār. Hin.
Opportunity comes not daily.

Samā kare (nar kyā kare ?) samen sam-n kī bāt. Kisī same ke din bare, kisī same kī rāt.
Each season does its seasonable work, and what can man do ? Some seasons make long days and some long nights.

Samajh kā ghar dūr hai.
It is a long way to understanding.

Samajhne-vāle kī maut hai.
It is death to those that understand.
(Where ignorance is bliss, I ween, 'tis folly to be wise.)

Samandar kyā jāne Dozakh kā azāb ? Mah.
What can the salamander know of the pains of Hell ?
(Because it lives in the fire.)

Samandar-sokh ko daryā kyā ?
What's a river to the sea convolvulus ?
(*Samandar-sokh*, is the *convolvulus argenteus*: a pun on the words here which also mean—one who swallows the ocean)

Same same kī bāt hai.
Each season has its own work.
(There is a time for every thing.)

Same same kī bāt; bāj par jhapte bagulā.
It is a sign of the times : the heron preys upon the hawk.

Same same sundar sabhī; rūp ku-rūp na koë.
Every thing is beautiful at its own time and nothing ugly.
(Every dog has his day.)

Samjhā aur patthar huā.
Who understands becomes a stone.
(*i. e.*, is not easily turned from his opinion.)

Samjhāë samjhe nahīn, man nahīn dhartā dhīr. Prohlād pahle banī, pāchhe banā sarīr.
They cannot understand, and are not patient. First was fate created and then man's body.

Samjhe so gadhā : anārī kī jāne balā ?
Who understands is wretched : the ignorant does not care.

Samjho, nā būjho : khūntā le-ke jhūjho.
You neither know nor see: you can only whirl about a club.
(Strength without skill: brute force: metaphor drawn from *gad kā-bāzī* or fencing.)

Samman, aisī prīt kar, jaisī kare kapās: Jīte to hurmat rakhe, aur mūë chalegī sāth.
O Samman, love as the cotton loves : That keeps up thy honor in life and goes with thee to thy grave.
(*i. e.* as clothes, it adds to your dignity, and as a cere cloth, it shrouds your corpse: Samman was a *sādhū* or saint and these are sayings popularly attributed to him.)

Samman ! aisī prīt kar jaise shakkar ghī : Jāt bhāt pūchhe nahīn, jis se mil jāë jī.
Samman, your love should be like butter and sugar; Have no distinction of caste with those with whom your life is cast.

Samman ! aisī prīt kar jūn Hindū kī joë : Jīte jī to sang rahe, mare pe sattī hoë !
Samman ! let your love be as a Hindu wife : With you in life and with you at death !
(By committing *satti* and burning at the husband's pyre.)

Samman, chūrī kānch kī : kaurī kauri dekh : Jab gal lāgī pīū ke, lākh take kī ek. Wom.
Samman, bangles of glass are but a farthing each, But when they clasp a husband's neck they are worth a million each.

Samman, dhāgā prem kā jin toro chatkāë : Tore par jo jor ho, bīch gānth par jāë.
O Samman, break not the chord of friendship : For when broken there will be a knot where it is joined.

Samman ! sānjh andher mān mūl bāt mat chāl; Jān ganvāve ek din, sang ganvāve māl.
Samman ! go never out in the darkness of night, Or some day you will lose your life and property.

Samman, sānsā mat karo ! sir par hai Sāīn ; Jo kuchh likhā lilāt men, bhejenge yanhīn.
O Samman, have no doubts ! There is a God above, Who will send thee whatever is written in thy fate.

Samman, voh din kaunse, jo sukh se lāë pīt ? Ab dukh de nīyāre bhāë, kaun gāon kī rīt ? Wom.
Samman, where are gone those days when you loved me with joy ? Now you keep aloof, and give me pain; what manners are these ?

Samman, voh phal kaunse, jo pakke pe karvās ? Kachche lagen suhāvne, gaddar karen mithās ?
O Samman, what fruits are those, which become bitter by ripening ? Are pleasant when green, and sweet when half ripe ?
(*Answer :* human life, in its three stages of youth, manhood and old age.)

Sāmne pānī bharā kalsā ā-jāë, to achchhā shagūn hotā hai. Superstition.
To meet a jar full of water is a good omen.

Sampat kī jorū; bipat kā yār. Hin.
In prosperity a wife, and in adversity a friend.
(*i. e.* a wife will stick to you in prosperity and a true friend in adversity : Indian habits.)

Sampat se bhetā nahīn, daliddar se tūtan. E.
No friend to prosperity and an enemy to adversity.
(A stupid man.)

Sānbhar jāë alonā khāë !
Go to Sānbhar and eat without salt.
(The Sānbhar lake is the chief place for

the manufactory of salt in Central India: To live in the meat market and have no meat.)

Sāṅbhar meṅ non kā toṭā!
Scarcity of salt in Sāṅbhar!

Sāṅbhar meṅ paṛā so sāṅbhar huā.
What falls into salt becomes salt.

Sāṅch barābar tap nahīṅ, aur jhūṭ barābar pāp. Jā ke man meṅ sāṅch hai, tā ke man meṅ Āp.
No penitence like truth, and no sin like a lie. Who keepeth truth in his heart, God dwelleth in him.

Sāṅche gurū kā bālhā mare na mārā jāë.
The perfect teacher's disciple can never die or be killed.

Sāṅchī bāt Gopālā bhāve.
God loves the truth.

Sāṅchī bāt Sādu'llah kahe, sab ke man se utrā rahe.
Sādu'llah speaks truth, and is disliked by all.
(The candid friend.)

Sāṅch ko āṅch nahīṅ.
Fire burns not the truth.
(The innocent have nothing to fear. The allusion is to the common ordeal by fire in India, the idea being that fire will not injure the innocent.)

Sāṅchoṅ koī na māne, jhūṭhoṅ jag patyāë.
No one heeds the truth, and all believe in lies.

Sandal ke chhāpe muṅh ko lageṅ.
May your face be bright with sandal wood.

Saṅg āmad o sakht āmad. Per.
When a stone hits it hits hard.
(Misfortunes never come singly: used also in the sense of 'difficult times require severe measures.')

Sangat achchhī baiṭhīye, khāīye nāgar pān; Khoṭī sangat baiṭh-ke kaṭāë nāk aur kān.
Form intimacy with the good, and eat the best betel; Form intimacy with the bad, and lose both nose and ears.
(Good will come of the former, and evil of the latter.)

Saṅgat kā parbhāo hai.
It is the influence of society.
(As the society so the man.)

Sangat kī phūṭ kā Allāh belī!
God protect the people from internal strifes.
(From all sedition, privy conspiracy and rebellion, Good Lord, deliver us.)

Sangat se phal hot hai; vohī til vohī tel, Jāt pat sab chhor-ke pāyā nām phulel.
Companionship bears this fruit: oil is from oilseed, But leaving its kind it becomes scent.
(*i. e.* by being mixed up with flowers and other ingredients.)

Saṅg soī, to lāj kyā? Wom.
After sleeping with a man what shame is left her?

Sāṅjhī chalī sāṅjh se sāth Basantā put: Mādho bhī to jāt hai, bāṅdh kamar ke sūt.
Sāṅjhī went in the evening and Basantā her son with her: And now Mādho goes away with all the thread round his waist.

Sāṅjh jāë aur bhor āë, Voh kaise na chhināl kahāë?
If a woman goes out in the evening and comes back at dawn, Is she not a harlot?

Saṅkh bajāo, sovo, sādhū, jo sukh pāve kāyā!
Sound your conch, and sleep, O saint, that your body rest in peace.
(Every cobbler to his last.)

Saṅkh bāje sattar balā bhāje. Hin. Superstition.
When the conch sounds, seventy misfortunes fly.
(The *saṅkh* is sounded as a call to prayer in Hindū temples.)

Sāṅp aur chor dabe par choṭ kartā hai.
A snake and a thief will not hurt you till they are hard pressed.

Sāṅp aur chor kī ḍhāk baṛī hotī hai!
Great is the fear of snakes and thieves!

Sāṅp kā bachchā sapoliyā!
The young of a snake is a snakeling!
(*Sapoliyās* or young snakes are supposed to be worse for poison than old ones. *Moral*: don't let a sinner off on the ground of his being a young one.)

Sāṅp kā kāṭā pānī nahīṅ māṅgtā.
Bitten by a snake needs no water.
(He will die before he can get it.)

Sāṅp kā kāṭā rassī se ḍartā hai.
Bitten by a snake dreads a rope.
(Burnt child fears the fire.)

Sāṅp kā kāṭā sove: bichchhū kā kāṭā rove.
Bitten by a serpent sleeps (dies): bitten by a scorpion weeps.

Sāṅp kā sir bhī kabhī kām ātā hai.
Even the head of a snake may be of use.
(Waste not want not.)

Sāṅp kā sir hī kuchalte haiṅ.
A snake's head is made to be crushed.

Sāṅp ke mūṅh meṅ chhachhūndar: nigle to andhā, ugle to koṛhī.
Like a muskrat in a snake's mouth: if he devours it he becomes blind; if he vomits it he becomes leprous.
(On the horns of a dilemma: the proverb expresses a common superstition that the snake to escape out of such difficulties has to go into water.)

Sāṅp kī sī kenchlī jhāṛnā.
He casts his skin like a snake.
(To recover from sickness.)

Sāṅp kī to bhāp bhī burī. Superstition.
Even the breath of a serpent is bad.
(Because it can scorch.)

Sāṅp, satāvā, dhokyā, tīnoṅ jīv nikāz: Jab lag pār basāë, baiṭh na in ke pās.
A serpent, an enemy, and a cheat, these three are the bane of life: As long as you can help it sit not near them.

Sānp, singh jit deh pakhāleṅ, Ḍhor, manukh hālan jūṅ hāleṅ. Rus.

Where snakes and tigers lay their limbs
Men and cattle shake like an earthquake.

Sānp mare, nā lāṭhī ṭūṭe.

(i) Let the snake die, but let the stick not be broken.

(In removing one evil, take care not to incur another.)

(ii) Neither let the snake die, nor the stick break.

(An amicable settlement of a quarrel.)

Sānp nikal gayā :—lakīr pīṭā karo !

The snake has gone off :—now destroy his [track !

(Too late to beat the shadow.)

Sānpoṅ kī sabhā meṅ jībhoṅ kī lapā lap.

In a company of snakes tongues do wag.

(Said of a company of great talkers and little doers.)

Sānp sab jagah ṭeṛhā chaltā hai, par apne bil meṅ sīdhā jātā hai.

The snake's course is always crooked, but he goes straight to his own hole.

(Crooked with others, true to one's own.)

Sāṅsā bhalā na sāṅs kā,
Aur bān bhalā nā kāṅs kā.

Anxiety even for a moment is not good,
Like a rope of *kāṅs* grass.

(Which is of no use.)

Sāṅsā mat kar, mūrkhā, ki sir par hai Kartār;
Vohī hai sab jagat kā sāṅsā meṭan-hār.

Fond fool, have no care when God is with thee, For he alone is the remover of the cares of all the world.

Sāṅsā Sāīṅ meṭ de, aur na meṭe koe. Jab ho kām sandeh kā, to nām usī kā lo.

God can cure all care, and none else. When thou hast an anxious business trust in him alone.

Sāṅsā sudh budh sabhī ghaṭāve. Sāṅsā sukh kā khoj miṭāve.

Care destroyeth sense and wisdom. Care destroyeth rest and ease.

(*Post equitem sedet atra cura.*)

Sāṅs sāṅs meṅ jītab ghaṭe, bāḍhā mūl na ho ; Is jītab par phūl kar mat bhūlo Hari ko.

Life wanes with every breath, and increases never ; Puffed up with pride of life forget not God.

Santan kī bānī sune prem sahit jo koë, Gangā ādī tīrath phal bin asnāne hoë.

Who listens with all his heart to the discourse of saints, Will obtain the reward of the Ganges and other holy places without bathing.

Sāṅṭe kī sagāī sedhe, tel kī miṭhāī sedhe.

A double marriage and sweetmeats fried in oil are both bad.

(*Sāṅṭe kī sagāī* means to exchange daughters in marriage : A gives his daughter to B's son and B his to A's son. This is done to save expense.)

Santokh kaṛvā, par phal mīṭhā hai.

Contentment is bitter, but its fruit is sweet.

Sapūtī rove ṭūkoṅ ko, nipūtī rove pūtoṅ ko. Hin. Wom.

The mother with a son cries for food, and the mother without one for a son.

(Every one cries for the moon.)

Sapūtoṅ ke kapūt, aur kapūtoṅ ke sapūt hote āë haiṅ.

Good men do have bad sons, and bad men [good ones.

Sārā dhaṛ dekh nāche morvā, pāoṅ dekh lajāë.

The peacock is delighted with his body, but ashamed of his feet.

(It has ugly feet.)

Sarāë kā kuttā har musāfir kā yār.

The dog of the inn is the friend of every traveller.

Sārā gāoṅ jal gayā, kāle meghā pānī de.

The whole village has been burnt, and now the black clouds rain.

Sārā ghar jal gayā jab chūṛyāṅ pūchhīṅ. Wom.

After the whole house had been burnt to ashes my bangles were noticed.

☞ A showy woman once put on a new set of glass bangles and went out to see her neighbours, hoping that they would be admired. But none of her neighbours took any notice of them, and so in her mortification she set her house on fire, upon which a great crowd assembled at the spot where the woman stood artfully wringing her hands in despair. One of the spectators, however, noticed her bangles at last and said "you have new bangles on to-day !" on which the woman replied in the words of the proverb.

Sarāhal bahuṛyā ḍom gharjāë. E. Wom.

Praise a daughter-in-law and she will go with a sweeper.

(*i. e.* praise will turn her head.)

Sārā jātā dekhiye, to ādhā dīje bāṅṭ.

When you see your all going, share half [of it.

Sārā khel taqdīr kā hai.

It is all the sport of fate.

Sārā navardā phirdī, kūāṅ dekh ḍardī. Panj.

After wandering through the whole desert, she is frightened at a well.

(*Navardā*, a desert, a terrible solitude: proverb alludes to the uncertain nerves of women.)

Sārang ne sārang gaho, sārang bolo āë ; Jo sārang sārang kahe, sārang mūṅh te jāë.

A peacock caught a snake, while clouds their thunder rolled ; When the peacock screamed the snake let go its hold.

(The peacock is said to scream and dance with joy at the sound of thunder : the saying contains elaborate puns on the word *sārang* which means a peacock, a snake, thunder, and the peacock's cry : it also means a musical measure, a cloud and a frog.)

Sārā shahar jal gayā, Bībī Fātima ko khabar hī nahīṅ. Mah. Wom.

The whole city burnt down and still my Lady Fātima is ignorant of it.

(Said of the selfish and indifferent to the affairs of those about them.)

Sāras kī sī jorī.
Like a pair of cranes.
(Inseparable friends.)

Sāras kī sī jorī ; ek andhā ek korhī !
They are like a pair of cranes ; one blind, the other leprous !
(Two bad people closely connected: *Arcades ambo.*)

Sardārī kā ḍanḍā aṭkā hai.
The badge of office still sticks to him.
(Said to one who won't condescend to take a lower place than that he formerly held.)

Sardhā ḍhāl jo pahne khāve, Vā ke ṭoṭā kadhī na āve.
Who eats and wears as his means permit, Will suffer no loss.

Sardhā lāgal kailoṅ bhatār, Ohu niksal jāt ke Chamār. E. Wom.
With great eagerness I took a husband, And then he turned out to be a Chamār.
(Chamārs are a very low caste : marry in haste and repent at leisure.)

Sardī kā mārā panaptā hai, an kā mārā nahīṅ panaptā.
Frozen out revives, starved out dies.

Sāre dhaṛ kī sūī nikāle, so koī nahīṅ ; āṅkh kī sūī nikāle, so sab koī. Wom.
Who takes out the pins out of the whole body is nothing; but who takes the pins out of the eyes only is every thing.
☞ Women especially are wont to have recourse to magicians in order to revenge themselves on their enemies; and one plan is to make an effigy of flour, prick it all over with pins and leave it in the *marghaṭ* or place of cremation, in the belief that the object of enmity will be similarly pierced and die. If, however, the pins are again extracted from the figure by the aid of magic, the dead person returns to life. The story goes that once upon a time the wife of a man thus slain, having extracted all the pins but those in the eyes, was obliged to suspend her work in order to go to prayer, the hour for which had arrived. A slave-girl, however, happening to come in drew out the remaining pins. The man returned to life, and believing that it was the slave-girl that had drawn out all the pins, forthwith married her and repudiated his wife.

Sāre ḍīl meṅ zabān hī halāl hai.
The tongue is the purest member of the body.
(An advice to speak the truth.)

Sāre din pīsā pīsā, chapnī bhar bhī na uṭhāyā. Wom.
She ground all day and filled not even the [pot lid.
(To describe one who has labored much to no advantage : he toiled all night and caught no fish.)

Sāre din ūnī ānī, rāt ko charkhā pūnī. Wom.
Idle all day, she begins at night to spin.
(To describe one who lets slip the proper time for work.)

Sāre nagar meṅ do hī; dhunakkar yā bhunakkar.
In the whole city only these two; carders and weavers.
(Low company.)

Sarese kā ṭaṭṭū banā phirtā hai.
He struts about like Indra's nag.
(Saresa is Indra : there is infinite contempt thrown into the proverb by the use of the word *ṭaṭṭū*, a worthless pony, a nag.)

Sāre shahar meṅ ūṅṭ bad-nām.
The camel is notorious throughout the city.
(Give a dog a bad name and hang him.)

Sarfiyāṅ rā magz bāyad chūṅ sagāṅ ; Nahviyāṅ rā magz bāyad chūṅ shahāṅ. Per.
A dog's brain for the Accidence, But a king's brain for the Syntax.
(Said of Arabic.)

Sārī choṭ nihāī ke sir.
It's the anvil that gets well hammered.

Sārī deg meṅ ek hī chāval dekhte haiṅ. Mah.
One grain tests the whole pot full.
(To see if the rice is boiled : judging the whole by the sample.)

Sārī khudāī ek taraf, Fazal Ilāhī ek taraf.
The whole creation on one side, and God's grace on the other.

Sārī khudāī ek taraf, jorū kā bhāī ek taraf.
The whole world on one side, the wife's brother on the other.
(Please the wife please her brother : love me love my dog.)

Sārī kuṛiāṅ mar gaī, nānī se rāh chale ? Panj.
Are all the young women dead, that you run after your grand-mother ?

Sārī Rāmāyan sun-ke pūchhā 'Sītā kis kī jorū thī ?' Hin.
After listening to the whole *Rāmāyan*, he asks whose wife Sītā was.
☞ Expresses one who from stupidity or inattention, after appearing to listen to a discourse betrays a total ignorance of the subject. Every Hindū knows the leading incidents in the *Rāmāyan*, as every Englishman knows those in the *Bible*, so that not to know who Sītā was would be like not knowing who the Virgin Mary was.)

Sārī rāt kahānī sunī, subeh ko pūchhe 'Zulekhā aurat thī yā mard ?' Mah.
He has been all night listening to the story, and in the morning asks, 'Was Zulekhā a man or a woman ?'
(*Zulekhā, vulgo Zulekhāṅ*, was Potiphar's wife; a story as well known in the East as in the West. The point of the proverb lies in the chance masculine termination of her name as vulgarly and commonly pronounced, Zule Khāṅ.)

Sārī rāt mimyānī, aur ek hī bachchā byānī. E. Wom.
The goat bleated all night, and produced only one kid.
(Great cry and little wool : goats usually produce two kids at a birth.)

Sārī rāt roī, aur ek hī marā. Wom.
She mourned the whole night long, and still one only had died.
(The conventional mourning for the dead is measured by time ;—to mourn *all* night

would mean the death of more than one person—hence this proverb has the same sense as the preceding.)

Sārī rāt soē, ab subeh ko bhī na jāgeṅ?

I have slept all night and shall I not wake in the morning?

(Better late than never.)

Saṛī sāhibī aur gach kā sonā.

Shabby gentility and sleeping upon a plastered roof.

(Applied to a mean person who aspires to great things.)

Sārī umar bhāṛ hī jhokā.

He fed the oven for the whole of his life.

(Passed his life unprofitably in menial occupation.)

Sārī umar kāṭh meṅ rahe, chalte vaqt pāoṅ se gaē.

He remained a life-time in the stocks, and in the end he lost his leg.

(In his hurry to get out of them.)

Sarkār se milā tel, palle hī meṅ mel.

If a ruler gives you oil, take it in your wrapper.

(Royal gifts are no inheritance: take it and be thankful.)

Sār parāī pīr kī kyā jāne an-jān?

What does one man know of what gives another pain?

(The wearer only knows where his shoe pinches.)

Sār sarāvat nā kareṅ byāh kāj ke bīch; Is meṅ dhan ko yūṅ samjh jaise kankar kīch.

Be not economical at a wedding; Look then on money as on dust and mire.

(A saying of the Brāhmans to encourage that extravagance at weddings by which they prosper.)

Sarsoṅ phūle Phāg meṅ aur sāṅjhī phūle sāṅjh. Nāh kadhe phūle phale, jo tiryā ho bāṅjh.

Mustard blooms in February, and twilight comes in the evening. But a barren woman shall never bear.

(It is a great abuse to a woman to be barren in India.)

Sāsaṛ kāran baid bulāyā, Sauk kahe terā dhagṛā āyā. Wom.

I called in the doctor for my mother-in-law, And my co wife says he is my lover!

Sāsaṛ sāṅsā mat kare, dekh thuṛairā kām: Thoṛe ko bahotā kare, den lage jab Rām. Wom.

Mother-in-law, grieve not because business is slack: When God is favorable little becomes much.

Sās bahū kī huī laṛāī, Kare paṛausan hāthā pāī. Wom.

When a bride and her mother-in-law fall out The neighbours intermeddle.

Sās, bahū kī huī laṛāī, Sir ko phoṛ marī hamsāī.

In a quarrel between mother and daughter A neighbour gets her head broken for nothing.

(To burn one's finger in another's porridge.)

Sās bin kaisī susrāl; Lābh bin kaisā māl? Wom.

Without his mother it is no husband's house; without gain there is no business.

Sās gaī gāoṅ, bahū kahe, 'maiṅ kyā kyā khāūṅ?' Wom.

The mother-in-law is gone to her village, and the bride thinks of what she shall eat.

(That is, what luxuries she shall enjoy in her absence: when the cat's away the mice may play.)

Sās jhāṅke ṭūīṅ ṭūīṅ, bahū chalī Baikunṭh. Hin. Wom.

The mother-in-law peeps out meekly and the daughter-in-law goes to Heaven.

(Said as a skit on a young wife who makes pilgrimages and leaves the old woman at home: by Hindū custom the young women live at home and old women go abroad.)

Sās kā oṛhnā, bahū kā bichhaunā. Wom.

The covering of the mother-in-law is the bedding of the daughter-in-law.

(Things upside down:—the Hindū bride is below her husband's mother in the household.)

Sās ke āge bahū ko kyā baṛāī? Wom.

In the presence of the mother-in-law, what is the rank of the bride?

(See preceding.)

Sās ke oṛhnā, patoh ke bichhonā. E. Wom.

The mother-in-law's covering is the daughter-in-law's bedding.

(See *Sās kā oṛhnā, bahū kā bichhaunā.*)

Sās kī cherī, sab kī jaṭherī. Wom.

The mother-in-law's maid is the mistress of all.

(*i. e.* all the women in the house are afraid of her.)

Sās kī rīsī patoh ke māthe. Wom.

The habits of the mother-in-law are copied by the daughter-in-law.

(Boys ape their teachers as monkeys copy their keepers.)

Sās ko nahīṅ pāeṅche, bahū chāhe tanbū aur sarāche! Wom.

The mother-in-law has not even drawers, and the bride wants a tent and screens.

(*i. e.* to be a grand lady, her position being below that of her mother-in-law; hence the sting of this proverb.)

Sās koṭhe, bahū chabūtre. Wom.

If the mother-in-law goes into the hall, the daughter-in-law will go out into the entrance.

(In imitating her she will exaggerate her follies; modest Indian wives should always stay at home.)

Sās, koṭhe par kī ghās. Wom.

A mother-in-law is like the grass on the roof.

(A worthless thing.)

Sās lukkā lukkā, bahū bukkā bukkā. Wom.

What the mother-in-law does secretly, the daughter-in-law does openly.

(See *Sās koṭhe, bahū chabūtre.*)

Sās mar gaī apnī arvāh tombe men chhoṛ gaī. Wom.

When my mother-in-law died she left her soul in the gourd.

☞ It is related of a strict woman, who had always kept her daughter-in-law in great restraint, that on her death bed she told her, that after she was dead she could deposit her spirit in a gourd, of which the girl was always to take advice. When the old woman was dead and gone the girl was in great fear of the gourd, and whenever she wanted to do any thing she first asked its advice as her mother-in-law had enjoined her. One day a neighbour, happening to come in when she was consulting the gourd, dashed the gourd to the ground and broke it into pieces, and thenceforth the girl enjoyed full liberty.

"*Sās morī mare, sasur morā jīe,*" *naī bahuṛyā ke rāj bhaē.* Wom.

When her mother-in-law dies and her father-in-law lives the bride reigns supreme.

Sās mūī, bahū betā jāyā; Vā kā paltā vā men āyā. Hin.

The mother-in-law died, and the daughter-in-law gave birth to a son; And so the account was balanced.

Sās na nandī, āp hī ānandī. Wom.

There is neither mother-in-law nor sister-in-law, so she is happy by herself.

(A sister-in-law is no less a disturber of the wife's peace in an Indian home than is her mother-in-law.)

Sāsrā, sukh bāsrā! Wom.

In your husband's house you will live in comfort!

(Advice to a young bride.)

Sāsre tere sāg, māthe tere bhāg: Bāp ke tere rāj, tū baiṭhī baiṭhī jhānk. Hin. Wom.

Comfort in your husband's house, and good fortune is to you: Royalty in your father's house, and you may only look on.

(A mother-in-law's rebuke to her daughter-in-law, when the latter extols her father's easy circumstances and deprecates her husband's petty means: a daughter has no claim to her father's estate according to Hindū law.)

Sās, ptsās, tujhe peṭ kā dukh; pahle chūlhā hī yād āyā. Wom.

Mother-in-law, your stomach is a trouble to you; your first thought is the kitchen.

Sās se bair, parausan se mātā. Wom.

An enemy to her mother-in-law, and a friend to her neighbour.

(A foolish woman.)

Sās se toṛ, bahū se nātā Wom.

Cuts with mother-in-law, and attached to the daughter-in-law.

(A foolish woman: the *sās* has the power in a Hindū house, not the *bahū*: always worship the rising sun.)

Sastā gehūn, ghar ghar pūjā. E.

When wheat is cheap, there are offerings in every house.

Sastā hansāve, mahngā rulāve. Agric.

Cheapness moves to laughter, dearness to tears.

Sastā rove bār bār, mahngā rove ek bār. Mercantile.

Cheap weeps oft, dear but once.

(Cheap and nasty.)

Sasta ūnt, mahngā paṭṭā.

A cheap camel and a costly collar.

(Said when a thing costs more than it is really worth.)

Saste ko dekh bhālke lenā chāhiye. Mercantile.

Think twice over a cheap bargain.

Sastī bheṛ kī ṭāng uṭhā-uṭhā-ke dekhte hain. Mercantile.

Lift up the leg of a cheap sheep.

Sāsū chhoṭī, bahū baṛī.

The mother-in-law small, and the daughter-in-law tall.

(The allusion here is to a second marriage with a small girl of a man, who has already a grown up son with a grown up wife.)

Sās udhalyā, bahū chhinalyā, susrā bhāṛ chukāve, Phir bhī dulhā sās bahū ko Sītā satī batāve.

Though his wife be a harlot and her mother a strumpet and father a scullion, Still will the bridegroom call them chaste as Sītā.

(A man will never speak ill of his own female relatives:—its an ill bird that fouls its own nest.)

Sasurār sukh kī sār: Jo rahe dinā do chār!

A father-in-law's house is the abode of rest,
If one live there for two or three days!

(Never outstay your welcome)

☞ It is said that once a *Kāyath* visited his father-in-law's house and finding that all his creature comforts were well attended he wrote down the first line of the above proverb. His brother-in-law judging from this that his sister's husband had taken a fancy to the house and not wishing him to outstay his welcome wrote the second line under it as a hint.

Sāte kī sagāī, aur biājū rupae kā ehsān kyā? Mercantile.

A betrothal for a consideration and money lent on interest confer no obligation.

Sāṭhā nāṭhā.

A man of sixty is a bull.

(Virility is supposed to last sixty years.)

Sat hārā aur gayā mārā.

Who eschews truth (or spirit) is ruined.

Sāṭhā so pāṭhā, bīsī so khīsī.

A man of sixty is a young elephant and a woman of twenty is past her prime.

(For explanation see above.)

Sāt hāth hāthī se rahiye, pānch hāth singhāre se,
Bīs hāth nārī se rahiye, tīs hāth matvāre se.

Keep seven yards off an elephant, five yards from a horned bull, Twenty yards from a woman and thirty yards from a drunkard.

(Drunkenness is self made madness.)

Sāṭh gāon bakrī char gaī.

A goat has eaten up the sixty villages.

The story is told of a king, who returning from the chase much fatigued, happened to go in into a beggar's hut. The owner showed him all the hospitality he was capable of, and welcomed him to his frugal fare. The king was much pleased with him, wrote him out on the leaf of a tree a grant for sixty villages in recognition of the hospitality he had recieved and started for his capital. Unfortunately a goat ate up the leaf and next day the beggar appeared at the royal court and shouted out the words of the proverb. The king recognized him and gave him a new grant.

Sāthī aisā chāhiye, jo sārā sāth nibhāē. Sāth na us kā lījiye jo dukh bich kām na aē.

A friend is he that is ever with thee. Hold him not for friend that is useless in trouble.

(A friend in need is friend indeed.)

Sāthī to vohī bhalā jo dhur de tujhāṅ puchā; Vā ko sāthī mat kaho jo chhoṛ adham māṅ jā.

He is a true friend that carries thee to the end; Call not him a friend that will leave thee half way.

Sāth jorū khasam kā.

Husband and wife make a good partnership.

Sāth kaun kisī ke jātā hai?

Who goes with any one (to his grave)?

Sāth ke līye bhāt chhoṛā jātā hai.

Food is deserted for the sake of company.

Sāth koī āyā, na koī jāē.

Nobody came with you, and nobody will go with you.

(Naked came I out of my mother's womb and naked shall I return thither. *Job* I. 21. We shall carry nothing away with us when we die.)

Sāṭh sās, nanad hoṅ sau, Mā kī hor na in sūṅ ho. Wom.

If a woman have sixty mothers-in-law and a hundred sisters-in-law, None will be like her own mother.

Sāth soī, bāt khoī. Wom.

When she slept with him, her honor was gone.

Sāth sonā, aur mūṅh chhupānā! Wom.

Sleep with a man, and hide your face!

Sāth so, peṭ kā dukh. Wom.

Sleep with a man, and be troubled in your belly.

Sāth to hāth kā diyā hī chaltā hai.

What you give with your hands will go with you (to the next world).

(A saying of the mendicants.)

Satī kuchā, patang māṅri, kesarī kes, gajdant, Sūr katārī, bipr dhan, mare pe lāge hast.

A chaste woman's breasts, a serpent's gem, a lion's hair and an elephant's tusks; A brave man's sword, and a Brāhman's wealth are not obtained till they are dead.

Sāt māmā kā bhānjā bhūkā hī bhūkā pukāre. Hin.

The nephew of seven uncles goes hungry.

(*i. e.*, no one feeds him or looks after him: everybody's business is nobody's business.)

Sāt māmā kā bhānjā, nautā hī nautā phire.

The nephew of seven uncles lives on invitations.

(See above.)

Sat mat chhāḍe, he piyā! sat chhāḍe pat jāē! Sat kī bāndhī Lachchhmi pher milegī āē. Wom.

Don't give up truth, my love; by leaving truth you will lose your credit; Fortune guarded by truth will come again.

(Conselation on losses by a wife to her husband.)

Sāt pānch kī lākṛī, ek jane kā bojh.

Sticks from several people make a load for one.

(Spoken when several persons each contribute a little towards the relief of one.)

Sāt pānch mil kīje kāj, hāre jīte na āve lāj.

When half a dozen do a job, no one gets the credit of loss or gain.

Sāt pānch pakuā, na ek gūlar. E.

One Indian fig is better than half a dozen *pakuās.*

(*Pakuā* is a wild tasteless fruit.)

Satrā bahatrā.

Seventy or seventy two.

(Fit for nothing: in his dotage.)

Sāt sau chūhe khā-ke billī haj ko chalī. Mah. Wom.

After eating up seven hundred rats, the cat is going on a pilgrimage (to Mecca).

(Spoken of a very wicked person, who pretends to have become penitent and religious: applied to old prostitutes who take a religious turn.)

Sattar chūhe khā ke billī haj ko chalī.

After devouring seventy rats the cat went on a pilgrimage (to Mecca).

(First sin then prayer: see preceding *Sāt sau chūhe khāke, etc.*)

Sattar kīne sāt ke, aur solah ke kiye sau. Byāj burā, re bālke; yā sūṅ rākho bhau.

Seven grows to seventy, and sixteen to a hundred. Usury is a bad thing, my lad; always fear it.

Sāt tavoṅ se mūṅh kālā karnā. Wom.

To blacken one's face with seven frying pans.

(To disgrace another, or one's self exceedingly: one *tavā* would of course be enough.)

Satt mān-ke bakrā lāē, kān pakaṛ sir kāṭā: Pūjā thī so mālan le gaī, mūrat ko dhar chāṭā.

True faith brought the goat and cut off its head; But the gardener's wife got the offering, and so the idol was none the better for it.

(A skit at idolatry attributed to Kabīr.)

Sattū bāndh-ke pīchhe paṛnā.

To tie up your provender and go on.

(To follow up an object persistently.)

Sattū khā-ke shukr kyā? Mah.
Why give thanks (to God) for a feast of *sattū?*
(*Sattū* is the flour of parched pulse and is the food of the very poor.)

Sattū man-bhattū, jab ghulbā, jab khaibā, jab jaibā; dhān bichāre bhalle, kūṭe khā- challe. E.
Pulse-meal is a pleasant thing; you knead, and eat and go your way; but rice is a pleasanter thing, for you simply husk and eat and go your way.
(Proving two and two make five, or black is white: specious argument: it takes very little time to prepare and eat *sattū*, but husking rice and then cooking it is a laborious task.)

Satvantī kā lāj baṛ, chhinārī ke bāt baṛ. Wom.
A chaste wife is very bashful and a bad one a great talker.

Satyā rahegā sab maregā.
The truthful will live, all else will die.

Sau aibon kā ek aib nā-dārī hai.
Poverty is as bad as a hundred faults.

Sau bairī katvān kahe, mastak likhā so hoë,
Lekh likhe ko, bālke, meṭ na sakke koë.
Though my enemies may speak ill of me, what is written in my fate will be;
What is written in my fate, my son, none can efface.

Sau bār terī, to ek bār merī.
If a hundred times be yours, one time will be mine.
(Said to thieves: you will be caught at last.)

Sau bāt kī ek bāt yeh hai.
There are a hundred words in this one word.
(*Multum in parvo.*)

Sau bharve maren to ek chammach-chor paidā ho; sau randī maren to ek āyā.
It takes a hundred pimps to make one stealer of spoons, and a hundred harlots to make one *āyā*.
(The "stealer of spoons" means the *khidmatgār* of European households in India: both these, and the *āyās* or maids are of notoriously bad character.)

Saudā achchhā lābh kā, aur rājā achchhā dāb kā.
Let a bargain be profitable and a king terrible.

Saudā bik gayā, dūkān rah gaī.
The goods are sold, the shop remains.
(Her bloom is gone, the frame remains.)

Saudā kar, nafā hogā.
Buy and sell and you will get profit.

Saudā līje dekh-kar, aur roṭī khāīye sek-kar.
Test your article before you buy it, and toast your bread before you eat it.

Sau ḍanḍī na ek Bundelkhanḍī!
A hundred clubs to one Bundelkhandī!
(The Rājpūts of Bundelkhand are reputed to be powerful men.)

Saudā saudāiyon, bāt nafe men.
Bargain for bargain and the flattery for profit.
(Allusion to the habits of native merchants to induce their customers to buy.)

Sau Dillī ujaṛ gaī, tau bhī savā lākh hāthī.
Though Dehlī has been ruined a hundred times, there are still a million and a quarter elephants in it.
(The elephant in India is a sign of wealth.)

Sau din chor ke to ek din sāh kā.
A hundred days are the thief's, but one day is the merchant's.
(A rogue may often escape detection, but will be caught at last. The pitcher goes often to the well, but breaks at last.)

Sau gāliyon kā ek gālā banāyā aur uṛā diyā.
I made a ball of his abuses and cast it to the winds.
(Forbearance: water off a duck's back. There are puns here—*gālī* means an abusive expression, a bad name: *gālā* a viler expression still and also a flake of cotton.)

Sau gāṛī na ek chhakṛā; sau harām-zāde na ek magrā.
One waggon is equal to a hundred carts, and one sulky man to a hundred black-guards.

Sau gāṛī na ek chhakṛā, sau sote na ek machlā.
One waggon is as good as a hundred carts, and one drowsy man as a hundred sleepers.
(None are so blind as those that won't see.)

Sau gaz vārūn, aur gaz bhar na phārūn.
I will sacrifice a hundred yards and will not give away one.
(Words without deeds.)

Sau gulāmon ghar sūnā. Mah. Wom.
Although there be a hundred slaves, the house is empty.
(If the master be absent.)

Sau gunḍā na ek muchh-munḍā. Panj.
One man with a shaven moustache will match a hundred reprobates.

Sau hāthī laṭ gayā, tau bhī savā lākh ṭake kā.
Though an elephant be old and decrepit, still he is worth a million and a quarter.

Sau jīvon kā ek bachāvā.
A hundred lives and one to preserve them.
(Reference to the working member of the Hindū joint family, on whom all the others depend for support and who has no right to any more than his own share in the total earnings.)

Sau kāliyon kā ek kālā.
He is as black as a hundred black men.
(A very great black-guard.)

Saukan burī hai chūn kī, aur sājhe kā kām.
Kānṭā burā karīl kā, aur badrī kā ghām. Wom.
A co-wife is bad though made of dough, and bad is a joint concern. Bad is the thorn of the acacia and the heat of a cloudy day.
☞ The *chūn kī saukan* of the proverb is founded on the story of a man who set up a flour model of an ideal co-wife, which he covered with rich dress and precious jewels and caressed and worshipped every day, in order to vex his living wife.

Saukan chūn kī bhī burī. Wom.
A co-wife though of flour is intolerable.
(See *Saukan burī chūn kī*, etc.)

Saukan gaī aur āṅkh chhoṛ gaī. Wom.
The co-wife is gone, but she has left her eyes (sons).

Sau kapūt se ek sapūt bhalā.
One good son is better than a hundred bad ones.

Sāū kā sāth bhalā, Aur rāt kā ghāt bhalā.
A true friend for companionship and the night for wickedness are the best.

Sau kavvoṅ meṅ ek baglā bhī nares hai.
One heron amongst a hundred crows is a prince.
(Both the heron and the crow are the types of what is bad in India.)

Sau ke rah gaë saṭh, ādhe gaë naṭ : das deṅge, das dilā deṅge, das kā denā kyā ?
Sixty remains of the hundred, let us remit half: ten I give, ten I'll get given and the other ten are not worth giving.
(Rebuke to a debter who shilly-shallies over payment of a debt.)

Sau khoṭoṅ kā voh sardār jis kī chhātī ek na bāl.
He is a rogue in hundred rogues who has no hair on his chest.
(A bodily defect is supposed to create mental vice.)

Sau kī hānī sahassar bakhānī.
A hundred lost is called a thousand.
(Men are apt to exaggerate a loss.)

Sau kosā aur ek masosā barābar hai. Wom.
One forbearance is equal to a hundred curses.

Sau lagīṅ tau kyā ? hazār lagīṅ tau kyā ?
If it be a hundred what does he care? If it be a thousand what does he care?
(Reference to blows with a shoe: the saying is applied to one who runs inconsiderately into debt; or to one who has already been frequently disgraced.)

Sau laṭhait na ek paṭait.
One foil equals a hundred cudgels.
(Skill has the advantage over brute force.)

Sau māre aur ek na gine.
Hit him a hundred times and count it not one.
(He is fit for nothing but a sound thrashing.)

Sau māre aur ninnānve se bhūl jāë.
Give him a hundred blows, but forget when you are at ninety-nine.
(So that you may go on.)

Sau meṅ phūlā ; hazār meṅ kānā ; Savā lākh meṅ ēṅchā tānā.
Wall-eyed against a hundred; one-eyed against a thousand; Squint-eyed against a million.
(Degrees of evil in people who are effected in the eyes.)

Sau naktoṅ meṅ ek nāk-vālā nakkū.
Among a hundred noseless men, one with a nose is called a *nakkū*.
(*i. e.* one with a great nose: a good man in a bad company is the worse for it.)

Saut bhalī, sautelā burā. Wom.
A co-wife may be good, but her child never.

Saut chūn kī bhī burī. Wom.
A co-wife even of dough is intolerable.
(See above *Saukan chūn kī*, etc.)

Sautiyā ḍāh mashhūr hai.
The malice of a co-wife is notorious.

Saut jāë, saut kā nāṛā na jāë ! Wom.
May the co-wife go away, but not her petticoat string!
(*i. e.* her husband.)

Saut kī mūrat bhī burī. Wom.
The very statue of a co-wife is intolerable.
(See above *Saukan chūn kī*, etc.)

Saut par saut aur julāpā ! Wom.
Co-wife upon co-wife and heart-burnings!

Savāb na azāb ; kamar ṭūṭī muft meṅ.
Nor sin nor virtue; my back has been broken for nothing.
(Said of unprofitable labour.)

Savāl dīgar, javāb dīgar.
Question one way, and answer another.
(Cross purposes and crooked answers.)

Sāvan ghoṛī, Bhādoṅ gāë, Māgh mās jo bhaiṅs biyāë, Jī se jāë ki khasme khāë. Superstition.
A mare that bears in August, a cow that bears in September, A buffalo that bears in January, Are sure to die or kill their owner.

Sāvan hare, na Bhādoṅ sūkhe.
Nor green in summer, nor dry in autumn.
(Always the same: an equable temperament.)

Sāvan kaisā sāṅthrā ? Poh, māh kaisā pāṅkhṛā.
A mattrass of straw in the autumn and a fan in winter.
(Are useless: the *sāṅthrā* is supposed to be a cool bed of straw among the poor.)

Sāvan ke andhe ko harā hī harā sūjhe.
Every thing is green to him who goes blind in summer.
(Applied in contempt to an official out of office, as implying that he regrets that he has no longer opportunities for filling his pocket.)

Sāvan ke rapṭe, aur hākim ke ḍapṭe kā kuchh ḍar nahīṅ. Hin.
It is no harm in slipping in Sāvan, or in being snubbed by a master.
(Sāvan being the rainy month in India all the roads get miry and slippery: usually it is very unlucky for a Hindū to slip.)

Sāvan khīr jo khāë sakāre, Mirag ḍhāl kurchāleṅ māre. Rus.
Who eats milk and rice in August Will bound about like a deer.

Sāvan kī nā sīt bhalī : jātak kī nā pūt bhalī.
Butter milk in August is not good; nor is the love of begetting children.

Sāvan mās bahe purvaiyā, Becho bardā, kīno gaiyā. E. Agric.
When east winds blow in August, Sell off your oxen and buy cows.
(East winds in Sāvan mean a good rainy season and when the rains are plentiful oxen will not be required for irrigation, and there will be ample fodder for milch cows.)

Sāvan mās chale purvaiyā, Khele pūt, balā le maiyā. Agric.
When East winds blow in August, The children play and the mothers cheer them on.
(See preceding.)

Sāvan meṅ hue siyār, Bhādoṅ meṅ āī bāṛ, "aisī bāṛ kabhī nahīṅ dekhī thī"!
In August the jackal was born, and in September he sees a flood and says "never in my life have I seen such a flood."
(Said of one who makes a great deal of what he has never seen before.)

Sāvan meṅ karelā phūlā; nānī dekh navāsā bhūlā.
The *karelā* blossomed in August, and the grandson's head was turned over his grandmother's (wealth).

Sāvan sāg na Bhādoṅ dahī, Kuār mīn, na Kātak mahī.
Eat not greens in August, nor tyre in September, Nor fish in October, nor curds in November.

Sāvan Sivā upās.
August is a fast to Siva.
(In the month of Sāvan the Hindūs, especially the worshippers of Siva, keep a fast in honor of Mahādev.)

Sāvan sove sāṅthre, aur Māh khurairī khāṭ, Ap hī voh mar jāeṅge, jo Jeṭh chalenge bāṭ.
Who sleeps on straw in September, on a plain cot in January, and travels in May, dies on purpose.
(In North India September is damp, January cold, and May excessively hot.)

Sāvan suklā saptamī, chhipke uge bhān, Kahe Ghāg, 'sun Ghāgnī, barkhā deo uṭhān'.
If the sun rises out of clouds on the seventh of the bright half of *Sāvan*, Saith Ghāg to Ghāgnī 'the rains are over.'
(*Suklā* is bright and the *krishnā* the dark half of the Hindū lunar month; the date in the proverb would be about the 22nd of July. Ghāg is the Hindū Hodge.)

Savere kā bhūlā sāṅjh ko bhī āve, to bhūlā nahīṅ kahlātā. Hin.
If what was forgotten in the morning is remembered in the evening there has been no forgetfulness.
(*Moral:* overlook a mistake that has been repaired.)

Savere kā ṭahalnā din bhar kī khushī.
A walk in the morning gives cheerfulness for the day.

Seh kā kāṅṭā ghar meṅ mat rakkho, laṛāī hogī.
Superstition.
Don't keep a porcupine's quill in the house or it will create strife.

Sej kī makkhī bhī burī. Wom.
Even a fly is insufferable on the marriage bed.
(*i. e.*, a co-wife however insignificant is intolerable.)

Seṅdur na lagāeṅ, to bhatār kā man kaise rakkheṅ? E. Hin. Wom.
If I am not to put the red-spot on my forehead, how am I to please my husband?
(The red-spot is the sign of coverture.)

Seṅdur ṭikulī jaral, to peṭo meṅ bajjar paral?
E. Wom.
If I have no red-spot, must my stomach starve?
(See explanation of *seṅdūr* in the preceding.)

Seṅt kā chūnā, dādā kī qabar. E. Mah.
Building a grandfather's tomb with unpaid for cement.

Seṅt kā māl, hirdā nirdaī. E.
The heart has no pity on easily gotten wealth.
(Easy come easy go.)

Ser kī hāṅḍī meṅ savā ser paṛā aur uphnī.
Put an ounce and a quarter into an ounce pot and it bubbles over.
(A light head is soon turned by a little success in the world.)

Ser ko dūdh, adhaun ko pānī, Ghammar ghammar phire matānī.
A pint of milk and a gallon of water, And swish swish goes the churn.

Ser ko savā ser.
There is a pound and a quarter somewhere for every pound.
(Every oppressor has some one who can suppress him.)

Ser meṅ pūnī bhī nahīṅ katī hai.
Of the pound of cotton not a skein is yet spun.
(Very little of the work has been as yet done.)

Ser meṅ panserī kā dhokhā. Mercantile.
He 'll cheat you five pounds out of every pound.
(A great rogue.)

Seṭh kyā jāne sāban kā bhāo?
What does a banker know of the price of soap?
(He deals in money only.)

Sevā aisī lābh de jūṅ gāṅḍā de ras. Sevā kī thī Dom ne, hue ek ke das.
Service yields profits as a sugar cane yields juice. A musician once did service and made tenfold profit by it.
(In India service is valued according to the picking attached to it.)

Sevā kare, so mevā pāve.
Who works will get the fruit.
(No gains without pains.)

Sevak saṭh, nirap kirpan, kunārī, Kapṭī mitr sūl sam chārī.

A stupid servant, a niggardly king, a bad woman, and a treacherous friend, are all as thorns.

Sevak soī jāniye, rahe bipat men sang; Tan-chhāyā jūn dhūp men, rahe sāth ek rang

He is a true servant, who remains with you in adversity, Like the shadow of the body that remains with you in the sun.

Shābāsh, miyān, tujh ko! Tū ne moh liyā mujh ko! Mah. Wom.

Bravo, my dear sir! You have taken my fancy!

(Ironical: also an assignation.)

Shabad bhed ko lakhā nahīn, to kyā ho pushtak chīnh līye? Jo dil dil-bar se milā nahīn, to kyā ho karvā kopīn līye?

What boots it to a man to read if he doth not understand the book? If the heart obtain not its desire what signify the bowl and *faqīr's* rags?

(A saying of the *sādhus*.)

Shādī gamī sab ke sāth hai.

Pain and pleasure are with all of us.

Shādī hai, kuchh guṛyon kā byāh thoṛā hī hai. Wom.

A marriage feast is not a doll's wedding.

(It is an expensive affair: also used when a man spends but very little at a wedding.)

Shādī, khānā abādī.

Marriage is the house of procreation.

Shāgird qahar, ustād gazab.

The oppressive servant of a tyrant master.

Shahad kī chhurī.

A knife of honey.

(A hypocrite: fair words and foul deeds.)

Shahad lagā-kar chāṭo.

Spread honey on it and lick it.

(Said of a paper or document which is no longer of use: a dead letter.)

Shahad, suhāgā, ghī marī dhāt kā jī.

Honey, borax and *ghī* are the essence of refined metal.

(All these are used as tonics in the native pharmacopea.)

Shahar kā gunḍā hai.

He is a city rake

Shahar kā salām, dehāt kā dāl bhāt.

The citizen makes a salute, but the villager gives pot-luck.

Shahar men ūnṭ bad-nām.

The camel has a bad name in the city.

(Give a dog a bad name and hang him.)

Shāhid vār vār, muqadme-wāle pār pār.

The witnesses are on this side and the parties to the suit on that.

(Cross purposes and crooked answers)

Shāhjahān būṛhe, bagal men chhaṛī, Khāte pīte bipat paṛī.

When Shāhjahān was old, and required a crutch, In the midst of plenty misfortune befell him.

(He was deposed and confined by his son Aurangzeb, in 1656 A.D.)

Shāhjī kī amaldār hai.

These are the days of Shāhjī.

(Shāhjī was the father of Sivājī, the great Marhaṭā, and was a thorn in the side of Shāhjahān and his successor Aurangzeb between 1635 and 1663.)

Shāh kā māl bhūīn paṛe dūnā.

When a banker's wealth falls on the ground it doubles.

(The wealth of a king is doubled by tillage.)

Shāh ke dūne.

The banker's profits are double.

Shaitān jān na māre, to hairān to zurūr kare. Mah.

If the devil will not kill, he will at any rate torment.

Shaitān ke kān bahre. Mah. Wom.

May the devil be deaf.

(May this not reach the ears of those, who will found a calumny on it.)

Shaitān ke kān kāṭe. Mah.

He has cut off the devil's ears.

(He surpasses him in iniquity.)

Shaitān kī ānt. Mah.

The guts of the devil.

(Said of a very long thing.)

Shaitān kī khālā. Mah. Wom.

The devil's aunt.

(Said of a very wicked woman, as a caution.)

Shaitān ne bhī laṛkon se panāh māngī hai. Mah.

The devil even seeks refuge from boys.

(That dreadful boy: it was the boy that did it.)

☛ The story goes that the Devil, who took a peculiar pleasure in playing with boys, one day appeared amongst them in the shape of a donkey, whereupon four boys got on his back; and a fifth, for whom there was no room, rode on a stick which he inserted *in anum*. This was too much for the Devil, who forthwith vanished and forswore their company ever after.

Shaitān se zyādah mashhūr. Mah.

More notorious than the devil.

Shaitān sir par chaṛh rahā hai. Mah.

The devil is riding on his head.

(He is under the influence of the devil.)

Shaitān tūfān se Khudā nigahbān. Mah. Wom.

May God protect us from the devil and his calumnies.

(Used towards a great and very artful calumniator.)

Shakal bhūt kī sī, nāon Albele Lāl!

As ugly as a goblin, and Beauty his name!

Shakal churail kī, mizāj paryon kā. Mah. Wom.

Ugly as an ogress and imperious as a fairy.

Shākir ko shakkar, mūsī ko ṭakkar. Mah.

Rewards for the grateful, and blows for the ingrate.

Shakkar dīye mare, to zahar kyon dīje?

If sweets can kill him, why give poison?

Shakkar-khore ko Khudā shakkar hī detā hai. Mah.
God gives sugar to the sugar-eater.
(God tempers the wind to the shorn lamb.)

Shakkar-khore ko shakkar hī miltī hai.
He that eats sugar will get sugar.
(See preceding.)

Shalīte meṅ mekh na rakkhe, lashkar meṅ Shekh na rakkhe.
Do not put a peg into a sack, nor a Shekh into a regiment.
(There are four classes of Musalmāns, Sayyids, Mugals, Paṭhāns, and Shekhs; of whom the last make the worst soldiers, being usually low-caste converts or descended from such.)

Shamā kā pusht aur rū barābar hai. Mah.
The front and back of a candle are the same.
(Said of an honest character, whilst an insincere man is compared to the earthen lamp (*chirāg*), the back of which casts a shadow.)

Shamā ke sāmhne chirāg kī kyā zarūrat?
Before a candle an earthen lamp is not needed.
(As it gives less light.)

Shamā kī raushnī jalte talak, aur dīye kī raushn Mahshar talak. Mah.
The light of the candle lasts while it burns, the light of a lamp till the day of Judgment.
(Pun on the word *diyā* which also means charity.)

Shām bhaī, din ḍhal gayā, chakvī dīnī roē, "Chal chakve vā des meṅ, jāṅ shām kadhī na hoē."
Night comes, the day declines, and *chakvī* weeping calls, "Come, *chakvā*, to that land, where evening never falls."
☞ *Chakvā* and *chakvī* are the male and female of the ruddy goose or *anas casarca*, which frequent river banks and have a plaintive cry at night. The natives have a legend that they are the embodiments of a pair of lovers, who "loved not wisely but too well" in life and so were cursed to be separated and to cry out to each other all night. The cry is "*Chakvā, maiṅ āūṅ?*" "*nā, Chakvī*" "*Chakvā*, may I come"? "no, *Chakvī*"—To which is replied "*Chakvī, maiṅ āūṅ?*" "*nā, Chakvā*"—"*Chakvī*, may I come? no, *Chakvā*.

Shām ke murde ko kab tak roē? Hin.
How long will you weep for him who died in the evening?
(*i. e.* it will be a long time before the corpse is carried to the burning place, as Hindūs do not burn their dead at night. So a man who has died in the evening, must of course, be waited upon till the next morning.)

Shamlā ba-miqdār-i-ilm. Pers.
His turban is as great as his learning.

Shunīda kaē bawad manind-i-dīda. Pers.
Hearing is not like seeing.

Shankā ḍāyan, mansā bhūt. Hin.
Our fears create giants, and our thoughts phantoms.

Shān meṅ kyā jufte paṛeṅge? Mah.
What detriment will your dignity suffer?
(Said to one too indolent or haughty, to help himself: also to one who thinks much of himself, or is above his work.)

Sharābiyoṅ se dūr hī bhale.
It is best to keep one's distance from a drunkard.

Sharāb Kāēthoṅ kī ghuṭṭī meṅ paṛtī hai.
Drinking comes to Kāiths with their mother's milk.

Sharāb-khār, hamesha khuār.
Wine bibers are always wretched.
(They spend what they can lay their hands on in drink.)

Sharāb se sab nashe nīche haiṅ.
Wine is the best of all intoxicants.

Shara meṅ sharm kyā? Mah.
What shame is there in lawful dealings?

Sharan gurū kī āē-ke, jo sumre Siyā Rām, Yahāṅ rahe ānand se, ant base Hari Dhām. Hin.
Who follows a prophet and calls on God,
Will be happy in this world and go to God's home in the next.
(Siyā is Sītā the wife of Rāma, now a synonym for God. Hari is Vishnū, also God: *gurū* is a religious teacher, a prophet in the sense of the *Old Testament*.)

Sharmāī billī, khambā noche.
A cat ashamed scratches at the pillar.)
(To hide one's shame: look foolish.)

Sharm che kuttist ki pesh mardāṅ biāyad. False Pers. [men?
Is shame a bitch that she should come to
(Said by the *literati* towards a shameless person.)

Sharm kī bahu nit bhūkhī mare. Wom.
A bashful bride is always hungry.
(When she goes to her husband's house: the bashfulness of native girls in a strange house sometimes prevents their eating properly.)

Shatranj nahīṅ, sad ranj hai.
It's not chess but a hundred cares.
(Allusion to the deep thought required by the game.)

Shauq dād Ilāhī hai.
Taste is a gift of God.
(*De gustibus non disputandum.*)

Shauqīn bahuryā, chaṭāī kā lahṅgā. E. Wom.
A gay bride with a mat for gown.

Shauqīn bībī, kammal kī cholī. Cholī meṅ āg lagal, tahlal phirī. E. Wom.
My fair lady has a blanket for bodice. The bodice is burnt into holes and still she struts about.

Shekh Chanḍāl na chhoṛe makkhī, na chhoṛe bāl.
Shekh Chanḍāl leaves neither flies nor hair.
(Applied sarcastically to a glutton. Greedy as a hog. Hindūs will not eat food with flies or hair in it. Chandāls are free-thinking *faqīrs*, who will eat any kind of food.)

Shekhī aur tīn kāne!
Bragging over three mites!

Shekhī kā muṅh kālā.
Brag has a black face.
(*i. e.* is disgraced. Pride goes before a fall.)

Shekhī-khore se kahā, 'terā ghar jaltā hai.' Kahā, 'balā se, merī shekhī to mere pās hai.'
Said one to Mr. Dignity "your house is on fire." Said he "never mind, my dignity remains!"
(Applied to one whose pride is not abated by external misfortunes.)

Shekhī seth kī, dhotī bhāre kī!
The dignity of a millionaire in a borrowed loin cloth!

Shekh kyā jāne sāban kā bhāo?
What does a nobleman know of the price of soap?

Shekh ne kachhue ko bhī dagā dī hai.
A Shekh can deceive even a tortoise.
(Spoken contemptuously of a deceitful person.)

Shekh ne kavve ko bhī daga dī hai.
A Shekh can deceive even a crow.
(In India the crow is noted for its cunning.)

☞ The story goes that a Shekh once planned a scheme to catch a crow, which was in the habit of drinking water out of his water pot and thus spoiling it. He put some butter on his mouth and lay on his back stopping his breath as if he were quite dead. The crow came and pecked at his mouth, when the Shekh instantly pinned its beak firmly between his teeth. The crow finding no escape asked him what his caste was, thinking to escape when he opened his mouth to answer. But the Shekh was too clever to be thus out-witted so he replied between his teeth pressing them down more firmly than before '*Shekh*.'

Shekhon kī Shekhī, Paṭhānoṅ kī ṭar. Yahāṅ na dhovenge, dhovenge ghar.
The brag of a Shekh and the pride of a Paṭhān. "If I am not to wash here, I'll wash at home."

Shekh Saddo kā bakrā hai.
It is a goat devoted to Shekh Saddo.
(Shekh Saddo is a malignant sprite much feared and worshipped by women.)

Shekh Sādī Shīrāzī ashiqoṅ ke bādshāh, mashūqoṅ ke qāzī. Mah.
Shekh Sādī of Shirāz was the king of lovers, and the judge of the beloved.
(Allusion to his erotic writings which are universally known in the East.)

Sher bakrī ek ghāṭ pānī pīte haiṅ.
The tiger and the goat drink at the same spring.

Sher kā ek hī bhalā.
One cub is enough for a tiger.
(One son is sufficient.)

Sher kā jūṭhā gīdaṛ khāā.
The jackal eats the leavings of the tiger.
(Popularly in India every tiger has a jackal to lead him to his prey.)

Sher ka khājā bakrī.
The goat is the prey of the tiger.

Sher ke burqe meṅ chhīchhṛe khāte haiṅ.
He eats offal in the vesture of a lion.
(To get a dishonest livelihood.)

Sheroṅ kā mūṅh kis ne dhoyā?
Who ever washes a tiger's mouth?
(Allusion to the dirty faces of little native children. The practice, however, arises from the notion that a dirty face is a protection against *nazar*, or the evil eye.)

Sheroṅ ke sher hī hote haiṅ.
Tigers beget tigers.

Sher Shāh kī dāṛhī baṛī, yā Salīm Shāh kī?
Which had the longest beard, Sher Shāh or Salīm Shāh?
(Said in reproof of ridiculous quarrels about trifles. Sher Shāh Sūr and Salīm Shāh Sūr were father and son, and Emperors of Dehli between 1542 and 1554 A. D.)

Shikārī shikār khelen, chūtiyā sāth phiren.
The huntsmen go for their sport and fools follow them.

Shikār ke vaqt kutyā hagāī.
When it's time to go hunting the bitch is purged.
(Spoken of one, who keeps out of the way when wanted under a false pretence.)

Shikār ko gaē, aur khud shikār ho gaē.
He went out to hunt, and was hunted himself.
(The biter bit.)

Shīn ke shaṭakke yā shaṛappe.
Gulping down *sh.*
(Said in reproof of one, who pronounces *s* as *sh.*)

Shiv japeṅ, nā Rām japeṅ, na Hari se lāveṅ het, Woh nar aise jāeṅge, jūṅ mūlī ke khet.
Who worships neither Siva nor Rāma nor Hari (Vishṇu), Will be ruined as ruthlessly as a field of radishes.

Shugl behter hai ishq-bāzī kā, Kyā haqīqī o kyā majāzī kā?
To be in love is a good thing, Whether spiritually or carnally.

Shukkar-vār kī bādlī, rahī Sanīchār chhāē: Aisā bole Bhaḍḍarī, 'bin barse nahiṅ jāē.' Agric.
Clouds on Friday and again on Saturday, Bhaḍḍarī says, will never pass away without rain.

Shuk sāro rākheṅ sabai, kāg na rākhe koē; Mān hot hai gunan teṅ; gun bin mān na hoē.
All keep parrots, no one keeps crows: Respect is shown to goodness; without goodness there is no respect.

Shutar gamze karte haiṅ.
They are making camels' eyes.
(They look upon us disdainfully or haughtily.)

Siār auroṅ ko shugan de, āp kuttoṅ se ḍare.
A jackal gives luck by meeting others; but let him beware of a dog.
(To meet a jackal is an omen of good luck.)

Siār ke mantrī kavvā :—chhoṛ dahale hāṛ chām, khāhale masvā. Bhoj.

The crow's advice to the jackal :—leave the bones and the skin and eat up the flesh.

☞ Todar Mal is said to have made a similar remark as to his financial operations in the Kāngrā Valley for his master Akbar. He took certain lands for the crown and the rest he allowed the loyal chiefs to keep ; and regarding these lands he remarked, that he had taken the flesh and left the chiefs the skin and the bones.

Sidhā ghar Khudā kā.

There is nothing crooked about the house of God.

(Spoken of a court of justice, easy of access to all.)

Sīdhī rāh chhoṛ-ke ṭeṛhī rāh mat chalo.

Don't leave a straight road for a crooked one.

Sīdhī ungliyon ghī nahīn nikaltā. Mercantile.

Straight fingers bring no butter.

(Natives put their hands into a butter pot and bend the fingers to get it out: hence this action, which is universal, is used as a metaphor to express that exertion is required for any result however trifling.)

Sīdhī ungliyon ghī nikle, to ṭeṛhī kyon kīje?

If you can get out butter with a straight finger, why bend it?

(When a case can be amicably settled why go to law? See preceding.)

Sifle kī maut Māgh.

January is death to the poor.

(Because of the cold.)

Sift bhī ho, muft bhī ho, baṛe pane kā bhī ho.

Stout and wide and for nothing.

(A good bargain.)

Sih-bandī ke pyāde kā āgā pīchhā barābar.

The future and the past are the same to a man on six pence a day.

Sīh, sānp se het kar, bhūton ke gal lāg ; Rānghaṛ uṭhe navāj ko to kos pachāse bhāg.

Be in love with tigers and serpents and embrace goblins and demons; But when a Rānghaṛ is going to prayer fly fifty miles from him.

(A skit at the Rānghaṛ tribe, who are very quarrelsome and quick to take life and property.)

Sikhāē pūt darbār nahīn jāte.

A son who has to be taught should never go to Court.

(*i. e.*, coached up witnesses never win a case.)

Sīkh det aurān ko Pānḍā, Ap bhare pāpon kā bhānḍā.

The Pandit preaches to others And fills up for himself a pot full of sins.

(Practise what you preach.)

Sīkhegā nāū kā, kaṭegā baṭāū kā.

A barber learns by cutting travellers.

(To express that every one seeks his own advantage, regardless of the injury it may inflict on others : a barber learns by shaving fools.)

Sikhī, sīkh paṛausan ko, ghar men sīkh jiṭhānī ko. Hin. Wom.

She teaches what she has been taught to her neighbour and her sister-in-law.

(Borrowed knowledge.)

Sikhnā na sikhānā, nāhaq sir phoṛnā.

He neither learns nor teaches, he simply worries his head.

Sikho, beṭā, soī, jā men hanḍyā khudbud hoī.

Learn, my son, what will keep the pot boiling.

(A father's advice to his son on entering school.)

Sīkh usī ko denī āchhī, jo terī sikshā māne sānchī.

He is worthy of your advice that trusts in it.

Sīkh to vā ko dījye, jā ko sīkh suhāē. Bandar ko kyā dījye, baye kā ghar hī jāē.

Teach him who can be taught. What's the good of teaching the monkey that destroyed the weaver bird's nest?

☞ The story goes that a weaver bird invited a monkey to build himself a shelter from the rain, in the following words : "*Mānas ke se hāth pāon, mānas kī sī kāyā, Chār mahine barkhā bītī, chhappar kyon nahīn chhāyā*"? "With man's hands and feet and a man's body, How come you to sit four months in the rain without a thatch over you?" He then taught the monkey how to weave a nest after his own fashion, but the result was that the monkey destroyed the weaver bird's nest in order to make one for himself without of course succeeding in doing so.

Sīlwant gun nā taje, augun taje na gulām ; Hardī zardī nā taje, khaṭras taje nā ām.

The virtuous never give up their virtue, nor the vicious their vice : As turmeric never gives up its yellowness, nor the mango its acidity.

Sīmāb kī khāsyat rakhtī hai.

Like quick-silver.

(Unstable as water, he shall not withstand.)

Sīncho ham hit jān-ke, in na karī kuchh kān, Chhātī pe painḍā kiyā, ochhe kī pahchān.

I nourished him gently as a friend but he heeded not, And made a way on my breast, this is the way of the low.

(The above couplet is put in the mouth of water, which nourishes wood in the form of trees,and these when grown and strong make their way in the form of boats and ships on the surface of the water in spite of all the advantages received from it: ungratefulness.)

Sīng kaṭā bachhṛon men milnā.

To drop the horns in order to mix with the heifers.

(Said of second childhood, and of a person who acts childishly.)

Sīng kī ke hūk? aur aranḍ kā ke rūkh?

Can you make a hook out of a horn? Or a tree out of a castor plant?

(*Hūk* is English and is now a universally used word in India.)

Sing parāē des meṅ, nit māreṅ nit khāēṅ.
A lion in a foreign country will ever prey and eat.
(Natives believe that lions leave their homes for prey! The proverb means that great robbers have to go to a distance for their victims.)

Sing se sarbar kare siyār.
A jackal vying with a tiger.
(Society upside down.)

Siṅkh sarappe to Lālājī ke sang gae; ab to dekho aur khāo. Hin.
Licking the broomstick is gone with my father; now you can only look and eat.
☞ It is said of a miser that he allowed his family only as much butter as could be drawn up on a broomstick out of a gallipot; when he was dead, he was outdone by his son, who used to place a sealed up pot of butter before his family to be looked at only. There is also a story of a Bangālī miser who sat by the river side with his platter of rice and at each mouthful, pointing to the river, consoled himself exclaiming "ā mashli, ī bhāt. There's the fish and here is the rice."

Sipah-garī ke chhattīs fan haiṅ.
There are thirty-six arts in the soldier's profession.
(Native notion on the subject.)

Sipāhī kā māl, jhāṅṭ kā bāl.
A soldier's property is not worth a hair.
(He possesses very little.)

Sipāhī kī jorū hamesha rāṅḍ.
A soldier's wife is ever a widow.

Sipāhī kī roṭī sir beche kī.
The soldier gets his bread by selling his head.

Sipāhī ko ḍhāl dharne ko jagah chāhiye.
A soldier only wants room for his shield.
(He will soon make the room required for himself.)

Sīpī se samudr khālī karnā.
Baling out the sea with a shell.
(A foolish act.)

Sir baṛā sardāroṅ kā, pair baṛā paldāroṅ kā.
Great men have good heads, and porters good feet.

Sir diyā okhlī meṅ, to mūsloṅ se kyā ḍarnā?
When your head is in the mortar, why fear the pestle?
(When a man is engaged in a pursuit which he knows to be perilous, he ought not to shrink from danger.)

Sire hī kī bheṛ kānī.
The very first sheep is blind.
(Wrong at the very outset.)

Sir gail sirvāhā hai.
As the head so the turban.
(To express that without a leader the people fall into ruin and confusion.)

Sir gālā, mūṅh bālā.
A white head and childish speech.
(Second childhood.)

Sir gāṛī, pair pahiyā, kare to roṭī miltī hai.
Make your head into a cart and your feet into wheels and you 'll get your bread.

Siṛī hai to kyā? par bāt ṭhikāne kī kahtā hai.
He may be a fool, but his words are wise.

Siṛī siṛī chhat par chaṛhte haiṅ.
Step by step the ladder is won.

Sir jhāṛ, mūṅh pahāṛ.
The head a bush, the face a hill.
(Said of a forbidding countenance.)

Sir kā bāl ghar kī khetī hai.
The hair of the head is one's own plantation.
(It grows and is pulled out at will.)

Sir kā nahāyā pāk. Mah.
He that bathes his head is pure.
(Applied to a decision, which comes from the fountain-head, or supreme power.)

Sir kā pāoṅ, aur pāoṅ kā sir.
The head and feet have changed places.
(Without order or regularity: upside down: topsy-turvy.)

Sir kā pasīnā eṛī ko ānā.
The sweat of the head reaches to the heels.
(The sweat of the brow.)

Sir meṅ bāl nahīṅ, bhāl se laṛāī. Wom.
No hair on her head and she fights with the bear.
(*i. e.*, she fights without proper preparation; being bald headed she is liable, so the native women think, to be more scratched than if she had hair.)

Sir muṇḍā-ke fazīhat hue.
Brought infamy on himself by shaving his head.
☞ It is said that a man shaved his head to become a *faqīr* in the expectation of getting his livlihood easily, but experience taught him that begging was harder work than working and he was thus put to shame: out of the frying-pan into the fire. Also, Hindūs shave their heads when a pilgrimage is accomplished and the proverb is a skit at a man who shaved his head without doing the pilgrimage and so brought ridicule on himself when found out.

Sir muṇḍā-ke kyā ghuṭnā muṇḍāoge?
After shaving your head, will you shave your knees?
(There will be no more left for you.)

Sir muṇḍāte hī ole paṛe.
His head was no sooner shaved than it hailed.
(Misfortune overtook his first venture.)

Sir nahīṅ yā sarohī nahīṅ.
Either no head or no sword.
(*i. e.*, may my enemy lose his head or I my sword: death or glory: pistols for two, coffee for one.)

Sir naqad, naukrī udhār.
Your head in cash, your wages on credit.
(I want your work now and will pay your wages hereafter.)

Sir par āre chal gaē, tau bhī Madār hī Madār. Mah. Wom.
The saw is across her head, yet she cries "Madār Madār!"
(Shekh Madār is a celebrated saint. The first sentence of the proverb is an idiom,

meaning to be in great distress, and the whole means that if you want to get out of trouble exert yourself.)

Sir par jūtī, hāth men roṭī. Mah. Wom.
Blows on the head and the bread in the hand.
(Disgrace endured, a meal secured.)

Sir sahlāven, bhejā khāven.
Pats the head and eats the brains.
(To pick the brains.)

Sir salāmat, to pagṛī pachās.
If your head be safe, you may wear fifty turbans.

Sir se kafan bāndhe phirte hain.
He wears a cerecloth on his head.
(Said of a desperate character, who is reckless of his own life and of course ready to take another's also: he carries his life in his hands.)

Sir se khāyā bhārī.
His testicles are heavier than his head.
(A big hat on a small head.)

Sir se utre bāl gū men jāo yā mūt men.
The hair once off the head may go into the excrement or urine.

Sir sijde men man badiyon men. Mah.
Bowings of the head and evil in the heart.
(Said of a hypocrite.)

Sir sir aqal, gur gur biddyā.
To every head its own brains and to every master his own teaching.
(As many men so many minds: *quot homines tot sententiæ.*)

Sir to nahīn khujāyā hai?
Your head has not been scratched yet.
(Said to one whose acts require chastisement.)

Sir to nahīn phirā hai?
Is not your head turned?
(Why do you talk nonsense?)

Sisakte gaē, bilakte āē.
He went sobbing and came back roaring.
(An unwilling or sulky servant.)

Sīs kāṭe, bāl kī rakshā.
To cut the head and protect the hair.

Sītal rakh sansār ko, jo tū bhī sītal ho; Tanak āg, re bālke, phūnk det jag ko.
Keep the world cool if thou wouldst be cool: A little spark, my son, can set the world on fire.
(In India coolness is synonymous with pleasure.)

Sīt, dūdh jis ne de Sāīn, vā ko to Baikunṭh hai yāhīn.
To whom God hath given curds and milk hath a heaven in this world below.

Sītla kā khājā.
The food of small-pox.
(Said of a man who is much pitted with small-pox.)

Sītlā kā pujāpā.
An offering to small-pox.
(Applied to a person, whose members are disproportioned or ill put together. Sītlā is the goddess of small-pox, and "offerings" are usually made of worthless things, hence point of the proverb.)

Sītlā kā thārā.
The abode of small-pox.
(Said of a man much pitted with small-pox.)

Sivaīyon bin Īd kaisī? Mah. Wom.
It is no Īd without vermicelli.
(It is no Christmas without plum cake. At the *Idu'lfitr*, or festival at the close of the *Ramazān* fast, Muhammadans eat *sivaiyāṅ* or *semīān*, a kind of vermicelli.)

Siyāhī bālon kī gaī, dil kī ārzū na gaī.
The blackness has gone from his hair, but not desire from his heart.
(An amorous old rake.)

Siyāh karo yā safaid.
Do it black or white.
(*Carte blanche.*)

Siyālkoṭī, harām boṭī.
The very bones of the Siyālkoṭīs are wicked.
(A skit at the people of Siyālkoṭ in the Panjāb.)

Siyām na chhoṛo, chhoṛo na set: Donon māro ek hī khet.
Leave nor black nor white; But kill them both at once.
☞ The story goes that a man had two co-wives, who died and turned into black and white kites, and haunted a third wife he married later. The proverb embodies her advice to him.

Siyānā kavvā khe khāē.
A wise crow will eat dung.
(To describe a person who conceives himself to be very prudent, but falls into a palpable blunder.)

Siyāne kā gūh tīn jagah.
A clever man's ordure goes into three places.
(Applied to one, who pretends to superior wisdom, and falls into a ridiculous mistake. The phrase supposes one of this description to have trodden on some ordure, and not being satisfied with the first impression and with wiping his foot on the grass, to examine it accurately, by first putting to his hand and then his nose to it.)

Siyāne to hain bahut se, sab se siyānā chho; Hīnā dekh ho chaugunā, ṭhāḍe par kam ho.
There are many wise, but the wisest of all is wrath, Which falls four-fold on the weak and gently on the strong.

Soā so chūkā.
Who sleeps fails.

Sobhā lāven manukh ko surat, phurat aur gyān: Jis men yeh tīnon nahīn, ve nar ḍhor pahchhān.
Wit, smartness and wisdom are the ornaments of man: Who hath not these is no better than a beast.

Sobhā ran kī sūrmā, ghar kī sobhā bīr, Raj kī sobhā chāndnī, bhojan sobhā khīr.
The warrior is the beauty of the battle field, the wife of the house, The moon-light of the night and rice and milk of food.

Soch-ke chalnā, musāfir, yeh ṭhagoṅ kā gāoṅ hai.
Mind your steps, wayfarer, this is a village of murderers.

Sochnā jī mochnā.
Anxiety gnaws at the heart.

Sohbat kā asar hai.
The effects of companionship.
(A man is known by the company he keeps.)

Sohnī būā, aur chaṭāī kā lahṅgā! Wom.
A handsome old lady and a mat for her gown!

So jāē supne meṅ prānī, dhan daulat ko pāve;
Jāg paṛe jaise ko taise, hāth kachhū nahīṅ āve:
Supne kī sī māyā jis ko apnī batlāve.
A man may sleep and dream of wealth and riches; But when he wakes he finds himself as before with nothing in his hands: So are but a dream the riches which man calls his own.

Somin pūchhe som se, kahe badan malīn?
Kā gāṅṭhī se gir paṛā? Kā kāhū ko kuchh dīn?'
'Nā gāṅṭhī se kuchh gir paṛā, nā kāhū ko dīn;
Dete dekhā aur ko, tāte badan malīn.'
Saith a miser's wife to a miser, 'why look you so sad? Have you dropped aught from your pocket, or given aught away?' 'Naught have I dropped from my pocket, naught have I given away; I saw another give, and for this am I so sad.'

Sonā chāṅdī āg hī meṅ parkhe jāte haiṅ.
Gold and silver are best tried in the fire.
(Trouble tests the quality of men.)

Sonā chhūe to maṭṭī ho jāē.
If he touches gold it turns to clay.
(An unfortunate man.)

Sonā jāne kase, aur mānas jāne base.
Gold is tested by the touch-stone, and a man by living with him.

Sonā-jhonā kuchh zāt nahīṅ. Wom.
Wealth is not caste.

Sonā kahe sunār se, 'uttam mhārī jāt.
Kāle mūṅh kī ghūṅgchī tule hamare sāth'!
'Ham lāloṅ kī lālṛī, lāl hamārā raṅg;
Kālā mūṅh jab se huā, tulī nīch ke saṅg.'
Says gold to the goldsmith, 'I am of the highest caste, And yet a black-faced weight is weighed with me!' (Answered the carat) 'I am the best of rubies, and red my hue, My face has become blackened by being weighed with the low.'
(There are elaborate puns in this saying: gold is weighed against carats in India made of small red black-faced weights called *ghūṅgchī*. *Lāl* red also means ruby.)

Sonā le-ke maṭṭī bhī nahīṅ detā. Mercantile.
He would not return even clay for the gold he had borrowed.
(A bad debt.)

Sonā lene pī gae, aur sūnā kar gaē des; Sonā milā, na pī phire: rūpā ho gae kes.
My husband went for gold and made my home dreary; I neither got my gold nor has he returned: only my hair has gone (silver) white.

Sonā nīk, to kān pharāe ke? E. Wom.
If gold is good, it will not tear the ear.

Sonā pānā aur khonā dono bure. Superstition.
To find gold or lose it are both bad.

Sonā sugandh hai.
It is golden and fragrant.
(It is very excellent.)

Sonā sunār kā, abhran sansār kā.
The ornament is the wearer's, but the gold remains with the goldsmith.

☞ It is said that a king once asked a goldsmith, how many *ānās* in the rupee he was wont to appropriate. He replied the whole sixteen. To put him to the test, the king ordered him to make a golden image, and caused a strict watch to be placed over him night and day during the execution of the work. Before entering on his task within the palace walls, the goldsmith made a brass image, which he left at his own house in his wife's pot of tyre. When the golden image was made, the goldsmith said to the watchmen, 'Now one thing only is wanting. It must be immersed in an acid.' Accordingly, by previous arrangement his wife at that moment passed by calling "*lo dahī*" (Who will buy my tyre?), and was called in by the goldsmith who pretended to buy her tyre for his acid, and slipped his golden image into the pot and took out the brass he had placed there.

Sonā uchhālte chale jāo.
You can go along tossing gold.
(Used to express the security in which the subjects live under a good government.)

Sone kā garvā aur pītal kī peṅdī.
A golden pot with a brass bottom.
(Spoken of persons or things which possess excellent qualities along with great defects.)

Sone kā nivālā khilāiye, aur sher kī nazroṅ se dekhiye.
Rear and nourish with kindness, but chastise with severity.
(Spare the rod, spoil the child.)

Sone kī aṅgūṭhī, pītal kā ṭāṅkā, māṅ chhināl, pūt bāṅkā.
A ring of gold patched up with brass, is a harlot's son that is a fop.

Sone kī baṛerī, phūs kā chhappar!
A golden ridge pole for a thatched roof!

Sone kī chiṛyā hāth lagī hai.
A bird of gold has come into our hands.
(To meet with a liberal patron or benefactor: also said by pleaders and court officials, (*amla*) when a rich man comes into their clutches: also said by begging Brāhmans at the death of a rich man when they receive largesses.)

Sone kī chiṛyā hāth se uṛ gaī.
The bird of gold has flown out of my hands.
(The converse of the above.)

Sone kī kaṭārī ko koī peṭ meṅ nahīṅ mārtā.
No one stabs himself even with a golden dagger.
(Life is too precious to be risked for gold.)

Sone kī kaṭorī meṅ kaun bhīk na degā ?
Who would not give alms into a golden cup ?
(A handsome young woman finds no difficulty in getting a husband; also, people are ready enough to lend money to the rich.)

Sone ko salām, rūpe ko alek, bhūke ko na dekh.
Say *salām* to gold, and *alek* to silver; but don't look at the poor.
(Salute the rich, but not the poor: *salām alek*, a corruption of the Arabic *salām alaikum*, peace be upon thee, is the usual form of salutation among Muhammadans.)

Sone meṅ pīlī, motiyoṅ meṅ dhaulī. Wom.
She is yellow with gold and white with pearls.
(Richly decorated with ornaments.)

Soṅṭā bal bin kām na āve, Bairī chhīn tujhe judkāve.
Your club is of no use without strength, For then enemy can snatch it away to thrash you with.

Soṅṭā hāth deh meṅ hāṅgā, Us ne bheṅṭe sab kuchh māṅgā.
With a club in his hand and strength in his body, He can get whatever he asks for.
(Might is right.)

Soṅṭe, chal, ab terī bārī.
Go on, club, it's your turn.
☛ It is said that Shekh Chillī, a typical fool, once asked his mother to cook him some food for a short trip, which he intended to make. His mother made him four loaves which he took for his journey. At the end of first stage he seated himself in the cool shade of a tree (which happened to be haunted by four fairies) and placing the four pieces of bread before him said to himself "I may eat one, I may eat two, I may eat three, or I may eat all four." The four fairies thought him to be some great demon who intended to eat up all of *them* and so they begged him to spare them and promised to give him some wonderful thing. To this Shekh Chillī agreed. So they gave a magic frying pan and told that it would supply him with as much bread as he might want. Shekh Chillī returned with the booty and on his way home stayed at an inn, to the keeper of which he boastingly revealed the secret virtue of the frying pan. The innkeeper being a great rogue and Shekh Chillī, a fool, the latter was cheated out of the frying pan, which was replaced by another. The next morning when Shekh Chillī came to his mother in great glee and revealed the hidden mystery of the frying pan, she took it with hesitation and put it on a stove for trial. It did not of course answer her expectations and Shekh Chillī was greatly mortified. Next day he resolved to go again on the same road and asked his mother to bake him another four loaves. She did so and he started. When he came to the same tree he repeated his former words to his four loaves of bread. This greatly shocked the fairies who rightly conjectured that he must have been cheated out of their former gift. So they gave him a rope, and a club, telling him that by their means he would recover his stolen property. Shekh Chillī on his return put up at the same inn and threw down the rope at full length, saying "Fasten all the men present, you rope." The rope instantly tied up all the men. Next he cast down his club and said "Now, club, it is your turn," whereon the club began to pommel all the men present, till the innkeeper owned his fault and gave up the miraculous frying pan, which Shekh Chillī brought home in great triumph.

Sone se ghaṛāī mahṅgī.
The workmanship is dearer than the gold.

Soraṭh mīṭhī rāgnī, ran mīṭhī talvār, Jāṛe mīṭhī kāmlī, sejoṅ mīṭhī nār.
Sweet is the *soraṭh* tune, sweet a sword in the battle-field, Sweet a blanket in winter, and sweet a woman in bed.

Sotā nāg jagānā.
To wake a sleeping snake.
(To wake a sleeping lion: let sleeping dogs lie.)

Sote kā kaṭṛā, jāgte kī kaṭyā.
The bull buffalo for the sleeper and the cow for the wide awake.
(To sleep is to lose. A female buffalo is more valuable on account of her milk than a male one, which is only used for carrying burdens.)

Sote kā mūṅh kuttā chāṭe.
A dog can lick the sleeper's mouth.
(When the cat's away, the mice may play.)

Sote ko sotā kab jagātā hai ?
How shall a sleeper wake a sleeper ?
(Shall the blind lead the blind ?)

Sote laṛke kā mūṅh chūmā, na māṅ khush na bāp khush.
To kiss a sleeping child is no pleasure to its father or mother.
(To do a man a favor without his knowledge brings no thanks.)

Sotī bhiṛ jagānā.
To wake sleeping wasps.
(Let sleeping dogs lie.)

Sotī ṛāṛ jagānā.
To wake up a sleeping quarrel.
(See preceding.)

Sotī thī, par kātā nahīṅ, jo kātā to pāṅch pāo. Wom.
I was sleeping and did not spin, but when I began, I spun one and a quarter.
(A skit at an idler.)

Sot kā pānī pāk.
Running water is purest.

Sove bhāṛ par, supnā dekhe dharohaṛ kā.
He sleeps on the oven, and dreams of treasures.
(*Bhāṛ par sonā*, idiom for extreme poverty. *Chateaux en Espagne.*)

Sovegā so khovegā, jāgegā so pāvegā.
Who sleeps loses, who wakes gets.
(To sleep is to lose. Early to bed and early to rise Makes a man healthy, wealthy and wise.)

Sove rājā kā pūt yā jogī abdhūt.
You must be a prince or an ascetic to sleep soundly.
(Ordinary natives have a notion that princes are free from care !)

Soyā aur mūā barābar.
Sleep and death are the same.
(The sleeping and the dead are but as pictures: sleep the twin brother of death.)

Suāṅs suāṅs meṅ Krishn raṭ, suāṅs birthā mat kho: Nā jānūṅ yā suāṅs kā yehī ant na ho.
Call on God with every breath, don't pass a breath in vain: Who knows but that this will be your last breath.

Suarg se utrā, babūl meṅ atkā.
It descended from heaven, but stuck in an acacia.
(The *babūl* is a very thorny tree. The saying is used of Government officials who are apt to stick to money that passes through their hands.)

Sūā semal dekh-ke, sabhī gaṅvāī budh:
Phūl dekh-ke ram rahe, phal kī rahī na suddh.
A parrot seeing a *semal* flower lost his senses: Stuck to the flower and forgot the fruit.
(The *semal* tree with its beautiful flowers and want of shade and fruit is a standing synonym for what is delusive in the world.)

Suāt-būṅd sīpī mukat. kadlī bhayo kapūr,
Kāre ke mukh bikh bhayo; sangat sobhā, Sūr.
The rain-drop in Suāt makes pearls in shells, camphor in plantains, And poison in a snake's month: (behold the effect of) association (saith) Sūr Dās.
☞ The proverb embodies a series of superstitions associated with rain which falls during the lunar asterism Swāti (Arcturus). Sūr Dās was a celebrated Bhagat or a Mediæval (religious) Hindū reformer.

Subah hī subah Khudā kā nām lo! Mah.
Begin the day in the name of God.
(Said in reproof of one who begins the day with a lie on his tongue, or says or does anything improper.)

Subah hotī hai shām hotī hai! Umr yūṅhī tamām hotī hai.
Now morning and now evening! Thus pass our lives.
(Fleeting life.)

Subah kā bhūlā, shām ko āve, tau bhī bhūlā nahīṅ kahlātā.
If what was forgotten in the morning be remembered in the evening it cannot be called forgetfulness.

Subah kī bohnī, aur Allāh miyāṅ kī ās. Mercantile.
Take the morning handsell and put your trust in God.
(It is a common superstition that it is very unlucky to refuse handsell.)

Subah kī nāṅh achchhī nahīṅ. Superstition.
Nay in the morning bodes no good.
(A saying of the Banyās—never refuse handsell: see preceding.)

Sudh aur chho kā bair hai, chho āvat sudh jā:
Uhī nar bhar-pūr hai, jo sudh na det gaṅvā.
Wisdom and anger are at variance; when anger comes wisdom goes: He is a perfect man that lets not wisdom go.

Sudh budh apnī ṭhīk rakh, jab tujhe āve chho: Chho hai bhūt bigāṛvā: is kā mīt na ho.
Anger is a devil; have no love for it; If anger seize thee keep thy senses straight.

Sudh budh nā kho āpnī, bāt ne merī mān. Is dunyā rahnā nahīṅ; mat nā ho anjān.
Put not away thy sense, but listen to my words. Thou shalt not remain in this world: forget not this.
(A saying of *faqīrs*.)

Sūdhe kā mūṅh kuttā chāṭe.
A dog may lick the face of the simple.

Sudh sūṅ sudhreṅ kār sab, sudh bin hot bigāṛ:
Aisā sudh bin hai manukh jaisā pāthar, jhāṛ.
It is skill that does the work, without skill it is spoilt: A man without skill is like a stone or a bush.

Sufaid bāl maut kā paigām.
Hoary hairs are the harbinger of death.

Sufaid bāl javānī kā zavāl.
White hair is the sign of declining years.

Sufārish bagair rozgār nahīṅ miltā.
Without interest you cannot get a berth.

Sugandh lagāūṅ to ūbh marūṅ, ūbh marūṅ pahne tan sārī, Hār chaṅbelī kā bhārī lagat, tum jānat ho tan kī sukhvārī!
Scent is a nuisance and my gown is a nuisance And a flower garland is heavy upon me—as I am so delicate!
(Affected delicacy)

Sughaṛ balaiyāṅ susrā le, Bail māṅg bahū ke de. Agric.
If the bride be clever her father-in-law will caress her, And get her oxen on credit.

Sughaṛ sughaṛ haṅs gaīṅ phūaṛoṅ ko āyā hāṅsā. Wom.
The simpleton laughs aloud where the wise woman smiles.

Suhāgan kā pūt pichhvāṛe khele hai.
The married woman's child plays at the back of the house.
(If a child dies, a married woman has hopes of supplying his place. The phrase is used when speaking of losses sustained by a person who has a good income, and is able soon to repair them.)

Suhāg bhāg arzānī, chūlhe āg na ghaṛe pānī. Mah. Wom.
Wedlock's joys are cheap, but there's no fire in the hearth nor water in the pitcher.
(An unhappy marriage.)

Sūhā jog suhāg kā aur kūp jog hai nīr, Gur biddyā kā jog hai; soch samajh, re bīr.
The red spot becomes coverture, and water becomes a well, Learning becomes a teacher; remember this, my brother.
(A red spot on the forehead is a sign of coverture among Hindū women.)

Suhāte kī lāt, na-suhāte kī bāt.
Better the kicks of a pleasant man than the speech of an unpleasant one.

Sūhe kī rīt nahīṅ, mashrū kī taufīq nahīṅ.
Wom.
Red garments are not customary, and silk not procurable.
(The horns of a dilemma.)

Suī chor, so bajjar chor.
Steal a needle, steal a thunderbolt.
(The sin is in the fact, not in the amount.)

Suī jahāṅ na jāē, vahāṅ sūā ghuseṛte haiṅ.
Where a needle cannot pass, they thrust in a skewer.
(To strain at a gnat and swallow a camel.)

Suī kā bhālā ho gayā.
Making a spear of a needle.
(Making a mountain out of a mole-hill.)

Suī kahe 'maiṅ chhedūṅ chhedūṅ,' pahle chhed karāē.
The needle says "I'll pierce, I'll pierce," but first it's pierced itself.
(He sees the mote in his neighbour's eye, but perceives not the beam in his own eye.)

Suī, katarnī, gaz, unglaiṭā rakhe, so darzī kā beṭā.
Who keeps a needle, scissors, yard and thimble, is a tailor's son.
(A tree is known by the fruit.)

Suī ke nāke se sab ko nikālā hai.
All are drawn through the eye of a needle.
(Said of one who is no respecter of persons.)

Sūjhe na biṭaurā, Chāṅd se "Rām Rām."
He can't see the (village) dunghill and salutes the New Moon.
(Natives always salute the New Moon.)

Sūjhe nahīṅ, aur gulel kā shauq !
He can't see and is fond of shooting !

Sūjī phūlī jaise ghī kā kuppā.
Swollen and puffed up like a butter bag.
(*Kuppā* is a leathern receptacle for holding *ghī*.)

Sūī satkā kapṛā phaṭak.
Putting in the needle tears the cloth.
(Said of a mischievous man.)

Sūkhā ḍhāk, baṛhaī kā bāp.
Dry *dhāk* wood is the carpenter's father (master).
(*Ḍhāk* wood when dry is very hard.)

Sukhan-goī mushkil nahīṅ, sukhan fahmī mushkil hai. Ped.
It's not hard to speak well, the difficulty is to understand.

Sukhan unhoṅ par ḍālye, jo haṅs haṅs rākheṅ mān. Wom.
Beg only of them who smile and show you due respect.

Sukhār, duhār, āsmānī farmānī haiṅ. E. Agric.
Drought and inundation are the works of God.

Sūkhā sākhā Bāman hogayā phūl phāl Chugattā.
The thin Brāhman has turned into a fat Mugal.
(To describe one who from poverty has acquired great wealth.)

Sukh baṛhe, muṭāpā chaṛhe.
When ease comes corpulence comes.
(Very true in India, where fatness is often synonymous with respectability.)

Sukh dukh meṅ jo rahe sahāī, sajjan vā ko bolīṅ, bhāī.
He is a true brother, my friend, that is true through weal and woe.
(A friend in need is friend indeed.)

Sūkhe dhāṅoṅ pānī paṛā.
The rain fell just as the rice was withering.
(In the nick of time.)

Sūkhe lakṛī kī tarah, khāē bakrī kī tarah.
Thin as a stick he eats like a goat.

Sūkhe māṅ jhaṛ ber ghane hoṅ : Sammat māṅ an ḍher ghane hoṅ. Agric.
In draught wild plums are plentiful, And in a good season corn.
(The appearance of a heavy crop of *bers* is a sign of a dry season.)

Sūkhe Sāvan, rūkhe Bhādoṅ. Agric.
A dry Sāvan means a barren Bhādoṅ.
(Sāvan is July—August and Bhādoṅ is August—September. The autumn harvest which is cut in Bhādoṅ depends on the rain in Sāvan.)

Sūkhī chināī karteṅ haiṅ ?
He builds with dry mortar.
((1) To do a business badly. (2) A skit at the Brāhmans, who will eat without drinking at a feast, so that they may eat the more.)

Sukhī rahegā voh sadā, jin chho dīnā mār : Jag māṅ bhalā kahāt hai chho kā māran-hār.
He will be ever happy that stilleth his wrath : The suppressor of anger is ever praised in the world.
(A soft answer turneth away wrath.)

Sukh kāran sāgar tajo, ān bindh āyo ang, Motī nar yūṅ kampiyāṅ, tū haṅsi aur ke sang.
For happiness sake it leaves the ocean and is bored through: Like a pearl man trembles when a woman laughs.

Sukh ke baṛe jodhā rakhvālī haiṅ. Hin.
Happiness is guarded by bold warriors.
(*i. e.* happiness is difficult to reach.)

Sukh ke sab sāthī haiṅ.
Prosperity has many friends.

Sukh māno to sukh hai ; dukh māno to dukh :
Sachcha sukhyā voh hai, jo sukh māne na dukh.
Take it for pleasure and it is pleasure; take it for pain and it is pain : The truly happy is he who minds neither pleasure nor pain.

Sukh meṅ āē Karam Chand, lage muṅḍāvan ganj.
Karam Chand came in raptures to have his bald head shaved.
(Said of a prosperous man, who foolishly injures himself.)

Sukh meṅ Sāīṅ ko bhajo, jo dukh mūl na ho: Sādh kaheṅ, re bālke, sīkh mān jas lo.
Call on God in pleasure that pain come not to thee: Hear this my sons, saith the saint, and be respected.
(Remember now thy Creator in the days of thy youth, while the evil days come not: nor the years draw nigh, when thou shalt say: I have no pleasure in them. *Ecclesiastes* xii. 1.)

Sukh sampat kā sab koī hai.
All associate with the prosperous.

Sukh se dukh bhalā, jo thoṛe din kā ho.
Trouble is better than ease, if it last but for a while.

Sukh sove horū, jis ke gāē na gorū.
He will sleep soundly, who has no cattle.

Sukh sove kumhār, jā kī chor na leve maṭyā.
The potter sleeps soundly, for thieves will not steal his clay.

Sukh soveṅ Shekh, aur choran bhāṅḍe le.
The mendicant sleeps soundly, while thieves walk off with his pots.
(The *Shekh* here is a wandering bard of the *bhaṛāiṅ* class, who sing songs in honor of saints. They are poor and of course their pots are not worth stealing.)

Sukh sove Shekh, jin ke ṭaṭṭū na mekh.
Happy sleeps the mendicant, who has nor horse nor tether.
(See preceding.)

Sūlī par bhī nīnd ātī hai.
Sleep comes even at the stake.
(The horribly cruel punishment of impalement was common enough in former times in India.)

Sūlī par kī roṭī khāte haiṅ.
He eats bread at the stake.
(To earn one's livelihood by hazardous means: always liable to punishment: to live on a volcano.

Sūm ke ghar kuttā jāē na jāne de.
The dog at a miser's gate, neither goes in himself nor lets others pass.
(A skit at the niggardly servants of a rich miser: the dog in the manger.)

Sūm kī thātī.
The deposit of a miser.
(1) Describes one so avaricious as to spend absolutely nothing.
(2) Describes something to be taken special care of: as a miser is sure to try and cheat about his deposits with another, in the hope of gaining by it.)

Sumran kar meṅ, surat na Hari meṅ, kaho, bhek yeh kaisā hai? Ūpar se to sidh ban baiṭhā, bhītar paisā paisā hai.
Beads in hand, no thoughts of Hari (God): say, what sect is this? Without he is a holy saint, within nothing but pence.

Sūnā ghar bhiroṅ kā rāj.
The empty house is the wasps' estate.

Sūnā khet, kulachhnā, hirnā hī chug jāē.

Khet birānā boē-ke bīj akārath jāē. Agric.
Deer will graze the unguarded field, thou fool.
And seed sown in another's field, profits nothing.

Sunār apnī māṅ kī nath meṅ se bhī churātā hai.
The goldsmith will steal a piece of his own mother's nose-ring.
(He would cheat his own father.)

Sunāṛī becheṅ kāṅṭū, anāṛī becheṅ māṅchhū. E.
The wise man sells the bones, the fool his fish.

Sunār kī khaṭāī, aur darzī ke band.
The goldsmith's acid and the tailor's tag.
(Said of an evasive answer.)
☞ These classes are habitually behind hand with their work: the first tells you your jewels are ready and just put into the acid to be cleaned, and the second that your clothes are ready and only the tags remain to be tacked on.

Sūne māṅ mat chīz rakh, lejā chor chakār:
Khau hai dhan aur jīv kā sūnā aur ujāṛ.
Place not thy goods in a lonely place, for thieves will steal.
A wilderness and a desert are the bane of life and property.

Sūnī sej se markhanā bail bhī bhalā. Wom.
A butting ox is better than a lonely bed.
(Better a bad tempered husband than none at all. Widows in India have a very rough time of it: hence proverb.)

Sunī sunāī bāt kī, gaṭhrī bāṅdhe khūṅṭ:
Barchhin kī mār paṛī, kakṛin kī bhaī lūṭ.
He believes implicitly all he hears:
(For instance) a man was speared for stealing cucumbers.
(Cucumbers being of no value in India: it would be absurd to put a man to death for stealing them.)

Suniye sab kī, kījiye apne man kī.
Listen to all, but do as your mind desires.

Sun koī hazār kuchh sunāve, Kīje vohī jo samajh meṅ āve. Qābū ho to kīje na gaflat. Ājiz ho to hāriye na himmat, Ātā ho to hāth se na dīje: Jātā ho to us kā gam na kīje.
Listen to a thousand plans, But do what you understand. As far as you can make no mistakes. Let not disappointment destroy your courage. Give not up what comes to your hand: And grieve not for that which leaves you.

Sunnī na Shīa, jī meṅ āyā so kīyā. Mah.
Neither a Sunnī nor a Shīa, I do as I like.
(Said by a free-thinker: the Sunnīs and Shīas are the two main sects of the Muhammadans and are always at daggers drawn.)

Sun re ḍhol bahū ke bol. Wom.
Hear, drum, my lady's voice.
(Spoken by one to whom another has made many professions of kindness, which have not been fulfilled.)
☞ The story goes that a mother informed

her son of the bad conduct of his wife, but he did not believe her. His wife afterwards fell sick and the family priest advised her to confess all her sins, as her last moments were approaching, which she consented to do. While she was preparing herself for the difficult task the old woman contrived to put her son within a large drum which she placed next to the sick bed. While the sick woman was giving over her sins one by one, the old mother kept on beating the drum to the words of the Proverb.

Sun sun-ke teri bāt, sahelī, soch huā mere man ko: Kar-ke byāh gharen nahīn rakhte bābal apnī dhī ko. Wom.

My maid, I have heard and my heart grieves, That after marrying her off a father keeps not his daughter at home.

(In India girls are well treated in the parents' and badly in their husbands' homes: hence the point of this saying.)

Sun sun mīṭhī bolgat, baiṭh na bairī pās: Dahī bhulāve, bāore, khāē kadhī kapās?

Keep not company with thy enemy, misled by his honeyed words: Thou fool, thou mayest not eat any time cotton for curds.

Sūp bole so bole, chhalnī bhī bole jis men bahattar chhed.

The winnowing-fan may speak, but the sieve with its seventy two holes never.

(Those who live in glass houses must not throw stones.)

Suphal hot man kāmnā, Tulsī, prem partīt: Apno aepan lāē-ke tiryā pūjat bhīt.

Tulsī, the heart's desires are fulfilled through love and faith: A woman worships a wall for her own ends.

(Faith can heave mountains. Tulsī Dās was the celebrated author of the Hindī *Rāmāyan*.)

Supne kī sī māyā, jis ko apnī batlāve.

Our possessions are but the illusions of a dream.

Supne men rājā bhae, din ko vohī ahvāl.

Though a king in your dreams at night, in the day you will be as you were.

Supne men suāmī mile kar na sakī do bāt: Sovat thī, rovat uṭhī, maltī rah gai hāth.

I saw my lord in dream and could not talk with him: I awoke from my sleep weeping and wringing my hands.

Supurdam ba tū māya-i-khesh rā: Tū dānī hisāb-i-kam-o-besh rā. Pers.

I have made over my property to you: You now know all its good and bad points.

(A preface to books.)

Sūraj bairī grahn hai, aur dīpak bairī paun, Jī kā bairī kāl hai; āvat roke kaun.

The enemy of the sun is an eclipse, the enemy of the lamp is the wind, And the enemy of life is death: who shall avert it?

Sūraj dhūl ḍālne se nahīn chhuptā.

The sun is not hidden by throwing dust on it.

Sūraj ko kyā ārsī le-ke dekhte hain?

Do you want a glass to look at the sun?

(To show a lantern to the sun.)

Sūraj ne bhān ubhārī, rain ghar ko sidhārī.

When the sun comes out, the night goes home.

Sūrā kāṭe aur bil men ghus jāē.

A brave man will cut a hole and escape through it.

(Discretion is the better part of valour.)

Sūrā, ran men jāē-ke lohā karo nisank. Nā mohe charhe randāpro, nā tohe charhe kalank. Wom.

Go, warrior, to the battle-field, and fearless wield your sword. Your death will bring no widowhood to me, nor cavil at your name!

(A woman's advice to her husband when starting for war.)

Sūrā so pūrā.

The brave are the full.

Sūrat churail kī sī, mizāj pariyon kā sā.

The face of a goblin, and the airs of a fairy.

Sūrat men aise, sīrat men aise.

Such without and such within.

(Altogether bad.)

Sūrat mere mitr kī man men rahī samāē, Jūn menhdī ke pāt men lālī lakhī na jāē.

The image of my love fills my heart within, As their redness is not seen in the myrtle leaves.

(*Menhdī* leaves are used for dying the palms and nails red, but are themselves green. The saying has a spiritual and allegorical meaning.)

Sūrat na shakal, bhāṛ men se nikal.

Nor face nor shape, as if just out of an oven.

(Said of an ugly woman.)

Sūr Dās janam ke nahīn āndhar!

Sūr Dās was not born blind!

(Sūr Dās was a Bhagat or free-thinking Hindū reformer. He is said to have blinded himself to avoid contamination with a woman, with whom he had fallen in love.)

Sūrmā chanā bhāṛ nahīn phoṛ saktā.

The hardest grain of pulse won't split the oven.

(It is in vain to strive against greatly superior force: *chanā* or pulse is parched in ovens in India; hence point of proverb.)

Surmā sab lagāte hain, par chitvan bhānt bhānt. Wom.

All apply antimony, but their manners differ.

(Manners make the man: *surmā* antimony is used for beautifying the eyes.)

Sur men Isar base.

God dwells in music.

Sur, nar, muni kī yehī rītī: Suārath lāē karen sab prītī.

This is the way of gods and men and saints: To love their own ends.

Surtīlā so phurtīlā.

Witty is smart.

Sussā, gādaṛ, lomṛī, ḍarpok tū, inko jān; Mānas kūkar dekh kar tajne lagen prān.

The hare, the jackal, and the fox are of a

timid sort; Their lives begin to go at sight of man or dog.

Susson jāūn yā goson jāūn?

Shall I go for a hare or for forest dung?

☛ A country woman whose daily avocation was to collect forest dung for fuel, one day happened to catch a hare. She concluded that hares would come to her every day and hence proverb.

Susti burī, re bālke, yā kuṅ jī se ṭār; Rattī bojhā sust ko lāge bojh pahāṛ. Rus.

Idleness is a bad thing, my lad, thrust it from thy life; An ounce weight to an idle man is as heavy as a mountain.

Sust mūnakh kā koī na lāgū, Phurtīle ke sab le bhāgū.

None befriends the lazy; But all men love the active.

Sutā jo rākhe chorī par; to pagṛī-pat rakh morī par.

Who sets his heart on thieving stakes his own good name.

Sūt ke binaule ho gaë.

All the thread is turned into cotton seed.

(*i. e.* the whole work is spoilt, or all the plans are thwarted.)

Sūt kī aṇṭī, aur Yūsuf kī kharīdārī! Mah.

Purchasing Joseph with a skein of thread.

☛ The Muhammadan story is that when Joseph was being sold as a slave in Egypt, an old woman came forward to purchase him for a skein of cotton.

Sūt na kapās, kolī se laṭṭham laṭṭhā.

Neither thread nor cotton and quarrels with the weaver.

(To describe one who quarrels without any reasonable pretence.)

T

Tab lag jhūṭ na boliye, jab lag pār basāë.

Lie not if you can help it.

Ṭahaliye ko ṭahal sohe, bahaliye ko bahal sohe.

Service befits a servant, and his caste befits a man of caste.

(Every cobbler to his last.)

Ṭahal karo faqīr kī, jo deve tumheṅ asīs;
Rain dinā rāzī raho jog meṅ bisvā bīs.

Serve the holy that thou mayest be blessed,
And pass thy days in all happiness.

Ṭahal karo mā bāp kī, jo hoeṅ sampūran ās.
Yā ṭahal sūṅ jo phireṅ Narak unhoṅ kā bās.

Serve thy father and thy mother that thou mayest obtain all thy desire. Who doeth not such service shall dwell in Hell.

(Honor thy father and thy mother that thy days be long in the land the Lord thy God giveth thee.)

Ṭahal na ṭakorī, lāo 'majūrī morī!'

Nor service nor work done and he asks for his wages!

Taī kī terī, khapṛī kī merī.

What's on the platter is yours, what's in the basket is mine.

(What is being cooked is yours, what is ready cooked is mine: selfishness.)

Tairāk hī ḍūbte haiṅ.

It is only swimmers that sink.

Tairegā so ḍūbegā.

Who swims will sink.

(Sooner or later: don't go out of your depth.)

Ta'allī ko takrār nahīṅ.

There is no disputing what's evident.

Ṭakā ho jis ke hāth meṅ, voh baṛā hai zāt meṅ.

Who hath a penny in his pocket is of high caste.

Ṭakā karāī, aur ganḍā davāī.

A penny for the article and two pence for the repairs.

(Penny wise, pound foolish.)

Takalluf meṅ hai taklīf sarāsar!

Verily ceremonies are troublesome!

Takalluf meṅ rel chal dī.

While ceremony squabbles the train is off.

☛ The story goes that two punctilious native gentlemen on the platform of the Railway Station at Lucknow would out-do each other in politeness; said one, '*Hazrat savār hūjiye!*' '*Qiblā āp!*' '*Nahīṅ, qiblā āp!*' 'Be seated, your highness, 'After your reverence!' Nay, after your excellency!' Meanwhile the train went off. Observe the English word *rel* in a recognized proverbial saying.

Takā parāyā hāth aur gayā Narak.

Who depends on other's hands will go to Hell.

Ṭakā roṭī ab le, chāhe tab le.

You may take your bread and your penny now or when you choose.

(You are not to expect more.)

Ṭakā sā javāb de dīyā.

He gave a penny answer.

(A flat denial.)

Ṭake kā sārā khel hai.

It's money that makes all the fun.

Ṭake kī lauṅg Banyāyan khāë; kaho, ghar rahe ki jāë?

When a Banyā's wife takes to two-penny cloves: say, will he be ruined or not?

(A skit at the proverbial niggardliness of the Banyās.)

Ṭake kī murgī, chha ṭake mahsūl.

A penny for the fowl and six pence for the tax on it.

Ṭake tītar gailā par, pāṅch rupayā par. Bhoj.

A partridge for a penny in poverty is (as expensive as one for) five rupees in prosperity.

Takhtī par takhtī; mīyāṅjī kī āī kambakhtī.

Superstition.

When slate is on slate, there's bad luck for the master.

(A school phrase: it embodies a superstition that if one of the *takhtīs* or writing boards happens to lie upon another it brings bad luck to the master.)

Tāk-jhāṅk-kar chāl mat; yeh hai burā subhāo. Jār kahen, yā chortā, yā kahen ūdbilāo.
Don't go about looking and staring; it is a bad habit. People will call you a rake, or a thief, or a fool.

Takle kā sā bal nikal gayā.
The twist has been taken out of him, as out of a spindle.
(Said of a naughty boy made to behave himself by punishment: he has learnt a lesson.)

Tak tiryā ko apnī, par tiryā mat tāk: Par nārī ke tākne pare sis māṅ khāk.
Look on your own wife; never on another's: Looking on strange women will lay your head in the dust.

Tālam tolā mat kare, kīye bachan bhugtā: Jo nar bachnoṅ se phire, voh pat det ganvā.
Evade not and keep thy word: Who goes back in his word loses his honor.

Tāl bajā-ke māṅge bhīk, Us kā jog rahā ke thīk.
Who rings a bell to beg for alms, His mendicancy prospers not.
(A skit at the mendicants who go about begging alms with bells in their hands.)

Tāl batā us ko na tū, jis se kiyā qarār: Chāhe ho bairī terā, chāhe hove yār.
Disappoint him not to whom thou hast made a promise; Be he your enemy, or be he your friend.

Tal dhār, ūpar dhār. E. Agric.
Above and below it's all a stream.
(Raining cats and dogs.)

Tale Dhartī, ūpar Rām.
By the Earth below and God above.
(An oath.)

Tale kā dam tale rah gayā, ūpar kā ūpar.
The inner breath remained inside and the outer outside.
(Dazed by bad news.)

Tale gherā, ūpar sehrā.
A ring below and a chaplet above.

Tale ke dāṅt tale rah gaē, aur ūpar ke ūpar.
The lower teeth remain below, and the upper teeth above.
(That is, the jaw is set with fear: used to express being shocked at any thing.)

Tale parī kā mol kyā?
What is the value of what's under your feet?
(Said by a meek and obedient wife. Used also to express the inutility of wasting time in the discussion of matters which are past: reviving the dry bones of a discussion. Also that what is in one's power is not valued.)

Tale tāṅg, ūpar māṅg.
The legs below, and the head above.

Tālā bin kaisā tālā? Jorū bin kaisā sālā?
No lock without a key: No brother-in-law without a wife.

Tālī dou kar bāje. E.
It requires two hands to clap.
(It takes two to make a quarrel.)

Tāl meṅ chamke tāl machharyā, ran chamke tarvār, Tanbuā chamke saiyāṅ pagaryā, sej pe bindyā hamār.
Fish look well in a lake, and a sword on the battle field, My husband's turban in a tent, and my spangles on my bed.
(Every thing has its place.)

Tal mundyā, Pātāl dhuṅdyā.
Looking for Hell with his head down.
(A great rogue always plotting mischief.)

Tāl na bhūke ko kabhī, jo de tujhe Khudā. Ādhī meṅ se pās bhī, use bāṅt-kar khā.
Refuse not the hungry what God hath granted thee. If thou have but half a loaf, share that half with him.

Tāl na talīyā, bovo singhāre, bhaīyā. Agric.
Nor tank nor lake and he wishes to sow water caltrops my friend.

Tāl se talaīyā gahrī, sāṅp se sanpolā jahrī. Superstition.
A lake is deeper than a pond and a young serpent more poisonous than a large one.

Tāl sūkh patpar bhayo, hansā kahīṅ na jāē. Mare purānī pīt ko, chun chun kankar khāē.
The lake hath dried up but the swan goes not away. Out of its old love it lives on pebbles and stones.
(Home sweet home.)

Tāl to Bhopāl Tāl, aur sab talaiyāṅ haiṅ.
The only lake is Bhopāl Lake, the rest are but ponds.
(*Tāl* is one of those artificial lakes called "tanks" by Europeans in India.)

Tāl ujhal kar ujhleṅ kyār, Jab barkhā ho pūrām pār. Agric.
Lakes and ponds will overflow, When rains are heavy.

Talvār kā ghāo bhartā hai, bāt kā ghāo nahīṅ bhartā.
A wound from a sword can be healed, but the wound from a word never.
(Thy tongue like a sharp razor worketh deceitfully. Psalms, lii, 2.)

Talvār kā khet harā nahīṅ hotā.
The field destroyed by the sword never revives.

Talvār kī āṅch ke sāmhne kol birlā hī thairtā hai.
It wants a brave man to stand up against the flash of a sword.

Talvār māre ek bār, ehsān māre bār bār.
The sword slays once, but kindness oft.
(Mistaken kindness.)

Talvaryā vā ko mat kaho jo khāṅḍā le-kar hāth, Ran se bhāge eklā, chhoṛ ṭol kā sāth.
Don't call him a swordsman who takes his sword with him, As he runs from the battle field and leaves his comrades behind.

Talvaryā vohī bhalā, jo ran meṅ hāth dikhāve, Bairī ke ṭukṛe kare, aur āp turat bach jāve.
He is a true swordsman who can use his sword in the field; Cuts down his enemies and so saves himself.

Talvoṅ kī sī kahūṅ, yā jībh kī sī? E.
Shall I judge according to the soles of my feet, or according to my tongue?

☞ The story goes that a judge received bribes from both parties to a suit. One presented something eatable, and the other slipped a gold *mohar* under his feet; and hence the dilemma described in the proverb. It is applied to the difficulties of a bribe-taker.

Talvoṅ se lagī hai.
She is stuck to the soles of his feet.
(Said of prostitutes.)

Talvoṅ se lagī, sir meṅ se nikal gaī.
It entered my heel, and comes out of my head.
(I am burning with rage from head to foot.)

Tālyāṅ bajā le, banno, byāh hogā.
Clap your hands, my child, you will be soon married.
(Said to amuse children.)

Tamāchā māre muṅh lāl rakhte haiṅ.
A slap on the face keeps the cheeks red.
(People punished recollect the punishment: to hide one's poverty with a good grace.)

Tama ra seh harf ast, har seh tihī. Pers.
Avarice has three letters and all three empty.
(In Persian writing there are no dots to the three letters of the word *tama*, avarice.)

Tām-jhām lage!
Bring the sedan!

☞ It is related of a man, who became the fortunate owner of a sedan, that he used to ride about in it upon the slightest occasion. At last he determined to do his own marketing and to thus call the sedan continually into service. "I want pepper" says the wife. "Bring the sedan" says her husband. "Oh I forgot the salt." "Bring the sedan." The proverb is used to express silly vanity.

Tānā bānā sūt purānā.
The warp and the woof are both of old thread.
(To labor in vain.)

Tānā Shāh dīvānā, jis ke chiṭṭhī na parvānā.
Tānā Shāh is a fool, who does no business in writing.
(And so gets himself mixed up in needless disputes.)

Tāṅbā dekhe chālnā, man dekhe beopār. Mercantile.
Seeing money settles, seeing the person does business.
(Business is transacted face to face or for cash payments.)

Tan de, man le.
Give your body, and get money.
(Work and you will get.)

Tandurustī hazār nemat hai.
The health is equal to a thousand blessings.
(Health is better than wealth.)

Taṅgī gaī, farākhī āī.
Poverty gone, and plenty come.

Taṅgī ke sāth farākhī, aur farākhī ke sāth taṅgī lagī huī hai.
Plenty waits on poverty and poverty on plenty.
(The mutability of the affairs of this world.)

Ṭāṅg ke nīche se nikāl diyā.
Kicked from beneath the feet.
(Subdued.)

Ṭāṅg pakaṛ ke lāē aur pūṅch pakaṛ ke bahā diyā?
Pull him in by the leg and kick him out by the tail!

Tan gudṛī, man dhāgā: koī kuchh hī lakhe, man lāgā.
The body is a clout and the mind a thread: say what they will, this is my opinion.
(A saying of the *faqirs*: the mind keeps the body together.)

Ṭāṅg uṭhe nā, chaṛhal chāhe hāthī.
He cannot lift his leg, and he wants to mount an elephant.
(Attempting beyond one's powers.)

Tānī ghāṭ ki bānī ghāṭ?
Which is in fault: the warp or the woof?
(Both are: faults on both sides.)

Tan kā bairī tāp hai, aur man kā bairī neh; Jis tan meṅ yeh doū rame, to gae jīū aur deh.
Fever is the enemy of body and love the enemy of heart; The man possessed by both loseth heart and body.

Ṭāṅkā pānā mil gayā.
The pieces have been joined again.
(To express a quarrel having been settled.)

Tan kasrat meṅ, man aurat meṅ.
The body in exercise and the heart set on women.
(The native notion is that the two are incompatible!)

Ṭāṅkī baj rahī hai.
It resounds with chisels.
(The building is going on rapidly.)

Tan kī kar le tuntunī, aur man ke kar le tār. Phir jas gā Hari nām ke, jo turat mile Kartār.
Make your body into a guitar, and your heart the strings for it. Then play the sweet hymns of God upon it and you will find the Creator soon.

Tan kī tanak sarāē meṅ nek na pāyo chain; Sāṅs naqārā kūṅch kā, bājat hai din rain.

The body is ever moving and has no rest at all; The marching-drum of the breath is beaten night and day.

(We are always on the road to death.)

Tan ko kapṛā, na peṭ ko roṭī.

Nor covering for the body, nor bread for the stomach.

Tan lagī dhupṛī, to balā chhāẽ jhupṛī?

When the sun warms his back, who cares to put up a hut?

(To forget the necessity for a want the moment it ceases to press.)

☞ The story goes that a man in the cold of the night swore to put up a hut in the morning, but as soon as the sun warmed him he forgot all about it.

Tan milā to kyā huā, man kī b ujhī na piyās, Jaise sīp samudr men kare "tirās tirās."

What boots it to have a body when the heart is not appeased, And like a pearl-shell in the sea cries out "I am athirst, athirst."

(The natives say that pearls are formed by rain-drops falling into the shells of oysters during the time of Swāti (Arcturus).)

Tan par chīr na ghar māñ nāj: Dad-susre kā ropā kāj!

No clothes to her body, nor grain in the house: And celebrating the funeral of her wretched old grandfather!

(Which would cost much money.)

Tan par sohe kāpṛā, aur ran sohe ranjīt. Bīr purakh vohī bhale, jo sab se rākhen prīt.

Clothes befit the body and heroes a battle field. Those men are good that love all men.

Tan phūaṛ kā bhaiṅs sūṅ bhārī: Kahe "kaho mohe Nājo Pyārī." Rus.

The ninny is heavier than a buffalo, And asks to be called Miss Slip.

(Nājo is a slim and slender girl; a slip of a girl.)

Tan pinjrā, man tītrā, sāṅs jīvan kā sūl. Jab tītar uḍ jāt hai, to ho jā pinjar dhūl.

The body is a cage, the soul a partridge in it and breath the means of life. When the partridge flies the cage it turns to ashes.

Tan putlā hai khāk kā, ise dekh mat bhūl. Ek din aisā hoegā mile dhūl men dhūl.

Be not proud of thy body; it is but a bag of dust; And one day it will turn to dust again.

(Dust unto dust, and ashes to ashes. The above is a well known saying of the *bhagats* or religious reformers, and is to be found every where in endless variation.)

Tan sītal ho sīt sūṅ, aur man sītal ho mīt sūṅ.

Milk pleases the body and friendship the heart.

Tan sukhāe pinjar kare, dhare rain din dhyān: Tulsī, miṭe na bāsnā, binā bichāre gyān.

They reduce their bodies to skeletons and night and day they meditate: But, Tulsī, avarice will not go till they get heavenly knowledge.

Tan sūkhā, kubṛī pīṭh huī, ghoṛe par zīn dharo, bābā! Ab maut-naqara bāj chukā, chalne kā fikr karo, bābā.

Your body thin, and your back bent, you should now saddle your horse, sir! Your death march is being beaten, and you had better think of going, sir!

Tan sukhī to chain hai, Nā to dukh din rain hai.

If there is health there is pleasure, If not there is pain day and night.

Tan sukhī to man sukhī.

The body at ease, the mind at ease.

(*Mens sana in corpore sano.*)

Tan tājā, to qalandar rājā.

When his belly is full, the beggar is a king.

(*Qalandars* are Muhammadan mendicants: in India many of them carry about performing monkeys.)

Tan takiyā, man bisrām: Jahāṅ par rahe, vahāṅ ārām.

When your body is your pillow and your mind your inn, You will find rest wherever you may sojourn.

(A saying of the mendicants.)

Ṭanṭā mat kar, jab talak bin ṭanṭe ho kām. Ṭanṭā bis kī bel hai; yā kā mat le nām.

Never quarrel as long as you can do without it. A quarrel is a poisonous creeper; never even take its name.

Tāṅt bājī rāg pāyā.

We get the note by striking the string.

Tānṭe se nāṭā bhalā, jo deve turat jabāb. Voh ṭānṭā kis kām kā, jo barson kare kharāb?

The churl that refuses at once is better than he that argues. What is the use of an argument, that spoils your life for years?

Tāṅt sī deh, pāoṅ nā hāth, Laṛan chalī sūran ke sāth?

A body like a catgut, and no hands and feet, And still he goes to fight with heroes!

(Said in reproof of one who evinces preposterous desires without means to fulfil them)

Tan ujlā, man sāṅolā, bagle kā sā bhek: To se to kāgā bhalā, bāhar bhītar ek.

Fair of body and foul of mind, you are like a heron: A crow is better than you that is the same within and without.

(The heron standing stately and motionless watching for its prey is the conventional Indian simile for a hypocrite, and the crow for all that is objectionable in appearance and fact.)

Tanūr-bāzī aur Allāh rāzī. Mah.

Living on baker's bread pleases God.

(Muhammadan religious mendicants are the

chief frequenters of public bakers' shops in India and hence point of saying)

Tāolā so bāolā, dhīrā so gambhīrā.

Haste is madness, patience wisdom.

(More haste less speed.)

Tape Jeth to barkhā ho bhar peṭ. Agric.

A hot July brings plentiful rains.

Tape nakhat Mirgshirā joē, Ṭab barkhā pūran jag hoē. Agric.

Heat in *Mirgshirā* and the world will be filled with rain.

(*Mirgshirā*, a lunar asterism, falls in June-July.)

Tapke kā ḍar hai.

There is much fear of a leak.

☞ The story runs that an old soldier, who had seen better days, once came riding tattered and torn on a weary hack to a little hut in the vicinity of a village haunted by tigers and asked the old woman of the hut if there was anything to be afraid of in it, to which the lady replied that *tapkā*, or leakage, was greatly to be feared. A tiger standing in the rear of the hut overheard the woman saying this and supposed that the *tapkā* must be stronger and more ferocious than himself and became very much afraid of it. After nightfall there came on a storm, and when it thundered and lightened the poor soldier's pony got loose. The soldier with a stick in his hand went out in search of it, and in the darkness of the night mistaking the tiger for his pony gave him a sound thrashing, brought him into the hut and tied him to the tether. The tiger, taking him for a *tapkā*, made no resistance. Early in the morning the report that a tiger had been tethered with a rope spread till it reached the king of the place, who came to see what had happened, and being much pleased with the valour of the old soldier, gave him a robe of honor and appointed him the chief commander of his army.

Tāqat kamar meṅ chāhiye aulād ke liye. Rakhte nahīṅ haiṅ sirf bharosā Madār kā.

Strength in the loins is necessary for offspring. It is not enough to put reliance in Madār.

(Shāh Madār, the great saint of Makanpūr, died in 1433 A. D.)

Taqāze kā huqqā bhī nahīṅ pīyā jātā.

Even a borrowed pipe is unpleasant.

(Natives generally lend a *huqqā* if asked for it. *Moral*—never borrow anything.)

Taqdīr ke āge nahīṅ, tadbīr kī chalā.

Scheming avails not against fate.

Taqdīr ke likhe ko tadbīr kyā kare? Gar hākim khafā ho, vazīr kyā kare?

What schemes avail against the decrees of fate? If the king be angry what can his minister do?

Taqdīroṅ bāzī hai.

It is gambling with fate.

Taqdīr sīdhī hai, to sab kuchh.

If fate be propitious all will go right.

Tāq par baiṭha ullū, māṅge bhar bhar chullū.

The owl sits in the niche, and demands by handfuls.

(Spoken of a mean person, who gives orders to his superiors; *chullū* is as much water as can be taken into the hand made into a cup.)

Ṭarāzū se khaṛe ho-kar na tolo : barakat jātī hai.

Mah. Wom. Superstition.

Don't use your scales standing : you will lose your luck.

Tarkash meṅ to tīr nāhīṅ, par sharmā sharmī laṛte haiṅ.

Not an arrow left in his quiver, but he fights on for very shame.

(Hoping against hope.)

Taṛke kā bhūlā sāṅjh ko āē, to bhūlā nahīṅ kahātā.

If what was forgotten in the morning be remembered in the evening it cannot be called forgetfulness.

(Another interpretation is,—If one who had gone astray in the morning came home safe in the evening he cannot be said to have gone astray.)

Taṛke uṭhkar khāṭ se, chhoṛ chhāṛ sab kām, Mālā le kar hāth māṅ, jab Sāīṅ kā nām :

When you rise from your bed in the morning eschew all work, Till you take your beads in your hand and call on God.

Tarvar āchhā chhāoṅlā aur rūh sūhānā sāṅolā.

Good is a shady tree and good is a brunette.

Tasalvā tor ki mor? Tir.

Is the pan yours or mine?

Tasbīh pherūṅ, kis ko gherūṅ? Mah.

Counting my beads, whom shall I cheat?

(Put into the mouth of a hypocrite.)

Tāsh par mūṅj kā bakhiyā. Wom.

Rope lace upon brocade.

(To put the beggar on the gentleman. *Mūṅj* is a grass of which ropes are made.)

Tas Makund, tas pādan ghoṛī : Bidhī ne ān milāi joṛī. E.

As Makund, so his roaring mare : Fate has made a rare match of them.

Tātā, tītā, āmlā, tīnoṅ dhāt bināś.

Hot, warm, and sour destroy virility.

Tāte dūdh bilār nāche.

The cat dances about the hot milk.

(As she cannot drink it.)

Ṭāṭ, kāmlā, dolrā, tīnoṅ jāt gulām ; Jit chāhe, jit baiṭh-kar turat karo bisrām. Rus.

Canvass, blanket and bedding are lowly things, On which thou canst take thy rest when thou wilt.

Ṭāṭ kāmle ghar māṅ ghāle ; Bār batāve sāl dusāle. Rus.

He keeps canvass and blankets at home. And abroad calls them shawls.

Ṭāṭ kī aṅgyā, mūṅj kī tanī ; Dekh, mere deorā, main kaisī banī? Wom.

A canvass boddice and strings of straw; See, brother-in-law, how beautiful am I?

Tatṛī ne dīyā, janam—jalī ne khāyā ; jībh jalī na savād āyā. Hin. Wom.

The miserly hussy gave it, and the helpless

fellow ate it; but it had neither pungency nor flavor.

(No good can come of what two unlucky people do for each other: the saying is also used of a very small quantity of food given to eat.)

Tattā kaur nigalne kā, na ugalne kā.

A scalding morsel, neither to be swallowed nor spat out.

(*i. e.* in company: Scylla and Charybdis.)

Ṭattar khol, nikhaṭṭū āē.

Open the door, the idle fellow is come.

(Great boast, little roast.)

Tattī khichṛī ghī na pāyā; ab kā syālā yūṅ hī gayā.

Hot *khichṛī* without *ghī*: this is how my winter was passed.

(*Khichṛī* is pulse and rice which is unpalatable without *ghī*; hence proverb means great poverty. It is usually eaten in winter.)

Ṭaṭṭī kī oṭ shikār khelte haiṅ.

They hunt behind the curtain.

(To have secret vices.)

Ṭaṭṭū ko koṛā aur tāzī ko ishārah;

The sorry horse requires a whip; but a sign is enough for the generous steed.

(A word is enough to the wise, but a rod for the fool's back.)

Taubah baṛī sipar hai gunehgār ke liye. Mah.

Repentance is the best shield for a sinner.

Taubah kā darvāzah khulā hai. Mah.

The door of repentance is ever open.

(It is never too late to mend.)

Taubah kar, bande, is gande rozgār se. Mah.

Forbear, my friend, from such a dirty trade.

Talvā chaṛhā aur jīv baṛhā.

When the frying pan is on the fire the heart is warmed.

Tavā chaṛhā baiṭhī misrānī, Ghar meṅ nāj, agan-nā pānī!

The cook-maid has placed the frying-pan on the stove, though there is neither corn nor water, nor fire in the house.

Tavāef ke bichhaune par banā hai kām sone kā Na ṭhairegā, mulammā hai; abas hai sar ke khone kā?

The gold that's spent on a harlot's bed, Remains not and is mere gilt; so why throw away your gold?

Tāval mat kar kār māṅ, dhīrā dhīr banā; Tātā bhojan, bālke, devat jīv jalā.

Haste not over your work, do it slowly; A hot morsel, my son, will scorch your tongue.

Tavā na kūṅḍā nā chulhārī! Kahe nār 'maiṅ hūṅ bhaṭyārī'! Wom.

She has no frying pan, no oven and no fire; And the woman would be called an inn-keeper!

Tavā na tagārī, kāhe kī bhaṭyārī?

No cooking pots nor pans and an inn-keeper all the same!

Tavā, tagārī, āg, jal, an, iṅdhan, jit hoeṅ, Bārā dūn ujāṛ māṅ bhuke manukh na roeṅ.

Where there is a frying-pan, a kneading pan, fire, water, corn and fuel, Even if it be a mighty wilderness there is no starvation.

Tave kī terī, hāth kī merī.

The cake on the fire is yours, that in the hand is mine.

(To express that the person spoken to is in a great hurry. See next.)

Tave kī terī, tagārī kī merī.

What's on the fire is yours, what's in the plate is mine.

(To express hurry and impatience: also selfishness.)

Tavele kī balā bandar ke sir.

The misfortunes of the stable are on the monkey's head.

(Allusion to the superstition according to which a monkey is always kept in a stable in order to transfer evil from the horses to the monkey.)

Tave par kī būṅd.

A drop on a hot frying-pan.

(Soon expended or of no avail: the phrase alludes to the practice of testing the heat of an iron plate, on which bread is to be baked by sprinkling drops of water on it, whilst heating it over a fire.)

Ṭāyar bhalā nā lāṅgṛā; rūkh bhalā nā jhāṅgṛā.

A lame hack is not good, nor is a thorny tree.

Ṭāyar, ṭaṭṭū, gaj, gau, pūt, mīt, dhan māl, Ko bhī sang na jāt hai, jab leṅ jīū nikāl.

Thy mare, pony, elephant, cow, son, friend and goods, Go never with thee when thy life departs.

Tāzī ko mārā, aur Turkī kāṅpā.

When the Arab horse is whipped the Turkish is cowed.

(One example sets many aright: *pour encourager les autres.*)

Tāzī mār khāē, Turkī ash pāē.

The Arab (horse) is whipped, while the Turkish is fed up.

(The good and able are in distress and those less worthy are in prosperity. Desert and reward seldom go together.)

Tāzīm-i-kārīgarāṅ muāf! Pers.

Working men are excused.

(From conventional formalities.)

Ṭek unhoṅ kī rakhe Sāīṅ, gabar kapaṭ nahīṅ jin ke māṅhīṅ.

God keeps their honor safe that have no pride nor treachery within them.

Telan se kyā dhoban ghāṭ; is ke mūsal us ke lāṭh. Wom.

The washerman's wife is no worse off than the oilman's; this has a pestle, that a rod.

(*i. e.* both are equally bad: *Arcades ambo.*)

Tel ḍāl, kamblī kā sājhā.

By sprinkling a little oil, he became a partner in the blanket.

☞ It is customary when a blanket is finished, to rub oil on it to give it a gloss, and the story is that when one man had prepared a blanket another dropped a little oil on it, and on the strength of that claimed a share in the blanket. The proverb is used to express a person laying claim to a share in the property of others by making a trifling addition of his own.

Tel dekho, tel kī dhār dekho.

Look at the oil, or look at it flowing.

(Examine the matter; also wait for the issue.)

☞ It is said that a certain prince had four friends, a soldier, a priest, a camel driver, and an oilman. When the reigning monarch, his father died, and he succeeded to the throne he made his four old friends his ministers. The adjoining rulers and governors shortly afterwards finding the new prince given to luxury and indolence and his companions ignorant of their duties marched against him. The prince hearing of their advance called a meeting of his ministers and asked each one for his advice. The soldier at once advised war: the priest advised peace at any price: the camel driver said that there was no occassion for hurry and that it was always best to wait and see on which side the camel sits. (*Dekhiye ūnt kis kal baiṭhtā hai?* Proverb.) Whereupon the fourth minister, the oilman, in approval of the last opinion said "Let us first look at the oil and then see it flowing," *i. e.* there is no hurry.

Telī joṛe palī palī, Rahmān luṛhāve kuppe.

The oilman stores by ladles, and God spills by cans full.

(*L' homme propose, Dieu dispose.*)

Ṭelī kā bail ho gayā.

He has become an oilman's ox.

(*i. e.*, working like a galley slave. The oilman's ox is the embodiment in India of hard and thankless toil for another's benefit.)

Ṭelī kā bail le-ke kumhāin saṭṭī hoē. E. Wom.

The potter's wife dies for the oilman's ox!

(Wasted sympathy.)

Telī kā kām tamboli kare, chūlhe meṅ āg uṭhe.

If the betel vendor does the oilman's work, he will set the chimney on fire.

(Every cobbler to his last.)

Ṭelī kā tel, bhagat Bhaiyājī kī.

The oil is the oilman's, and the saintship is the Saint's.

(This expression is used when one person gets the credit of a work performed at the expense of another. The point is that the oilman gave the oil burnt at the shrine of the saint, for which of course the saint only got the credit.)

Telī kā tel girā hīnā huā, Baniye kā non girā dūnā huā.

When an oilman's oil is spilt it lessens, and when a Baniyā's salt spills it doubles.

(In the latter case dust gets mixed up with the salt and so increases its bulk.)

Telī kā tel jale, mashālchī kā dil jale.

While the oilman's oil burns, the torch-bearer's heart burns.

(The servant grieves over the oil which might have been his gain.)

Telī ke bail ko ghar hī kos pachās.

The oilman's ox travels 50 miles in his own [stall.

(Allusion to his going round in a circle while working at the mill.)

Telī ke tīnoṅ mareṅ, aur ūpar se ṭūṭe lāṭh.

All three of the oilman's may die and his (oilpress) beam break.

(*i. e.*, the two oxen that move the mill and the man who drives them may be ruined, for aught I care: I have no concern with them.)

Telī khasam karā aur rūkhā khāyā! Mah. Wom.

Marry an oilman and live on dry bread.

(Applied to one who attaches himself to some powerful person and yet remains in distress.)

Ṭelī kyā jāne mushk kī sār.

What can an oilman know of the odours of musk.

Telī rove tel ko, Maqsūdan rove khalī ko.

The oilman weeps over his oil, and Maqsūdan over her oil-cakes.

(Each is interested in what concerns him. *Maqsūdan* is here a fanciful name for a menial servant.)

Ṭel jal chukā.

The oil is consumed.

(All the wealth is dissipated: there is no more to spend.)

Tel jale ghī, ghī jale tel.

Oil boils to butter, butter boils to oil.

(Native notion.)

Tel kī jalebī mūā dūr se dikhāē. Mah. Wom.

The wretch shows his oily sweetmeats at a distance.

(Applied to one who promises fair, but does not perform: sweetmeats fried in oil instead of *ghī* are very indigestible.)

Tel na miṭhāī, chulhe dharī kaṛhāī. Wom.

Without sugar or oil, the frying-pan is put on the fire!

Tel tiloṅ hī meṅ se niklegā.

Oil certainly comes from oil-seed.

(The tax falls on the consumer. *Or*, the people pay.)

Ṭeṅṭ ānkh meṅ, mūṅh khurdīlā; Kahe piyā 'morā chhail chhabīlā.'

A cataract in his eye, and his face pitted with small pox, And yet his love calls him her handsome husband.

Teṅṭ bārvā kāl ke mīt: Khāēṅ kisān aur gāveṅ gīt. Agric.

Wild fruits are the friend of famine: The laborer eats and rejoices.

Terā ḍhakā rahe, merā bik jāē. Mercantile.

Let yours remain covered up, till mine be sold.

(Applied to a selfish person.)

Terā hāth aur merā mūṅh. Wom.
Thy hands and my mouth.
(Earn and feed me: selfishness.)

Terā kīyā tere āge āve!
May thy ill-deeds overtake thee!

Terā māl so merā māl, merā māl so—heṅ heṅ!
What's yours is mine, but what's mine—hā hā!

Terā pānī main bharūṅ, mere bhare kahār. Hin. Wom.
I draw water for you and the water-bearer [for me.
(Put into the mouth of a vain servant.)

Terā pī to meṅ base, jūṅ patthar meṅ āg; Dekhā chāhe dīdār ko, chakmak ho ke lāg.
Your love lives within yourself as fire within a flint; If you want to see your love, be like a flint.

Terā thā so merā huā, barāë Khudā ṭuk dekhne de. Mah. Wom.
What was mine is now yours, for God's sake let me see him for a while.
(Said by a mother to her son's wife, who has acquired great influence over her son.)

Tere baiṅgan, merī chhāchh.
Your egg plant for my butter milk.
(Said of one who claims much in return for little, the *baiṅgan* being very much more expensive than *chhāchh*.)

Tere dayā dharam nahīṅ man meṅ, Mukhṛā kyā dekhe darpan men?
When within thy heart is nor mercy nor compassion, Why look at thy face in a glass?

Tere jau, terī darāṅtī; chāhe jaise kāṭ.
Yours the barley, and yours the sickle, cut it when you please.
(It does not concern me.)

Tere mere sadqe meṅ, us kī jorū peṭ se.
His wife is pregnant on our charity.
(Said by her family to the ill-conducted wife of an impotent man when in the family way.)

Tere mūṅh meṅ ghī shakkar.
Sugar and butter for your mouth.
(Said to one who brings good news.)

Terhvī sadī meṅ sharā kī bāteṅ koī nahīṅ māntā. Mah.
In the thirteenth century none minds religious precepts.
(The century of the Muhammadan era that has been very lately completed.)

Terī ḍar yā tere gusaiyāṅ kī?
Am I afraid of you or your master?
(Put into the mouth of an insolent servant.)

Terī āvāz Makke Madīne meṅ. Mah. Wom.
May your voice be heard in Makkā and Madīnā.
(A benediction on one who brings good tidings: also used to one who shouts when he speaks.)

Terī god meṅ baiṭhūṅ, aur terī hī ḍāṛhī nochūṅ.
I'll sit in your lap, and pluck out your beard.
(Put into the mouth of an ungrateful person.)

Terī karnī tere āge, merī karnī mere āge.
May thy deeds overtake thee, and mine me!
(Let us each reap the reward of what we have done; said as a curse to a person returning good for evil.)

Terī qudrat ke āge koī zor kisī kā chale nahīṅ. Chīṅṭī par hāthī chaṛh baiṭhe, tab voh chīṅṭī mare nahīṅ.
Might availeth not against Thy wondrous power (O God!). An elephant may mount an ant and still the ant not die.

Terī qudrat ke qurbān!
I sacrifice myself to Thy power (O God)!

Ṭer ṭer-ke rove, apnī lāj khove. Mercantile.
Who weeps and cries aloud loses his credit.
(Keep your losses to yourself.)

Tetar ke mūṅh Lachchhmī.
Fortune dwells in the third man's mouth.
(Used when the parties to a dispute refer it to the arbitration of a third person.)

Tete pāoṅ pasāriye, jetī lambī sauṛ.
Stretch your leg according to your coverlet.
(Cut your coat according to your cloth.)

Tetrī beṭī rāj rajāve, tetrā beṭā bhīk maṅgāve. Hin. Superstition.
A daughter after two sons, brings prosperity; a son after two daughters, brings beggary.

Ṭhag na dekhe, dekhe kalvār.
If you've never seen a *ṭhag* look at a publican.
(A *ṭhag* is a member of a gang of criminals banded together for the purpose of robbery by means of murder.)

Ṭhag nā dekhe, dekhe qasāī; sher na dekhe, dekhe bilāī.
If you've never seen a *ṭhag* look at a butcher; if you've never seen a tiger look at a cat.
(For explanation of *ṭhag* see above.)

Thailī meṅ rupayā, mūṅh meṅ guṛ.
Money in your purse and honey on your tongue.
(The two requisites for a happy life in the world.)

Thailyāṅ bhī silā līṅ?
Have you a bag ready sewn for it?
(Said mockingly to one who asks for money.)

Ṭhair ṭhair-ke chāliye, jab ho dūr paṛāo: Ḍūb jāt andhiyāo māṅ dauṛ chalantī nāo.
Walk slowly and surely when the halting place is far off: Fast going boats are often upset in a storm.
(The hare and the tortoise.)

Thakal pairākū phen chāṭe. E.
The exhausted swimmer licks the foam.
(His capital all spent, on paltry jobs intent.)

Thakā ūṅṭ, sarāë taktā hai.
The weary camel looks to the inn.

Thake bail, gon bhaī bhārī; ab kyā lādoge beopārī?
The ox is tired, and your sack is heavy; what will you load up now, you carrier!

Thākur patthar, mālā lakkaṛ, Gangā Jamnā, pānī; Jab lag man meṅ sāṅch na upje, chāroṅ Bed kahānī.

Idols are stone, beads are wood, the Ganges and the Jamnā are water; All the four Vedas are but tales, if truth finds no place in the heart.

(A saying of the free-thinking *Bhagats*.)

Ṭhālī banyā kyā kare? Is koṭhī ke dhān us koṭhī meṅ bhare.

What will the unemployed shopkeeper do? Remove his rice from one barn into another.

(Doing nothing is more painful than doing something.)

Thālī girī, jhankār sab ne sunī. Hin.

When the brazen dish falls, all hear the clang.

(There's no smoke without a fire: the spreading of a report.)

Thālī par se bhūkā nahīṅ uṭṭhā jātā. Hin.

The hungry man does not leave the platter.

Thālī phūṭī na phūṭī, jhankār to sunī.

Whether the platter was cracked or not, I heard it clink.

(Give a dog a bad name and hang him.)

Thanḍā hai barf se bhī, mīṭhā hai jaise olā; Kuchh pās hai to dejā; nahīṅ pī jā rāhe Maulā.

Colder than ice, sweeter than sugar; Give, if you have any thing; if not drink in the name of God.

(*i. e. gratis*: the water carrier's cry.)

Ṭhanḍā lohā garam lohe ko kāṭtā hai.

Cold steel cuts the hot.

(Patience will prevail in the long run: a cool man will always get the better of a passionate one.)

Ṭhanḍī chhāoṅ jo baiṭhtī jal jātā voh rūkh: Jaltī baltī maiṅ phirūṅ, ban meṅ detī kūk. Wom.

Had I sat under the cool shadow of a tree, it would have burnt up: Consuming and burning I roam about and cry out in the woods.

(To express great misfortunes.)

Ṭhāoṅ gun kājal, ṭhāoṅ gun kālak.

In one place it is a beautiful spot, in another a black stain.

(What's one man's meat is another man's poison: *kājal* is lamp-black used for brightening the eyes—it becomes some women and not others.)

Thā soch jo kuchh avval, ākhir vohī pesh āyā.

First thoughts are best.

(Used to express the intelligence of the speaker:—didn't I say so?)

Ṭhāṭhar khol, nikhaṭṭū āyā. Wom.

Open the wicket, the earn-nothing has come!

(Used by women towards idle husbands.)

Ṭhaṭhere ṭhaṭhere badlāī! Mercantile.

One brazier exchanging with another!

(Used generally of a quarrel between persons of the same profession: who is to decide when doctors disagree?)

Ṭhekā le us kām kā, jo tujh se hove ṭhīk.

Contract for that which you are sure about.

Ṭheke kā kām phīkā.

Work on contract is unsatisfactory.

Ṭheṅge thām, labede hazār. E.

Stand my ridicule, or a thousand blows.

Ṭhes laje, budh baṛhe.

Stumble and get sense.

Ṭhīk nahīṅ ṭheke kā kām: Ṭhekā de, mat khov dām:

Work on contract is never to be trusted. Don't give on contract and lose your money.

Ṭhīkrā hāth meṅ hogā aur bhīk māngtā phiregā.

May you ever have a potsherd and wander from door to door.

(A curse: the *ṭhīkrā* is the potsherd used by mendicants to receive alms.)

☞ Gālib, the witty poet of Dehlī, relates that one day he heard his servant murmuring over the *chilam* (pipe) which he had filled with live coals from the *ṭhīkrā* (fire place, also potsherd) for his master: so he enquired of him what he had been saying to the *ṭhīkrā*. The servant replied that he had been explaining that he had had no pay for eight months. "And what did the potsherd say?" "Never mind, *I* am with you!"

Ṭhīkrā hāth meṅ aur us meṅ sattar chhed!

May you carry a potsherd and may there be seventy holes in it.

(A curse: see preceeding.)

Ṭhīkre kā sukh, kharchī kā dukh.

Plenty of land but no money to spend.

(Said by prostitutes when badly paid.)

Ṭhokar khāve, budh pāve.

Stumble and get sense.

Ṭhokar lagī pahāṛ kī, toṛeṅ ghar kī sil.

Kicked by the mountain he breaks the grindstone at home.

(Applied to one, who having suffered injury from another he is unable to cope with, wreaks his vengeance on his own family and dependents: passing on the rebuke with interest.)

Ṭhok bajā le bast ko, ṭhok bajā de dām: Bigṛat nāhīṅ, bal ke, dekh bhāl kā kām.

Buy your goods carefully and give a proper price: The work, my son, which is done carefully is never spoilt.

Ṭhoṅgeṅ mār kiyā sir ganjā, kahe 'mere hai hāth na panjā.'

He has made my head bald with his blows and says he has no hands and fingers.

Ṭhoṅṭ chiterā man meṅ jhīṅke.

The maimed painter mopes.

(Applied to express the regret of one who sees himself excluded from an employment for which he is capable.)

Thoṛā āp ko, bahut gair ko.

Little to his own and much to outsiders.

(Said of one who does not favor his relatives,

which is quite subversive of all that is proper to the native mind.)

Thoṛā denā, bahut ārzū karnā.

Little giving and great entreaties.

Thoṛā kareṅ Gāzī Miyāṅ, bahut kareṅ ḍafālī.

Gāzī Miyāṅ could do little, but his followers do much (for him.)

(Gāzī Miyāṅ or Gāzī Sālār, the great saint of Bahṛāich in Oudh, was the nephew of Maḥmūd of Ghaznī and being killed at Bahṛāich in a disturbance, in A. D. 1033, is now considered to be a martyr and to work miracles. The proverb is a skit at the pretensions raised up for the many saints of India by their modern adherents.)

Thoṛā khānā aur Banāras meṅ rahnā. Hin.

Little to eat and a life at Benares.

(The wish of a pious Hindu, who hopes to obtain salvation by the penance of fasting and by living in the holy city of Benares: metaphorically, it is better to earn small pay at home than large pay abroad.)

Thoṛā khānā, izzat se rahnā.

Eat moderately, and live with honor.

(Used in reproof to one, who spends his all on his stomach.)

Thoṛā khānā javānī kī maut.

Eat little and die early.

Thoṛā khānā sukhī rahnā.

Eat little and live in health.

Thoṛā thoṛā hī kar-ke bahut ho jātā hai.

Little by little makes much.

(Many a little makes a mickle.)

Thoṛe dhan meṅ khal itrāē.

Little money turns the head of a fool.

Thoṛe mol kī kāmlī kare baṛoṅ kā kām, Mahmūdī aur bāftah sab ke rākkhe mān.

A cheap blanket can render service to the great, And be as useful as silks and satins.

Thoṛe pānī meṅ ubhre phirte haiṅ.

Swaggering on small means.

(Little fishes disport in little water. Said of the *nouveaux riches*: *pānī* "water" here means "money.")

Thoṛī ās Madār kī, bahut ās gulgulon kī.

Little trust in Madār, but great in sweets.

Madār or Shāh Madār is the great saint of Makhanpūr, who died in 1432 A D. At his festival sweets are distributed and hence the point of the proverb.)

Thoṛī pūṅjī khasmoṅ khāē. Mercantile.

A small capital ruins the master.

Thothā chanā, bāje ghanā.

An empty pea makes a great noise.

Thothe phaṭke uṛ uṛ jāeṅ.

Winnow empty grain and all will fly away.

Thūk bilonā.

To churn spittle.

(To talk nonsense.)

Thūk dāṛhī, phiṭṭe mūṅh! Panj.

I spit in your beard and say fie! to your face!

Thūk-kar chāṭnā.

To lick up one's own spittle.

(To turn back on one's word.)

Thūkoṅ sattū nahīṅ sante.

You can't make dough with spittle.

(Empty words buy no barley.)

Ṭiḍḍī kā ānā kāl kī nishānī. Agric.

When locusts appear, famine is near.

Tīj paṛe khet meṅ bīj. Agric.

On *tīj* the seed is sown.

(*Tīj* is a Hindū festival held in the month of Sāvan or July.)

'*Tik tik' samjhe, 'ā ā' samjhe, kahe sune se rahe khaṛā; Kaheṅ Kabīr, suno, bhāī sādho, as mānas se bail bhalā.*

An ox that understands '*tik tik*' and '*ā ā*' and stands still when told, Saith Kabīr, hear O Saints, is better than a man who will not listen.

('*Tik tik*' and '*ā ā*' are the noises made to bullocks by their drivers.)

Ṭikulī sendur gail, to khāne meṅ bhī bajjar paṛab? E. Hin. Wom.

Because my red spot is gone, am I to lose my food as well?

(Married women during coverture wear a red spot on their foreheads, which they are obliged to drop on becoming widows.)

Til chor, so bajjar chor.

Steal a pin, steal an anvil.

(As will be hanged for a sheep as a lamb.)

Til-guṛ bhojan, Turak mitāī, Āge mīṭh, pāchhe karvāī.

Sesamum, molasses, and a Musalmān's love, Are sweet first and afterwards bitter.

(Allusion to the ease of divorce among Musalmāns.)

Til kī ojhal pahāṛ.

A sesamum seed can hide a mountain.

(If it be held near enough to the eye: the sesamum seed is very small.)

Til rahe to tel nikle.

As long as there is oilseed, there will be oil.

Til, tīkhur, dānā, ghī, shakkar meṅ sānā; khāē buḍḍhā, hoe javānā.

Sesamum, linseed and the poppy-seed mixed with sugar and butter, will make an old man young.

(The above recipe makes a nutritive caudle.)

Ṭīm ṭām kī pagṛī bāṅdhī, voh bhī sadqa jorū kā, Nek pāk kā chaukā dīnā gobar gāē gorū kā.

To plaster with cow-dung to make a place pure, Is like wearing a smart turban out of your wife's wedding presents.

Tīn bulāē terah āē, de dāl meṅ pānī.

Three were invited and thirteen have come, so water the porridge.

(To make it enough to go round: allusion to the habit of many natives of taking their relatives and servants to a feast to which they themselves only are invited.)

Tīn bulāē terah āē; dekho yahāṅ kī rīt: Bāharvāle khā gaē, aur ghar ke gāveṅ gīt!
Three were invited and thirteen have come; such is the custom here:—Outsiders eat and the family have only the songs!
(Which accompany the feast: see preceding.)

Tīn bulāē terah āē; suno gyān kī bānī. Rāgho Chetan yūṅ kaheṅ, "tum do dāl meṅ pānī"!
Three were invited and thirteen have come, hear the wisdom of this speech. Saith Rāgho to Chetan,—"put water into the porridge."
(See preceding proverb.)

Tīn din ke chhokrā, hameṅ sikhāvat bāt! Jable voh liheṅ ṭhīkrā, table mārab lāt! Bhoj.
A three days' old boy and teaching me! When he picks up his pebble I'll give him a kick.
(Teaching your grandmother to suck eggs.)

Tīn din qabr meṅ bhī bhārī hote haiṅ. Mah.
Even in the grave, there are three days of trouble.
(Musalmāns believe that during the first three days after death the deceased has to answer to God for all his doings in life.)

Tīn dīye aur terah pāē; Kaise lobh byāj kā jāē. Mercantile.
I gave three and got thirteen: How the love of usury does increase!
(The proverb is a skit at the usurers.)

Tīn gunāh Khudā bhī bakhshtā hai. Mah.
Even God forgives three sins.
(How oft shall my brother sin against me and I forgive him? Till seven times? I say not unto thee until seven times but until seventy times seven. *Mathew* xviii, 21, 22.)

Tīn haiṅ sāh kisān ke; jāṅḍ, jāl aur kair. Agric.
The three bankers of the husbandman: the *jaṅḍ*, the *jāl*, and the *kair*.
(These three trees are the last resource of the starving cultivator in seasons of famine.)

"Tīn kachaurī, nau barātī, khāo chūram chūr"! Aē ghar-basī! tere byāh hai, yā luṭam lūṭ?" "Bandī jab kartī hai, jab aisā hī karte."
"Three cakes and nine wedding guests and gobble them all up! My lady, is it a wedding or a robbery?" "When I do it—I always do it like this."
(A Barmecide feast.)

Tinkā girā gaind mukh, nek na ghaṭo ahār! So le chalī papīlkā pālan ko parivār.
If straw fall from an elephant's mouth, his food is in none the worse for it: But an ant can take in and live on it.

Tinkā ho to toṛ lūṅ; pīt na toṛī jāē. Pīt lagat chhūṭat nahīṅ, jab lag maut na āē.
Were it a straw I could snap it, but love cannot be broken. When love once grasps it leaves not until death comes.

Tīn kā ṭaṭṭū terah kā zīn.
The nag worth three rupees and the saddle thirteen.

Tinkā utāre kā ehsān hotā hai.
To take away a straw confers an obligation.

Tinke kī chaṭāī, nau bīgahā phailāī.
Stretching a mat of straw over nine acres.
(Promising more than can be performed.)

Tinke kī oṭ pahār. Wom.
A mountain can be hid by a straw.
(See above, *Tīl kī ojhal pahāṛ.*)

Tīn lok se Mathurā niyārī. Hin.
Mathurā is apart from the three worlds.
(Eccentricity.)

Tīn meṅ, nā terah meṅ, na ser bhar sutlī meṅ, na karvā bhar rāī meṅ.
Nor one of the three, nor one of the thirteen, nor on my string, nor in my mustard pot.
☞ The story goes that a certain courtesan sorted her admirers into grades—first came three, then thirteen, then those she noted by knots on a string, and last the common herd represented by the seeds of mustard in a mustard pot. Hence the proverb expresses a person of no value at all.

Tīn narī meṅ terah gaz.
Three kids' skins stretch thirteen yards.

Tīnoṅ tirlok dekhāī de-gaē.
I saw all there was in the three worlds.
(And found nothing to eat: said by the hungry.)

Tīn pāo bhītar, to deotā aur pītar. Hin.
We remember the gods and ancestors, when the stomach is full.
(Hunger makes a man neglect his religious duties: three quarters of a *ser* of grain makes a full meal in the native notion.)

Tīn pāo kī tīn pākāīṅ, savā ser kī ek; Jeṭh nipūtā tīnoṅ khā gayā, maiṅ santokhan ek.
Three of three quarters and one of one seer and a quarter: My greedy brother-in-law ate the three and I was content with one.
(This is ironical: the small loaves my brother-in-law ate and I was content with one, but that was a very large one.)

Tīn peṛ bakāin ke, miyāṅ bāgbān!
Three *bakāyan* trees, and my gentleman a [gardener!
(The *bakāyan* or *melia azidarach* is a very shady tree.)

Tīn ṭāṅg kī ghoṛī, nau man kī ladnī!
A lame mare and nine hundred weight on her back!

Tīn terah ho gaē.
Gone to threes and thirteens.
(Dispersed and scattered: cast to the winds: used especially of a Hindū joint family that has separated.)

Tīn thān, chauthā maidān.
Three stalls, and the fourth the plain.

Tīn thān, chauthī jān, un kā Allāh nigahbān! Mah.
Three children and the fourth myself: God keep them safe!

Tīn ṭikaṭ mahā bikaṭ, aur chār kā mūṅh kālā, pāṅch ho to bhalā. Wom.
Three stares are bad, four disgrace and five ruin.

Tīn Tirhūtiyā mile, paknā rah gayā. [cook.
When three Tirhūtis meet, there's no one to
(A skit at the strong caste prejudices of the Tirhūti Brāhmans.)

Tīn tilālā, chauthe kā mūṅh kālā.
Three are cheats, and the fourth a blackguard.

Tīrath gaē, muṇḍāē sidh.
If you go on a pilgrimage, you have to shave.
(Shaving the head is one of the ceremonies at Prāg (Allahabad) and other holy places.)

Tīrath, mūrat pūj-kar mat nā umar gaṅvāe. Pūjā kar Kartār kī, jo turat mukat ho jāē.
Waste not thy life in pilgrimages and worshipping of idols. Worship thy Creator that thou mayest quickly be saved.
(A saying of the *bhagats* or reformers.)

Tiretā ke bījoṅ ko pahuṅch gaē. E.
It has run to seed in the Third Age.
(The *Tretā Jug* or Third Age of the world was the one that immediately preceded the present one. In it mankind was three parts bad.)

Tīr judāī ā lagā, diyā kalejā chhed. Pī apnā pardes māṅ, kis se kahiye bhed?
The arrow of loneliness hath pierced my heart. My love is abroad, to whom shall tell my secret.

Tīr, kavve, tīr!
Arrow, crow, arrow!
(Crows are commonly scared by shouting *tīr*, arrow.)

Tīr na kamān; kāhe ke paṭhān. Mah.
Neither bow nor arrows; what kind of Paṭhān is he?
(Said of one who pretends to qualifications, which he does not possess. *Paṭhān* is here used to mean a soldier or warrior.)

Tīr na kamān, mere chachā khūb laṛe.
My uncle fought famously, though he had neither bow nor arrows.
(Vain glory see preceeding.)

Tīr na kamān; miyāṅ kā Allāh nigahbān! Mah.
He has neither bow nor arrows, may God protect him!

Tīr, turumtī, istrī, chhūṭat bas nā āeṅ; Jhūṭ jo māne yeh bachan ve nar kūṛh kahāeṅ.
An arrow, an eagle and a woman once out of hand come never back; Who disbelieves this saying is certainly a fool.

Tiryā bhalī vohī hai, bhāī, jo purkhā sang kare bhalāī.
The woman that doeth a man good, my friend, is a good woman.
(O woman, in our hours of ease, fickle, vain and hard to please: When pain and anguish wring the brow, A ministering angel thou!)

Tiryā bhī nar bin hai aisī, Binā dhanī ke khetī jaisī.
A woman without a husband is as a field without an owner.

Tirya bin to nar hai aisā, rāh baṭāū hove jaisā.
A man without a wife is as a traveller on the road.
(*i. e.* he has no fixed abode.)

Tiryā bis kī bel hai: yā saṅg bach-kar chāl Yā kā nehā khoṭ hai dīn, dharam, dhan, māl.
Woman is a poisonous creeper; avoid her company: Her love destroys faith, caste, wealth and money.

Tiryā chalitr, aur chor kī ghāt, Pāī paṛe na, kah gaē Nāth.
Women's wiles and thieve's tricks Cannot be fathomed: so say the Saints.

Tiryā charitr jāne nahīṅ koē; Khasam mār-ke satī hoē. Hin.
None knows the wily tricks of women; They kill their husbands and then burn themselves.
(To prove their innocence! *Satī* is burning at a husband's pyre, and is the act of the best women only.)

Tiryā jāt kamān hai, jit chāhe tit tān.
Women are like bows; they can bend as much as they please.
(Changeable as the moon: *varium et mutabile est fœmina.*)

Tiryā purakh bin hai dukhī, jaise an bin deh; Jale bale hai jīvṛā, jūṅ khetī bin meṅh.
A wife is troubled without her husband, as the body without food; She is burnt and dried up as a field without rain.

Tiryā rove purakh binā, khetī rove meṅh binā. Agric.
A woman weeps without a husband and a field without rain.

Tiryā terah, mard aṭhārah. Hin.
A woman at thirteen and a man at eighteen.
(Make a fair match.)

Tiryā thirakat jo chale, vāko bhalā na jān: Jaise hāth likher kā kāṅpat ho nuqsān.
Don't think her good who goes with mincing gait: If the painter's hand trembles, it spoils his work.

Tiryā to hai sobhā ghar kī, Jo ho lāj rakhāvā nar kī.
A woman is indeed the ornament of the house, When she upholds honour of her husband.

Tiryā, tujh meṅ tīn gun, augun haiṅ lakh chār: Maṅgal gāve, sat rache, aur kokan upjeṅ lāl.
Woman, thou hast three good qualities and four hundred thousand bad: To sing, to burn (as *satī*), and to produce sons.

Tiryā tujh se jo kahe, mūl na tū voh mān: Tiryā mat par jo chaleṅ voh nar haiṅ nir gyān.
Never listen to your wife's advise: Who takes his wife's advice has no sense.
(Madame, we look to you to give us heirs, but not advice.)

Tisī ke khet meṅ jolhā bhutlāne. E.

The weaver loses his way in the linseed field.

(Through his stupidity: the stupidity of the weaving classes is a standing joke in India.)

Tis-mār Khāṅ bane phirte hai.

He struts about like a Tīsmār Khāṅ.

☞ The story goes that once an idle husband and a soldier by birth, being much goaded by his wife to earn a living, resolved to go to a distant land. His wife, a day previous to his march, prepared 30 sweet-meat balls or *laḍḍūs* as provisions for one month, but she unknowingly crushed a poisonous insect into them. The next day the man set out and had not reached the first stage before thirty thieves attacked him. They got nothing in plunder but the thirty poisonous *laḍḍūs*, which they very eagerly ate up, as they had been starving for the two previous days. No sooner had they eaten them than the poison made them torpid. When the soldier saw the condition of the thieves he cut off their noses and went his way. He came to a city where he was suspected of some heinous crime and apprehended. He boldly and frankly told what he had done and explained the whole truth. The king set an enquiry on foot and finding that the thieves were thirty out-laws, who had been banished from the country and had incessantly harrassed the people, he gave him a suitable reward, with the title of Tīsmār Khāṅ and appointed him his councilor.

Tīsre din murdah bhī halāl hai. Mah.

On the third day even a dead body is lawful.

(To a man who has fasted three days or is nearly dying of hunger any kind of food is allowed by Muhammadan law.)

Tītar bāveṅ bol jā to sagre kār hoṅ ṭhīk; Dāhne bolat nā bhalā, sāṅch jān yeh sīkh.

Superstition.

If a partridge cry on the left all your wishes will thrive; If it cry on the right believe me it is not a good omen.

Tittar bittar ho gae sagar Dom ke kām; Nimaṛ gae, jijmān, jab gāṅṭh girah ke dām.

All the musician's business goes to the dogs, When the money in his pocket is gone, my patron.

(Empty words buy no barley: a saying of the ḍoms or public singers.)

Tīvan bin nā roṭī sohe; Gūṅdhe bin nā choṭī sohe.

Bread unseasoned is not good, Nor hair unbraided.

Tohrā būte kan bhūsā ekko na chhuṭī. E. Wom.

You don't know chaff from wheat.

(You have no discernment: not to know B from a Bull's foot.)

To ko levan maiṅ chalī, tū mohe gherī ā; Ab tū mo ko chhoṛ de, maiṅ tohe chhoṛ diyā.

Wom.

I came to take thee and thou didst win me; But now that thou leavest me, I leave thee.

(Once I loved a maiden fair But she did deceive me......now I do abhor her.)

To ko na bhunāūṅ, torā bhaīyā aur bandhāūṅ. E.

I'll not change you; I'll get more of your brothers for you.

(A skit at the proverbial avārice of the true Pūrbiyā.)

☞ A Pūrbiyā had occasion to change a Rupee, but was loth to part with it. So he turned away from one shop after another till the perspiration broke out in the hand in which he held the rupee. Touched by what he pictured to himself as tears shed by his dear rupee he addressed it in the words of the Proverb.

Tolā bhar kī ārsī, nānī bole Fārsī.

The thumb-ring weighed an ounce, and the grandmother spoke of it in Persian.

(Hyperbole: tall talk.)

Tolā bhar kī chār kachaurī, khurmā māshe ḍhāī kā, Lālājī ne byāh rachāyā, dhablā bech lugāī kā. [Hin.

With four thin cakes and tiny sweets, My gentleman has held a marriage on the proceeds of his wife's petticoat.

(A skit at the pretensious marriages of the poor.)

Tolā bhar kī tīn chapātī: Kahe jimāne chālo hāthī.

With three cakes weighing on ounce, He says he is going to feed an elephant.

Tolā ke peṭ meṅ ghuṅgchī.

A dram goes into the belly of an ounce.

(The large fish eat the small ones.)

Ṭolan māṅ ghar ṭol bhalā: Sab bājan māṅ ḍhol bhalā.

One's own household is the best of company, And a drum the best of music.

Toran āē chārā, aur khet par ijārā.

Come for forage and claims the field.

(Said of a preposterous claim.)

Toṛ ḍāl tāgā; tū kis bhaṛve ke mūṅh lāgā.

Mah. Wom.

Break the marriage thread; what blackguard have you been talking with?

(*Tāgā* is the marriage thread: used to a woman who goes wrong soon after her marriage, as the *tāgā* cannot last long.)

Torī banat banat ban jāī, tū Hari se lāgā raho, re bhāī.

By and bye you will succeed, stick then to Hari (God), my friend.

Torī hoelo mūrī khar, paṭvā bhailo sāg: Agvāre pichhvāre baiṭhlo, so ho bhailo sardār. E.

Radishes and weeds for vetches and their leaves for spinach: He has become a gentleman who was but a dependent.

(*Torī* is the pod of a kind of edible vetch: the Indian radish is looked on as of no value.)

Ṭoṭā karde mūṅh nūṅ kālā; Ṭoṭe vāl jagat dā sālā. Mercantile: Panj.

Ruin blackens the face, And the ruined is the brother-in-law of the world.

(A blackened face implies disgrace: *sālā* or brother-in-law is a strong term of implied abuse or contempt.)

Ṭoṭā ṭalā nā ṭale, jab lag miṭe na lekh: Sādh kaheṅ, re bālke, lākh jatan kar dekh.
Poverty cannot be removed, as long as fate's writing is not effaced, Though thou contrive a thousand plans, my son: so say the saints.

Ṭoṭā ṭāmak, ṭotrū chhāne raheṅ na mūl. Yūṅ parghaṭ hoṅ jagat māṅ, jūṅ lashkar kī dhūl.
A loss, a drum, and a dove cannot be concealed; They betray themselves in the word as doth the dust of an army.

Tote chashm ādmī hai.
His eyes are like a parrot's.
(*i. e.* restless and uncertain: said of a fickle man.)

Tote kī sī āṅkheṅ pher letā hai.
He turns his eyes about like a parrot.
(Said of one insensible of kindness, because a parrot, however petted, will fly away at the first opportunity.)

Ṭoṭe mārā banjyā bhar jogī kā bhes, Hāṅḍe bhichchā māṅgtā ghar ghar des bides.
The bankrupt merchant puts on the mendicant's robes and begs from door to door at home or abroad.
(A skit at the interested motives from which men turn mendicant.)

Ṭoṭe se ho ghar kā ṭībā; Ṭoṭā gayā to khulā nasībā. Mercantile.
Misfortune will ruin a house, But when misfortune goes good fortune comes.

Tū bhī rānī main bhī rānī: kaun bharegā pānī? Hin. Wom.
I am a queen and you are a queen: so who is to fetch the water?
(Said to an idle servant.)

Tū chāh merī jāī ko, main chāhūṅ terī khāṭ ke pāē ko. Wom.
Love my daughter and I will love the foot of your bed.
(*i. e.* the very ground you tread on: said by a mother of the bride to the bridegroom: *also*, love me love my dog.)

Tū chhūē aur main mūī. Wom.
Touch me and I die.
(Affectation of delicacy.)

Tūfān, Shaitān, Allāh nigah-bān!
God keep us from calumny, and the Devil!

Tū gadhī kumhār kī, tujhe Rām se kauth?
You are a potter's ass, what have you to do with Rām?
(*Rām* here means any thing important: the saying is a rebuke.)

Tū gor khod mo ko, main gāṛ āuṅ to ko.
You dig a grave for *me* and I'll bury *you* in it.

Tūī to mūī: nahīṅ tūī to mūī.
If she miscarries she suffers: if she miscarries not she suffers.
(Loss or suffering in any case: a bad job.)

Tujhe parāī kyā paṛī? apnī nabeṛ tū.
Why do you meddle with others? Do your own business.

Tujh par paṛe jo audhsā dil bich mat ghabrā. Jab sāīṅ kī ho dayā kām turat ban jā. Rus.
Let not thy heart be downcast when adversity overtaketh thee. When God shall have mercy thy work will quickly prosper.

Tū kahe so sach hai, buddhī! tū kahe so sach! Superstition.
What you say is true, old lady! What you say is true.
(Old women are supposed to speak the truth.)
☞ The story goes that some men having robbed an old woman bound her to a stretcher and so bore her through the streets, replying to her cries that she was plundered, in the words of the Proverb. Thus the people were deluded into the idea that the procession was one of the mimic representations commonly exhibited in India about the Holī season.

Tū kanr ke māre phirat, kyoṅ man meṅ pachhtāyo? Jis ne jaisā diyo hai, tis ne taiso pāyo.
Why dost thou pine for want of bread? As a man gave (in a former birth) so he receiveth now.
(Hindū belief.)

Tū kar apnā kām, tavalyā bhusan de. E.
Do your work quickly and let the curs bark.

Tukhm tāsīr: sohbat kā asar.
As the seed so the result; as the society so the man.
(A tree is known by its fruits and a man by the company he keeps.)

Tū khol merā maknā, main ghar sanbhālūṅ apnā! Mah. Wom.
Lift up my (bridal) veil, for I must manage my house.
(Said in reproof to a young bride, who is too eager to interfere in the affairs of her husband's house. An imprudent act according to native ideas.)

Ṭuk jīyā to kyā jīyā.
To live for a moment is not worth living.
(Respite under the sword.)

Ṭukṛā-toṛ javāb de denā.
To give a short answer.

Ṭukṛe de de bachhṛā pālā, sīṅg lage jab māran āyā.
I brought the calf up on my own food, and as soon as his horns grew he turned upon me.
(Ingratitude.)

Ṭukṛe khāē din bahlāē, kapṛe phāṭe ghar ko āē. Wom.
He eats his meals and wastes his days and comes home in rags.
(An idle husband.)

Ṭukṛoṅ kā pālā huā hai.
Brought up on leavings.
(A slave.)

Ṭuk ṭuk kar-ke man bhar khāve, Tanak Begmān nām batāve! Wom.
Little by little she eats a hundred weight,

and yet she calls herself Miss Delicate-eater!

(A habit by no means confined to the women of India.)

Tulsī, āh garīb kī Hari se sahī na jāē! Marī khāl kī phūṅk se lohā bhasam ho jāē.

O Tulsī, God even cannot bear the sighs of the poor! Bellows of leather will turn iron to ashes.

Tulsī, aise jīv kī kahā kare koī sākh, Le-ke de chāhat nahīn, kiryā karat hain lākh?

Tulsī, who would credit the man, That takes and returns not, though he swore a thousand oaths?

Tulsī, aise jiv kyon Narak-kuṇḍ na jāēn, Man ke kapṭī mintr hain, pagyā utāro chāhen?

Tulsī, why should not such men go to Hell, That betray and dishonor their friends?

Tulsī, aise mitr ke koṭ phānd ke jāē, Āvat hī to hans mile, aur chalat rahe murjhāē.

Tulsī, climb over a fort to go to that friend, Who meets you with a smile and leaves with a heavy heart.

Tulsī, aise nalan kī kaise gat mat hoē, Bāp ne rākhī pāturī, tā ke ḍhig rahe soē?

Tulsī, how shall that man be saved, That sleeps with the concubine of his own father?

Tulsī, aise nalan se man phāṭe jas dūdh, Nīke kām ko nā chalen, bure ko har dam ūdh.

Tulsī, from such men the heart is turned like milk, That are loth to do good but eager to do evil.

(A pun here on the word *phaṭnā*, which means turning of the heart, as well as of the milk.)

Tulsī, aise patit ko bār bār dhirkār, Rām bhajan ko alsī, khaibe ko taiyār.

Tulsī, accursed be such a sinner base, That is slow to worship God and quick to eat!

Tulsī, aisī pīt kar jaise bhor talā: Jhol-jhāl-ke pī liyā, pher lagā galā.

O Tulsī, let thy love be as the scum upon a pond: Men part it to drink and then it joins again.

Tulsī, ām kulīn hai, nave barappan jān: Ochhā per hai renṛ kā rahe sīs dhar tān.

Tulsī, the mango is a noble tree, that knows its worth and bows: The castor is a mean tree that lives with its head in the air.

Tulsī, anchhar karm ke meṭ na sakke Rām: Meṭe to achraj nahīn, par samajh kiyā hai kām.

Tulsī, even God cannot efface the writing of fate: It would be no wonder if He could, but He hath ordained thus of a purpose.

(God obeys his own laws.)

Tulsī, apne Rām ko bhajiye jaise lūṭ:
Yeh tan gharā hai kānch kā chhin men jāgā ṭūṭ.

Tulsī, call on God as (heartily as) you would plunder: This body is a vessel of glass that may break at any moment.

Tulsī, apne Rām ko khīj bhajo yā rījh: Khet paṛen sab ūpjen ulṭe sīdhe bīj.

Tulsī, repeat the name of God willingly or unwillingly: All the seeds that fall into a field are sure to germinate whether right or wrong side up.

Tulsī apno jān ke, kinī thī parīt. Dhoko de niyāre bhae: bhalī nibhāī pit!

Tulsī, mistaking him for a friend I believed in him. He cheated me and went off: how well he returned my love!

(Said by a woman when her lover, who had promised to live always with her, breaks his promise.)

Tulsī, besvā dekh-ke karan lage tāk jhānk: Āvat dekho sant ko, mūnh linho jhaṭ ḍhānk.

Tulsī, they ogle at women and cast side long glances, And when they see a coming saint they hide their faces.

Tulsī, bharose Rām ke līye pāp bhar moṭ, Jūn bibhīchārī nār ko baṛī khasam kī oṭ.

Tulsī, relying on God I have committed a full load of sins: Like an unchaste wife who trusts to her husband's protection.

(The illegitimate child of a married woman can be fathered on her husband, while a widow or maid has no such advantage.)

Tulsī, bides jo jāt hain, karen samān anant: Nā jānūn parlok ko kaise nar nishchant?

Tulsī, he who goes abroad takes much supplies with him: Who knows why men are indifferent about the next world?

Tulsī, birvā bāg ke sīchat hū kumhlāēn: Rām bharose jo rahen, parbat par haryāēn.

Tulsī, the watered trees of the garden will die: But that which trusts in God will flourish on the mountain.

(Natives of the plains of India believe that trees don't flourish on mountains!)

Tulsī, buro na māniye jo ganvār kah jāē: Sāvan kī sī naddua burā bhalā bah jāē.

Tulsī, don't take ill what a fool may say: A torrent in the rains takes good and bad with it.

Tulsī, chandan biṭap basī, bin bikh bhayo na bhuang: Nich nichāī nā taje, jo pāve sat sang.

Tulsī, the snake gives not up its poison by living in a sandal tree: So the base give not up their baseness, though they dwell with the righteous.

Tulsī, chhal bal chhāṛ-ke kīje Rām se neh; Antar pat sūn hai kahā jin dekhī sab deh?

Tulsi, give up all artifice and deceit, and love God; Why hide from a husband that hath seen thy whole body?

Tulsī, dayā na chhāḍiye jab lag ghaṭ men prān; Kabhūn to Pirbhū Dīn-dayāl ke bhanak paṛegī kān.

Tulsī, give not up mercy, while there is breath in thy body, That (thy prayers) may reach the ears of the Lord of Mercy.

Tulsī, dhīraj ke dhare kunjar man bhar khāē ; Ṭūk ṭūk ke kārne suān ghar ghar jāē.
Tulsī, patiently the elephant eats his hundred weight, While the dog runs from door to door for his crusts and crumbs.

Tulsī, Hari kī bhakt bin ye āve ke kāj, Arab kharab loṅ Lakshmī, ude ast loṅ rāj ?
Tulsī, without devotion to God, what avails it To possess millions of wealth and dominion from East to West ?

Tulsī, jag meṅ āē-ke augun taj de chār : Chorī, jārī, jāmnī, aur parāī nār.
Tulsī, in this world eschew four bad things : Theft, incest, suretyship and a stranger's wife.

Tulsī, jag meṅ āēke nehche bhajiye Rām : Manukh majūrī det haiṅ, kyoṅ rākheṅ Bhagvān ?
Tulsī, having come into the world thou must ever call on God, When man gives wages, will not God ?

Tulsī, jag meṅ āēke sīkh ūkh se leo : Jo tum ko anrath kare, vā ko ras tum deo.
Tulsī, in this world learn this lesson from the sugar cane : To give them pleasure that injure thee.
(Whosoever shall smite thee on thy right cheek turn to him the other also. *Matthew* v, 39.)

Tulsī, jag meṅ jas rahe, yā rahe Rām ko nām.
Tulsī, in this world reputation lasts and so does God's name.

Tulsī, jape to Rām jap, aur nām mat le : Rām nām shamsher hai jam ke sir meṅ de.
O Tulsī, worship Rām, if you want to worship : take not another name : The name of Rām is a sword to strike at the head of Death.

☞ It is said that Tulsī Dās, the author of Hindī *Rāmāyan*, was a bigoted worshiper of Rām. Once upon a time he came to visit Mathurā, where he was greatly shocked to hear every body worshiping Krishna and his wife Rādhā, whereupon he made the following couplet : "*Tulsī, yā Brij bhūm meṅ kahā Rām se bair ?" Rādhā Krishna raṭat āk ḍhāk aur kair.* O Tulsī, what enmity there is with Rām in this land of Brij (Mathurā). That every leaf and leaflet calls on Rādhā and Krishna. "But when he entered one of the temples of which there is no end, and espied the splendid image of Krishna in his majestic beauty he said half yielding and half retiring : "*Kahā kahauṅ chkab āj kī, bhale bane ho, Nāth ! Tulsī mastag jab nive jab dhanush bān lo hāth.* What can I say, O Lord, of thy grace and beauty to-day ? But Tulsī will bow his head to thee when thou takest a bow and arrow in thy hand." The image was transformed at once, holding a bow and an arrow, with all the grace of Rāmchandar, whereupon Tulsī Dās expressed himself in the following couplet and bowed down : *Kit murlī kit chandrikā, kit Gopin kā sāth ! Tulsī Dās ke kārne Nāth bhaē Raghū Nāth.* Where hath gone the flute and where the crown and where the milk maids (the emblems of Krishna) ? for the sake of his worshiper Tulsī, the Lord became Raghū Nāth.

Tulsī, kadhī na chhāḍiye, chhimā, sīl, santosh, Gyān, garībī, Hari bajan, komal bachan adosh.
Tulsī, give not up mercy, virtue and content, Wisdom, meekness, the worship of God, sweetness and innocence.

Tulsī, kahat pukār-ke, sune sakal de kān : Hemdān, gaj-dān se, baṛā dān sanmān.
Saith Tulsī aloud, let all give ear : Courtesy is a better gift than gold and elephants.

Tulsī, kāhū chor ne chorī jāē karī : Mos mās ke dhan liyo, pūrī nāhīṅ parī.
Tulsī, a thief went out to steal : He squeezed men of their property and still he did not thrive.

Tulsī, kālī kāmlī chaṛhe na dūjā rang.
Says Tulsī, the black blanket takes no other hue.
(Shall the leopard change his spots or the Ethiopian his skin.)

Tulsī, Kaljug ke samae, dekho yeh kartūt ; Rām nām ko chhoṛ-ke pūjan lage ab bhūt !
Tulsī, behold the customs of the Evil Age, Men leave the true God to worship devils !

Tulsī kā pattā kaun chhoṭā kaun baṛā. Hin.
Is one leaf of the *tulsī* tree better than another ?
(Every leaf has equal virtue and alike confers future felicity. The proverb is said of individuals of like rank and worth.)

Tulsī, kar se karm kar, mukh se bhaj le Rām : Aisā sama na pāē go je lākhoṅ kharche dām.
Tulsī, work with thy hands, and call on God with thy mouth : Thou wilt find no better times though thou spend millions.

Tulsī, mīṭhā boliye, sab se kar ke prīt, Kareṅ prem tā se sabhī, lakhī kokil kī rīt.
Tulsī, speak pleasantly and bear love to all, And all will love thee, as they do the cuckoo.

Tulsī, mīṭhe bachan se sukh upje chahūṅ or : Basī karan yeh mantr hai, taj de bachan kaṭhor.
Tulsī, pleasant words please the whole world : The charm for success is giving up harsh words.

Tulsī, mūrakh māne nahīṅ jab lag khatā na khāē : Jaise bidhuā istrī garabh rahe pachhtāē.
Tulsī, a fool listens to no advice until he suffers loss ; Like a widow who repents when she is pregnant.
(Pregnancy being an unquestionable proof of a widow's unchastity.)

Tulsī, paisā pās kā sab se nīko hoē : Hote ke bahan aur bāp haiṅ, an-hote kī joē.
Tulsī, to keep you, penny by you is the best of all : Your father and sister (befriend you) when you have it and (only) your wife when you have it not.

Tulsī, par ghar jāē-ke dukh na kahīye roe : Bharam ganvāve āpno, bāṅṭ na sakke koē.
Tulsī, bewail not thy woes in a strange

house: Thou wilt betray thy secret where none will share them.

Tulsī, pichhle pāp se Hari charcha na suhāē; Jaise jur ke ans meṅ bhūk bidā ho jāē.

Tulsī, the old sins make the worship of the God unacceptable: As fever destroys the appetite for food.

Tulsī, pirtimā pūjibo, jyoṅ guṛyoṅ kā khel: Bheṭ bhaī jab pīv se dhare pitārī mel.

Tulsī, the worship of idols is like playing with dolls, Which a girl gives up when she goes to her husband.

(*i. e.* idol worship is mere childishness. When I was a child, I spake as a child, I understood as a child, I thought as a child; but when I became a man I put away childish things. I. *Corinthians* ii, 13.)

Tulsī, Rām kī bhakti bin dhik ḍāḍhī, dhik mūṅchh: Pasū gharante nar bhayo, bhūlo sing aur pūṅchh.

Tulsī, without the love of God, beard and whiskers are worthless things; A man grows out of beasts, and wants only horns and tail.

(To make an animal of him.)

Tulsī, saran hai Rām kī, sun le merī ṭer: Gaj ko chhuṛāyo grāh se merī bār kyoṅ der?

Saith Tulsī, I am thy slave, O God, hear my prayer: Thou didst save the elephant from the crocodile, wilt delay then to save me?

(Allusion to a struggle for life between an elephant and a crocodile in Hindū mythology.)

Tulsī, tab hī jāniye Parmeshuar se prīt, Harakh uṭhe, ādar kare, āvat dekh atīt.

Tulsī, know that a man loves God, When he stands up cheerfully and welcomes a coming mendicant.

Tulsī, tahāṅ na jāiye jahāṅ janam bhūm kā ṭhāoṅ: Āo bhagat jāneṅ nahīṅ, dhare pāchhlā nāoṅ.

O Tulsī, go not to your native place: Where they 'll show you no respect, and call you by your nickname!

(No man is hero to his valet. A prophet is not without honor save in his own country and in his own house. Matthew xiii, 57.)

Tulsī, tahāṅ na jāiye jahāṅ na barn bibek! Rāṅg, rūp, rūā, bhūā, set set sab ek.

O Tulsī! go not to that place where there is no distinction of caste! Tin, silver, cotton and grass flowers are all white.

(But differ in quality. Tulsī Dās was the author of the Hindī *Rāmāyāṇa* and a Brāhman and hence the saying.)

Tulsī, tum to kahat ho, sangat se sab hot: Bich ukh meṅ rām-sar, tehī ras kāhe na hot?

Tulsī, thou sayest that companionship effects all things; But where is the sweetness of grass in the midst of sugar-canes?

Tulsī, voh doū gae, paṇḍit aur girhast: Āte ādar nā kiyā, jāt diyā na hast.

Tulsī, both are bad, layman and priest: That are not courteous on coming and go without giving help.

(Respect to whom respect is due.)

Tulsī, yā sansār meṅ pākhanḍī kī mān: Sidhoṅ ko sīdhā nahīṅ, jhūṭoṅ ko pakvān.

Tulsī, in this world all believe in hypocrites: Saints get no uncooked food, and the liars live on sweets.

Tulsī, yā sansār meṅ, pāṅch ratn haiṅ sār: Sādhu milan aur Hari-bhajan, dayā, dharm, upkār.

Tulsī, in this world are five chief gems: communion with saints, worship of God, mercy, faith and kindliness of heart.

Tulsī, yā sansār meṅ sab se milye dhāē: Nā jānūn kis bhes meṅ Nārāyan mil jāē.?

Tulsī, in this world run to meet all men: You cannot say in what disguise you may meet God.

(Be all things to all men.)

Tulū aur gurūb ke vaqt sijda manā hai. Mah. Superstition.

At actual sunset and sunrise you must not kneel to pray.

Tum ant gae, ham ant kar āyo, māroṅ chūn kūtan ne khāyo. E.

While you went one way, and I the other, the dogs ate up the dough.

(When the members of a family fall out, outsiders benefit by the quarrel.)

Ṭūm baiyar kī pat badhāve: Ṭūm tujhe dhanvant kahāve.

Ornaments exalt the credit of a woman: Ornaments will make a rich man.

(The tailor makes the man.)

Tum baṛā nannhā kātti ho. Wom.

You spin a fine thread.

(Over economy: skinning a flint.)

Tum bhī kahoge "koī mujhe joru kare."

You also shall say "who will marry me?"

(Said of one who is proud of superior acquirements.)

Tum bhī kahoge "mujhe charkhā le de"?

Can you ask any one to buy you a spinning wheel?

(*i. e.* more fit for a woman's work than a man's work: said to a foolish man.)

Tum bhī kore chālīs sere ūt ho.

You are a forty *ser* fool.

(Ūt, a lad who dies unmarried, is used in the sense of the English 'cow' or 'calf': forty *sers* being a complete *man* is used as an idiom meaning completeness.)

Ṭūm binā baiyar hai aisī, bin pānī ke khetī jaisī.

A woman without ornaments is like a field without water.

Tum bin aisī gat bhaī, sun merī, aē pīū: Jaise khāl luhār kī, sāṅs let bin jīū.

Without thee, my husband, my body Is like the blacksmith's bellows that breathe without life.

Tum ḍāl ḍāl, ham pāt pāt.

If you go on every branch, I will go on every leaf.

(Whatever stratagems you practise, I will be a match for you.)

Tum, Dātā, dukh bhanj ho, morī suno, Nāth, guhār: Hauṅ aprādhī janm ko, nakh sikh bharo bikār.

O God, Thou remover of pain, hear my prayer, O Lord, I have been a sinner from my birth, full of vice from top to toe.

(I will arise and go to my father and will say unto him, Father, I have sinned against heaven and before thee and am no more worthy to be called thy son. Luke, xv, 18, 19.)

Tū mere bāle ko chāhe, to maiṅ tere būṛhe ko chāhūṅ.

You cherish my infant, and I will take care of your old man.

(You scratch my back and I will scratch yours.)

Tū merā laṛkā, khilā, maiṅ terī khichṛī pakāūṅ. Wom.

You amuse my child, and I'll cook your food.

Tumhāre bail, hamāre bhaiṅsā: tumhāre hamāre phir sāth kaisā.

You have an ox and I a buffalo: how can you and I keep company?

(An ox travels faster than a buffalo, which is a very heavy animal.)

Tumhāre chāṭe to rūkh bhī nahīṅ rahe haiṅ.

Even the trees cannot stand your licking.

(Metaphor from the action of locusts; said to an extortioner.)

Tumhāre farishtoṅ ko bhī khabar nahīṅ hai. Mah.

Even your angels have no knowledge of it.

(Every man has two guardian angels that live on his shoulders and take note of all he does.)

Tumhāre laṛke bhī kabhī ghuṭniyoṅ chaleṅge? Mah. Wom.

When will your children crawl on their knees.

(When will you speak the truth or perform your promise?)

Tumhāre mare des khāk, hamāre mare des pāk.

Your death will destroy the land, but mine will purify it.

(Humility: the following proverb is its reverse.)

Tumhāre mare des pāk, hamāre mare des khāk.

Your death will purify the land, but my death will destroy it.

(Foolish pride.)

Tumhāre mūṅh kā ugāl, hamāre peṭ kā ādhār.

The droppings from your mouth are food for my stomach.

(Fed on the crumbs from the rich man's table.)

Tumhāre mūṅh meṅ ghī shakkar!

May your mouth be filled with *ghī* and sugar!

(Said to one who brings a good news or comes at a propitious time.)

Tumhāre mūṅh meṅ kae dāṅt haiṅ, yeh to koī pūchhtā hī nahīṅ.

No one asks, how many teeth you have in your head.

(A phrase used to imply good government and security of life and property.)

Tumhāre pān kā ugāl, hamāre peṭ kā ādhār.

The remains of your betel is food for my stomach.

(That which you can easily spare without missing it, will be of the greatest service to me.)

Tumhāre peṭ meṅ chiṅṭe kī gāṅṭh hai.

There's an ant's joint in your stomach.

(You eat so little!)

Tumhārī barābarī voh kare, jo dauṛte hiran ko pakṛe.

He is your equal, who runs and catches a deer.

(*i. e.* a dog: said in contempt.)

Tumhārī barābarī voh kare, jo ṭāng uṭhā-kar mūte.

He is your equal, who lifts up his leg to make water.

(*i. e.* a dog: see preceding.)

Tumhārī bāt kā etebār kyā?

There's no trusting in your word.

Tumhārī bāt meṅ band kyā?

There is no reliance on your speeches.

(See preceding.)

Tumhārī bāt thal kī ma beṛī kī.

Your speech neither belongs to land nor water.

(It is incongruous and inconsistent.)

Tumhārī bāt uṭhāī jāe na dharī jāe.

Your words can neither be taken up or put down.

(They don't go down.)

Tumhārī jūtī aur tumhārā hī sir.

Your shoes are on your own head.

(The expenditure is met by the income.)

Tumhāre bhatār na hamāre joe: as kuchh karo ki beṭvā hoe. E.

You have no husband and I no wife; let us so act that we may have a son.

(A frank way of asking a widow's hand in marriage by a widower.)

Tum jāno, tumhārā kām jāne.

You know your own business best.

(I'll have nothing to do with it.)

Tūm kāpṛe jis ghar pāveṅ, ek chhoṛ das baiyar āveṅ.

Not one but ten women will flock to house where jewelry and clothing are to be had.

Tum kāṭo merī nāk aur kānī, Maiṅ na chhoṛūṅ apnī bānī. Mah. Wom.

You may cut off my nose and ears, But I'll not give up my ways.

(Said by an obstinate woman in reply to her husband's threats.)

Tum kis khet ke bathve ho?
From what field came this weed?
(Said to a boaster.)

Tum kis khet ki mūlī ho?
From what field came this raddish?
(See preceding.)

Tum ko ham sī anek haiṅ, ham ko tum sā ek: Ravī ko kaval anek haiṅ, kavalan ko ravi ek.
Wom.
You have many like me, I have but one like you: The sun sees many lotuses, but the lotuses only one sun.
(An obedient wife to her husband.)

Tum kyoṅ phaṭe meṅ pāoṅ dete ho?
Why do you thrust your feet into the torn place?
(Why do you bring another's quarrel on to your head? They who in quarrels interpose will often wipe a bloody nose.)

Tum ne uṛāīṅ. ham ne bhūn bhūn khāīṅ.
You made it fly away, I fried and ate it.
(Teach your grandmother to suck eggs.)

Tum rūṭhe: ham chhūṭe! Mah. Wom.
You are angry: I am free!
(Reference to the ease of divorce under Muhammadan law.)

Tum sarīke saiṅkṛoṅ phirte haiṅ.
A lot of men like you wander here and there.
(You are no great shakes.)

Tum thūkte ho, ham thūkte bhī nahīṅ.
You may spit, but I can't.
(*Noblesse oblige.*)

Tum to aql ke pīchhe laṭh liye phirte ho.
Why do you pursue your good sense with a club?
(To destroy it! Said to a man acting rashly.)

Tum to jab mā ke peṭ se bhī nahīṅ nikle hoge.
You were not come out of your mother's womb then.
(Does your mother know you 're out?)

Tum to kuchh jānte hī nahīṅ, auṅdhe mūṅh dūdh pīte ho.
You know nothing, sucking up milk on your face.
(*i. e.* you are acting like a baby.)

Tum to mujhe chheṛoge!
You 'll lay your hand on me!
(I am afraid you are going to kiss me: sham modesty.)

☞ The story goes that a woman with an empty pitcher on her head met a man carrying pigeons in his two hands: "Don't take liberties with me" said she. "How could I?" he replied—"Oh you could put them into my pitcher."

Tū mujh ko, to maiṅ tujh ko.
You love me and I 'll love you.

Tū ne kī Rāmjanī, maiṅ ne kīyā Rāmianā.
You 've got a mistress and I have got a lover.
(Rebuke of a wife to a debauched husband.)

Tūṅ kithoṅ dā Khakkhā Sāhab haiṅ?
Where are you the Lord of?
(Are you any body in particular? *Khakkhā* is the letter *kh*, beginning *Khāṅ* or Lord, in the Gurmukhhī character of Panjābī.)

Tuntunī bajāte: mīyāṅ khāte shakkar ghī; Naukrī kī aisī taisī, ab ke bache jī.
Blowing the trumpet my lord lived on sugar and *ghī*: but the service may be accursed if he save his life this time.
(The glory and danger of soldiering.)

Tū raho rī, hauṅ hī lakhūṅ: chorh na aṭā, Brij bāl: Binā same sashī ke ugahe paṛhāīṅ aragh akāl. Hin. Wom.
Stop, I'll go up to see: you must not mount the balcony my maid of Brij, Or libations will be poured out without a moon.
(*i. e.* people will mistake your face for the moon: a mother's advice to her beautiful daughter. It is customary for Hindūs to pour out libations to the moon on fast days before taking their food.)

Turaī kaddū; lānat har dū!
Gourd and pumpkin; a curse upon both!
(*Arcades ambo.*)

Turak kā ke mīt, sarap se kā pīt.
The love of a Muhammadan is the friendship of a serpent.

Turak, talaiyā, totrā, na yeh kisī ke mīt: Bhīṛ paṛat mūṅh pher leṅ, rāhkheṅ na pirīt.
Rus.
A Musalman, a wasp, and a parrot are no body's friend: In time of difficulty these go away and show no love.

Turat bhalāī voh nar pāve, jo dhan Dātā nām luṭāve.
Who spends his money in the name of God will soon get a good name.

Turat dān mahā kallyān. Hin.
Ready alms is sure salvation.

Turat dān mahā pun.
Ready alms is a great virtue.
(See preceding.)

Turat fateh ho us ke tāīṅ, jis kā hāmī hove Sāīṅ.
He soon conquers whom God helps.

Turat hī poö, turat hī khāo: Bāsī khā mat, ojh baṛhāo.
Quickly bake and quickly eat: Eat not stale food or your belly will swell.
(Said of the *chapātī* or unleavened cake of the natives, which must be eaten fresh.)

Turat majūrī jo parkhāve, vā kā kār turat ho jāve.
Who pays ready wages gets his work done quickly.

Turat phurat hoṅ sagre kām, jab hoveṅ muṭṭhī meṅ dām.
When you have money in your hand your work is soon done.

Turat phurat ho voh bhī kār, madad kare jis kā Sarkār.

His work is very soon done whom the Government helps.

Turfatu'l-ain meṅ.
In the twinkling of an eye.

Turkī pīṭe tāzī kāṅpe.
When the Turkish (horse) is whipped the Arab (horse) trembles.
(The punishment of one is a warning to others: *pour encourager les autres.*)

Turkī pīṭe tāzī ke kān hoṅ.
When the Turkish (horse) is whipped the Arab horse) takes warning.
(See preceding.)

Turkī tamām huī.
His Turkish is come to an end.
(He has got to the length of his tether: can talk no further.)

Turtā phurti kām māṅ achhī nāhīṅ jān : Sāṅch kahā hai sādh ne ; jaldī māṅ nuksān.
Too much haste in work is not a good thing: The saints have truly said that haste makes waste.

Tūr, tel, tāpnā, Jāṛ māns ko āpnā.
Cotton, oil and a fire will conquer Winter.

Turuk hū hue, tau bhī nā. E.
I have turned Muhammadan and have still gained nothing by it.
(Allusion to the former custom of Muhammadans giving their daughters in marriage to Hindū converts.)

Tū sachchā aur terā gurū sachchā !
You are true and so is your teacher!
(Said to a truthful man.)

Ṭuṭā mat rah ṭol sūṅ rāh bhīr ke bīch ; Ek akele manukh ko sūjhe ūṅch na nīch.
Don't lose your company on a journey or in a fight; One man alone can never think of all the ins and outs.
(Union is strength.)

Tū telī kā bail; tujhe kyā sair ? lagā raho ghānī se.
You are an oilman's ox; what have you to do with pleasure? stick to your oilmill.
(Said as a taunt to one who drudges night and day.)

Ṭūṭī bāṅh gale paṛe.
A broken arm goes round the neck.
(*i. e.* it is worn in a sling: a native of India will never desert his relatives, however badly they may turn out.)

Tūtī, chuge to ūṅch chug, nīch chugan mat jā : Kule lajāve āpne, kaheṅ Akabbar Shāh.
O parrot, if you have to take, take from a lofty place: Otherwise, saith King Akbar, you will disgrace your family.
(If you have to place yourself under an obligation choose an honorable man for the purpose.)

Ṭūṭī hai to kisī se juṛtī nahīṅ : aur juṛī hai to koī toṛ saktā nahīṅ.
What is broken none can join, and if it be joined, none can break it.
(Consolation to a very sick person.)

Ṭūṭī kā kyā joṛnā ? Gāṅṭh paṛe aur na rahe.
How can you join the broken? You may make a knot, but it won't last.
(A quarrel between friends is never really made up.)

Ṭūṭī kamān se ḍareṅ nau jane !
Nine men afraid of a broken bow!

Ṭūṭī kī būṭī batā do, hakīmjī !
Show me, doctor, the cure for the broken!
(Said when all hope of life is abandoned.)

Ṭūṭī kī kyā būṭī !
There is no remedy for the broken.
(*i. e.* against death.)

Tūtī pāleṅ chūtyā aur āshaq pāleṅ lāl : Kabūtar pāleṅ choṭṭe, jo take parāyā māl.
Fools keep parrots and lovers keep sparrows: Thieves keep pigeons that look to other's wealth.
(The *lāl* is a little red bird emblematic of beauty: pigeons of course are easily detached from their flocks.)

Ṭūṭī ṭāng, pāoṅ nā hāth ; Kahe 'chalūṅ ghoṛan ke sāth.'
A broken leg, and no feet nor hands; And he says 'I can run with horses.'
(Said of a fool who presumes a great deal on himself and ventures to undertake what his betters have failed to achieve. Fools rush on where angels fear to tread.)

Ṭūṭle telī, to kamar meṅ adhelī.
The ruined oilman has but eight annas round his waist.
(*i. e.* no capital.)

Ṭūṭ na rakh, re bālke, sab se mil kar chāl : Ṭūṭā ḍhobar det haiṅ gām galī māṅ ḍāl.
Be not quarrelsome, my son, but be friends with all: The broken vessel is thrown into the village lane.

U

Uddam se diladdar ghaṭe.
Poverty declines before labor.
(Industry is the key to prosperity.)

Udhār barī hattyā hai. Mercantile.
Debts are a great trouble.

Udhār denā, laṛāī mol lenā.
Give on loan and buy a quarrel

Udhār dīje, dushman kīje. Marcantile.
Give a loan and make an enemy.

Udhār dīyā, gāhak khoyā. Mercantile.
Sell on credit and lose you customer.
(Because he will then desert you for fear of being pressed for his money.)

Udhār dīyā gāhak gayā : sadqa dīyā rad balā. Mercantile.
Sell on credit and lose your customer; make an offering and avert evil.
(It is better to give than to lend.)

Udhār kā khāyā koī nahīṅ bhūltā.
Money borrowed is never forgotten.

Udhār khāe baiṭhe hain.
They have borrowed money to do it.
(To be set upon a thing.)

Udhār khānā, aur phūns kā tāpnā barābar hai.
To live on credit is to warm one's self at a straw fire.
(Which wont last long.)

Udheṛ ke roṭī na khāo, nangī hoti hai. Superstition. Mah. Wom.
It is not good to peel off the upper layer of bread and eat it.

Udhlī bahū balaiṅḍe sānp dikhāve. Wom.
The gadding wife sees a snake in the roof.
(i. e. makes an excuse for running out of the house.)

Ūdho, ban āē kī bāt. Hin.
It is luck that has done this, Ūdho.
(Spoken of one who has been prosperous beyond his merits.)

Ūdho kā len, na Mādho kā den. Hin.
I owe nothing to Ūdho, and Mādho owes nothing to me.
(I am independent.)

Udhyāil satvā pitran ke dān. E.
Spoilt flour is offered to the ancestors.
(Offerings to the ancestors are obligatory on Hindūs: hence the sting of this saying.)

Ugat uge, mah bhare, bisvat uge jāë. Agric.
What comes up in a month if it come up easily will soon wither.

Ugle to andhā, khāve to korhī. Superstition
If he vomits it goes blind, if swallows it becomes leprous.
(To be on the horns of a dilemma.)

☞ The notion is that if a snake gets a muskrat into its mouth it will become leprous if it eat it, and blind if it vomits it. Its remedy is to go into water with it.

Ūjaṛ gāon men murār mahton.
The oil press is lord of the deserted village.
(It being too heavy to be carried away.)

Ūjaṛ ho ghar sās kā, jo bair kare har bār!
Pīhar ghar sūbas base, jab lag hai sansār. Wom.
May the house be destroyed of the mother-in-law that quarrels all day! My father's house may thrive as long as the world lasts.

Ūjaṛ kheṛā, nāo na beṛā.
A deserted village has neither boat nor raft.

Ūjaṛ men Gūjar nāche, ḍhāk dekh Bairāgī, Khīr dekh ke Bāman nāche, tan man ho gayā rājī.
The Gūjar rejoices in the wastes, the mendicant at the ḍhāk tree, the Brāhman at rice and milk with a happy heart.
(Gūjars are herdsmen, the ḍhāk is a sacred tree, and the greediness of Brāhmans is proverbial, hence the point of the proverb.)

Ujjal baran, adhīntā, ek charan do dhiyān: Ham jāne tum bhagat ho, nire kapaṭ kī khān.
White of colour, and meek on one leg, but of two thoughts: I thought you to be a saint, but you are a very pit of deceit.
(The *baglā bhagat* or heron standing on one leg, the picture of dignity, while all the while it is merely intent on its prey is the conventional Indian synonym for hypocrisy.)

Ujlo ujlo sab bhalo, ujlo bhalo na kes: Nārī nive na rip ḍare, na ādar kare naresh.
Every thing white is good, except white hair, Which no woman respects, nor enemy fears, nor king acknowledges.

Ujṛe ghar kā baleṅḍā.
The ridge pole of a deserted house.
(Spoken contemptuously of a very tall, thin and awkward person.)

Ukhlī men musrā, māë bāp bisrā. E.
The pestle in the mortar, and the parents forgotten.

Ukhlī men sir dīyā, to mūslon kā kyā ḍar?
When your head is in the mortar why dread the pestle?
(In for a penny, in for a pound.)

Ūkh se ganḍerī pyārī, guṛ se pyārā gāṅḍā: Mān bahan se jorū pyārī, jis se hoe guzārā.
Cuttings are sweeter than the sugarcane, lolly pops than sugar: A wife is sweeter than mother and sister that makes life go.

Uktānī kumhārī nākhūn se maṭṭī khode.
The sorrowful potter's wife will dig mud with her nails.
(To scratch the earth with the nails is a sign of sorrow.)

Ulajh jāëgā to sulajh hī rahegā. Hin.
When once entangled he will be disentangled.
(i. e., when once entangled by marriage he will be disentangled from his wild ways: advice to the parents of a wayward son, who is sowing too many wild oats: marriage will sober him.)

Ulajhnā āsān, sulajhnā mushkil.
To entangle is easy, to disentangle is hard.

Ūl men se nikal-kar chūl men paṛnā.
Out of the pivot and into the socket.
(Out of the frying pan into the fire.)

Ulṭā chor kutvāle ḍāṅḍe.
The thief threatens the constable.
(Turning the tables.)

Ulṭe bāns Barelī ko.
Bamboos to Bareilly.
(Coals to Newcastle.)

Ulṭī Gangā bahnā.
The Ganges is flowing the wrong way.
(Spoken on the occurrence of something improbable.)

Ulṭī Gangā pahāṛ ko chalī.
The Ganges is flowing up hill.
(See preceding.)

Ulṭī khoprī andhā gyān.
When your head is down you will gain hidden knowledge.
(A saying of the *faqīrs*: be humble to gain knowledge unto salvation.)

Ulṭī mālā phernā. Hin. Superstition.
To tell beads backwards.
(To call down curses: see following.)

Ulṭī saifī paṛhnā. Mah. Superstition.
To say the *saifī* backwards.
☞ *Saifī* is a form of imprecation against an enemy. A naked sword is placed erect before the person pronouncing the curse, who blows upon it after every sentence. The effect is said to be the death or ruin of the person so cursed.

Ulṭī ṭāṅgeṅ gale paṛīṅ.
Twining his own legs round his own neck.
(Bringing misfortune on himself.)

Ulṭī ṭopī, guṛ chane. Children.
His cap's the wrong way round: let's have sugar and pulse.
(As a forfeit: a children's saying.)

Ulṭī vā kī rīt hai, ulṭī vā kī chāl, Jo nar bhoṅḍī rāh men apnā khove māl.
Depraved his habits and evil his ways,
That loseth his wealth in the paths of folly.

Unais bīs to bhaile chāhe. Bhoj.
It is always at nineteens and twenties.
(In nature no two things are quite alike.)

Ūṅch baṛerī, khokhar bāṅs; rin khailoṅ bārah mās.
To live all the year round on borrowed money is to have a high ridge pole made of hollow bamboos.
(Which will soon break.)

Ūṅche chaṛhke dekhā, to ghar ghar yehī lekhā.
When I looked down from on high, all the houses were of a height.
(All trees are of one height, when you look down from the moon.)

Ūṅchī dukān phīkān pakvān.
A lofty shop and bad food.
(Great boast little roast: a whited sepulchre.)

Ūṅch nīch meṅ boī kyārī, Jo upjī so bhaī hamārī.
If you sow on unlevel ground, You will only get what grows.
(*i. e.* very little: you wont get much out of bad work.)

Ūṅcho ūṅcho sab chaleṅ, nīcho chale na koē.
Tulsī! nīcho voh chale jo garabh se ūṅcho hoē.
All like to go up on high, no one likes to go below. Tulsī! he loves to go below that is above pride.

Ūṅghte ko ṭhelte kā bahānā.
The drowsy man falls and says, that some one shoved him.
(The slightest action on the part of another is made an excuse for transferring the whole blame to him.)

Ungliyān nachānā achchhā nahīn.
It is not good to play with one's fingers.
(*i. e.* to gamble.)

Ūnī bastr meṅ dosh nahīṅ!
Woolen cloth is always clean!
(*i. e.* it won't stand washing.)

Unke peshāb meṅ chirāg jaltā hai.
His very water holds a burning lamp.
(Said of persons of great influence or haughty temper.)

Unnīs bīs kā to farq hotā hī hai.
There is always the difference between nineteen and twenty.
(In nature no two things are alike.)

Ūnṭan ko kin chhappar chhāē? gaj kā mār-ghaṭ kamr banāē?
Who ever thatched sheds for camels, or made a burning place for elephants?
(Camels are always kept in the open and elephants owing to their weight are burnt where they die.)

Ūṅṭ balbalāne se laṛtā hai.
When the camel fights it gurgles.
(Allusion to the habits of the animal: a quarrel always makes a noise.)

Ūṅṭ baṛṛātā hī ladtā hai.
A camel always snarls when being loaded.
(Applied to a person whose complaints are disregarded by those who oppress him: allusion to the habits of the animals which invariably make a snarling noise while being loaded up. The proverb is also used towards an unwilling servant.)

"*Ūṅṭ balaiyāṅ le gaī,*" "*hāṅjī hāṅjī*" *kīje.*
If they say a cat carried off a camel, you must say "Yes sir, yes sir."
(Very like a whale.)

Ūṅṭ buḍḍhā huā, par mūtnā nā āyā.
The camel has grown old, yet he knows not how to make water.
(Said of a foolish old man grown in years, but not in sense.)

Ūṅṭ chaṛke būṅṭ māṅge.
Mounted on a camel he wants to pluck [vetches.
(*i. e.* he attempts impossibilities: the Indian vetch being a low plant.)

Ūṅṭ chaṛhe, kuttā kāṭe.
Mounted on a camel, yet bitten by a dog.
(Misfortune has long arms for the unfortunate.)

Ūṅṭ ḍūbeṅ khachchar thā māṅge.
The camels drown and the mules would wade through.
(He would bend the bow of Ulysses: he would rush where angels fear to tread.)

Ūṅṭ ḍūbeṅ, meṅḍkī thā māṅge!
The camel drowns and the frog wants to wade through!
(See preceding.)

Ūṅṭ ghoṛā bhas gaēl, gadhā pūchhe, 'kitnā pānī'?
Horse and camel are drowned, and the ass asks if it is deep!

Ūṅṭ jab bhāge jab pachchham ko.
A camel when runs, it runs to the west.
(*i.e.* towards its desert home in Arabia.)

Ūṅṭ jab tak pahāṛ ke nīche nahīṅ jātā hai, tab hī tak jāntā hai, 'mujh-se koī baṛā nahīṅ.'
The camel thinks himself the tallest thing there is, till he comes to a hill.
(A giant amongst dwarfs.)

Ūṅṭ kā pād, na zamīn kā, na āsmān kā.
When the camel breaks wind, it reaches neither to the earth nor to the sky.
(Always hanging half-way: imperfect.)

Ūṅṭ ke gale meṅ billī.
The cat tied to the camel's neck.
☞ A man who had lost his camel made a vow that if he found him again, he would sell him for a penny. In order to keep his vow and yet save his pocket, he tied a cat to the neck of the camel and he made it a condition that the purchaser of the camel for a penny should also buy the cat, which he priced at the real value of both.

Ūṅṭ ke mūṅh meṅ zīrā.
A caraway seed in the mouth of a camel!
(A pinch of grain to a famished creature!)

Ūṅṭ kī chorī aur jhuke jhuke.
You can't creep to steal a camel.

Ūṅṭ kī chorī sir par khelnā.
Steal a camel and risk your life.
(As it is difficult to hide so large an animal.)

Ūṅṭ kī pakaṛ, kutte kī jhapaṭ.
The grip of a camel and the bite of a dog.
(Are both very hard in their way.)

Ūṅṭ kī pakaṛ, kutte kī jhapaṭ se Khudā bachāe.
God preserve us from the grip of a camel and the spring of a dog!

Ūṅṭ kis kal baiṭhe?
Let us see on which side the camel sits.
(See *dekhiye ūṅṭ kis kal baiṭhtā hai?*)

Ūṅṭ ko kis ne chhappar chhāē haiṅ?
Who has ever thatched a roof for camels?
(None regards the welfare of the poor.)

Ūṅṭ lade begārī.
Camels work for nothing.

Ūṅṭ Makke hī ko bhāgtā hai.
Even the camel runs to Makkā.
(See explanation under *ūṅṭ pachchham ko bhāgtā hai.*)

Ūṅṭ marā kapṛe ke sir.
The dead camel is charged to the cloth on its back.
☞ It is related that a merchant, who was lamenting the loss of his camel, was consoled by a wayfarer, who suggested that he could recoup the value of the camel from the sale of its burden.

Ūṅṭ makkhī ko bhī haṅkātā hai.
A camel drives off even flies.
(Never despise your enemy.)

Ūṅṭ re ūṅṭ, terī kaun kal sīdhī?
O thou camel, hast thou one straight bone in thy body?
(Said of one who has no good in him.)

Ūṅṭ sā qad to baṛhā liyā, par shaūr zarā bhī nahīṅ.
You have grown as tall as a camel, but you have no sense at all.

Ūṅṭ to dāgte the, makṛī (yā meṅḍkī) ne bhī ṭāng phailā dī!
When the camels are branded, the spider (or frog) too must put up his leg!
(*c. f.* the fable of the Frog and the Bull.)

Ūpar kā dhaṛ bhāī, aur nīche kā alkhudāī.
Above a brother or friend, but below the Lord knows what.
(Spoken of a hypocrite of fair external appearance, concealing a wicked or profligate mind.)

Ūpar se 'Rām Rām', bhītar qasāī kā kām.
Outwardly a psalm-singer, inwardly a very butcher.
(Fair without and foul within.)

Upṛe jhāṅṭ Madār kī, Shujā chale Ajmer?
What loss is it to Madār, if Shujā go to Ajmer?
(The shrines of Shāh Madār at Makhanpur and of Muinuddīn Chishti at Ajmer attract large crowds of pilgrims.)

Uṛad kahe "mere māthe ṭīkā; Mo bin byāh na hove nīkā."
Saith the pulse, "I bear a mark on my forehead, Without me it is no marriage."
(*Uṛad* pulse is eaten by the guests at a marriage. 'I bear a mark on my forehead' means 'I am a thing of importance'.)

Uṛad ke āṭe kī tarah aiṅṭhtā hai.
He turns and twists like the dough of the *uṛad* pea.
(Which is a very sticky substance.)

Uṛ, bhaṅbhīrī, Sāvan āyā.
Up, butterfly, it is August.
(Make hay while the sun shines.)

Uṛ chal, panchhī, pī ke des. Wom.
Fly away, bird, to my husband's country.

Uṛdī uṛdoṅ kī bhalī, aur ras kī āchhī khīr; Lāj jo rākhe pīv kī, woh bhī āchhī, bīr. Rus.
Pease-pudding of peas is best, and sweetened *khīr* is best: She is the best woman, friend, that upholds her husband's honor.

Uṛdū kā muhāvra Dillī par khatam hai.
Uṛdū idioms are confined to Dehli.
(Compare "the Queen's English.")

Uṛtā gappā.
A flying shot.
(Applied to a lucky hit.)

Uṛte ke par kāṭte haiṅ.
He clips the wings of flying birds.
(He puts salt on their tails.)

Uṛtī uṛtī tāq chaṛhī.
Flying and flying it has rested on the shelf.
(The report is confirmed.)

Us bastī meṅ tū kadhī kījyū mat bisrām; Jo ho nāmī des meṅ ṭhag choran kā gām.
Take not thy rest in that town, That is known to be the abode of thieves and robbers.
(A man is known by the company he keeps.)

Us din bhūleṅ chaukṛī, volī, nabī aur pīr, Lekhā leve jis dināṅ Qādar Pāq-qadīr. Mah.
Saints and prophets and hermits will look blank on that day, When the Almighty God shall call them to account.
(The Day of Judgment.)

Use to dhonī bhī nahīṅ ātī.
He cannot even wash himself.
(A real fool.)

Usī gharī tāhde use, jo bairī tujh ghar āë; Aisā nā ho dhoe se baiṭhe pair jamāë.
Drive away your enemy the moment he comes to your house, Lest he get possession of it by treachery.

Usī kī jūtī, usī kā sir.
His own shoes on his own head.
(The Engineer hoist with his own petard : to take the arrows from his own quiver.)

Usī rāh par chal tū, jo tūjhe gurū batāë; Jo biddyā ke thān par turat ṭhikānā pāë.
Follow that road which the priest pointed out, That thou mayest quickly reach the abode of learning.

Usī rūkh par hai chadhā, usī kī jaṛ katvāë, Voh mūrakh to ek din gir dab-kar mar jāë.
The fool who cuts the roots of the tree upon which he sits, Will one day fall and be crushed by it.
(To cut away the branch upon which you are sitting.)

Us jātag par pyār jatāo, māt pitā bin jis ko pāo.
Love the child that hath nor mother nor father.

Us jātag sūṅ karo na yārī, jis kī mātā ho kalhārī.
Never befriend the child of a wrangling jade.

Us ke āge sīs nivāo, baḍā baḍerā jis ko pāo.
Always bow to a good old man.

Us ke bhāg baḍe albele, jo daulat meṅ khāve khele.
Very great is his good fortune that is born to wealth.
(Born in the purple : born with a silver spoon in his mouth.)

Us ke kān pe ek jūn nahīṅ chaltī.
No louse creeps in *his* ears.
(He won't yield.)

Uske rāj meṅ gābhan gābh ḍāle.
In that reign pregnant women miscarried.
(Through fear, as of Nādir Shāh, 1747—1772 A. D.)

Us kī girah kā kyā jātā hai?
What falls from *his* pocket?
(Said of a bad servant, the loss is always his master's and not his own.)

Us kī razzāqī hai.
God provides for all.

Us kī ṭāṅgeṅ, usī ke gale meṅ.
His own legs are round his own neck.

Us kī sikh na sikhiyo, jo gur se phir jāë, Biddyā sūṅ khālī rahe, phir pāchhe pachtāë.
Follow not him that hath turned against his priest: For such are void of learning and will at the last repent.

Us kī tūtī bol rahī hai.
His parrot is now talking.
(Said of a prosperous man.)

Us kī sāt vohdahū lā sharīk hai. Mah.
God is one and has no equal!

Us ko sīkh na do nadhī jo ho kaṭṭar nīch; Loh mekh nāhīṅ ghise kadhāṅ pāthar bīch. Rus.
Never advise the cruel and base; An iron peg will never pierce through a stone.

Us ko sab kī fikr hai.
God takes care of all.

Us ko to patthar māre, maut nahīṅ.
You may stone him, but you can't kill him.
(The wicked hath a long rope : the cat's nine lives.)

Us ko vahāṅ māre, jahāṅ pānī bhī na mile.
Slay him where no water can be had.
(Said of the incorrigibly bad.)

Us kūkar se bach-kar jānā, jā ko jagat kaṭ khānā.
Avoid the dog that is known to bite.

Us mānas ko dūrāṅ tāho, jā ko kapṭī tum sun pāo.
Eschew him that is reported to be treacherous.

Us mānas ko ho ati labhā, jā ke bura na lāge dhābā.
Whose character is not stained prospereth greatly.

Us mānas ko tū kadhe na apne pās biṭhā, Jār ujaggar des meṅ jo mānas ho jā.
Let not that man sit beside thee, That is a notorious rake.
(A man is known by the company he keeps. Blessed is the man that walketh not in the counsel of the ungodly nor standeth in the way of sinners. *Psalms* I. 1.)

Us mānas se milnā bhūṅḍā, chho aur kapat kā jo ho ḍūṅḍā.
It is not good to dwell with him that hideth anger and hypocrisy in his heart.

Us mānas se milo re bhāī, jā ke jī meṅ base bhalāī.
Dwell with him in whose heart dwelleth goodness.

Us nar ke bhī ek din paṛe gale meṅ phaṅd, Jis ne chorī lūṭ par leī kamaryā bāndh.
That man shall one day put his neck into a snare, Who girdeth his loins for theft and robbery.

Us nar ko nā sīkh suhāve, Neh phand meṅ jo phaṅs jāve.
He listens not to any advice, That hath fallen into the snares of love.

Us nar se tum milo na koī, Jā ko dekho kapṭī dhoī.
Have no dealings with the man, That is known to be a treacherous hypocrite.

Us purkhā kā nāh bharosā, jo le chīz dikhāve thosā.
Never trust him that takes and returns not.

Us purkhā kī bāt par nāh bharosā rākh ; Bar bar bole jhūṭ jo din bhar māñ sau lākh.

Trust not in that man's words, For he tells a hundred thousand lies a day.

Usar khetī meṅ kesar ?

Saffron from a barren soil.

(Said when a man has chance good luck: also of the worthy sons of unworthy parents.)

Us setī mil daur-kar, jo nar gyānī ho : Dānā dushman bhī bhalā, kah gae yeh sab koe.

Hasten to meet a wise old man; All the world says it is good to have a wise man even for an enemy.

Ustād, hajjām, nāī, maiṅ, aur merā bhāī ; Ghoṛī, aur ghoṛī kā bachherā, aur mujh ko to āp jānte hī haiṅ.

The barber, the shaver, and the beard-scraper, I and my brother, the mare, and her colt, and me, you know.

(Applied to one who pretends at a distribution of provisions to receive shares for several people, which are in fact all for himself.)

Utar gaī loī to kyā karegā koī ?

When my blanket (honor) is off, who can do any thing ?

Utāolā so bāolā, dhīrā so gambhīrā.

Hasty is mad, slow is sure.

Utāro Nāth pār morī naīyā !

Take my boat over, O Lord !

Ūtar pātar : maiṅ miyāṅ, tū chākar.

Now we are quits; you are my slave, and I your master.

(Said by children when a debt is paid or an obligation returned.)

Utārū hākim, aur dupahre dahī nuqsān kartā hai.

A hasty judge and curds at noon do harm.

Ut aukhad kuchh kām na āve, maut pakaṛ jī jis kā leve.

No medicine avails when death takes possession of a life.

(No remedy for death.)

Ut bhī bhalā hai baiṭhnā, jit kar kesubh-gyān, Mullā panḍit baiṭh-kar bāñche Bed Qurān.

It is well to sit there, where, in the fullness of knowledge, *Mulla* and *Panḍit* propound their Scriptures.

(*Mulla* is a Mahommedan priest and *Panḍit* a Hindu priest.)

Ut bhī mūl na jā, re bhāī, jit hotī ho mār pīṭāe.

Never go to that place where a fight is going on.

(They who in quarrels interpose, Will often wipe a bloody nose.)

Ut bhī tauṅh mat baiṭh piyāre, jit baiṭhe hoṅ bairī sāre.

Dwell not, my friend, where thy enemies dwell.

Ut Dātā deve use jo le Dātā nām ; It bhī sagre ṭhīk hoṅ, us ke kartab kām.

In the next world God will reward those who call on Him, And will also make all their business here to prosper.

Uṭh gae nā jāniye, jo ṭaṭṭī de gae bār.

Don't think a man has left (for good) because his door is closed.

Uṭhā babūlā prem kā, tin kā chaṛhā akās : Tin kā tin meṅ mil gayā, tin kā tin ke pās.

The impulse of love hath fled and gone to heaven, To meet Him whose it was, and to be with Him whose it is.

(Said of the soul of a dead man.)

Uṭhāo merā maknā, maiṅ ghar saṅbhālūṅ apnā. Mah. Wom.

Lift up my veil, and let me examine my house.

(A satire on a bride, who exhibits haste in assuming her role of mistress; whereas Hindū conventionalities require her to remain completely veiled during the first four *chālās*, (periods of 40 days) after her marriage.

Uṭhāū chūlhā.

A moveable fire place.

(Said of a person, who has no fixed abode: a rolling stone: the rolling stone gathers no moss.)

Uṭh jā taṛke uṭh, re bhāī, Jit tanne dikhe lābh bhalāī.

Get up early and go thither, my friend, Where good and profit are.

Uṭh-kar phalī sarīkī to phoṛtī hai hī nahīṅ.

She won't even get up to open a pod.

(He won't even raise his hand to his mouth.)

Uthlī rakābī, phul phulā bhāt; lo panchoṅ hāthoṅ hāth.

The dish is shallow and the rice cooked; take it, friends, in your hands.

Uṭhte hī ṭāng ṭūṭī.

He no sooner rose than he broke his leg.

(A very unfortunate man.)

Uṭhte lāt, baiṭhte ghūṅsā. Wom.

When he is up he kicks her, and when he is sitting he hits her.

(A bad husband.)

Uṭhtī javānī, māṅjhā ḍhīlā!

The bloom of youth in a flabby body !

(An idle young man.)

Uṭhtī paiṅṭh.

The market is almost over.

(Spoken of one who was rich or powerful, but is now decaying.)

Uṭhtī paiṅṭh āṭhveṅ din.

Market day comes but once a week.

(Make hay while the sun shines: Christmas comes but once a year.)

Utī ke ninnānve, bārah panje sāṭh !

The ninety nine of the fool is twelve times five.

Ut kā jānā nāhīṅ achhā, jit gunḍan kā hove bāsā.

Never go to that place where vagabonds do abound.

Ut mat gehūṅ buā re chele, Jit hoṅ thāl aur pāthar ḍhele. Agric.

Never sow wheat my son, Where clods and stones abound.

Ut mat kadhe na baiṭh tū jit kunyāī log: Nyāo bhūl kunyāo kā bāṅdheṅ milkar jog.

Sit not with the unjust, That have forgotten justice and unite to do unjustice.

Ut mat kadhī na jā, re mītā, Jit rahtā ho singh aur chītā.

Go not thither, my friend, where tigers and leopards do abound.

(Don't put your head into the lion's mouth.)

Ut mat ro apnā dukh jā kar, jit āveṅ bairī umḍā-kar.

Never weep over your sorrows before your enemies.

(A wise man keeps his troubles to himself.)

Utrā chhitrā jo huā, vā kī sār na ho, Sādh kahe, re balke, lākh jatan kar lo.

Who loses his credit will never regain it, Say the saints, my lad, though he try a hundred plans.

(Give a dog a bad name and hang him.)

Utrā ghāṭī, huā māṭī.

(i) Down the throat, is turned to clay.

(Is digested into the body: said as a consolation to the poor.)

(ii) No sooner carried to the place of cremation than it turns to dust.

(Said of a dead body.)

Utrā Kabīr sarāē men, gaṭh katre ke pās, Jas karsī tas pāvasī: tū kyoṅ bhayo udās.

When Kabīr puts up in an inn with a pickpocket, Why should he grieve; for as one does, one is rewarded.

Utrā shahnā, mardak nām.

Out of place, out of grace.

Uttam gānā, maddham bajānā.

Singing is best, playing next.

Utre jī se chīz jo, vā kī sor na ho. Tū aisī mat kījyū, jo jagat bisāre toe.

What hath once fallen in esteem hath never value more. Therefore act not so that the world despise thee.

Ut se andhā āē hai, it se andhā jāē: Andhe se andhā milā kaun batāē rāē?

A blind man starts from there and a blind man starts from here: When the blind man meets the blind man, who shall show the onward way!

Uttam khetī, maddham bān, nikhad sevā, bhīk nidān.

Best is tillage, middling trade, bad is service, and worst begging.

Uttam se uttam mile, mile nīch se nīch; Pānī se pānī mile, mile kīch se kīch.

Good mingles with good, and bad with bad; water with water, mire with mire.

Uttar gurū Dakkan māṅ chelā; Kaise biddyā paḍhe akelā?

The teacher in the North and the pupil in the South: How shall he learn his lesson?

Uttar-har jo barkhā hove, to kāl pichho-kaṛ jā-kar rove. Agric.

If rains fail in the North there will be no famine.

Uttar jāo kī Dakkhan, vohī karam ke lakkhan.

Go North or go South and your fate will follow you.

(*i. e.* never travel: Hindū good advice!)

Uttar kī ho istrī Dakhan byāhī jāē; Bhāg lagāve jog jab, to kuchh nā pār basāē.

A woman from the North shall marry into the South: If fate so wills she has no power.

(Expresses the great reluctance still entertained by natives to travelling)

Uttar, pātar; maiṅ miyāṅ, tū chākar.

Off, father; I am lord and you servant.

(A son to his old father, who is keeping him out of his inheritance.)

Uttar rahe batāve Dakkhan, vā ke āchhe nāhīṅ lakkhan.

Who lives in the North and says he comes from the South cannot have a good character.

Ut tauṅh buā bājrā bhāī, jit hove thal kī muktāī. Agric.

Sow millet in a porous soil.

Ut terā jānā mūl na sohe, jo tane dekhat kūkur hove.

Never go to the house of him who feels jealous of you. [*ḍerā.*

Ut terā jānā nipaṭ bhalerā, jit hove tere mīt kā

It is altogether wise to go whither thy friend doth dwell.

(This expresses a wide-spread notion among natives. Nothing distresses a native so much as to be obliged to go to a place where he will have only himself to look to for his welfare, and where he knows he has no one to back him up in his aims.)

Uzr-i-gunah bad-tar az gunah. Per.

An excuse for a sin is worse than the sin.

(*Qui L'excuse s'accuse.*)

V

Vadā khilāfī burī bāt hai.

Breach of promise is a bad thing.

Vā din dekhe jāēṅge bhale bure sab kār, Jā din lekhā legā vo Qādir Kartār.

On that day will all our bad and good deeds be tried, When Almighty God shall take His account.

(A saying of *faqīrs.*)

Vahāṅ us ke ghar basant hai, yahāṅ mere ghar basant.

There is joy in his home and joy in mine.

(So why should I go there!)

Vahāṅ farishtoṅ ke bhī par jalte haiṅ.
Even angels would burn their wings there.
(There angels fear to tread.)

Vahāṅ talak haṅsye jo na roiye.
Laugh so that you may not weep.

Vāh, bahu, terī chatrāī, Dekhā mūsā kahe, 'bilāī.'
Bravo, my clever wife, you see a rat and call it a cat.

Vāhī nar ko jān tū pūrā apnā mīt, Jo rākhe bin lābh ke tujh se pīt parīt.
Believe him to be a true friend, That loveth without hope of gain.
(Greater love hath no man than this that he lay down his life for another *John* xv., 13.)

Vāh, Miyāṅ Bāṅke, tere dagle meṅ sau sau ṭāṅke.
Bravo! my noble swell, your jacket is patched in a hundred places.
(A sarcastic address to a tattered beau.)

Vāh, Miyāṅ Kāle; khūb rang nikāle.
Well done, Mr. Black! you have changed your colour well.
(Turned over a new leaf.)

Vāh Miyāṅ Nāk-vāle!
Bravo, my Lord Long-nose!
(*Nāk* is metaphorical for fame: ironical.)

Vahm kī dārū hī nahīṅ.
There is no remedy for caprice.

Vahm kī dārū to Luqmān ke pās bhī nahīṅ.
For caprice even Luqmān had no cure.
(Luqmān is the Esculapius of the Musalmāns as Dhanvantara is of the Hindūs.)

Vāh Pīr Aliyā; pakāī thī khīr, ho gayā dalyā.
Brāvo, Saint Aliyā; I cooked milk and rice, and it has turned to gruel.
☞ Aliyā was a saint at Hānsi who on one of his begging rounds saw an old woman cooking something. He enquired of her what it was. She said she was cooking gruel, whereas really she was cooking milk and rice. Whereupon the saint said "let it be so," and went his way. When the woman uncovered the pot she discovered that her milk and rice had been turned into gruel and shouted out the words of the proverb.

Vāh purkhā mere chātar gyānī! Māṅgī āg uṭhā lāyā pānī!
Bravo, my clever and wise man! I sent for fire and you have brought water!

Vāh, purkhā, terī chatrāī: Chūn, bech-kar gājar khāī!
Hurrah for your wit, my friend: you bought carrots with your flour.
(Carrots are worthless in India.)

Vāh, purkhā terī chaturāī: Māṅgā guṛ lādī khaṭāī!
Hurrah for your wit, my friend. I asked for sweet and you gave me bitter!
(If his son ask for bread will he give him a stone? Matthew vii. 9.)

Vāī nar bharpūr kahāve, apne āp ko jo bisrāve.
Call him a perfect man that hath no care for himself.

Vaisā hī to ko phal mile, jaisā bīj buāe. Nīm boe ke, balke, gāṅḍā koī na khāe.
As you sow the seed so shall you obtain the fruit; Who ever tasted sugarcane, my boy, by planting *nīm* tree.
(The leaves and fruit of the *nīm* tree are very bitter. Make your own bed and lie on it.)

Vā kī gat vā hī jāne.
He alone knows his own heart.

Vakīloṅ kā hāth parāī jeb meṅ.
A counsel's hands are always in some one's pocket.

Vā ko achchhā mat kahe jo tere dhore āe: Kare burāī aur kī apne taīṅ badhāe.
Think him not a good man that cometh to thee To detract from others and extol him.

Vā ko sīkh na dījye jo ho mūṛh gaṅvār. Golī maṭh par ḍāl do, pakṛe na qarār.
Never give counsel to an ignorant fool. Throw a ball on to a dome and it will never stick there.

Valāyat meṅ kyā gadhe nahīṅ hote?
What, are there no asses abroad?
(There are fools every where.)

Valī kā beṭā shaitān!
A devil begot of a saint!
(A bad son of a good father.)

Valī ke ghar shaitān.
A devil in the saint's house.
(See preceding.)

Valī ko valī hī pahchāntā hai.
A saint only knows a saint.
(Set a thief to catch a thief.)

Valī sab kā Allāh, ham to rakhvālī haiṅ.
God is the master of all; I am only its keeper.
(Put into the mouth of a miser.)

Vā nārī ko mat kūṛh batāo, jā sūṅ din din labhā pāo.
Don't call him a fool, who brings your daily gains.
(Don't slay the goose that lays the golden eggs.)

Vā nar se mat mil, re mītā, Jo kadhe mirag, kadhe ho chītā.
Never be friends with him, my friend, Who is one moment a deer and the next a leopard.

Vā purkhā kī din din khuārī, jā kī tiryā ho kalhārī.
His days are wretched that hath a quarrelsome wife.

Vā purkhā ko jagat sarāhve, Jo Harī nām ke bal bal jāve.
The whole world praises him who devotes himself to the name of God.

Vaqt kā gulām, aur vaqt hī kā bādshāh.
At one time a slave and at another a king.
(Swimming with the tide: said of a timeserver.)

Vaqt kā ronā be-vaqt ke hansne se behtar hai.
It is better to weep in season than to laugh out of season.

Vaqt kī khūbī hai.
It is the virtue of the time.
(Ironical: sufficient unto the day is the evil thereof.)

Vaqt nikal jātā hai, bāt rah jātī hai.
Time passes, the matter remains.
(Said of help declined: or a grievance unredressed.)

Vaqt par bhāg jānā mardāngī nahīṅ hai!
It is not brave to run away when you ought to fight.

Vaqt ko ganīmat jāniye.
Learn the value of the time.
(Make hay while the sun shines.)

Vaqt pare par jāniye ko bairī ko mīt?
Adversity shows both friends and foes.

Vaqt par gadhe ko bāp banāte haiṅ.
Make a father of an ass when it serves your purpose.

Vaqt par gāṅṭh kā paisā hī kām ātā hai.
Your own money will serve you best in time of need.
(Saving against a rainy day.)

Vaqt par jo ho jāe, so ṭhīk hai.
What is done in time is the best.

Vaqt par koī kām nahīṅ ātā.
No one befriends you in the time of need.

Vaqt par kuchh ban nahīṅ ātī.
You can do nothing at the critical moment.
(Said of a man who is apt to lose his head.)

Vaqt par sab kuchh karnā paṛtā hai.
Every thing should be ready at the proper time.

Vaqt pīrī shabāb kī bāteṅ, Aisī haiṅ jaise khuāb kī bāteṅ.
To talk like a youth in old age is like talking in a dream.

Vaqt sab kuchh karā letā hai.
Necessity makes us do all things.
(Necessity is the mother of invention.)

Vaqt vaqt kī rāgnī hai.
There is a time for every tune.
(Allusion to the modes of native music, which are conventionally appropriated to different times and seasons. There is a time for everything.)

Vārī gaī, pherī gaī: jalve ke vaqt ṭal gaī.
Mah. Wom.
She is very affectionate, but is absent at the time of need.

Vārī pherī jab gaī, jab neo dharāī. Aur mūṅh moṛe bāteṅ kare jab tākhoṅ aī. Bāṅdh munḍerī ūtrā jam diye dikhāī.
She served most devotedly when the foundation was laid; When the building came up to the niches she turned away her face; The mason was described as a hell-hound when the coping of the walls was finished.
(When we get up to the roof we kick the ladder.)

Vārī sove, uṭhe savere, vā ko nāh diladdar ghere.
Who sleeps late and rises early will never know poverty.
(Early to bed and early to rise, Makes a man healthy, wealthy and wise.)

Vār kaheṅ utpār hai, pār kaheṅ itvār: Pakaṛ kinārā baiṭh raho, yehī pār yehī vār.
This side is called that side, and that side this; stick to one side and it will be both sides.

Vār karat pī jāt hai, pher na āvat hāth: Beg charan pī ke gaho, jo mūl na chūṭe sāth.
Put off your love and he will go to come back no more, Quickly clasp his feet that he may never love you.

Vār na pūr adham māṅ naiyā, Khevā kahe kī: 'utro, bhaiyā!'
No (shore) this side nor that: the boat is in the open (sea.) And still the boatman says 'get out, my friend!'

Vār-vāle kaheṅ pār-vāle achchhe, pār-vāle kaheṅ vār-vāle achchhe.
Those on *that* side call *this* side the best, and those on *this* side call *that* side the best.
(No one is contented with his own: every body wants to be some body else.)

Vār vār pānī pīte haiṅ. Wom.
Each drinks water in her turn.
(Each takes the advantage of his opportunity: also allusion to the marriage custom of a mother's drinking water from her son on his marriage: so "every women has to do so in her turn" is the meaning: every dog has his day.)

Vasīlā baṛī chīz hai.
Interest is a great thing.

Vasīle binā rozgār nahīṅ miltā.
There is no livelihood without interest.
(In the opinion of the Indian middle classes.)

Vā tiryā sang baiṭh na, bhāī, jā ko jagat kahe har jāī.
Have no truck with the woman, my friend, who is known to be bad.

Vā tiryā to ek din bhāje, jā kī āṅkh kadhāṅ nā lāje.
That woman will one day run away who feels no sense of shame.

Vazīrī chunī shahar-yārī chunāṅ. Pers.
As the minister so the king.
(Because the king works through him.)

Voh apne dam se achchhā hai.
He only is good.
(Not the rest of his family.)

Voh bāt koson gaī.
That opportunity is now far off.

Voh bhalā-mānas kaisā jis ke pās nahīṅ paisā!
He is no gentleman who has no money.
(Money makes the gentleman.)

Voh bhī aise gae, jaise gadhe ke sir se sing.
Lost and gone, like the horns from a donkey's head.
(Hindūs believe that originally asses had horns and horses wings.)

Voh bhī kuchh aisā to na thā.
He was not so bad as all that.
(The devil is not so black as he is painted.)

Voh billī pūj-ke chalte hain.
He worships his cat before setting out.
(Said of an over-superstitious person: arising from the notion that cats are the embodiments of deceased Brāhmans and should therefore never be killed.)

Voh būnd Multān gaī.
That drop is gone to Multān.
(Said of a lost opportunity: the idea is taken from that of a drop of rain water running down to Multān through one of the five rivers of the Panjāb, which are all confluent, before reaching it. See also. *Voh pānī Multān gaī.*)

Voh būnd valāyat gaī.
That drop has flown to a far country.
(See preceding.)

Voh daftar gāo khurd ho gae.
That office has become cow's food.
(They make hay there.)

Voh darbā hī jal gayā.
The place itself is burnt to ashes.
(Nothing more to be expected there.)

Voh din ḍubbe, jab ghoṛī charhe kubbe. Panj.
Accursed be the day, when the hunchback rides a horse.
(An imprecation.)

Voh din gae, jo bhains pakauṛe hagtī thī.
The days are gone, when buffaloes passed sweetmeats.
(Said of a man no longer extravagant.)

Voh din gae, jo Khalīl Khān fākhtā mārte the.
The days are gone when Khalīl Khān shot pigeons.
(The days of his prosperity are over.)

Voh ḍūben manjdhār; jin par bhārī bojh.
He sinks midstream, who bears too a heavy load.
(My sin is greater than I can bear.)

Voh guṛ nahīn, jo chiūntiyān khāen.
This is no treacle for the ants to eat.
(You can't impose upon me.)

Voh guṛ nahīn, jo makkhī baiṭhe.
This is no sugar for the flies to sit on.
(See preceding.)

Vohī apnā, jo apne kām āve.
That's yours, which you can use when you please.

Vohī baḍā jag bīch hai, jin pūjā Kartār. Bin pūjā to mānush se āchhe māṭī rākh.
He only is great in the world that worshippeth God. Dirt and mire are better than a man that doth no worship.

Vohī baṛā hai jagat men, jin karnī ke tān, Kar līnā hai āpnā Mahārāj Bhagvān. Hin.
He is indeed a great man that by the power of his good deeds Hath made the great God his own!

Vohī bhalā hai mere lekhe, Haq nā-haq ko jo nar dekhe.
I think him to, be a good man That knoweth right and wrong.

Vohī ḍhāk ke tīn pāt.
He is a very *ḍhāk* tree with three leaves.
(Do what I will I can never get any more:—usually said by domestics and subordinate officers whose pay is never raised: the *ḍhāk* tree has a very scanty foliage.)

Vohī kannyā, jis ke ablaq bāl!
Is she a virgin, who has grey hairs?
(Used to express something very wonderful or impossible: every Hindū woman in India is married.)

Vohī mānas de sake rājan ko sikh gyān, Jo na rākhe lobh dhan aur dhare hāth par jān.
He alone can give wise counsel unto kings, That hath no love for lucre, and carrieth his life in his hands.
(*i. e.* fears not death. To advise the great is a dangerous thing.)

Vohī manush dhanvant hai, vohī manush balvant, Jo Sāīn ke nām par baiṭhā hove nichant.
He is rich, and he is strong, Who hath confidece in the name of God.
(Blessed is the man whose delight is in the law of the Lord. *Psalms* I. 2.)

Vohī man, vohī chālīs ser.
Call it a *man*, or call it forty *sers*.
(Six of one and half a dozen of the other: a *man* contain forty *sers* of 2lbs. each.)

Vohī phūl jo Mahesh charhen.
Those are truly flowers which are presented to the Gods.
(Used of a present to a superior, which has been accepted, implying, that by such acceptance, it has acquired a value which it had not before.)

Vohī rāg gānā.
To sing the same old song.
(To repeat a thing often: the tune the cow died of.)

Vohī rahegā chain men lobh kiyā jin dūr; Sāīn kā kar āsrā, rākhā jī bharpūr.
He shall live ever at ease that escheweth avarice: Confident on God shall he dwell and contented in his heart.

Vohī rānḍ kī rānḍ, vohī bābā pūṭī.
Call her the widow's daughter, call her a fatherless orphan.
(Six of one and half a dozen of the other.)

Vohī tīn bīsī, vohī sāṭh, vohī chārpāī vohī khāṭ.
Call it three-score or call it sixty: call it a bedstead or call it a cot.
(See preceding.)

Voh kamlī hī jātā rahī, jis men til bandhte the.
The blanket is gone, in which the sesamum was tied up.
(Said in reply to one who solicits any thing after the opportunity has passed: some sesamum is commonly tied up in the bride's kerchief after the marriage is over.)

Voh kaunsī kishmish hai, jis men tinkā nahīn?
Was there ever a raisin without a stalk?
(There is no rose without a thorn.)

Voh kaunsī taprī, jo ham se chhaprī?
Where is the house that I have not seen?
(Are you going to teach me?)

Voh kīmiyā-gar kaisā, jo mange paisā?
He is no alchemist, who has to beg for coppers

Voh kuchh nāhar to nahīn, jo khā jāegā,
He is not a tiger that he will eat you up.

Voh kyā merī khālā kī khal bachchī hai?
Is she my aunt's daughter? Mah. Wom.
(Is she any relation to me?)

Voh mānas nit sukh pāve, Sikh badon kī jo chi lāve.
Who minds the counsel of his elders Will be happy all his life.

Voh mandhī hī jātī rahī, jahān atīt rahte the.
The shrine is gone, where the saint used to live.
(Said of those who used to live on the dead man's charity.)

Voh mar gae, hamen marnā hai.
He is dead and we must die.

Voh nārī bhī din din rove, jā kā purakh nikhattū hove.
She will ever grieve, whose husband earns nothing.

Voh pānī Multān gaë.
The water is now gone to Multān.
☞ It is said that the celebrated Gurū Gorakh Nāth once paid a visit to Rāe Dās the Bhagat who was a *chamār* or leather worker. Gurū Gorakh Nāth during his visit felt thirsty and asked Rāe Dās for some water, but recollecting that he was of a low caste, he did not drink it but, put it into his cup. Afterwards Gorakh Nāth went to see Kabīr, who asked him what he had got in his cup. He replied that it was some water given to him by Rāë Dās, which he could not drink: on this Kamālī the daughter of Kabīr, who was well acquainted with the supernatural powers of Rāë Dās, took the pot and drank off the water and with it she learnt all the mysteries of nature. When Gorakh Nāth, much to his surprise, saw the change that came over her, he went back to Rāë Dās with great impatience and asked him for some more water; but in the interval, Kamālī had been carried away by her husband to his house in Multān. Rāë Dās, having discovered through his supernatural powers what had happened, replied in the following coupled:—*Piyāve he jab piyā nahīn, tab tum ne bahū abhī mān kiyā: Bhalā jogī, phire divāna; voh pānī Multān gayā.* When I gave you to drink, you did not drink and were very proud. *Jogi* thou art gone mad: the water has gone to Multān.

Voh purkhā bhī ati dukh pāve, Sikh badon se jo phir jāve.
Who listens not to the advice of elders, Will ever be troubled in life.

Voh purkhā bhī mūl hai khotā, pāve lābh batāve totā.
He is a really bad man, who calls his profits a loss.

Voh purkhā din din pachhtāve, jo āmad se dugnā khāve.
That man will ever lament, who spends twice his income.
(Outrunning the constable.)

Voh purkhā ek din pachhtāve, dayā dharam jo jī se tāhve.
That man will one day grieve, who drives mercy and faith from his heart.

Voh purkhā le nipat bhalāī, jis ko hove khauf Ilāhī. Mah.
The man that fears God hath ever a good name.

Voh purkhā to phale aur phūle, jo Dātā ko mūl na bhūle.
Who forgets not God will ever prosper.

Voh rājā martā bhalā, jis men niyāo na ho; Marī bhalī voh istrī, lāj na rakhe jo!
Perish the king that hath no justice in him; Perish the woman that hath no shame in her.

Voh same hī nahīn rahe.
Those days are no more.
(The good old days: *laudator temporis acti.*)

Voh shaitān se ziyādah mashhūr hai.
He is better known than the devil!

Voh sharāb pānī kī tarah pītā hai.
He drinks wine like water.
(He drinks like a fish.)

Voh tiryā to nit sukh pāve, jā kā purkhā vā ko chāhve.
That woman is ever happy whose husband loves her.

Voh tiryā pat nāhh ganvāve, jā kī bar bar ānkh lajāve.
That woman will never lose her honor who casts down her eyes and is modest.

Voh to Shaitān se bhī ek darjah ziyādah hain.
He is a point more wicked than the devil.

Y

Yā base Gūjar, yā rahe ūjar.
May Gūjars live in his fort or it remain empty!
☞ There is a myth that when Muhammad Tughlaq, the king of Delhi, was building the fort of Tuglaqābad near Delhi,—(1391 A. D.), Nizāmuddin Aulea, the celebrated Sūfi Saint (died 1325, A. D.) began to sink a large well in the vicinity of it, by which the progress of the royal work was greatly impeded as all the labourers and workmen flocked to the saint's well to work there. The king being

much offended ordered all labourers procurable to go to his fort and would not allow one work at the well. The workmen therefore laboured at the fort in the day time, and at the well at night thinking it a good work.

One day the king happening to come to see the progress of the fort noticed some of the men dozing and heavy with sleep, and asked them the reason of it. The men frankly admitted the cause of their sleepiness. Whereupon the king prohibited all the shopkeepers from selling any oil to Nizāmuddin, thinking that without oil it would be impossible for him to carry on the work at night. But a stream of water gushed out of the well the same day, and Nizāmuddin ordered his men to use the water of the stream instead of oil, which gave out a bright and clear light, and thus his work went on smoothly and satisfactorily.

The next time when the king again saw his men sleepy, and learnt after enquiry how it was that the saint's well was making progress, he thought him to be a magician and demanded his head.

A man thereupon sent to Nizāmuddin with a large water melon in which was conveyed the meaning of the royal demand.

When the saint had made out the sentence he proclaimed the following curse—"May lightning strike the Tughlaq ; may Gūjars live in his fort or it remain empty."

Immediately a black cloud arose from the horizon and thundered over the king's fort ; and Tughlaq was instantly struck dead by lightning. The fort is still in ruinous state, half inhabited by Gūjars and low caste Muhammadans, whence proverb.

Yā be-hayāī ! Mah. Wom.
What shamelessness !
(Common exclamation.)

Yā be-īmānī terā hī āsrā hai !
In fraud is my hope !
(Put in the mouth of a great cheat.)

Yā bhainsā bhainson men, yā qasāī ke khūnṭe par.
Let the bull buffalo be among the cows or tied to the butcher's peg.
(The two uses to which it can be put.)

Yād bhalī Bhagvān kī aur bhalī na koe ; Rājā kī kar chākri, jo parjā tābe hoe. Hin.
To remember God is better than all things ;
He that serveth the king all the people obey.
(This image is peculiarly applicable in India, where Government service in any shape means personal power and hence respect.)

Yād karī Bhagvān kī to ho gae bhagat Kabīr. Jhūṭe Vā kī yād bin sab hain pīr faqīr.
By remembering God Kabir became a Saint.
Monks and Saints are nought if they remember Him not.
(Kabir was the great reformer of the 15th century.)

Yād rakho is bāt ko, jo hai tum men kuchh gyān ; Sāin jā ko hogayā, vākā sagar jahān.
O thou that hast knowledge, bear this in thy heart. That the whole world is with him on whose side is the Lord.

Yahān achchhon ke par jalte hain.
Here the wings of even the accomplished burn.
(Said of a very strict superior.)

Yahān farishton ke par jalte hain.
An angel's wings would burn here.
(See preceding.)

Yahān fikr maishat hai, vahān dag dag-i-hashr. Āsūdgī harfest, na yahān hai na vahān hai.
In this world is the trouble of livelihood, in the next the dread of the Day of Judgment.
Happiness is a word unknown to either.

Yahān Hazrat Jibrāil ke bhī par jalte hain. Mah.
Even the wings of the Angel Gabriel would burn here.
(See yahān achchhon ke par jalte hain.)

Yahān ke bābā Ādam hī nirāle hain.
The Adam of this place is a strange being.
(Applied to eccentricity.)

Yāhān kyā terī nāl gaṛī hai ?
Is your navel string buried here ?
(Said to one who is reluctant to leave a place.)

Yahān parinda par nahīn mār saktā.
There is no bird to flap its wings here.
(An absolute desert)

Yahān sab kān pakaṛte hain.
Every one here is caught by the ear.
(No one is master here.)

Yā hansā motī chuge, yā langhan kar jāen.
The swan feeds on pearls or fasts.
(The swan (*hansā*) will only eat pearls according to native superstitions : *noblesse oblige.*)

Yahān to ham bhī hairān hain.
I am quite at a loss here myself.
(Said when advice is asked in a difficult matter.)

Yahān tumhārī dāl nahīn galegī.
Your pulse cannot be boiled here.
(You cannot expect any thing from me.)

Yahān tumhārī ṭikkī nahīn lagegī.
Your loaf cannot be baked here.
(Your schemes won't take here : see preceding.)

Yahān ulṭī Gangā bahtī hai.
Here the rivers run backwards.
(Eccentricity.)

Yahān zarūr kuchh dāl men kālā hai.
There is surely something black in the pulse here.
(To smell a rat : something rotten in the Stat of Denmark : there's a screw loose some where.)

Yā idhar ho, yā udhar ho.
Either be on this side or on that.
(Don't hesitate or evade.)

Yā kare dard-mand, yā kare garaz-mand.
Suffering and need do all things.

Yā khāe ghoṛā, yā khāe roṛā.
Horses and houses eat up (your wealth).
(Building is sweet impoverishment : Fools build houses for wise men to live in.)

Yā Khudā khair ! bachā hāth pair !
Thank God ! my limbs are safe !

Yā Khudā khair kar, khair kā berā pār kar!
God preserve us, and take the boat of virtue across!

Yā Khudā; Tū de, na main dūn?
O God, thou mayest give, but not I.
(Said by a miser.)

Yak man ilm rā dah man aql mībāyad. Pers.
An ounce of learning requires a pound of sense.

Yak na shud, do shud. Pers.
It was not one, but two.

Yā kisī ko kar rahe, yā kisī kā ho rahe.
Either make another yours or be his.
(Moral: don't try and get on by yourself! This is a deeply rooted notion among the middle class natives.)

Yā māre sājhe kā kām, yā māre Bhādon kā ghām.
A joint undertaking and an August sun will equally destroy.

Yaqīn barā rahbar hai. Ped.
Certainty is a sure guide.

Yā Rabb, merī ābrū vā din rakhiyo to Jā din sab sansār kā nirmal lekhā ho?
O God do Thou uphold my honor on that day, When Thou shalt take a strict account from the whole world!
(A saying of the *bhagats* or reformers.)

Yārān chorī, na pīrān dagābāzī. Mah.
There is no hiding from your friends, and no cheating your priest.

Yār Dom ne Banyā kīnā, Das le karaj sainkrā dīnā.
A singer made friends with a Banyā: He borrowed ten of him and repaid a hundred.
(A skit at the usurious habit of the Banyā caste.)

Yār Dom ne Jāt banāyā, Sīt dūdh in muklā pāyā.
A minstrel made friends with a Jāt, And in return got milk and tyre in plenty.
(*Jats* generally keep quantities of milch cows.)

Yār Dom ne kīnā Gūjar, Churā churā ghar kar diyā ūjar.
A minstrel made friends with a Gūjar, Who plundered his home.
(A skit at the thieving propensity of the Gūjar tribe.)

Yār Dom ne kīnā Kanjar, Har liyā palā palāyā kūkar.
A minstrel made friends with a gipsy, Who carried off his tamed dog.
(Kanjars or gipsies are very fond of keeping dogs.)

Yār Dom ne kīnā Nāī, kaudī de nā bāl mundāī.
A Dom made friends with a barbar and got shaved for nothing.

Yār Dom ne kiyā julāhā, Tan dhākan ko kaprā pāyā.
A singer made friends with a weaver, And thus found clothing for his body.

Yār Dom ne kiyā Rangharyā, Aur na dekhā vaisā haryā.
A minstrel made friends with a Rānghar, And found no worse thief than he.
(The *Rāngharş* are bastard Rājpūts of little reputation.)

Yār Dom ne kiyā sipāhī, bāt bāt mān kare larāī.
A Dom made friends with a soldier and quarrelled over word he uttered.

Yārī karen so bāore, aur kar-ke chhoren kūrh, Yā to or nibāhiye yā is se rahiye dūr.
Who form an attachment are fools, and who break them are idiots, Either put up with them or keep them at a distance.

Yā rind rinde yā fatah chande.
Be as poor as a beggar, or rich as a conqueror.

Yār-i-shātir kūn, na bār-i-khātir. Ped.
A friend should make you glad, not make you sad.

Yār kā dil yār rakkhe, to yār kā bhī rakhiye; Yār ke ghar khir pakke, to tanak sī chakhiye; Yār ke ghar āg lagī, to pare pare takiye.
If your friend please your heart, please his; If your friend has a good dinner, taste a little of it; If your friend's house catches fire, look on at a distance.
(Said of friendship formed on selfish motives a fair weather friend.)

Yār kā gussa bhatār ke ūpar.
Angry for her lover against her husband.
(Said of an unchaste wife.)

Yār karūn, pyār karūn. Chūlar tale angār dharūn, jal jāe to kyā karūn?
If I make a friend I love him. If I should put him on a fire and he is burnt, how can I help it?
(Applied to one, who makes professions of friendship, but is secretly hostile: a false friend.)

Yār kī yārī se kām, yā yār ke felon se?
Is our concern with the affections, or with the actions of our friends?
(The answer is obvious.)

Yār ko karūn pyār, khasam ko karūn bhasam, larke ko karūn chatnī!
I 'll caress my lover, burn my husband, and destroy my son!
(Said of a bad woman.)

Yār vohī hai pakkā, jis ne man yār kā rakkhā.
A true friend is he, who studies his friend's wishes.

Yār vohī, jo bhīr men kām āve.
A friend in need is friend indeed.

Yār zindah, sohbat bāqī.
As long as friends are living a meeting may be expected.

Yā sansār men karam pardhān.
In this world the strongest of all things is fate.

Yā sukh-nīnd soö, yā mālā japo.
Sleep quietly, or count your beads.
(Do one thing or other; you can't do two things at once.)

Yā to bhar māṅg sendur, yā nipaṭ ho rāṅd.
Either have a large quantity of the red paint, or be a widow outright.
(The red paint is the peculiar sign of the *feme covert.*)

Yeh āp ke farmāne kī bāt hai!
This is *your* view!
(A common rebuke. I call him George Washington, *you* may call him what you please.)

Yeh baṛ miṭṭhā, yeh baṛ khaṭṭā.
This is very sweet and that is very sour.
(Said of a person in a state of uncertainty of mind: to get into two minds about a thing.)

Yeh bāteṅ mat kījyo kadhe na tū, ae yār, Jin bātoṅ meṅ rūs jā Sāīṅ aur sansār.
Never do, my friend, such deeds, As offend God and the world.

Yeh bāt sharāfat se baīd hai.
This is unworthy of a gentleman.

Yeh bāt voh bāt, ṭakā dhar more hāth.
We have said this and that, and so down with your coppers.
(Said of avaricious persons, especially Brāhmans, who after each word of advice ask for money.)

Yeh bachan merā ṭhīk hai, sāṅch ise tū jān. Mare binā chhūṭe nahīṅ jī se bhūṅḍī bān.
This my saying is true believe me. A bad habit will not leave you till death.

Yeh bel mandhe chaṛhtī nazar nahī ātī.
I can't see that this creeper grows.
(Said of a man not likely to succeed. He wil never set the Thames on fire.)

Yeh bhī apne vaqt ke Hātim Tāī haiṅ.
He is the Hātim of the age.
(Hātim Tāī is the conventional Arab hero of all that is generous.)

Yeh bhī dām gulāmoṅ khāë; Yeh bhī baingan kāṭ pakāë.
As to the money it has been spent by the slaves: As to the egg-fruit it has been peeled and boiled.

Yeh bhī kisī ne na pūchhā, ki tere mūṅh meṅ kai dāṅt haiṅ?
No one ever asks how many teeth there are in your head.
(Said to express total neglect of a stranger or teacher in any village or neighbourhood: also said of good government, where safety of life and property is insured.)

Yeh bhī merī bāt tū jīv bīch dhar le:
Gaṅjā de gajvāl ko; par jīv bhed mat de.
Let this my advice sink into thy heart: Confide thy treasure to the treasury, but never the secret of thy heart.

Yeh bhī sikshā nāth jī kah gae ṭhīkam ṭhīk: Khoveṅ ādar mān ko dagā, lobh, aur bhīk.
This is sound advice from the saints: Deceit, avarice and beggary destroy a man's self respect.

Yeh bis kī gāṅṭh hai.
This is a knot of poison.
(Said of a vicious or wicked person.)

Yeh ḍāṛhī dhoke kī ṭaṭṭī hai.
This beard is a screen for imposture.
(Said of a hypocrite: The robe does'nt make the clergyman.)

Yeh dīde na-dīde haiṅ dīdār ke.
These eyes are very fond of seeing.

Yeh din sab ke vāste hai.
This day cometh to all.
(Said in consolation to the relatives of one recently deceased.)

Yeh dunyā din chār hai, sang na tere jā: Sāīṅ kā rakh āsrā, aur Vā se hī neh lagā.
This world is but for a few days, and goeth not with thee: Trust therefore in the Lord and love Him only.

Yeh *Gangā kis kī khudāī hai?*
By whom was *this* Ganges dug?
(Spoken in reproof of one, who boasts of his possessions and used in two senses: (1) that they are the gift of God, or (2) that he owes them to the speaker.)

"*Yeh ghoṛā kis kā?*" "*Jis kā maiṅ naukar.*"
"*Tū naukar kis kā? Jis kā yeh ghoṛā.*"
"Whose is this horse?" "His whose servant I am." "Whose servant are you?" "His whose this horse is."
(Arguing in a circle.)

Yehī bhalā hai, mīt jī, jhūṭ kadhe na bol: Bāṅg na sonā ho kadhī, phirat sunahrī jhol.
Never tell a lie, is sound advice, my friend: Tin will never become gold, though gilded a hundred times.
(Honesty is the best policy.)

Yehī bharosā ṭhīk hai, ki Dātā de to lūṅ.
Auran kā kar āsrā jī tarsāve kyoṅ?
It is best to trust in God and take when He giveth to thee. Why trouble thy heart by expecting from others?
(Hope deferred maketh the heart sick. Blessed are they that expect nothing for they shall never be disappointed.)

Yehī gau aur yehī maidān.
This is the cow and this is the field.
(Cause and effect.)

Yehī gaunā, bahur nahīṅ aunā.
This is a real parting, for there is no return.

Yehī lachchhan mār khāne ke haiṅ.
These are the marks of a whipping.
(Proof positive of an evil nature: the cloven hoof.)

Yehī mūṅh, yehī masālah.
Such sauce for such a mouth.
(More nice than wise: let it alone, it is meat for your master.)

Yeh javānī, mujhe na bhāve: sing ḍulāve hansī āve.

This youthful levity does not suit me: you laugh at the wagging of a horn.

Yeh kai fāqoṅ meṅ sīkhe the?
After how many fasts did you learn this?
(Said in reproof of a witty saying, of which the author is very proud.)

Yeh kavvā phaṅsne kī chāl hai.
This scheme is likely to catch crows.
(Said of a cunning fellow: crows are proverbially difficult to catch.)

Yeh kisī kā bhī sagā nahīṅ.
He has kinship with no one.
(He keeps faith with no one.)

Yeh *kuttā nahīṅ māṅtā.*
You can't control *this* dog.
(By 'dog' understand the belly.)

Yeh merī sīkh mān, re mītā; Bhīṛ sameṅ mat rah hat-rītā.
Hear this my advice, my friend: Never be empty handed in a row.

Yeh merī sikshā mān, piyārā; Saudā kadhe na bech udhārā. Mercantile.
Hear this my advice, my friend; Never sell anything on credit.

Yeh merī sikshā mān, re chelā; Kadhe bāṭ mat chāl akelā.
Hear this my advice, my brother; Heal a quarrel as far as you can.
(A soft answer turneth away wrath).

Yeh merī siksikshā mān, re bīrā; Kapṭī sang nā rākho sīrā.
Hear this my advice, my brother; Have no dealings with the treacherous.

Yeh merī sikshā mān, re chelā; Kadhe bāṭ mat chāl akelā.
Hear this my advice, my pupil; Never take a journey alone.

Yeh merī sikshā mān, re chele, Vā sūṅ mat mil jūā jo khele.
My friend, learn this lesson from me, Never associate with a gambler,

Yeh merī sikshā mān, sahelī; Par nar sang nā baiṭh akelī Wom.
Listen to this my advice my friend; Never sit with a strange man alone.
(By 'strange man' understand a man of another family).

Yeh tū sikshā sādh kī nehche chit meṅ lā; Bhed na apne jīv kā auran ko batlā.
Bear even this council of the saint in thy heart; Tell not the secret of thy heart to another.

Yeh merī sikshā nipaṭ hai āchhī; Roṭī mūl na khā adh kāchī!
Hearken ever to this my advice:
Never eat of half-baked bread!

Yeh merī sikshā, piyā, chit lāo; Par nārī ko dūr se tāko.
Keep this advice, my husband, in thy heart; Ever hold thyself aloof from another's wife.

Yeh mūṅh aur gājreṅ!
Carrots for such a mouth!
(The carrot in India is emblematical of what is worthless.)

Yeh mūṅh aur masūr kī dāl!
Peas for such a mouth!
(*Masūr kī dāl* is a valuable commodity.)

Yeh mūṅh pān joga?
Is this a mouth fit for betel?
(Used to express incongruity between the situation and the desires or pretentions of a person: *pān* is an expensive article: See preceding proverb.)

Yeh *paṭṭī nahīṅ paṛhe.*
I have never learnt *this* lesson.
(Said by one who declines compliance with an unreasonable request.)

Yeh tīn kāṅre, aur yeh pau bārah.
This is the three and this the ace and twelve.
(The three is a unlucky and the ace and twelve a lucky throw at *chaupaṛ*.)

Yeh to achchhe the, ūpar-vāloṅ ne bigāṛ diyā.
He was a good man till his associates spoilt him.

Yeh voh faqīr nahīṅ, jo khākar duā deṅ.
This beggar will not bless you for your dole.
(Said of an ungrateful person.)

Yeh voh gur nahīṅ, jo chiūṅṭī khāe.
There is not enough treacle in this to give to an ant.
(There is never enough where nought leaves.)

Yūṅ mat jāne, bāore, ki pāp na pūchhe koe: Sāīṅ ke darbār meṅ ek din lekhā hoe.
Think not: O fool, that none enquireth of thy sins: One day an account will be taken in the Court of God.
(The Day of Judgment.)

Yūṅ mat jī meṅ jān tū ki manukh badā jag bīch: Yād binā Kartār kī hai nīchan kā nīch.
Think not that a man as he is is great in this world: He is the basest of the base that remembereth not God.

Yūṅ mat mān gumān kar, ki 'Maiṅ hūṅ sher jawān', Tujh se is sansār meṅ lākhoṅ haiṅ balvān.
Be not so proud of heart as to say, 'I am a great man', : There are thousands greater than thee in this world.

Z

Zabān hī halāl hai, zabān hī murdār hai.
The tongue is lawful, and the tongue is unlawful.
(The tongue no man can tame: the tongue is an unruly member full of poison. *James* iii., 8.)

Zabān hī hāthī chaṛhāve, zabān hī sir kaṭvāve.
The tongue may help you to an elephant, or put your head in peril.

Zabānī jamā kharch batānā.
To credit and debit by word of mouth only.
(Said as a reproof to one who talks much and does little.)

Zabān jane ek bār; māṅ jane bār bār.
The tongue giveth birth but once; a mother often.
(Never go back from your word.)

Zabān ke āge lagām nahiṅ.
No curb on his tongue.

Zabān ke āge lagām zarūr chāhiye.
Always keep a curb on your tongue.

Zabān ke nīche zabān hai.
He has a tongue under his tongue.
(Said of the double tongued.)

Zabān kyā chalī? do hal chal-gae.
He wagged his tongue like ten ploughs going at once.
(Said to one who talks without consideration.)

Zabān mat phero.
Don't twist and turn your words.

Zabān se beṭā beṭī parāē ho jāte haiṅ.
Your own children can be made another's by the tongue.

Zabān se khandaq pār.
He can jump over a ditch with his tongue.

Zabān shīrīṅ mulk gīrī, zabān ṭeṛhī mulk bāṅkā.
A sweet tongue will conquer the whole world, and a crooked tongue will estrange it.
(Have honey on your tongue and money in your pocket.)

Zabar-dast kā ṭheṅgā sir par.
All feel the strong man's thumb.
(By 'thumb' understand 'power,' as in English.)

Zabar-dast ke bīsoṅ bisve.
The strong man usurps the whole twenty *bisvās*.
(*i. e.* the whole village; a *biswā* is a share in village lands held in common between hereditary shareholders.)

Zabar-dast kī lāṭhī sir par.
The strong man's club is on the head.
(All bow to the strong.)

Zabar-dast māre aur rone na de.
The tyrant will smite and will not let you weep.
(Under a bad Government you are never allowed to disclose the injustice done to you.)

Zabar-dast sab kā jaṅvāī.
The strong man is every body's son-in-law.
(His behests are obeyed.)

Zāhid kā kyā Khudā hai, hamārā Khudā nahiṅ?
Whose God is the saints', that He is not my God?
(God provides for all.)

Zāhir ābād, bāṭin kharāb.
Fair to see and foul of speech.

Zāhir Rahmān kā, bāṭiṅ Shaitān kā.
A Saint to look at, but a Devil to talk.

Zakhmī dushmanoṅ meṅ dam le to mare, na dam le to mare.
If a wounded man in his enemy's power breathe he dies; if he breathe not he dies also.
(To be put on the horns of dilemma; to fall between two stools.)

Zālim kā paiṅḍā hī nirālā hai.
The tyrant has the road all to himself.

Zālim kā zor sir par.
The tyrant's power is on my head.

Zālim kī jaṛ bhī ukhaṛ jātī hai.
Even a tyrant can be uprooted.

Zālim kī rassī darāz hai.
A tyrant has a long rope.
(Threatened men live long.)

Zālim kī umr koṭā.
The tyrant's term of life is a short one.
(He is liable to be assassinated by one of his sufferers.)

Zamīn āsmān ke qullābe milāte haiṅ.
He knits together the wings of the earth and the sky.
(Said of a great liar.)

Zamīn-dārī dūb kī jaṛ.
An estate is like the roots of the *dūb* grass.
(*i. e.* it is always productive.)

Zamīn-dār kī jaṛ harī.
A landowner is ever flourishing.

Zamīndār ko kisān, bachche ko masān.
A tenant is to a landlord, what weaning is to children.

Zāmin de yā dilāē. Mercantile.
A surety must either pay or make (his principal) pay.

Zāmin, dunyā pāp hai, tiryā hai mahā pāp Donoṅ ko tū phūṅk de, nām Niranjan jāp.
Zāmin, the world is sinful, and women very sinful, Eschew them both and take the name of God.
(Keep thyself unspotted from the world.)

Zāmin honā dhan kā khonā.
To be a surety is to lose your money.

Zāmin mat ho bāp kā, bhalā jo chāhe āp kā.
Never be surety even for your own father, if you wish well for yourself.
(Never back another man's bill.)

Zāmin mat ho chor kā, Aur siṅg pakaṛ mat ḍhor kā.
Never be surety for a thief and never hold a cow by the horn.

Zāmin na hūjiye, girah kā dījiye.
Better give from your pocket than become surety.
(It is better to give than to lend.)

Zamīn sakht aur āsmān dūr hai.
The earth so hard, the sky so far.
(Whither shall I fly?)

Zāmnī podnī kī kyā?
What security can a tomtit give?
(*Podnī* is a small bird: here used to imply any insignificant person.)

Zarā nā zahūr; 'gāṅṭh merī bhar-pūr'!
He possesses nothing at all, and says his pocket is full!

Zarā sā khāve bahot batāve, voh hai bahū sugh-railī: Bahotā khāve kam batlāve, voh bahuaṛ bigvailī.
Who eats a little and calls it much is a good house-wife: Who eats much and calls it little is a bad house-wife.

Zarā sā muṅh baṛā sā peṭ.
A little mouth with a large belly.
(Said of a glutton or an avaricious child.)

Zarā sā muṅh baṛī bāteṅ!
A little mouth and mighty words.
(Precocity; an old head on young shoulders.)

Zarā zarā sā kar liyā aur apnā pallā bharliyā.
Little by little will fill your pocket.

Zar bal na zor bal.
Neither strength nor money.

Zar-dār kā saudā hai, be-zar kā Khudā hāfiz.
The rich can procure all things, but God alone is the protector of the poor.

Zardār kā saudā hai: be-zar kā Khudā hāfiz! Pardār paṛe uṛte haiṅ: be-par kā Khudā hāfiz!
The rich can procure all things: God help the poor! Winged birds can fly: God help the wingless!

Zar dīje hazār, magar dil na dīje: Ulfat burī balā hai; kisī se na kīje!
Give your thousand, but never give your heart: Love is a wretched thing; never love at all.

Zar gayā, zardī chhāī; zar āyā, surkhī āī.
Money gone the face is pale: money come the face is flushed.

Zar hai to ghar hai, nahīṅ to khaṅḍar hai.
If there is money it is a home, if there is none it is a ruin.

Zar hai to nar hai, nahīṅ panchhī be-par hai.
If he has money he is a man, otherwise he is as a featherless bird.
(A man without money is not worth a straw.)

Zar hazār zeb lagātā hai, Be-zar bigṛā nazar ātā hai.
Money makes a hundred ornaments, Without money every thing looks ugly.

Zar kā to zarra bhī āftāb hai: Be-zār kī maṭṭī kharāb hai.
A little money maketh a sun: No money maketh a wretched earth.

Zar kā zāyal karnā, jīte jī hai marnā.
To lose your money is to die before your death.

Zar kā zorā pūrā hai, aur sab adhūrā hai.
The strength of money is a full strength, all else is naught.

Zar ko zar hī khenchtā hai. Mercantile.
Money draws money to itself.
(To him that hath shall be given.)

Zar nest ishq ṭeṅ ṭeṅ.
Without money your suit is nothing.
(Money makes the mare to go.)

Zar phailāyā aur kār barāyā.
Open your purse and your work is done.

Zarūrat ke vaqt gadhe ko bhī bāp banā lete haiṅ.
In time of need they will call even an ass father.

Zar, zamīn, zan, jhagṛe kī jaṛ haiṅ.
Money, land, and women are the roots of quarrel.
(*Effodiuntur opes irritamenta malorum.*)

Zar zor Khudā dād hai.
Strength and wealth are the gifts of God.

Zāt bhāṅt pūchhe nahīṅ koī: Hari ko bhaje, so Hari kā hoī.
Let none trouble about caste and creed; Who calleth on God is called of God.

Zāt bhāṅt pūchhe na koī; janeū pahan ke Bāman hoī.
No one troubles about his caste or tribe; he has put on the string and is therefore a Brāhmaṇ.
(The *janeū* is the sacred string of the Brāhmaṇs.)

Zāt bhāṅt pūchhe nā koī: kurtī penhī tilangā hoī.
Nobody asks about caste and clan: who puts on uniform is a soldier.

Zāt ganvaulon, peṭ na bharal. E. Wom.
A lost caste and an empty stomach.
(Said sometimes by insincere converts to Christianity.)

Zāt kā bairī zāt, kāṭh kā bairī kāṭh.
Caste is enemy to caste: wood is enemy to wood.
(Intruments for cutting wood are useless until provided with wooden handles: hence the point of the proverb.)

Zāt ke bulāiye barābar biṭhāiye: kam zāt ke bulāiye nīche biṭhāiye.
When you invite a man of your own caste seat him level with yourself: when a man of lower caste seat him lower than your self.
(Observe the rules of social etequette: in Rome do as Rome does.)

Zāt Khudā kī be-aib hai. Mah.
God is without a flaw.

Zāt kī beṭī zāt hī ke jātī hai. Wom.
High caste brides for high caste bride-grooms.

Zāt mad pīye mālūm hoe.
His caste will be known when he is drunk.
(An appeal from Philip sober to Philip drunk.)

Zāt meṅ Turuk aur bāje meṅ buruk.
Muhammadans among castes and a drum among instruments.
(Are the most noisy.)

Zauq meṅ shauq dastūrī meṅ larkā.
A son for perquisite is the height of delight.

Zeroṅ se sher hote haiṅ.
A tiger comes from a cub.
(Strength from weakness grows.)

Zor ke āge zarb nahīṅ chaltī.
Blows don't hurt strength.

Zor kī lāṭhī sir par.
The club of the strong falls on the head.

Zor na zulm; aql kī kotāhī.
Neither oppression nor tyranny; only want of understanding.
(None are so cruel as the ignorant.)

Zor thoṛā, gussā bahut, mār khāne kī nishānī.
A hot temper and little strength are precursors of a good beating.

Zyādah jī kar kyā, Āqbat ke boriye sametoge?
Do you want a long life that you may count your bags on the Day of Judgment?

Zyārat-i-buzurgān, kafārah-i-gunah. Per. Mah.
Respect for the old is an atonement for sin.
(Honor thy father and thy mother that thy days may by long in the land the Lord thy God giveth thee.)

ADDENDA.

Ādmī chane kā mārā martā hai.
A blow with a beanstalk will kill a man.
(The uncertainty of life.)

Adhūre kām aur jantī lugāī ko kadhī na dekhe: nafrat ho jātī hai!
To see a job half done and a woman in the act of delivery is disgusting.

Āg, jaṅvāsā, āgrī, chauthā gāṛīvān; Jiūṅ jiūṅ chamke bijlī, voṅ voṅ taje pirān.
The fire, the *janvāsā*, the salter, and the cartman, All do greatly grieve when the lightning flashes.
(*The janvāsā* is a thorny bush, which dies after the first rain. Lightning in India is always the precursor of rain.)

Āṅkh, nāk, mukh, mūṅdke nām Niranjan le. Bhītar ke paṭ jab khuleṅ, jab bāhar ke paṭ de.
Shut your eyes, your nose and your mouth, and then call on God. Your inner doors will open when your outer doors are shut.
(This saying is in support of the doctrine that contemplation on atheism leads to salvation.)

Āpā taje, to Harī ko bhaje.
Who gives up himself calls on God.
(See preceding.)

Āp ḍūbā so ḍūbā, aur ko bhī le ḍūbā.
He drowned himself and another with him.
(To drag down others with your own fall.)

Āp mile so dūdh barābar, māṅg mile so pānī; Kahe Kabīr, voh rakt barābar, jā meṅ enchā tānī.
If it comes of its own accord, it is like milk; if it comes by begging, it is like water; And if it comes by extortion it is like blood, saith Kabīr.

Asauj meṅ jo barse Dātā, Nāj niyār kā rahe na ghāṭā. Agric.
When God gives rain in November, There will be no scarcity of corn and fodder.

Āsmān kī chīl, zamīn kī asīl. Mah. Wom.
The kite of the sky, and the slave girl of the earth.
(Are both bad.)

Ās pās barse, Dillī paṛī tarse.
It rains here, it rains there, but still Dehlī moans.
(A drought in Dehlī and luxuriance all around.)

Ātā hai hāthī ke mūṅh, jātā hai chiūṅṭī ke mūṅh.
It comes through an elephant's mouth and it goes through an ant's mouth.
(Said of illness.)

Baḍoṅ ko hove dukh baḍā, chhoṭoṅ se dukh dūr: Tāre sab niyāre raheṅ, gaheṅ chandr aur sūr.
Great men have great troubles, which little men escape: All the stars remain apart, while sun and moon are eclipsed.
(Uneasy lies the head that wears a crown.)

Bagal thā sipārā, to pūt thā hamārā; Jab kamar huā katārā, to kanth huā tumhārā.
When he had a book under his arm, he was my son: Now that he has a dagger round his loins, he is your husband.
(A mother-in-law remonstrating with her son's wife, who is too jealous of her husband to allow him to visit his mother.)

Bahū navelī aur gau dudhelī. Rus.
A fresh wife and a milch cow are the best.

Bairī ho nā āpnā, lākh jatan kar dekh: Meṭe se miṭte nahīṅ, jūṅ Karman ke lekh.
Try you ever so much an enemy will never be a friend, As the lines of Fate can never be effaced.

Bairī lāge hāth, to chhoṛ na lekar māl; Us kī jaṛ ko mūl hī bāhar phek nikāl.
If your enemy fall under your clutches never give him up for money; Take him root and branch and cast him away.

Bairī sang na baiṭhiye pīkar mad aur bhang; jī khovā hai baiṭhnā jab bairī ke sang.

Never sit with your enemy when you are drunk with spirit or hemp, because thus you will endanger your life.

Bājrā kahe "main hūn allelā; Do mūsal se larūn akelā: Jo merī nājo khichṛī khāb, To turat boltā khush ho jāē."

Saith the millet, "I am a warrior, Fighting betwixt two pestles: When beauty hath a dish of me, She soon chatters with delight."

Bal se rājā rāo hai; bal bin baḍā na ko. Sānch baḍere kah gae, 'bal bin baḍā na ho.'

By might kings are monarchs; without might none is great. Truly have our forefathers said, 'Without might there is no greatness.'

Bal sūn nāmī ho gaē Rustam, Arjūn, Bhīm. "Bal bin kaisī hākīmī" kah gae sānch hakim.

Strength gained a name for Rustam, Arjun and Bhīm. Truly said our doctors 'without strength there is no governing.'

(Rustam is a hero of Persian romance, and Arjuna and Bhīma of (Sanskrit) Indian romance.)

Banī banāve Bāniyā, banī bigāṛe Jāṭ; Mūnḍen sīs sarā-hkar ḍom, kabīsar, bhāṭ.

Baniyās improve, and Jats spoil their possession: Bards, poets and minstrels live by flattery.

Banjī aur baṭāūā sukh pāwen jis gām, Vā ko to chau-khūnt men karen nek sarnām.

The tradesman and the wayfarer will extol highly that place throughout the world, where they are well treated.

Bante der lagtī hai, bigaṛte der nahīn lagtī.

It takes time to prosper, but no time to be ruined.

(Slow to rise and quick to fall; *facilis descensus Averni.*)

Bāp ḍom aur ḍom kī dādā; Kahe miyān "main shurfa-zādā!"

A bard his father and a bard his grandfather, And he thinks himself of noble birth!

Bārah baras ke ko Bed kya? Aur aṭṭhārān baras ke ko qaid kyā?

There is no teaching a man of twelve, and no controlling a man of eighteen.

(According to the native ideas a boy can think for himself at twelve, and is beyond control at eighteen!)

Baṛe ādmī ne dāl khāī, to kahā 'sādā mizāj hai': garīb ne dāl khāī, to kahā 'kangāl hai.'

If a great man eat *dāl*, they say he is a fool: but if a poor man eat *dāl*, he is called a wretch.

(One air for the rich and another for the poor.)

Bāṛ lagāī khet ko, bāṛ khet ko khāē. Rājā ho chorī kare, niyāo kaun chukāē?

A hedge is put up to protect the field, but the hedge eats it up. When the king steals, who is to do justice?

Bāton hāthī pāe, bāton hāthī-pāē.

Words bring one an elephant and words bring one under an elephant's feet.

(Here the pun is on the word *pāē*, which means (1.) get, (2.) feet. To be trampled under an elephant's feet is an old Indian punishment.)

Bāt par bāt yād ātī hai.

One word leads on to another.

Beṭā jan kar niv chale, sonā pahan-kar ḍhak chale. Wom.

Walk lowly after giving birth to a son and veil closely when you wear gold.

(A warning to women never to be proud of their sons or vain of their ornaments.)

Bhāgvān to jagat mān vāsā koī na ho, Jo koī rājā niyāu men sagar umar de kho.

No man so charitable as the king, Who spends his whole life in administering justice.

("Charity" in India involves doing "good works unto salvation.")

Bhains kahe "gun merā pūrā. Merā dūdh pī hove sūrā. Jis ke ghar men main bandh jāūn, Dūdh dahī kā nāl bahāūn." Rus.

Saith the buffalo, "I am full of virtues. Who drinks my milk is strong. Into the house where I am tied up, There flows a stream of milk and butter.

Bhūkā chāhe roṭī dāl; Dhāyā kahe "main joṛūn māl."

The hungry wants but bread and pulse, but the satiated wants to hoard money.

Biddyā to voh māl hai, jo kharchat dugnā hoē; Rājā, rāo, chorṭā chhīn na sakke koē.

Learning is a property that doubles as it is spent; Nor king, nor lord, nor thief can steal it.

(In modern England, however, there is a process known as "picking the brains.")

Chāk kunam! girah kunam! dekho merā hunar!

Behold my art! I can cut! and I can sew!

Chanā pakat hai Chait mān, aur gehūn Baisākh bichār; Kātak pāke bājrā, aur Mangsir pāke juār. Agric.

Gram ripens in March, and wheat in April, millet in October, and maize in November.

Chappe jitnī koṭhṛī aur Miyān Mahalle-dār!

A poky house and the owner a very landowner.

(A taunt to a showy person.)

Chirāg se chirāg jaltā hai.

One lamp is lighted by another.

(This proverb alludes to the old Native custom of lighting one lamp with another before the introduction of lucifer matches, and it means 'an heir begets an heir'.)

Dekh jagat meṅ audsā mat ḍar aur mat ro: Binā hukam Bhagvān ke bāl nā binkā ho.
Never fear nor weep when you meet with hardship in the world; Because without the order of God not a hair of your head can be hurt.

Devā ko rin mile suhelā, An-devā ko mile na dhelā. Mercantile.
A good paymaster can borrow easily, But a bad paymaster not a farthing.

Dhan joran ke dhiyān meṅ yūṅ hī umar na kho. Motī barge mol ke kadhī na ṭhīkar ho.
In hoarding wealth waste not your life. Pebbles never can be rated with pearls.
(*i. e.* The riches of this world are as pebbles to pearls in comparison with the riches of the next.)

Dhān kahe "maiṅ hūṅ Sultān; āē gaē kā rākhūṅ mān." Rus.
"I am the king of corn" saith the rice, "For I honor the guest."
(Rustic guests are usually feasted with rice and sugar.)

Dharam pāp sab manukh ke dhovat hai is taur, Jal sālan jūṅ dhovat haiṅ sab kapṛan kā ghor.
Charity washes off the sins of men, as soap washes the dirt of clothes.

Dhaule bhale haiṅ kāpre, dhaule bhale nā bār: Kālī ạchhī kāmlī, kālī bhalī na nār.
White clothes are good, but not white hairs: A black blanket is good, but not a black woman.

Dhobī ke ghar paṛe chor: voh na luṭā, luṭe aur.
When a washerman's house is attacked by thieves, it is not he, but others that are plundered.
(Because the clothes that are stolen belong to his customers.)

Donoṅ bairī dīn ke Rāṅghaṛ aur Shaitān: Burā karāveṅ aur se aur āp bure se kām.
Both the Rāṅghaṛs and the Devil are enemies of the faith: They sin themselves and make others to sin.

Dūr gae kī ās kyā?
What hope is there from him that is afar?

Ek āsāmī sau arzīyāṅ!
One post and a thousand applications for it.
(True in the East and the West.)

Ek boṭī sau kutte.
One piece of flesh and a thousand dog's for it.
(See preceding.)

Ek jhūṭ ke sabūt meṅ sattar jhūṭ bolne paṛte haiṅ.
Seventy lies are required to prove one.
(One lie leads to many.)

Ek pāpī sārī nāo ko ḍabotā hai.
One sinner drowns the whole boat.
(A Jonah.)

Ek sher mārtā hai, sau lomṛiyāṅ khātī haiṅ.
One tiger kills and a hundred foxes eat (the carcass).
(One man earns and his whole family live by it.)

Gadhā marā kumhār kā aur dhoban satī ho.
The potter's ass is dead and the washerman's wife burns herself (as a widow).
(Misplaced sympathy.)

Gāḍī to chaltī bhalī, nā to jān kabāṛ.
It is a cart if it goes well, otherwise it is but timber.

Gālī mat de kisī ko, gālī kare fasād: Gālī sūṅ lākhoṅ hue laṛ-bhiṛ kar barbād.
Never give abuse; abuse breeds quarrels: Through abuse thousands have fought and been ruined.

Gehūṅ āchhā nahar kā, aur chāval āchhā ḍahar kā. Agric.
Wheat grown near a canal is good and so is rice in lowlands. [*kā mīr.*

Gehūṅ kahe "suno, re bīr, Maiṅ hūṅ sab nājan
Says the wheat "hear ye, my brothers, I am the chief of all the corn."

Ghar kā khet na khetī bāṛī, Kahe "miyāṅ, merī nambardārī." Agric.
He possesses nor field nor garden, And pretends to be the head of the village.

Ghar kī jorū kī chaukṣī kahāṅ tak?
How far can you look after your own wife?

Ghar kī khāṅḍ kirkirī; chorī kā guṛ miṭhā.
The householder's sugar is gritty, but the thieve's is sweet.
(Stolen kisses are sweetest.)

Ghar kī sobhā gharvālī ke sāth.
The splendour of the house lies with the housewife.

Ghī khāvat bal tan mān āve: Ghī āṅkhan kī jot badhāve.
Butter strengthens the body and the eyesight as well.

Ghūnghaṭvālī dekhkar bhalī bīr mat jān.
The thickly veiled is not always good.

Gurbā kushtan roz-i-avval. Pers.
The cat should be killed on the very first day.
(A story relates that a man killed a cat on his wedding day in order to terrify his young wife, whence the proverb.)

Hālī āchhā hāṅglā, aur baldā āchhā chāṅglā. Agric.
If the ploughman goads well, the ox pulls well.
(*Experientia docet.*)

Hāṭ bhalī na sīr kī, aur sangat bhalī na bīr kī.
A partnership shop is bad and so is the companionship of a woman.

Hīnā bairī jānkar mat niḍar ho, yār; Kīṛī barkar sūṅḍ māṅ de hāthī ko mār.
Never despise your enemy because he is weak: An ant can kill an elephant by entering its trunk.

Hoṛ līje goṛ, udhār dīje chhoṛ.
Bets must be paid, though debts run on.
(Bets are 'debts of honor' in India, as well as in England.)

Hote kī bahn aur bāp hain; bin hote kī joē: Tulsī, rupayā pās kā sab se nīkā hoe!
Father and sister befriend in prosperity and a wife in adversity; But, saith Tulsī Dās, the money in your pocket is your best friend.

Hūs phere, chūme mere. Hin.
When the marriage ceremony is over he can suck my thumb.
(*i. e.* He have no longer any control over his daughter's life.)

Jahān gāē, vahān gāē kā bachchā.
Where the cow is, there is her calf.
(Wheresoever the carcass is, there shall the eagles be gathered together. *Matthew*, xxiv, 28.)

Jahān gul hogā, vahān khār bhī zurūr hogā.
Where is the rose, there is the thorn.
(There is no rose without a thorn.)

Jaise ke sang taisā kare, āchhā nahīn kām. Bure ke sang nekī kare, nekī ko parnām.
It is not righteousness to do to another as he deserves. To do good to a bad man is righteousness indeed.

Jaisī Lakkho bandaryā, vaise Manvā bhānd.
Like Lakkho the monkey, like Manvā the juggler.
(Six of one and half a dozen of the other.)

Jaisī sardhā ho terī, vaisā hī bojh uṭhā: Hāthī bojhā chiūntī thāvat dab mar jā.
Take up a burden that you can bear: the load of an elephant will surely crush an ant.

Jaisī sevā kare, vaisā mevā pāē.
As you do service, so will you get the fruit of it.
(As you serve so will you be served: learn to obey that you may learn how to rule.)

Jaldī kām Saitān kā, aur der kām Rahmān kā.
Quickly for the Devil, slowly for God.

Jal kī machhlī jal hī men bhalī.
The fish of the water is best in the water.
(*Cf.* the English: "Fish out of water.")

Jal se agnī bujhat hai; jal barsat thanḍ ho; Jal se dhobī mail ko dūr karat hai dho.
Water quencheth fire, and water maketh the season cool; With water also the washerman washeth away the dirt.

Jane jane se mat kaho kār bhed kī bāt.
Never let out the tricks of your trade.

Jāp ke birte pāp.
Sinning on the strength of his devotions.
(Sanctimoniousness: charity shall cover a multitude of sins.)

Jeṭh, jiṭhānī, deorā, sab matlab ke mīt: Matlab bin to koī bhī rākhe nā prīt. Rus. Wom.
My husband's elder brother and his wife and his younger brother are all interested friends: Without self-interest no one keeps up a friendship.

Jeṭh tapaī ho barkhā gahrī; Hanse bāngrū, roven nahrī. Agric.
A hot July sends plenty of rain, When the highlands laugh and the lowlandsweep.

Jhānsī gale kī phānsī; Datyā gale kā hār; Lalitpur nā chhāḍiye jab lag mile ahār.
Jhānsī is a noose for your throat; Datyā a wreath for your neck; But never leave Lalitpur while you can get your bellyful.
(Jhānsī, Datyā and Lalitpur are three cities in the Central Provinces and the above proverb illustrates the public estimation in which each is held.)

Jhūṭe kī kyā dostī? Langre kā kyā sāth? Bahre se kyā bolnā? Gūnge kī kyā bāt?
No friendship with a liar; no company with a cripple: No speaking with the deaf; no words with the dumb.

Jhūṭī to hotī nahīn kadhī bhī sānchī bāt, Jaise tahnī ḍhāk mān lage na chauthā pāt.
A lie can never be the truth, As a *ḍhāk* tree can never bear more than three leaves on a twig.

Jhūṭ kahnā aur jhūṭ khānā barābar hai.
To tell a lie is to eat leavings.
(According to Hindū custom no one but a man of very low caste will eat food, of which a portion has been eaten by another.)

Jī jalāne se hāth jalānā behtar hai.
A burnt hand is better than a burnt heart.
(Headache is better than heartache.)

Jin molon āī, un hī molon gaīvāī.
Ill got is ill spent.

Jis bahuar kī bairan sās, Vā kā kadhī na ho gharvās. Wom.
The wife that hath a scolding mother-in-law, Will never know the comforts of a home.

Jis ghar baḍe na bujhiyen, dīpak jale na sānjh; Voh ghar ūjaṛ jāenge, jin kī tiryā bānjh.
The house where the elders are not heeded, the lamp is not lit in the evening, and the wife is barren, will be ruined.

Jis kā ghoṛā us ke bār.
A horse should be kept at his owner's door.

Jiv kisī kā mat satā, jab lag pār basāe; Kānṭe hain is rāh men, is batyā matjā.
Worry no man's life out if you can help it: There are thorns in this path; traverse it not.

Jo bairī hon bahot se, aur tū hove ek; Mīṭhā bankar nikas jā: yehī jatan hai nek.
When your enemies are many and you are alone, pass them courteously: this is good advice.

Jogī kis ke mīt? Aur pātar kis kī nār?
The mendicant is nobody's friend and the harlot nobody's wife.

Jo Īshwar kirpā kare, to khaṛe hilāven kān arhar ke khet men.
If God be kind, a donkey will shake his ears in my field of pulse.
(The story goes that a man who was driving

some asses laden with treasure lost one of them in a field of pulse. The next day the ass was found by the owner of the field, who took away all the money and drove it off.)

Jo jal Sāḍh lagat hī barse, Nāj niyār bin koī na tarse. Agric.

If it rains in June, No one will feel the want of corn and fodder.

Jo kosat bairī mare aur man chītve dhan hoe; Jal mān ghī niksan lage, to rūkhā khāē na ko.

If curses could kill an enemy and wishes could bring us wealth, and if butter could be made from water, who would eat dry bread?

Jo main aisā jāntī, pīt kare dukh hoē: Nagar ḍhaṇḍerā phertī "pīt na kariyū koē." Wom.

Had I known before that pains do dwell in love, I would have proclaimed by the beat of drum that no body should love.

Jo Sāīn ke hukm se mūnh na phere to, Tere bhī phir hukm se mūnh na phere ko.

If thou turn not thy face from the commands of God, No one shall turn his face from thy commands.

Jo Sāvan men barkhā hove, Khoj kāl kā bilkul khove. Agric.

When it rains in July, The footprints of famine disappear.

Jote hal, to hove phal. Agric.

Who drives the plough gets the fruit.

(Who sows mows.)

Jo tūhī rājā huā apnā sukh mat ṭhān; Phakkar aur phakīr ke dukh sukh par kar dhyān.

Though you be a king never look to your own pleasurs But look to the pain and hardships of the poor and the beggar.

Jyūn jyūn bāo bahe purvāī, Tyūn tyūn atī dukh ghāyal pāī.

As long as the East wind blows, The wounded greatly suffers.

(When the wind is in the East 'tis neither good for man nor beast.)

Kājal kī kajlauṭī aur phūlon kā hār!

Black as the lampblack phial she decks herself with flowers.

(Said of a very ugly woman who adorns herself richly.)

Kālā hiran mat māryo, re, sattar ho jāēngī rānd.

Never kill a black buck, or seventy does will be widowed.

Kallar khet rahe jis pās, Vā ke hoe nāj na ghās. Agric.

Who owns a barren field gets nor corn nor grass.

Kāl kā mārā, sab jag hārā.

Against death the whole world is powerless.

(No remedy against death.)

Kāl karante āj kar, āj karante ab: Pal men parle hot hai pher karegā kab?

Do to-day what you would do to-morrow and do now what you would do to-day: A moment may bring death and then when will you do it?

Kāman to vohī bhalī, jo par-ghar kadhī na jāē: Bhaē rākhe yūn nāh kā, jūn galkaṭ se gāē.

That wife is best, who never goes to another's house, and fears her husband, as a cow fears the butcher.

Kānā, yānā, lāḍlā; tīnon haṭ kī khān! Andhā, gūngā, kāērā, hain pūre shaitān.

A one-eyed man, a minor, and a spoilt child are all three accursed things: But the blind, the bald and the squint-eyed are real devils.

Kān Kāshī, kān Kāshmīr, kān Khurāsān, Gujrāt? Tulsī! yahān to jīv ko parālabdh le jāt.

Where is Kāshī (Benares) and where Kashmīr, where Khurāsān and where Gujrāt?

Saith Tulsī: Man's destiny takes him to every place.

Karnā hai so āj kar, 'kal' 'kal' mat nā kar. Challā phirtā ādmī chhin mān jāve mar.

What you have to do, do to-day, and never say 'to-morrow.' Even a man walking may die in a moment.

Karnī hī sang jāt hai jab chhuṭ jāē sarīr: Koī sāth na de sake māt—pitā, sut, bīr.

Your deeds will follow you when your soul departs: None will accompany you, neither parents, nor son, nor brother.

Kātag mān jo sīt ko piye, so lābhā pāē: Bhādon mān jo koī piye, to deve tāp chaḍhāē.

Who drinks butter-milk in October will enjoy it: Who drinks it in August will get fever.

Kaṭ mar jāēnge ek din, jo nar rākhen bair; Bakrī kī mān kad talak rahe manātī khair?

They will be one day destroyed and die, who bear enmity: How long shall a kid's mother expect it to live?

Khāt sanvāre khet ko, aur sīkh sanvāre pīt ko. Agric.

Manure improves the fields and example strengthens friendship.

Khet bhalā nā jhīl kā, aur ghar āchhā nahīn sīl kā. Agric.

A lowland field is not good, nor is a damp house.

Khet jo tanne bhete nahrī, vā ke milte mat le dahrī. Agric.

If you can get a field by a canal, Never exchange it for a low-lying one.

Kurlā kare na dātan phere, phir kaise hon dānt nikhere?

Who never rinses his mouth nor uses a tooth-brush, how can his teeth be clean?

Lāj bhalī hai, bālke, yā mat jī se khoē: Lāj binā aisā manush, khasam binā jūn joē.

Modesty is a good thing, my son, never dismiss it from thy mind: A man without modesty is like a wife without a husband.

Lālach mat kar, bāore; lālach burī balā: Turat pakāerū jāl mān lālach sūn phans jā.

Never covet, fond fool, avarice is a vice: It is through greed that birds fall into the net.

Lāvan bin nā sohe roṭī, bin gūndhe nā sohe choṭī.

Bread is the better for relish, and the hair for braiding.

Main hūn aisā chātar siyānī, Chātar bhare mere āge pānī.

I am such a clever man that a clever man fetches my water.

(Does me homage self applansr.)

Mandar mān sahī sanj se rākho dīpak bāl: Sānjh andhere baiṭhnā hai atī bhonḍī chāl.

Light the lamp early in the evening in your house: It is unlucky to sit in the dark.

Māpā, kaniyā aur paṭvārī, Bheṭ liye bin karen na yārī.

The surveyor, the assessor, and the village accountant will never be friend you you without a bribe.

Marnā hai bad nek ko; jīnā nāp sadā: Behtar hai jo jagat mān nek nām rah jā.

Both good and bad will die; none will live for ever: So it is best to leave a good name hehind.

Maut dījo, par maur na dījo!

Better death than a marriage.

Maut dījo, par mor na dījo! Mercantile.

Better death than a dull market.

Mele men jo jāē tū, to nāvān kar men ṭānk, Chor, juārī, gaṭhkaṭe ḍāl saken na ānkh. Rus.

When you go into a fair keep your money in your pockets, That nor thief, nor pickpocket nor gambler may see it.

(Common village gamblers are often also thieves.)

Millat mān atī lābh hai; sab se milkar chāl: Mākhī jab hon ekṭhī, to deven sahad mahāl.

In companionship profit dwells; keep company with all you meet: It is a company of bees that makes a hive and produces honey.

Mintar se antar nahīn, bairī se nahīn neh; Pītam se pardā nahīn, jīn nirkhī sarī deh? Wom.

No hiding from a friend, no loving an enemy; No screening from the husband who has seen the whole body.

Mīt banāē nā bane bairī, singh aur nāg: Jaise kadhe na ho saken ek ṭhaur jal āg. Rus.

An enemy, a lion and a serpent will never be a friend, as fire and water cannot exist together in the same place.

Mūl na vā sūn bhāē karo, jo nar kaṭe garūr: Jo nar Sāīn se ḍare vā se ḍaro zarūr.

Never fear the man that boasts and vaunts, But fear the man that fears God.

Mūrakh ko mat saunp tū chatrāī kā kām: Gadhā bikat miltī nāhīn badh ghoṛe ke dām.

Never teach an ingenious art to a fool: A donkey will never sell at the price of a horse.

Mūrakh mūndh ganwār ko sikh na dījo koē: Kūkar bargī pūnchhṛī kadhī na sīdhī hoē. Rus.

Never throw away your advice upon a village boor: A dog's tail can never be straightened.

Nahākar khāē aur khākar sove, Us ke ausak kadhe na hove.

Who eats after bathing and sleeps after eating will never know an ache.

Nikaṭ hain ek ānkh se dhoī, dhobī, dhān: Achhe bhonḍo ko gaē sab kartab ke tān.

Cheat, washerman and rice, all begin with the same letter; But every one is good or bad according to his deeds.

(*Dhoī* is "cheat": *dhobī* is "washerman," *dhān* is "rice.")

Ninnānve ghaṛe dūdh men ek ghaṛā pānī kiyā jānā jāē?

One pitcher of water cannot be recognised in ninety pitchers of milk.

☞ The story goes that Akbar once enquired of Bīrbal which was the most untrustworthy class. The minister replied that milkmen were, and in order to prove the truth of this he ordered all the milkmen in Āgrā to fill a tank with pure milk. Every milkman, thinking to himself that if he were to put into the tank a pitcher of water instead of milk, no body would know of it. So each man with this notion in his head poured a pot full of water instead of milk into the tank, and when next day the king went to see it he found the whole of it filled with pure water only.

Nipat savere khet man jākar hal ko bāh: Jab sūraj ho shikar mān baiṭh chhāon men jā. Agric.

Early in the morning go to your field and plough your land: When the sun rises to the zenith sit quietly under a shade.

Pābandī ek kī bhalī.

It is well to be bound to one person only.

(A multitude of masters ruins a servant.)

Pair jo pachhvā mān barsāve, Vohī nirmal rās uṭhāve. Agric.

Who threshes corn when the west wind blows will get a clean heap.

Paise bin mātā kahe "jāmā pūt ku-pūt": Bhāī bhī paise binā māren lakh sir jūt.

When you have no money your mother calls you bad, and your very brothers beat you with shoes.

Panḍit aur mashālchī donon ulṭī rīt; Aur dikhāve chāndnī, āp andhere bīch.

A doctor and a torch-bearer are both upside down; Both throw light upon others while they are themselves in the dark.

(*Pandit* here means one who but does not act up to his preaching.)

Pāp ḍabove dharam tirāve : Dharmī kadhī nāṅh dukh pāve.

Sins perish and goodness thrives : So a good man will never know pain.

Parāī badshugnī ke vāste apnī nāk kaṭāī.

To cut off your own nose to cause an ill omen to another.

(It is an ill omen to see a person without nose when setting out on a journey. To bite your nose to spite your face.)

Parāyā khāiye gā bajā ; apnā khāiye ṭaṭṭī lagā.

Use others' things with joy and merriment : use your own with shut doors.

Paṛhe ke āge ṭokrā ḍālā, us ne kahā "mujhe uploṅ ko bhejā."

When a basket is put before a man of learning, he understands that he is meant to bring fuel.

(A hint is enough for the wise.)

Paṛhtum te martum ; nā paṛhtum te martum.

Learn and you'll die; learn not and you'll die.

(Learn or not learn, die you must.)

Parjā bhāje chhoṛke kunniyāī kā gām ; Chahūṅ or jag māṅ kare pher use bad nām.

The people fly from the tyrant's rule, And spread an evil report of him over all the world.

Parjā jaṛ hai rāj kī, rājā hai jūṅ rūkh ; Rūkh sūkhkar gir paṛe, jab jaṛ jāve sukh.

The subjects are the roots of the kingdom, and the king the tree : The tree will dry up and fall if the roots drie.

Pat chāhe to, bālke, paṛh biddyā bharpūr ; Bin-biddyā ke ādmī haiṅge jaise būr.

If you want honor, acquire learning, my son ; Without learning a man is but the refuse of society.

Pīr miyāṅ bakrī, murīd miyāṅ bāṅgā ; Ā gāī bakrī chab gāī bāṅgā. E.

The priest is a goat and his disciple cotton ; When the goat comes it gobbles up the cotton.

(The priest lives upon the earnings of the disciple.)

Qānūṅgo kī khoprī marī bhī dagā de !

Even the skull of a dead lawyer will cheat you !

Qāzī ba-do gavāh rāzī. Mah.

The judge is satisfied with the evidence of two witnesses.

(Under Muhammadan law.)

Qāzī jī apnā āgā to ḍhāko, pīchhe kisī ko nasīhat karnā. Mah.

Reverend doctor, first cover your own nakedness, and then preach to others.

(Act first and then advise.)

Qāzī jī bahoterā harāeṅ, maiṅ hārtā hī nāhīṅ.

Let the judge confute me ever-so-much I'll never be confuted.

(Stubbornness.)

Qāzī ke marne se kyā shahar sūnā ho jāegā ?

Will the Qazi's death empty the city ?

Rājī rākh kisāṅ ko, jo hālā bhar dhan de ? Rājī huā majūr to mukta kām kare. Rus.

Keep happy the husbandman that bring you your produce, For a satisfied laborer works hard.

Sej chaṛhte hī rāṅḍ. Hin.

Widowed on the marriage-bed.

(Death in the moment of victory : to fail on the verge of success : there's many a slip 'twixt cup and lip.)

Sukh, sampat aur audsā sab kāhū ko ho ; Gyānī kāṭe gyān se, murkh kāṭe ro.

Ease, plenty and affliction befall every man ; A wise man receives them with wisdom and a fool with cries.

Sūnā khet jaunḍiyā sove, Kyoṅ na khetī ujaṛ hove ?

When the field is unwatched and the watchman sleeps, the crop is sure to be destroyed.

Tujh dhore jo chākrā deve umar gaṅvā, Būḍhā vā ko jān-kar dhore se mat tāh.

Never drive him away in his old age, Who hath spent his life in thy service.

Ūṅṭ kī barsāt meṅ kambakhtī.

The rainy season is a calamity to the camels.

Uṛad kahe "maiṅ sab se nīkā ; Sab panchoṅ mil dīnā ṭīkā. Jab mere hoṅ uṛdī baṛe, To gabrū khā jāeṅ khaṛe khaṛe." Rus.

"I am the best grain of all" saith the pulse, "and every community hath installed me king. When fried cakes are made of me, young dandies haste to eat them."

AGRICULTURAL.

Ādhe Asāṛh to bairī ke bhī barse. [field.
The July rains fall even on the enemy's
(Equal justice.)

Agil khetī āge āge, pachhilā khetī bhāg jāve.
A crop in time and good produce, a crop too late and failure.

Bail badhiyā sājhe adhiyā.
The bull and the ox go half shares.
(For explanation see page 26 col. I.)

Baisākh Jeṭh dutiyāyām, Uttar ūncho chand,
Yeh nehche kar jāniye, pirthī meṅh sulabh.
If the new moons of April and May have the northern horns high, there will be plenty of rain for the earth. [*chār dukhārī.*

Ban, bālak, aur bhains, ukhārī, Jeṭh mās yeh
Trees, babies, buffaloes and sugarcanes, These four suffer in the month of May.
(From the hot winds.)

Barse Asauj to hojā nāj kī mauj.
September rain and plenty of grain.

Barse Sādh to banjā ṭhāṭ.
Rain in July and every thing blooms.

Barse Sāvan to hoṅ pāṅch ke bāvan.
Rain in August and five becomes fifty two.
(Crops increase tenfold,)

Basāo shahr kā aur khet nahr kā.
A house in a city and a field by a canal (are the best of their kind).

Bhādoṅ donoṅ sākh kā rājā hai.
August is the king of the two harvests.
(The most profitable crop is that in autumn.)

Bhādoṅ kā jhallā ek sing gīlā ek sūkhā.
In August showers one horn is wet and the other dry. (See page 33 col. I.)

Bhādoṅ ke meṅh se donoṅ sākh kī jaṛ bandhtī hai.
With August rains both harvest thrive.

Bhādoṅ meṅ barkhā hoë, kāl pachhokaṛ jā-kar roë.
When the rains fall in August famine steps aside and weeps.

Bhūlā pire kisān jo Kātag māṅge meṅh. [vember.
It is a mad peasant that wants rain in No-

Bhūn boyā upaṭ gayā.
The burnt seed came to nothing.
(Said of a child who turns out ill.)

Bhūrā bhainsā, chāṅdlā joë Pūs mahāvaṭ birle hoë.
A brown buffalo, a bold wife and rain in December are indeed rare.

Chaṛhte barse Ardrā, utrat barse Hast,
Kitnā Rājā ḍanḍ le, rahe anand girhast.
If rain falls in July and October the peasants will be happy, however much the king may tax them. [*chale to lenā na denā.*

Chenā jī kā lenā; chaudah pānī denā, byār
Millet eats up the heart: give it fourteen floodings, and then comes the hot wind, and there is nothing to give or take.
(See page 54 col. II.)

Ḍābar ḍūbe jag tire, jag ḍūbe ḍābar tire.
When the low lands are flooded the world swims (with plenty); when the world is drowned (with drought) the low lands swim (with rich produce).

Dhān kā gāoṅ puāl se jānā jātā hai. [about).
The rice village is known by the straw (lying
(The tree is known by its fruit.)

Dhān, pān, panyaule, nāṅh jāt latiyaule.
Rice, and betel must be well watered or they will not thrive.

Ek mās ritū āge dhāve.
The season runs a month ahead.
(Its character is seen a month previously.) [*pātī.*

Ek pān jo barse Suātī, Kurmiu pahire sone kā
When showers fall in September, the farmer's wife wears golden rings.
(For explanation see page 79 col. II.)

Gadhoṅ se hal chale to bail kaun bisāe? [oxen.
If donkeys could draw ploughs who would buy
(Which are of a higher price.)

Hālī kā peṭ suhālī se nahīṅ bhartā. [crisp cakes.
The ploughman's stomach is not filled with
(For explanation see page 95 col. II.)

Harī khetī, gyābhan gāë, mūṅh paṛe tab jānī jāë.
The standing crop and the pregnant cow are your own when they yield.
(The uncertainty of the future.)

Hathiyā barse, Chitrā maṅḍrāë, ghar baiṭhe kisān ririyāë.
Rain in October and clouds in November and the peasant sits at home and weeps.

Hathiyā barse tīn hot haiṅ shakkar, shālī, māsh;
Hathiyā barse tīn jāt haiṅ tillī, kodoṅ, kapās.
Rain in October and three things prosper sugar-cane, rice and pulse; Rain in October and three things die, sesamum, millet and cotton. [*bāo.*

Jab āve barsan kā chāo, pachhvā give, na parvā
When it means to rain it will rain whether east or west wind blows.

Jaisā bo, vaisā kāṭ.
As you sow so you mow.

Jin baṛhā har charo, so kaise chareṅ puār.
How should the animal that has lived on green grass eat straw.
(Accustomed to luxury, reduced to misery.)

Jis kā tej us kā bhej.
Who has the power has the rent. [*kar roe.*

Jo Bhādoṅ meṅ barkhā hove kāl pachhokaṛ jā
When rain falls in August famine goes behind a wall and weeps.

Jut Jut mareṅ bailvā baiṭhe khāeṅ turang.
The oxen work to death, the horses feed in their stalls.
(The poor work that the rich may thrive.)

Kāl kaṛhāū kisān kā khāū.
Famine and dearth are the death of farmers.

Kallahr kā khet jaise kapṭī kā heth.
A traitor's friendship is a barren field.

Karam-hīn khetī kare bail mare yā sūkhā paṛe.
If an unlucky man become a cultivator, his oxen die or there comes a drought.

Kar khetī pardes ko jāë, tā ko janam akārath jāë.
Who tills the soil and goes abroad wastes his life.

Karo khetī aur bharo ḍanḍ.
Raise a crop and pay a fine.
(For explanation see page 132 col. I.)

Karo khetī aur boo bail.
Plough a field and sow oxen.
(A good breed of oxen is becoming extinct.)

Kāṭne vāle ko thoṛā, baṭorne vāle ko bahut.
Little to the reapers and much to the sheaf makers.
(Because the latter get the gleanings,)

Khāt paṛe to khet nahīṅ to bhūṛ kā ret.
Manure it and it is a field, otherwise it is sandy desert.

Khāye chanā, rahe banā.
Eat pulse and keep your health.
(For explanation see page 137, col. ii.)

Khet bārānī, jaise niām rājānī.
An irrigated field is like the gift of a king.
(For explanation see page 138. col. i.)

Khet bigāṛe khartuā aur sabhā bigāṛe dūt.
Back biters ruin society, as weeds ruin the field.

Khet gae kisān.
He is a husbandman that goes to the field.
(For explanation see page 138, col. i.)

Khetī kar-kar ham mare, bahore ke koṭhe bhare.
I worked myself to death in the fields, and it was the banker that filled his granary.
(For explanation see page 138, col. i.)

Khetī rāj rajāë, khetī bhīk mangāe.
Husbandry makes kings, and beggars both.
(For explanation see page 138, col. i.)

Le liyā palla aur bīnan lagī sillā.
The gleaner brings her baskets and begins.
(Said to one who acts without previous permission.)

Māghe jāṛ na Pūse jāṛ batāse jāṛ.
December and January make no winter, but the wind does.

Māgh kā jāṛā, Jeṭh kī dhūp, Baṛe kashṭ se upje ūkh.
With frost in February and heat in June, The sugar-cane grows with difficulty.

Mahāvaṭ barsī aur sādhī sarsī.
With winter rain the spring crop thrives.

Mātā ke parse, Bhādoṅ ke barse se peṭ bhartā hai.
The meal served by a mother, like August rains, fills the stomach.

Mat bo chāpaṛ, ujṛe ṭābaṛ.
So not on a stony soil, or you will ruin your family.

Mirg, bāndrā, tītar, mor ; ye chāroṅ khetī ke chor.
The deer, the monkey, the partridge, and the peacock, these four are the thieves of the field.

Pachhvā chale, khetī phale.
When the west wind blows, the harvest thrives.
(For explanation see page 175, col. ii.)

Pahle bo pahlë, kāṭ.
Early sow, early mow.
(Early bird gets the worms.)

Phāorā na kudār, borā khet hamār.
Nor hoe ,nor spade, and a big field is mine.
(Undertaking what is beyond one's power.)

Sādhī kī sākh aur pīpal kī lākh.
The spring crop and the lac on *pīpal* trees.
(Are the best.)

Sastā haṅsāve, mahṅgā rulāve.
Cheapness moves to laughter, dearness to tears.

Sāvan mās bahe purvaiyā, Becho bardā, kīno gaīyā.
When east winds blow in August, sell off your oxen and buy cows.
(For explanation see page 216, col. i.)

Sāvan mās chale purvaīyā, khele pūt bolā le maiyā.
When east winds blows in August, the children play and the mothers cheer them on.

Shukkar-vār kī bādlī, rahī Sanichar chhāë. Aisā bole Bhaḍḍorī, bin barse nahīṅ jāë.
Clouds on Friday and again on Saturday, Bhaḍḍarī says, will never pass away without rain.

Sughaṛ balaiyāṅ susrā le, Bail māṅg bahū ke de.
If the bride be clever her father-in-law will caress her, And get her oxen on credit.

Sukhār, duhār, āsmānī farmānī haiṅ.
Drought and inundation are the works of God.

Sūkhe meṅ jhaṛ ber ghane hoṅ : Sammat māṅ an ḍher ghane hoṅ.
In draught wild plums are plentiful, and in a good season corn.
(For explanation see page 226, col. ii.)

Sūkhe Sāvan, rūkhe Bhādoṅ.
A dry Sāvan means a barren Bhādoṅ.

Sūnā khet kulachhnā hirnā hī chug jāë Khet birānā boë-ke bīj akārath jāë.
Deer will graze the unguarded field, thou fool, And seed sown in another's field, profits nothing.

Tal dhār, ūpar dhār.
Above and below it's all a stream.
(Raining cats and dogs.)

Tāl na talyā bovo singhāṛe, bhaīyā.
Nor tank nor lake and he wishes to sow water caltrops my friend.

Tāl utihal kar ujhlen kyār, jab barkhā ho pūram pār.
Lakes and ponds will overflow, When rains are heavy.

Tape jeṭh to barkhā ho bhar peṭ.
A hot July brings plentiful rains.

Tape nakhat. Mirgshirā jāë, Tab barkhā pūran jag hoë.
Heat in *Mirgshirā* and the world will be filled with rain, *Mirgshirā*, a lunar asterism falls in June-July. [*gīt.*

Tenṭ bārvā kāl ke mīt: khāen kisām aur gāven
Wild fruits are the friend of famine: The laborer eats and rejoices.

Ṭiḍḍī kā ānā kāl kī nishānī.
When locusts appear, famine is near.

Tīj pare khet men bīj.
On tij the seed is sown.
(For explanation see page 238, col. ii.)

Tīn hain sāh kisān ke; jānd, jāl aur kair.
The three bankers of the husbandman: the *jānd*, the jāl, and the kair.
(For explanation see page 238, col. i.)

Tiryā rove purakh binā, khetī rove menh binā.
A woman weeps without a husband and a field without rain.

Ugat uge, mah bhare biswat uge jāë;
What comes up in a mouth if it come up easily will soon wither.

Ut mat gehūn buā re chelā, jit hūn thal aur pathar ḍhele.
Never sow wheat my son, Where clods and stone abound.

Ut taunh buā bājrā bhāī jit hon thal kī muktāī.
Sow millet in a porous soil.

BHOJPURI PROVERBS.

Abre ke bhains byāil, sagro gāon maṭyā le dhāil.
When the poor man's buffalo calves every one runs with his pail (for milk).
(Grinding the poor and defenceless.)

Āile gaile, goṛ halukaile, pile kaur haluk.
With coming and going his knees shook, and what little he got he vomited.
(To work hard and fail.)

Āil teharvā, kharchae ke gharbā, na koī chīnhe jāne, nahīn etibarvā.
The cost of the festival has come on us, but no one knows and trusts us here.
(For explanation see page 6, col. ii.)

Akelvā gaīl maidān phire, loj kahil ki harāë gaile.
If she go out by herself they say she is with a stranger.
(For explanation see page 9, col. i.)

Andhar ke gāë byāil, ṭahrī leke daurlan.
The blind man's cow calved, and every one ran with his milk-pail.

Āpan bhal hoit, to jagattar parīt yārī.
If you are good, the whole world is your friend.

Āpan de-ke, buṛbak bane ke!
Give up your all, and be a fool!
(Benevolence spells bankruptcy).)

Āpan khet bambh loṭe, pāhī jote jāī lā.
His own field lie fallow while others' lands he ploughs.

Āpan māmā mar mar gailan, jolhā dhunyā māmā bhailan.
Leave your own uncles and make uncles of weavers and carders.
(See page 15, col. i.)

Apnā bail kulhāṛī nāthab.
My own oxe's nose I can bore with an axe.
(See page 16, col. i.)

Apnā ke juṛe nā, ankā ke dānī.
With nothing of his own, he is generous to others.

Bābhan ke babuā kahle, nān jāt laṭyāole.
Call a churl a gentleman and he kicks his own brethern.
(See page 23, col. ii.)

Bāgho ke munh kehū dhoal he?
Who ever washed a tiger's face?
(For explanation see page 24, col. ii.)

Bāg lāgal nā, mangrā derā del.
The garden not laid out and mendicant has pitched his tent.
(For explanation see page 24, col. ii.)

Ban ke pāt, ban ke khaṛikā, Kerī karat Bāṛī ke larikā.
The woodman's children play with forest leaves and forest stalks.
(i. e. with what is most easily procurable.)

Baṭur hāth dusmanven logo.
Strike your enemy with your clenched fist.
(If you strike at all strike hard.)

Bhagle chor kaṭhaṛyā hāth.
A flying thief takes away even a wooden cup.
(Any worthless thing.)

Bhāī aisan hit nā, bhāī aisan bairī nā.
No friend like a brother, no foe like a brother.

Bhail bīyāh, mor karbā kā?
My marriage is over, what more can they want of me?
(Allusion to the custom of the bridegroom paying for his bride.)

Bhojpur men jaihā mat, jaihā to khaiyā mat, khaihā to soihā mat, soihā to ṭoihā mat, ṭoihā to roihā mat.

To Bhojpur town go not; or if you go, eat not, or if you eat, sleep not; or if you sleep, (your bag) feel not; or if you feel it, cry not.

(A skit at the thieving propensities of the town.)

Bhūlal bhāṛ Divālī gāve.

It is a mad bard that sings at the Divālī.

(For explanation see page 43, col. i.)

Burbak bar ke sāṅjhe bichaunā.

A stupid bridegroom goes to sleep in the evening.

(To sleep before dark is considered very unlucky.)

Burbak Dās gae harvāī, dūī bail men eko nāhīn.

Mr. Fool went to plough and lost both his oxen.

(By ill treatment and folly.)

Burbak debī ke kulthī ke achchhat.

Linseed is offered to a foolish goddess.

(For explanation see page 48, col. i.)

Burbak dhanaī kā rahikā bās, koṭhī men chāur, ghar men upās.

Riches don't give pleasure to a fool; rice in his barn, and his house without food.

(He can't learn to spend.)

Burbak ek gae baṛ gāon, ḍerā pāin ūnche ṭhāon, bahe beār, āṛ nahīn pāven, phāṭe gāṅṛ malār gāven.

A fool went to a great village, and got a lodging in a high place; the wind blew hard and no shelter could he get; so as miserable as possible he whistled and sang the song of rain.

Burbak gaile, machhlī māre, tāp aile ganwāë.

A fool went to fish and lost his rod.

Chhajjū gaile chha janā, Chhajjū aile nau janā.

When Chhajjū went there were six of them when he returned there were nine.

(Don't be too ready to make friends.)

Chhūchhā kā sang na sāthī, bhailā duāre jhūmle hāthī.

No friends for the empty handed, but elephants at the rich man's gates.

Chor ko angārī miṭh.

Live coals taste sweet to a thief.

(For explanation see page 60, col. i)

Dimakā ke khāil peṇṛ, soch ke maral deh, kavano kām ke na rahe.

A tree eaten by white ants, and a body worn with care are nothing worth.

Ek kā tīte, tino tīt.

One bitter, all three bitter.

Ghar men khāë nahīn aṭārī par dhūān kare.

Nothing to eat in the house, and he raises a smoke on the balcony.

(Vain show.)

Hisāb leb, ki Banyā ḍāṅrab?

Are you taking an account, or fining the Baniyā?

(Are you dealing fair or cheating.)

Je bakut dhadhalā, so āg men parelā.

Who makes a bonfire will fall into the fire.

(Playing with edged tools.)

Jekar maiyā pūā pakāve, tekar dhiyā lilke.

The girl whose mother makes cakes must cry for them.

(For explanation see page 115, col. i.)

Jekar puṛkhā na dekhal poë, tekā ghar khur bandī hoë.

Shall the man who never saw a potherb have a horse shod in his stable.

(For explanation see page 115, col. i.)

Jekrā bīghā ehar kapās, tekrā ḍaṅre darā nā.

You can fine him who has a cotton field.

(Because he can pay.)

Jekre ghurvā baiṭhen, tekre āṅṛ dāgīn.

He injures him whose horse he rides.

(Ingratitude.)

Jekrī joe tekre pās dekhan-hārā tāke ās.

The wife is his who has her, the looker on can only hope.

Je morā lal ke nā, se kaunā kām ke?

If he be not my son, what has he to do with me.

Je mūṅh chīrelā, se to āhār dele chāhe?

Shall He not give the mouth food that opened it.

Kiryā aur tarkārī khāne hī ke bā.

Greens and oaths are made to be taken.

Lachchhmī se bheṭ na, daridr se bair!

He can not get prosperity and quarrels with adversity.

Lajādhur bahoryā, sorāe men ḍerā!

A shameful wife and an abode in an inn!

Lajāil laṛikā, ḍhoṅṛhī ṭohve.

A boy ashamed looks at his own stomach.

Langoṭ parle ughār ke pāle.

The shameless has fallen into the power of the naked!

Madhūre āṅche, roṭī miṭh.

A slow fire makes the bread sweet.

(Slow and sure.)

Man karbe moṭā khaiben sonṭā; man korben menhin, sagre tehīn.

Be niggardly and get blows, be generous and get everything.

Navā dekhle kāṅkhe bār.

On seeing a barber he finds hair under his armpit.

Pakle gūlar kavve ke nīnd āvā le.

How can a crow slep soundly when the figs are ripe?

(Crows are very fond of this fruit.)

Puryā bahal sūkhal ghāo phaphandal.

When the east wind blows healed sores break out.

(For explanation see page 187, col. i.)

Rām ke bhakt, kāṭh ke guṛiyā.
Din bhor ṭhak ṭhak, rāt ke ghuskuriyā.

The worshipper of Ram is a wooden doll:
Praying all day and resting at night.
(A skit at the vaishnava pujaris or priests.)

Samaë chūk phir kā pachhtānī?
Why regret a lost opportunity?
(Why weep over spilt milk?)

Siar ke mantrī kavva:—chhoṛ dahale hāṛ chām, khāhale masvā.
The crow's advice to the jackal:—leave the bones and the skin and eat up the flesh.
(For explanation see page 220, col i.)

Tīn din ke chhokrā, hamen sikhāvat bāt!
Jable voh lihen ṭhīkrā, table mārab lāt!
A three day's old boy and teaching me!
When he picks up his pebble I'll give him a kick.
(Teaching your grandmother to suck eggs.)

Unais bis to bhaile chāhe.
It is always at nineteens and twenties.
(In nature no two things are quite alike.)

EASTERN PROVERBS.

Ab ke muṛiheṅ, ho rājā.
Come back and be king.

Abrā kī joṛū sab kī bhaujāī.
The poor man's wife is every one's sister-in-law.
(For explanation see page, 1 col. ii.)

Ādī ke chandan, lilār charcharāë.
Put ginger for sandalwood, and your forehead will smart.
(Pounded sandalwood is a common cooling remedy)

Ādī mirchāī kā kaun sāth?
Chillies don't go with ginger.

Aghānā bagulā pothyā tit.
To the surfeited heron all fish is bad.
(Said of the *blasé*; sick of a good thing.)

Aile joṛlā, parkhore.
A relative has come, go and recognize him.
(Look before you leap.)

Aisan buṛbak kaun hai, jo khāt nahīṅ aghāë?
Every fool knows when his stomach is full.

Aisan suhāg morā nit uṭh holā.
May such good fortune be ever mine!

Āj baservā niar, kal baservā dūr.
To-day's home is near, to-morrow's home is far.
(This world and the next.)

Ajīran ke ajīran hī ṭhele, nahīṅ sir chauhaṭṭe.
Let the strong contend with the strong, or your head shall be a foot-ball for the way-farer.

Ām jhaṛe patāī, laṛikā rove dāī dāī!
Only the mango blossoms are falling, and the child cries 'give give! (mangoes)'
(Crying for the moon.)

Āṅdhar kūkar batāse bhūke.
The blind dog howls at the wind.

Āṅdhar kūṭe, bahar kūṭe, chāval se kām.
Whether a blind man pound or a deaf man pound, the rice is pounded.
(The work is done who ever does it.)

Ankā gorvā dhoe naunyā, āpan dhovat lajāë.
The barber washes others feet, but is ashamed to wash his own.

Ankar chukkar, ankar ghī, pāṅḍe bāp kā lagā kī?
Another's flour, another's butter, what do they cost the cook?
(See page 12, col. ii.)

Ankar sendūr dekh, āpan kapār phore!
Seeing another's position he ruins himself.

Annukh ghar men nātī bhatār.
In a stranger's house the grandson is lord.
(Be civil to a cock on his own dung hill.)

Apnā haiye hī nā, dusre ke dānī.
With nothing of his own he is generous to others.
(A vain boaster.)

Apnā ke bīrī bīrī, dūsre ke khīr pūrī.
She drives people away herself and begs dainties from others.

Apnā mīṭh, ankar tīt.
Your own is sweet, another's bitter.
(One's own geese are always swans.)

Apnā ṭeṭar dekhen nahīṅ, dūsre kī phullī nī hāren.
He can't see the cataract in his own eye, but he sees the stye in another's.
(For explanation see page 17, col. i.)

Apnā ṭhīk nā, ankar nīk nā.
His own is not right, nor another's good.
(A fool himself he takes no advice.)

Apnī ber ko gholam ghālā, hamrī ber ko bhūkam bhākā.
You make cakes for yourself, but starve.

Aql na gyān, thappaṛ khāī samajh bihān.
Nor sense nor wisdom, but he'll learn by blows.

Arkā nāin, bāṅs ki naharnī!
The inexperienced barber has bamboo nail-scissors.
(These should be of steel.)

Armān bharī ghūghā.
A shell full of desires.

Asal kahe so dārī jār.
Speak the truth and be abused!

Bābājī kā ṭhevas baṛ.
My lord has a very long thumb. (He is overweening.)

Bāhar mīyāṅ chhail chikanyā, ghar men lībṛī joë.

Abroad my lord goes in gorgeous array with a naked wife at home.

Bandar kyā jāne ādī kā savād?
What does a monkey know of the flavour of ginger.

Ban par tīn bilārī, mūsā kahelī, je hamrī joē.
When the cat is away in the forest the rat says 'she's my wife.'
(When the cat's away the mice may play.)

Bāole kī byāhī gāē, sab metī le vā ke dhāē.
When the fool's cow calves all the neighbours run with their cans for the milk.
(Said of an oppressed pepole.)

Bāp marihen, to pūt rāj karihen.
When the father dies the son reigns.
(*Le roi est mort: vive le roi!*)

Bāp marle kuṅar, māē marle tuar.
Father dies and you are a bachelor, mother dies and you are an orphan.
(For explanation see page 31, col. ii.)

Bāṛī men bārah ām, haṭṭī men aṭṭhārah ām.
Twelve mangoes (for a penny) in the orchard, and eighteen in the market.
(upside down.)

Bar ke na mile bhūsā, baryātī māṅge chūrā!
The bridegroom has not even straw and the guests are asking for sweets!
(Used when a preposterous request is made.)

Bāsī bhāt men Allah Miyān kā kaun nihorā?
Why be grateful to God for stale rice?

Bāṭe ghāṭe kutiyā marī, nāth kahe merī bāch'ā parī.'
If a bitch die on the road or by the river side, the *jogi* says, 'my words have taken effect.'
(He takes credit to himself for any chance event.)

Beche ke sāg, kare motiyon kā dām!
He sells pot-herbs, and bargains for pearls!

Be-dharmā bhāī, aur behnā ke sāth men!
I become a pervert to marry a wool carder!
(See page 36, col. ii.)

Be-gharnī ghar pādat hai, hai gharnī ghar gājat hāi.
Without a wife the house doth howl, with a wife the house doth joy.
(The pleasures of married life.)

Beṭī sasurā na jātī, man man gājatī.
The daughter goes not to her father-in-law's house and frets and fumes to herself.
(A common incident in native life.)

Bhains ke āge bīn bajāve voh, baiṭhī pagurāve.
If you play the harp before a buffalo, she will still chew the cud.
(Casting pearls before swine.)

Bhal janmal, bhal paṇḍit bhail.
Happy his birth who turns out a *pandit.*
(*Pandit*, a man learned in the Scriptures.)

Bhal marulas, bhal pillū paral.
Stone dead and worm eaten.

Bhal māth muraulan; bhal bel girlain!
It was well that he shaved his head; it was well that the wood apple fell on it!
(Great ill-luck.)

Bhang, gāṅjā jan deū gavāran ke, Hathṛhiyā bhar bhāt sanghāran ke.
Don't give *bhang* and *gāṅjā* to the village boor, Or he will eat up a bucket full of your rice.
(For explanation see page 40, col. i.)

Bijulik māral, luāṭh dekh bhūge.
Singed by lightning he runs from a burning stick.
(A burnt child dreads the fire.)

Bisunī bilār ḍabrī men ḍerā.
The unexpected cat sits on the dish.
(For explanation see page, 46, col. i.)

Biyāh kā ashgun malūm bhae, lahore men āē bhaṭṭā!
It bodes ill for the marriage, when rubbish is sent for the first present!

Bulāve na chalāve, mor tīn bakhre.
Nor called nor invited, she claims three shares for herself.

Būnṭ baṛā hoe, to bhansār na phoṛe.
One grain, howsoever big, cannot break the oven.

Chaltā phirtā na maral, baiṭhaū mar jāū.
Walking and wandering don't kill, sitting still does kill.

Chām ke chandū chalal pahāṛ, pīchhal ṭangṛī ṭūṭal kapāṛ.
A man of leather (weak) went up a hill, he missed his footing and broke his pate.

Chene ke bans men sapūt bhae māṛhā.
Parched maize is the excellent offspring of millet.
(For explanation see page 54, col. ii.)

Chhānī par phūns nahīn, ḍeoṛhī par nāch.
No straw on his thatch and dances at his door!
(Living for apearances.)

Chhātī par bāl nahīn, bhāl se laṛāī.
No hair on his breast, and he is going to fight the bear.
(For explanation see page 55, col. ii.)

Chhoṭī sī gauraīyā bāghon se nazārā.
A little sparrow staring at the lion.
(Little roast, great boast.)

Chhūṭal ghoṛā bhusaule ṭhāṛh.
The loose horse makes for his stall.

Chīnṭī sasarne ko jagah nahīn.
No room even for an ant to creep in.

Chor aur moṭ kas ke bāndhe ke chāhe.
A thief and a bundle should be tied tightly.

Chor ko panhai dūr hī se sūjhe hai.
The thief spies the shoe from afar.
(With which he is to be beaten.)

Chorvā ke man base kakṛī kā khet.
The petty thief's mind is running on the cucumber field.

Dādā mariheṅ to bhoj kariheṅ.
When the grandsire dies we'll have a good feast.

Dāde rāj na khāē pān, dāṅt dikhāvat gae pirān.
He never tasted betel leaf even in the time of his grandfather; but fatigued himself to death in showing his teeth.
(For explanation see page 62, col. i.)

Dāge ke sāṅr, to dāge le lohār.
If the bull is to be branded, let the blacksmith do it.
(Every cobbler to his last)

Dahī kī gavāhī chūrā.
The fried rice proves the curd.
(As it cannot be used without them.)

Damṛī kī lāī Banyāiṅ khāē! "ye ghar rahe ki jāē?"
The shopman's wife ate a farthing's worth of parched rice, (and quoth he) "the house will be ruined."

Damṛī kī murgī, nau ṭakā nikāī.
A farthing for the hen and three half pence for its plucking.

Dānā chhitrānā tahāṅ jānā zarūr hai.
Where your grain (food) is scattered, there should you go.

De dāl meṅ pānī, paigā bah chale chuhānī.
Put enough water into the pea soup to float a log.
(To prevent your neighbours from sponging on you.)

Deh meṅ na latlā, lūṭe ke Kalkatta!
Without a rag on his body, he intends to plunder Calcutta!

Dekhne ko bulbul nigalne ko domaryā bṛṛ.
A nightingale to look at, he can swallow wild figs.
(For explanation see page 67, col. i.)

Dhāke ke Bangāl, kūze ke kangāl.
At Dhākā in Bengal the paupers have no goblets.
(For explanation see page 68, col. ii.)

Dhāl talvār sirhāne, aur chūtaṛ bandī khāne!
Sword and shield on the pillow, and his legs in the prison!
(A coward.)

Dhān bichāre bhalle, jo kūṭā khāyā chalie.
Rice is a very good thing; pound it, eat it, and go your way.
(Pounded rice is very soon cooked.)

Dhan nātī hukkā, posāk nātī juluph.
A pipe for property, and hair for clothing.
(Wretchedly poor.)

Dhobī ke ghar byāh, gadhe kā chhuṭṭī bhail.
On the wedding of a washerman, the donkeys have a holiday.

Dhobī, dhāī bheṅrī pāṅke lagī.
When the sheep was washed and cleansed she went into the mud again.

Ḍhove ke ṭokrī, gāve ke gīt.
He works as a laborer and sings songs.
(A light heart.)

Dūlah ke pattal na, bajaniye ke thār!
No platter of leaves for the bridegroom, and the musician wants a brass dish!

Dulārī biṭyā, īṅṭe ke laṭkan!
A darling daughter, and bricks for her earrings!

Dūsre kā seṅdūr dekh, apnā lilār phoreh.
Seeing the vermillion spot on another's forehead, she cuts her own open.
(For explanation see page 77, col. i.)

Ek āṅkh maṭar kā biyā, voh bhī āṅkh Bhavānī liyā.
She had an eye no bigger than a pea, and even that was taken by (the Goddess) Bhavānī.

Ek bakhiyā more palle, kaun pinaute hoke challe.
I have only a quilt upon my back, what care I where I go?

Ekī dāl, eki chaur, karai gun aur baur.
The same pea and the same rice agree with one and disagree with another.
(One man's food is another man's poison.)

Ek janā ghar mardā bhel, chār janā mil khāṭī lel, Āp āp ke sabhī malūk, jhāṅṭ ukhāṛe murdā halūk.
In a certain house a man died and four men went with the bier; they were so delicate that they lightened the body by cutting off the hair!

Ek peṛ haṛre, sagre gāoṅ khāṅsī.
There is one myrabolan tree, and the whole village has a cough.
(For explanation see page 80 col. i.)

Ek to gareṛan, dūsre lassan khāē.
A shepherdess that eats onions.
(For explanation see page 80 col. i.)

Ero ke chero, navvā ke barāhil.
Slavery to the slave and shampooing to the barber.
(For explanation see page 81 col. i.)

Gāchh meṅ kaṭhal, honṭh meṅ tel.
The jack-fruit on the tree, and oil on the lips.
(For explanation see page 82 col. i.)

Gadhā ke khāil khet, na har-loke ke, na-par loke ke.
If an ass eats up your field, it is neither good for this world, nor the next.
(For explanation see 82 col. ii.)

Gāē na āve bachve lāj.
A cow is not ashamed of her calf.

Gāle hāth Gopālak māē.
Gopāl's mother always has her hand to her cheek.
(For explanation see page 83 col. ii.)

Gāṅṛ na dhoe so ojhā hoē.
Who won't wash his loins will be a wizard.

Gāṅth khule na, bahuryā dubras !
The bride is so delicate that she cannot untie the knot !
(Refers to the marriage ceremony.)

Gāṅth meṅ dām na, paturya dekh ruāī āe.
With no money in his pocket he weeps to see a woman.
(Being unable to wed her.)

Gāṅth meṅ paisā nahīṅ Bankipur kī sair.
With no money in his pocket he goes to Bānkipur.

Garas parlā se ādmī burbak hota hai.
His own interests make him mad.

Genṭhī saṅbhār, madhurī chāl, āj na pahoṅchab pahoṅchab kāl.
Look to your baggage and go slowly, and if you don't reach to-day you will to-morrow.
(Slowly does it : the tortoise and the hare.)

Ghāeṅ ghāeṅ torā, manhān bāje morā.
In private he is yours, public he is mine.
(i. e. my husband is your paramour, a taunt of one woman to another.)

Ghar baiṭhal ādhā bhalā.
Half at home is better (than all abroad).

Ghar kā bhed jab kī pāyā, chauk pūran ko ḍhaknā āyā.
The household resources were found out, when they brought an earthen vessel for the house-warming.
(For explanation see page 88 col. i.)

Ghar meṅ kharach nā ḍeoṛhī par nāch.
Not a penny in the house and dancing in the porch.

Ghar phūṅk-kar birrā mārnā.
To burn a house in order to kill a wasp.
(For explanation see page 89 col. ii)

Gīd gīd gilaunḍā khāē, ber ber mahue tal āē.
Grown tame on the *gilaunḍā* he makes to the *mahuā*.
(For explanation see page 91 col. I.)

Gor chamāin, gorbhe mātal.
A fair cobbler's wife is proud of her complexion.

Guṛ barā haṅsyā, khāte bane na ugalte.
A sickle covered with treacle cannot be swallowed nor vomited up.

Hai gharnī ghar gājat hai, nahīṅ gharnī ghar pādat hai.
With the housewife the house is lively, without the housewife the house is dull.

Hāṅḍī meṅ achchhat nā, 'chalā samdhī jeṅve.
Not a pinch of rice in the pot and he says 'come friend, feast with me.'

Hansā chalal bhāg, keo na sangae lāg.
When the swan (soul) flies, none goes with it.

Haṅs gun pāve, tevar lāge.
What is given with smiles he receives frowns.

Haṅsī meṅ bikhelī bhail.
Jest leads to earnest.

Haṅsvā chākh. na khurpā bhotar.
Nor sickle sharp nor axe blunt.
(For explanation see page 97 col. II.)

Haṅsva ke byāh, khurpā ke gīt.
The sickle is to be wedded, and the song is of the axe.
(Irrelevancy.)

Haq na pāve inām !
He cannot get his rights and wants a present !

Har kā māne, par kā na māne.
A disappointed man can be appeased, a snubbed one never.

Harkāyā bhal i parkāyā na bhalā.
Better disappoint than snub.

Hathiyā chale nā paiyā, baiṭhe de Gusaīyāṅ.
He cannot stir his hands or feet (and says) 'God save me as I sit.'
(Sad of a lazy fellow.)

Hāth ke saṅkal muṅh ke piyār.
Handcuffs on his hands and loving words upon his lips.
(Sham affection.)

Hosnāk burhiyā chaṭāī kā laṅhgā.
A gay old woman with a mat petticoat.
(A person with more inclination than means.)

Hunḍār chīnhe Bāmhan kā pūt ?
A wolf won't spare a Brahman's son.
(For his piety.)

Hunḍrā re, bakrī charaibe pathru samet.
O wolf, graze this goat and its kid !

Īd, Baqrīd, Shabrāt kuṭnī ; Dāhā kare hāē hāē Phagvā bisnī.
At the Id, Baqrīd and Shabrāt they have procuresses ; at the Dāhā they mourn and at the Holī they have prostitutes.

Ikkā, vakīl, gadhā, Paṭnā shahar meṅ sadā.
Ikkas, pleaders and donkeys abound in Paṭnā.
(An Ikkā is a conveyance drawn by one pony.)

Jabar kī joē mahtārī hoē, nibal kā joē merī sārī.
The strong man's wife is treated as a mother and the weak man's wife as a sister-in-law.
(i. e. chaffed and jested with.)

Jab din āē bhale, tab laḍḍū marai chale.
When good times come you enjoy sweets.

Jab lau kuṭhlā meṅ nāj, tab lau julahṭū ko rāj.
As long as there is corn in the bin, the weaver's son is a king.

Jab le sakhā ke bhāo āī, tab le pūte ke āṅkhe jāī.
The son will lose his eyes before the brother comes to believe.

Jāhī teṅ kuchh pāiye, kariye tākī ās.
Expect where you get.
(For explanation see page 110, col. i.)

Jaisā deve vaisā pāve : Pūt bhatār ke āge āve.
As you give you shall get, even to your sons and husband.
(For explanation see page 110, col. i.)

Jaisan dekhe gāoṅ kī rīt, taisan kare log se prīt.
Be friendly with the people in the fashion of the village.

Jaise kī sevā kare, taisī āsā pūr.
As the master you serve, so the fulfilment of your hopes.

Janam ke dukhiyā, karam ke hīn, tin kā Deo tilangvā kīn.
Wretched from birth and unfortunate are those of whom God hath made soldiers.
(For explanation see page 113, col. i.)

Jānelā chilam jin kō par charhelā aṅgārī.
The pipe knows what it is to bear the fire.

Jāo Naipāl sōth jaĕ kapāl.
Go to Naipāl and your fate will follow you.

Jare jāĕṅ sūjhe sūkar.
Going to the burning place and thinking of (the planet) Venus.
(For explanation see page 114, col. i.)

Jatne kī tīn roṭī tatne kī ṭikrī alag karo tīn roṭī ene lāvā ṭikrī.
One loaf is equal to three cakes, so let go the three cakes and bring the one loaf.

Jau ko gae, satuāaī ko āĕ.
Started for barley comes for barley flour.
(Unfair demand: a shilling's worth for six pence.)

Javāṅ jāĕ pāttāl burhiyā māṅge bhatār.
The maidens are dying and the grandmothers demanding husbands.
(Upside down: topsy turvy; incongruity.)

Jekrā harī aisan Thākur, tekrā jam ke ḍar?
Why should he fear the Angel of Death who has such a (merciful) God?

Je pūt pardesī bhaile, deo pittar sab se gaile.
The sons who have gone to foreign lands have gone from the worship of Gods and ancestoras.

Je Pāṅṛe ke patrā meṅ, se Paṅṛidiṅ ke aṅchrā meṅ.
What is writ in the Pandit's book, his wife hath in her wrapper.

Jhīṅgar baiṭhe bakucha par kahas ki 'ham hīṅ mālik haiṅ.'
The cricket sitting on a bundle of clothes says "I am the owner."

Jitnā maṛve meṅ āvelā, otnā kohbar meṅ na āve.
All that sit at the marriage feast cannot enter the marriage chamber.

Julāhā churāve nalī nalī, Khudā churāve ekke berī.
The weaver steals a reel at a time; but God makes him lose all at once.
(Of all his ill gotten gains: poetical justice.)

Jūṅ jūṅ bāo bahe purvāī, tūṅ tūṅ ati dukh ghāil pāī.
When the wind is in the East, the pains of wounds are much increased.

Kājal gayā Bihār, bahoryā naṛere hī hai.
They have gone to Bihār for the lamp-black and the bride is on the tip-toe of expectation.
(For explanation see page 127, col. ii.)

Kānī āṅkh maṭar kā bīyā, voh bhī āṅkh Bhavānī līyā.
Even my one eye, small as a pea, hath the Goddess of small-pox taken.

Kānī gāĕ Bāman ke dāṅ!
A one-eyed cow for the Brahman's alms!
(For explanation see page 130 col. I.)

Kānī gāĕ ke alge tathān?
Has the one-eyed cow a separate stall.
(For explanation see page 130, col. i.)

Karain Kallu bharain Lallū.
Kallu does the deed, and Lallū pays for it.
(The cat's paw.)

Karne ko chākrī sone ko ghar.
Service is for work, the house for sleep.
(For explanation see page 132, col. i.)

Karyā Bāman, gor chamār, tekrā sang na utre pār.
A black Brahman and a fair chamār won't do you any good.
(For explanation see page 132, col. ii.)

Kehū ke jeṭh pūt, kehū ke lekhe kanvā.
To some he is an elder son, to others only a boy.
(For explanation see page 134, col. ii.)

Kekar kekar dharo nāoṅ, kamra oṛhle sāre gāoṅ.
The whole village wears a blanket, whatever you choose to call it.
(For explanation see page 134, col. ii.)

Kekarnī kare, kekrā sire bite.
One does the act, and another is called to account for it.

Khalyā sās kin sāsoṅ meṅ? Kodoṅ kā bhāt kin bhātoṅ meṅ?
The wife's aunt is no mother-in-law, as millet is no rice.

Khirādī kā gāṅṭh kāhe hī kaṭe.
The turner's tool cuts through every thing.

Koṛhī ko dāl bhāt kamāsut ko phuṭhā.
The lazy lives on rice and pulse, the hard-working only on peas.
(For explanation see page 142, col. i.)

Koṭhī meṅ chāur ghar meṅ upās.
Grain in the barn, hunger in the house.
(Said of a fool or a miser.)

Kumhār kā gadhā, jahīṅ ke chūtar, māṭī dekhe, tahīṅ ke pīchho daure.
The potter's ass runs after any one whose breeches are muddy.
(He takes him for his master.)

Kuttā ke āṭā hoĕ to liṭṭī lage ke khāĕ.
If the dog had flour he would have baked bread for himself.

Lajānā bakū mūṅh bidore.
The shame-faced goat shows his teeth.
(For explanation see page 148, col i.)

Laṭe kī joë sāre gāoṅ kī sarhaj.
The wife of a poor man is the sister-in-law of the whole village.
(For explanation see page 150, col. i.)

Lūr na ūr, chalā miyāṅ Jagdīspūr.
Nor sense nor skill and he goes to Jagdispur.

Maral bhachhiyā Bāman ke dān.
(Said of a useless gift.)

Mard jekrā gāṅṭh rupaiyā.
A man with silver in his pocket.
(Born with a silver spoon in his mouth.)

Māreṅ mehar aur bhāge paṛausin.
The wife is beaten, and the neighbour flies through fear.
(For explanation see page 157, col.).)

Marihoṅ par ṭarihoṅ nāhīṅ.
I'll die before I budge from here.

Māṛ na juṛe māṅge tāṛī!
He has no right even to butter-milk and demands tāṛī.
(For explanation see page 157, col. ii.)

Maskharī ke chūṛā bhar bhar gāl.
Filling his cheeks with flattery's cakes.
(Said of a toady.)

Mastānī bakrī bok kā mūṅh chūmtī hai.
The she-goat on heat kisses the buck-goat's mouth.

Māthe gaṭhrī, madhurī chāl; "āj na pahoṅchab pahoṅchab kāl."
A bundle on his head, and easy his gait; and "I'll reach to-day or at any rate to-morrow.
(An easy going man.)

Māthe kā muraundā, bel ka khisnā.
No sooner was his head shaved, than a bel fruit fell on it.
(For explanation see page 159, col. i.)

Māth par moṭrī, Basant ke gīt.
With a bundle on his head, he sings the songs of spring.
(For explanation see page 159, col. i.)

Milkī na kahe dil kī, paiṭheṅ darvāze nikleṅ khiṛkī.
The wealthy keep their own cousel, going in by the front door and out by the back.
(For explanation see page 161, col. ii.)

Miyāṅ hāth aṅgūṭhī, bīvī ke kan pāt,
Lauṅḍī ke dāṅt missī, tīnoṅ kī ek bāt.
The ring on a husband's hand, the ring in a wife's ear, the black on a slave-girl's teeth, are all alike.
(For explanation see page 162, col. i.)

Mūlī aur mūlī ke patvātoṅ par lon kī ḍalī!
Radishes and radish-leaves with a pinch of salt!
(For explanation see page 164, col. i,)

Nāch tān yeī nā, "āṅgan bāṅkṛe"
Rāṅdhnā yeī nā, "olī lāṅkṛā."
Not knowing how to dance (he says), "the floor is uneven!" Not knowing how to cook (he says), "the greens are tough!"
(A bad workman quarrels with his tools.)

Na dauṛī chalaiṅge, na thas lagegī.
Who runs not, stumbles not.
(Look before you leap.)

Nainā det batāē sab hīye ko het ahet,
Jaise nirmal ārsī burī bhalī kah det.
The eyes show the love and hatred of all hearts, As a clear glass showeth both fair and fowl.

Nām baṛā ūṅchā, kān donoṅ būchā.
A great name, and both ears cut off.
(A stain on the family escutcheon.)

Nauā ke ghar chorī bhel, tīn choṅgā bār gel.
There was a theft in the barber's house and three cups full of hair stolen.

Naukar ko chākar, maṛaī ko usārā!
A servant to a servant is a shed to a hut.
(The one is as absurd as the other.)

Nau kūṅḍe aur das negī.
Nine platters, and ten to receive them.
(For explanation see page 172 col. i.)

Nayā nau gaṅḍā, purānā chha gaṅḍā.
For the new nine for the old six.

Nayā nayā rāj bhail gagrin anāj bhail.
Changes of government fill the pitchers with grain.
(i. e. they create many posts.)

Neotal Brahman, shatrū barābar.
To invite a Brahman is to call an enemy.
(A skit at the greediness of the class.)

Nikauṛiyā gaē hāṭ, kakṛī dekh jīrā phāṭ.
Without a farthing he went to the mart, saw a cucumber and broke his heart.

Padnī āil na peṭhyā lāgal.
It is no market without the shameless wench.
(For explanation see 175, col. ii.)

Pāhan meṅ ke mārbe chokhā tīr nasāī!
If you shoot at a stone, you will spoil a good arrow.
(For explanation see page 175, col. ii.)

Pahāṛ ke aṭhgan silūt.
The support of the hill is a stone.

Pahle pīve bhakvā, phir pīve tamakhvā, pīchhe pīve chilam-chaṭ.
The first puff is smoke, the second is tobacco, and the third is clearing the pipe.
(For explanation see page 176, col. i.)

Pānī meṅ machhlī, nau nau ṭukṛā hissā.
The fish in the water, and is being divided into nine shares.
(For explanation see page 178, col. i.)

Paṛhiye, bhaiyā, soī jā meṅ handyā khud bad hoī.
My son, learn those things that will keep the pot boiling.

Parkā dhan gauraiyā mār.
Sparrows may eat up another's wealth.
(For all I care,)

Parkal ghoṛ bhusaule ṭhāṛh.
The tame horse runs to its stall.

Petahā chākar, ghasahā ghoṛ, khāë bahot kām kare thoṛ.
A pot bellied servant, and a fat horse eat much and work little.

Phar na pharī, bagīchā ke nāoṅ !
Nor fruit, nor vegetables, and called a garden !

Pharyā na sārī, baṛī sobhā hamārī !
No gown and no petticoat and great credit is mine.

Phir, muṛle bel tale.
Again, you shaven-head, have you come under the *bel* tree.
(For explanation see page 183, col. ii.)

Pūjle deotā, chhoṛle bhūt.
Worship the gods and give up the devils.

Qaraz kāṛh kare beohār, mehrī se jo rūṭhe bhatār, be bulaval bole darbār, yeh tīnoṅ pashām ke bār.
Who trades on borrowed money, who quarrels with his wife, who speaks at Court without being spoken to; these three are as cast off hair.

Rahab bhukle, chalab ṭihukle.
I may starve, but I will not stoop.

Rahe ke bhusahul, nāoṅ leve ke dharohar. !
He lives in a straw hut, and calls himself a banker !

Rah rah, beṅgnā, hore de bihān, tujh par sājeṅge tīr kamān.
Stay, stay, you frog, until it is dawn, that I may shoot you with an arrow.

Rām na māre, apai marai de ku-matichaṛ hāë.
God did not kill him, but his own folly did.
(His own worst enemy.)

Roṭiyā chākar, ghasyā ghor ; khāë bahut, chale thoṛ.
An ill-paid servant and a badly fed horse eat much and work little.

Sab gun kë āgar, phūṭal gāgar.
Full of every virtue, but only a broken goblet in the house.

Sabzī mat deo gavāran ko, hanḍyā bhar bhāt bigāṛan ko.
Don't give *bhaṅg* to village boors, they will simply spoil a pot-ful of rice.
(For explanation see page 200, col. ii.)

Sampat se bhetā nahīṅ diladdar se ṭūṭan.
No friend to prosperity and an enemy to adversity.
(A stupid man.)

Sastā gehūṅ ghar ghar pūjā.
When wheat is cheap, there are offerings in every house.

Sāt pāṅch pakwā, na ek gūlar.
One Indian fig is better than half a dozen *pakuās*.
(Pakvā is a wild tasteless fruit.)

Sattū man bhattū, jab ghulbā jab khaibā, jab jaëbā ; dhān bichāre bhalle kūṭe khāë challe.
Pulse meal is a pleasant thing ; you knead, and eat and go your way ; but rice is a pleasanter thing, for you simply husk and eat and go your way.
(For explanation see page 214, col. i.)

Seṅt kā māl hirdā nirdaī.
The heart has no pity on easily gotten wealth.
(Easy come easy go.)

Sunārī bechen kāṅṭū, anāṛī bechen māṅchhū.
The wise man sells the bones, the fool his fish.

Tālī doū kar bāje
It requires two hands to clap.
(It takes two to make a quarrel.)

Talvoṅ kī sī kahūṅ yā jībh kī sī ?
Shall I judge according to the soles of my feet, or according to my tongue ?
(For explanation see page 231, col. i.)

Tas Makund, tas pādanghorī : Bidhī ne ān milāī joṛī.
As makund, so his roaring mare : Fate has made a rare match of them.

Thakal pairākū phen chāṭe.
The exhausted swimmer licks the foam.
(His capital all spent, on paltry jobs intent.)

Theṅge thān, labeḍe pazār.
Stand my ridicule, or a thousand blows.

Tiretā ke bījoṅ ko pahoṅch gaë.
It has run to seed in the third age.
(For explanation see page 240, col. i)

Tīsī ke khet meṅ jolhā bhutlāne.
The weaver loses his way in the linseed field.
(For explanation see page 241, col. i.)

Tohrā būṭe kam bhūsā ekko na chhuṭī.
You don't know chaff from wheat.
(For explanation see page 241, col i.)

To ko na bhunāūṅ, torā bhaīyā aur baṛhāūṅ.
I'll not change you ; I'll get more of your brothers for you.
(For explanation see page 241, col. ii.)

Torī hoelo mūṛī khar, patvā bhailo sāg : Agvāre pichhvāre baiṭhlo, so ho bhailo sardār.
Radishes and weeds for vetches and their leaves for spinach : He has become a gentleman who was but a dependent.
(For explanation see page 241, col. ii.)

Tū kar apnā kām tavalyā bhusan de.
Do your work quickly and let the curs bark

Tum ant gāë ham ant ko āë, māṛaṅ chūn kūtan ne khāyo.
While you went one way, and I the other, the dogs ate up the dough.
(For explanation see page 245, col. ii.)

Tum'āve bhatār na hamāre joë as kuchh karo kī hitvā hoë.

You have no husband and I no wife; let us so act that we may have a son.
(For explanation see page 246, col. ii.)

Turuk hũ hue, tau bhī nā.
I have turned Mahommadan and have still gained nothing by it.
(For explanation see page 348, col. i.)

Udhyāil satvā pitran ke dān.
Spoilt flour is offered to the ancestors.
(For explanation see page 249, col. i.)

Ukhlī men musrā, māī bāp bisrā.
The pestle in the mortar and the parents forgotten.

HINDOO PROVERBS.

Ab ke sāhe, ham na byāhe : phiṭ paro voh sāhe !
The marriage season come and I not wed
Out on the season that hath sped !
(Cursing the stick that beats you.)

Ād Hindū, bād Musalmān,
First Hindū, then Musalmān.
(For explanation see page 3, col. i.)

Āē Kanāgat phūlā kāns, Bāman uchhlen nau nau bāns.
When the *kanāgats* come, the long grass blooms, and the Brāhman dances nine poles high.
(For explanation see page 3, col. ii.)

Aintvār jab jāniye jab haṭṭī līpen bāniye.
Know it's Sunday when the shopman leeps his shop.
(It being the invariable custom.)

Āj kāl kī kannyā apne mūnh se bar māngtī hain.
The girls of the period choose their own husbands.
(Very shocking in India.)

Andar chhūt nahīn, bāhar kahen 'dūr, dūr.'
Within no abstinence, without he says 'away.'
(Hypocrisy.)

Baqal men chhurī mūnh men 'Rām Rām.'
A dagger in his bosom, and politeness in his mouth.
(For explanation see page 24, col. i.)

Baṛī bahū, baṛā bhāg.
Older the wife, greater the good fortune.
(For explanation see page 33, col. i.)

Baṛī bahū ko bulāo, jo khīr men nūn ḍāle.
Run for the elder brother's wife, she 'll put salt in the *khīr*.
(For explanation see page 33, col. i.)

Baṛī bhābī mān ke thānak.
The elder brother's wife ranks with the mother.
(According to custom.)

Baṛī nāk-vāle.
A man with a great nose.
(of great honor.)

Banjāre kī 'Rām Rām,' Jam kā sandesā.
The traders' salute is a message from the Devil.
(i. e. a dun.)

Beche so banjārā, rakkhe so haṭṭiyārā.
Who sells (grain) is a merchant, who hoards it is a murderer.
(For explanation see page 36, col. i.)

Bharmā bhūt, sankā ḍāyan.
Imagination is a devil, and fear a witch.
(Therefore be brave and sensible.)

Bhūke ko kuchh dījiye, yathā shakt jo hoe.
Feed the hungry as much as in you lies.

Bhūle Bāman gāē khāī, 'ab khāūn, to Rām duhāī.'
The forgetful Brāhman ate beef (and said) 'I will never eat it again, by God !'
(For explanation see page 43, col. i.)

Bin parche parīt nahīn.
No belief without proof.

Birādrī ko na khilāyā, chār kāndhī hī jimā-diye.
The kinsfolk have not been feasted, only the corpse bearers have been fed.

Biyāh pīchhe pattal bhārī.
When the marriage feast is over, even the leaf plates are a heavy expense.
(Plenty ceases with the feast.)

Chhabbe hone gae the, Dubbe bhī na rahe.
Wanting to become a Chhabbe he loses even his original rank of Dubbe.
(For explanation see page 54, col. ii.)

Chhatar-patī ghaṭe pāp aur baṛhe ratī.
O goddess forgive his sins and increase his fortune.
(Said when a child sneezes.)

Chhattīs parkār ke bhojan men sattar do bahattar rog bhare hain.
In thirty six dishes are seventy two complaints.

Chhattrī kā bhagat, na mūsal kā dhanak.
You can no more make a monk out of a Chhatrī (soldier) than a bow out of a pestle.

Chhāyā baṛī māyā hai.
Shade is a great blessing.
(*Chhāyā*—also roof over your head.)

Chhīnkat nahāiye, chhīnkat khāiye, chhīnkat rahiye so ; Chhīnkat kisī ke na jāiye chahe sarb sone kī ho.
You may sneeze and wash, eat, and sleep ;
But you must not sneeze and go to another's house, though all of gold.

Chhoṭī sī bachhiyā, baṛī sī hattiyā.
The calf is small, but the sin is great.
(As well be hanged for a sheep as a lamb.)

Chinḍāl na chhoṛe makkhī na chhoṛe bāl.
The low castes leave neither hair nor flies.
(For explanation see page 57, col. ii.)

Chīrā hai jis ne, vohī nīregā.
Who opened the mouth will feed it.

Dān, bit samān.
Be charitable according to your means.

Darshan moṭā, paiṅḍā khoṭā.
Great object, but a bad road.
(Such as a pilgrimage to Badri Nāth in the Hills.)

Dāsī karam kahār se nīche.
To serve is worse than to be a scullion.
(Service is another name for slavery.)

Dātā ke tīn gun ; de, dilāve, deke chhīn le.
God has three qualities, to give, to make others give, and to take back what He has given.
(Said also of a king or master.)

Debī din kāṭe, log parchā māṅgeṅ.
Devī (goddess) spends her days (in care), and man is ever demanding a miracle.

De, dilāve, de de kare, so pirānī bhausāgar tare.
He that gives, causes to be given, and persuades others to give, passes through the sea of this world.

Deh dhare ke ḍanḍ haiṅ.
The penalty for being created.
(Disease and suffering; no body no pain : Adam's legacy.)

Deh meṅ anek rog bhareṅ haiṅ.
Innumerable maladies lurk within the body.

Deotā bāsna ke bhūke haiṅ.
The gods hunger after the smell only.
(For explanation see page 68, col. i.)

Dhāo, jo bidh likhā soī pāo.
Rush on, but you 'll only meet your fate.

Dharm hār dhan koī khāë.
Any body can make money by dishonesty.

Dharam kī jaṛ sadā harī.
The root of faith is ever green.

Dharnī kī mā sāṅjh.
Evening is the mother of patience.
(See page 69, col. ii.)

Dhāvegā so pāvegā.
Who runs gets, or who worships gets.

Dhūnī pānī kā sanjog hai.
There is some connection between his fire and water.
(For explanation see page 71, col. i.)

Dīyā dān māṅge Musalmān.
Musalmans will claim back the given alms.
(For explanation see page 73, col. i.)

Donoṅ khoe jogyā mudrā aur ādes.
The jogī lost both his ear-ring and his salute.
(For explanation see page 74, col. ii.)

Dunyā dhund kā pasārā hai.
The world is but an expanse of vapour.
(The world is a mirage: all chaos.)

Ek din pāhonā, dūsre din ann-khāonā.
One day a guest, the second day a sponge.

Ek gurū ke bālke.
Disciples of one teacher.
(For explanation see page 78, col. i.)

Ek lakh potā savā lakh nātī us Rāvan ke dīyā na bātī.
With a thousand sons' sons and a million daughters' sons, nor wick nor lamp to such a Rāvan.
(For explanation see page 79, col. i.)

Gae Dakkhan vohī karam ke lakkhan.
He went to the south, and had the same fortune.

Gangā gae, muṅḍāë sidh
When gone to the Ganges, shaving is necessary.

Gangā gae muṅḍāë sir.
Gone to the Ganges and shaved his head.

Gangā kar gaur garībau kī.
O Ganges, hear the prayer of the poor !

Gangā ko ānā thā, Bhāgīrath ko jas.
Fate made the Ganges flow, but Bhāgirath gets the credit.

Ganjī sattī, ūt pujārī.
A bald pigeon and a dwelling in a palace.

Garabh karnte Rāvan hāre.
Rāvan was humbled for his pride.
(Allusion to the story in the Ramayan.)

Garabh kā sir nīchā hotā.
Pride goes before a fall.

Ghar āī Lachchhmī ko lāt mārnā achchhā nahīṅ
Never kick good fortune when she comes to you of her own accord.
(Never decline a spontaneous offer of marriage or of a post.)

Ghar āyā nāg na pūje bāṅbī pūjan jāī.
They do not worship the snake in the house, but they go to worship at his hole.
(For explanation see page 87, col. i.)

Ghaṛī meṅ gāoṅ jale nau ghaṛī bhaddrā.
The village burns in an hour, and in nine hours comes the lucky moment.
(For putting it out : a skit at the astrologers.)

Ghaṛī meṅ ghaṛyāval hai.
The clock strikes differently every hour.
(Uncertainty of the fortune.)

Ghar kā bhedī Lankā ḍhāve.
A domestic foe would ruin Lankā.
(For explanation see page 88, col. i.)

Ghar kā jogī jognā ann gāoṅ kā siddh.
A jogī is a beggar at home and a saint abroad.
(For explanation see page 88, col. i.)

Ghar ke khīr khāeṅ aur deotā bhalā māneṅ.
The house-folk eat the offering of milk and rice and the gods are propitiated all the same.
(For explanation see page 88, col. ii.)

Ghoṛā chāhiye bidāāgīko, sarā phirtā sā āyo.
A horse is wanted for the bridegroom, so bring it quickly.
Ginī ḍalyāṅ haiṅ.
Each bit is counted.
Gūdaṛ meṅ gindauṛā.
A sweet cake in a rag.
(For explanation see page 92, col. ii.)
Hari kī māyā chhin meṅ dhūp chhin men chhāyā.
God's wonderous deeds, one moment sunshine, and another moment shade.
Hāth bechā hai, kuchh zāt nahīṅ bechī.
I have sold you my limbs, not my caste.
(For explanation see page 99, col. ii.)
Hindī na Fārsī lālā jī Banārsī.
With neither Hindī nor Persian, he is a scholar from Banāras.
(Benares is noted for its Sanskrit scholars.)
Hom karat hāth jare.
Burning the hand in making a sacrifice.
(To be injured by a good action.)
Indar rājā garjā, mhārā jīā larjā.
My heart trembles when the clouds thunder.
(For explanation see page 105, col. i.)
Issar āē, diluddar bhāge.
When good fortune comes poverty runs away.
Issar se bheṭā nahīṅ, diladdar se bigāṛ.
Good fortune he has not and quarrels with misfortune.
(Making the matter worse.)
Is tarah kāṅptā hai jaise qasāī se gāē.
He is trembling like a cow before a butcher.
Jab prajā nahīṅ, to rājā kahāṅ. !
When there are no subjects where is the king!
Jahāṅ Gang vahāṅ rang.
Where Ganges flows are gala shows.
Jaisā deotā vaisī pūjā.
As the God so the worship.
Jā ko Rām rachchhak tā kā kaun bhachchak.
Whom Ram protects none can slay.
Jam se burī janet.
Better Hell than the plagues of a marriage procession.
Jas dūlah tas banī barāt.
As the bridegroom, so the wedding party.
Jā se jā ko kām, soī tāko Rām.
He is thy God, whom thou hast to serve.
Jeṭh jeṭhe Āsāṛ heṭe.
(The weather is) best in Jeṭh and worst in Āsāṛh.
(Jeṭh is May—June, *Asāṛh*, July—August.)
Jeṭh ke bharose peṭ.
Pregnant on expectations from her husband's elder brother.
(For explanation see page 115, col. ii.)
Jis kī yahāṅ chāh unkī vahāṅ bhī chāh.
Who are loved in this world are loved of heaven.
(i. e. They die early whom the gods love.)

Jis ke dhī nahin us kī dehlī dhī.
Who has no daughter, looks upon his threshold as his daughter.
(For explanation see page 118, col. ii.)
Jitne muṅḍ utne pinḍ.
As many heads (sons), so many offerings to your manes.
(For explanation see page 121, col. i.)
Jo bole so kunḍā khole.
Who speaks first must open the door.
(For explanation see page 122, col. i.)
Kālī gāē Bāman ko dān.
A black cow given in alms to a Brahman.
(For explanation see page 128, col. ii.)
Khāṅḍ binā sab rāṅḍ rasoī.
Without sugar a dinner is like a widow.
(For whom no one in India has any regard.)
Khāne ko pīchhe, nahāne ko pahle.
Bathe before eating.
Khudā kā mārā harām, apnā mārā halāl.
Killed by God is unlawful, killed by yourself is lawful food!
Kutte ko haḍḍī bhalī lagtī hai.
Dogs best love a bone.
(Hindū skit at the Muhammadans.)
Māī bāp ke lātan māre, mehrī dekh juṛāē,
Chāroṅ dhām jo phiri āve, tabhūṅ pāp nā jāē.
Who kicks his parents to please his wife,
His sin will cleave to him though he makes all the pilgrimages.
(For explanation see page 152, col. ii.)
Mard ke chār nikāh durust haiṅ.
It is lawful for a man to have four wives.
(Hindu chaff of the Muhammadans.)
Mūī bachhiya bāman ke dān.
A starving heifer given in alms to a Brahman.
(A useless gift.)
Nāī, dāī, baid, qasāī in kā sūtak kadhī na jāī.
Barber, mid-wife, leech and butcher; these four are always defiled.
Nayā atīt peṛū per aldo.
The unversed ascetic squats on his haunches.
(For explanation see page 172, col. ii.)
Pahle hī gasse meṅ bāl āyā.
Hair in the very first morsel of food.
(For explanation see page 176, col. i.)
Panch jahaṅ Panmeshuar.
Where is the jury, there is God.
(For explanation see page 177, col i.)
Pānī pīje chhān-ke gurū kīje jān-ke.
Strain your water before you drink it, and test your priest before you retain him.
Pāoṅ lo bintī sau lo gintī.
Prostration is the end of bowing, as a hundred is of reckoning.
Parāē dhan par Lachchhmī Narāyān.
He is the Lord of Wealth on others' property.
(i. e. he wastes it.)
Pardes kales nareshan ko.
Even kings suffer in strange land.

Parhā na likkhā nām Bidyā-dhar.
He can neither read nor write and named Mr. Doctor.
(For explanation see page 180, col. i.)

Par kī khetī par kī gāē, voh pāpī jo māran jāē.
The field is another's and so is the cow : he is a sinner who drives it away.
(For explanation see page 183, col. ii.)

Pasū kā satānā, nirā pāp kamānā.
To torture an animal is a great sin.

Pheroṅ kī gunahgār hai.
The marriage tie is her only sin.
(For explanation see page 183, col. ii.)

Prem kahānī kahat hūṅ, suno sakhī rī āē,
Pī ḍhūḍan ko ham gaīṅ, āīṅ āp harāē!
I tell thee a tale of love, come near, my love, to hear. I went in search of my love, and lost myself!
(For explanation see page 186, col. i.)

Pūre gurū ghanṭāl haiṅ.
An old priest is only a bell ringer.
(Allusion to the services in Hindu temples.)

Pūt supūt to kyoṅ sanche? pūt kapūt to kyoṅ sanche?
If your son is a good son you need not collect money; If your son is a bad son you need not gather wealth.
(For explanation see page 187, col. ii.)

Rākhan -hār bhae bhuj chār, to kyā bigṛe bhuj do ke bigāṛe.
When he that has four hands (Vishnū) is my protector, what harm can his enmity do me that has only two?

Rupae vāle ko rupae kī ās, mo ko Rām kī ās.
The rich man trusts in his wealth, and I in my God.
(The self consolation of the poor.)

Sāban dīye mail kaṭe, Gangā nahāī pāp.
Soap cleans from dirt, and bathing in the Ganges from sin.

Sabhī bāt khoṭī sire dāl roṭī.
Best is pulse and bread; all else is bad.
(Pulse and bread are wholesome and cheap.)

Sādhoṅ ko kyā savād? Guṛ nahīṅ batāshe hī sahī.
What cares a saint for relishes? If there be no sugar then give him sugar candy.
(For explanation see page 202, col. i.)

Sāhū bahe na jāēṅ, gauṅ se jāēṅ.
The banker is not being carried away, he is going down for some object of his own.
(For explanation see page 203, col. i.)

Sājhe kī Holī sab se bhalī.
Partnership at the Holī is a good thing.
(For explanation see page 206, col. i.)

Sājhe kī mā Gangā na pāē.
The mother of several sons will never reach the Ganges.
(For explanation see page 206, col. i.)

Samae samae ke dātā Rām
God gives in every clime and time.

Samae na bāram bār.
Opportunity comes not daily.

Sampat kī jorū; bipat kā yār.
In prosperity a wife, and in adversity a friend.
(For explanation see page 207, col. ii.)

Sārī Rāmāyan sun ke pūchhā Sītā kis kī jorū thī?
After listining to the whole Ramāyan, he asks whose wife Sītā was.
(For explanation see page 210, col. ii.)

Sās mūī, bahū beṭā jāyā; vā kā paltā vā meṅ āyā.
The mother-in-law died, and the daughter in-law gave birth to a son; and so the account was balanced.

Sāt māmā kā bhanjā bhukā hī bhūkā pukāre.
The nephew of seven uncles goes hungry.
(For explanation see page 213, col. ii.)

Sāvan ke ṛapṭe aur hākim ke ḍapṭe kā kuchh ḍar nahīṅ.
It is no harm in slipping in Sāvan, or in being snubbed by a master.
(For explanation see page 215, col. ii.)

Savere kā bhūlā sāṅjh ko bhī āve, to bhūlā nahīṅ kahlātā hai.
If what was forgotten in the morning is rembered in the evening there has been no forgetfulness.
(For explanation see page, 216, col. i.)

Shām ke murde ko kab tak roē?
How long will you weep for him who died in the evening?
(For explanation see page, 218, col. i.)

Shankā ḍāyan, mansā bhūt.
Our fears create giants and our thoughts phantoms.

Sharan gurū kī āē ke jo sumre Siyā Rām,
Yahāṅ rahe ānand se ant base Hari dhām.
Who follows a prophet and calls on God,
Will be happy in this world and go to God's home in the next.
(For explanation see page, 218, col. ii.)

Siṅkh saṛappe to Lalji ke sang gae; ab to de-kho aur khāo.
Licking with broomstick is gone with my father; now you can only look and eat.
(For explaxation see page, 221 col. i.)

Sukh ke baṛe jodhā rakhvālī haiṅ.
Happiness is guarded by bold warriors.
(*i. e.* happiness is difficult to reach.)

Thālī girī jhankār sab ne sunī.
When the brazen dish falls, all hear the clang.
(For explanation see page, 237, col. i.)

Thālī par se bhūkā nahīṅ uṭhā jātā.
The hungry man does not leave the platter.

Thora khānā aur Banaras meṅ rahnā.
Little to eat and a life at Benares.
(For explanation see page, 238, col. i.)

Tīn lok se Mathurā niyārī.
Mathurā is apart from the three worlds.

Tīn pāo bhītar, to deotā aur pītar.
We remember the gods and ancestors, when the stomach is full.
(For explanation see page, 239, col. ii.)

Tiryā charitr jāne nahīṅ koī khasam mār ke sattī hoī.
None knows the willy tricks of women: They kill their husbands and then burn themselves.
(For explanation see page, 240, col ii.)

Tiryā terah mard aṭṭhārah.
A woman at thirteen and a man at eighteen.
(make a fair match.)

Tolā bhar kī chār kachaurī, khurmā māshe ḍhāī kā, Lālā jī ne byāh rachāyā dhablā bech lugāī kā.
With four thin cakes and tiny sweets, my gentleman has held a marriage on the proceeds on his wife's petticoat.
(A skit at the pretentions marriages of the poor.)

Tulsī kā pattā kaun baṛā kaun chhotā ?
Is one leaf of the tulsi tree better than another?
(For explanation see page, 244, col. ii.

Turat dān mahā Kallyān.
Ready alms is sure salvation.

Turat dān mahā pun.
Ready alms is a great virtue.

Ūdho, ban āē ke bāt.
It is luck that has done this Udho.
(For explanation see page, 249, col. i.)

Udho kā len na Mādho kā den.
I owe nothing to Udho, and Mādho owes nothing to me.
(I am independant.)

Ulojh jāīgā to sulajh he rahegā.
When once entangled he will be disentangled.
(Far explanation see page, 249, col. ii.)

MERCANTILE PROVERBS.

Bāzār us kā jo le-ke de.
The market is his who pays.

Bhāī na de, bhāo de.
Sell at the market rate, not for friendship's sake.
(Benevolence spells bankruptecy.)

Bhārī byāj mūl ko khāē.
High interest means loss of principal.

Bhūl chūk lenī denī.
All mistakes should be given and taken.
(Errors excepted; the E. E. of the English traders.)

Biyāj motā mūl kā ṭotā.
High interest loses the capital.

Bohnī ṭohnī, rad balā.
Cash for handsell puts away misfortune.

Detā bhūle na letā.
Neither giver nor taker can make a mistake about it.
(Said of an easy and plain calculation.)

Ek hāth lenā, ek hāth denā.
Take with one hand and pay with the other.
(Ready money.)

Ek ke dūnā se sau ke savāī bhal.
A hundred and quarter for a hundred is better than the two for one.
(For explanation see page 79, col. i.)

Gāhak aur maut kā ṭhīk nahīṅ kab āve ?
Who knows when death or a customer will come?

Ghar bhāṛe, hāṭ bhāṛe, pūṅjī ko lāge byāj, Munim baiṭhā roṭiyāṅ jhāṛe, divālā kāṛhe kāiṅ lāj.
His house hired, his shop hired, his capital borrowed. His owner eating up his goods; no shame to him if he became bankrupt.
(Said of the improvident.)

Ghaṛe se gharā nahīṅ bharā jātā
You cannot fill a jar with a jarful.
(i. e. on account of wastage.)

Hāth kā denā; aur bair bisānā.
Lend your money and make an enemy.

Hāthoṅ hāth bik gayā.
Sold from hand to hand.
(A rapid sale.)

Is hāth lenā us hāth denā.
Give with one hand and receive with the other.
(Cash dealings.)

Itnā nafā khāo, jitnā āṭe meṅ non.
Make as much profit as there is salt in flour.
(Don't exceed safe limits in speculating)

Jab bhae sau to bhāg gayā bhau.
(i) When it (debt) reaches to a hundred he no longer fears it.
(Owe a man £10,000 and you are his master.)
(ii) When a hundred join together fear flies from them.
(The bundle of sticks: union is strength.)

Jhūṭ se kām nahīṅ chaltā.
Business can't thrive on lies.

Jis kā āṅḍū bike voh badhiyā kyoṅ kare [him ?
If the entire bull will sell, why castrate

Khol gharā kar be dharā.
Open the jar, and get ready the scales.
(For explanation see page 138, col. ii.)

Kyā udhār kī mā marī hai?
Is the race of credit extinct?
(For explanation see page 147, col. i.)

Maṭṭī kā ghaṛā bhī ṭhonk bajā-kar lete haiṅ.
Even an earthen pot is rung before it is bought.
(For explanation see page 159, col. ii.)

Maut aur gāhak kā etebār nahīṅ, jāne kis vaqt ā jāē.
None can tell when death or a customer will come.

Mūl se byāj pyārā hotā hai
The interest is dearer than the principal.
(For explanation see page 164, col. ii.)

Mūṅh māṅge dām nahīṅ milte.
The price asked for cannot be had.
(For explanation see page 165, col. i.)

Ochhī pūṅjī khasmoṅ khāe.
A small capital ruins its master.

Pahlī bohnī Allah Miyāṅ kī ās.
After handsell my hope is in God.
(For explanation see page 176, col. i.)

Pāsang kā chor tīn jagah daṅḍāē;
Jhuktā tole, rukan de, pāsang dikhāve.
The thief with false weights gets punished in three ways; Giving over weight, making a bad bargain, and showing the difference in his scales.
(For explanation see page 181, col. ii.)

Pūrātol chāhe maṅhgā bech.
Let the weight be right, whatever the cost

Rakho is maqūle pe dār o madār, Ki nau naqd achchhe na terah udhār.
Depend upon this motto: That nine in cash are better than thirteen on credit.
(A bird in hand is worth two in the bush.)

Rakh pachhtāvā kuchh nahīṅ, bech pachhtāvā achchhā.
It is useless to repent that you have kept, and well to repent that you have sold.
(For explanation see page 191, col. i.)

Rupaē kā kām rupae se chaltā hai.
Money carries on the business that requires money.
(Money makes the mare to go.)

Rupae ko rupayā kamātā hai.
Money begets money.

Sach bol pūrā tol.
Speak the truth, and give full weight.

Sāh ke savāē, kambakht ke dūne!
The banker's interest is twenty-five per cent: the userer's is cent per cent!

Sāhū baṭṭe voh bhī sāh
Who sells at cost price is still a merchant.
(For explanation see page 203, col. i.)

Sāhūkār ko kisān aur bālak ko mosān.
A farmer is to a banker, what wasting is to a child.
(For explanation see page 203, col. ii.)

Saiṅkṛon ke vāre niyāre ho gae.
It is a gain of hundreds.
(Said of large and lucrative contracts.)

Sājhā bhalā na bāp kā aur tāo bhalā na tāp kā.
Partnership even with a father is not good, Nor is a burning fever.

Sājhā sadhe na bāp kā.
Partnership even with a father is not lasting.
(For explanation see page 205, col. ii.)

Sākh lākh se bhalī.
Credit is better than a fortune.

Sastā rove bār bār, maṅhgā rove ek bār.
Cheap weeps oft, dear but once.
(Cheap and nasty.)

Saste ko dekh bhāl ke lenā chāhiye.
Think twice over a cheap bargain.

Sastī bheṛ kī tāṅg uṭhā uṭhā ke dekhte haiṅ!
Lift up the leg of a cheap sheep.

Sāṭe kī sagāī aur biyājū rupae kā ehsān kyā
A bethrothel for a consideration and money lent on interest confer no obligation.

Ser meṅ panserī kā dhokā.
He 'll cheat five pounds out of every pound.
(A great rogue.)

Sīdhī uṅglioṅ ghī nahīṅ nikaltā.
Straight fingers bring no butter.
(For explanation see page 220, col. i).

Sonā le ke maṭṭī bhī nahīṅ detā.
He would not return even clay for the gold he had borrowed. (A bad debt.)

Tāṅbā dekhe chītnā, man dekhe beopār.
Seeing money settles, seeing the person does business.
(For explanation see page 231, col. ii.)

Terā ḍhakā rahe, merā bik jāē.
Let yours remain covered up, till mine be sold.
(Applied to a selfish person.)

Ṭeṛ ṭeṛ ke rove apnī lāj khove.
Who weeps and cries aloud loses his credit.
(Keep your losses to yourself.)

Ṭhathere ṭhathere badlāī!
One brazier exchanging with another!
(For explanation see page 237, col. i.)

Thoṛī pūṅjī khasmoṅ khāē.
A small capital ruins the master.

Tīn diye aur terah pāē; kaise lobh byāj kā jāē.
I gave three and got thirteen; How the love of usury does increase!
(The proverb is a skit at the usurers.)

Ṭoṭe se ho ghar ka ṭībā; Ṭoṭā gayā to khulā nasībā.
Misfortune will ruin a house, But when misfortune goes good fortune comes.

Udhār baṛī khattyā hai.
Debts are a great trouble.

Udhār denā laṛāī mol lenā.
Give on the loan and buy a quarrel.

Udhār dīje, dushman kījē.
Give a loan and make an enemy.

Udhār dīyā, gāhak khoyā.
Sell on credit and lose your customer.
(For explanation see page 248, col. ii.)

Udhār diyā gāhak gayā: sadqā dīyā rad balā.
Sell on dredit and lose your customer; make an offering and avert evil.
(It is better to give than to lend.)

MUHAMMADAN PROVERBS.

Ādhe Qāzī Quddūh, ādhe Bābā Ādam.
Half the world are Bābā Ādam's and half are Qāzī Quddūh's.
(For explanation see page 2, col. ii.)

Ādmī ko ḍhāī gaz zamīn kāfī hai.
Man wants but seven feet of earth.
(His grave).

Āh-i-mardān na ūhī zanān.
Not a man's *āhe* nor a woman's *ūhī* in him.
(See page 6, col, i.)

Āī hai jān ke sāth, jāegī janāze ke sāth.
Come with your life, it leaves but with your corpse.
(A bad habit.)

Aisā kīyā dil gurdah, ki rupayā kīyā khurdah !
Such spirit and liberty ! he has actually changed a rupee !
('Bang went six pence!')

Aise hote to Īd Bakrīd ke kām āte.
Had you been of any use you would have been used at the Īd and Bakrīd.
(For explanation see page 7, col. i.)

Āī to rozī, nahīn to rozah.
Earn and dine, or else fast.

Akelā Hasnū rove, ki qabr khode.
Let lonely Hasnū weep or dig the grave.
(You can't do two things at once.)

Al bal Khudā bal.
God's strength is the greatest strength.

Al farbah khwāh-makhwāh mard-i-ādmī.
A fat man is undoubtedly one of the first consequence.
(In appearance.)

Alif Allah.
God is Alif.
(For explanation see page 9, col. ii.)

Allāh Allāh karo khair māngo.
Call on God and ask his blessing.

Allāh Allah, khair sallah.
Thank God, it is well over.
(All's well that ends well.)

Amānat men khayānat to zamīn bhī nahīn kartī.
Even the earth does not commit breach of trust.
(*i. e.* it yields what is sown in it.)

Andhā hādī, bahrā murshid.
A blind guide and a deaf follower.

Apnā 'Bis'mi'llah,' dūsre kā 'nauz bi'llah.'
One's own 'God bless him !' to the other's 'God preserve me from him !'
(Allusion to the rhyming Arabic sayings.)

Aṛī dhaṛī Qāzī ke sir paṛī.
Whatever happens the Qāzī is responsible.
Shifting responsibility on to others' shoulders.)

Āyā banda, āī rozī, gayā banda, gaī rozī.
Come man, come food, gone man, gone food.
(For explanation see page 23, col. i.)

Āyā Ramzān, bhāgā Shaitān.
When Ramzān comes, the Devil flies.
(For explanation see page 23, col. ii.)

Banda ājiz hai.
Man is but man.
(Apt to err.)

Bas ho chukī namāz musallāh baṛhāīye.
The prayer is over, so put away the carpet.
(Said when any work is finished.)

Bi'smi'llah hī galat.
Wrong at the very *Bi'smi'llah.*
(For explanation see page. 46, col. i.)

Bi'smi'llah ke gumbad men baiṭhe hain.
He resides under the dome of *Bi'smi'llah.*
(For explanation see page 46, col. i)

Boyā na jotā Allāh Miyān ne diyā potā.
Without sowing or ploughing God gave him a grandson.
(See page 47, col. i.)

Bure kahne-vāle par t'n harf.
For evil speakers three letters.
(See page 47, col. ii.)

Chirāg raushan, murād hāsil.
The lamp is lighted and the wishes are fulfilled.
(For explanation see page 58, col. i)

Chugal-khor, Khudā kā chor.
The tale-bearer is God's enemy.

Dah dar dunyā, sad dar ākhirat.
Ten in this world is a hundred in the next.
(Street cry of Muhammadan beggers.)

Ḍāṛhī Khudā kā nūr hai.
The beard is the light of God.

Dar-i-tauba bāz hai.
The door of repentence is open.

Dastar-khān ke bichhāne men sau aib : na bichhāne men ek aib.
Who spreads his table hath a hundred faults : who spreads it not hath only one.

Dastar-khān kī billī.
The cat of the banquet.
(For explanation see page 65, col. i.)

Ḍeṛh īnṭ kī masjid judī hī banāte hain.
They built a separate mosque of their own with a brick and a half.
(Going their own way.)

Din Īd, rāt Shab-barāt.
Each day was an Īd, and each night a Shab-i-barāt.
(For explanation see page 72, col. i.)

Diyā fātehā ko lage luṭāne.
He squandered away what was given him as an offering.
(For explanation see page 73, col. i.)

Do dil rāzī, to kyā karegā Qāzī ?
When two hearts agree what can the Qāzī do ?
(For explanation see page 73, col. ii.)

Do Mulla meṅ murgī harām.
Between two Mullas the fowl remained unlawful meat.
(For explanation see page 74, col. i.)

Do qasāīyoṅ meṅ gāē murdār.
Between two butchers the cow died a natural death.
(And so became unlawful food.)

Dunyā murda pasand hai.
The world praises the dead.
(*De mortuis nil nisi bonum.*)

Ek din mehmān, do din mehmān, tisre din balāē jāṅ.
One day a guest, two days a guest, the third day a nuisance.

Ek hammām meṅ sab naṅge.
In one bath all are naked.
(For explanation see page 78, col. i.)

Fālūdah khāte dāṅt ṭūṭeṅ to balā se.
If the teeth be broken by eating pudding it is of no consequence.
(For explanation see page 81, col. i.)

Fāl zabān yā fāl Qurān.
Divination by word of mouth, or divination by the scripture.

Fātehā na darūd khāne ko maujūd.
He is in too great a hurry to eat to say grace.

Fikr aur zikr donoṅ chāhiyeṅ.
Meditation and prayer both are required.
(Of a mendicant.)

Gae bichāre roze rahe ek kam tis.
When one day of the fast is over twenty nine remain.
(For explanation see page 83, col. i.)

Gae the rozah chhuṛāne, namāz gale paṛī !
He went to be freed from the fast, and prayers were added to it !

Garīb kī jorū aur Umdah Khānam nām.
The wife of a pauper and named my Lady Excellent.

Garib ne roze rakkhe din baṛe hue.
When the poor fast, the days lengthen.
(For explanation see page 86, col. i.)

Gāzī Miyāṅ, Dam Madar, khichchaṛ pakkā ham taiyār.
By Gāzi Miyān and Dam Madār, I am ready to eat the cooked dinner.
(For explanation see page 86, col. ii.)

Ghar ke pīroṅ ko tel kā malīdā.
For the house priest only cakes of oil.
(For explanation see page 88, col. ii.)

Ginī boṭī napā shurvā.
The bits of meat are counted and the soup is measured.
(For explanation see page 91, col. i.)

Gosht khā lete haiṅ, haḍḍiyāṅ pheṅk dete haiṅ.
Flesh is eaten and bones are thrown away.
(Take what is good for you.)

Haj kā haj nij kā nij.
Pilgrimage is pilgrimage, and trade is trade.
(For explanation see page 95, col. i.)

Halvāī kī dukān aur dādā jī kī fātehā.
To celebrate a grand-father's obsequies at a comfectioner's shop.
(For explanation see page 96, col. i.)

Haq Allāh pāk zāt Allāh.
God is truth and God is pure.

Haq kā razī Khudā hai.
The guardian of truth is God.

Haq kar halāl kar, din meṅ sau bār kar.
Do the right and lawful, and do it a hundred times a day.

Haq kā sāthī Khudā.
God sides with the truth.

Haq nām Allah kā.
The true name is God.

Harām khānā aur shalgam !
Unlawful food and a turnip at that !
(As well be hanged for a sheep as a lamb.)

Har nivāle bismillah.
Every mouthful in the name of God.
(For explanation see page 99, col. i.)

Hātam kī gor par lāt mārī.
He has kicked the tomb of Hātam.

Hāth pāoṅ kī ālkasī our mūṅh meṅ mūchheṅ jāēṅ.
His moustaches go into his mouth for very laziness.
(For explanation see page 101, col. ii.)

Hāzri ke mele meṅ koī ho.
Any one may be present at the breakfast meeting.
(For explanation see page 102, col. ii.)

Hirī phirī bal gaī, jalve ke vaqt ṭal gaī.
She is always at hand for the benediction, but steals away when she should make a present (to the bride.)
(For explanation see page 102, col. ii.)

Hujjatī lā ummatī.
Argument is scepticism.
(To doubt is to go to hell.)

Hukmī bandah jannat meṅ.
Obedience on Earth (leads to) a place in Heaven.

Idhar Qiblah Quṭab, udhar Khatījah, mūtūṅ kidhar.
This side the Mecca, the other Khatījah, where I am to make water ?
(For explanation see page 104, col. i.)

Īd ke chāṅd ho gae.
He is become the moon of the Īd.
(For explanation see page 104, col. ii.)

Jaise Hasan vaise Husain.
As is Hasan, so is Husain.
(For explanation see page 110, col. ii.)

Jaise murde pe sau man miṭṭī, vaisī hazār man.
One ton of earth on a corpse is as good as a hundred tons.

Jaisī rūh vaise farishte.
As the soul, so the angels.
(For explanation see page 111, col. ii.)

Jaisī terī phāphaṛ kodo, vaisī merī hīng.
As your millet, so my assafœtida.
(For explanation see page 111, col. ii.)

Jis ke hoveṅ assī voh kare khassī.
Who has eighty Rupees must sacrifice a goat.
(For explanation see page 118, col. ii.)

Jorū kā ḍhablā bech-kar tandūrī roṭī khāī hai.
He has enjoyed a loaf on the proceeds of his wife's gown.
(Downright selfishness.)

Julāhe kī tarah Īd Bakrīd ko pān khā lete haiṅ.
He enjoys the luxury of betel leaf like a weaver at the Īd and Bakrīd.
(For explanation see page 124, col. ii.)

Kachchī peṅdī dastar-khuān kā zarar.
The under baked-pot will soil the cloth.
(For explanation see page 126, col. ii.)

Kachchī peṅdī dastar-khuān kā zarar.
An unripe melon is a disgrace to the table.
(For explanation see page 126, col. ii.)

Kālī jumerāt ka vādā karnā.
To promise on black Thursday.
(For explanation see page 128, col. ii.)

Kauṛī ke vāste masjid ḍhate haiṅ.
He would let the mosque go to ruin to save a penny.

Khālā jī kā ghar nahīṅ hai.
It is not your aunt's house.
(For explanation see page 135, col. i.)

Khālā kā dam aur kivāṛ kī joṛī.
Only an aunt alive and a pair of door flaps.
(Said to a boaster.)

Khālā kā rutbā mā ke barābar.
An aunt is as a mother.
(For explanation see page 135, col. ii.)

Khālā kī mehmānī hāth ḍāl pachhtānī.
To accept the invitation of an aunt and repent of it.
(For explanation see page 155, col. ii.)

Khāne ko bi'smi'llah, kām ke istagfir'allah.
Ready for the grace before meat, but for work "God forbid."

Khizar mile jī Khizar mile!
I have found Kizar.
(For explanation see page 136, col. ii.)

Khudā ke ghar meṅ chor kā kyā kām?
What business has a thief in the house of God!

Khudā ke ghar meṅ sab kuchh.
In the house of God there is every thing.
(With God all things are possible.)

Khudā ke ghar se phire haiṅ.
They have returned from the house of God.
(For explanation see page 189, col. ii.)

Kutte ko masjid se kyā kām?
What business has a dog in the mosque.

Kutte kī maut āve to masjid meṅ mūt jāve.
Death approaches the dog, when he makes water in the mosque.
(As he will be severely punished.)

Likhe sāī paṛhe Mūsā.
Moses only can read the writings of Jesus.
(Said of an illegible hand.)

Likhe Mūsā paṛhe Khudā.
i. God only can read the writings of Moses
ii His writing is so scratchy that only he himself can read it.
(For explanation see page 151, col. i.)

Mā chhoṛ mausī se mazāq.
You can flirt with your aunt; but not with your mother.

Makke gaë na Madine gaë, bich hi bich meṅ hājī bhaë.
He went to neither Makka nor Madina, but became a pilgrim half way.

Makke meṅ rahte haiṅ, par haj nahīṅ karte.
Living in Makka he never made the pilgrimage.
(The nearer the church, the further from God.)

Mare to shahid, māre to qāzī.
A martyr if killed, a *qāzī* if he kills.
(For explanation see page 157, col. ii.)

Mar gaë mardūd, jin kī fātihā na darūd.
The wretch has died without ceremony or burial.
(Without extreme unction.)

Mārte khāṅ se sab ḍarte haiṅ.
Every one fears my lord Tyrant.

Mās binā sab sāg rasoī.
Without meat a dinner is but greens.

Maulā hāth baṛhāīyāṅ, jis chāheṅ tis deṅ.
Greatness rests with God; He gives to whom he pleases.

Maulā yār to beṛā pār.
If God be kind you will succeed.

Mīrāṅ kī boṭī hai.
A dish of offerings to Mīrāṅ.
(For explanation see page 161, col. ii.)

Mue par sau durreh.
A hundred stripes on the dead.
(For explanation see page 163, col. i.)

Muflis se savāl harām hai.
It is wicked to beg from the poor.

Muft kī dāvat meṅ sirf roṭī hī bhāt hai.
A feast of bread which costs nothing is as (good as) meat.
(Never look a gift horse in the mouth.)

Muft kī sharāb Qāẓī ko bhī halāl!
Even the Qāẓī may drink of a present of mine.
(For explanation see page 163, col. ii.)

Muharram kī paidāyash.
Born at the Muharram.
(For explanation see page 163, col. ii.)

Mullājī kyā kahenjī ākhunjī āge hī samjhe hue hain.
What can the priest teach, that the high priest has not learnt before?

Mullā kī dāṛhī tabarruk men gaī.
The Mullā's beard goes in relics.
(For explanation see page 164, col. i.)

Mullā na hogā to kyā masjid men azān na hogī?
If there be no priest, will there be no call to prayer in the mosque?

Murdah bahist men jāē yā dozakh men, yahān to halve māṇḍe se kām.
The dead may go to heaven or hell, my concern is with the sweets and cakes.
(For explanation see page 166, col. i.)

Murgā hazam bakrī par dam.
He has gobbled up a fowl, and is waiting for a goat.
(A greedy man.)

Murgā pasham, bheṛ bhasam.
What's a fowl to one who has swallowed a sheep?

Murgī kī azān kaun suntā hai.
Who minds the crowing of a hen?
(For explanation see page 166. col. ii.)

Murgī kī bāng kā kyā etebār?
What trust is there in a crowing hen?
(For explanation see page 166, col. ii.)

Musalla pasār bagal men yār.
Kissing a girl over the praying carpet.
(Said of a hypocrite.)

Musalmānī abādānī.
Where there are Musalmāns, there is population.
(For explanation see page 166, col. ii.)

Musalmānī men ānā kānī kyā?
There should be no reserve among Musalmans.
(For explanation see page 166, col. ii.)

Mūzī ko namāz chhoṛ-ke māre.
You may leave your prayers to kill an obnoxious beast.

Nae namāzī aur boriye kā tahmad!
A new Musalmān and a mat for apron.
(For explanation see page 167, col. ii.)

Namāzī kā ṭakā.
The holy man's penny.
(For explanation see page 165, col. ii.)

Namāz chhuṛāne gaë the, roze gale paṛe!
They went to get rid of their prayers and were obliged to fast as well.
(For explanation see page 169, col. ii.)

Na rahe mān, na rāhe mānī, ākhir dunyā fānā fānī.
Nor respect, nor pride can last for ever, for all the world will die at last.

Nau sau chūhe khāke billī haj ko chalī.
After eating nine hundred rats the cat went on a pilgrimage.
(A death-bed repentence: at the eleventh hour.)

Nayā Musalmān "Allah hī Allāh" pukāre.
A Musalmān convert cries "Allah Allah."
(Allusion to the proverbial zeal of all converts.)

Nek andar bad, bad andar nek.
Good out of evil, evil out of good.
(For explanation see page 173, col. i.)

Nekī barbād gunah lāzim.
The good is forgotten, and returned for it.
(Evil for good.)

Nikāhī na byāhī; munḍo bahū kahān se āī.
There was no marriage ceremony, so whence came this scald-head to be a wife.
(For explanation see page 173, col. ii.)

Nīyat sābit manzil āsān.
Honesty makes the journey easy.

Pahle ghar men to pīchhe masjid men.
First at home, and afterwards at the mosque.
(Charity begins at home.)

Pahle hī bismillah galat.
Wrong from the very beginning.
(For explanation see page 176, col. i.)

Pāk nām Allāh kā.
Only God is pure.

Pāk rah be-bāk rah.
Be innocent and fear not.
(Innocent actions carry their warrant with them.)

Panch māne Khudā, Khudā māne panch.
The jury believes in God, and God believes in the jury.

Panch mil Khudā, aur Khudā mil panch.
God is with the jury, and the jury with God.

Parāë māl pe, yā Husain!
Invoking Husain with another's property.

Parāyā sir Qurān kī jagah.
Another's head is instead of the Qurān.
(For explanation see page 179, col. i.)

Paṛhā na likkhā, nām Mahammad Fāzil.
He can neither read nor write, and named Mr. Doctor.
(For explanation see page 180, col. i.)

Paṛhī na qazā kī.
Who does not know, cannot fail to pray.
(For explanation see page 180, col. ii.)

Peshā habībullāh, jo na kare so lānatullah.
The love of God on those who work and the curse of God on those who won't.
(For explanation see page 182, col. i.)

Qabr kā munh jhānk kar āë hain.
I have just peeped into my grave.
(Snatched from the jaws of death.)

Qabr men bhī tīn din bhārī hote hain:
There's three days misery even in the grave.
(For explanation see page 187; col. ii.)

Qabr men pāon laṭkāe baiṭhā hai.
He has one foot in the grave.

Qabr men rakh ke khabar ko na āyā koī, mūe kā koī nahīn jīte jī kā sab koī.
When I am laid in the grave, no one will come to see me. None is for the dead: all are for the living.

Qabr par qabr nahīn hotī.
Grave upon grave is not proper.
(For explanation see page 187, col. ii.)

Qadr ullū kī ullū hī jāntā hai;
Humā ko kab chugad pahchāntā hai?
Owls know the value of owls, But how shall the owl know the value of the phœnix?
(For explanation see page 188, col. i.)

Qāzī ke mūsal men nārā.
The Qazi's pestle has a string (for drawers)
(For explanation see pape 188, col. ii.)

Qurān par Qurān rakhne kā kyā muzāeqā hai?
What harm is there if you put one Qurān upon another.

Ramzān ke namāzī, Muharram ke sipāhī.
In Ramzān a worshipper, in Muharram a soldier.
(For explanation see page 192, col. ii.)

Rizālā mast huā; khudā ko bhūl gayā.
When a blackguard is puffed up he forgets that there is a God.

Roze khor, Khudā ke chor.
Who eats during a fast pilfers from God.

Roze ko gae namāz gale paṛī.
We went to be relieved of fasting and prayers were added to it.
(For explanation see page 197, col. i.)

Roz roz kī davā bhī gizā hozātī hai
Medicines taken daily become a part of your diet,
(For explanation see page 197, col. i.)

Rupayā to shekh nahīn to julāhā.
If you've wealth you are a Shekh; if not you are a weaver.
(For explanation see page 197, col. ii.)

Sabaq aur tabaq donon mavjūd hain.
Learning and food are both before you.
(For explanation see page 198, col. i.)

Sabr kā ajar Khudā degā.
God will requite the patient heart.
(Every thing is his who knows how to wait.)

Sābir o shākir dono jannatī hai.
Patient and grateful are both for Heaven.
(For explanation see page 179, col. i.)

Sab pīr chhūṭe, pakṛī gaīn Bībī Nūr.
All the other saints have escaped and only Lady Nūr is caught.
(For explanation see page 199, col. ii.)

Sachāī men Khudā kī sūrat hai.
Truth is in the image of God.

Sadā Īd nahīn, jo halvā khāe.
Every day is not a holiday in which to eat sweets.
(The Id is the chief musalman festival.)

Sahrī bhī na khāūn to kafir na ho jāūn.
If I were not even to eat breakfast I should be an infedel
(For explanation see page 203, col. i.)

Sahrī khāe so rozā rakkhe.
Who eats the morning meal, must keep the fast.
(For explanation see page 203, col. i.)

Sakhī kā sar buland, mūzī kī gor tang.
The head of the bountiful shall be exalted, and the miser's grave shall be narrow.
(Beggar's cry.)

Sālī ādhī nihālī solhaj pūrī joē.
A wife's sister is half a wife, a brother-in-law's wife in a full wife.
(For explanation see page 206, col. ii.)

Samandar kyā jāne dozakh kā azāb?
What can the salamander know of the pains of Hell?
(Because he lives in the fire.)

Sārī deg men ek hī chāval dekhte hain.
One grain tests the whole pot full.
(For explanation see page 210, col. ii.)

Sārī rāt kahānī sunī, subeh ko pūchhe Zulekhā aurat thī yā mard?
He has been all night listening to the story, and in the morning asks, was Zulekha a man or a woman?

Sattū khā-ke shukr kyā?
Why give thanks (to God) for a feast of *sattū*?
(For explanation see page 214, col. i.)

Sent kā chūnā, dādā kī qabar.
Building a grandfather's tomb with unpaid for cement.

Shaitān jān na māre; to hairān to surūr kare.
If the devil will not kill, he will at any rate torment.

Shaitān ke kān kāṭe.
He has cut off the devils ears.
(He surpasses him in iniquity.)

Shaitān kī ānt.
The guts of the devil.
(Said of a very long thing.)

Shaitān ne bhī laṛkon se panāh māngī hai.
The devil even seeks refuge from boys.
(For explanation see page 217, col. ii.)

Shaitān se zyādah mashhūr:
More notorious than the devil.

Shaitān sir par chaṛh rahā hai.
The devil is riding on his head.
(He is under the influence of the devil.)

Shākir ko shakkar mūzī ko takkar.
Rewards for the grateful, and blows for the ingrate.

Shakkar-khore ko Khudā shakkar hī detā hai.
God gives sugar to the sugar-eater.
(God tempers the wind to the shorn lamb.)

Shamā kī pusht aur rū barābar hai.
The front and back of a candle are the same.
(For explanation see page 218, col. i.)

Shamā kī raushnī jalte tak, aur dīye kī raushnī mahshar tak.
The light of the candle lasts while it burns, the light of a lamp till the day of Judgment.
(For explanation see page 218, col. i.)

Shāh men kyā jufte parenge?
What detriment will your dignity suffer?
(For explanation see page 218, col. ii.)

Shara men sharm kyā?
What shame is there in lawful dealings?

Shekh Sādī shīrāzī, āshiqon ke bādshāh, māshūqon ke qāzī.
Shekh Sādī of Shīrāz was the king of lovers, and the judge of the beloved.
(For explanation see page 219, col. i.)

Sir kā nahāyā pāk.
He that bathes his head is pure.
(For explanation see page 221, col. ii.)

Sir sijde men man badiyon men.
Bowings of the head and evil in the heart.
(Said of a hypocrite.)

Subah kī subah Khudā kā nām lo!
Begin the day in the name of God.
(For explanation see page 225, col. i.)

Sunni na shiā, jī men āyā so kiyā.
Neither a Sunnī nor a Shiā, I do as I like.
(For explanation see page 227, col. ii.)

Sūt kī antī aur Yusuf kī khorīdārī!
Purchasing Joseph with a skein of thread.
(For explanation see page 229, col. i.)

Tanūr bāzī aur Allāh rāzī.
Living on baker's bread pleases God.
(For explanation see page 232, col. ii.)

Tasbīh pherūn, kis ko gherūn?
Counting my beads, whom shall I cheat?
(Put into the mouth of a hypocrite.)

Taubah barī sipar hai guneh-gār ke liye.
Repentance is the best shield for a sinner.

Taubah kā darvāzah khulā hai.
The door of repentance is ever open.
(It is never too late to mend.)

Taubah kar bande is gande roz-gār se.
Forbear, my friend, from such a dirty trade.

Terhvīn sadī men sharā kī bāten koī nahīn māntā.
In the thirteenth century none minds religious precepts.
(For explanation see page 236, col. i.)

Tīn din qabr men bhī bhārī hote hain.
Even in the grave, there are three days of trouble.
(For explanation see page 239, col. i.)

Tīn gunah Khudā bhī bakhshtā hai.
Even God forgives three sins.
(For explanation see page 239, col. i.)

Tīn thān, chauthī jān, un kā Allah nigahbān!
Three children and the fourth myself: God keep them safe.

Tīr na kamān, kāhe ke pathā.
Neither bow nor arrows, what kind of Pathān is he?
(For explanation see page 240, col. i.)

Tīr na kamān; miyān kā Allah nigahbān!
He has neither bow nor arrows, may God protect him!

Tīsre din murdah bhī halāl hai.
On the third day even a dead body is lawful.
(For explanation see page 241, col. i.)

Tumhāre farrishto ko bhī khabar nahīn hai.
Even your angels have no knowledge of it.
(For explanation see page 246, col. i.)

Us din bhulen chaukrī valī, nabī aur pīr.
Lekhā leve jis dinan Qādar Pāk-qadīr.
Saints and prophets and hermits will look blank on that day, when the almighty God shall call them to account.
(The day of judgment.)

PERSIAN PROVERBS.

Āb na dīdah mozah kashīdah.
No water to be seen, and his stockings pulled off.
(Crying out before you are hurt.)

Āqilān pairavī-i- nuqat na kunand.
The learned don't need the dots.
(For explanation see page 19, col. i.)

Aql chih kuttist kī pesh-i-mardān bi-āyad.
Who is that bitch, sense, that she should come to heroes!
(Brute force.)

Arzān ba-illat, garān ba-hikmat.
Cheap and nasty, dear and good.

Avval taām, bādhū kalām.
Eat first and talk afterwards.

Avval khesh, bādhū darvesh.
First yourself, then the beggar.
(Charity begins at home.)

Ayān racheh bayān?
Why explain the obvious?

Be-adab, be-nasīb; bā-adab, bā-nasīb.
Ill-mannered is unfortunate; well-mannered is fortunate.

Buvad ham-pesha, bā ham-pesha dushman.
Two of a trade can never agree.

Chahār chīz ast tohfa-i-Multān :
Gard, garma, gadā o goristān.
Multan is famous for four things, Dust, heat, beggars and graves.

Chārpāe baro kitāb-i-chand.
A quadruped with some books on its back.
(Originally from the Gulistān.)

Chashm-i-mā raushan, dil-i-mā khush.
Light of my eyes and my heart's delight.
(A son.)

Chih nisbat khāk rā ba ālam-i-pāk ?
What connection is there between Earth and Heaven ?

Dārū-i-gazab khāmoshī.
Silence is the best cure for anger.
(*Compare.* A soft answer turneth away wrath.

Dīvānah bakār-i-khud hūshyār.
Mad, but in his interests wise.

Evaz māvaz gilā na dārad.
One thing for another prevents complaints.
(Exchange is no robbery.)

Faqīr rā ba mujādla che kār ?
What has a friar to do with fighting.

Galla chūn arzān shavad, imsāl sayyid mīshavam.
If corn were to grow cheaper I would turn sayyid.
(For explanation see page 84, col. i.)

Gam na dārī buz bakhar.
If you have no cares buy a goat !
(And cares will soon follow.)

Gandum az gandum biroyad, jau zi jau.
Wheat grows wheat, and barley barley.
(As you sow you shall reap.)

Guzashta rā salvāt !
Blessings on what is past !
(Let by-gones be by-gones.)

Guzasht unche guzasht.
Past is past.

Hājit-i-mushshātah nest rūē dil ārām rā.
A fair face needs no paint.
(Beauty unadorned is adorned the most.)

Ham khurma o ham-savāb.
Both the palm fruit and its virtues.
(For explanation see page 96, col. ii.)

Ham-piyāla o ham-nivāla.
Eating and drinking together.
(Bosom friends.)

Har kase maslahat-i-khesh niko mīdānad.
Every one knows his own interests best.

Har kamāle rā zavāle.
All maturity is destined to decay.

Har kāre o har marde.
Every man to his own business.

Har roz Īd nest, ki halvā khurad kase.
Every day is not Īd, that one may eat cakes.
(There is a time for every thing.)

Hikmat-i-Chīn, hujjat-i-Bangāla.
China for art, Bengal for litigation.

Himmat-i-mardān madad-i-Khudā.
Endeavour is man's, help is God's.
(God helps those that help themselves.)

Hisāb-i-dostān dar dil.
Friend's accounts are kept in the head.

Hukm-i-hākim marg-i-mafājāt.
The ruler's order is sudden death.

Huqqa yak dam, do dam, sih dam bāshed, Na kī mīrās-i-jadd o am bāshad.
Take one, two or three puffs at a pipe, but don't use it as an heirloom.
(For explanation see page 104, col. i.)

Ilm dar sīnah, na dar safīnah.
Knowledge is in the heart, not in books.

Iqrār-i-jurm islāh-i-jurm.
A fault confessed is half redressed.

Isā ba dīn-i-khud, Mūsā ba dīn-i-khud.
Let Jesus stick to his faith and Moses to his.
(Religious toleration.)

Jau-farosh gandum-numā.
He shows you wheat and sells you barley.
(A swindler.)

Javāb-i-jāhilān bāshad khamoshī.
Answer the ignorant with silence.

Kam kharch bālā nashīn.
Small cost and great show.

Khud kardah rā ilāje nest.
There is no remedy for one's own actions.

Khud rā fazīhat, dīgre rā nasīhat.
A scoundrel himself he preaches to others.

Khufta rā khufta kai kunad bedār ?
How shall a sleeping man awake a sleeping [man ?

Khurda na barda, muft dard gurda.
Nothing for eating and drinking, but a stomach-ache all the same.

Koh kandan o kāh bar āvurdan.
To dig up a hill to find a straw.
(To look for a needle in a bundle of hay.)

Kunda-i-nā tarāsh.
An unlopped trunk.
(A blockhead.)

Kushtah kushtah mekund.
I. Alchemy kills. II. Alchemy strengthens.
(For explanation see page 144, col. ii.)

Mārāche azīn qissa ki gāo āmad o khar raft.
What is it to me that a cow hath come and a donkey gone ?
(For explanation see page 156, col. ii.)

Marzī-i-Maulā az hamah aulā.
God's will before all things.

Muft rāche guft !
Why cavil at a gift !

Mulāzim-i-nau tez-rau.
A new servant is very active.
(A new broom sweeps clean.)

Mulk-i-Khudā tang nest, pāē marā lang nest.
God's universe is wide enough, no helpless cripple am I.
(For explanation see page 164, col. ii.)

Murabbī byār o murabba bikhur.
Get a patron and eat dainties.

Murdah badast-i-zindah.
The dead are at the mercy of the living.

Musalmānāṅ dar gor, va Musalmānī dar kitāb.
The Musalmāns are in their graves and their faith in their books.
(No true Muhammadans are left.)

Mushk āṅ ast ki khud boyad, na ki attār goyad.
Musk is known by its smell, not by the praise of the perfumer.
(Good wine needs no bush.)

Mushkil-i-nest ki āsāṅ na shavad Mard bāyad ki hirāsāṅ na shavad.
No difficulty so great but it may be overcome: a true man never sinks under it.

Namūd be-būd.
Show without substance.

Naqal rā che aql?
Imitation is not intelligence.

Naql-i-kufr, kufr nabāshad.
To copy an infidel is not to be infidel.
(For explanation see page 171, col. i.)

Narm chob rā kirm mī-khurad.
We evils eat soft wood.

Nīm hakīm khatra-i-jān! Nīm mullā khatra-i-imān!
Half a doctor and danger of life Half a priest and danger to the faith!
(A little knowledge is a dangerous thing.)

Parā-gandah rozī porā-gandah dil.
An uncertain living makes an uncertain mind.
(The miseries of a hand to mouth life.)

Pesh-i-tabīb marau, pesh-i-kār-āzmūdan birau.
Don't go to the doctor, go to the experienced.
(Experience beats learning.)

Pīrāṅ na-mīparand, murīdāṅ mī parānand.
The holy man can't fly, but his disciples can make him.
(For explanation see page 185, col. i.)

Pir shau biāmoz.
Be old and learn.
(Never too late to mend.)

Qadam-i-darveshāṅ radd-i-balā.
The feet of the holy scare away evil.

Qadr-i-afiyat kase dānad, ki ba musībat-i-griftār āyad.
He knows the value of ease who once falls into difficulty.

Qahr-i-darvesh bar jān-i-darvesh.
The poor man's rage only hurts himself.

Qaul--mardāṅ jāṅ dārad.
Un honest man's words carry weight.

Sabr talkh ast, va lekin bar-i-shīrīṅ dārad.
Patience is bitter but its fruit is sweet.

Safar kardah bisyār goyād darog.
Travellers tell many a lie.
(Traveller's tales)

Salāh na shud balā shud.
It was not an invitation but a misfortune.

Sang āmad o sakht āmad.
When a stone hits it hits hard.
(For explanation see page 208, col. i.)

Sarfiyāṅ rā magz bāyad chūṅ sagāṅ; Nahviyāṅ rā magz bāyad chūṅ shahāṅ.
A dog's brain for the accidence; But a king's brain for the syntax.
(Said of Arabic.)

Shamlā ba-miqdār-i-ilm.
His turban is as great as his learning.

Shanīdā kae bavad mānind-i-dīdā.
Hearing is not like seeing.

Sharm che kuttist ki pesh mardāṅ biāyad.
Is shame a bitch that she should come to men?
(For explanation see page 218, col. ii.)

Supurdam ba to māyā-i-khesh rā: Tū dānī hisāb-i-kam o besh rā.
I have made over my property to you: You now know all its good and bad points.
(A preface to books.)

Tama ra seh harf ast, har seh tihī.
Avarice has three letters and all three empty.
(For explanation see page 231, col. i.)

Tāzīm-i-kārī garāṅ muāf!
Working men are excused.
(From conventional formalities.)

Uzr-i-gunāh bad tar az gunāh.
An excuse for a sin is worse than the sin.
(Qui L'excuse s'accuse.)

Vazīre chunī shahr-yāre chunāṅ.
As the minister so the king.
(Because the king works through him.)

RUSTIC PROVERBS.

Ādhe Māghe kamlī kāṅdhe.
In the middle of February coats go over the shoulders.
(The winter is past.)

Aggam buddhī Bāniyā, pachchham buddhī Jāṭ.
The most wit to the Banyā, the least wit to the Jāṭ.

Andhrī gaiyā, dharam rakhvālī.
A blind cow, and faith her keeper.

Aṅḍva bail jūī kā savāl.
An entire ox is the worry of one's life.

Bahut atahtāī, jūī ke kāl hā.
A great oppressor is always in danger of his life.

Bāṅs kī jaṛ meṅ ghamoe jāme hue.
A prickly shurb grows in the roots of the bamboo.

Be-menh ke dānvrī, ghorā binā lagām,
Be-māth ke lashkar, tīnon bhail na-kām.
Ploughing the soil without rain, having a horse without a bridle, and an army without a leader, are three evil things.

Bhains dūdh jo karhvā pīve,
Hāngā ghate na jab lag jīve.
Who drinks boiled buffalo's milk will keep his strength through life.

Bhūke ber aghāē gānde.
Berries for the hungry, sugarcane for the full.
(To him that hath shall be given.)

Chākī pherī huī chūn kī dherī.
It is the turning of the mill and you 'll get flour.
(You 'll get nothing for nothing.)

Chamāron ke kose dhor nahīn marte.
Cattle don't die of the currier's curse.
(For explanation see page 51, col. i.)

Chha mahīne mimyānī to ek bachcha biyānī.
The she-goat was six months pregnant and produced one kid.
(Great boast, little roast)

Chikne galvā malvā ke.
The smooth cheek of a rich man.

Dāndā balā jādā ṭalā.
When the log burns the cold goes away.
(Care leads to success.)

Dhūl kī rassī baṭnā.
To twist a rope of sand.
(To draw blood from a stone.)

Gādar ānī ūn ko, baiṭhī chare kapās.
The sheep came to be shorn, but ate up the cotton field.

Ganvār kā pānsā toṛe pānsā.
The (practical) joke of a clown will break a rib.

Gānv bhāge, paghiyā lāge!
The village deserted, and the harvest on!

Ghar men hal na baldyā, mānge īkh haldyā!
Without a plough or oxen, he demands sugar-cane for his ploughing foe.

Ghar men nahīn tāgā albelā mānge pāgā.
There is not a thread in the house, and the blockhead wants a turban.

Goēnṛā khetī, sīkhā sānp, māī bhae kāran bādī bāp.
A field by the village, a man-eating serpent, a terrible mother, and a disagreeable father are bad things.

Her pher āve to kākṛī maṭkāve.
If I can get again, I'll again enjoy cucumber.
(For explanation see page 102, col. i.)

Honṭ hile na jibbhyā kholī, bhī sās kahe baḍ bolī.
Nor opened her lips, nor moved her tongue, and still the old woman scolded her.

Jab bhājan ko hoe lugāī toṛe koṭ aur phānde khāī.
When a woman wills to run away she will break the fort and leap over the ditch.
(For explanation see page 107 col.)

Jis ghar hoe kuchalyā nārī; sānjh bhor ho us kī khuārī.
The house that has a bad wife is on the eve of ruin. [kā dalyā.

Jis ghar hoe purakh kuchalyā us ghar hove khīr
The house that has a bad husband gets gruel for its milk and rice.
(For explanation see page 118, col. i.)

Jis ghar nārī phūṛī oh ghar jāno kūṛī.
The house of a slut is no better than a dunghill.

Jis ke bārah bigah bāngā, us kī kamar men ḍorā nahīn.
Who has twelve acres of cotton field, has not a rag to his back.

Jo koī khāē chane kā ṭūk pānī pīve sau sau ghūnṭ.
Who eats pease-pudding will drink a hundred gulps of water.
(For explanation see page 123, col. i.)

Jo koī khāē nibāh ke juār, mūl bane voh mūndh ganvār.
Who hath eaten millet from his birth, Hath been clodhopper from the beginning.
(Millet (juār) is very coarse food.)

Kamānī na pahiyā, " gāṛī jot mere bhaiya."
Nor spring nor wheels, and says he, " bring up the cart, friend "

Kān par ekjun nahīn chaltī.
Even a louse does not venture on his ears.
(Spoken of one who does not yield to advice.

Karkā sohe palī ne, bārah sohe mālī ne.
Pastorals suits the shepherd, and the song of the well the gardener.
(For explanation see page 131, col. ii.)

Kharsā pyārā bījnā, siyāle piyārī āg, Barkhā piyārī tīn chīz, kambal, chhāvā, rāg.
In summer I like a fan, in winter a fire,
In the rains a blanket, a roof and a song.

Khasam, devor donon, ek sās ke pūt yeh huāyā voh huā.
Your husband and his younger brother are sons of one mother; if it is not the former, then it is the latter.
(For explanation see page 137, col. i.)

Mātā bargī mamtā, saukan bargā bair;
Dūjā ko rākhe nahīn, dekhā sānjh saver.
A mother's love, a co-wife's hate; There is nothing like them, though thou search from morn to eve.

Mathvā, madārī kā kyā sāth?
What has a Hindoo to do with a Muhammadan!

Nāt kā na got kā bānṭā mānge poth kā.
Nor relative nor clansman, and he has the assurance to ask for a share.
(In the hereditary property.)

Rab na rābṛī, le uthe khābṛī!
(I never said a word) sweet or sour, and he drew his sword!

Sādh bhagat den jinhān asīs, sukhī rahen ve bis-ve bīs.
Whom saints and prophets bless, will surely be happy.

Sādhū kī jin sangat kīnī unhan kamāī pūrī kīnī
Who dwell with the holy reap a full reward.

Sānp singh jit deh pakhālen, Dhor, manukh hālan jūn hālen.
Where snakes and tigers lay their limbs, Men and cattle shake like an earthquake.

Sāvan khīr jo khāe sakāre, Mirag ḍhāl kur-chālen māre.
Who eats milk and rice in August will bound about like a deer.

Sustī burī re bālke, yā kūn jī se ṭār; Ratī bojhā sust ke lāge bojh pahāṛ.
Idleness is a bad thing, my lad, thrust it from thy life; Anounce weight to an idle man is as heavy as a mountain.

Tan phūar kā bhains sūn bhārī: Kahe "kaho mohe Nājo Pyārī."
The ninny is heavier than a buffalo, And asks to be called Miss Slip.
(Nājo is a aslim and slender girl; a slip of a girl.)

Tāṭ kāmlā, dolṛā, tinoṅ jāt gulām; Jit chāhe jit baiṭh kar turat karo bisrām.
Canvass, blanket and bedding are lowly things, On which thou canst take thy rest when thou wilt.

Tāṭ kāmle ghar mān ghāle; Bār batāve sāl dushāle.
He keeps canvass and blankets at home, and abroad calls them shawls.

Tujh par pare jo audhsā dil bich mat ghabrā Jab sāīn kī ho dayā kām turat ban jā.
Let not thy heart be downcast when adversity overtake thee. When God shall have mercy thy work will quickly prosper.

Turak, talaiyā, tol rā, na yeh kisī ke mīt. Bhīṛ paṛat mūnh pher len, rakhen na parīt.
A musalman, a wasp, and a parrot are nobody's friend: In time of difficulty these go away and show no love.

Urdī urdon kī bhalī, aur ras kī āchhī khīr; Lāj jo rākhe piv kī, voh bhī āchhī, bīr.
Pease-pudding of peas is best, and sweetened *khīr* is best: She is the best woman, friend, that up-holds her husband's honor.

Us ko sīkh na de khadhī jo ho kuttar nīch; Loh mekh nāhīn ghise kadhān pāthar bīch.
Never advise the cruel and base; An iron peg will never pierce through a stone.

SUPERSTITION.

Din ko sove rozī khove.
Who sleeps in the day-time loses his livelihood.

Divālī jīt, sāl bhar jīt.
Win at Divālī, win all the year round.
(For explanation see page 72, col. ii.)

Divālī kī rāt ko būnṭī bunṭī pukartī hai.
On the night of the Divālī every herb and plant finds tongue.

Donoṅ vaqt mile nahīn sīle sūraj kī ānkh phūṭ jāegī.
One should not sew when day meets night, as it puts out the eye of the day.

Dūbegā bhāṛū kā bhāṛū, rāt same ne de sae jhāṛū.
You will be utterly ruined if you sweep out your house at night.

Fajar fajar kī nānh kuchh nahīn.
No'in the early morning bodes no good.
(For explanation see page 61, col. i.)

Gine ginave totā pāve.
Who counts loses.

Girah apnā phal kar hī jātā hai.
Each star yields its fruit.

Jahān kuttā hotā hai, vahān nekī kā farishtah nahīn ātā.
Where the dogs are no good angels will come.

Jeṭhe laṛke laṛkī kī shādī Jeṭh men nahīn karte.
The first born is never wed in the month of Jeṭh (May and June).

Jummā chhoṛ, sanīchar nhāe, us kā sanīchar kadhī na jāe.
Who omits Friday and bathes on Saturday misfortune will never leave him.

Kāle ke āge chirāg nahīn jaltā.
No lamp will burn before a black snake.
(For explanation see page 128, col. i.)

Kanjā bhāgvān hotā hai.
Blue-eyed is fortunate.

Kaun kisī ke ave jāve? dānā pānī lātā hai.
No one visits another; it is the prospect of food that takes him there,

Kutte kī sī pasli phaṛke.
My heart beats like a dog's.
(For explanation see page 145, col. i.)

Maggah men marnā, agle janam men gadhā bannā.
Who dies in Maggah will be an ass in his next life.
(For explanation see page 152, col. i.)

Mūsī kā māl, nikle phūṭ ke khāl.
The miser's wealth breaks out in sores.
(It is unlucky and brings evil on his heir.)

Olti tale kā bhūt sattar purkhen kā nām jāne.
The ghost under the eaves has known the names of seventy ancestors.

Pichhlī roṭī khāē, pichhlī mat āē.
Who eats the last cake will be a fool.
(For explanation see page 184, col. ii.)

Rāt kī nīyat harām!
Plans made at night are wicked!

Rāt ko jhāṛū denī manhūs hai.
It is unlucky to sweep the house at night.

Rāt ko sānp kā nām nahīn lete hain.
Don't mention a serpent at night.
(For explanation see page 194, col. ii.)

Richh kā ek bāl bhī bahut hai.
One hair of a bear is enough.
(For explanation see page 195 col. i.)

Sadqā diye rad balā.
To give alms is to avert evil.

Samne pānī bharā kalsa ā-jāē, to achchhā shagūn hotā hai.
To meet a jar full of water is a good omen.

Sankh bāje sattar balā bhāje.
When the conch sounds seventy misfortunes fly.
(For explanation see page 208, col. ii.)

Sānp kī to bhāp bhī burī.
Even the breath of a serpent is bad.

Seh kā kānṭā ghar men mat rakkho, laṛāī hogī.
Don't keep a porcupine's quill in the house or it will create strife.

Sonā pānā aur khonā dono bure.
To find gold or lose it are both bad.

Subah kī nānh achchhī nahīn.
Nay in the morning bodes no good.
(For explanation see page 225, col. i.)

Takhtī par takhtī; miyānjī kī āī kambakhtī.
When slate is on slate, there's bad luck for the master.
(For explanation see page 229, col. ii.)

Tāl se talaīyā gahrī, sānp se sanpolā jahrī.
A lake is deeper than a pond, and a young serpent more poisonous than a large one.

Tarāzū e khaṛe ho-kar na tolo: barakat jātī hai.
Don't use your scales standing: you will lose your luck.

Tetrī beṭī rāj rajāve, tetrā beṭā bhīkh mangāve.
A daughter after two sons brings prosperity, a son after two daughters, brings beggary.

Tītar baveā boljā to sagre kār hon ṭhīk; Dahne bolat na bhalā, sānch jān yeh sīkh.
If a partridge cry on the lefs all your wishes will thrive, If it cry on the right believe me it is not a good omen.

Tū kahe so sach hai, buddhī! tū kahe so sach!
What you say is true, old lady! What you say is true.
(For explanation see page 242, col. ii.)

Tulū aur gurūb ke vaqt sijdā mana hai.
At actual sunset and sunrise you must not kneel to pray.

Udher ke roṭī na khāo, nangī hotī hai.
It is not good to peel off the upper layer of bread and eat it.

Ugle to andhā, khāve to koṛhī.[becomes leprous.
If he vomits it goes blind, if swallows it
(To be on the horns of a dilemma.)
(For explanation see page, 249, col. i.)

Ulṭī mālā phernā.
To tell beads backwards.

Ulṭī saifī paṛhnā.
To say thesaifi backwards.
(For explanation see page 250, col.i.)

WOMENS PROVERBS.

Ab satvantī hokar baiṭhī lūṭkar sansār.
She sits a saint, grown rich on a world's plunder.

Āe Chait suhāvan, phūlar mail chhuṛāvan.
When April comes her dirt leaves her.
(For explanation see page 3, col. ii.)

Āegā kuttā to pāegā ṭikkā.
When the dog comes he will get his share. (Who works gets.)

Ae mere agle, man māne so karle.
My husband, you can do with me as you choose.
(For explanation see page, 4, col. i.)

Āge hāth, pichhe pāt.
A hand before and a leaf behind.
(For explanation see page 5, col. i.)

Āī na gaī chhochho, ghar kī men rahī.
A chance guest, she stuck to the house.
(A piece of good luck.)

Āī na gaī, kaule lag gyāban huī.
A chance passenger, she leant against the pillar and became pregnant.
(For explanation see page 6, col. ii.)

Āī na gaī, kaun nāte bahin!
Never even seen, how is she sister?

Aisan suhāg morā nit uṭh holā.
May such good fortune be never mine!

Aise pe to aisī: kājal diye pe kaisī?
So beautiful! How will she be with her eyes touched up with lamp black?

Aisī aisī chaṛī bal bal jāīn, nau nau patrī bhatāīn khāīn.
Accept the invitation where you 'll get nine plates of rice.

Aisī bahū syānī, je painchā mānge pānī!
Such a clever wife! She asks for water on loan!

Aisī hotī kātan hārī, to kāhe phirtī mārī mārī?
Had you spun well, would you have been deserted and forlorn?

Aisī laṭkī, ki bhuī men paṭkī.
So degraded as to touch the earth.

Āj napūtī, kal napūtī, ṭesū phūlā sadā napūtī.
To-day barren, to-morrow barren; even when the *palās* tree blossoms still barren.
(For explanation see page 8, col. ii.)

Akelī lakṛī kahān tak jale?
How long will a single stick burn?
(One man cannot do the work of ten.)

Ālā, de nivālā.
O niche, give a morsel.
(For explanation see page 9, col. i.)

Alā lūn, balā lūn, sahnak sarkā lūn.
I'll love you, and I'll serve you, but I'll steal your dinner.
(Said of a hypocrite.)

Albelī ne pakāī khīr; dūdh kī jagah ḍālā nīr.
The ninny made *khīr* of water instead of milk.
(*Khīr* is a dish made of rice and milk.)

Al gaī, bal gaī, jalve ke vaqt tal gaī.
She loves and she serves, but in the time of need she 's off.

Āmne sāmne ghar karūn, aur bīch karūn maidān.
I will take up my abode right in front, and there shall be no screen between us.
(Said of an impudent, shameless woman.)

Āṅkh eko nahīn, kajrautī dau ṭhāīn!
Eyes she has none, but she has ten pots of lamp-black (for her eyes)!

Āṅkh na dīda kāṛhe kashīda!
Blind of the eyes the needle plies!

Āṅkhon sukh, kaleje ṭhanḍak.
The delight of the eye, the joy of the heart
(A son.)

Āṅkh pharke dahnī, māyā mile ki bahnī:
Āṅkh pharke bāīn, bhaiyā mile ke sāīn.
When the right eye throbs it's mother or sister coming.
When the left eye throbs it's brother or husband coming.

Anokhī jurvā sāg men shurvā.
The silly hussy has made broth of the greens.
(*Shorbā* is soup made of meat.)

Antṛī men rūp buqchī men chhab.
Your beauty is in your stomach, and your grace is in your bundle.
(For explanation see page 15, col. i.)

Ā, paṛausan laṛen.
Come neighbour, let us fight.
(For explanation see page 15, col. ii.)

Āp paṛausan, mujh sī ho!
Come, neighbour, and be as I am.
(For explanation see page 15, col. ii.)

Āp hī nāk choṭī giriftār hain.
His very nose and hair are captives.
(He is hemmed in with difficulties.)

Apnā ke roṭī tīn gīt gāutī!
With one loaf for herself only she sings a song of three!

Apne bāolon roīye, aur ke bāolon hanṅiye.
Cry over your own idiot (son); but laugh over another's.

Ane ko nā, ante, khablā khablā bante.
He gives to others and not to his own, and so is boiling water.
(For explanation see page 17, col. ii).

Apne pūt kuāre phiren, paṛausī ke phere.
Leaving her own sons bachelors she marries off other's sons.

Apnī kokh ka pūt nausādar.
The son of your own womb is invaluable.
(For explanation see page 18, col. ii.)

Apnī ṭāṅg ughāṛye aur āp hī lājon marye.
Expose your own leg and die of shame.
(To wash the family dirty linen in public.)

Aur kī bhuk na jāne, apnī bhūk āṭā sāne.
She cares nought for others' hunger, for herself she kneads the flour.

Bāhar ke khāen ghar ke gīt gāen.
While strangers eat, the household starves.
(For explanation see page 25, col. i.)

Bāhar miyān alalle talalle, ghar men chūye pakken.
Abroad my lord has cakes and wine, at home he cooks rats.

Bāhar miyān chhail chikaniyā, ghar men libṛī joē.
My lord abroad is a dandy, but at home there is a draggle-tailed wife.

Bāhar Miyān jhaṅg jhaṅgāle, ghar men naṅgī joē.
Abroad my lord goes in gorgeous array with a naked wife at home.

Bāhar Miyān Panjhazārī, ghar men bīvī karmon kī mārī.
Abroad he is my Lord Governor, at home his wife is a victim of fate.
(A poor miserable creature.)

Bāhar miyān sūbedār, ghar men bīvī jhoke bhāṛ.
My lord abroad is a captain, but at home his wife feeds the oven.
(The occupation of a menial.)

Bahuṛyā ke baṛ dulār, hānḍī bāsan chhūahī na pāvās!
Many caresses to his wife, but she must not touch the house vessels!
(Sham love.)

Bāl bāl gunahgār.
Faulty in every hair.
(Tor explanation see page 27, col. i.)

Bālon hāth chhinālā aur kāgon hāth sandesā.
An assignation through a child and a message through a crow.

Bandī jab shādī kartī hai, tab aisī hī kartī hai.
When her slave celebrates a wedding she does it as well as this.
(Said in contempt of an entertainment.)

Bāndī ke āge bāndī āī, logon ne jānā āndhī āī.
A slave girl got a handmaid, and the people thought a storm had come!

Bāṅdī ke āge bāṅdī meṅh gine nā āndhī.
When a slave girl gets a handmaid she takes no thought of rain or storm.
(For explanation see page 28, col. ii.)

Band ke jāë band meṅ nahīṅ rahte.
Born in bondage does not remain in bondage.
(Misfortune will not always cling to one.)

Bāṅh chhuṛāë jāt ho, nibal jāṅke moë; Hirde meṅ se jāoge to mard badūṅgī toë.
Shake yourself off and go, and think me powerless; If you go out of my heart then think yourself a man.

Banī ṭhire besvā, khole phire kesvā.
A woman with her hair down is a harlot.

Bāṅj achchhī ekaunj burī.
Better be barren than bear once.
(The barren woman is spared the loss of an only child.)

Bāṅj bajauṭī Shaitān kī langoṭī.
A barren woman is the Devil's breeches.
(The most wretched thing on earth.)

Bāṅj byānī soṅṭh uṛānī.
To expend dry ginger for the delivery of a barren woman.
(Great cry little wool.)

Bāṅj kyā jāne parsūtī kī pīṛā ?
What does a barren woman know of the pains of child-birth ?

Bāp kā nām Damṛī, beṭvā kā nām Chhakuṛyā, nātī kā nām Pachkauṛiyā, tīn pursā bītī chhadām na pūrā bhayā.
The father Damṛī, the son Chhakauṛī, the grandson Pachkauṛī, three generations passed and a *chhadam* was not complete.
(For explanation see page 31, col. i.)

Baṛoṅ kā baṛā hī bhāg.
Great men have great fortune.

Barsāt bar ke sāth.
The rainy season is best for living with one's husband.

Bāsī mūṅh phokā pānī augun kare hai.
Plain water is bad for a stale mouth.

Bāsī phūloṅ meṅ bās nahīṅ, pardesī balam terīas nahīṅ.
As there is no fragrance in a withered flower, so is there no hope of aid from a husband in a foreign land.

Bas-kar miyāṅ bas-kar ; dekhā terā lashkar !
Enough good sir, enough; I have seen your army.
(Said in derision to a boaster.)

Baṭyā āūṅ, baṭyā jāūṅ, khetak charāūṅ na bālī khāūṅ.
By the footpath I come, by the footpath I go, on the edge I graze, and destroy not one ear of the corn.
(For explanation see page 34, col. ii.)

Battīs dāṅt kī bhākhā khālī nahīṅ jātī.
The words of thirty-two teeth will never fail.
(For explanation see page 35, col. ii.)

Bech bech, merī pakhnī kā byāh.
My tomboy is married off by the sale of all my property.
(For explanation see page 36, col. i.)

Be-dard qasāī kyā jāne pīṛ parāī !
What knows the merciless butcher of the pain of others ?

Be-dharmā bhaī, aur behnā ke sāth meṅ !
I became a pervert to marry a wool-carder !
(For explanation see page 36, col. ii.)

Begāne kāran lūlī ṭore ṭāṅg.
To lose a leg in another's cause.

Bejṛā ke pīsan-hārī gehūṅ kī gīt gāveṅ.
Grinding coarse grains she sings the song of wheat.
(She talks very big : draws the long bow.)

Be-lajjī bahuryā par ghar nāche.
A shameless wife dances at others' houses.

Beṭā lāegā chamārī, voh bhī kah lāegī bohū hamārī.
If my son should marry a low woman, she would still be called my daughter-in-law.
(Make the best of a bad bargain.)

Beṭā mariyo, par tissar na paṛiyo.
May my son die, rather than I get a third.
(For explanation see page 37, col. ii.)

Beṭī sasurā na jatī, man man gājatī.
The daughter goes not to her father-in-law's house and frets and fumes to herself.
(A common incident in native life.)

Be-vaqt kī shahnāī, mūë kūṛh ne bajāī.
The fool plays the pipe at the wrong time.
(For explanation see page 38, col. i.)

Bhādoṅ kī chhāchh bhūtoṅ ko ; Kātak kī chhāchh pūtoṅ ko.
Buttermilk in August for the devil, in October for your children.

Bhājī kī bhājī ; kyā dūsre kī mohtājī ?
A present for a present, what more can one require.
(Short debts long friends.)

Bhalā huā didī gaune gaī, dīde kī pharyā maī kā bhaī.
It is well that my husband's sister is married and gone, for I shall get her gorgeous clothes.
(For explanation see page 39, col. i.)

Bhal bhail piyā ke bhāgh māral, je begārī se bachal.
It is good that my husband has been devoured by a tiger, for I am saved from working for him.

Bhale bābā, band paṛī, gobar chhoṛ kashīde paṛī.
Father dear, I am a prisoner, and instead of picking upcowdung, I makeembroi- dery.
(For explanation see page 39, col. ii.)

Bhalo bhayo merī maṭukī ṭuṭī, maiṅ dahī bechan se chūṭī.
It is well, that my pot is broken, for I am saved from selling the tyre.

Bhar hāth chūṛī paṭ sūṅ rāṅṛ !
Bracelets on her arms and a widow withal !
(For explanation see page 40, col. ii.)

Bharī thālī meṅ lāt mārnā.
To kick over the plate full of food.
(To quarrel with one's bread and butter.)

Bhāt bin rah jāve, piyā bin rahā na jāve.
You can go without your dinner, but not without your lover.

Bhāt khāte, hāth pirāë!
She can't eat rice because it makes her hand [ache!
(She is so delicate.)

Bhat pare voh sonā, jis se tūṭeṅ kān.
Fire burn the gold that splits the ears!
(For explanation see page 41, col. i.)

Bhīt hogī to leo bahotere chaṛh raheṅge.
While the wall stands it receives lots of whitewash.
(While the bones last flesh there will be.)

Bhojan na bhāt, naihar kā samād!
Nor bread nor rice at home, or at my father-in-law's.
(The widow, who is ill-treated wherever she be.)

Bhūl gaī nār, hīng ḍāl diyā bhāt meṅ.
The woman has blundered and put the asafœtida into the rice.
(For explanation see page 43, col. i.)

Bhūlī, re Rāghuā, terī lāl pagiyā par.
I was taken in, Rāghuā, by your gay red [turban.
(For explanation see page 43, col. ii.)

Bhus meṅ chīngī ḍāl Jamālo dūr kharī!
Jamālo fired the straw and stood aloof!
(A mischief maker: a fire brand: an incendiary.)

Bhattā kā bhagvā, mūṅjakdorī, bīvī dusoī chhat naihā mor!
With a gown of sack cloth, and a thick rope for the strings she thinks none like her!

Bībī haiṅ bharmālī kān pītar kī bālī!
My lady is very consequential on the strength of a brass ear-ring!

Bībī Khailā, do chitte, ek mailā.
Madam Slut has two white and one dirty [(skirt.)
(A whited sepulchre.)

Bībī Khailā, do jaṭṭī ek melā.
Madam Slut and two farmers' wives make [a fair.
(Three women and a goose make a market.)

Bībī ko bāndī kahā, haṅs dī; bāndī ko bāndī kahā ro dī.
Call a lady a slave and she will laugh; call a slave a slave and she will fret.

Bībī Makke na gaiṅ, lāḍlī ho āīṅ.
My lady did not go to Mecca, yet she became a darling.
(Kissing goes by favor.)

Bībī vāre bāndī khāë, ghar kī balā kahīṅ na jāë.
The wife gives alms, the slave girl takes them, and the misfortunes of the family still remain in the house.
(For explanation see page 4, col. i.)

Bībī nek bakht damṛī kī dāl tīn vaqt.
A careful housewife makes a penny worth of peas serve for three meals.

Bī Daultī apne tehe meṅ āp hī khaultī.
Madam Purse-proud boils in her own flames.
(Fries in her own fat.)

Billī ke bhāgoṅ chhīṅkā ṭūṭ paṛā.
It was the cat's luck that the net broke.
(For explanation see page 44, col. ii.)

Bin bulāë ahmaq le dauṛe sahnak.
The fool has come uninvited with a platter.
(For explanation see page 45, col. i.)

Bin bulāī Domnī laṛke bāle samet āī.
Uninvited the songstress comes with all her children.

Birachh kī chhāyā aur purush kī māyā.
The shade of a tree and the influence of a man (go with them.)

"*Bīvī, bīvī, īd āī.*" "*Chal, haram-zādī, tujhe kyā?*"
"My lady, my lady, the feast has come!" "Go along you wretch, what has it to do with you?

"*Bīvī bīvī īd āī,*" *Chal, murdār, tujhe apnī tikyā se kām?*"
"My lady, my lady" the feast has come!" "Go you wretch, and mind your loaf of bread!".

Bole ke na chāle ke, maiṅ to sūte ke bhalī.
No good for talk or company, I'm the one for [sleep.
(For explanation see page 46, col. II.)

Bolī boli to ye bolī, "Merī jūtī bole."
When she did speak all she said was, "May my shoe speak."
(She would not talk at all.)

Boyā na jotā, Allah Miyāṅ ne diyā potā.
Without sowing or ploughing God gave him a grandson.
(For explanation see page 47, col. i.)

Bulbul kā sā choṅḍā.
Hair braided like a crested shrike.
(For explanation see page 47, col. ii.)

Burhā chochlā janāze ke sāth.
An old woman's wantonness ceases at her [funeral.

Būṛh bhaī guïyāṅ, dimāg mor vaise.
My friend has grown old, but her airs are the same.
(Skittishness in old age.)

Būṛh bhail, buṛh ghaus na chhūṭal.
He has grown old but his childishness has not left him.

Būṛh na savād ghiū khichṛī.
An old man has no taste for dainties.

Chabokar so laṛokar.
Joking leads to fighting.

Chāhe kodoṅ dalāle, chāhe maṅḍvā pisāle.
Be it wheat or be it corn, I'll grind and pound it for you.
(For explanation see page 49, col. i.)

Chāh karūṅ, pyār karūṅ, chūlhe tale aṅgār dharūṅ, jal jāë to maiṅ kyā karūṅ?
I'll love him, and I'll caress him, and I'll put fire under him; if it burn him, what can I do?
(Sham affection.)

Chakkī pherī huī chūn kī ḍherī.
It is the turning of the mill that makes the flour heap.

Chakkī men kaul ḍāloge, to chūn pāoge. [flour.
Throw grain into the mill and you'll get
(You'll get nothing for nothing.)

Chakkī tale ghar terā nikal, sās, ghar merā.
Get out, thou mother-in-law, thy house is under the mill stone; this house is mine.
(For explanation see page 49, col. ii.)

Chakmak dīda, khāë malīda.
Wanton eyes are on dainties fed.
(Said of harlots.)

Chal chakhe! mere mūnh mat lag.
Away! avaunt! don't stick to my mouth.
(Don't talk with me.)

Chal, chhāon, main āī hūn, jumla pīr manāī hūn. [invoked all the saints.
Go on, shadow; I will follow, for I have
(For explanation see page 50, col. i.)

Chale na jāne, āngan ṭeṛhā. [crooked.
Can't walk because, forsooth, the yard is
(A bad workman quarrels with his tools.)

Chalī chalī āī saut ke pīhar. [co-wife.
She went for refuse to the family of the
(For explanation see page 50, col i.)

Chalnī men gaī dohne; karmon ko kā dosh?
She went to milk with a sieve, so what blame to fate?

Chale na jāe, gaṭhrī murautho.
He can't walk and a bundle on his head.

Chalo, sakhī, wahān chalen jahān basen Brij Rāj;
Goras bechat, Hari milen; ek panth do kāj.
Come, friend, let us go to the place where the sovereign of Brij lives, To sell our milk and meet with Krishna, and thus kill two birds with one stone.

Chanbelī chāo men āī, Bakhtāvar reoṛiyān bānṭe.
The jasmine has begun to bloom, for Bakhtāvar is dispensing sweets.
(For explanation see page 51, col. ii.)

Chanbelī chāo men āī, Bakhtiyāre sāth lāī.
Show my Lady Jasmine favor; And she'll bring her whole family.

'*Chaonḍī, ghar līpegī?*' '*Nahīn, nigoṛe, khodūngī.*'
'*Chandī, ghar khodegī?*' '*Nahīn, nigoṛe, lipūngī.*'
'You shrew, will you plaster the floor?' 'No, you wretch, I'll dig it.' 'You shrew, will you dig the floor?' 'No, you wretch! I'll plaster it.'
(Mary, Mary, so contrary.)

Chanechirunjī ho gae, gehūn ho gai dākh; Ghar men gahne tīn hain, charkhā, pīṛhī, khāṭ.
Peas dear as almonds, wheat as raisins, And three ornaments only in the house, a spinning-wheel, a stool and a bed.
(Hard time.)

Chapnī likhkar sir par dharī, nikal paṛā yā nikal paṛī.
The inscribed platter is placed upon her head, a fairy boy or fairy girl will come out.
(For explanation see page 52, col. ii).

Chār din kā rang chang: chhoṛ dahī jarvā, morā sang!
Your love lasts four days only: none of your company, you mean brute! [bhaiyā.

Chār ghar-chau bhaiyā, tekrā bīch men bhikhon
Four brothers dwell in four houses, and one of them is a beggar.
(The inequality of men.)

Charhī karhāī tel, na āyā to kab āegā?
The oil may keep away, if it comes not when the frying pan is on the fire.

Chhab gaṭhrī men, joban rakābī men.
Show in his bundle, and youth in his platter.
(Fine feathers make fine birds.)

Chhadām men laṛāī, paise men sughaṛ bhalāī.
A half penny will settle a row about a farthing.
(For explanation see page 54, col. ii.)

Chhāj bole so bole, chhalnī bhī bole jis men bahattar sau chhed.
If the winnowing fan speak, it is well, but if the seive full of holes speak, what then?
(For explanation see page 54, col. ii.)

Chhāvat manḍvā gāvat gīt, piyā bin lāgat sab anrīt. [seemly without a lover.
Singing songs and making a bower is all un-

Chhelī jī se gaī, khāne-vālon ko savād na āyā.
The goat lost its life, but the eaters were not pleased,
(Said of unappreciated self sacrifice.)

Chhīle chār, baghāre pānch.
She peeled but four, and brought ont five.
(Said tauntingly to a conceited daughter-in-law.)

Chhināl kā 'beṭā babuā, re babuā'
A harlot's child is every body's darling.
(For explanation see page 56, col. i.)

Chhiṭāk chūn, chaubāre rasoī! [top.
An ounce of meal and a feast on the house

Chhoṛ jhāṛ, mujhe ḍūban de.
O bramble! let me down.
(For explanation see page 56, col. i.)

Chhoṛo, Bī Billī, chūhā lanḍūrā hī jiegā.
Let go the rat, my Lady Cat, he will live though he has lost his tail.

Chhoṭā ghar, baṛā samdhiyānā.
A small house and large connections.

Chhoṭī nanad angyā kā band, baṛī nanad bijlī basant.
My younger sister-in-law is as my bodice strings, my elder sister-in-law is as the summer lightning.
(For explanation see page 56 col, ii.)

Chhurī bhalī na kaṭārī.
The knife is no better than the dagger.

Chhūṭ bhalāī sāre gun.
He has all the qualities except goodness.

Chikanyā faqīr, makhmal kā langoṭ!
A foppish beggar with velvet breeches!

Chikna dekh phisal pare.
A fair appearance misleads.

Chikne gāl tilinyāṅ ke aur jare bare bhurjinyāṅ ke.
The oilman's cheeks are smooth and shiny, the grain-parcher's burnt brown.

Chillar chunne se bhagvā halkā hove?
The breeches won't grow lighter for picking out the lice.
(Cheese paring won't result in large savings.)

Chirāg meṅ battī aur āṅkh pe paṭṭī.
A wick in the lamp and a bandage over the [eyes,
(Said of a sleepy head.)

Chiryā apnī jān se gaī, khāne vāle ko savād na āyā.
The sparrow lost its life and still the eater [was not satisfied.
(For explanation see page 58, col. ii.)

Chīz na rākhe āpnī aur choroṅ gālī de.
He takes no care of his things and then abuses the thieves.

Chor chorī se gayā, to kyā herā-pherī se bhī [gayā?
The thief has left off stealing, but has he also left off hunting?
(For explanation see page 58, col. ii.)

Choṭ lagī pahāṛ kī aur toreṅ ghar kī sil.
Hurt by the hill he goes home to break the grind-stone.
(Said of one vents his rage on his wife.)

Chūhā bil meṅ samātā na thā, kānoṅ bāṅdhā chhāj.
The rat was already unable to enter his hole and he tied a winnowing far to his ears.
(For explanation see page 60 col, ii.)

Chūhe hāth lagī haldī kī girah, pansārī hī ban baiṭhā.
The mouse got hold of a piece of turmeric and set up a druggist's shop.

Chūlhe āg na ghare pānī, ūpar hī ūpar jā gai [bānī!
No fire in her grate, no water in her jar, may she fly away above!

Chūlhe, chakkī, sab hī kām pakkī.
She is quite up to the hearth and the mill.
(For explanation see page 60, col. ii.)

Chūlhe kā rāo 'lāo hī lāo' pukāre.
The king of the kitchen always cries 'more, [more.'
(Said of a gormandiser.)

Chūlhe kī, na chakkī kī.
Nor fit for the hearth, nor fit for the mill.
(She can neither bake nor grind flour.)

Chūlhe pīchhe soveṅ aur taihrī ko toheṅ.
He sleeps behind the hearth and feels the empty plate.
(Living from hand to mouth.)

Chuniye, khudiye poslon dhīyā, Ail damdā, le gail dhiyā.
Bring up a daughter on cakes and tarts,
And a son-in-law comes and takes her away.

Churāve na th-vālī, nām lage chīr-kuṭhī vālī kā.
A nose-ringed woman steals, and a ragged wench is charged with it.
(For explanation see page 61, col. ii.)

Chuṭiyā ko tel nahīṅ, pakauroṅ ko jī chāhe.
No oil for her locks and she longs for fried cakes.
(For explanation see page 61, col. ii.)

Dādā mareṅge to potā rāj kareṅge.
When the grandsire dies, the grandsons reign.
(*Le roi est mort, vive le roi.*)

Dahī bechan chalīṅ, pīṭh pichhārū kamoiyā.
She goes out to sell her tyre, and hangs the pitcher down her back.
(Ashamed to put it on the head: above her work.)

Dāī jāne apnī hāī.
The midwife knows her own feelings.
(For explanation see page 12, col. ii.)

Dāī ke sir pān phūl.
On the head of the nurse are betel and flowers.
(For explanation see page 62, col. ii.)

Dāī se peṭ chhupānā.
To hide the belly from the midwife.
(For explanation see page 62, col. ii.)

Dāī se peṭ nahīṅ chhiptā.
You can't hide the belly from the mid- [wife.

Dakkhan gaē na bāore, rahe Chanderī chhāē.
Who went to the Dakkhan never returned but took up his abode at Chanderī.
(For explanation see page 62, col. ii.)

Daliddar ghar meṅ non pakvān.
Salt is a delicacy in the house of poverty.

Damṛī kī arhar, sārī rāt kharar.
A farthing's worth of peas, and the sound of grinding all night.
(Great cry and little wool.)

Damṛī kī dāl, āp hī kuṭnī āp hī chhināl.
With only a farthing's worth of split peas, I must be host and guest myself.
(There is not enough for one person.)

Damṛī kī dāl, "būā patlī na ho."
A farthing's worth of pease, and "be careful sister, that (the soup) be not thin."
(To express a miser who exacts impossibilities.)

Damṛī kī ghoṛī chhā paserī dāna.
A farthing mare wants thirty sers of corn.
(Which would be worth a rupee.)

Damṛī kī guṛyā ṭakā ḍolī kā.
A penny for fetching a half-penny doll.
(Said of the weddings of the poor.)

Damṛī kī nihārī meṅ ṭāṭ ke ṭukṛe.
Farthing soup is made of (soaked) can- [vas.

Ḍaṛhyālā dhan.
A treasure of a beard.
(For explanation see page 64, col. ii.)

Ḍar na dahshat, utār phirī khishtak.
Nor fear nor awe, she goes about naked.

Darvāze par āī barāt, samdhan ko lagī haqās.
The marriage procession has arrived at the gate, and the bride's mother feels a call of nature.

Dasoṅ ungliyā, dasoṅ chirāg.
Her ten fingers are ten lamps.
(She is highly accomplished.)

Dātā datār sutnī utār.
(My husband) is so liberal that he would even take off my trousers to give them away.

Ḍāyan bhī das ghar chhoṛkar khātī hai.
Even a witch will pass over ten houses before she fastens on her prey.
(For explanation see page 66, col. i.)

De duā samdhāne ko, nahīṅ phirtī do do dāne ko.
Call blessings on the marriage relati ons, but for whom you would have been a beggar.
(Honor to whom honor is due.)

Dekhā na bhālā sadqe gaī khālā.
The aunt is devoted to the nephew whom she has never seen.
(For explanation see page 66, col. ii.)

Dekhā so khāyā, na mūṅh pāoṅ jogā.
He ate what he saw and nothing saved for his face or feet.
(Living from hand to mouth.)

Dekhe ke baurahiyā, āve pāṅchoṅ pīr.
In appearance she is mad, but she knows how to invoke the five *pīrs.*
(For explanation see page 66, col. ii.)

Dekhe ko buḍḍhī, kām ko āṅdhī.
An old woman to look at, but a whirl-wind at her work.
(Not much to look at, but a devil to go.)

Dekhī, pīr, terī karāmāt!
Your miraculous powers are known, my saint!
(We know the length of your tether.)

Dekhī 'Rām!' terī kartūt.
I know 'Rām!' thy wondrous works.
(See preceding.)

Dekhiye dīdār aur māriye paizār.
Look at them, but don't touch them.
(For explanation see page 67, col. i.)

Dekhnā so pekhnā.
To see is to desire.

Dekho re, Ahirinyāṅ ke ḍiṭhā, Chhaṅṭlas chāur, paroslas pīṭhā.
Look at the perversity of the cowherd's wife; She takes out grains and serves the husk.

Dekho Miyāṅ ke chhand band, phāṭā jām tīnp, band.
Look at this gentleman's consequentialirs a and his tattered robe with three stra ps.
(Whereas it ought to have eight or nine.)

Dekh paṛausan jal marī.
My neighbour saw and died with envy.

Ḍeṛh pāo āṭā, pul par rasoī.
A pound of flour and a dinner on the bridge.
(In a public place: a vain show.)

Dhable meṅ khāk.
Dust on her skirt.
(An abuse.)

Dhadhāegā so butāegā.
A blazing fire is soon out.
(Pride goes before a fall.)

Ḍhāk tale kī phūaṛ, Mahve tale kī sughaṛ.
A blockhead under a Ḍhāk tree is as good as a clever fellow under a Mahvā.
(For explanation see page 68, col. ii.)

Dhān, pān, pānī Kātag; suād jānī.
Rice, betel and water taste best in October.

Dhān sūktā hai, kavvā taṛtaṛātā hai.
As long as the rice is drying the crows will keep on cawing.
(For explanation see page 69, col. i.)

Dhāo dhāo karam likhā, soī pāo!
Work on and get what's in your fate!
(For explanation see page 69, col. i.)

Dhī beṭī apne ghar bhalī.
Daughters are best in their own houses.
(i. e. their husbands' houses.)

Dhī mūī, jaṅvāī chor.
The daughter dead, the son-in-law is as a thief.
(That is, no more seen.)

Dhī na beṭī, udhal gaī samdheṭī.
Nor child, nor daughter, and she cries out that her daughter's sister-in-law has done wrong.
(For explanation see page 70, col. i.)

Dhī na dhiyānā, āp hī kamānā, āp hī khānā.
Nor daughter-in-law nor son-in-law, whatever he earns goes into his own stomach.

Dhīyā pūt ke na gātī, bilaiyā ke gātī.
No clothing for his son or daughter, but for his cat (mistress).

Dhobī chhoṛ saqqā kiyā, rahī Khizar ke ghāṭ.
She left the washerman, and wedded a water-bearer, but still her fate is connected with water.
(For explanation see page 70, col. ii.)

Ḍhol bāj; dammāme bāje.
The large drums followed the small ones.
(For explanation see page 70, col. ii.)

Dhotī thī do pāoṅ, dhone paṛe chār pāoṅ.
There were but two feet to wash, and there are now four.
(For explanation see page 71, col. i.)

Din ko ūnī ūnī, rāt ko charkhā pūnī.
She saunters all day to spin at night.
(For explanation see page 72, col. ii.)

Divāl rahegī, to leo bahotere chaṛh rahenge.
While there is a wall lots of the plaster will adhere.
(While there is life, flesh will grow.)

yā Dīdār se, lāgī hāth khāne.
He gave her (food) at a distance and she sat down to eat it on the spot.
(For explanation see page 73, col. i.)

Dīyā na bātī, muṇḍo phire itrātī.

There is neither lamp nor candle and the widow is strutting about.
(For explanation see page 73, col. ii.)

Dīye kī raushnī mahshor tak.
The lamp's light extends to the day of judgment.
(For explanation see page 73, col. ii.)

Ḍolī, āī ḍolī āī, mere man meṅ chāo ; Ḍolī meṅ se nikal paṛā bhoṅkṛā bilāo !
The *ḍolī* comes, the *ḍolī* comes and my heart longs (for her) ; But out of the *ḍolī* has come an ugly old cat.
(For explanation see page 73, col. ii.)

Ḍolī na kahār, bīvī hūī haiṅ taiyār.
Nor palanquin nor bearers, and my lady is ready dressed.
(For explanation see page 74, col. i.)

Ḍūb kanth bharose tere !
Rieliance on you has ruined me, my husband!

Dūdhoṅ nahāo, pūtoṅ phalo.
May you bathe in milk and be fruitful in children.

Ḍug ḍug bāje, bahut nīke lāge, Nawā neg māṅge, uṭhā baiṭhī lāge !
It is pleasant to listen to the music, But how fidgety one gets when the musician wants his fee.

Dukhiyā dukh rove, sukhiyā jeb ṭove.
While the wretched weep, the happy feel their pockets.
(For explanation see page 75, col. ii.)

Dūr ke ḍhol suhāone.
Drums at a distance sound well.
(For explanation see page 76, col. ii.)

Ek bolī, do bolī, merī naktī satā saṭ bolī.
For a word or two my graceless offspring answers me at once.

Ek kauṛī gāṅṭhī, "chūṛā pahinūṅ ki māṭhī ?
One farthing's all she's got, and "shall I buy bangles or armlets ?"
(Foolish extravagance.)

Ek mere ghar annā, dūsre ravanā.
A servant girl I keep and eke an errand boy.
(How rich I am !)

Ek to kānī beṭī kī byāhī, dūsre pūchhne-vāloṅ ne jān khāī.
First I married my son to a one-eyed girl and now they worry me with questions.
(As to the looks of the bride.)

Ek to kānī beṭī, māī, dūsre pūchhne-vāloṅ ne jān khāī.
First I am the mother of a one-eyed girl and then I am worried by questions about her.
(When it comes to arranging her marriage)

Ek to Mīrāṅ the hī, dūje khāī bhāṅg.
He was already possessed by (the evil spirit) Mīrāṅ, and then he took to bhang.
(For explanation see page 80, col. ii.)

Fāl kī kauṛiyān mulla ko halāl.
Divination's fee the divine may lawfully take.
(Money earned is money lawfully got.)

Fātehā na darūd, khā gae mardūd.
The reprobate has eaten without saying grace.
(For explanation see page 82, col. i.)

Gandī boṭī kā gandā shorbā.
Stinking meat makes stinking broth.

Gāṅṭh na muṭṭhī, phar pharāë uṭṭhī.
Her heart is in a flutter (to buy), but she has no money in pocket or hand.

Gāo bajāo, banne ke lo!e kī nahīṅ.
You may play and sing, but you won't please the bridegroom.
(Work till you sweat, you 'll nothing get.)

Gāo bajāo, kauṛī na pāo.
Sing and play, but you won't get a farthing.
(More kicks than half-pence.)

Gauṅḍe āī barāt, bahū ko lagī hagās !
The bridegroom's procession has arrived and the bride has a call of nature.

Gāūṅ na gāūṅ, to birhā gāūṅ.
I'll sing of the pangs of love, if I am to sing at all.

Ghāī kī merī, tave ke terī.
What is in the pot is mine, what is on the plate is yours.
(Selfishness: *I* take what is cooked, *you* take what is still raw.)

Ghar-bār tumhārā koṭṭhī kuṭhle ke hāth na lagānā.
The whole house is your's but do not touch any thing in it.
(Sham love: sham professions of hospitality.)

Ghar-bār hansyā, na nigalne kā, na thūkne kā.
The house is full of sickles, and there is nothing to swallow or throw up.
(The house is full of knicks-knacks of no sort of utility.)

Ghar bhī baiṭho aur jān bhī khāo !
You stick at home and eat up lives.
(Jān-khānā, to worry to death: said to an idle son.)

Ghar chhoṛ hazīrā qāyam.
He has left his house to lodge in a mean place.
(A foolish fellow.)

Ghar ghar yehī lekhā.
In every house there is this one regulation.
(Every community has its peculiar customs.)

Ghar ghar yehī maṭyāle chūlhe haiṅ.
Every house has an earthen kitchen.
(All are alike.)

Ghar jalgayā jab, tab chūṛiyāṅ pūchhīṅ.
When the house was burnt they admired her bangles.
(For explanation see page 88, col. i.)

Ghar kāj, bahū gīndoṅ ko.
There is work in the house, but the bride is in the court-yard.

Ghar kī bībī hāṅḍnī, ghar kuttoṅ jogā.
When the mistress of the house is always gadding, the house becomes fit for the dogs.

Ghar meṅ āī joē, ṭeṛhī pagṛī sīdhī hoe.
When the bridle comes home, the crooked turban is soon put straight.
(For explanation see page 89, col. i.)

Ghar meṅ bhūnī bhāng nahīṅ, aur bahār neote sāṭh. [sixty guests invited.
Not even parched *bhang* in the house and
(Parched *bhang* is a worthless article.)

Ghar meṅ dekho chhalnī na chhāj; bāhar Miyāṅ Tīr-andāz.
At home nor sieve nor winnowing fan, and abroad my Lord Archer!
(For explanation see page 89, col. i.)

Ghar meṅ dhān na pān, bīvī ko baṛā gumān!
Nothing to eat or drink in the house, and the lady of it very proud!

Ghar meṅ diyā na bātī, mundo phire itrātī.
In the house nor lamp nor wick, but the shaven-head (widow) proudly strutting.

Ghar meṅ diyā, to masjid meṅ diyā.
Light your lamp first at home and afterwards at the mosque.
(Charity begins at home.)

Ghar meṅ ghar laṛāī kā ḍar. [quarrels.
With close neighbours there is a fear of

Ghar meṅ kharch nahīṅ, aṅṭhī pahirtī pokhrāj-jaṛal dāhaë. [ring.
Not a rap in the house, and sports a topaz

Ghar meṅ nahīṅ būr, beṭā māṅge motī-chor.
Not even bran in the house, and the son wants lollypop.

Ghar miltā hai to bar nahīṅ miltā, bar miltā hai to ghar nahīṅ miltā.
If you can get a good house you cannot get a good husband, if you can get a good husband you cannot get a good house.
(To marry your daughter.)

Ghar na bar.
Nor husband nor home.

Ghar se bāhar bhalā.
Better abroad than at home.
(Said to an idle or quarrelsome husband.)

Ghī kahāṅ gayā? Khichṛī meṅ. Khichṛī kahaṅ gaī? Piyāroṅ ke peṭ meṅ.
Where is the butter gone? Into the Khichṛī. Where is the Khichṛī gone? Into my dear one's stomach.
(For explanation see page 90, col. ii.)

Ghī saṅvāre kām, baṛī bahū kā nām.
The flavor is in the ghī, but the eldest daughter-in-law gets the credit.
(Of being a good cook.)

Gin poiṅ, saṅbhāl khāiṅ.
She counts (her cakes) and bakes them, and then eats them with care.
(Living from hand to mouth)

Gobar kī sāṅjhī bhī pahrī oṛhī achchhī lagtī hai.
Even a *sāṅjhī* of cow dung looks well when dressed up.
(For explanation see page 91, col. ii)

Godī kā laṛkā mar jāë, peṭ kī āg bujhāë.
When the lapling dies, the belly quenches the fires of grief.
(*i. e.* all sorrow for the child gives way to hunger.)

God kā chhoṛ peṭ ke kī ās?
Losing one child in her lap she depends on her womb for another
(A bird in hand is worth two in the bush.)

Gojhe kā ghāo, rānī jāne yā rāo.
The hidden wounds only the king or the queen can know.
(The skeleton in the cupboard.)

Gond, panjīrī aur hī khāeṅ, Jachhā rānī paṛī karhāen. [in woman simply groans.
The strangers eat the candle and the lying

Gudṛī se bībī āīṅ, 'Shekhjī, kināre ho!'
The lady comes in from the market and says 'out of the way, sir!'

Guṛiyoṅ ke byāh meṅ chīoṅ kī bel. [seeds.
At a doll's marriage the gifts are tamarind
(Said of the very poor.)

Hagāse laṛke ke nathne pahchāne jāte hoiṅ.
The child's nostrils show when it wants to go to stool.

Hāl kā na qāl, kā ṭukṛā roṭī chamchā dāl kā
Nor enthusiasm nor doctrine; a bit of bread and a spoonful of peas is all he is fit for.

Halke pichhoṛe, uṛ uṛ jāeṅ. [away.
Winnow hollow grain and it will all fly

Hal na sakūṅ mere sau bakhre.
I can't move, but I claim a hundred shares.
(Applied to one who is lazy and greedy.)

Hamāre hāṅ se āg lāī nām rakhā basandar.
She brought fire from my house, and called it *basandar*.
(For explanation see page 96, col. ii.)

Hamārī bismellah aur ham par hī chhū.
My own charm practised on me.

Ham se bahū baṛī syānī painchā māṅge pānī.
The bride is cleverer than me, she asks for water on loan!

Hāṅḍī na ḍoī sab pat khoī.
Nor pot nor spoon, and all my credit gone.

Haṅs haṅs khāīye phūaṛ kā māl.
Enjoy the ninny's wealth and laugh at her.
(A fool and his money are soon parted.)

Haṅsvā dūr, ki paṛausin kī nāk?
Which is furthest off, the sickle or the neighbour's nose?

Haṅsvā re! tūṅ ṭeṛh kāhe? a to apnā gauṅ se?
'Sickle, why are you crooked?' Because it suits me!'

Haq kahe so dārī jār.
Tell the truth and be abused.
(The candid friend.)

Hardegī chamchā.
A spoon for every pot.
(A jack of all trade: also a faithless husband.)

Hari gun gāve dhakkā pāve, chūtaṛ hilāve ṭakā pāve.
Sing psalms and you will be pushed aside, have a wanton gait and you will get money.

Hāth dekhan ko ārsī kyā?
Why keep a glass to look at the hand?
(For explanation see page 99, col. ii.)

Hāth kangan ko ārsī kyā hai?
To see the bracelet on your arm needs no mirror.
(For explanation see page 100, col. ii.)

Hāth kashīdah, āsmān dīdah.
Needle work in her hands and her eyes towards the sky.
(Want of proper attention: in the clouds.)

Hāth men lānā pāt men khānā.
Brings it in his hands and eats it from a leaf.
(To live from hand to mouth.)

Hāth men, na gāt men, main dhanvantī jāt men.
Nothing in her hands, and nothing on her body, and I am of a great caste!

Hāth na gale, nāk men, nāk men piyāz! ke ḍale!
Nothing on hands and neck and pieces of onion in her nose.
(For explanation see page 101, col. i.)

Hāth na muṭṭhī halbalā uṭhī.
With nothing in her fist she gets up in a hurry to buy.
(For explanation see page 101. col. i.)

Hāthon menhdī, pāvan menhdī, apne lachchhan aurān dendī.
She has stained her own hands and feet with *hinā* and recommends the same practice to others.
(For xplanation see page 101, col. i.)

Hāth pāon hilā, Bagwān degā.
Labor, and God will give.
(God helps those that help themselves.)

Hūr bhī saukan ko ḍāyan se burī hai.
To a co-wife a fairy is uglier than a goblin.

Īd pīchhe chāṅd mubārak?
Congratulation after the Īd.
(For explanation see page 104, col. ii.)

Īṅṭ kā ghar maṭṭī kar dīyā!
She has brought his brick house to dust.
(A bad manager.)

Itne kī kamāī nahīn, jitne kā lanhgā phaṭ gayā.
The earning will hardly cover the rents of the petticoat.

Jab bhūk lagī bharve ko tandūr kī sūjhī, aur peṭ bharā us kā to phir dūr kī sūjhī.
When he was hungry the rascal had his eyes on the kitchen, but when he was satisfied his eyes began to wander.
(Cupboard love.)

Jab se uge bāl, tab se yehī ahvāl.
He has been like this ever since his hair began to grow.
(For explanation see page 107, col. ii.)

Jab tak bahū kuārī, tab tak sās vārī;
Bahū āī god men, lāḍ gayā haud men.
As long as a maid is not wed the would-be mother-in-law is devoted to her. No sooner is she brought to her arms, than all her love goes down into the pit.
(Observation of Indian domestic life.)

Jab tak jīnā tab tak sīnā.
While we live we must sew.
(Work while we live.)

Jab tak karūn bābū bābū, tab tak karūn apne qābū.
While I call him "my lord my lord" I can keep him under my thumb.

Jachchā aur bachchā donon jīen!
May the lying-in-woman and her child both live.
(For explanation see page 108, col. i.)

Jag jalā to jalne de, main āp jaltī hūn.
If the world suffer, let it suffer, for I am suffering.

Jahān dekhen gunnā pūrī tahān jāen lurhī lurhī.
Wherever the cakes and sweets are she soon slips in.

Jahān dekhī roṭī, vahān mundāī choṭī.
She would shave her head for the sake of the bread.
(For explanation see page 109, col. i.)

Jahān dekhe tavā parāt, vahān gāve sārī rāt.
Wherever she sees plate and dish she sings the whole night.
(Said of a greedy person.)

Jaisā sūt, vaisī pheṭī; jaisī mā vaisī beṭī.
As the thread so the skein; as the mother so the daughter.

Jaise kanthā ghar rahe vaise rahe bides:
Jaisī orhī kāmlī, vaisā orhā khes.
It is all one to me whether my husband stay at home or live abroad. As I would as soon wear a blanket as a shawl.
(Contentment.)

Jaisī gaīn thīn vaisī āīn, haq mahar kā boriyā lāīn.
She came back as she had gone, and brought a mat for her marriage portion.
(Ill luck.)

Jaisī dāī āp chhināl, vaisī jāne sab sansār.
As a wet-nurse is wanton, so she thinks every woman a wanton.

Jaisī māī vaisī jāī.
As the mother, so the daughter.

Jaisī terī til-chaulī, vaisā merā gīt.
As your fee, my song shall be.

Jā ke kāran pahrī sārī vohī ṭāng rahī ughārī.
The same leg is exposed for which I had put on the skirt.
(Position not improved by marriage.)

Jā kī sās āchhī vā kā hī ghar vās;
Jā kī nakarā sās vā kā nahīn gudra.
Who has a good mother-in-law has the whole house; Who has a bad mother-in-law cannot live long in the house.

Jale pāon kī billī.
A cat with a burnt paw.
(For explanation see page 112, col. ii.)

Jal men khari piyāson mare.
Standing in water she dies of thirst.

Jannā aur marnā barābar hai.
The throes of childbirth are as the agonies of death.

Jān na pahchān "Khālā bari salām." [aunt."
Nor known nor recognized and "good morrow,

Jānte kā dil an-jānte kā kalejā. [foolish.
The soul of the wise and the heart of the
(For explanation see page 114, col. i.)

Jāo pūt Dakkhan vohī karam ke lakkhan.
My son if you go to Deccan, your fate will still be the same.

Jeore se nārā ghisnā hai. [neck with.
It is a thick rope that I have to rub my
(For explanation see page 115, col. i.)

Jijā ke māl par sālī mat vālī.
The sister-in-law vain of her brother-in-law's wealth.
(It is nothing to her : folly.)

Jis kā dar vohī nahīn ghar.
Whom most I fear is not at home.
(i. e. my husband, so now I can do as I like.)

Jis kā guiyān nahīn us kā kūkar guiyān.
Who has no friend has a dog for her friend.

Jis kā khāiye an pānī us kī kīje awādānī.
Bless him whose food you eat.

Jis kā marvā us gīt.
The songs are in his praise whose is the marriagebower.
(Who pays the fees hears the song)

Jis ke kāran jogan bhaī, voh saiyān pardes.
For whom I am turned a Jogan (female ascetic) is gone abroad.
(Unrequited love.)

Jis ke nahīn pūt, voh kyā jāne mayā.
Who has no son knows no motherly feelings.

Jis ke pās dhibuā, vohī hamārā babūā.
Who has the pence is 'your honor.'

Jis kī khāiye chandyā us kī kījiye bandyā.
Be the slave of him whose bread you eat.

Jive merā bhāī galī galī bhaujāī.
While my brother lives there's a wife for him in every lane.
(For explanation see page 121, col ii.)

Jo bar dekh tap muhe āve vohī bar mujhe biyahan āve!
Such a bridegroom is come to marry me, as I cannot look on without fever!

Kājal to sab lagāte hain par chitvan bhānt bhānt. [differ.
They all apply lamp-back, but their glances
(Beauty unadorned is adorned the most.)

Kal ka līpā deo bahāe, āj kā līpā dekho āe.
Wash off yesterday's plaster and look to to-day's.
(Let by-gones be by-gones.)

Kamāe na dhamāe, mo ko bhūj bhūj khāe.
He neither earns nor gets, but feeds on me.
(A lazy husband or son.)

Kamar na būtā sānjhe sūtā!
No strength in his loins and early to bed!

Kamāū āve dartā, nikhattū āve lartā.
The bread winner comes home quietly, and the earn-nothing quarrelsome.

Kamāū khasam kis se na chāhe!
Who would not wish for a hard-working husband?

Kamāū pūt kaleje sāl. [breast.
The son who earns lies on his mother's
(He is the darling of his mother.)

Kām kare nath vālī, pakrī jaē chirkut-vālī.
The bejewelled woman did it and the ragged woman was taken up.
(For explanation see page 129 Col. ii.)

Kānā mujh ko bhāe nahīn, kāne bin suhāe nahīn.
I dislike the one-eyed rogue and yet I cannot do without him.
(Said by a woman of a husband she dislikes.)

Kanth na pūchhe bāt, merā dhanā suhāgan nām.
My husband never speaks to me, yet I am called a happy married woman.
(For explanation see page 130, col. ii.)

Kā par karūn singār, piyā mor āndhar?
For whom should I deck myself, when my husband is blind?
(The blind man's wife needs no paint.)

Karā aur kar na jānā main hotī to kar dikhātī.
She did it, but didn't know how to do it; if I had been there I would have shewn her.
(For explanation see page 131, col. i.)

Kātā aur le dauṛī.
Off to the market as soon as she has spun.
(To be in a needless hurry.)

Kātā sūt paretan ko, pakkī roṭī juṛyāve ko.
She can reel off the spun thread, and manage the baken cakes.
(For explanation see page 132, col. i.)

Kaunā kamāī par tel bukvā? [metics?
On what income do you expect oil and cos-

Kaune rūp par etnā singār.
On the strength of what beauty do you deck yourself thus?

Kavvā ṭar-ṭarātā hī hai, dhān sūkhte hī hain.
The crows keep on cawing, but the corn dries all the same.
(For explanation see page 134, col. i.)

Khāe na khilāe; khālā dīdon āge pāe!
My aunt neither eats nor gives me to eat, may she lose her eyes and legs!
(A curse.)

Khair kī jūtī, khairāt kā nāṛā, paṛhde Mullā aqd udhārā.
My shoes and breeches were got as alms, so Mullah, marry me on credit.
(For explanation see page 135, col. i.)

Khālī kharī tī pūrī fazīhatī.
An empty purse is a great curse.

Khānā na kapṛā saiṅ kā bhatrā. [name.
Nor food nor raiment, a husband but in

Khasam kā khāēṅ bhāī kā gāēṅ.
She is supported by her husband, but gives her brother the credit of it.
(A habit among native women)

Khasam kiyā sukh sone ko paṭṭī lag kar rone ko.
I took a husband to live with and have only a wall to weep against.
(For explanation see page 137, col. i.)

Khāvind rāj buland rāj, pūt rāj dūt rāj.
The husband's reign is a great reign, the son's reign is the devil's reign.
(For explanation see page 137, col. ii.)

Khon baṛā, khon posh baṛā, khol-ke dekho, to ādhā baṛā.
The tray is large and so is the cover; take it off and you will find only half a cake in it.
(A pun on the word baṛā, great, and also a cake.)

Khon pāk, khon-posh pāk; khol-ke dekho to khāk hī khāk.
The try is clean and so is the cover; take it off, and you will see nothing but dust.

Khudā laṛne kī rāt de, bichhaṛne kā din na de!
God grant us the night of fighting, but never the day of separation.

Khundā Nathiyā aur kiyā huā bhatār, kisī k kām nahīṅ ātā.
A blunt tool and a paramour are of no use.
(For explanation see page 140, col. i.)

Kis birte pe tattā pānī!
On what account do you want warm water.
(For explanation see page 140, col. ii.)

Kiyā par kar na jānā, main hotī to kar dikhāīt
She did it, but did not know how to do in had I been there I would have showt, her how.
(Based on a story in the *Alif Lailā*)

Koī bhī mā ke peṭ se to lekar nahīṅ niklā hai.
No one was taught in his mother's womb.

Kokh kī āṅch sahī jātī hai par peṛū kī āṅch nahīṅ sahī jātī.
The pain of the womb can be borne, but not the pain of the pelvis.
(For explanation see page 142, col. i.)

Kokh māng se ṭhandī rahe! [head !
May you ever be happy both in womb and
(For explanation see page 142, col. i.)

Kos chalī nā bābā pyāsī. [athirst.
Not a mile travelled and father, I am
(For explanation see page 142, col. ii.)

Koṭhī kuṭhle ke hāth na lagāo, ghar bār sab tumhārā. [whole house is yours.
Except the cupboard and the wardrobe the
(For explanation see page 142, col. ii.)

Kuārī khāē roṭiyāṅ byāhī khāē boṭiyāṅ.
The virgin daughter eats bread, but the married eats the (parents') bones.
(For explanation see page 143, col. i.)

Kuchāl sang hāṅsī, jeū jān kī phāṅsī.
To joke with the vicious is to hang yourself.

Kuchh to bāolī, kuchh bhūtoṅ khaderī.
Somewhat mad and somewhat possessed by evil spirits.
(Said of a silly and foolish woman.)

Kūd mue, kūd; terī nalyoṅ meṅ gūd.
Nikal gayā gūd, to rah gayā mardūd.
Jump, you rascal, jump, while marrow is in your bones. [better than a corpse.
When that marrow is gone, you will be no

Kuṭnī se to Rām bachāve! pyārī ho kar pat utrāve.
God protect you from a procuress! she will gain your heart and betray your honor.

Kyā pardesī kī pīt aur kyā phūs kā tāpnā?
Diyā kalejā kāṛh huā nahīṅ āpnā.
What is a fire of straw, and what is a stranger's love? Give him your heart and he is never your own.

Kyā ṭoṭkā karne āī thī.
Have you come to cast a spell?
(Said of a short visit.)

Lao sīpī, khukhor bhīt mere saīyāṅ par itnī bītī!
Bring me a shell to scrape the wall, my husband's substance must not be wasted thus!
(For explanation see page 149, col. i).

Larkan ke bhagvā nā, bilāī ke gātī. [cat.
Not a strip for the child, but a coat for the
(For explanation see page 149, col. ii.)

Laṛkā roe, khasam chillāve, laṛkauri mehariyā fazīhat hoe. [mother gets abuse.
The child cries, the husband roars and the
(A family quarrel.)

Laṛte to nahīṅ, muē mārte haiṅ.
They fight not, but speak ill of the dead.
(Said of back biters.)

Le lugṛī, chal gudṛī.
Take the old clothes and go to the market.

Lihāz kī āṅkh jahāz se bhārī.
No ship so heavy as a good reputation.

Luṭāyā bigānā māl: bandī kā dil daryāo.
It is another's property that is plundered; pitiless is the slave's heart.
(For explanation see page 151, col. ii.)

Mā beṭī gāne-vālī, bāp pūt barātī!
Mother and daughter for singers, and father and son for wedding procession!
(A poor man's marriage.)

Mā betiyoṅ meṅ laṛāī huī, logoṅ ne jānā bair paṛā! [think them enemies!
Mother and daughter quarrel and people
(Lover's quarrels; kiss and make up.)

Mā bhaṭyārī, pūt Fateh Khāṅ.
The mother an innkeeper and the son my Lord General.

Mā bhaṭyārī beṭā tīr-andāz. [archer.
The mother an innkeeper and the son an
(For explanation see page 152, col. i.)

Mā chāhe beṭī ko aur beṭī chāhe moṭe dhīng ko.
The mother on her daughter doats and the daughter on her stout lover.

Machhlī to nahīṅ ke saṛ jāegī.
It is not fish, that it should putrify.
(Said in deprecation of undue haste.)

Mā ḍāyan ho to kyā bachchoṅ hī ko khāegī?
Even an ogress will not devour her own child.

Maiṅ aur merā manus, tīsre kā mūṅh bhulas.
I and my husband; let every one else's face burn.
(Selfishness.)

Maiṅ bhalī, tū shābāsh!
I am all right and hurrah for you!
(Mutual praising.)

Maiṅ bhalī ki panethā?
Which is the simpleton, I or the peddlar?

Maiṅ hī pāl karā mustanḍā, moe hī māre le-ke ḍanḍā!
I brought him up to be a strong man and he beats me with his stick!
(A woman to her undutiful son.)

Maiṅ kab kahūṅ tere beṭe ko mirgī āve hai?
When did I ever say that your son has epileptic fits?
(For explanation see page 150, col. i.)

Maiṅ karūṅ terī bhalāī, tu kare merī āṅkh meṅ salāī.
I seek to do you good, and you would run a needle into my eye.
(Returning evil for good.)

Maiṅ kyā terī paṭṭī tole kī hūṅ.
Am I in any way your inferior.

Maiṅ to terī lāl pagyā pe bhūlī re Raghūā!
It was your red turban, Raghuā, that misled me

Maiṅ tujhe chāhūṅ aur tū kāle dhīṅg ko.
I love you and you a black paramour.
(For explanation see page 153, col. i.)

Māṅ kī sauk, na bāp se yārī,
Kis nāte kī tauṅ mahtārī?
Nor my mother's co-wife, nor my father's mistress, How come you then to be my mother?
(For explanation see page 153, col. ii.)

Māne na jāne, 'maiṅ bhī naushā kī khālā.'
Nor known nor recognized, and "I am the bridegroom's aunt."
(For explanation see page 154, col. ii.)

Māne to deo, nahīṅ bhūt kā leo!
Believe and he is a god, otherwise he is only plaster!
(Faith can move mountains.)

Mangnī ke satvā sās ke pinḍā.
Borrowed meal is offered to the mother-in-law.
(For explanation see page 155, col. i.)

Manganī kī chādar to par pachās kā ādar!
A borrowed sheet and she offers it to fifty different people.

Man hamārā pās dhan ūn kā pās.
My mind is mine, his wealth is his.
(Contentment: my mind to me a kingdom is.)

Man kare pahiran chautār, karam likhe bheṛī ke bār.
Her heart on satins, but her fate on sheep's wool.

Man kī mārī kā se kahūṅ? Peṭ masosā de de rahūṅ.
To whom shall I tell my grief? I can but press my belly!
(For explanation see page 155, col. ii.)

Man motiyoṅ byāh man chaoloṅ byāh.
A *man* of pearls and it is a marriage: a *man* of rice and it is a marriage!
(For explanation see page 156, col. i.)

Mān na mān, maiṅ dulhā kī chachī!
Believe me or not, I am the aunt of the bridegroom.
(For explanation see page 156, col. i.)

Mā Punhārī, bāp Kanjar, beṭā Mirzā Sanjar.
The mother a chamber wench, the father a basket maker, and the son my noble Lord!
(Said of an upstart.)

Mā pe pūt, pitā par ghoṛā bahut nahīṅ to thoṛā hī thoṛā.
The son is as the mother, the colt is as the sire; if not altogether, at least somewhat.
(For explanation see page 156, col. i.)

Mā pisanhārī achchhī, aur bāp haft-hazārī kuchh nahīṅ.
A mother that grinds corns is better than a father that is captain of seven thousand men.
(For explanation see page 156, col. i.)

Maran chalī aur sūkh sāmhne.
Going to her death and (the planet) Venus in front of her!
(For explanation see page 156, col. ii.)

Mard kā dikhāyā na khāīye, mard kā lāyā khāīye.
Eat not before your husband; but eat what he brings you!
(For explanation see page 156, col. ii.)

Mard kā kyā hai? ek jūtī pahnī, ek jūtī utārī.
It's nothing to the man: he puts on the new shoe and throws off the old one.
(For explanation see page 156, col. ii)

Marī kyoṅ? sāṅs na āyā!
Why did she die? for want of breath!

Mar mar na jāte to bhar ghar hote.
Had none of us died the house would have been full.

Mār mūe mār terī hatriyāṅ piṛāeṅ morī ādat na jāe!
Beat me, you wretch, beat me till your hands ache: but my habits will not leave me!
(Obstinate wife to her husband.)

Mathrā de bundā, lubhāve das gunḍā.
With spangles on her forehead she lures ten lecherous men.

Mat kar sās burāī tere bhī āge jāī.
Mother-in-law, don't ill-treat me: you too have a daughter to come after you.
(For explanation see page 160, col. i.)

Māṭṭhā māngan chalīn, aur malaīyā pīchhe lukāī.
She asked for butter-milk with butter behind her back!

Merā māthā usī vaqt ṭhinkā thā.
It was hammered into my forehead at that very time.
(For explanation see page 100, col. ii.)

Merā thā so terā huā; barāë Khudā ṭuk dekhne de!
He was mine and is yours: for God's sake let me see him some times.
(For explanation see page 161, col. i.)

Mere byāh, jījī ke ṭhik ṭhik.
The wedding is in my house, and my sister has the music.
(For explanation see page 161, col. i.)

Mere hai, so Rājā ke nahīn, aur Rājā merā māngtā.
I have what the Rājā has not, so he must come begging to me.
(For explanation see page 161, col. i.)

Mere hī se āg lāī nām dharā basandar.
She got the fire from me, and now she calls it sacred fire.
(For explanation see page 161, col. i.)

Mere lalā kī ulṭī rīt! Sāvan mās chunāveṅ bhīt!
The eccentricities of my husband! He builds his wall in August!
(For explanation see page 164, col. i.)

Mere lāl ke sau sau yār, dhuniā, julāhe, aur manihār!
My son has hundreds of friends; wool-carders, weavers, and bangle-sellers.
(For explanation see page 161, col. i.)

Mere miyāṅ ke do kapre suthan, nāṛā, bas.
A pair of trowsers and a string compose my husband's apparel!
(Great poverty.)

Merī ek bolī, do bolī, merī naktī satā sat bolī.
I speak once or twice, that impudent wretch speaks a hundred times.
(By 'speak' understand 'abuse.')

Missī, kājal kis ko? Miyān chale bhus ko!
For whom shall I stain my teeth or blacken my eye-lashes? My husband gathers straw!
(To express scanty means: *res angusta domi.*)

Miyāṅ ke miyāṅ gaë, bure bure supne āë.
My husband gone and bad dreams as well!
(Misfortune never comes singly.)

Miyān nāk kāṭne ko phireṅ, bīvī kaheṅ, "nath gharā do!
The husband comes to cut off her nose, and the wife says "buy me a nose-ring!"
(Cross-purposes.)

Miyāṅ ne ṭohī, sab kām se khoī.
Her master toyed with her and she ran-away.
(Losing a good servant by a foolish act.)

Miyāṅ phire lāl gulāl, bīvī kī haiṅ bure havāl.
My lord enjoying himself and my lady in distress!

Mo ko na to ko, le chūlhe meṅ jhoko.
Not for you, nor for me, take it, and throw it into the fire.

More bāp ke upjal kapās, more lekhe paral tusā
My father's cotton crop has come up, but for me there's only hail (misfortune).
(For explanation see page 162, col. ii.)

Morī kī īṅṭ chaubāre charhī.
The brick of the drain is raised to the terrace.
(For explanation see page 162, col. ii.)

Mor saiyāṅ chikanīā, pachās birā khāë; Āge pīchhe rinihā, dīvāna bane jāë.
My husband is a fop, eating 50 leaves (a day); and when his creditors surround him he feigns madness.
(Betel leaves are expensive luxuries.)

Muft kā chandan ghise jā, bilallī!
Thou fool, thou art grinding the sandal wood for nothing!
(For explanation see page 163, col. ii.)

Muft ke khāne vāle ham aur hamārā bhāī.
We two eat for nothing, I and my brother.
(For explanation see page 163, col. ii.)

Mūī kyoṅ? sāṅs na āyā.
Why did she die? For want of breath!
(A misfortune that cannot be avoided.)

Mūṅh kī mīṭhī hāth kī jhūṭī
A sweet tongue and a false hand.
(To excite false hopes.)

Mūṅh par mumānī pīṭ pīchhe sūar-khānī.
Relations to their faces, pigs behind his back.
(Said of a treacherous woman.)

Mūṅh par pūt, pīchhe harāmī mūt.
A son to his face and a bastard behind his back.
(See preceding)

Mūṅh se hazār chāvl khāī, nāke se eko nā.
With your mouth you may eat a thousand grains of rice, with your nose not one.
(For explanation see page 165, col. ii.)

Murgī apnī jān se gaī, khāne vāle kā mazā na āyā.
The fowl lost its life, and the eater was not satisfied.
(For explanation see page 166, col. ii.)

Murgī ko takle hī kā ghāo bās hai.
A wound from a needle is enough for a fowl.

Nāch na sakūṅ āṅgan ṭeṛha!
I can't dance because the floor is uneven.
(For explanation see page 167, col. i.)

Nāchne niklī to ghūṅgaṭ kaisā?
When you come out to dance, why be veiled?
(For explanation see page 167, col. i.)

Nāk ho to nathiyā sobhe.
The nose ring becomes a nose.

Nāk kaṭī mubārak, kān kaṭe sulāmat.
If her nose be off it is lucky, if her ear be off it is blessed.
(To describe a very impudent person.)

Nāk par supārī torte hain.
He cracks betel-nuts on his nose.
(He is very irascible.)

Nakṭe kā khāīye ukṭe kā na khāīye.
Better be fed by the noseless than by the disagreeable.
(*Ukṭā* is a man who reminds of an obligation.)

Nakṭī maiyā, pānī pilā!" Pūtā inhīn gunon se!"
"My noseless mother, give me some water." "What upon such language, my son."

Na main jalāūn terī; na tū jalā merī.
I will not burn yours, and don't you burn mine.
(I'll throw no dirt at you, don't you threw it at me.)

Na main kahūn terī, na tū kaho merī.
I speak not ill of you; don't you speak ill of me.
(Said after a quarrel is made up.)

Nām Basantī, mūnh kūkar as.
Her name Beauty and a dog's her face.

"Nām kyā?" "Shakar pārā." "Roṭī kitnī khāē?" Das bārah." "Pānī kitnā pīye?" "Maṭkā sārā." "Kāmkarne ko" "Laṛkā bichārā!"
"Your name?" "I'm Lollypop" you eat "Loaves ten or twelve." "You drink?" "A large jar full" "You work?" I am but a lad, you know!

Nanad kā nadoī, gale lāg lāg roī.
She embraces and weeps over her husband's sister's husband.
(For explanation see page 170, col. i.)

Nangī bhalī ki chhīnke pāon.
Is it best to go naked, or be hung up by the heels?
(Of two evils choose the least.)

Nangī bhalī ki ṭeṭ·k machvā.
Is it best to be naked or to create a row?

Nangī ho-ke kātā sūt, buḍḍhī ho ke jāyā pūt.
She spins when she is naked, and bears when she is old.
(For explanation see page 170, col. ii.)

Nānī ke āge nansār kī bāten!
She speaks ill of her grand-mother's relations before her grand-mother.
(Want of tact.)

Nānī khasam kare, navāsā chaṭṭī bhare.
The grand-mother goes astray, and the grand-son pays the fine.
(For explanation see page 170, col. ii.)

Nār sulakkhnī kuṭumb chhikāve, āp tale kī khurchan khāve.
A good housewife feeds the house hold well, and is content with the leavings for herself!

Na sūp dūse jog, na chhalnī sarāhe jog.
The winnowing-fan is not worth abusing, nor the sieve worth praising.
(Arcades ambo.)

Nātā na gotā khaṛā ho-kar rotā!
Neither kith nor kin, so what are you howling at!
(For explanation see page 171, col. ii.)

Na tel talī na ūpar palī.
Nor oil at the bottom, nor in the ladle.
(Said of a very small dole.)

Nātin sikhāve ājī ko, ki bārā ḍeoṛhe āṭh!
She is teaching her grand-mother that twelve times one and a half makes eight!
(Go and teach your grand-mother to suck eggs.)

Naumī Gūgā Pīr mānāūn, na charkhe ke hāth lagāūn.
At Gūgā Pīr's naumī I cannot spin my wheel.
(For explanation see page 172, col. ii.)

Nayā chikanyā, renḍī ke phulel!
A raw youth with caster oil for cosmetic!

Nikhaṭṭū āve laṛtā, kamāū āve ḍartā.
The ne'er do-weel comes home noisy, the bread-winner quietly.

Nīk nīk more bhāg, ek ek machhalyā kī do do machhalyā.
How fortunate am I, for every fish I have two.
(For explanation see page 173, col. ii.)

Nipūtī ke mūnh dekhle sāt upās.
To see a barren woman's face is to go seven days without food.

Niyāre chūlhe bal bal jāūn, sārā khātī ādhā khāūn!
I shall be so delighted to have a separate hearth, That half a meal will be a whole one to me!
(A young wife to her mother-in-law.)

Ochhe ke ghar khānā, janam janam kā tānā.
Dine with the mean, and be reminded of it all your life.

Ochhī ke hāth lagī kaṭorī pānī pī pī marī padorī.
A mean woman got a cup, and drank till she burst.
(For explanation see page 175, col. i.)

Onāmāsī na āve, "maiyā, pothī lā de!"
He knows not the alphabet and asks his mother to get him a book.

Oṛhī chādar huī barābar, "main bhī shāh kī khālā hūn.
She puts on a veil like a lady, and says, "I, too, am the king's aunt."
(For explanation see page 175, col. i.)

Paisā na kauṛī, bāzār men dauṛī.
Without a penny to her name, and off to the market.

Paise par dhar ke boṭiyāṅ uṛāūṅ tau bhī dard na āve.
I could break your bones on the grind-stones and feel no remorse.
(Parents to their children.)

Pāṅch mahīne byāh ko bīte peṭ kahāṅ se lāī.
How is it that she has a child after five months' marriage?

Panch-phūlā Rānī banī haiṅ.
She sets up to be a Panchphūlā Rānī.
(For explanation see page 178, col. i.)

Parāyā sir lāl dekh, āpnā sir phoṛ dāleṅge?
Shall I break my own head because I see the red spot on another's?

Parde meṅ zardā lagātī haiṅ.
She has thrown a stain on the curtain.
(For explanation see page 180, col. i.)

Pardesī balam, terī ās nahīṅ, bāsī phūloṅ meṅ bās nahīṅ.
There is no hope of a lover gone abroad, nor scent in stale flowers.

Pardesī kī pīt ko sab kā man lalchāē; Doī bāt kā khoṭ hai! rahe na sang le jāē.
All hanker after a stranger's love: But there are two drawbacks: he 'll neither stay, nor take you with him.

Parlī pīyā, tore bas; jinne chāhā tinne ghas.
I am fallen, husband, under your power; use me as you like.
(For explanation see page 181, col. i.)

Par mūī sāsū, esoṅ āē aṅsū.
Last year her mother in-law died, and now she is weeping.
(Crocodile's tears.)

Peṭ bhī khālī, god bhī khālī.
Womb and lap are both empty.
(Nor chick nor child.)

Peṭ meṅ paṛā chārā, kūdne lagā bichārā.
When he had filled his belly, he began to show his pranks.

Peṭ meṅ paṛī būnd nām rakhā Mahmūd.
No sooner she conceives than she calls the child Mahmūd.
(For explanation see page 182, col. ii.)

Phaṭe ko na siye, aur rūṭhe ko na manāē to kyoṅ-kar guzārā hoē?
If you don't repair rents and conciliate the offended how can you get on?

Phūar chāle nau ghar hāle.
When the ninny walks abroad, nine houses tremble.
(For explanation see page 183, col ii.)

Phūaṛ jurvā sāg meṅ shurvā.
The silly house-wife makes gravy of pot herbs.

Phūar kare siṅgār, māṅg īṅṭoṅ se phoṛe.
The ninny decks her forehead by rubbing brick-bats into it.
(For explanation see page 183, col. ii.)

Phūaṛ ke ghar ugī chaṅberī, Gobar māṅḍ usī par gerī.
A jessamine grew in a ninny's house, And she put her cow-dung cakes on it.
(i. e. She knew not the use of it.)

Phūaṛ sīne baiṭhe jab sūī toṛe.
When a ninny sews she breaks her needle.
(A bad workman quarrels with his tools.)

Phūl āē haiṅ to phal bhī āeṅge.
When you see the blossom, you may expect the fruit.
(For explanation see page 184, col. i.)

Phūlī phūlī gaune ko, ṭhasak nikal gaī raune ko.
Full of pride comes the bride to her husband; crest-fallen returns she from her father's house.
(For explanation se page 184, col. i.)

Phūṅke ke na phāṅke ke ṭāṅg uṭhā ke tāpe ke.
She 'll neither blow nor stir the fire, but she 'll warm her legs at it.
(Said of the selfish and idle.)

Pī ke pātan sir dharo, dharo charan par sīs Bāsā ho baikunṭh meṅ phir to bisve bīs.
Lay on your head your husband's shoes, and on his feet your head, and you will be sure of your place in heaven.
(For explanation see page 184, col. ii.)

Pīrjī kī sagāī Mīrjī ke yahāṅ.
The Pīrs are betrothed to Mīrs.
(For explanation see page 185, col. i)

Pīr ko na shahīd ko pahle nakṭe deo ko!
Not to priest, nor to saint, but to the worthless devil first!
(For explanation see page 185, col. i.)

Pīs lūṅ to pīṭūṅ.
When I have done grinding I will thrash you.
(Said to children. Don't think you 'll be let off.)

Pīs mūī pakā mūī āē lauṭhe khā gaē.
I ground and cooked and the louts came and ate it.
(A mother to her idle sons.)

Pīsne vāliyāṅ pīs le jāeṅge, kuchh hattā thoṛī ukheṛ le jāeṅgī.
When the corn-grinders have ground the corn, they don't take away the handle of the (hand) mill.
(For explanation see page 185. col. ii.)

Piyā kī kamāī mohe nahīṅ lahnā, Mope bāzū band nahīṅ aur sab gahnā.
My husband's earnings are no benefit to me: I have no armlets though all other jewelry.
(Unreasonable discontent.)

Pul bāndhal jāē, bahū kajrī khele.
The bride plays in the boat, while the bridge is being thrown across.
(For explanation see page 186, col. ii.)

Purakh kī māyā birachh kī chhāyā.
The reputation of a man is the shadow of a tree.
(As long as he lasts his reputation lasts.)

Pūt bhaē siyāne dukh bhaē birāne.
When the son grows up, discomforts depart.
(i. e. he is then able to support his parents.)

Pūt kupūt ho jāë to ho par mān kumān nahīn hotī.
A son may be a bad son, but a mother a bad mother never.

Pūt mānge gaīn bhatār letī āīn.
She went to get a son and found a husband.
(For explanation see page 187, col. ii.)

Pūt mīṭh, bhatār mīṭh kiryā keh kar khāūn ?
My child is dear and my husband is dear, which shall I swear by ?
(The horns of dilemma.)

Pūt na bhatār, pīchhohī ṭāën ṭāën.
Neither her son nor her husband, yet she howls at his absence.
(For explanation see page 187, col ii.)

Pūton rāt dulambhuī.
The begetting of a son is uncommon.

Qaras kāṛh mehmānī kī laundon mār dīvānī kī.
The feast is on credit, and the boys are driving me wild !
(By asking for dainties : a poor man's feast.)

Rahā Karimnā, to ghar gayā, Karimnā tau ghar gayā.
If the wretched Karim remain at home, the house is ruined : if he go aboad the house is ruined.
(For explanation see page 189, col. ii.)

Raho rī kutiyā merī ās, main āūn Kātak mās !
Wait for me, you bitch I'll be back in October.

Rājā āge rāj; chhalnī na chhāj.
While there is a king there is a kingdom, after him there is not even a sieve and a basket.
(Said by a widow.)

Rājā ke ghar gaī aur rānī kahāī.
When she enters a king's house, she becomes a queen.
(For explanation see page 190, col. i.)

Rājā rūṭhegā apnā suhāg legā, kyā kesī kā bhāg legā.
If the king be displeased he can take back his gifts, but he cannot deprive me of my fate.

Rakat le gailan sautin ke naihar.
Go for blood to a co-wife's mother's house.
(Deep hatred.)

Rām nām le so dhakkā pāve, chūtaṛ hilāve so ṭakā pāve.
Call on God and be punished about, skip and dance and make money.
(For explanation see page 192, col. i.)

" Rānḍ " ke āge gālī kyā ?
The height of abuse is " widow."
(For explanation see page 193, col. i.)

Rānī ko kaun kahe " āgā ḍhak " ?
Who will tell a woman to cover her breast ?
(who can counsel a great man !)

Rānṛ bhailā ke sukh kaun, jo nichant sūtal nā ?
What is the use of being a widow, if one cannot sleep soundly ?

Rāt ko Narbadā utrī subah ko kūā dekh ḍarī.
She crossed the Narbada at night, and was frightened next morning at a well !

Rātan kātūn kātnā sir par nahīn nātnā.
All night long she spins and still has nothing to cover her head.

Rāton roī aur ek hī mūā !
Long nights she cursed and only one man died !
(For explanation see page 194, col. ii.)

Rāt pare upāsī din ko khoje bāsī.
He passes the night hungry, and in the morning looks for the stale rice.

Rāt parī būnd nām rakhā Mahmūd.
She concieved last night, and has already named the issue Mahmud.
(For explanation see page 194. col. ii.)

Rattī bhar kī tīn chapātī,
Khāne vāle sāt sangātī.
Three cakes of a penny weight each, and all her friends to eat them.

Rattī dān na dhī ko dīyā ; dekho rī, samdhan kā hīyā !
Look at the liberality of the bride's mother; she has not given her a farthing !
(for dowry.)

Rīt na satvansā merā lāḍlā navāsā !
Nor seventh month rite nor feast, and yet he is her darling grandson !
(For explanation see page 195, col. ii.)

Rone ko to thī hī itne men ā gaë bhaiyā.
Just as she was about to cry, her brother came to see her.
(For explanation see page 196, col. i.)

Roṭī gaī mūnh men zāt gaī gūh men.
The bread went down his throat, and his caste into the filth.
(For explanation see page 196, col. i.)

Roṭī ko rove, chūlhe pīchhe sove.
Weeping for want of bread, and sleeping behind the hearth.
(A description of extreme poverty.)

Roṭī ko rove aur khaprī ko ṭohve.
Weeping for the bread, she caresses the platter.

Roṭī na kapṛā sent kā bhutrā.
Nor food nor raiment (from him); a husband in name only.

Rūp na singār Khatrānī kī sādh.
Without beauty or ornaments, she would be a Khatānī.
(For explanation see page 197, col. ii.)

Rūthe ko manāë nahīn, phate ko silāë nahīn, to kām kyon-kar chale ?
If you don't appease the offended or mend your rents, how will you get along ?

Sab din change, tihvār ke din nange.
Gay dresses every day, and ill clad on holi.
(For explanation see page 198, col. i.)

Sab gun kī āgar, dhīyā, nāk binā be-hāl.
You would be perfect, my child, if you had a nose.
(Great deal braggars, little doers.)

Sab gun pūrī, kaun kahe adhūrī.
Filled with good qualities, who shall call you imperfect?
(For explanation see page 198, col. ii.)

Sab-hī kūkar jo Kāshī jāeṅ, to pātar chāṭan kaun āeṅ?
If all the dogs were to go to Kāshī (Benares), who would there be to lick the platter?
(Dogs in India are the public scavangers.)

Sābit nahīṅ kān bāliyoṅ kā armān.
She has n't a whole, and yet she wants ear-rings.

Sab kāmoṅ meṅ pūrī, koī na kahe adhūrī.
You are perfect in all arts, no one can call you imperfect.
(Said as a snub to a boastful woman.)

Sab kehu bole to nīk lāgalā, kapūr bahu bole tihūk barelā.
When others speak it is pleasant, but when my daughter-in-law speaks it pricks me.
(For explanation see page 199, col. i.)

Sab koī jhūmur paire, langṛī kahe 'hamhūṅ.'
As all wear anklets, the lame girl wants one too.

Sab kuchh gaī miyāṅ terī chulbul na gaī.
Every thing is gone, husband, but your childishness.

Sab kuchh gayā, miyāṅ kī ṭākh ṭākh na gaī.
Every thing is gone, but my husband's ill humour.

Sab sadqe maiṅ alag.
I sacrifice all to you except myself.

Sab toṛen merā ek Rab na toṛe.
All may break with me, but God!

Sadā kī padnī urdoṅ dosh!
Always breaking wind, she lays the fault on the peas.
(For explanation see page 201, col. i.)

Sāg meṅ shurvā; aṇḍe meṅ pānī! Kyoṅ, Bībī Paṭhānī?
Soup out of grass, water out of eggs. How can it be, my lady Paṭhānī?
(For explanation see page 202, col. ii.)

Sagrī raiṅ ban ban phirī, bhor bhae kuāṅ se ḍarī.
She roamed the whole night in the wilds, And was frightened at a well in the morning.
(Sham modesty.)

Sahīh gae salāmat āē.
Sound he went and safe he returned.
(For explanation see page 203, col. i.)

Sāīṅ more āp birūjhal, log dihal pochārā.
Lāt mūkā ham sahlauṅ, aur sahlauṅ dugārā.
My husband was already vexed with me, and the people egged him on. I bore kicks and blows, and shower of abuse.
(Adding insult to injury.)

Sāīṅ terī sohlī aur ādār kare na koē, Durdur kareṅ saheliāṅ maiṅ murmuṛ dekhūṅ toē.
My Lord I am thy slave and none respecteth me: my friends keep me at a distance, and I can but look to thee.
(For explanation see page 204, col. ii.)

Saīyāṅ bhae kotvāl ab ḍar kāhe kā.
My husband's now Kotvāl, so what have I to fear?
(For explanation see page 204, col. ii)

Saīyāṅ gaē bides maiṅ to kāt kāt muī, Āgre kā charkhā Burhānpur kī rūī.
My husband gone abroad, I'm worn to death with spinning, with the wheel from Agra, and the cotton from Burhānpur.

Saīyāṅ gae ladnī, lādaiṅ jhaṛā jhaṛ: sau ke pachās kiye chale āe ghar!
My hundred went a trading and collected goods no end: But when he had made a hundred into fifty he came back home.

Saīyāṅ jā mat bides ko, kanthā haṭmat khol!
Hunar dekh mere hāth kā kā tūṅ sūt an mol.
Go not, my spouse, to foreign lands, nor open a shop, my husband! Behold my dexterous hands, I'll spin a priceless thread.

Saīyāṅ ke arjan bhaīyā ke nāoṅ; Pahan oṛh, maiṅ sāsar jāūṅ!
The earnings are my husband's, and the credit my brother's: I will dress myself and go to my husband's house!
(For explanation see page, 205, col. i.)

Saīyāṅ ne is dunyā meṅ lakhoṅ rupaiye baṭṭe; Kadhi na lāē laḍḍū peṛe, ber khilāē khaṭṭe.
In this world my husband has made a fortune of millions; But he brought no sweets for me, only plums, wild and sour.
(For explanation see page 205, col. i.)

Saīyāṅ tere kārne jal bal ho gaī rākh; Pat se maiṅ be pat huī, panchan meṅ gaī sākh.
For thy sake, my love, am I burnet to ashes, and have lost my honor, and been disgraced among my kind.

Sājan āvat hūṅ suno, kuchh neṛe kuchh dūr, Palk on hī se jhāṛ lūṅ un pāvan kī dhūr.
I hear my love approaching nearer and nearer; And I'll brush the dust off from his feet with my eye-lashes.

Sajan bin Id kaisī.
It is no festival without a husband!

Sājan dukiyā kar gae aur sukh ko le gae sāth; Ab dukh de niyāre bhae, merī baur na pūchhī bāt.
My husband has made me wretched, and taken my joys with him; He has made me wretched by leaving me, and has sent me never a word.
(A woman's lament over an absent husband.)

Sājan ham tum ek hoīṅ dekhat ke haiṅ do.
Man se man ko tol le do man kadhī na ho.
I and you my love are one, though seemingly we are two. *Man* weighed against *man* will never make two man.
(For explanation see page 205, col. i.)

Sajan pīt lagāē ke dūr des jin jāo:
Baso hamārī nagrī, ham māngeṅ tum khāo.
My love, once having loved, go not to foreign lands: Live you in my city, and I will beg that you may eat.

Sājan sājan milgae jhūṭe paṛe basīṭh.

When friend meets friend, the meddler is disgraced.

Sajan sakāre jāenge aur nain marenge roē, Bidhnā aisī rain kar ki bhor dadhī na hoē.

My love starts to-morrow and my eyes fade with weeping. O God, make such a night that there shall be no morn.

Sajan tum jhūt mat bolo! Khudā ko sānch pyārā hai. Kahāvat hai badon kī yūn, kadhī sānchā na hārā hai!

My husband do not tell a lie! For God loves the truth. It hath been said of old that truth injureth not?

Sājan voh din kaun the jo sukh se lāē pīt? Ab dukh de niyāre bhaē:—kaun gāon kī rīt.

My love, where are the days when you loved me with gladness? To beg and leave me in sorrow:—what manners are these?

Sājan yūn mat jāniyo toē bichhrat moe chain; Āle bin kī lākrī sulgat hūn din rain.

Don't believe, my love, that I have pleasure in your absence; Like a green-wood tree, I smoulder night and day.

Sājhā sadhe na bāp kā sae rāse kī khān, Ghar niyārā kar bālmā bāt merī tū mān.

Partnership will not last even with one's father; it is the root of strife: Keep a separate house, my spouse; please listen to my words.

(For explanation see page 205, col. ii.)

Sakhī na sahelī bhalī akelī. [that I am alone.

Neither friend nor companion; It is well

Shāh Khānam kī ān khen dukhtī hain dīve shahr ke gul kar do [the lights in the town.

Shāh Khānam has sore eyes, so put out all

(For explanation see page 206, col. ii.)

Salāmat rahe bahu jis kā borā bharosā.

Long life to my daughter-in-law, in whom I have great hopes.

(For explanation see page 206, col. ii.)

Salemo bin id kaisī?

It is no festival with out Salemo?

Samman chūrī kānch kī kaurī kaurī dekh jab gal lāgī piū ke, lākh take kī ek.

Samman, bangles of glass are but a farthing each, But when they clasp a husband's neck they are worth a million each

Song soī to lāj kyā? [left her?

After sleeping with a man what shame is

Sapūtī rove tūkon ko, nipūtī rove pūton ko.

The mother with a son cries for food, and the mother without one for a son.

(Every one cries for the moon.)

Sārā ghar jal gayā jal chūriyān pūchhīn.

fter the whole house had been burnt to Aashes my bangles were noticed.

(For explanation see page 209, col. ii.)

Sarāhal bahuryā dom ghar jāī

Praise a daughter-in-law and she will go with a sweeper.

(i. e. praise will turn her head.)

Sārā shahar jal gayā, Bībī Fātima ko khabar hī nahīn. [Lady Fātima is ignorant of it.

The whole city burnt down and still my

(For explanation see page 209, col. ii.)

Sardhā lāgal kailon bhatār, Ohu niksal jāt ke Chamar.

With great eagerness I took a husband, And then he turned out to be a Chamār.

(For explanation see page 210, col. i.)

Sāre dhar kī suī nikāle, so koī nahīn; ānkh kī suī nikāle, so sob koī.

Who takes out the pins out of the whole body is nothing; but who takes the pins out of the eyes only is everything.

(For explanation see page 210, col. i.)

Sāre din pīsā pisnā, chapnī bhar bhī na uthāyā.

She ground all day and filled not even the pot lid.

(For explanation see page 210, col. i.)

Sāre din ūnī ūnī rāt ko charkhā pūnī.

Idle all day, she begins at night to spin.

(For explanation see page 210, i.)

Sārī rāt mimyānī, aur ek hī bachchā byānī.

The goat bleated all night, and produced only one kid.

(For explanation see page 210, colii.)

Sārī rāt roī aur ek hī marā.[one only had died.

She mourned the whole night long, and still

(For explanation see page 210, col. ii.)

Sāsar kāran baid bulāyā sauk kahe terā dhagṛa āyā.

I called in the doctor for my mother-in-law, And my co-wife says he is my lover.

Sāsar sānsā mat kare dekh thuṛaırā kām, Thoṛe ko bahotā kare den lage jab Rām.

Mother-in-law grieve not because business is slack: When God is favorable little becomes much.

Sās bahū kī huī laṛāī kare paṛausan hāthā pāī.

When a bride and her mother-in-law fall out the neighbours intermeddle.

Sās bin kaisī susrāl. Lābh bin kaisā māl.

Without his mother it is no husband's house without gain there is no business.

Sās gaī gāon bahū kahe main kyā kyā khāūn.

The mother-in-law is gone to her village, the bride thinks of what she shall eat.

(For explanation see page 211, col. ii.)

Sās jhānke tūīn tūīn bahū chalī baikunth.

The mother-in-law peeps out meekly, and the daughter-in-law goes to heaven.

(For explanation see page 211, col. ii.)

Sās kā oṛhnā bahū kā bichhaunā.

The covering of the mother-in-law is the bedding of the daughter-in-law.

(For explanation see page 211, col ii.)

Sās ke āge bahū ko kyā baṛāī?

In the presence of the mother-in-law, what is the rank of the bride?

(See preceeding.)

Sās ke oṛhnā patoh ke bichhaunā.[in-law's bedding.

The mother-in-law's covering is the daughter-

Sās kī cherī sab kī jaṭherī. [of all.
The mother-in-law's maid is the mistress
(For explanation see page 211, col. ii.)

Sās kī rīsī patoh ke māthe. [the daughter-in-law.
The habits of the mother-in-law are copied by
(For explanation see page 211, col. ii.)

Sās ko nahīṅ paiṅche, bahū chāhe taṅbū aur sarāṅche !
The mother-in-law has not even drawers, and the bride wants a tent and screens.
(For explanation see page 211, col. ii.)

Sās koṭhī bahū chabūtre.
If the mother-in-law goes into the hall, the daughter-in-law will go out into the entrance.
(For explanation see page 211, col. ii.)

Sās koṭhe par kī ghar. [roof.
A mother-in-law is like the grass on the
A worthless thing.)

Sās lukkā lūkkā, bahū bukkā bukkā.
What the mother-in-law does secretly, the daughter-in-law does openly.
(See Sās koṭhe, bahū chabūtre).

Sās mar gaī apnī arvāh toṅ be meṅ chhoṛ gaī.
When my mother-in-law died she left her soul in the gourd.
(For explanation see page 212, col. i.)

" *Sās morī mare, sasur morā jīē" naī bahurīyā ke rāj bhaë.*
When her mother-in-law dies and her father-in-law lives, the bride reigns supreme.

Sās na nandī, āp hī anandī.
There is neither mother-in-law nor sister in-law, so she is happy by herself.
(For explanation see page 212, col. i.)

Sāsrā, sukh bāsrā. [comfort !
In your husband's house you will live in
(Advice to a young bride.)

Sāsre tere sāg, māthe tere bhāg : Bāp ke tere rāj, tū baiṭhī baiṭhī jhāṅk.
Comfort in your husban's house, and good fortune is to you ; Royalty in your father's house, and you may only look on.
(For explanation see page 212, col. i.)

Sās rī sās tujhe peṭ kā dukh, pahle chūlhā hī yād āyā
Mother-in-law, your stomach is a trouble to you ; your first thought is the kitchen.

Sās se bair, parauson se nātā. [to her neighbour.
An enemy to her mother-in-law, and a friend
(A foolish woman.)

Sās se toṛ, bahū se nātā. [the daughter-in-law.
Cuts with mother-in-law, and attached to
(For explanation see page 212, col. i)

Sāṭh sās nanad hoṅ sau, Mā kī hoṛ na inse ho.
If a woman have sixty mothers-in-law, and a hundred sisters-in-law, None will be like her own mother.

Sath soī bāt khoī. [gone.
When she siept with him her honor was

Sāth sonā aur mūṅh chhupānā !
Sleep with a man and hide your face !

Sāth so, peṭ kā dukh. [belly.
Sleep with a man and be troubled in your

Sat mat chhūṭe he piyā ! sat chhāḍe pat jāe.
Sa kī bāṅ thī Lachchhmī pher milegī āē.
Don't give up truth, my love ; by leaving truth you will love your credit ; fortune guarded by truth will come again.
(For explanation see page 213. col. ii.)

Sat sau chūhe khā ke billī haj ko chalī.
After eating up seven hundrep rats, the cat is going on a pilgrimage. (to Mecca.)
(For explanation see page 213, col. ii.)

Sāt tavoṅ se mūṅh kālā karnā.
To blacken one's face with seven frying pans
(For explanation see page 213. col. ii.)

Satvantī kā lāj bar, chhīnārī ke bāt bar.
A chaste wife is very bashful, and a bad one a great talker.

Sau gulāmaṅ ghar sūnā. [house is empty.
Although there be a hundred slaves, the
(If the master be absent.)

Saukan burī hai chūn kī, aur sājhe kā kām
Kāṅṭā burā karī kī, aur badrī kā ghām.
A co-wife is bad though made of dough, and bad is a joint concern. Bad is the thorn of the acacia, and the heat of a cloudy day.
(For explanation see page 214, col. ii.)

Saukan chūn kī bhī burī.
A co-wife though of flour is intolerable.

Saukan gaī aur āṅkh chhoṛ gaī. [eyes (sons).
The co-wife is gone but she has left her

Sau kosā aur ek masosā barābar hai.
One forbearance is equal to a hundred curses

Saut bhalī, sautelā burā.
A co-wife may be good; but her child never.

Saut chūn kī bhī burī.
See above saukan chūn etc.

Saut jāē saut kā mārā na jāē ! [ticoat string !
May the co wife go away but not her pet-
(i. e. her husband.)

Saut kā mūrat bhī burī.
The very statue of a co-wife is intolerable.

Saut par saut aur jalāpā !
Co-wife upon co-wife and heart-burnings !

Sej kī makkhā bhī burī.
Even a fly is insufferable on the marriage bed
(For explanation see page 216, col.ii. ii)

Sendur na lagāeṅ to bhatar kā man kyoṅ-kar rakkheṅ !
If I am not to put the red-spot on my forehead, how am I to please my husband !
(The red-spot is the sign of coverture.)

Seṅdur ṭikulī jaral, to peṭo meṅ bajjar paral !
If I have no red-spot must my stomach starve!

Shābāsh miyāṅ tujh ko, tū ne moh liyā mujh ko !
Bravo, my dear sir ! you have taken my fancy.
(Ironical : also an assignation .)

Shādī hai, kuchh guryoṅ kā byāh thoṛā hī hai.
A marriage feast is not a doll's wedding.
(For explanation see page 217, col. i.)

Shaitān ke kān bahre.
May the devil be deaf
(For explanation see page 217, col. ii.)

Saitān kī kālā.
The devil's aunt.
(Said of a very wicked woman, as a caution)

Shaitān tūfān se Khudā nigahbān.
May God protect us from the devil and his calumnies [niator.)
(Used towards a great and very artful calum-
Shakal churail kī mizāj pariyoṅ kā.
Ugly as an ogress and imperious as a fairy.
Sharam kī bahiū nit bhūkī mare.
A bashful bride is always hungry.
(For explanation see page 218, col. ii)
Shauqīn bahuryā, chaṭāī kā lahṅgā
A gay bride with a mat for a gown.
Shauqīn bībī. hammal kī cholī. Cholī meṅ āg lagal, tahlul phīrī.
My fair lady has a blanket for a bodice. The bodice is burnt into holes and still she sturts abount.
Sīkhī sīkh-p reausan ko, ghar meṅ sīkh jiṭhānī ko
She teaches what she has been taught at her neighbour and her sister-in-law.
Sir meṅ bāl nahīṅ, bhāl se laṛāī. [bear.
No hair on her head and she fights with the
(For explanation see page 221 col. ii)
Sir par āre chal gae tau bhī Mādār hī Madār.
The saw is across her head, yet she cries "Madār Madār!"
(For explanation see page 221, col. ii.)
Sir par jūtī hāth meṅ roṭī. [hand.
Blows on the head and the bread in the
(For explanation see page 222, col. ii.)
Sivaīyoṅ bin Id kaisī?
It is no Id without vermicelli.
(For explanation see page 222, col. ii.)
Sohnī būā, aur chaṭāī kā laṅhgā! [gown!
A handsome old lady and a mat for her
Sonā jhonā kuchh zāt nahīṅ.
Wealth is not caste.
Sonā nīk, to kān phaṛāē ke?
If gold is good, it will not tear the ear.
Sone meṅ pīlī, motiyoṅ meṅ dhaulī. [pearls.
She is yellow with gold, and white with
(Richly decorated with ornaments.)
Sotī thī, par kātā nahīṅ, jo kātā to pāṅch pāo.
I was sleeping and did not spin, but when I began, I spun one and a quarter.
(A skit at a idler)
Sughaṛ sughaṛ hans gaīṅ phūhaṛoṅ ko āyā hāṅsā.
The simpleton laughs aloud where the wise woman smiles.
Suhāg bhag arzānī, chū'he āg na ghaṛe pānī.
Wedlock's joys are cheap, but there's no fire in the hearth nor water in the pitcher.
(An unhappy marriage.)
Sūhe kī rīt nahīṅ, mashrū kī ṭaufīq nahīṅ.
Red garments are not customary, and silk not procurable.
(The horns of a dilemma.)
Sukhan unhoṅ par ḍāliye, jo hans hans rākheṅ māṅ. [due respect.
Beg only of them who smile and show you
Sūnī sej se markhanā bail bhī bhalā.
A butting ox is better than a lonely bed.
(For explanation see page 227, col. ii.)
Sun re ḍhol bahū ke bol.
Hear, drum my lady's voice.
(For explanation see page 227, col. ii.)
Sun sun ke terī bāt, saheli, soch huā mere man ko. Kar-ke byāh gharoṅ nahīṅ rakhte bābal apnī dhī ko.
My maid, I have head and my heart grieves, that after marrying her off a father keeps not his daughter at home.
(For explanation see page 228, col. i.)
Sūrā ran meṅ jāē ke lohā karo nisank. [laṅk.
Nā mohe chaṛhe randāpro, nā tohe chaṛhe ka-
Go, warrior, to the battle-field, and fearless wield your sword. Your death will bring no widowhood to me, nor cavil at your name!
(For explanation see page 228, ii.
Surmā sab lagāte haiṅ par chitvan bhāṅt bhāṅt.
All apply antimony, but their manners differ.
(For explanation see page 228, col. ii.)
Tāsh par mūṅj kā bakiyā.
Rope lace upon brocade.
(For explanation see page 233, col. ii.)
Tāṭ kā āṅgyā mūṅj kī tanī ; Dekh, mere deorā main kaisī banī?
A canvass boddice and strings of straw; See, brother-in-law, how beautiful am I?
Tatrī ne dīyā janam jalī ne khāyā ; jībh jalī na savād āyā.
The miserly hussy gave it, and the helpless fellow ate it; but it had neither pungency nor flavor.
(For explanation see page 234, col. i.)
Tavā na kūṅḍā na chulhārī! Kahe nār "maiṅ hūṅ bhaṭyārī"!
She has no frying pan, no oven and no fire; And the woman would be called innkeeper!
Telan se kyā ḍhoban ghāṭ; is ke mūsal us ke lāṭh.
The washerman's wife is no worse off than the oilman's; this has a pestle, that a rod.
(*i. e.* both are eqally bad : *Arcades ambo.*)
Telī kā bail le-ke kumhāiṅ satti hoē.
The potter's wife dies for the oilman's ox.
(Wasted sympathy.)
Telī khasam kiyā aur rūkhā khāyā!
Marry an oilman and live on dry bread.
(For explanation see page 235, col. ii.)
Tel kī jalebī mūā dūr se dikhāve.
The wretch shows his oily sweetments at a [distance.
(For explanation see page 235, col. ii.)
Tel na miṭhāī, chūlhe dharī kaṛhāī.
Without sugar or oil, the frying-pan is put on the fire!
Terā hāth aur merā mūṅh.
Thy hands and my mouth.
(Earn and feed me : selfishness.)
Terā pānī main bharūṅ, mere bhaie kahār.
I draw water for you, and the water bearer for me.
(Put into the mouth of a vain servant.)
Terā thā so merā huā, barāē Khudā ṭuk dekhne de. [let me see him for a while.
What was mine is now yours, for God's sake
(For explanation see page 236, col. i)

Terī āvāz Makke Madīne meṅ. [Madīnā.
May your voice be heard in Makkā and
(For explanation see page 236, col. i.)

Thandī chhāoṅ jo baiṭhtī jal jātā voh rūkh; Jaltī baltī maiṅ phirūṅ, ban meṅ detī kūk.
Had I sat under the cool shadow of a tree, it would have burnt up: consuming and burnig I roam about and cry out in the woods.
(To express great misfortunes.)

Thāṭhaṛ khol nikaṭṭā āyā.
Open the wicket, the earn-nothing has come.
(Used by women towards idle husbands.)

Tīkulī sendur gail, to khāne meṅ bhī bijjar paṛab?
Because my red-spot is gone, am I to lose my food as well?
(For explanation see page 238, col. ii.)

Tinke ki oṭ pahāṛ.
A mountain can be hid by a straw.
(See Til kī ojhal pahāṛ.)

Tīn tikaṭ, mahā bikaṭ, aur chār kā mūṅh kālā, pāṅch ho to bhālā.
Three stares are bad, four disgrace and five ruin.

To ke levan maiṅ chalī. to mohe gherī ā; Ab tu moko chhoṛ de, maiṅ to he chhoṛ diyā.
I came to take thee and thou didst win me, but now that thou leavest me, I leave thee.
(For explanation see page 241, col. i)

Toṛ dāl tāgā tū kis bharve ke mūṅh lāgā.
Break the marriage thread; what blackguard have you been talking with?
(For explanation see page 241, col. ii)

Tū bhī rānī maiṅ bhī rānī, kaun bharegā pānī?
I am a queen and you are a queen: so who is to fetch the water?

To chāh merī jāī ko, maiṅ chāhūṅ terī khāṭ ke pāī ko.
Love my daughter and I will love the foot of your bed.
((For explanation see page 242, col. i)

Tū chhūē aur maiṅ mūī.
Touch me and I die.
(Affectation of delivery)

Tū khol merā maknā, maiṅ ghar saṅbhālūṅ apnā!
Lift up my (bridal) veil, for I must manage my house.
(For explanation see page 242, col. ii.)

Ṭukre khāē din bahlāē, kapṛe phāṭe ghar ko āē.
He eats his meals and wastes his days and comes home in rags.
(An idle husband.)

Ṭuk ṭuk kor ke man bhar khāve, Tonak Begmāṅ nām batāve!
Little by little she eats a hundred weight, and yet she calls herself Miss Delicate eater!
(A habit by no means confined to the women of India.)

Tum baṛā nannhā kātī ho.
You spin a fine thread.
(Over economy: skinning a flint.)

Tū merā laṛkā khilā maiṅ terī khichṛī pakāūṅ.
You amuse my child, and I'll cook your food.

Tumhāre laṛke bhī kabhī ghutniyoṅ chaleṅge.
When will your children crawl on their knees.
(When will you speak the truth or perform your promise)?

Tum kāṭo merī nāk aur kānī, maiṅ na chhoṛūṅ apnī bānī.
You may cut off my nose and ears, But I'll not give up my ways.
(Said by an obstinate woman in reply to her husband's threats.)

Tum ko ham sī anek haiṅ, ham ko tum sā ek Ravī ko kaval anek haiṅ, kavlan ko ravī ek.
You have many like me, I have but one like you: The sun sees many lotuses, but the lotuses only one sun.
(An obedient wife to her husband.)

Tum rūṭhe ham chhūṭe!
You are angry; I am free!
(For explanation see page 247, col. i)

Tū raho rī, hauṅ hī lakhūṅ chaṛh na aṭā Brij-bāl: Binā same sashī ke ugah parhaiṅ aragh akāl.
Stop I'll go up to see: you must not mount the balcony my maid of Brij, Or libations will be poured out without a moon.
For explanation see page 247. col. ii.)

Udhlī bahū balaiṅde sāṅp dikhlāve.
The gadding wife sees a snake in the roof.
(i. e. makes an excuse for running out of th house.)

Ujar ho ghar sās kā, jo bair kare har bār! Pīhar ghar sabas base, jab lag hai sansār.
May the house be destroyed of the mother-in law that quarrels all day! My father's house may thrive as long as the world lasts.

Uṛ chal panchhī pī ke des.
Fly away, bird, to my husband's country.

Uṭhāo merā maknā maiṅ ghar saṅ bhālūṅ apnā.
Lift up my veil, and let me examine my house.
(For explanation see page 253, col. ii.)

Uṭhte lāt, baiṭhte ghūṅsā.
When he is up he kicks her, and when he is sitting he hits her.
(A bad husband.)

Vārī gaī pherī gaī jalve ke vaqt ṭal gaī.
She is very affectionate, but is absent at the time of need.

Vār vār pānī pīte haiṅ.
Each drinks water in her turn.
For explanation see page 256, col. ii.)